The Archaeology of Warfare

UNIVERSITY PRESS OF FLORIDA

Florida A&M University, Tallahassee
Florida Atlantic University, Boca Raton
Florida Gulf Coast University, Ft. Myers
Florida International University, Miami
Florida State University, Tallahassee
University of Central Florida, Orlando
University of Florida, Gainesville
University of North Florida, Jacksonville
University of South Florida, Tampa
University of West Florida, Pensacola

The Archaeology of Warfare

Prehistories of Raiding and Conquest

EDITED BY

ELIZABETH N. ARKUSH AND MARK W. ALLEN

University Press of Florida
Gainesville/Tallahassee/Tampa/Boca Raton
Pensacola/Orlando/Miami/Jacksonville/Ft. Myers

11 10 09 08 07 06 6 5 4 3 2 1

A record of cataloging-in-publication data is available from the Library of Congress.

ISBN 0-8130-2930-9

The University Press of Florida is the scholarly publishing agency for the State University System of Florida, comprising Florida A&M University, Florida Atlantic University, Florida Gulf Coast University, Florida International University, Florida State University, University of Central Florida, University of Florida, University of North Florida, University of South Florida, and University of West Florida.

University Press of Florida
15 Northwest 15th Street
Gainesville, FL 32611-2079
http://www.upf.com

Contents

Part III. Themes in the Archaeological Study of Warfare

Figures

Tables

Preface

This project emerged from two symposia held at the 66th annual Society for American Archaeology meeting in New Orleans in 2001. The first, organized by the editors of this volume, was called "The Archaeology of Pre-State and Early State Warfare," and aimed for a global, anthropologically informed perspective on warfare. At the same meetings we were delighted to attend a symposium organized by Rachel Kluender and titled "Peopling a No-Man's Land: Anthropological and Archaeological Approaches to Pre-State Conflict," which focused on closely similar concerns with a particular emphasis on North American archaeology. Scholarly and public interest in the archaeology of warfare had been mounting for several years, spearheaded most visibly by the publication in 1996 of Lawrence Keeley's *War Before Civilization*, and it is perhaps no coincidence that these two sessions emerged at the same time. The papers presented in them offered fresh perspectives on early warfare and on how warfare might change over centuries of cultural development.

Participants from both sessions were enthusiastic about the possibility of combining papers in a single, geographically balanced volume. In particular, Steven LeBlanc and Jonathan Haas, the discussants at our session, were instrumental in encouraging us to proceed with the project. Rachel Kluender was also very supportive of the idea and generously allowed us to solicit additional participants from her session. Papers were also invited from Anne Underhill on warfare and state development in China and from Chapurukha Kusimba on warfare and slavery in East Africa to round out the volume geographically.

We thank all the contributors to the volume for their thoughtful revisions and their patient, timely cooperation on the long and sometimes winding path this project took before its completion. John Byram of the University Press of Florida was supportive of the book from the beginning, and his assistance has been greatly appreciated. The comments of the two anonymous manuscript reviewers led to significant improvements in the final product. We would also very much like to thank two special people who supported us in this five-year endeavor: Kwame Burroughs and Nancy Allen.

1

Introduction

Archaeology and the Study of War

MARK W. ALLEN AND ELIZABETH N. ARKUSH

Warfare has been with us for a long time. Recent archaeological studies have shown that in many times and places in the pre-modern and prehistoric past, warfare was a constant and overwhelmingly important fact in peoples' lives (Carman and Harding 1999; Demarest et al. 1997; Haas 1990, 2001; Keeley 1996; Lambert 1997, 2002; LeBlanc 1999; Martin and Frayer 1997; Milner 1999; Osgood et al. 2000; Raaflaub and Rosenstein 1999; Rice and LeBlanc 2001; Walker 2001; Webster 2000; Wilcox and Haas 1994). War altered peoples' fates, shaped their worldviews, and affected their decisions large and small, from everyday matters of whether to go out to collect firewood, to some of the most important ones: where to locate settlements and how to build them, how much authority to confer on whom, when and with whom to engage in trade and marriage, how to conceptualize gender and age, and how to expend collective labor. These studies have established the disturbing fact that the prehistory and history of our world has been intimately bound up with the course of war. However, we still lack a deep understanding of the causes and conditions that make war likely, that influence its practice, and that shape its long-term effects on the societies that engage in it.

The purpose of this volume is to provide insight on warfare by examining the long-term evolution of societies and regions that existed in changing contexts of war. By including perspectives from non-Western areas, prehistoric societies, and incipient states at the moment of conception, we aim to offer a better understanding of the true range of variation in the way warfare and societies have shaped each other.

This is a task better suited to archaeology than history. Historians and, specifically, military historians have produced several insightful studies of the history of warfare in the West (for example, Ferril 1985; Garlan 1975; Handel 2001; Hanson 2001; Keegan 1993; Kern 1999; Lynn 2003; McNeill 1982; O'Connell 1995; Toynbee 1950; van Creveld 1991a). However, these texts often misread, downplay, or neglect warfare in prehistoric periods and non-Western regions. For example, the military historian John Keegan's (1993) *A History of Warfare* and recent works by classicist Victor Davis Hanson (1989, 2001) downplay the impact of warfare in non-state and non-Western societies, treating it as ritualistic, game-like, and "irrational," in contrast to a distinctive "Western way of war" whose unique efficiency has led to Western domination. Unfortunately, neither author effectively incorporates anthropological or archaeological perspectives on the variability of warfare in non-Western cultures and prehistoric periods (Lynn 2003).

Thus, theoretically informed studies of long-term patterns of warfare in pre-state and early state societies are still relatively rare, especially outside the West. This volume is intended to redress this problem. Archaeologists also have the unique ability to examine the changing face of warfare as it existed on the fringes of European colonial expansion, where written accounts are sketchy and one-sided. Such archaeological studies offer a valuable perspective, not only on what causes war or peace, but on how societies shape war and how war shapes societies over long time periods. The varied trajectories presented here demonstrate that this co-evolution has been complex and multilinear.

Causes and Consequences of Warfare

When considering the long-term relationship between warfare and society, researchers, including those in this volume, often take one of two major and equally valid perspectives. The first approaches war as a *cause* of fundamental social change—especially the rise of sociopolitical complexity. The second perspective sees warfare as an *effect*, sparked or shaped by factors ranging from environmental changes, shifting populations, and new technologies, to internal sociopolitical processes such as ideological change and factionalism. This second focus is related to that most basic of questions, what causes war? Both have a long pedigree in anthropology and archaeology. Because each of the chapters in this volume relates to one or the other or both of these questions, it is relevant here to briefly discuss this scholarship.

Causes of War

The causes of war have understandably been a major concern for anthropologists. Over the past few decades, scholars have debated whether innate, psychological, material, structural, or ideological causes are responsible for outbreaks of war (Carneiro 1970, 1981; Conrad and Demarest 1984; Dickson 1981; Durham 1976; Ferguson 1984, 1990; Kelly 2000; Robarchek 1990). Archaeological studies have been valuable in this issue, for archaeologists are uniquely able to track resource abundance and subsistence practices along with intensity of warfare over long time periods. Where the data exist, interesting correlations can be noted between warfare and resource stress, especially as a result of environmental instability and crisis (for example, Allen 1996; Ember and Ember 1992; Haas 1999; Jones et al. 1999; Lambert 1997; LeBlanc 1999; Milner 1999; Vayda 1960). Population pressure has traditionally been seen as a powerful explanation for warfare, with some support from both archaeological and ethnographic cases (Hallpike 1977; Keeley 1996; Nolan 2003). However, it should be noted that wars for materialist gain need not be conducted in a context of scarcity; more surplus and labor power may also be the incentives (Kang 2000). Rich polities use violence to protect their trade interests in valuable commodities, including slaves. Leaders may depend on tribute wealth to remain in power (Wolf 1987).

The question of war's causes has led to debate over the timing of the first appearance of warfare in human societies. Some scholars contend that warfare is as old as our species or even older (Gat 1999, 2000; Keeley 1996; Otterbein 2004; Walker 2001; Wrangham 1999; Wrangham and Peterson 1996); others consider prevalent warfare to have arisen at the transition to sedentary lifestyles (Haas 1999, 2001; Jones et al. 1999; LeBlanc 1999; Milner 1999; Roper 1969, 1975; Vencl 1999), or even later, as the first states formed (see Otterbein 2004). The question presents methodological difficulties, since data from the pre-sedentary past are fewer and the evidence for warfare necessarily slimmer—mobile bands build no fortifications and they use no specialized weapons, so skeletal data is often the only evidence for war (Vencl 1999). The rather spotty archaeological evidence for pre-sedentary violence in comparison to later periods can be seen as either an absence of warfare or an artifact of sampling size; in consequence, this debate is likely to remain unresolved for some time yet.

Archaeologists may neglect social and ideological factors in warfare because they cannot see them as easily as material factors, such as environmental change and population growth. However, there is no question that patterns of warfare are greatly influenced by non-material factors. Cross-cultural comparisons of ethnographic cultures reveal correlations between warfare and aspects of social structure such as virilocality and fraternal interest groups (Otterbein 1970, 2004). A recent theory of the origin of warfare by Raymond Kelly (2000) proposes that a logic of social substitution in segmented societies led to war—an attack on a group member became an attack on the entire group. Socialization for warfare is well documented by anthropologists (Chagnon 1983; Ferguson 1999:406; Robarchek and Robarchek 1998); children, especially boys, may be inculcated with values of fierceness and taught they must avenge slights; warrior prowess may be emphasized as an essential aspect of masculinity. Such factors may be quite difficult for archaeologists to detect. On the other hand, the archaeological record is rich in evidence linking warfare to ideologies of elite power, and archaeologists have perhaps underestimated the force of such ideologies in shaping elite decisions.

While changing military technology may not cause outbreaks of war by itself, there is ample evidence for the importance of technology in the transformation or evolution of war. Examples include the effect of the bow and arrow on warfare in North America and Europe (Blitz 1988; Keeley 1996); of chariots and horse-riding in the ancient Near East and Europe (McNeill 1982); of bronze and iron metallurgy throughout the Old World (Keegan 1993); and, obviously, of gunpowder across the entire globe (for example, van Creveld 1991a, 1991b). Historical and ethnographic studies demonstrate the dramatic power of new military technologies such as firearms to transform not only the practice of war, but whole political and social landscapes (Earle 1997; Ferguson and Whitehead 1992; Keegan 1993; Otterbein 1994; Vayda 1976). Such transformative military technologies also include fortification, discussed below.

Other social and technological changes may exacerbate or alter warfare at different levels of political complexity, but their effects are only beginning to be understood. Does the intensity or practice of warfare alter when agricultural practices intensify? How do changing storage technologies alter military logistics and enable new kinds of warfare? How does the development of wealth finance systems shape raiding, alliance-making, and conquest? How do internal social factions use or cause warfare?

Consequences of War

A large body of scholarship has centered on the idea that war facilitates the development of social complexity in certain contexts, or up to a certain stage (Carneiro 1970, 1981, 1998; Cohen 1984; Earle 1997; Ferguson 1984, 1999; Haas 1987, 1992; Johnson and Earle 1987; Mann 1986; Redmond 1994a; Webster 1975). War allows polities to extend their reach through domination and conquest (Carneiro 1970, 1981). The wealth taken in booty or tribute from the losers, and the management of wealth and subject populations, can necessitate and support elites and governmental hierarchies. War that involves the capture of slaves can amplify social stratification by creating a slave underclass, as in the northwest coast societies of North America (Ames 2001). Warfare also opens unique avenues to political opportunists. Emergent leaders can exploit plundered goods or captured slaves, manage collective actions like the building of fortifications, negotiate peaces and alliances, and make themselves useful to their communities as war leaders in a context in which defense is of desperate importance (Allen 1994, 2003; Feil 1987; Hayden 1995; Kracke 1978; Redmond 1994a; Sillitoe 1978; Webster 1975).

But warfare does not always work in these ways. Chronic warfare can also fragment regions and make further political consolidation nearly impossible (Allen 2003). It is clear from ethnographic studies that in many regions, intense warfare is or was practiced without corresponding political consolidation. Indeed, endemic chiefdom warfare can be viewed as "the political failure of chiefs to organize stable regional systems" (Earle 1997:109). Many of the chapters in this volume demonstrate that warfare may be related to episodes of both consolidation and fragmentation.

When societies do expand and become more politically centralized, the goals and tactics of war change fundamentally (Carneiro 1990; Johnson and Earle 2000; Keegan 1993; Keeley 1996; Otterbein 2004; Redmond 1994a, 1994b; Reyna 1994; Service 1968; Turney-High 1971). In complex societies, it is often a single leader or a small group of elites who make decisions about war in pursuit of their own objectives (Reyna 1994). Smaller-scale societies usually rely on discussion, consensus, and shared risks and rewards in their approach to war (Sillitoe 1978). States and some powerful, centralized chiefdoms practice war that results in the control of people's labor through the conquest of groups. Conquest requires institutionalized leadership for command and warrior recruitment, surplus to fuel armies, and organizational hierarchies, infrastructure, and wealth finance systems for the control of subject populations and the extraction and use of tribute wealth from them. Where these are lacking, as in many smaller-scale societies, land may sometimes be captured in warfare, but permanent dominance over subject peoples is not established. Instead, raiding warfare may be practiced for plunder, prestige, revenge, and vacated territory (and, of course, for defense against enemies with similar goals). However, it is worth pointing out that some of the largest empires ever carved out through military action were those of steppe horse warriors with only ad hoc leadership and little infrastructure (Barfield 1994). Finally an intermediate form of warfare might be characterized as indirect conquest. Indirect conquest results in the subordination of neighboring polities with their chiefs and the flow of tribute, prestige, and labor from them to a paramount center, but it does not involve the annexation and direct governance of these subordinate chiefdoms, and the resulting power arrangements are often unstable and easily toppled (Anderson 1994; Kirch 1984; Webster 1998).

The tactics, as well as the aims of war, differ between smaller-scale, politically decentralized societies and populous, centralized ones. Raiding warfare tends to be conducted so as to harass, decimate, and terrorize the enemy group. Surprise attacks on villages, ambushes of work parties, and hit-and-run raids are common, while organized battles may be relatively bloodless, with projectile fire but little hand-to-hand combat. Centralized societies usually have better command and control, allowing commanders to conscript more soldiers and engage in higher-casualty situations, such as shock (hand-to-hand) combat and storming forts. They have better supply and logistics, allowing longer campaigns and, sometimes, extended sieges. On the other hand, these same organizational strengths of centralized societies can function as defensive weaknesses since they require firmly located and vulnerable facilities, while smaller, decentralized societies are often difficult and unattractive candidates for conquest (see Goldberg and Findlow 1984).

One major effect of warfare may be to further the development of institutions, ideologies, and social patterns that encourage more warfare. As warfare affects settlement patterns, trading networks, and gender ideologies, as new technologies develop or spread, and as warriors gain influence or soldier classes arise, societies may entrench themselves in a cycle of warfare that cannot be broken without threatening their own dissolution. Thus, as Ferguson (1999:427) states, "A society in a system evolved for war is ready, even waiting, for war . . . in many cases war is so woven into the fabric of social life that a given polity could not survive without it." These themes of cause, consequence, and coevolution are taken up and reconsidered to a greater or lesser extent by every author included in this volume. Sometimes the authors lend their weight to one or another established view; sometimes they present new perspectives.

Tools for the Archaeological Study of War

We would argue that one of the main contributions of this volume is that it displays the full variety of analytical and descriptive methods in the archaeological tool kit for studying warfare in the past. An overarching pattern among the chapters is a reliance on multiple methods and the synthesis of information from a variety of sources. While the story told about warfare by any one class of evidence (changing weaponry, for example) tends to be patchy and incomplete, different kinds of evidence and different sources of analogy can be combined to reveal detailed, long-term patterns of warfare. The case studies of this volume rely on the synthesis of multiple sources and techniques, almost without exception. In so doing, they reveal both obvious and more subtle changes in the practice or intensity of warfare over hundreds or thousands of years. This synthetic approach also enables the authors to present richly detailed pictures of the societal contexts that surrounded these trajectories of warfare. Indeed, it is the archaeologist's ability to get at long-term context that allows his or her work to speak to the questions of war's causes and consequences. As a result, these case studies go far beyond simple forensic arguments that merely demonstrate the presence of warfare in the past.

Many of the analytical methods used in this volume have been used throughout the discipline's history, but some are innovative, or are combined in innovative ways:

- Analysis of changes in fortifications or other defensible settlement patterns as a reliable indicator of changes in warfare
- The re-examination of archaeological excavations and collections with new interpretive techniques and approaches
- The judicious use of ethnohistory, oral history, and ethnography to supplement archaeological evidence about violence
- The use of analogy from cross-cultural ethnography and even military science to provide insights

One of the most obvious indicators of warfare or the threat of war is the presence of fortifications or other defensive settlement patterns. Every chapter in this volume includes some discussion of fortification. Archaeologically highly visible, but ethnographically neglected, fortification may have had the potential to alter regional political landscapes dramatically. Fortifications are essentially omnipresent in the archaeological record of many if not most cultural regions. While all fortification makes raiding, conquest, and the stable control of territory much more difficult, the effect of fortification on warfare differs at different levels of sociopolitical complexity, having far more impact for societies without the organization, manpower, or surplus to besiege forts. Middle-range societies that fortify their settlements may find it extremely difficult to conquer one another, because such societies commonly lack the logistical infrastructure to set prolonged sieges or the military control to storm forts effectively (Allen 2003). Put simply, their defenses outpace their offensive capabilities. However, fortifications tend to become less effective as polities develop large, mobile armies and techniques for rapid expansion. Fortification's effect on warfare is a promising area for research, as are the reasons why fortification may spread, die out, or change its form. The fortifications noted in this volume from various regions around the world range from simple palisades to elaborate defensive systems capable of withstanding all but the most determined sieges. In all regions, they offer vital evidence for the conduct of war over time.

Similarly, several chapters look to the edges of polities to study the causes and effects of warfare. Buffer zones have long been noted as important markers of at least potential hostilities, if not outright endemic warfare (Allen 1994; LeBlanc 1999; Marcus and Flannery 1996). Here, LeBlanc proposes an intriguing general process in which warfare creates underutilized buffer zones, which then become the incentives for warring groups and leaders to pursue conquest and political consolidation. Another important contribution is made by Connell and Silverstein, who shed light on the crucial, precarious role of frontier polities caught in the middle of long-term rivalries between larger states, demonstrating the political complexity of large-scale conflict.

A third important tool used in this book is the reevaluation of existing archaeological data sets with an eye for evidence of warfare or peace. One of the clearest illustrations of the impact of Lawrence Keeley's (1996) book *War Before Civilization* is the widespread reanalysis of such data by archaeologists since the late 1990s. This could almost be called a paradigm shift, as warfare or its significance was often not commonly addressed by archaeologists in the past, even in some cases which seem obvious in hindsight, such as the American Southwest. The ability to reevaluate older information with new technologies, analytical tools, or research questions is a key strength of archaeology. The importance of these data is likely to increase significantly in the future, as the pace of site destruction accelerates, and as archaeology itself moves toward less intrusive investigations in both the lab and the field. As the authors assembled here show, considerable insight has already been gained by the reexamination of existing collections, reports, and publications.

A fourth tool used to good effect in this volume is the judicious use of whatever supplementary sources are available for a particular region. In particular, the use of ethnohistory and ethnography is well illustrated by the chapters in this volume and by many previous archaeological studies of war. Oral history and tradition likewise commonly provide archaeologists with insights into the goals and methods of warfare. Here, Kusimba discusses the traces of warfare visible in traditional African folk tales, used both to control and educate children on the dangers beyond their village's borders. Allen obtains insight on Maori warfare from the exploits of the Maori Battalion during the Second World War. Such sources provide a much needed balance to the archaeological study of war. The material archaeological record is very good at revealing connections among warfare, environmental change, nutritional stress, and population growth, but less suitable for detailing the complex texture of incidents, emotions, and motivations that lead to conflicts in ethnographic accounts. Likewise, some aspects of social structure such as residence patterns are very hard to detect in the ground. Ideology can be notoriously difficult for archaeologists to grasp, at least beyond the recognition of symbols and their contexts. Combined together, however, the material remains of archaeology and the supplemental sources of ethnohistory, ethnography, and oral history often enable rich insight into the practice of war.

Finally, archaeologists sometimes use ethnographic analogy to better assess the patterns revealed through the material record. Solometo extensively mines ethnographic analogy to help reconstruct warfare in the prehistoric Southwest, following Kelly's theory (2000), which was derived through cross-cultural ethnographic research. Likewise, Connell and Silverstein apply insights from their experience in recovering American military MIAs in Laos to better understand how warfare between large powers affects the places located between them. But the sources of ethnographic analogy need not be limited to ethnographic research or personal experience, because many societies wrote their own descriptions and treatises about war. At least a few anthropologists and archaeologists have advocated the use of ancient or modern military science to gain insight into the tactics, strategy, and practice of warfare (Allen 2003; Ferguson 1984; Turney-High 1971; Wilcox et al. 2001). These pioneering attempts reveal the potential of analogy to better illuminate long-term changes in warfare.

The Chapters

This book is composed of ten case studies of particular regions and two theoretical contributions that assess evidence from around the globe. The case studies are loosely organized into two parts: six chapters address warfare among autonomous villages to chiefdoms, and four concern warfare in early states and nascent empires. Concluding chapters apply evidence from multiple regions to central questions about warfare: the origin of warfare, and the relationship between warfare and sociopolitical evolution.

The leading chapter by Solometo expands the archaeological focus from simply determining the presence or absence of warfare to examining several important variables of the conduct and effect of non-state warfare revealed by ethnographic studies: social scale, social distance, tactics, and the frequency/duration/predictability of war. Her case study of prehistoric east-central Arizona investigates fortifications of different types to shed light on these variables, concluding that social distance was the critical factor that shaped how war was conducted.

Bamforth reevaluates the well-accepted model that changing climate in the late prehistoric Great Plains led to warfare between two different cultural groups identified by archaeology: the Middle Missouri culture, and Initial Coalescent cultural groups who migrated into the area. He reanalyzes available radiocarbon dates against climatic data with a finer scale of analysis and carefully separates fortified sites with short term occupation from those with long, complex histories. His analysis indicates that escalations of warfare in the Great Plains were not only tied to periodic, localized drought conditions, but also to the incursion of Coalescent newcomers. This case is an excellent illustration of multiple causes for warfare.

Dye examines changes among four different regions of the Southeastern United States. In each case, he assembles a wealth of archaeological evidence from paleopathology, settlement patterns, fortifications, weaponry, and iconography, to trace the development of warfare from Late Woodland roots through the rise and fall of Mississippian chiefdoms. His analysis demonstrates that shared traits such as fortifications, buffer zones, and the elaborate warrior cult iconography of Mississippian chiefs played key roles in the growth of chiefdoms. However, the trajectories of these four regions differed based on variables such as environment, resources, elite strategies, and population size.

Liston and Tuggle present a model of long-term patterns of war in the islands of Palau, related to subsistence and settlement changes. They document a shift from small inland polities with numerous clusters of earthwork fortifications separated by buffer zones, to a later pattern of coastal villages characterized by elaborate stone architectural features. This shift accompanied a major transformation of the environment, as inland deforestation and erosion expanded areas of coastal wetlands suitable for intensive taro cultivation. The authors also draw extensively on ethnographic and ethnohistorical information to argue that Palau has long been characterized by a rigid social structure which emphasized competition for status. While they interpret hill-forts and coastal stone defenses as a means of displaying community or leader status (as well as pragmatic forms of defense from attack), Liston and Tuggle are convinced that in Palau, warfare acted as a leveling mechanism rather than as a consolidating force.

Allen traces the evolution of war over time in New Zealand, assembling evidence from ethnohistorical sources, weapons, skeletal paleopathology, areal excavations, and settlement patterns. Like Liston and Tuggle, Allen draws on ethnographic information about Polynesian *toa* warfare to conclude that this ancestral institution likely represented a means for obtaining higher social status. But a fundamental shift in New Zealand warfare occurred with the development of *pa*, thousands of hill-forts located in those limited areas where horticulture was just feasible. Allen argues that Maori chiefdoms of a limited scale formed around the construction of fortified settlements and refuges overseen by ambitious leaders. However, these fortified sites also inhibited any type of regional consolidation. After European contact, the introduction of muskets led to further transformations of warfare as these new weapons permitted destruction on an unprecedented scale. These changes took decades, showing the stubbornness of ideology and the contingency of warfare's conduct on context and history.

Kusimba asks two questions. First, what were the causes of post-sixteenth century warfare in Africa? Second, what is the relationship between warfare and the slave trade in East Africa? This chapter breaks new methodological ground in demonstrating how slavery in Africa, an archaeologically neglected topic, can be detected through the ripple effects of warfare and fortification. Kusimba also examines how patterns of warfare and social interaction were affected by Portuguese colonies, repeated droughts, and a complex cycle of unintended consequences in which the slaughter of elephants for the ivory trade led to increases in insect-borne disease as forests spread. Finally, Kusimba turns to his own fieldwork on fortified sites in Kenya to show how archaeology can study these processes.

Underhill evaluates the causes and consequences of war in the Yellow River Valley in China, from the Longshan period to the Qin empire, drawing on evidence from fortifications, weaponry, and oracle bone divination. She argues that war increased markedly in this region after the development of state level organization, and that advancing military technology was a crucial part of this process: the development of weapon forms, the war chariot, and new methods of fortification, as well as the institutionalization of effective military organization. But she also illustrates how militaristic elite ideology and lineage competition were key motivations of warfare in China, and how social distance was often employed as a justification for war and conquest.

Arkush examines warfare in the later Andean highlands, showing how war's conduct and consequences changed over the course of a millennium. War included expansion and competition between rival states (Wari and Tiwanuku), led by elites who monopolized a set of symbols of military power; after the collapse of these states, war was related to political fragmentation and the building of large numbers of fortifications; finally, under the Incas, a new kind of conquest warfare that relied on brilliant logistical capabilities and a strategy of divide and conquer rapidly integrated the entire Andean region into an empire. Arkush uses this sequence to question the relationship between warfare and the rise of sociopolitical complexity.

Redmond and Spencer assemble an impressive array of archaeological, ethnographic, and ethnohistorical data to study the roles of raiding and conquest warfare in the development of chiefdoms and states in prehistoric Oaxaca. They make full use of decades of extensive regional survey data and intensive excavations to reconstruct the transition from Zapotec chiefdoms to the Monte Albán state. One of their key findings is that Monte Albán became a state by first conquering and incorporating distant groups. These forays into conquest brought in new resources and enabled the development of an institutionalized military organization in Monte Albán. With these in place, this state eventually overcame its nearest neighbors who had successfully resisted conquest for some time. This fine-grained sequence sheds light on the process of state emergence and its relationship to warfare.

Connell and Silverstein use the analogy of the Vietnam War to argue that we may need to look at peripheries rather than cores to see war between large powers. These peripheries are not only military frontiers, but vital avenues or channels of communication, trade, and travel. Connell and Silverstein consider two Mesoamerican examples of places caught in the middle: western Belize between the cities of Tikal and Calakmul, and northern Guerrero between the Aztec and Tarascan states. They employ political geography and emphasize spatial relationships in order to get at state level warfare in these two cases. Their innovative approach demonstrates the importance of studying war on a variety of scales, including small local communities vying with each other to garner favor from rival "superpowers."

The final two chapters are not case studies but theoretical treatments of particular questions. LeBlanc builds on Carneiro, developing a model to explain why war-related centralization happens in some places, but not in others. His innovative model links conquest and consolidation to the existence of a productive buffer zone which allows for a bonanza of resources if it can be acquired by removing or incorporating adjoining rival polities. LeBlanc supports this model with several archaeological examples from the literature.

Ferguson addresses three issues in his chapter: how anthropology has approached war in the past, how the Western world affected war in the tribal zone, and how warfare originated, based on archaeological evidence from early societies around the globe. His review of this extensive literature indicates increasing warfare after the transition to sedentism, suggesting that investment in a particular territory, higher population densities, and some degree of storable surplus may be, if not preconditions, strong encouragements for warfare. Increasing trade and social competition are also tied to escalating warfare in some regions. One of Ferguson's main points is that archaeology does not reveal constant war in all times and places. He cautions archaeologists to be careful when considering ethnographic data on warfare, as it may reflect alterations to the practice, tactics, or aims of warfare caused by colonial contact. Finally, he rightly argues for continued theory-building through collaboration between archaeologists, cultural anthropologists, and others.

Themes of the Volume

It seems useful to conclude this introduction by outlining some of the shared themes found within this volume. Several authors examine the role of ecology or environmental change in transformations of warfare. As noted above, archaeology often works happily enough on this issue within the confines of the material record. In some times and places the evidence is overwhelming that environmental fluctuations such as droughts led to rapid and substantial increases in the duration, frequency, and intensity of war. The chapters in the volume that point to relationships between warfare and ecology or environmental change (Bamforth, Liston and Tuggle, Allen, Kusimba, Arkush, and Ferguson) support one of the major anthropological camps on the causes of warfare—the materialist approach, which typically sees warfare as an expedient and contingent choice in a context of material need (Ferguson 1984, 2001).

However, another important theoretical perspective represented in the volume sees warfare as dependent on cultural, ideological, or social-structural rather than (or as well as) material factors. Solometo argues that a logic of social substitution and distance is appropriate for the study of war in the Southwest. Several other authors (Bamforth, Underhill, and Connell and Silverstein) see social distance or situational ethics as an important factor in the practice or intensity of warfare. Most of the chapters include some discussion of the use of militaristic symbols, often prestige weapons or metaphors of fierce predatory animals, as a form of ideological power to support or extend the positions of elites. By creating and continually reaffirming the link between elite power and victory in war, elites constrained themselves and their descendants to repeatedly engage in military exploits to legitimize themselves. Allen points out that traditional concepts of Maori warfare, such as what he calls "mutually assured revenge" to avenge any slight or insult, were so embedded in the conduct of war that they could not be dropped despite the disastrous consequences of the introduction of firearms. Thus, an important thread that runs through this volume is the effect of cultural history on the goals, tactics, and strategies of warfare at any given time and place. Simply put, traditions of war shape how war is fought. This naturally includes practical lessons learned, such as occurs when modern military forces use Clausewitz and Sun Tzu to teach tactics and strategy to junior officers. But it also includes such notions as how enemies are regarded, what constitutes proper conduct of war, and even the purpose of war itself. Traditions interact with changing conditions, such that in the case studies in this volume, warfare rarely remains static for long periods of time, despite the continuity of some tactics, goals, and other concepts.

A third major theme is one that can be traced to the seminal theory of Robert Carneiro that warfare led to centralization in the form of chiefdoms and states. Dye, Underhill, Arkush, and Redmond and Spencer all point to the political aims of elites who wage war to advance their own positions or expand their polities. LeBlanc's model of conquest and the incorporation of buffer zones is an extension of Carneiro's argument. On the other hand, several of the chapters in the volume note that warfare may lead to stalemate rather than conquest, and thus inhibit rather than encourage centralization. Solometo, Dye, Liston and Tuggle, Allen, and Arkush all discuss the relative effectiveness of defensive measures to resist attacks in prehistory before the development of complex chiefdoms or states with the enhanced ability to besiege or invest fortifications. Certainly, the relationship between war and power, and the role of conquest warfare in the origin of sociopolitical complexity, are issues that will continue to capture the attention of archaeologists.

A closely related issue is the difference between raiding and conquest warfare, and several chapters in this volume illustrate how archaeology can reveal the often rapid transition from raiding to conquest. Dye shows how complex Mississippian chiefs, with the offensive capability of missile weapons to overcome walls, went to war against one another to lay claim to commoners and their tribute. Underhill believes that warfare escalated drastically with the origin of states empowered by new weapons. Arkush describes how the Inca were able to overcome the limitations of earlier chiefdoms as they built an empire through conquest and intimidation. Redmond and Spencer show how vital the ability to wage conquest warfare was for Monte Albán. These examples suggest that the raiding-conquest model of warfare is a useful approach to understanding both the variation and evolution of warfare.

A last theme to highlight revolves around the two major perspectives noted earlier in this introduction. Warfare is usually treated by anthropologists either as a dependent or an independent variable in social transformation over time, that is, either as an effect (for example, of population pressure, sedentism, statehood, collapse, etc.) or as a cause (for example, of greater sociopolitical complexity, or alternately, of dispersal and fragmentation). The necessarily simplified worlds of these theoretical models can obscure the fact that warfare actually operates continually as both cause and effect of social transformations. Warfare facilitates social transformations, such as the growth and political centralization of polities, which change the aims, tactics, and practice of war itself. This circular evolutionary process has been used as an explanatory framework for both the evolution of complex societies and the concomitant transformation warfare undergoes (Redmond 1994a). In other words, war can be fundamentally altered by the same social transformations it fosters. This becomes particularly clear when we examine long cultural sequences. The case studies in this book illustrate several such causal cycles, in which warfare was tied to ideological, technological, political, and social changes that themselves altered patterns of warfare.

Around the globe, societies and warfare patterns have coevolved in complex, historically contingent, and often unique ways. Like our distant ancestors, we the living both inherit and remake a world troubled by devastating collective violence. As states, factions, and patterns of warfare continue to transform themselves, studying their trajectories in the past offers hope for understanding the present.

References

Allen, M. W. 1994. Warfare and Economic Power in Simple Chiefdoms: The Development of Fortified Villages and Polities in Mid-Hawke's Bay, New Zealand. Unpublished Ph.D. dissertation, Department of Anthropology, University of California, Los Angeles.

———. 1996. Pathways to Economic Power in Maori Chiefdoms: Ecology and Warfare in Prehistoric Hawke's Bay. *Research in Economic Anthropology* (17):171–225.

———. 2003. Hillforts and the Cycling of Maori Chiefdoms: Do Good Fences Make Good Neighbors? Manuscript on file, Department of Geography and Anthropology, California State Polytechnic University, Pomona, Pomona, CA.

Ames, K. M. 2001. Slaves, Chiefs and Labour on the Northern Northwest Coast (North America). *World Archaeology* 33(1):1–17.

Anderson, D. G. 1994. *The Savannah River Chiefdoms: Political Change in the Late Prehistoric Southeast*. Tuscaloosa: University of Alabama Press.

Barfield, T. J. 1994. The Devil's Horsemen: Steppe Nomadic Warfare in Historical Perspective. In *Studying War: Anthropological Perspectives*, edited by S. P. Reyna and R. E. Downs, 157–182. Langhorne, PA: Gordon and Breach.

Blitz, J. H. 1988. Adoption of the Bow in Prehistoric North America. *North American Archaeologist* 9(2):123–145.

Carman, J., and A. Harding (editors). 1999. *Ancient Warfare: Archaeological Perspectives*. Phoenix Mill, UK: Sutton Publishing Ltd.

Carneiro, R. L. 1970. A Theory of the Origin of the State. *Science* 169:733–738.

———. 1981. The Chiefdom: Precursor of the State. In *The Transition to Statehood in the New World*, edited by G. D. Jones and R. R. Kautz, 37–79. Cambridge: Cambridge University Press.

———. 1990. Chiefdom Level Warfare as Exemplified in Fiji and the Cauca Valley. In *The Anthropology of Warfare*, edited by J. Haas, 190–211. Cambridge: Cambridge University Press.

———. 1998. What Happened at the Flashpoint? Conjectures on Chiefdom Formation at the Very Moment of Conception. In *Chiefdoms and Chieftaincy in the Americas,* edited by E. M. Redmond, 18–42. Gainesville: University Press of Florida.

Chagnon, N. 1983. *Yanomamö: The Fierce People*. New York: Holt, Rinehart and Winston.

Cohen, R. 1984. Warfare and State Formation: Wars Make States and States Make Wars. In *Warfare, Culture, and Environment*, edited by R. B. Ferguson, 329–358. Orlando: Academic Press.

Conrad, G., and A. Demarest. 1984. *Religion and Empire: The Dynamics of Aztec and Inca Expansionism*. Cambridge: Cambridge University Press.

Demarest, A., M. Mansky, C. Wolley, D. van Tuerenhout, T. Inomata, J. Palka, and J. Escobedo. 1997. Classic Maya Defensive Systems and Warfare in the Petexbatun Region: Archaeological Evidence and Interpretations. *Ancient Mesoamerica* 8:229–254.

Dickson, D. B. 1981. The Yanomamö of the Mississippi Valley? Some Reflections on

Larson (1972), Gibson (1974), and Mississippian Period Warfare in the Southeastern United States. *American Antiquity* 46(4):909–916.

Durham, W. 1976. Resources, Competition, and Human Aggression, Pt. 1: A Review of Primitive War. *The Quarterly Review of Biology* (51):385–415.

Earle, T. 1997. *How Chiefs Come to Power: The Political Economy in Prehistory*. Stanford: Stanford University Press.

Ember, C. R., and M. Ember. 1992. Resource Unpredictability, Mistrust, and War: A Cross-Cultural Study. *Journal of Conflict Resolution* 36(2):242–262.

Feil, D. K. 1987. *The Evolution of Highland Papua New Guinea Societies*. Cambridge: Cambridge University Press.

Ferguson, R. B. 1984. Introduction: Studying War. In *Warfare, Culture, and Environment*, edited by R. B. Ferguson, 1–81. Orlando: Academic Press.

———. 1990. Explaining War. In *The Anthropology of Warfare*, edited by J. Haas, 26–55. Cambridge: Cambridge University Press.

———. 1999. A Paradigm for the Study of War and Society. In *War and Society in the Ancient and Medieval Worlds*, edited by K. Raaflaub and N. Rosenstein, 389–437. Cambridge, MA: Center for Hellenic Studies, Harvard University.

———. 2001. Materialist, Cultural, and Biological Theories on Why Yanomami Make War. *Anthropological Theory* 1(1):99–116.

Ferguson, R. B., and N. L. Whitehead (editors). 1992. *War in the Tribal Zone: Expanding States and Indigenous Warfare*. Santa Fe, NM: School of American Research Press.

Ferril, A. 1985. *The Origins of War: From the Stone Age to Alexander the Great*. London: Thames and Hudson.

Garlan, Y. 1975. *War in the Ancient World: A Social History*. London: Chatto and Windus.

Gat, A. 1999. The Pattern of Fighting in Simple, Small-scale, Prestate Societies. *Journal of Anthropological Research* 55(4):563–584.

———. 2000. The Human Motivational Complex: Evolutionary Theory and the Causes of Hunter-Gatherer Fighting, Part I: Primary Somatic and Reproductive Causes. *Anthropological Quarterly* 73(1):20–34.

Goldberg, N. J., and F. J. Findlow. 1984. A Quantitative Analysis of Roman Military Operations in Britain, *circa* 43 to 238. In *Warfare, Culture, and Environment*, edited by R. B. Ferguson, 359–385. Orlando: Academic Press.

Haas, J. 1987. The Exercise of Power in Early Andean State Development. In *The Origins and Development of the Andean State*, edited by J. Haas, S. Pozorski, and T. Pozorski, 31–35. Cambridge: Cambridge University Press.

———. 1990. Warfare and the Evolution of Tribal Polities in the Prehistoric Southwest. In *The Anthropology of Warfare*, edited by J. Haas, 171–189. Cambridge: Cambridge University Press.

———. 1992. *The Evolution of the Prehistoric State*. New York: Columbia University Press.

———. 1999. The Origins of War and Ethnic Violence. In *Ancient Warfare: Archaeological Perspectives*, edited by J. Carman and A. Harding, 11–24. Phoenix Mill, UK: Sutton Publishing Ltd.

———. 2001. Warfare and the Evolution of Culture. In *Archaeology at the Millennium*, edited by G. M. Feinman and T. D. Price, 329–350. New York: Kluwer Academic Publishers.

Hallpike, C. R. 1977. *Bloodshed and Vengeance in the Papuan Mountains*. Oxford: Clarendon Press.

Handel, M. I. 2001. *Masters of War: Classical Strategic Thought*. London: Frank Cass.

Hanson, V. D. 1989. *The Western Way of War: Infantry Battle in Classical Greece*. New York: Knopf.

———. 2001. *Carnage and Culture: Landmark Battles in the Rise of Western Power*. New York: Doubleday.

Hayden, B. 1995. Pathways to Power: Principles for Creating Socioeconomic Inequalities. In *Foundations of Social Inequality*, edited by T. D. Price and G. M. Feinman, 15–86. New York: Plenum Press.

Johnson, A. W., and T. Earle. 2000. *The Evolution of Human Societies: From Foraging Group to Agrarian State*. 2nd ed. Stanford: Stanford University Press.

Jones, T. L., G. M. Brown, L. M. Raab, J. L. McVickar, W. G. Spaulding, D. J. Kennett, A. York, and P. L. Walker. 1999. Environmental Imperatives Reconsidered: Demographic Crises in Western North America During the Medieval Climatic Anomaly. *Current Anthropology* 40(2):137–170.

Kang, B. W. 2000. A Reconsideration of Population Pressure and Warfare: A Protohistoric Korean Case. *Current Anthropology* 41(5):873–881.

Keegan, J. 1993. *A History of Warfare*. New York: Knopf.

Keeley, L. H. 1996. *War Before Civilization*. New York: Oxford University Press.

Kelly, R. 2000. *Warless Societies and the Origin of War*. Ann Arbor, MI: University of Michigan Press.

Kern, P. B. 1999. *Ancient Siege Warfare*. Bloomington, IN: Indiana University Press.

Kirch, P. V. 1984. *The Evolution of the Polynesian Chiefdoms*. Cambridge: Cambridge University Press.

Kracke, W. 1978. *Force and Persuasion: Leadership in an Amazonian Society*. Chicago: University of Chicago Press.

Lambert, P. M. 1997. Patterns of Violence in Prehistoric Hunter-Gatherer Societies of Coastal Southern California. In *Troubled Times: Violence and Warfare in the Past*, edited by D. L. Martin and D. W. Frayer, 77–110. Amsterdam: Overseas Publishers Association.

———. 2002. The Archaeology of War: A North American Perspective. *Journal of Archaeological Research* 10(3):207–241.

LeBlanc, S. A. 1999. *Prehistoric Warfare in the American Southwest*. Salt Lake City: University of Utah Press.

Lynn, J. A. 2003. *Battle: A History of Combat and Culture*. Boulder, CO: Westview.

McNeill, W. H. 1982. *The Pursuit of Power: Technology, Armed Force, and Society Since A.D. 1000*. Chicago: University of Chicago Press.

Mann, M. 1986. *The Sources of Social Power*. Cambridge: Cambridge University Press.

Marcus, J., and K. V. Flannery. 1996. *Zapotec Civilization: How Urban Society Evolved in Mexico's Oaxaca Valley*. London: Thames and Hudson.

Martin, D. L., and D. W. Frayer (editors). 1997. *Troubled Times: Violence and Warfare in the Past*. Amsterdam: Overseas Publishers Association.

Milner, G. E. 1999. Warfare in Prehistoric and Early Historic Eastern North America. *Journal of Archaeological Research* 7(2):105–151.

Nolan, P. D. 2003. Toward an Ecological-Evolutionary Theory of the Incidence of Warfare in Preindustrial Societies. *Sociological Theory* 21(1):18–30.

O'Connell, R. 1995. *Ride of the Second Horseman: The Birth and Death of War*. New York: Oxford University Press.

Osgood, R., S. Monks, and J. Toms. 2000. *Bronze Age Warfare*. Phoenix Mill, UK: Sutton Publishing Ltd.

Otterbein, K. 1970. *The Evolution of War.* New Haven: HRAF Press.

———. 1994. Why the Iroquois Won: An Analysis of Iroquois Military Tactics. In *Feuding and Warfare: Selected Works of Keith F. Otterbein*, edited by K. Otterbein, 1–8. Amsterdam: Gordon and Breach.

———. 2004. *How War Began*. College Station: Texas A&M University Anthropology Series.

Raaflaub, K., and N. Rosenstein. 1999. *War and Society in the Ancient and Medieval Worlds*. Cambridge, MA: Center for Hellenic Studies, Harvard University.

Redmond, E. A. 1994a. External Warfare and the Internal Politics of Northern South American Tribes and Chiefdoms. In *Factional Competition and Political Development in the New World*, edited by E. M. Brumfiel and J. W. Fox, 44–54. Cambridge: Cambridge University Press.

———.1994b. *Tribal and Chiefly Warfare in South America*. Ann Arbor, MI: Museum of Anthropology, University of Michigan.

Reyna, S. P. 1994. A Mode of Domination Approach to Organized Violence. In *Studying War: Anthropological Perspectives*, edited by P. Reyna and R. E. Downs, 29–65. Langhorne, PA: Gordon and Breach.

Rice, G. E., and S. A. LeBlanc (editors). 2001. *Deadly Landscapes: Case Studies in Prehistoric Southwestern Warfare*. Salt Lake City: University of Utah Press.

Robarchek, C. 1990. Motivations and Material Causes: On the Explanation of Conflict and War. In *The Anthropology of Warfare*, edited by J. Haas, 56–76. Cambridge: Cambridge University Press.

Robarchek, C., and C. Robarchek. 1998. *Waorani: The Contexts of Violence and War*. Orlando: Harcourt Brace.

Roper, M. 1969. A Survey of the Evidence for Intrahuman Killing in the Pleistocene. *Current Anthropology* 10:427–459.

———. 1975. Evidence of Warfare in the Near East from 10,000–4,300 B.C. In *War, Its Causes and Correlates*, edited by M. A. Nettleship, D. Givens, and A. Nettleship, 299–344. The Hague: Mouton.

Service, E. 1968. War and Our Contemporary Ancestors. In *War: The Anthropology of Armed Conflict and Aggression*, edited by M. Fried, M. Harris, and R. Murphy, 160–167. Garden City, NY: Natural History Press.

Sillitoe, P. 1978. Big Men and War in New Guinea. *Man* 13(2):252–271.

Toynbee, A. J. 1950. *War and Civilization*. New York: Oxford University Press.

Turney-High, H. H. 1971 [1949]. *Primitive War: Its Practice and Concepts*. Columbia, SC: University of South Carolina Press.

van Creveld, M. 1991a. *Technology and War: From 2000 B.C. to the Present*. London: Brassey's.

———. 1991b. *The Transformation of War*. New York: Free Press.

Vayda, A. P. 1960. *Maori Warfare*. Wellington, New Zealand: A. H. and A. P. Reed.

———. 1976. *War in Ecological Perspective*. New York: Plenum.

Vencl, S. 1999. Stone Age Warfare. In *Ancient Warfare: Archaeological Perspectives*, edited by J. Carman and A. Harding, 57–72. Phoenix Mill, UK: Sutton Publishing Ltd.

Walker, P. L. 2001. A Bioarchaeological Perspective on the History of Violence. *Annual Review of Anthropology* 30:573–596.

Webster, D. 1975. Warfare and the Evolution of the State: A Reconsideration. *American Antiquity* 40:464–470.

———. 1998. Warfare and Status Rivalry: Lowland Maya and Polynesian Comparisons. In *Archaic States*, edited by G. M. Feinman and J. Marcus, 311–351. Santa Fe, NM: School of American Research Press.

———. 2000. The Not So Peaceful Civilization: A Review of Maya War. *Journal of World Prehistory* 14(1):65–119.

Wilcox, D. R., and J. Haas. 1994. The Scream of the Butterfly: Competition and Conflict in the Prehistoric Southwest. In *Themes in Southwestern Prehistory*, edited by G. J. Gumerman, 211–238. Santa Fe, NM: School of American Research Press.

Wilcox, D. R., G. Robertson Jr., and J. S. Wood. 2001. Antecedents to Perry Mesa: Early Pueblo III Defensive Refuge Systems in West-Central Arizona. In *Deadly Landscapes: Case Studies in Prehistoric Southwestern Warfare*, edited by G. E. Rice and S. A. LeBlanc, 109–140. Salt Lake City: University of Utah Press.

Wolf, E. R. 1987. Cycles of Violence: The Anthropology of War and Peace. In *Waymarks: The Notre Dame Inaugural Lectures in Anthropology*, edited by K. Moore, 127–150. Notre Dame, IN: University of Notre Dame.

Wrangham, R. 1999. Evolution of Coalitionary Killing. *Yearbook of Physical Anthropology* 42:1–30.

Wrangham, R., and D. Peterson. 1996. *Demonic Males: Apes and the Origins of Human Violence*. Boston: Houghton Mifflin.

I

Warfare in Middle Range Societies

2

The Dimensions of War

Conflict and Culture Change in Central Arizona

JULIE SOLOMETO

Recent efforts to identify war in the archaeological record have demonstrated the prevalence of conflict throughout prehistory (Carman and Harding 1999; Keeley 1996; Lambert 2002; Martin and Frayer 1997). In the American Southwest, these efforts have made it possible to recognize temporal and spatial patterns in the incidence of war over an approximately 1,600-year period (LeBlanc 1999; Lekson 2002; Rice and LeBlanc 2001). The Southwest thus provides an ideal setting to address long-standing anthropological questions concerning war, including the circumstances that promote war or peace, the conditions that permit the spread of war, and the effects of war on processes of culture change. This latter issue is a subject of ongoing debate among Southwest archaeologists. The correlation of periods of widespread violence with episodes of aggregation, abandonment, and migration in the Southwest suggests that conflict played a role in these much-studied social transformations. As more researchers recognize this correlation they have begun "factoring warfare into . . . equations" of culture change (Wilcox and Haas 1994:237). Nevertheless, many recent models of population reorganization in the Southwest either explicitly reject war's influence or omit it from consideration entirely, creating a sharp rift between those who view war as an important explanatory variable and those with persistent doubts that conflict is a key factor in processes of culture change. This chapter seeks to contribute to the resolution of this debate by explicit examination of the relationship between the conduct and consequences of war in both ethnographic and archaeological contexts.

The continued reluctance of Southwest archaeologists to acknowledge war as a force of culture change can be traced to multiple sources. One difficulty is an inability or unwillingness to reconcile conflict in the past with the dominant explanatory framework in Southwest archaeology, which emphasizes the integrative potential of Southwestern social relations and religious practice. However, mechanisms of social integration and conflict need not be seen as contradictory (Haas 1990; McGuire 1986; Plog and Solometo 1997). The potential for conflict to integrate groups and to define identities at multiple social scales is demonstrated by numerous ethnographic studies (Levine 1999; Turton 1979).

Another major obstacle to war's acceptance as an explanatory variable, by no means unique to Southwesternists, is continued confusion about the conduct and consequences of conflict in non-centralized societies. Despite ethnological and archaeological arguments to the contrary, many Southwest archaeologists continue to view *all* war among non-centralized groups as limited in scale, fatalities, and impact. For these archaeologists, the result of this kind of conflict—often characterized as "just raiding"—is minor inconvenience, with little effect on human groups when compared to the powerful pull of integrative social institutions and religions. Given these perceptions of conflict in non-centralized societies, recent claims for a Southwest prehistory dominated by highly organized fighting forces, large-scale battles, and far-reaching social and demographic consequences (LeBlanc 1999; Turner and Turner 1999; Wilcox 1993; Wilcox et al. 2001a) have fallen on deaf ears. Clearly, explanations of culture change in the ancient Southwest cannot accommodate these contrasting viewpoints (McGuire 2002).

If explanatory consensus about the role of war in culture change is to be built in the Southwest and in other areas of the world, the conduct and effects of war in non-centralized societies must be explicitly studied. I contend that much of the dissension about the role of war in the past stems not just from widespread underestimation of the effects of conflict, but from an underappreciation of the immense variability of war in non-centralized societies. Lawrence Keeley's *War Before Civilization* has done much to counter the former problem, so I focus here on exploring the latter. The rich ethnography of "tribal" conflict reveals that war among these societies can take many forms, from short-lived, small-scale feuding to enduring long-distance and large-scale hostilities, as well as a host of other behaviors. These different forms of conflict can have distinctively different effects on the distribution and composition of social groups. The complexity apparent in ethnographic cases of war—including the variety of war's conduct and the wide range of possible outcomes—is likely to characterize the past as well. Therefore, archaeologists must attempt to distinguish among different forms of past conflict.

In this chapter I use ethnographic evidence to explore the range of variability of war among non-centralized societies. I characterize the conduct of war along a number of variables or dimensions and produce a model of non-centralized conflict that describes a relationship between several dimensions of war. Ethnographic data are also used to explore the relationship between the conduct and consequences of conflict. The archaeological implications of the ethnographic study are explored, and the final portion of the chapter demonstrates how the conduct of war—and its possible effects—can be identified in the archaeological record using a case study from the American Southwest.

War in Non-Centralized Societies

The anthropological study of war provides ample data to explore war's variability. I confine my discussion here to war among non-centralized societies, societies in which decision-making is largely by consensus and people are compelled to fight not by force but by personal and community-wide sentiment. Although some anthropologists still object to the application of the term "war" to conflict among non-centralized societies, I retain it here on the basis of current definitions of war (Ferguson 1984; Kelly 2000) and anthropological usage over the past 60 years (Otterbein 1999). Because continued confusion about the definition of war results in dissension and confusion about its presence in prehistory, it is worthwhile to fully explore war's most salient features. R. Brian Ferguson (1984) and Raymond Kelly (2000) provide particularly comprehensive definitions of war.

Ferguson (1984:5) succinctly defines war as "organized, purposeful group action, directed against another group involving the actual or potential application of lethal force." War is "organized" and "purposeful" in that it is premeditated and planned by the community or its warriors. In Kelly's (2000:4) words, the deaths that may result from war are not incidental or unexpected, but "are envisioned in advance" and are considered "morally appropriate and justified by circumstances or prior events." War also is a form of "action," but the action involved in war is not just combat itself. War is, in fact, "a period of armed hostility" (Meggitt 1977:10), with groups in a state of opposition to each other. This period of opposition may involve actual engagements (warfare proper), but also involves a state of readiness to fight and defend. Actual combat may be limited in its distribution, while mobilization of people and resources and other preparations for war are more widespread (Ferguson 1984). It is therefore likely, as others have noted (Haas 1990; Wilcox and Haas 1994), that evidence for mobilization for war will be more common in the archaeological record than evidence for violence and destruction. We can thus expect to see more indirect evidence of war, in the form of defensive settlement patterns and site plans, than the burned sites and unburied bodies that constitute direct evidence.

In some cases, the "lethal force" of Ferguson's definition includes not just the employment of weapons to kill, but also the intentional destruction or theft of resources, such as the burning of stored foods, fields, and homes (Keeley 1996; Kelly 2000). Groups reliant on stored foods and one annual growing season, such as those living in the northern Southwest, are particularly vulnerable to resource destruction; unlike many hunting-gathering populations and tropical horticulturalists who are able to quickly recoup losses of food, agriculturalists reliant on one annual harvest likely face starvation if their stored resources are destroyed or stolen (Raymond Kelly, personal communication 2002). Minimally, such tactics force victims to disperse, either to seek the economic support of relatives or to pursue more extensive subsistence strategies (such as foraging and hunting), in either instance resulting in the dissolution of the group (Keeley 1996; Wiessner and Tumu 1998:121).

Finally, perhaps the most important aspect of Ferguson's and other definitions of war is that it is a social activity carried out by *groups* against other groups. War thus excludes interpersonal violence, as well as actions explicitly carried out against individuals, such as capital punishment. The principle of "social substitution," defined by Kelly (2000), is at the root of the group nature of war. The logic of social substitution is that an injury to an individual (anywhere from petty theft to a homicide) constitutes an injury to that victim's entire group, demanding a group response. If peaceful means cannot be reached to redress the injury, retribution need not be carried out against the perpetrator but can be directed at *any member* of the perpetrator's group; the killing of any group member thus *substitutes* for the murder of the offender, despite the fact that the substitute is innocent or possibly even unaware of the initial offense. War thus includes most behaviors described as feuding or "blood vengeance"—the measured exchange of retaliatory deaths between groups—and tactics such as ambushes and murderous raids, as well as more familiar practices such as large-scale raids and arranged battles. It is the social context of conflict, not the size of warring parties, that determines the presence of war; if their actions are socially sanctioned, even small raiding parties seeking to ambush people away from their homes are conducting war. Given that war is waged only by groups, it is important for archaeologists to recognize that evidence of violent death alone (such as skeletal evidence of fatal injuries) is insufficient archaeological evidence for war; for war to be present, we must prove that groups were acting together to defend or attack.

The definition of war employed here encompasses a wide range of behaviors, from localized feuding to large-scale, long-distance hostilities between different cultural groups. It also includes war waged for a variety of reasons, from economic necessity to ideological mandate. This variability is evident in ethnographic comparisons of warring societies and can also be found within individual societies. Thus, groups that engage in conflicts with neighbors over access to resources or other common intergroup offenses (homicide, theft, wife abduction, etc.) may also pursue trophies or prestige in large-scale engagements with distant peoples. The consequences of these different patterns of conflict differ greatly and thus have varying effects on processes of culture change. If archaeologists are to understand the effect of war on culture change, they must first be able to distinguish among these different patterns in the conduct of war. In the following, I identify critical variables in the conduct of war that allow characterization of conflict in both the ethnographic and archaeological records.

Characterizing Conflict: Ethnographic Data on the Dimensions of War

Several characteristics or "dimensions" of war capture the variability of conflict in non-centralized societies. These dimensions include the *social distance* between groups, the size of participating social groups (*social scale*), the *tactics* employed and the instrumental *goals*, the *frequency* and *predictability* of engagements, and *duration* of war.[1] Ethnographic evidence, presented here, suggests that these dimensions strongly co-vary, producing distinct patterns of conflict. For example, among many non-centralized societies, discrete patterns of conflict are distinguished by participants on the basis of the degree of relatedness or social distance between opposing groups (Boehm 1984; Meggitt 1977; Otterbein 1968; Turton 1979). The Jívaro, for instance, recognize two different types of armed conflict: *ayambruamáktinyu*, or lengthy blood feuds waged against other Jívaro, and *meséta*, "wars of extermination" between neighboring tribes "that speak differently" (Harner 1972:183; Karsten 1923:16). Jívaro feuding is conducted by small war parties who are careful to kill only one person per engagement; deaths are limited, intended only to "settle the score" of the feud.[2] In contrast, the tactics of Jívaro intertribal wars aim to maximize casualties (and trophy heads); in these engagements large parties of up to 500 Jívaro surround and attack an enemy settlement at night or at dawn, killing and beheading men, women, and children. For the Jívaro, as for many other non-centralized societies, the identity of the enemy determines the choice of a specific course of conflict. Each dimension of war—and their interrelationships—is examined below.

Social Distance

Social distance refers to the strength of the relationship between groups engaged in hostilities. The strength of the relationship between groups can be measured by the number and nature of kinship ties (for example, are the links with affines or agnates?), perceptions of group or ethnic identity, the existence of trade partnerships, and the presence of a variety of other beneficial relationships, such as ceremonial cooperation and age-set membership.

Strong relationships between communities may prevent or limit war to brief episodes. Although close ties may also lead to frequent friction, groups linked by kinship, exchange, or ritual cooperation are less likely to risk endangering the lives of relatives, profitable trade relationships, and ritual efficacy by pursuing lengthy and deadly disputes (Koch 1974; Meggitt 1977). The intervention of community leaders and exhortations of other group members also put pressure on aggressors to resolve their quarrels quickly. With increasing social distance, shared interests decline; among unrelated groups there are fewer reasons to refrain from fighting and few mechanisms to achieve peace.

Social Scale

The social scale of war refers to the size of groups engaged in conflict. Warfare is waged at multiple scales, from small parties of two to three warriors to groups numbering in the hundreds. Some tactics require small war parties, as when secrecy and stealth are of primary importance, but in defensive and major offensive efforts, sheer numbers ultimately determine success. Groups at war are therefore anxious to recruit enough individuals to match or outnumber the size of enemy war parties. Recruitment involves increasing one's group size (be it a clan, village, or locality) and/or building alliances, that is, increasing the number of equivalent groups willing to cooperate in a given offensive or defensive effort.

The network of social ties between combatants directly influences the social scale of war by affecting the ease of alliance building. When close ties link multiple communities, potential allies may find their loyalties divided between combatants. If taking a side is likely to lead to armed conflict against affines or trade partners, third-party communities may choose to opt out of the conflict, preventing the escalation of hostilities beyond those most directly affected by the quarrel. In contrast, warriors with no binding relations to consider are more likely to join with allies in attacks on enemy groups, creating larger war parties capable of more devastating damage.

Tactics and Goals

The tactics of war include the size of the war party, the weapons employed, the size and location of the target of violent action (entire settlements, isolated work parties, travelers), and whether the engagement is to be a surprise attack or, more rarely, an arranged battle. After the war party engages the enemy, additional tactical choices include the nature of the injuries delivered (from slight wounding to fatal blows), the treatment of non-combatants, captives, the wounded, and the extent of property damage and looting.

Social distance also has a significant influence on the tactics employed in combat. For instance, warriors from related communities are more likely to avoid the deaths of non-combatants and to minimize property destruction than socially distant enemies. Shared ceremonial precepts may result in strict taboos on the destruction of an enemy's religious structures and sacred objects. Warring groups with any semblance of fellow feeling are also more likely to refrain from taking trophies (heads, scalps) or to commit other disrespectful acts. These forces of restraint are absent or tenuous among socially distant groups, however. At one extreme, the complete absence of ties between conflicting groups may result in the dehumanization of enemies, in effect sanctioning the maximization of deaths and property destruction and the most brutal treatment of noncombatants and captives (Bohannan 1958; Karsten 1923; Meggitt 1977).[3] These opponents are not immune from mutilation, "the ultimate expression of contempt for the victim's group" (Meggitt 1977:24). Thus cannibalism among the Jalé of western New Guinea is limited to socially and physically distant opponents, and prohibited against "people whose face is known" (Koch 1974:80). Similarly, mutilation can also signal the end of a social relationship, as occurred when the act of cutting an ear from a corpse terminated an alliance of Kofyar villages in northern Nigeria (Netting 1974).

The effects of social distance on war tactics are exemplified by Meggitt's (1977) analysis of the "modes of fighting" among the Mae Enga of highland New Guinea. Table 2.1 provides the tactics associated with the most common modes of Mae fighting: within clans, between clans of the same phratry, and between clans of different phratries. The bonds of "brotherhood" within clans and phratries demand conventions of battle that limit the extent of damage and death, such as providing fair warning of attack, avoidance of female casualties, and minimal property destruction and theft. In contrast, complete destruction of houses, resources, and ceremonial sites, as well as mutilation of enemy dead and attacks on women and children, are characteristic of conflict between phratries where "brotherhood" is absent.

The goals of conflict heavily influence the tactics of war. Ethnographers have documented numerous goals of war in tribal societies, including revenge, prestige, resource acquisition (including captives), territorial acquisition, and fulfillment of ideological objectives. War parties motivated by revenge or prestige are likely to pursue tactics resulting in a limited number of enemy fatalities to repay past offenses or to meet the requirements of a display of bravery. Groups exchanging single deaths are often content to ambush individuals away from their settlements, rather than mount attacks on residences. Warfare aimed at removing or annihilating enemies—whether due to social differences, failed

Table 2.1. Tactics Practiced by Mae Enga Warriors of Different Social Distance

Tactics	Intraclan	Intraphratry	Interphratry
Warning of engagement?	probable	yes	no
Type of engagement	battles	daytime battle	surprise raids, invasions
Non-combatants targeted	no	no	sometimes
Wounded targeted	no	no	yes
Mutilation	no	no	yes
Property damage	minimal	yes, but no sacred sites	yes, maximized, sacred sites targeted

Source: Data from Meggitt (1977).

partnerships, or territorial ambitions—entails large war parties, surprise attacks, deadly weapons, resource and settlement destruction, and the deaths of non-combatants.

Frequency and Predictability

The frequency of warfare refers to how often attacks occur or can be expected. The frequency of attacks among non-centralized societies is highly variable. During periods of hostility between neighboring groups, attacks can occur often, even on a monthly or weekly basis (Heider 1997), until some means are found to resolve the conflict. Attacks motivated by ethnic-based enmities or trophy-taking can occur from many times a year to a few times a generation; these types of conflict often appear to be dependent on ritual requirements and the cooperation of allies (Redmond 1994; Zegwaard 1959).

The frequency of actual or expected attacks significantly influences defensive strategies. When war is extremely infrequent and unpredictable, groups rarely expend the effort to defend themselves. The many economic and social disadvantages of preparing for attack—building new or fortifying old sites, relocating away from the threat, aggregating in larger groups, and establishing full-time watch posts—may outweigh the risk. In contrast, if warfare occurs on a regular, predictable basis, groups are strongly motivated to pursue defensive strategies. An analysis of data from Otterbein's (1970) cross-cultural study of war demonstrates a direct relationship between the frequency of engagements and one major defensive strategy—the use of fortified settlements—for "band" and "tribal" societies. Table 2.2 demonstrates that the majority of groups in the sample subject to "continual" war, that is one in which warfare occurs one or more times per year, fortify their settlements, while *all* groups that experience conflict less than once a year *do not* invest in fortifications. Clearly human groups are not willing to expend the effort to fortify in the absence of a regular

Table 2.2. Fortification and the Frequency of War for Non-centralized Societies

Frequency of War	Settlements are Fortified	Settlements not Fortified
Continual (n=15)	Albanians Amba[a] Fox Jívaro Motilon Orokaiva Santa Ana Tiv **Ila** *Comox*	Kurtatchi Timbira **Tibetans** **Yukagir** *Plains Cree*
Not continual (n=12)		Gisu Ingassana Mundurucu Trumai **Nandi** **Toda** *Abipon* *Andamanese* *Copper Eskimo* *Dorobo* *Tehuelche* *Tiwi*

Note: Hunter-gatherers in italics, pastoralists in bold, and intensive and shifting agriculturalists in regular type.

a. Otterbein (1970) codes the Amba as having unfortified residences. However, prior to the ethnographic present—when the threat of warfare was continual—"all of the inhabitants of the village lived together in one compact group of houses" and they "fought from a fortified position" (Winter 1956:85, 170).

threat. The societies in Otterbein's sample with continual engagements that do not fortify can be attributed to highly mobile settlement and subsistence strategies (Tibetans, Yukagir, Plains Cree), habitation of unfortified but defensible locations (Tibetans, Kurtatchi) and in the case of the Timbira, possible changes in settlement following pacification.[4] The strength of the relationship between warfare frequency and fortification has important implications for prehistorians. To Allen's (this volume) consideration of the social and economic effects of fortification, we must add the simple observation that archaeological evidence for defensive constructions indicates a high frequency of armed conflict in the past.

Strong ties between social groups also affect a group's ability to anticipate and mobilize for war. Groups aware of an imminent threat have the opportunity to prepare for armed conflict, whether by relocating beyond the range of their enemies, constructing defenses, manning watchtowers, or enlisting the help of allies. Even short notice of an attack can turn a potentially overwhelming defeat into a standoff or possibly a rout of the attacking war party. Groups that routinely fight their neighbors or other socially close foes, such as the Mae Enga of highland New Guinea, are intimately aware of the threat of attack, because they know who is "land-hungry" and who is seeking to redress a recent offense (Meggitt 1977). Although the generally hostile intentions of a neighboring group may be recognized, the exact timing of their attack and the participation of allies may not be known. Strict secrecy therefore surrounds all Mae Enga war preparations so that resident kinsmen and allies of the intended enemies do not divulge the date of the planned engagement.

In contrast, groups with little or no contact lack "informants" and may be utterly unaware of an enemy's intentions. In particular, long-distance attacks motivated by internal cultural objectives, rather than specific offenses known to both parties, are more likely to achieve complete surprise. Predictable raids by distant people are a possible exception to this pattern; these attacks are predictable because of their association with key points of cycles of exchange or ritual or with specific parts of the annual cycle (for example, after the harvest) (Rappaport 1968; Titiev 1944). In these instances, attacks may be anticipated within a discrete time frame, but advance word of the engagement is not guaranteed. For example, the residents of the Rio Grande Pueblos came to expect visits of Comanche during their trade fairs and after the harvest, visits that were as likely to involve raiding as peaceful exchange (Ford 1972).

Duration

Duration refers to both the length of individual engagements and the duration of hostilities between groups, which may involve a long series of engagements. The duration of individual attacks among tribal societies is generally brief. Although some exceptions exist (Keener 1999), tribal war parties typically lack the supply capability to finance lengthy sieges (Turney-High 1949). If the availability of food resources does not discourage this tactic, sieges can be prevented by investment in systems of communication with allies (through smoke signals, log drums, runners, and the like) who can come to the aid of besieged groups.

The duration of intergroup hostilities, or the period in which groups are in a "state of war," may be affected by a number of factors that either remove motivation or quickly decide a conflict, such as the relaxation of economic pressures or a decisive defeat. Duration is also strongly influenced by the social distance between combatants. As discussed above, close social ties provide both the motivations and the means to reconcile. Lengthy conflicts endanger relationships between relatives and trade partners, and over time mutual social and economic interests are likely to override reasons for continued conflict, building consensus to bring hostilities to an end. Related groups also are more likely to agree about the individuals and procedures that enable peacemaking, such as deference to the judgment of a respected leader, rituals formalizing the end of conflict, or shared ideas about the content and timing of compensatory payments. Conflict among related groups is thus likely to result in the cyclical alternation of war and peace (Kelly 2000:119).

In contrast, distant groups lacking the motives and mechanisms to end conflict are likely to remain in a continual state of war. Different languages, religious systems, and ideals preclude working toward peace, while the absence of mutual interests means that the decision to fight will always be driven by internal considerations. Marked cultural differences (particularly notable when trophy-taking is common) are instrumental in the perpetuation of war among many non-centralized societies, such as the Mohave and Pima (Stewart 1947), the Shuarä and Achuarä Jívaro (Bennett Ross 1984), and the tribes of the Great Plains (Biolosi 1984).

Summary and Archaeological Implications

The dimensions of war are important tools in understanding conflict in non-centralized societies. Identifying the states of these variables permits the characterization of war in single instances, while distinguishing it from the many other forms of conflict waged by human groups. Ethnographic evidence from a number of societies suggests that the dimensions of war often co-vary. In sum, the social distance, or strength of ties between groups, significantly influences how war is waged. Notions of shared identity and the desire to resume beneficial social, economic, and ceremonial relationships limit the deadliness and duration of fighting. Fierce tactics and various forms of disrespect for enemy bodies and property are reserved for socially distant enemies; with no beneficial relationships to resume, enmities between socially distant groups are more likely to persist. Finally, the frequency of engagements is not directly related to social distance, although it has a significant influence on defensive strategies, compelling groups to change settlement configurations and patterns of residence.

For any given episode of prehistoric conflict, a variety of classes of archaeological evidence can be used to identify the dimensions of war (Solometo 2004). For instance, based on the ethnographic evidence presented above, the presence of ancient fortifications indicates that warfare occurred frequently, on at least an annual basis. Estimates of the length of use of fortifications provide a measure of the duration of hostilities. The social scale of conflict can be determined by estimating the size of groups occupying defensive sites and by looking for either intervisible fortifications or site clustering, suggesting the cooperation of allies. Offensive and defensive tactics can be identified with a number of classes of evidence. If the weapons of war themselves are not found, they can be determined based on skeletal evidence, architectural evidence (for instance, the presence of bastions), or possibly in artistic representations. The extent and nature of site destruction indicates the intent of attackers (Were habitations destroyed? Were ritual structures destroyed? Were stored foods destroyed?), and skeletal evidence can do much to identify the tactics employed by aggressors (Were women and children targeted? Were bodies mutilated or trophies taken?). If the social distance between combatants is not readily apparent from the archaeological evidence, then we can use the states of the other variables and the interrelationships of war's dimensions evident in the ethnographic record to predict social distance. Clearly a pattern of minimal fortifications and the violent death of only males indicates an entirely different form of warfare (with entirely different consequences) than conflict resulting in the aggregation of population, long-term investment in defensive construction, and the deaths of non-combatants. I consider the consequences of different forms of warfare in the following section.

The Consequences of War in Non-centralized Societies

Just as war may be waged in different ways, it also has a wide range of consequences for groups engaged in combat. The potential outcomes of conflict range from demographic change and economic hardship to the alteration of social, political, and religious organizations. For the sake of brevity, I focus here on a subset of the demographic, economic, and social effects of war. Ethnographic data concerning the effects of war on political and religious institutions are scarce, suggesting that ideologies and leadership institutions change slowly, at a pace not observable in synchronic studies. I consider the effects of war and the impact of conflict on ideology in greater detail elsewhere (Solometo 2004).

The most immediate effects of war—on the organization and distribution of human groups and their resources—are heavily dependent on the tactics, frequency, and duration of conflict. Before discussing the influence of these variables, it must be stressed that much of war's effects will be dependent not only on how and how often engagements are fought, but on the relative *success* of engagements. While evenly matched opponents can fight lengthy wars of attrition with neither side gaining significant ground, sustained advantages in technology, numbers, and tactics can quickly produce a string of victories that radically alter the social landscape. Victories due to significant technological mismatches, though important in colonial contexts, were probably rare in prehistory; without evidence to the contrary, it can generally be assumed that combatant groups had relatively equal knowledge of and access to the implements of war. Numerical advantages were perhaps more likely in the past, particularly among culturally dissimilar opponents with different organizational capabilities and methods of war party recruitment. Finally, marked differences in the tactics employed on the battlefield can likewise produce a military imbalance. Whereas some tactics such as battle formations and defensive measures may change rapidly in response to experience, other tactical factors such as the nature of battlefield leadership and the treatment of non-combatants may change more slowly, thereby conferring advantages to the more "efficient" aggressors. Because some tactical choices are culturally determined, power imbalances are most likely to be present between groups who already possess marked cultural dissimilarities.

All other things considered equal, differences in the tactics of war can have markedly different demographic consequences. For instance, the practice of resource destruction may indirectly lead to increased mortality as defeated groups struggle to feed themselves. Perhaps the most important tactical choice affecting the overall demographic health of a warring population (or more properly, its opponents) is the treatment of non-combatant women and children. Female deaths, and the deaths of female children, have a greater impact on the overall population than do the deaths of males. As Kelly (2000:134) points out, female mortality results in reduced births and possibly the deaths of dependent children, the effect being a decrease in "the size of the population for two generations, because fewer females attain reproductive age fifteen years after the event."[5] In contrast, warfare resulting primarily in the deaths of males need not cause population decline, provided that surviving women are able to remarry and bear children. Widow remarriage and polygyny, where practiced, ensures that the reproductive potential of women is only temporarily affected (Kelly 2000:134; Meggitt 1977:111; Wiessner and Tumu 1998:117). These differences explain how the Mae Enga, reluctant to kill women even in the most lethal fighting, were able to increase in population at an estimated 1.25 percent per year prior to 1980 despite frequent warfare and a high (at least 25 percent) proportion of male combat deaths (Meggitt 1977:110; Wiessner and Tumu 1998:116). Early warning of attack and separate female dwellings also allowed Mae Enga women to escape direct assaults. In contrast, the nearby Etoro declined by as much as 50 percent between 1935 and 1975 due to repeated defeats by their Kaluli neighbors. Kaluli strategies of attacking work parties and burning entire longhouses occupied by men, women, and children caused significant female fatalities, which, in combination with other factors, resulted in population collapse (Kelly 1977).

A high frequency of conflict exacerbates mortality due to war, but even without significant victories, frequent conflict can alter the distribution of populations on the landscape while creating considerable economic stress. Fundamentally, frequent conflict necessitates a defensive response. As was demonstrated with Otterbein's cross-cultural data, frequent engagements typically result in the construction of fortifications. Similarly, steps to create "safety in numbers," such as aggregation in larger settlements and settlement clustering, are common responses to frequent conflict (Ferguson 1989; Rice 2001). Whether it is substantial investment in fortifications, a shortage of defensible locations, or fear of going it alone, defensive responses to a hostile environment often result in higher local population densities and significantly reduced mobility.

For populations reliant on extensive strategies of resource procurement, these defensive measures can have significant economic and social costs. Groups forced to aggregate face all the problems caused by elevated population densities: dwindling and less productive resources, increased distances to fields and hunting grounds, and mounting social tensions. Increased sedentism only exacerbates the negative effects of aggregation. Groups that choose to reduce fortification costs by retreating to defensible locations such as hilltops, islands, and cliffs also may have to leave productive gardens and fields behind. At the same time, defensive precautions increase the distance to resources and the risks of travel rise dramatically, limiting subsistence pursuits as well as interaction with relatives and trading partners (Bennett Ross 1984; Netting 1974). Although the effects of defensive settlement strategies can be costly to the economic and social well-being of communities, aggregation and increased sedentism in some circumstances may lead to innovations in resource production and to the adoption of novel solutions—such as centralized leadership—to emergent social problems (Adams 1996; Brandt 1994; McGuire and Saitta 1996; Plog and Upham 1983; Wilcox and Haas 1994).

Certainly the duration of war determines the overall impact of population loss and social and economic hardships. When a period of peace follows a brief war, groups have the chance to recover from their losses. With protracted conflict, however, there are far fewer opportunities to relocate closer to resources and to fill storerooms, and insufficient time to recruit new group members. Thus lengthy disputes lead to more dire consequences for warring populations.

In summary, lengthy conflicts with frequent engagements have the greatest economic and social impacts on human populations. Regular attacks necessitate a range of defensive measures—including the adoption of fortifications and defensive settlement strategies—that alter the distribution of people on the landscape and pose potential economic difficulties, such as local environmental degradation, increased travel time to resources, and reduced opportunities for trade. Lengthy conflicts result in the accumulation of economic hardships and in increased sedentism, which does little to alleviate pressure on resources. Tactics that include the targeting of non-combatants have the potential to produce population decline, particularly if one side is disproportionately successful and the pace of attacks exceeds the rate of demographic recovery. Because lengthy conflicts and the targeting of non-combatant women and children are most common between socially distant groups, war between distant foes is most likely to result in these negative consequences. These insights from the ethnographic record of warring societies provide archaeologists with the means to predict the impact of ancient conflict. By simply identifying the state of the dimensions of war for a given archaeological case and by considering the effect of defensive strategies and population loss, inferences about the impact of past conflict on human groups can be made and tested with additional evidence.

The Case Study: Conflict in East-Central Arizona

The remainder of this chapter presents a case study of prehistoric conflict from east-central Arizona. This case study demonstrates how archaeological data can be used to reconstruct the dimensions of past warfare, allowing us to examine the conduct of war and infer the consequences of conflict in terms of the ethnographic model developed above. A general consideration of the reconstruction of war's conduct from archaeological evidence is treated at length elsewhere (Solometo 2004). Explicit attention to variability in the conduct of war and to the ethnographic record is vital in order to make reasoned inferences about the effects of violent conflict on past cultures. Archaeological explanations that treat war as a unitary phenomenon (for instance, as "just raiding" or as "total war") too often reduce the consequences of war to simplistic formulations of either "minor inconvenience" or total cultural destruction. It is hoped that this model, and the case study provided here, will provide a more balanced approach to the problem of interpreting the effects of war on culture change.

The long history of research and ample recent attention to war in the American Southwest provide abundant data with which to explore the transmission and spread of conflict, the relationship between environmental stress and war, and the interdependence of war and ideology. These complex problems, which involve the examination of warfare at a large spatial scale, will one day be solved, but they will be solved only after we examine the conduct and consequences of conflict at the local level. The case study presented here examines one part of the northern Southwest that played a role in the transformation of the Southwestern cultural landscape. The study area, defined by two tributaries to the Little Colorado River (Figure 2.1), is of particular interest due to its placement at the juncture of the Mogollon, Ancestral Pueblo, and Sinagua culture areas. Always on the margins, and thus with high potential for conflict, the area is at the western limit of the distribution of Great Kivas (large ceremonial structures) tied to the Chacoan system (Herr 2001) and includes East Clear Creek, a substantial physical boundary believed to coincide with the eastern limit of Sinagua and western limit of Mogollon populations (Wilson 1969). Finally, the abandonment of the study area in the late thirteenth and early fourteenth centuries coincides with the development of aggregated villages and village clusters in neighboring areas, and the adoption of village plans with defensive advantages (LeBlanc 1999). If defensive concerns motivated these settlement changes, they may have had their roots in the warfare waged in the study area.

In the sections that follow, the defensive strategies pursued by the inhabitants of the study area between approximately A.D. 850 and A.D. 1250 are characterized in terms of five of the key dimensions of war—social scale, frequency, predictability, duration, and tactics—permitting a number of inferences about the goals of conflict and the social distance between warring groups. Although a variety of different types of archaeological evidence (skeletal evidence, weaponry, and iconography) can be used to characterize war, available data in the study area consist of defensive architecture, settlement patterns, and evidence of site destruction. These data indicate major changes in the conduct of conflict that must be considered as central factors in regional processes of population reorganization.

The Environmental and Cultural Setting

The study area includes the middle reaches of Chevelon Canyon, East Clear Creek, and Jacks Canyon, ephemeral drainages traversing the Mogollon Plateau from the Mogollon Rim northeastward to the Little Colorado River (Figure 2.1). These deeply entrenched canyons, as well as occasional lava-capped mesas and buttes, are the only features that punctuate the largely flat terrain of this portion of Arizona. Canyons and buttes provided the most favorable locations for defensive settlements so the area's residents fortified the handful of small prominences and "islands" created by the canyon's tight meanders or goosenecks. Similar, contemporaneous fortified sites are found to the east in the vicinity of Heber, Arizona and westward to Walnut Canyon, east of Flagstaff (Figure 2.1). Defensive sites are also reported at the summits of steep sided buttes in the Hopi Buttes region north of the Little Colorado (Gumerman and Skinner 1968). Prehistoric populations in the study area favored the middle reaches of the Chevelon and East Clear Creek drainages, from approximately

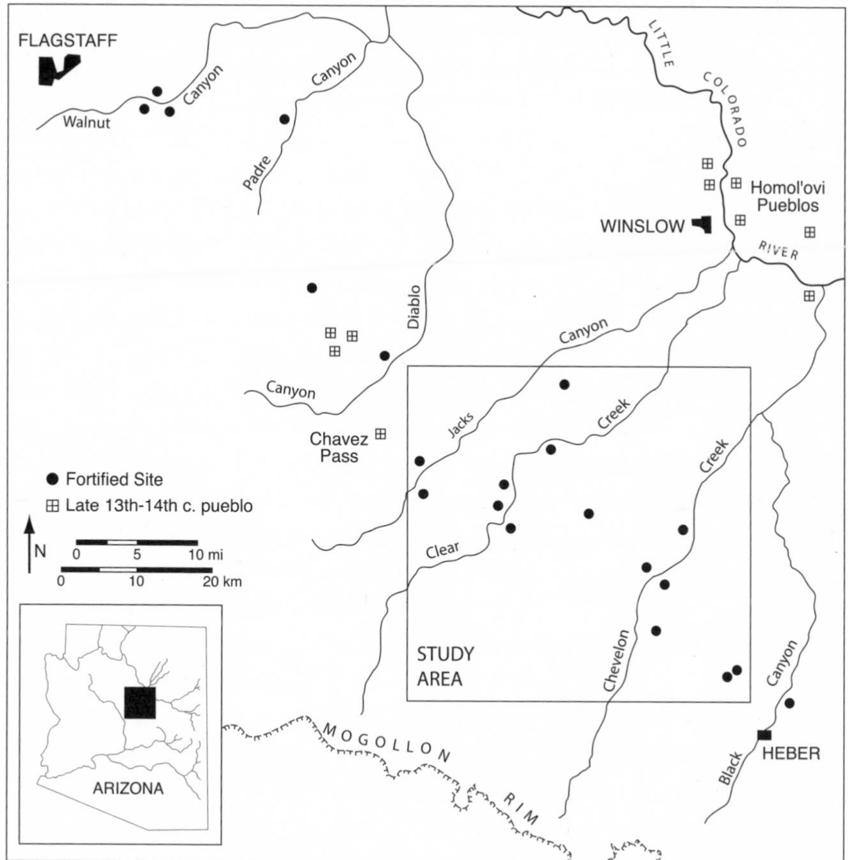

Figure 2.1. Distribution of fortified sites in east-central Arizona. Study area and large villages occupied in the late thirteenth and fourteenth centuries also shown.

1,830 m to 2,070 m (6,000–6,800 feet), where the wild resources of the pinyon-juniper woodland were found and where agriculturalists could strike a balance between length of growing season and precipitation (Plog 1978).

Early habitation of the area focused on the canyons, where game and other wild resources were abundant and cultigens were grown on small, sandy terraces in the canyon bottoms (Barton et al. 1999; Briuer 1977; Huckell et al. 1999). As the region's population grew and became increasingly dependent on agricultural products, they moved away from the canyons, exchanging flood-prone patches of canyon bottom and the shallow limestone-derived soils on canyon rims for secondary and tertiary drainages (also ephemeral) in the pinyon-juniper zone (Barton et al. 1999; Plog 1978; Riel-Salvatore 2000). The distribution of agricultural features such as terracing systems and check dams indicates a strong preference for shallow drainage bottoms and comparatively deep, sandstone-derived soils (Acker 1972; Gregory 1991; Plog 1978). The occupation of fortifications in the late twelfth and thirteenth centuries A.D. necessitated a return to the canyons, distant from these favored agricultural locations. The availability of defensible locations also appears to have driven populations slightly north of the densest areas of prior occupation, from thick pinyon-juniper forest to warmer, drier open woodland.

A small number of pit house villages, modest multiroom pueblos, and ceremonial facilities including large "communal" structures and Great Kivas are present in the study area, but the dominant site type from A.D. 900 to A.D. 1300 is a loose cluster of single masonry rooms (Plog 1974, 1978). The majority of these sites consist of two to three structures, although larger aggregates of rooms and small room blocks are occasionally found, particularly after A.D. 1050. The largest sites in the region, containing 15–30 freestanding and contiguous rooms, are either fortified or have ready access to fortifications. Sites with only one structure (and well-developed middens) are also common throughout the area's history, suggesting that entire households often resided in single rooms; given population/floor area constants appropriate to Southwestern contexts (Brown 1987; Hantman 1983; Hill 1970), the comparatively large size of Chevelon/East Clear Creek structures (16–35 m^2) suggests a figure of three to seven people per room.

The region's small sites are also found at low densities when compared with other portions of the Southwest. In the densely settled areas of the pinyon-juniper zone, population density increased through time, rising from an estimated 0.1 habitation sites/km^2 and 0.3 rooms/km^2 in the earliest phase of occupation to a maximum of three habitation sites/km^2 and 9.3 rooms/km^2 in the thirteenth century (Plog 1974). These figures, corrected for typical site-occupation spans (Hantman 1983) and assuming the minimum three people per room, suggest population densities of from less than one to a maximum of 14 people per square kilometer.

The study area was largely abandoned by the early fourteenth century, although it continued to be used by northern groups for resource gathering and ceremonial purposes into the twentieth century. The area's residents most likely joined clusters of large (200–1,000/room), growing pueblos at Chavez Pass and the Homol'ovi area, which were occupied from the mid-1200s into the late fourteenth and early fifteenth centuries (Figure 2.1). While the abandonment of the East Clear Creek area appears to have coincided with the abandonment of the area's fortified sites, in the Chevelon drainage occupation continued away from canyon locations for several more decades of unfortified settlement (Plog 1974, 1978).

Defensive Strategies

Early Period

The earliest archaeologically visible defensive strategies in the study region include large rectangular enclosures and enclosed plaza pueblos (Figures 2.2 and 2.3). Located away from the canyons, these rare sites are found in densely occupied portions of the pinyon-juniper woodland. Although these locations afforded few topographic advantages, enclosed site plans offered greater security than the characteristic aggregates of dispersed rooms.

Rectangular enclosures and enclosed plaza pueblos differ in their basic features. Rectangular enclosures are constructed of stone foundations and jacal superstructures, bounding an area of from 400 m² to 800 m². The entryways are small and inhibit direct access to the enclosure interior. Rectangular enclosures lack evidence for interior masonry rooms, although jacal structures may have been present at one site. Thus far, only two rectangular enclosures (CS 470, CS 689) have been found and are located within 800 m of each other in the midst of

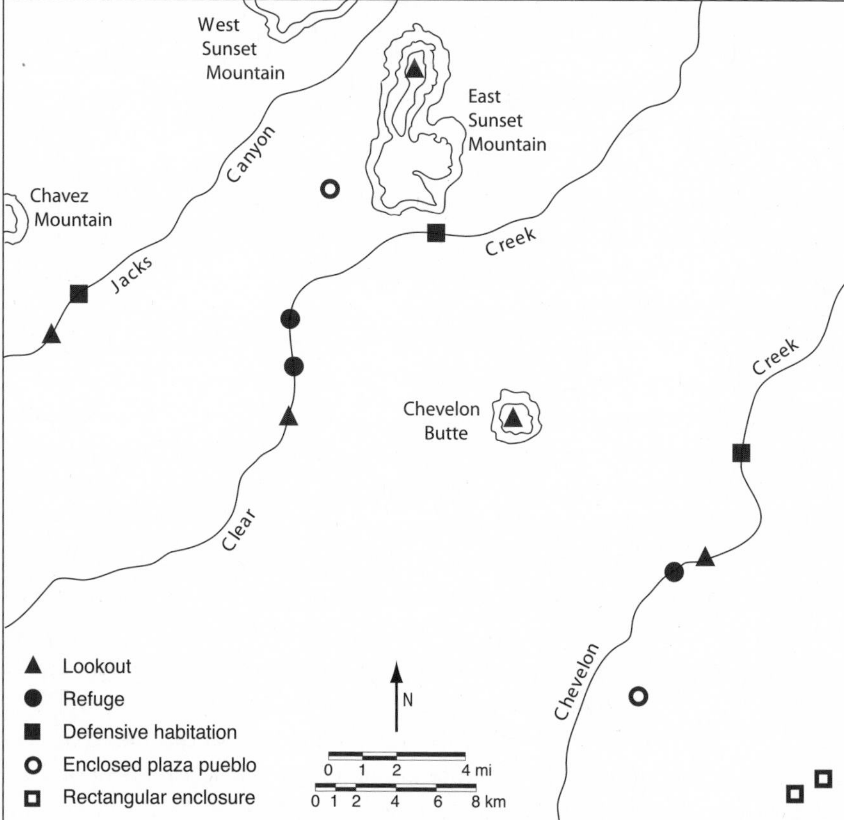

Figure 2.2. Distribution of fortified sites in the study area by site type.

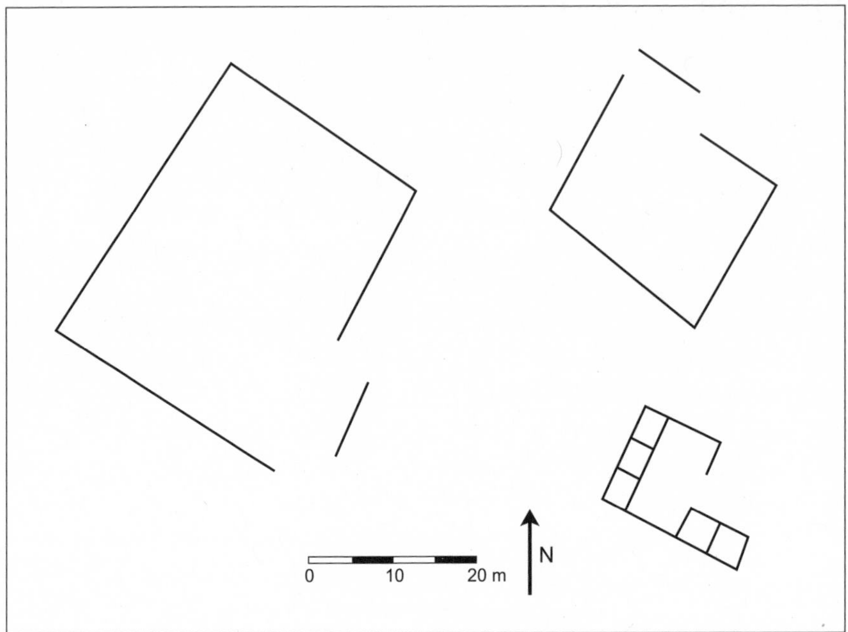

Figure 2.3. Early period fortified sites: rectangular enclosures (left, CS 470; right, CS 689) and an enclosed plaza pueblo (CS 2185).

a densely settled area of pit houses, small masonry habitations, and Great Kivas. Ceramic data indicate that both sites were in use for a lengthy period beginning as early as A.D. 850, with more intensive occupation in the late A.D. 1000s and early A.D. 1100s (Plog 1980).

In contrast to rectangular enclosures, enclosed plaza pueblos were clearly residential. The layout of rooms and walls limit access to these structures. Although later examples in the northern Southwest often contain two or more stories, enclosed plaza pueblos in the study region consist of a single masonry story. Enclosed plaza pueblos are also rare, with just a handful present in the study area and only one (CS 2185, Casa Perdida) thoroughly investigated. This site includes a few outlying rooms, access to multiple agricultural areas (including both extensive terracing and check dams), and proximity to a number of smaller sites. Casa Perdida was inhabited for a shorter period than the rectangular enclosures sometime in the early A.D. 1100s. The number of rooms at Casa Perdida and other known enclosed plaza pueblos indicate that the sites were occupied by larger co-resident groups than the unfortified settlements of the preceding century, with as many as four to five households present. The development of these kinds of temporary aggregates is a common response to conflict among groups living in small, dispersed settlements. Among the Jívaro, for example, aggregates of five to six households constructed fortified settlements for protection during short periods of intensified hostilities, dispersing after the relaxation of threat (Redmond 1994).

Both rectangular enclosures and enclosed plaza pueblos are rare, despite a number of large-scale, intensive surveys in the region. Although few examples exist, the longevity of rectangular enclosures suggests that they were nonetheless effective. Other populations in the area likely met the threat of conflict with less archaeologically visible defensive strategies, such as temporary aggregation in unfortified settlements, dispersal, or investment in advance warning systems. Future research aimed at determining the frequency of burning at small habitation sites and testing for the presence of wooden palisades may support the existing evidence for warfare in the early period.

Despite their apparent success into the early 1100s, patterns of dispersed settlement and early period fortifications were not adequate to withstand the violence of the mid-1100s. By A.D. 1150, most small sites were abandoned and both of the excavated early fortifications—one enclosed plaza pueblo and one rectangular enclosure—were destroyed by fire (Plog et al. 2001).

Late Period

From A.D. 1150 to A.D. 1250, topography became a crucial part of defensive settlement strategies. Sacrificing proximity to productive agricultural land, fortified settlements were built in highly defensible locations on canyon rims, in canyon walls, and on small promontories atop volcanic buttes and mesas in the open woodland zone. All fortified sites in this period supplemented topographic obstacles with architectural features to enclose habitation areas and control site access (White 1976).

The most typical site setting is a detached or semi-detached spur formed by a tight canyon meander or gooseneck (see Figures 2.6 and 2.7). Access to the site via the often broken, narrow bedrock "bridge" connecting the spur to the adjacent canyon rim is typically blocked by a substantial wall from 1.5 m to 2 m high (hereafter referred to as a "blocking" wall). The remaining margins of the landform are either bounded by sheer cliff faces or by enclosing walls built atop gentler slopes and breaks in cliff faces. Other defensive features include defended entries (Figure 2.6) and carefully constructed holes that pierce defensive walls; the function of these holes is uncertain, but they may have provided views of points of access, as well as protected positions from which to fire projectiles. Alternatively, they may have held supports for platforms for archers, although it is not clear why such supports would have to pierce the entire width of the wall, nor does it explain the fact that several of these potential loopholes are angled to "cover" points of comparatively easy access.

Figure 2.4. Aerial view of a lookout, NA 9033. A blocking wall and additional enclosing walls (not visible in photograph) inhibit access to the landform (photograph by Chris White).

In addition to the presence of possible loopholes, the placement of blocking walls strongly suggests the use of the bow and arrow as an element of defense. As seen in Figures 2.6 and 2.7, blocking walls are typically located not at the narrowest part of bedrock bridges (which would minimize construction costs), but 30–40 m back, placing attackers in optimal bow range at precisely the point where topography would force them to approach in single or double file (Raymond Kelly, personal communication 2000). Attack from these narrow bedrock bridges would have entailed significant casualties.

Although they share inaccessible topographic settings and defensive constructions, late period fortifications also differ in a number of respects, including the size of the enclosed area, the number and size of rooms, artifact density, and the nature of surrounding settlement (Table 2.3). These differences form the basis of a working typology of four fortified site types. Late period fortifications can be classed as lookouts, proximate refuges, isolated refuges, and defensive habitations (Solometo 2001, 2004). This typology is applicable to the other canyon-oriented sites in central Arizona and similar typologies have been proposed for fortified sites south of the study area below the Mogollon Rim (Spoerl and Gumerman 1984; Wilcox et al. 1999).

Lookouts consist of a single, small enclosure defined by enclosing and/or blocking walls (Figure 2.4). Lookouts lack internal rooms and have few artifacts.

Table 2.3. Fortified Site Types in the Late Period, A.D. 1150–1250

Site Type	Number of Rooms	Artifact Density	Surrounding Settlement	Inferred Function
Lookouts	0	none to very low	variable: absent, low density, or communicates with another fortified site	communication/ lookout, occasional refuge?
Refuge, proximate	5–8	low	large, long-lived communities of 20–30 rooms and communal structures	refuge for large community
Refuge, isolated	2 rooms, 1 communal structure, 1 storage room	moderate	absent	refuge for dispersed population
Defensive habitation	15–25, possible communal structures	high	variable: low density or large (25 room) community	year-round habitation or repeated use

Their name and function are inferred from the absence of evidence of habitation, as well as their commanding views of vast areas or of other canyon-oriented fortifications.[6] Lookouts would have provided effective places for a scout or group of scouts to spot raiding forces and signal or dispatch runners to allied settlements. The amount of effort expended in the construction and preparation of these sites suggests that they may also have been intended for use as short-term refuges, or that the individuals manning them expected to be attacked. Finally, lookouts may have been effective places from which to launch counterattacks on war parties assaulting neighboring fortified settlements. The division of forces mitigates the disadvantages of fortifications, which become traps once breached. The threat of being outflanked is a major deterrent to potential attackers—particularly when on foot in unfamiliar territory—and likely prevented many offensive forays or at least necessitated a hasty attack and hastier retreat (Fadiman 1982; Karsten 1923; Meggitt 1977).

Proximate refuges, in contrast to lookouts, show signs of at least short-term habitation and are found next to large, dispersed, and long-lived communities of 20–30 rooms. Proximate refuges occupy discrete and particularly inaccessible locations, such as rock shelters and small pinnacles, which restrict the extent of habitation. Storage facilities, also in easily defensible locations, are associated with these structures. Although too small to comfortably accommodate the resi-

Figure 2.5. A proximate refuge, NA 9032. Landform is approximately 40 m by 6 m (photograph by Chris White).

dents of the large communities for lengthy periods, refuges nonetheless contain from five to ten rooms, suggesting that they were used and occupied for longer than just the duration of individual attacks (in which case a single enclosure would seemingly be sufficient). The features of proximate refuges suggest that they provided extra security for both people and stored resources during brief periods of anticipated conflict. These sites may have been occupied during intervals when enemy groups were spotted in the area, or provided refuge to noncombatants during both offensive and defensive warfare.

NA 9032, a proximate refuge located on East Clear Creek, is shown in Figure 2.5. It is approximately 40 m by 6 m in size. Walls line the edges of the landform and define at least seven separate rooms on its summit. The remains of a granary are located on the terrace below the refuge walls. A loose cluster of 30 structures, including the largest community room known from the area, is 150 m away.

The isolated refuge category is represented by a single site in the project area (CS 58, Casa Blanca), located on Chevelon Creek (Figure 2.6). Like the proximate refuges, this site has a small number of rooms and a moderate density of artifacts. Unlike the proximate refuges, survey of the ten square kilometers (four square miles) surrounding the site failed to identify a large (or even a small) nearby community. It is unlikely, however, that only a small group of people occupied the site. Only a sizable resident population would have been able to

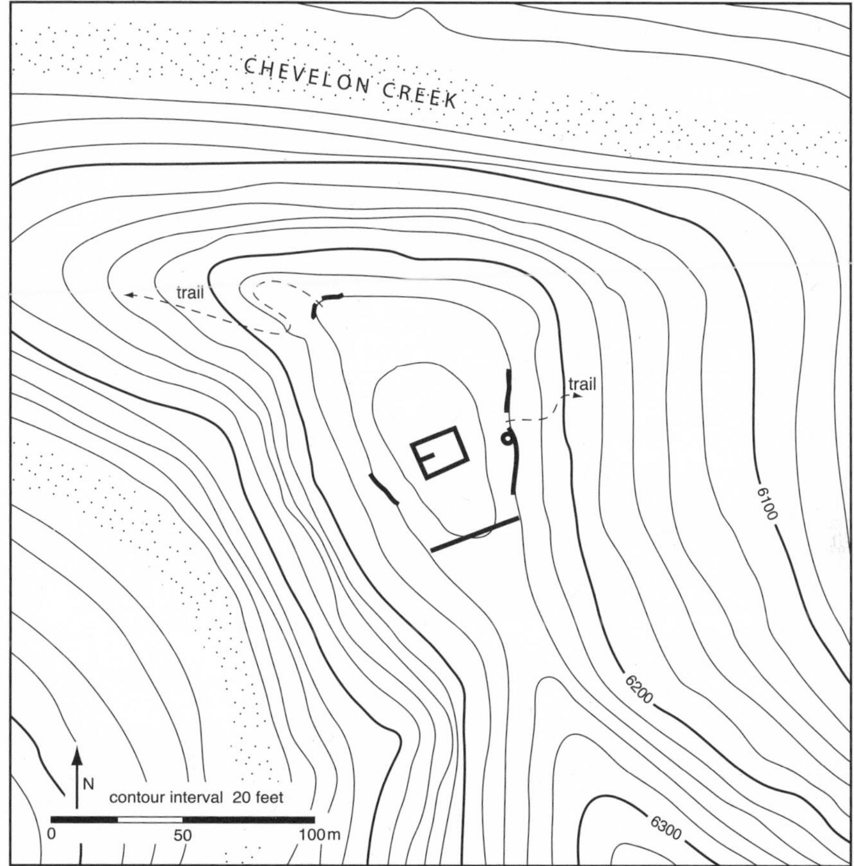

Figure 2.6. An isolated refuge, CS 58, Casa Blanca.

meet the considerable defensive requirements of this large site and its intervisible lookout. The refuge's primary structure, although relatively large, would not have accommodated many residents. The uncommon arrangement of sizable rooms and the scarcity of floor features in the primary structure suggest an unusual, possibly multipurpose, function for this building. Given the absence of convincing residential architecture, it is inferred that the site served only as a temporary refuge. More than a mile from permanent habitations, the refuge must have been used by groups with enough warning of attack to move families and necessary possessions within its walls.

Defensive habitations are located on large landforms, consist of from 15 to 25 rooms, and have dense artifact scatters (Figure 2.7). Single structures and contiguous units of two to five rooms are distributed throughout the defended area, preserving the dispersed layout of unfortified sites. The comparatively high density of artifacts on these sites suggests long-term, year-round use. Like proxi-

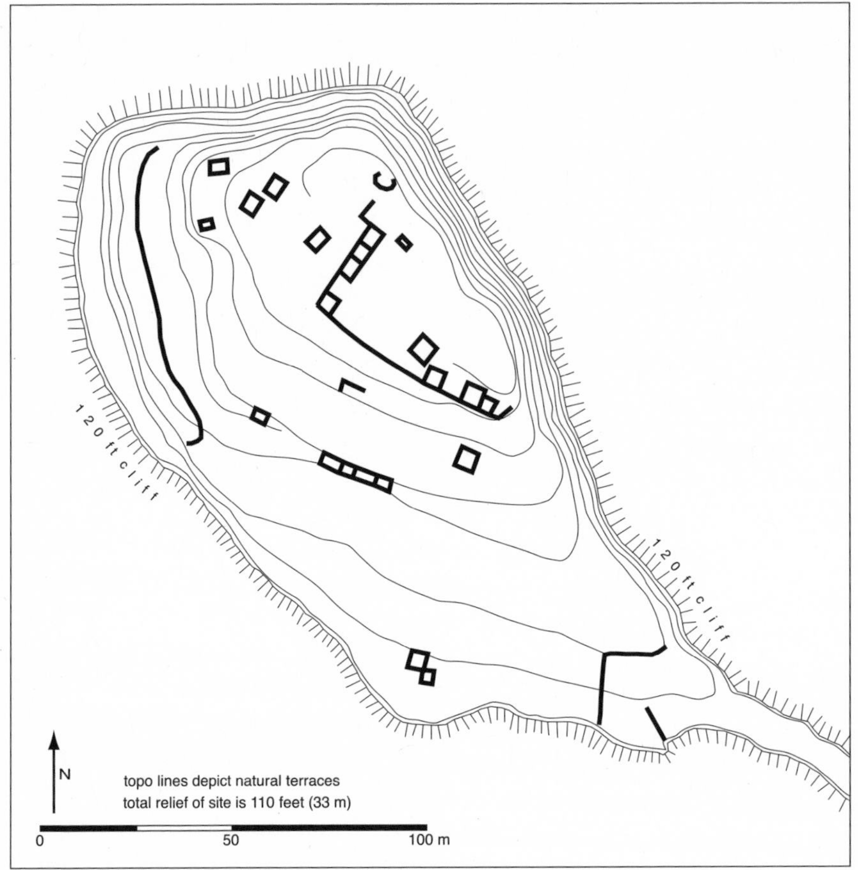

Figure 2.7. A defensive habitation, AZ P:1:9 (ASM).

mate refuges, use of defensive habitations indicates a long-term commitment to the defense of the community.

The considerable variability of fortifications in the study area is a result of multiple defensive strategies, from temporary aggregations of population in rectangular enclosures and the isolated refuge to relatively permanent communities of individuals committed to live within or close to fortifications. Movement to canyon locations at the outset of the late period also indicates a considerable shift in settlement strategy, an exchange of close proximity and ready access to productive agricultural land for the increased security of defensible landforms. The implications of these changes for the conduct and consequences of war in the study area are considered below.

Dimensions of War in East-Central Arizona

Identification of site types and settlement pattern data, in conjunction with the ethnographic model of conflict developed above, provide the means to characterize the conduct of war in the study area. Here I examine the social scale, frequency, and duration of war in the region, as well as the tactics employed in both the early and late periods. Table 2.4 summarizes the evidence for these dimensions of conflict and associated inferences about the conduct of war.

Social Scale

The size of sites and the nature of their defensive features provide estimates of the scale of groups engaged in conflict in the study area. Large-scale defensive cooperation was a characteristic response to conflict in both the early and late periods. The rectangular enclosures of the early period lack habitation features, but their large size and the comparatively high density of surrounding settlement suggest that they were designed for the protection of sizable groups, if only for

Table 2.4. Dimensions of War, Evidence, and Inference for Early and Late Period Fortified Sites in Study Area

Dimension	Evidence	Inference
Social scale	*early*: structure size, proximity to settlement (rect. enclosures), room counts (enclosed plaza)	*early*: unknown, but potentially large number of people in rectangular enclosures; multiple (4–5) households in enclosed plaza pueblo
	late: number of loopholes/defensive requirements, room counts	*late*: 20+ defenders, aggregation of 12 to 15 households (min.)
Frequency	*early*: use of fortifications *late*: use of fortifications, lookouts	*early and late*: continual war
Duration	*early*: use of rectangular enclosures, few early period fortifications *late*: long-term occupation of defensive habitations, proximate refuges	*early*: brief, infrequent episodes of conflict (alternating with peace) *late*: periods of peace rare or unpredictable
Tactics	*early*: burned sites *late*: burned sites, defendable or hidden storage	*early*: site destruction *late*: site destruction, resource destruction

brief intervals. If designed to serve residential needs for short periods, as many as 80–160 people could have fit within the walls of rectangular enclosures. A far larger number of occupants is possible if the sites were designed as strongholds used only during actual attacks. A much smaller group participated in early period efforts to construct habitable fortifications, but at approximately four to five households, groups living in enclosed plaza pueblos were nonetheless larger than the average residential unit in the study area.

Living within or close to fortifications is common in the late period, but the size of the co-resident group increases to a minimum of 12–15 households, nearly five times the size of the average Chevelon habitation site. Given the low population density and short distances between communities, it is likely that occupants of defensive habitations and refuges located on the same canyon were allies, providing valuable strategic assistance in defensive and offensive endeavors. The cooperation of closely related communities, common in the ethnographic record, therefore is likely in this period.

The number of people that occupied the isolated refuge is more difficult to assess. However, several lines of evidence support the inference that the isolated refuge was occupied by groups similar in size to those using other late period fortifications. First, the inclusion of a community room (100 m^2) and two larger-than-average rooms (with minimal floor features) in the primary structure suggests that this building was designed to accommodate large numbers of people for non-residential, non-domestic purposes. Further, defense of the site would require numbers greater than could be provided by even several households. Based on a Jívaro case study (Karsten 1923), the number of loopholes in the blocking wall at the isolated refuge can be taken as a measure of the number of people intended to defend it. Thus a total of 20 people would be required to defend this 35 m long, 2 m high, and 1 m thick wall. If 10 additional defenders were stationed at the two guarded entries and other enclosing walls on the site, a minimum group of 30 warriors would have been necessary to adequately protect the site. Assuming the refuge's occupants included families as well, the total site population may have been as large as 90–120 people.

These calculations further support the inference that the isolated refuge would have been used for relatively short periods. A large group would have been uncomfortable on this small landform and would have generated considerably greater quantities of artifacts had they lived there for an extended interval. Although uninterested in building masonry dwellings, the presence of contemporaneous, low-density artifact scatters in shallow rock shelters and open-air locations within 200–300 meters of the refuge suggests that the group using the site was instead content to occupy short-term, probably warm-season residences in the immediate vicinity of the fortifications.

Throughout the prehistory of the study area, populations combined for defense at scales greater than the average residential settlement. In the early period the inhabitants of small, dispersed sites constructed and used rectangular enclosures, structures that provided security for large numbers in the course of attacks or during brief episodes of conflict. The social ties that integrated these groups in times of war may have been forged in ritual interactions within Great Kivas, large structures used for communal ritual in several loci within the project area. The co-occurrence of a Great Kiva and a rectangular enclosure at a single site (CS 689) supports the notion that ceremonial partnerships translated to the coordination of defensive efforts.

The decision to combine for defense in permanent habitations did not come until the end of the early period, when at least a few groups of households chose to construct enclosed plaza pueblos. In the late period most fortified sites were built for year-round occupation (or access, in the case of proximate refuges) and accommodated large groups of people. As is true in many non-centralized societies, the need for defense drove people to aggregate above customary, "comfortable" levels. In addition to the co-resident group, defenders in the late period also are likely to have received support from nearby fortified communities on the same canyon. Distances between canyons may have been too great to permit cooperation once attacks were underway, but the residents of different canyons may have provided other kinds of support to each other, such as economic assistance and refuge to defeated groups.

Frequency, Predictability, and Duration

The analysis of cross-cultural data gathered by Otterbein, discussed above, indicates a direct relationship between the frequency of engagements and the presence of fortifications; investment in fortifications is undertaken by non-centralized societies only when attacks occur frequently, at least once a year. It is important to note that Otterbein documented the frequency of *actual* attacks on the political community or cultural unit, not the frequency of the *threat* of attack. Thus while there is no doubt that people build fortifications in anticipation of future conflict, they do so only after an offensive is launched on themselves or an allied group. The clear implication is that the presence of prehistoric fortifications demonstrates that warfare was frequent at some point in the past. Given their construction and labor costs, prehistoric investment in systems of advance warning and intersite communication, such as the construction of lookouts, appear also to be the result of episodes of frequent conflict. Although one might conclude that the construction of fortifications and lookouts was a response to a single attack (and threat of another), in the study area a lengthy interval of frequent violence is indicated by burned structures and long fortified site histories. Given that populations living in canyon-oriented sites sacrificed both their dispersed mode of settlement and access to agricultural land, their long-term commitment to life on the canyon rims suggests a constant threat.

Fortifications and lookouts indicate the frequency of past engagements or *warfare*, but give us few clues to the frequency of *wars* over a longer period. Likewise, the duration of individual wars is nearly impossible to assess given our coarse-grained chronologies. Using 50–100 year periods, archaeologists run the risk of confusing the material evidence of a lengthy war with annual engagements from that produced by a series of short, intense wars lasting on the order of weeks and months. Given these limitations, archaeologists are better able to estimate the total duration of time during which wars occurred, measured in decades and centuries. This dimension of conflict speaks more to long-term adaptations and pressures, modes of problem solving, and the ideological entrenchment of war than to the ability of warring groups to resolve their differences in single instances. Conflict was a factor in the lives of Chevelon/East Clear Creek populations for at least 400 years, from the construction of rectangular enclosures to the abandonment of canyon-oriented fortifications around A.D. 1250. The scarcity of early period fortifications suggests, however, that frequent warfare was less common in the interval from A.D. 850 to A.D. 1150 than during the late period, when larger numbers of people gathered in fortifications throughout east-central Arizona.

We can approach the question of war's duration from yet another angle. The fortified sites in the study area suggest two distinct kinds of defensive strategies. The groups using rectangular enclosures and the isolated refuge chose to inhabit these fortifications for brief periods only, returning to their homes after the danger of attack passed. While the construction and continued use of these sites indicates that engagements were frequent, their temporary occupation suggests that there were significant periods of the year when it was safe to live in unfortified settlements. In contrast, the strategy of the residents of enclosed plaza pueblos, proximate refuges, and defensive habitations was to live either within or immediately adjacent to fortifications, suggesting that the threat of conflict occupied much of the year, enough to discourage dispersal and (in the instance of the canyon-oriented sites) return to the area's most productive agricultural land.

A word must be added about the influence of the predictability of engagements on the design and use of the study area's fortifications. Because groups using the isolated refuge and rectangular enclosures had to travel for some distance (one mile or more) to reach them, some amount of advance warning was necessary for these sites to be effective adaptations to conflict. Those that chose to live within their fortifications were far less reliant on advance intelligence, however. It is possible that the occupants of enclosed plaza pueblos, proximate refuges, and defensive habitations chose to invest in permanent fortifications not only because the threat of engagements persisted throughout much of the year, but because attacks could not be reliably anticipated. If this was the case, a socially distant foe, whose actions and motives were unknown, is indicated.

The settlement data thus support two apparently contradictory interpretations of the duration and predictability of warfare during the year; although the isolated refuge and rectangular enclosures suggest brief, predictable hostilities, the enclosed plaza pueblos, proximate refuges, and defensive habitations indicate a response to lengthier intervals of conflict, and possibly a response to the threat of a socially distant foe. This contradiction can largely be explained by temporal factors. The apparent exceptions to this pattern, the early period enclosed plaza pueblos and late period isolated refuge, both appear to be borderline cases. The enclosed plaza pueblo was occupied during the latter end of the early period and may perhaps be seen as an initial (unsuccessful) attempt to incorporate residences and defensive construction. The isolated refuge, although definitely in use in the late period, also seems to have had earlier occupants. Ceramic frequencies indicate that the peak of this site's occupation was slightly earlier than those of the other late period fortifications and radiocarbon dates suggest even earlier use of the site. The temporary aggregation of populations at the rectangular enclosures and isolated refuge may represent a defensive strategy developed near the end of the early period when conflict was still brief and predictable.

Although at times indirect, evidence for the frequency, duration, and predictability of war in the study area suggests a transition from rare intervals of short-term, predictable warfare in the early period to as much as a hundred years of lengthy, unpredictable hostilities. Warfare in both early and late periods was at times frequent, occurring annually or more often, but intense conflict was less common and widespread in the early period. War likely alternated with long intervals of peace prior to A.D. 1100. War appeared to intensify sometime after A.D. 1100/1150 in the Chevelon/East Clear Creek area, resulting in a full-time commitment to defense.

Tactics and Goals

The tactics of war in the study area can be inferred from several classes of evidence. As discussed above, defensive tactics included early warning systems, the division of forces, and intercommunity cooperation. Fortification of residences, particularly in the late period, clearly suggests that offensive tactics included assaults directed at entire communities, rather than solely at individuals or work parties away from their homes. Evidence for site-wide burning at one enclosed plaza pueblo, one rectangular enclosure, and one defensive habitation sometime after the early A.D. 1100s supports this inference. Site-wide burning is common in the ethnographic record, where it is used to drive people from their homes, destroy their possessions, and increase the immediate difficulties of making a living in an already hostile social environment.

In the late period there is evidence that stored resources were increasingly a target of attack. Storage facilities were placed in defensible locations beside proximate refuges, hidden in canyon walls near defensive sites, and were occasionally burned. Attackers likely sought to destroy stored resources rather than capture them in the study area, given the lack of pack animals and the great difficulty associated with the transportation of large burdens under counterattack.[7] Destruction of stored goods would have had a devastating impact on the livelihood of small agricultural groups (Keeley 1996; Kelly 2000), and would have been particularly damaging for groups in the study area, a region characterized by a single short growing season each year. Ethnographic data suggest that groups in moderate climates experience only brief disruptions of their agricultural cycle after attacks targeting stored food resources (Raymond Kelly, personal communication 2002), whereas populations in the study area would probably be forced to rely on relatives or allies for extended periods. When stored resources aren't readily replaced, groups lacking the support of relatives face starvation; even those groups absorbed into other settlements would face the dissolution of their own communities and difficult conditions in new, ovecrowded settlements (Chagnon 1983; Haury 1958; Netting 1973).

Intentional resource destruction, like settlement destruction, indicates that one of the goals of war in the late period was the elimination of enemy groups. Ideological or political motives for late-period warfare seem more likely than direct economic goals, given the difficulty of resource acquisition and the poor quality of soils near the canyons. Paleo-environmental reconstructions support the conclusion that economic stress was not a major motivation for war. Tree-ring data show that the period from A.D. 1100 to A.D. 1250, when early period sites were burned and most canyon-oriented sites were founded and abandoned, was the most environmentally favorable interval in the region's history (Slatter 1979). The canyon-oriented fortified sites of east-central Arizona thus fail to support the direct relationship between environmental degradation and warfare proposed in the current Southwestern literature (Haas and Creamer 1996; LeBlanc 1999; Lekson 2002).

Change in Warfare, Culture Change

Understanding the dimensions of war is essential in order to reconstruct the changing conduct of prehistoric conflict in the Chevelon/East Clear Creek region from A.D. 850 to A.D. 1250. By defining the conduct of war in the past, it is possible to assess the potential outcomes of war in the study area, permitting a balanced consideration of the role of conflict in the changing social environment of east-central Arizona. The social distance between combatants, a dimension not immediately apparent from the archaeological evidence from Chevelon/East Clear Creek, can also be inferred based on comparison with a rich ethnographic dataset.

Defensive structures were present, but uncommon, during the early period of warfare from A.D. 850 to A.D. 1150. Groups in a portion of the study area responded to brief periods of conflict by leaving their small, dispersed habitations to aggregate in large rectangular enclosures. Although the threats were brief, the long use-life of rectangular enclosures suggests that warfare was a persistent problem during this three hundred year interval. Some temporary occupation of canyon locations is also possible during the early period. In the early decades of the A.D. 1100s, a few households chose to permanently combine for defense, living year-round in a few enclosed plaza pueblos in the study area. The bulk of early period settlement, however, consists of undefended locales lacking ready access to these unique defensive structures.

Given the rarity of hostilities, most groups in the early period chose not to fortify against attack. These groups may have counted on advance warning of their enemies' intentions so they could disperse, or relied on the cooperation of neighbors to meet advancing war parties outside settlements. Some form of advance warning also is indicated by the temporary use of rectangular enclosures. It is thus likely that early period war was waged by groups known to each other, groups that were linked by marriage or exchange yet also shared an extended history of conflict—involving actual or perceived injustices, insults, and interpersonal enmities—that could flare up on occasion. The presence of long-lived social ties between these opponents would result in the swift resolution of conflicts, matching the early period pattern of brief hostilities. Long intervals of peace meant ample recovery time for the area's population, minimizing the demographic and economic losses of war. The effects of early period conflict on settlement strategies also appear to have been minor; settlement location in this period appears to have been determined largely by access to the best agricultural land rather than by defensive factors. The necessity to combine for defense, even if sporadically, may have contributed significantly to the integration of groups sharing rectangular enclosures and Great Kivas. The possibility that these groups formed the basis of the aggregates of households living in late period fortifications must be considered.

The intensity of warfare appears to have increased significantly near the end of the early period, resulting in the construction of enclosed plaza pueblos, the most intense use of the rectangular enclosures, and the ultimate destruction of some early period defensive sites. Year-round occupation of enclosed-plaza pueblos also suggests that attacks may have become more frequent or unpredictable, necessitating constant vigilance. Movement to readily fortified locations along canyons and atop mesas in the mid-1100s confirms this change in the nature of conflict. Abandoning small, dispersed settlements and ready access to established fields, groups chose to aggregate in large villages of 15–30 rooms, five to ten times larger than the average site in the region. Construction of lookouts and the close spacing of some sites indicate complex systems of defense and intercommunity cooperation.

During the late period, attacks were frequent and anticipated throughout much of the year. Offensives were directed at settlements and their stored surpluses, but superior techniques of fortification and larger co-resident populations necessitated larger war parties, which would have tested the organizational abilities of attackers. Evidence for late period site destruction suggests that these organizational challenges were occasionally met, threatening communities with extinction. Distant from productive agricultural land and under constant threat of raids, the residents of fortified sites on the canyons also faced economic difficulties, making life in the region less attractive and perhaps untenable as stored surpluses dwindled, wild resources were depleted, and travel to trade with neighbors became increasingly dangerous. The conduct of war in the late period is suggestive of a socially distant enemy intent on driving away the residents of these sites. As discussed above, conflict in the late period is unlikely to have been caused by environmental stress or land shortage. Political or ideological motives are more likely, and a long-distance, ceremonially driven pattern of conflict cannot be ruled out. Evidence of scalping at Chavez Pass (Allen et al. 1985), a site founded shortly after the abandonment of the Chevelon/East Clear Creek canyon-oriented fortifications, suggests that trophy-taking may have been part of the region's war complex.

Later Developments

Ceramic and radiocarbon data strongly suggest that occupation of fortified sites in the Chevelon/East Clear Creek region ceased sometime in the mid-1200s. Available evidence indicates that the East Clear Creek drainage was abandoned at this time, while Chevelon populations left the canyons, but remained in the drainage until the early 1300s. Based on geographic proximity and similarities in plainware ceramics, the groups that left East Clear Creek most likely joined Chavez Pass and the other rapidly growing communities on Anderson Mesa, located approximately 10 miles to the west. In addition to poor local soils, the absence of farmable terraces in the canyon below the fortifications of East Clear Creek may have been responsible for economic failure and the decision to leave the area permanently. It is possible that the small patches of arable land at the bottom of Chevelon Canyon—favorites of the area's earliest agriculturalists—minimized the negative economic effects of late period hostilities, and thereby allowed Chevelon populations to remain in the area for an additional 50 years. In the latest phase of Chevelon occupation, the canyon is abandoned in favor of settlement strategies similar to those of the early period. Sites once again are located in the vicinity of sandstone-derived soils near smaller drainages and some early period sites are even reoccupied. Some concern for defense is indicated in the late A.D. 1200s, including a preference for locating communities on ridges and hilltops and building two-story structures, but these efforts pale in comparison to defensive strategies pursued in the canyons.

It is unclear at this point why the residents of the Chevelon drainage were able to return to more dispersed patterns of settlement. Their independence was likely risky as developments in the rapidly growing population centers at Anderson Mesa and at Homol'ovi, 30 miles north on the Little Colorado River, suggest that contemporaneous settlements were not only considerably larger, but were mobilized for war in the late thirteenth century. Both Chavez North, the earliest component of the ancestral Hopi town of Chavez Pass (*Nuvakwewtaqa*), and the earliest site in the Homol'ovi cluster (Homol'ovi IV) were built in the mid-1200s atop steep-sided hills (Adams 2002; Bernardini 2002). Several other villages established in the late 1200s were built on cliff edges, employed two-story construction and/or enclosed plaza plans, or (in one instance) were adjacent to canyon fortifications. Rapid population increase, continuing the trend of late period aggregation, occurred after A.D. 1250 in these areas, with villages growing from 20 rooms to as large as 200 rooms by A.D. 1300, and to as many as 700 rooms by A.D. 1350. So while communities 20–30 miles distant were growing rapidly in size, preparing for attack, and possibly recruiting warriors for defense (Bernardini 2002), groups in Chevelon were building small, vulnerable habitations. Understanding the relationship between the residents of these late sites and nearby village clusters will require further research. However, if alliances forged with groups at Homol'ovi and Anderson Mesa permitted the continued occupation of the Chevelon area, those alliances may have been short-lived. Occupation of the entire Chevelon drainage ceased by the early 1300s and abandonment of the area may have been precipitated by violence. Limited excavation at several late thirteenth- to early fourteenth-century sites suggests that a new kind of warfare was waged in this period, war that targeted religious structures and spared habitations. Understanding the dimensions of war in the decades prior to Chevelon's abandonment must await further fieldwork.

The Chevelon/East Clear Creek case study supports the observation that war among non-centralized societies not only takes many forms, but also is subject to change over time. In the study area, an enduring pattern of brief, infrequent engagements between socially linked groups gave way during the early- to mid-twelfth century to lengthy hostilities between socially distant groups, characterized by fiercer tactics and frequent and/or highly unpredictable engagements. Ethnographic data from numerous non-centralized societies suggest that these changes in the conduct of war accompanied major changes in social relationships between combatants, including the development of entrenched group identities and perhaps the dehumanization of enemy groups. In an uncertain and hostile social environment, populations in the Chevelon and East Clear Creek areas were anchored by defensive necessity to their canyon fortifications, where economic failures may have precipitated their decline.

The intense warfare in Chevelon and East Clear Creek from A.D. 1150 to A.D. 1250 immediately precedes the intensification of conflict on a much larger scale, a development extensively studied by Southwestern archaeologists (Haas and Creamer 1996; Kuckelman et al. 2000; LeBlanc 1999; Wilcox and Haas 1994). The ubiquity of conflict in the northern Southwest after A.D. 1250 is linked to a series of dramatic social changes, including population aggregation, regional abandonment, and the formation of ethnic identities. This study indicates that widespread war and the major social transformations of the late thirteenth century did not emerge in a vacuum. Rather, they developed over the course of the previous hundred years, as the appearance of a more socially distant foe led to new forms of conflict and transformed the social landscape of east-central Arizona. Much work remains to be done before we can determine the identity and motives of this socially distant enemy or understand how their actions reverberated through the northern Southwest. It is clear, however, that examination of the conduct and consequences of prehistoric conflict, even on a small scale, can contribute to an understanding of long-term processes of culture change.

Acknowledgments

Fieldwork in the Chevelon and East Clear Creek drainages was made possible by the United States Forest Service, the University of Virginia, the University of Michigan Department of Anthropology and Rackham School of Graduate Studies, and by a Sigma-Xi Grant-in-Aid of Research. Subsequent analyses were funded by a Wenner-Gren dissertation grant (Gr. 6753) and involved the cooperation of the Arizona State University Department of Anthropology and the Museum of Northern Arizona. I thank Ray Kelly, Steve Plog, John Speth, Chris White, and Matthew Chamberlin for the many productive exchanges of ideas that shaped this chapter. The text itself has greatly benefited from suggestions by Matthew Chamberlin, Joyce Marcus, Diane Solometo, Liz Arkush, Mark Allen, and two anonymous reviewers.

Notes

1. See Webster 1998 for an overlapping list of variables more appropriate to centralized societies.

2. The "interminable" nature of some Jívaro feuds, as well as the feuds of other groups, is often due to conflicting perceptions of the "score" (Boehm 1984). Unsurprisingly, the likelihood for disagreement about the score appears to be directly related to the social distance between the feuding parties (Peters 1967).

3. Important exceptions to the direct relationship between social distance and the severity of war tactics include "treacherous feasts" (Redmond 1994) or other kinds of surprise attacks between allies, such as the large-scale, deadly surprise raid conducted in 1966 by one member of a Dani alliance on another (Heider 1970). In these rare but devastating cases, explicit violation of the rules of engagement is *intended to express and to produce* social distance, terminating all previous ties.

4. Uncertainty about the Timbira stems from the fact that information about the frequency of war came from anecdotal evidence of periods before pacification, while the settlements described were those occupied at the time of fieldwork, that is, *after continual warfare had ceased*. Otterbein's Timbira source (Nimuendajú 1946) describes village plans in use *after* continual internecine war came to a close; the circular plan of Timbira villages in the ethnographic present may have formerly been fortified with the addition of an exterior palisade. The Timbira also formerly retreated to nearby hilltops in response to infrequent attacks by Neo-Brazilians.

5. It must also be noted that groups able to capture and incorporate enemy women pose a double demographic threat to their enemies. If one group is disproportionately successful, in very few generations they can significantly increase in size, while their victims are weakened by population decline.

6. The tight meandering of the canyons and shortage of hilltop locations in the study area make intervisible networks of defensive sites, such as those documented for other parts of the Southwest (Bremer 1989; Haas and Creamer 1993; Wilcox and Haas 1994; Wilcox et al. 2001b) impossible in the study area.

7. It would have been possible to remove resources only in the event of a total defeat. Given the emphasis on dividing forces between lookouts and fortified sites in the region, some defenders would likely survive even those attacks resulting in site destruction. As is often the case in the ethnographic record, the potential for survivors to regroup and at-

tack retreating war parties likely hastened their departure. Resource acquisition is much more likely for groups stealing mobile resources such as cattle or horses, or groups using pack animals or employing canoes. The drainages in the study region were almost certainly never navigable by watercraft.

References

Acker, C. 1972. Soil and Environment in the Explanation of Settlement. Manuscript on file, Department of Anthropology, Arizona State University.

Adams, E. C. 1996. The Pueblo III-Pueblo IV Transition in the Hopi Area, Arizona. In *The Prehistoric Pueblo World, A.D. 1150–1350*, edited by M. Adler, 48–58. Tucson: University of Arizona Press.

———. 2002. *Homol'ovi: An Ancient Hopi Settlement Cluster.* Tucson: University of Arizona Press.

Allen, W., C. F. Merbs, and W. Birkby. 1985. Evidence for Prehistoric Scalping at Nuvakweewtaga (Chavez Pass) and Grasshopper Ruin, Arizona. In *Health and Disease in the Prehistoric Southwest*, edited by C. F. Merbs and R. J. Miller, 23–42. Arizona State University Anthropological Research Papers No. 34. Tempe: Arizona State University.

Barton, M., M. McMinn-Barton, and E. Badal Garcia. 1999. Preceramic Land Use in the Middle Chevelon Creek Drainage. Paper presented at the 72nd Pecos Conference, Pinedale, Arizona.

Bennett Ross, J. 1984. Effects of Contact on Revenge Hostilities Among the Achuarä Jívaro. In *Warfare, Culture, and Environment*, edited by R. B. Ferguson, 83–110. Orlando: Academic Press.

Bernardini, W. 2002. The Gathering of the Clans: Understanding Ancestral Hopi Migration and Identity, A.D. 1275–1400. Unpublished Ph.D. dissertation, Department of Anthropology, Arizona State University, Tempe.

Biolosi, T. 1984. Ecological and Cultural Factors in Plains Indian Warfare. In *Warfare, Culture, and Environment*, edited by R. B. Ferguson, 141–168. Orlando: Academic Press.

Boehm, C. 1984. *Blood Revenge: The Anthropology of Feuding in Montenegro and Other Tribal Societies*. Lawrence: University of Kansas Press.

Bohannan, L. 1958. Political Aspects of Tiv Social Organization. In *Tribes Without Rulers: Studies in African Segmentary Systems*, edited by J. Middleton and D. Tait, 33–66. London: Routledge and Kegan Paul.

Brandt, E. 1994. Egalitarianism, Hierarchy, and Centralization in the Pueblos. In *The Ancient Southwestern Community*, edited by W. Wills and R. Leonard, 9–23. Albuquerque: University of New Mexico Press.

Bremer, J. M. 1989. Walnut Canyon: Settlement and Land Use. *Arizona Archaeologist* No. 23. Phoenix: Arizona Archaeological Society.

Briuer, F. 1977. Cultural and Noncultural Deposition Processes in Chevelon Canyon. Unpublished Ph.D. dissertation, Department of Anthropology, University of California, Los Angeles.

Brown, B. M. 1987. Population Estimation from Floor Area: A Restudy of Naroll's Constant. *Behavior Science Research* 21:1–49.

Carman, J., and A. Harding. 1999. *Ancient Warfare: Archaeological Perspectives*. Stroud, Gloucestershire: Sutton Publishing, Ltd.

Chagnon, N. 1983. *Yanomamo: The Fierce People* (3rd edition). New York: Holt, Rinehart and Wilson.

Fadiman, J. 1982. *An Oral History of Tribal Warfare: The Meru of Mt. Kenya*. Athens: Ohio University Press.

Ferguson, R. B. 1984. Introduction: Studying War. In *Warfare, Culture, and Environment*, edited by R. B. Ferguson, 1–81. Orlando: Academic Press.

———. 1989. Ecological Consequences of Amazonian Warfare. *Ethnology* 28:249–264.

Ford, R. I. 1972. Barter, Gift, or Violence: An Analysis of Tewa Intertribal Exchange. In *Social Exchange and Interaction*, edited by E. Wilmsen, 21–45. Anthropological Papers, Museum of Anthropology, University of Michigan No. 46. Ann Arbor: University of Michigan.

Gregory, D. 1991. Sand Draw South Cultural Resource Survey, Chevelon Ranger District, Apache-Sitgreaves National Forest, Coconino County, Arizona. Report submitted to the Apache-Sitgreaves National Forest, Springerville, AZ.

Gumerman, G. J., and A. S. Skinner. 1968. A Synthesis of the Prehistory of the Central Little Colorado Valley, Arizona. *American Antiquity* 33:185–199.

Haas, J. 1990. Warfare and the Evolution of Tribal Polities in the Prehistoric Southwest. In *The Anthropology of War*, edited by J. Haas, 171–189. New York: Cambridge University Press.

Haas, J., and W. Creamer. 1993. *Stress and Warfare Among the Kayenta Anasazi of the 13th Century A.D.* Fieldiana, Anthropology New Series, no. 21. Chicago: Field Museum of Natural History.

———. 1996. The Role of Warfare in the Pueblo III Period. In *The Prehistoric Pueblo World, A.D. 1150–1350*, edited by M. Adler, 205–213. Tucson, University of Arizona Press.

Hantman, J. 1983. Social Networks and Stylistic Distributions in the Prehistoric Plateau Southwest. Unpublished Ph.D. dissertation, Department of Anthropology, Arizona State University, Tempe.

Harner, M. J. 1972. *The Jívaro: People of the Sacred Waterfalls*. Berkeley: University of California Press.

Haury, E. 1958. Evidence at Point of Pines for a Prehistoric Migration from Northern Arizona. In *Migrations in New World Culture History*, University of Arizona Bulletin 29:2, Social Science Bulletin 27:1–8. Tucson: University of Arizona.

Heider, K. 1970. *The Dugum Dani: A Papuan Culture in the Highlands of West New Guinea*. Chicago: Aldine.

———. 1997. *Grand Valley Dani, Peaceful Warriors* (3rd edition). New York: Harcourt Brace.

Herr, S. A. 2001. *Beyond Chaco: Great Kiva Communities on the Mogollon Rim Frontier*. Anthropological Papers of the University of Arizona, No. 66. University of Arizona Press, Tucson.

Hill, J. 1970. *Broken K Pueblo: Prehistoric Social Organization in the American Southwest*. Anthropological Papers of the University of Arizona No. 18. Tucson: University of Arizona Press.

Huckell, L., B. Huckell, and S. Smith. 1999. Picking God's Pocket: The Final Chapter. Paper presented at the 72nd Pecos Conference, Pinedale, Arizona.

Karsten, R. 1923. *Blood Revenge, War, and Victory Feasts Among the Jibaro Indians of Eastern Ecuador*. Bureau of American Ethnology Bulletin No. 79. Washington, D.C.: Smithsonian Institution.

Keeley, L. H. 1996. *War Before Civilization*. New York: Oxford University Press.

Keener, C. S. 1999. An Ethnohistorical Analysis of Iroquois Assault Tactics Used Against Fortified Settlements of the Northeast in the Seventeenth Century. *Ethnohistory* 46:777–807.

Kelly, R. 1977. *Etoro Social Structure: A Study in Social Contradiction*. Ann Arbor: University of Michigan Press.

———. 2000. *Warless Societies and the Origin of War*. Ann Arbor: University of Michigan Press.

Koch, K-F. 1974. *War and Peace in Jalémó: The Management of Conflict in Highland New Guinea*. Cambridge: Harvard University Press.

Kuckelman, K. A., R. R. Lightfoot, and D. L. Martin. 2000. Changing Patterns of Violence in the Northern San Juan Region. *Kiva* 66(1):147–165.

Lambert, P. 2002. The Archaeology of War: A North American Perspective. *Journal of Archaeological Research* 10:207–239.

LeBlanc, S. A. 1999. *Prehistoric Warfare in the American Southwest*. Salt Lake City: University of Utah Press.

Lekson, S. 2002. War in the Southwest, War in the World. *American Antiquity* 67:607–624.

Levine, H. B. 1999. Reconstructing Ethnicity. *Journal of the Royal Anthropological Institute* (N.S.) 5:165–180.

McGuire, R. H. 1986. Economies and Modes of Production in the Prehistoric Southwestern Periphery. In *Ripples in the Chichimec Sea: New Considerations of Southwestern Mesoamerican Interactions*, edited by F. J. Mathien and R. H. McGuire, 243–269. Carbondale: Southern Illinois University Press.

———. 2002. Stories of Power, Powerful Tales: A Commentary on Ancient Pueblo Violence. In *The Dynamics of Power*, edited by M. O'Donovan, 126–147. Center for Archaeological Investigations, Occasional Paper No. 30. Carbondale: Southern Illinois University Press.

McGuire, R. H., and D. Saitta. 1996. Although They Have Petty Captains, They Obey Them Badly: The Dialectics of Prehispanic Western Pueblo Social Organization. *American Antiquity* 61:197–216.

Martin, D., and D. Frayer (editors). 1997. *Troubled Times: Violence and Warfare in the Past*. Langhorne, PA: Gordon and Breach.

Meggitt, M. 1977. *Blood is Their Argument: Warfare Among the Mae Enga Tribesmen of the New Guinea Highlands*. Palo Alto, CA: Mayfield.

Netting, R. 1973. Fighting, Forest, and the Fly: Some Demographic Regulators Among the Kofyar. *Journal of Anthropological Research* 29:164–179.

———. 1974. Kofyar Armed Conflict: Social Causes and Consequences. *Journal of Anthropological Research* 30:139–163.

Nimuendajú, C. 1946. *The Eastern Timbira*. University of California Publications in American Archaeology and Ethnology, Vol. 41. Berkeley: University of California Press.

Otterbein, K. 1968. Higi Armed Combat. *Southwestern Journal of Anthropology* 24:195–213.

———. 1970. *The Evolution of War: A Cross-Cultural Study*. New Haven: HRAF Press.

———. 1999. A History of Research on Warfare in Anthropology. *American Anthropologist* 101:794–805.

Peters, E. 1967. Some Structural Aspects of the Feud Among the Camel-herding Bedouin of Cyrenaica. *Africa* 37:261–282.

Plog, F. 1974. Settlement Patterns and Social History. In *Frontiers in Anthropology*, edited by M. Leaf, 68–91. New York: D. Van Nostrand Co.

———. 1978. An Analysis of Variability in Site Locations in the Chevelon Drainage, Arizona. In *Investigations of the Southwestern Anthropological Research Group: The Proceedings of the 1976 Conference*, edited by R. C. Euler and G. J. Gumerman, 139–148. Flagstaff: Museum of Northern Arizona.

Plog, F., and S. Upham. 1983. The Analysis of Prehistoric Political Organization. In *Development of Political Organization in Native North America*, edited by E. Tooker and M. H. Fried, 199–213. Washington, D.C.: American Ethnological Society.

Plog, S. E. 1980. *Stylistic Variation of Prehistoric Ceramics: Design Analysis in the American Southwest*. Cambridge: Cambridge University Press.

Plog, S. E., and J. P. Solometo. 1997. The Never-changing and the Ever-changing: The Evolution of Western Pueblo Ritual. *Cambridge Archaeological Journal* 7:161–182.

Plog, S. E., J. P. Solometo, W. Bernardini, and C. C. Heitman. 2001. Understanding Organizational Change in the Chevelon Drainage, Arizona: A Preliminary Report on the 1997–2000 Research of the Chevelon Archaeological Research Project. Report submitted to the Apache-Sitgreaves National Forest, Springerville, AZ.

Rappaport, R. 1968. *Pigs for the Ancestors*. New Haven: Yale University Press.

Redmond, E. 1994. *Tribal and Chiefly Warfare in South America*. Memoirs of the Museum of Anthropology, University of Michigan, No. 28. Ann Arbor: University of Michigan Museum of Anthropology.

Rice, G. E. 2001. Warfare and Massing in the Salt and Gila Basins of Central Arizona. In *Deadly Landscapes: Case Studies in Prehistoric Southwestern Warfare*, edited by G. Rice and S. A. LeBlanc, 289–329. Salt Lake City: University of Utah Press.

Rice, G. E., and S. A. LeBlanc (editors). 2001. *Deadly Landscapes: Case Studies in Prehistoric Southwestern Warfare*. Salt Lake City: University of Utah Press.

Riel-Salvatore, J. 2000. Human-environment Interaction in the Late Archaic and Early Mogollon/Anasazi of the Chevelon Creek Drainage. <http://archaeology.la.asu.edu/vm/southwest/chevelon/Page1.html>

Slatter, E. D. 1979. Drought and Demographic Change in the Prehistoric Southwest United States: A Preliminary Quantitative Assessment. Unpublished Ph.D. dissertation, Department of Anthropology, University of California, Los Angeles.

Solometo, J. P. 2001. Tactical Sites of the Chevelon and Clear Creek Drainages. In *The Archaeology of Ancient Tactical Sites*, edited by J. Welch and T. Bostwick, 21–36. Phoenix: Arizona Archaeological Council.

———. 2004. The Conduct and Consequences of War: Dimensions of Conflict in East-Central Arizona. Unpublished Ph.D. dissertation, Department of Anthropology, University of Michigan, Ann Arbor.

Spoerl, P. M., and G. J. Gumerman (editors). 1984. *Prehistoric Cultural Development in Central Arizona: Archaeology of the Upper New River Region*. Occasional Paper 5, Center for Archaeological Investigations. Carbondale: Southern Illinois University.

Stewart, K. M. 1947. Mohave Warfare. *Southwestern Journal of Anthropology* 3:257–278.

Titiev, M. 1944. *Old Oraibi: A Study of the Hopi Indians of Third Mesa*. Cambridge: Peabody Museum of American Archaeology and Ethnology.

Turner, C G., II, and J. A. Turner. 1999. *Man Corn: Cannibalism and Violence in the Prehistoric American Southwest*. Salt Lake City: University of Utah Press.

Turney-High, H. H. 1949. *Primitive War*. Columbia: University of South Carolina Press.

Turton, D. 1979. War, Peace and Mursi Identity. In *Warfare Among East African Herders*, edited by K. Fukui and D. Turton, 179–210. Senri Ethnological Studies No. 3. Osaka, Japan: National Museum of Ethnology.

Webster, D. 1998. Warfare and Status Rivalry: Lowland Maya and Polynesian Comparisons. In *Archaic States*, edited by G. Feinman and J. Marcus, 311–351. Santa Fe, NM: School of American Research Press.

White, C. 1976. Prehistoric Warfare in the Chevelon Creek Area: An Ecological Approach. In *Chevelon Archaeological Research Project, 1971–1972*, edited by F. Plog, J. Hill, and D. Read, 126–145. UCLA Archaeological Survey Monograph No. 2. Los Angeles: University of California Press.

Wiessner, P., and A. Tumu. 1998. *Historical Vines: Enga Networks of Exchange, Ritual, and Warfare in Papua New Guinea*. Washington, D.C.: Smithsonian Institution Press.

Wilcox, D. 1993. The Evolution of the Chaco Polity. In *The Chimney Rock Archaeological Symposium*, edited by J. M. Malville and G. Matlock, 76–90. Rocky Mountain Forest and Range Experiment Station, USDA Forest Service, General Technical Report RM-227. Fort Collins, CO: U.S. Department of Agriculture.

Wilcox, D., and J. Haas. 1994. The Scream of the Butterfly: Competition and Conflict in the Prehistoric Southwest. In *Themes in Southwest Prehistory*, edited by G. J. Gumerman, 211–238. Santa Fe, NM: School of American Research Press.

Wilcox, D., G. Robertson Jr., and J. S. Wood. 1999. Perry Mesa, A 14th Century Gated Community in Central Arizona. *Plateau Journal* 3(1):44–61.

———. 2001a. Organized for War: The Perry Mesa Settlement System and its Central Arizona Neighbors. In *Deadly Landscapes*, edited by G. Rice and S. LeBlanc, 141–185. Salt Lake City: University of Utah Press.

———. 2001b. Antecedents to Perry Mesa: Early Pueblo III Defensive Refuge Systems in West-Central Arizona. In *Deadly Landscapes*, edited by G. Rice and S. LeBlanc, 109–140. Salt Lake City: University of Utah Press.

Wilson, J. 1969. The Sinagua and Their Neighbors. Unpublished Ph.D. dissertation, Department of Anthropology, Harvard University, Cambridge, Massachusetts.

Winter, E. H. 1956. *Bwamba: A Structural-Functional Analysis of a Patrilineal Society*. Cambridge: W. Heffer and Sons Limited.

Zegwaard, G. A. 1959. Headhunting Practices of the Asmat of Netherlands New Guinea. *American Anthropologist* 61:1020–1041.

3

Climate, Chronology, and the Course of War in the Middle Missouri Region of the North American Great Plains

DOUGLAS B. BAMFORTH

Popular perceptions of the Indian peoples of the North American Great Plains derive largely from the well-documented nineteenth century conflict between Euroamericans and such hunter-gatherer groups as the Cheyenne and Lakota, and battles like those at Beecher Island and the Little Big Horn contributed significantly to widespread views of the American frontier. Popular views of Plains Indians were thus forged in warfare among hunter-gatherers and between hunter-gatherers and invading Euroamericans. However, for nearly a millennium prior to the period that so dominates our view of the Plains, the majority of Native Americans in the region, particularly in the eastern half of the region, were settled farmers rather than nomadic hunter-gatherers. As is widely known, and as I discuss in more detail below, the archaeology of these Plains horticulturalists shows some of the clearest evidence in the world for the existence of tribal warfare prior to Western contact.

The data on pre-contact Plains warfare (that is, Bovee and Owsley 1994; Brooks 1994; Lehmer 1971; Lintz 1986; O'Shea and Bridges 1989; Owsley 1994; Willey 1990) indicate clearly that levels of violence varied greatly in time and space. This chapter focuses on the Middle Missouri region of the northern Great Plains (Figure 3.1), where the available data suggest that warfare was most intense, and on the period from the initial settlement of this region by farmers in A.D. 1000 until A.D. 1650, just prior to Western contact. Archaeologists generally view warfare in the Middle Missouri region as a response to a combination of *in situ* population growth, in-migration of new populations from the Central Plains, limitations on arable land, and climatic deterioration. There are disagreements about the details of the interactions among these factors (Bamforth 1994; Willey 1990; Zimmerman and Bradley 1993), but all recent discussions of this issue have focused on the central role played by climate. These discussions particularly emphasize a shift from warmer/wetter "Atlantic interval" conditions between A.D. 900 and A.D. 1250 to cooler/drier "Pacific interval" conditions between A.D. 1250 and A.D. 1450 (Bryson et al. 1970; Wendland

and Bryson 1974); this shift would have seriously degraded conditions for dry-land horticulture, presumably creating extended periods of food shortage.

Osteological data from the victims of a massacre at the Crow Creek site in South Dakota provide the clearest linkage between warfare and Pacific period subsistence stress in the Middle Missouri region (Gregg and Zimmerman 1986; Kivett and Jensen 1976; Willey 1990; Zimmerman and Bradley 1993). Excavations at Crow Creek identified a town of some 50 houses that was destroyed by fire, and recovered the skeletons of a minimum of 486 individuals—essentially the entire population of the town—from a mass grave in one of the town's two fortification ditches. Marks on these individuals' bones leave no doubt that they were killed and mutilated, that the town was burned down around their bodies, and that they were intentionally buried after an extended period of exposure to carnivores. Importantly, analysis of these individuals' health status indicates that they had very high frequencies of growth-arrest lines and periosteal lesions, including lesions that were active at the time of the massacre. This population had clearly experienced severe biological stress repeatedly over an extended period of time and appears to have been actively malnourished at the time of the attack. Although there is disagreement about the identity of the attackers, radiocarbon dates from the fourteenth century, particularly an early date on charcoal associated with the bone bed, have been used to link the massacre to the Pacific interval.

As I discuss below, the Crow Creek villagers were part of a population of farmers that moved into an already well-populated Middle Missouri region at roughly A.D. 1300. Their poor health suggests that competition for arable land, either among these new migrants (Zimmerman and Bradley 1993) or between the migrants and previously resident farming groups (Bamforth 1994; Lehmer 1971), possibly exacerbated by Pacific interval climatic conditions, precipitated very high levels of violence. However, while this argument accounts for the Crow Creek data, it also implies that warfare should have been absent in the region prior to the onset of Pacific interval conditions and the in-migration of new population. The archaeological record of the period prior to A.D. 1300, though, leaves no doubt that warfare was common during this earlier period: victims of violence and undisputed fortifications are well-known from the interval between A.D. 1000 and A.D. 1300 (Lehmer 1971; Wood 1976), when climatic conditions are thought to have been well-suited to corn farming and populations should have been relatively low.

This chapter attempts to resolve this problem by reexamining evidence for violence in the pre-contact Middle Missouri region in combination with the results of recent paleoclimatic work. My goal here is to reconsider the relation between climatic deterioration, particularly drought, and warfare in this region by comparing recent reconstructions of drought and non-drought intervals between A.D. 1000 and A.D. 1650 with radiocarbon-dated evidence for episodes of violence and for intervals when violence appears to have been absent. I will argue that, while the currently available data are imperfect, they strongly suggest that drought did play an important role in determining the course of war on the northern Plains, although other factors, particularly changing social relations, were also important.

My discussion of these issues has four sections. First, I provide a brief overview of the recent environment and the culture history of the Middle Missouri region. Second, I summarize the traditional view of Middle Missouri region climatic change and the results of the recent work that challenge this view. Third, I discuss several important issues in the use of radiocarbon dates in sites like those considered here and examine the chronometric data on two particularly clear examples of violence in the region to illustrate these issues. Finally, I consider region-wide patterns in the timing and geographic distribution of evidence for violence to outline the historical development of war up to the time of contact.

Culture Historical Background

The Middle Missouri region of the Plains includes the stretch of the Missouri River that runs from north-central North Dakota to southeastern South Dakota (Figure 3.1). This portion of the river is also referred to as the "Missouri Trench," because the river has eroded its course deeply below the adjacent uplands. The effect of this for settled farmers is that arable land is found mainly in the floodplain, and extends like a ribbon of varying width along both sides of the river. Flooding of the river in the spring renews the soil and proximity to the water table greatly enhances plant growth; under natural conditions, the floodplain supports a dense hardwood forest, although this forest thins and largely disappears farther upstream. Importantly, the Missouri River gathers runoff from an enormous portion of North America, making the flow of water in it less dependent on rainfall in any of the local regions it passes through, thus buffering floodplain farmers from at least some of the effects of local environmental problems.

Although important details of the human history of this region remain to be worked out, the basic sequence of events for the period from A.D. 1000 to A.D. 1650 is fairly clear (Blakeslee 1994; Lehmer 1971; Roper 1995; Toom 1992a; Wedel 1986; Wood 1967). Horticultural ways of life appeared in the Middle Missouri area between A.D. 900 and A.D. 1000. Referred to as the Middle Missouri Tradition, this earliest farming occupation is marked archaeologi-

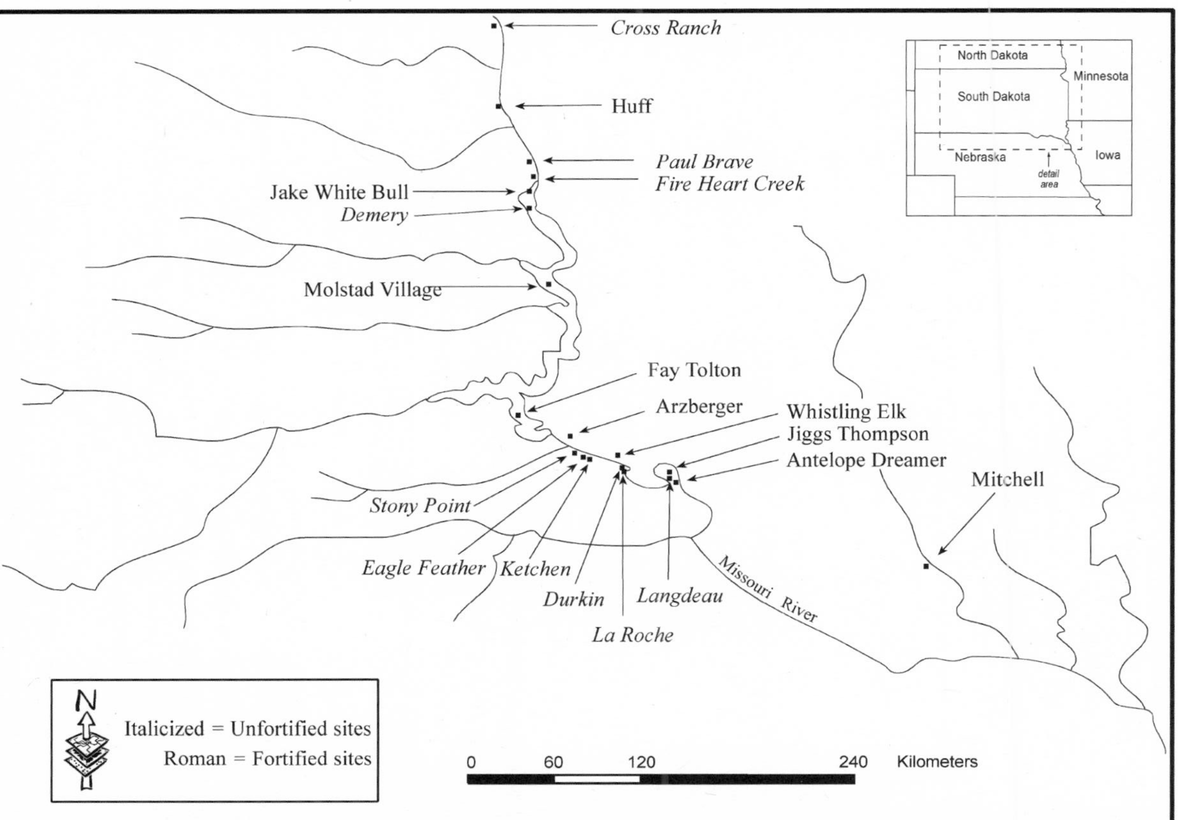

Figure 3.1. Location of the Middle Missouri region, showing locations of sites in Table 3.2.

cally by communities averaging roughly a dozen rectangular semi-subterranean earthlodges approximately 7 meters wide and 14 meters long, usually laid out in orderly rows. The available data indicate that these communities relied on a combination of horticulture (particularly corn, squash, and sunflower) and hunting and gathering (with bison providing the bulk of the wild food in the diet). Northern Plains archaeologists disagree about whether Middle Missouri populations represent an indigenous development or a movement of people up the Missouri from northwestern Iowa and southwestern Minnesota (Tiffany 1983; Toom 1992a, 1992b). Whatever the original source of this way of life, there is little doubt that it progressively spread northward up the Missouri valley and extended into North Dakota by A.D. 1200.

At roughly the same time, a second, archaeologically distinct, horticultural way of life developed in the Kansas River drainage on the Central Plains of Nebraska and Kansas. Referred to as the Central Plains Tradition, this occupation is marked by small, scattered clusters of square wattle and daub houses, particularly along secondary drainages. These communities grew a similar suite of cultigens to those along the Missouri, but seem to have relied on a wider array of locally available wild foods (although, as along the Missouri, bison were important). As in the Middle Missouri case, archaeologists have debated whether or not the Central Plains Tradition represents an indigenous development or a migration from the east, with recent work generally favoring the former interpretation (Blakeslee 1994; Roper 1995).

Archaeological and linguistic data and traditional histories of Native American groups indicate that the Central Plains farmers, referred to archaeologically as the Central Plains Tradition, were the ancestors of the Caddoan-speaking Arikara and Pawnee. Similarly, the northern Plains groups, referred to archaeologically as the Middle Missouri Tradition, were the ancestors of the Siouan-speaking Mandan and Hidatsa. The likelihood that these two occupations represent ethnically and linguistically distinct groups of people is particularly important here, because, during the latter part of the thirteenth century, Central Plains Tradition farmers largely abandoned the more southern and, particularly, western portions of their territory and moved north of the Platte River. These groups ultimately reached the Missouri River in northeastern Nebraska and, by the early 1300s, had moved upriver into South Dakota, where archaeologists refer to them as the Initial Coalescent Tradition. Initial Coalescent archaeological sites show some borrowing from the Middle Missouri groups already present in the Missouri Trench. However, the most significant difference between Initial Coalescent and Central Plains Tradition sites is their size: where Central Plains sites typically have no more than five to ten houses, Initial Coalescent sites often have as many as 50 houses, suggesting a significant increase in population aggregation (Lehmer 1971; Spaulding 1956).

Both Middle Missouri and Initial Coalescent sites show evidence for warfare in the form of ditch and palisade fortifications, often combined with construction of settlements in naturally defensible and/or physically inaccessible locations, and in the form of skeletal remains of obvious victims of violence. As noted above, recent discussions of this evidence have emphasized the period after the incursion of Coalescent groups into the Missouri Trench, and argue that warfare developed between indigenous and in-migrating groups, in part because of drought-induced deterioration in conditions for horticulture. As I show in the next two sections, though, this explanation oversimplifies both the evidence for the character of northern Plains climate between A.D. 1000 and A.D. 1650 and the evidence documenting the course of war in the region.

Reconstructing the Climate of the Middle Missouri Region from A.D. 1000 to A.D. 1650

While recent paleoclimatic work clearly documents the impacts of drought on the northern Plains region, it does not show the pattern of drought that the traditional climatic reconstruction proposes. I consider this reconstruction and then outline the results of more recent research.

The "Bryson Model" of Climate

Plains archaeologists have viewed the relation of environment to warfare in the Middle Missouri region within a framework that is often referred to as the "Bryson model" (Bryson et al. 1970; Wendland 1978; Wendland and Bryson 1974). This model rests primarily on pollen studies of ancient environments and evaluations of the global climatic conditions that should have supported the kinds of vegetation suggested by these studies. It views climatic history since the end of the Pleistocene in terms of a series of more or less steady-state periods separated by rapid transitions from one period to the next, with the dates taken as boundaries of climatic periods obtained by averaging radiocarbon dates thought to mark important climatic changes.

The Bryson model refers to the period from approximately A.D. 900 to A.D. 1250 or so as the "Neo-Atlantic" and reconstructs this interval as relatively warm and wet, conditions that should have lengthened the growing season and offered greater certainty that sufficient rain would fall to ensure a successful harvest. In contrast, the model sees the period from A.D. 1250 to A.D. 1450—the "Pacific interval"—as relatively cool and dry, which would have shortened the growing season and made dry land or floodplain horticulture less reliable. The evidence for active malnutrition among the victims of the Crow Creek massacre and the generally accepted date of that massacre in the early to middle 1300s (see below) fit this reconstruction nicely, and provide particularly clear evidence for the link between subsistence stress and war in the northern Plains.

Beyond the Bryson Model of Climate

Despite the popularity of this view of the Plains climate, though, there are both *a priori* and empirical problems with it. For example, pollen-based reconstructions are fairly imprecise indicators of climate, and often describe vegetational change at very coarse temporal scales. Furthermore, evidence for the pace of climatic change in any given region should derive from evidence from that region, not from hemisphere- or continent-wide averages of radiocarbon dates, and the Bryson model largely neglects such evidence.

Perhaps more importantly, the specific on-the-ground reconstructions proposed by the Bryson model are often contradicted by detailed empirical studies. In particular, precipitation reconstructions based on tree-rings from a variety of locations in and around the Plains (Cleaveland and Duvick 1992; Duvick and Blasing 1981; Stahle and Cleaveland 1988; Stahle et al. 1985, 2000; Stockton and Meko 1983; Weakly 1965; Woodhouse and Brown 2001) and on detailed studies of lacustrine sediments in North Dakota (Fritz et al. 2000; Laird et al. 1998), both of which span several of the supposedly homogeneous and rapidly changing climatic periods specified by the Bryson model, do not show either the steady-state climatic periods or the rapid transitions between such periods that the model proposes. The lacustrine studies do suggest an overall shift in climate at approximately A.D. 1200, but this shift appears to be towards less severe, not more severe, drought, and it is clear that the periods before and after A.D. 1200 were marked by substantial variation in drought conditions.

These data indicate that both severe droughts and extended periods of ameliorated conditions have been common in the northern Plains for at least the last 2,000 years, a conclusion that is incompatible with the literal interpretations of the Bryson model that dominate Plains archaeology. Simply put, all detailed empirical studies of northern Plains climate indicate unambiguously that the period from A.D. 900 to A.D. 1250 was not consistently wet, that the period from A.D. 1250 to A.D. 1650 was not consistently dry, and that both of these periods were characterized by significant climatic variation on the scale of decades. As might be expected given the degree of local variation in climate on the Plains and the different kinds of evidence these studies rely on, there is some variation in the specific drought sequences that different studies reconstruct. However, data from a variety of studies suggest that severe drought occurred on the northern Plains during the late 900s, mid to late 1100s, late 1200s and early 1300s, and mid to late 1500s (Fritz et al. 2000; Laird et al. 1998; Weakly 1965; Woodhouse and Overpeck 1998). Fritz et al. (2000) also reconstruct a possibly more localized drought in the area of the Dakotas in the mid-1400s.

Precipitation can vary greatly in different areas of the Plains and it is not unusual for one region to experience drought and another to experience average or above-average rainfall at the same time. To assess the impact of drought in any specific region, it is therefore important to rely on data gathered as close as possible to that region. Studies of lacustrine sediments from three lakes in North Dakota (Fritz et al. 2000; Laird et al. 1998) provide the best currently available data for the Middle Missouri region. Of these three, the Moon Lake sequence provides the best available combination of geographic proximity and chronological precision.[1] This sequence (summarized in Fritz et al. 2000:Figure 2) suggests that major droughts occurred in the Middle Missouri region from A.D. 1030 to A.D. 1090, A.D. 1150 to A.D. 1190, A.D. 1270 to A.D. 1330, A.D. 1430 to A.D. 1480, and A.D. 1550 to A.D. 1600. Significantly, at least three of these (those in the 1100s, the 1200s/1300s, and the late 1500s) correspond closely in time to droughts known more precisely by studies of tree-rings and other evidence in the American Southwest and elsewhere, and therefore likely document particularly widespread climatic events (Grissino-Mayer 1996; Jones et al. 1999; Laird et al. 1998; Stahle et al. 2000; Woodhouse and Brown 2001; Woodhouse and Overpeck 1998). The dates for this drought sequence are clearly approximate and the sequence as a whole must be considered a first estimate of the detailed climatic history of the region. However, the correspondence of these major events with similar events in other areas suggests that it provides a reasonable basis for this analysis.

Radiocarbon Dates, Duration of Site Occupation, and Chronology in the Middle Missouri Region

The heart of this chapter relies on a comparison of radiocarbon-dated evidence for periods of war and peace in the Middle Missouri region with the drought and non-drought intervals just noted. Plains archaeologists have relied on radiocarbon for virtually all of their culture histories, and there is a fairly extensive corpus of dated sites from the area at issue here on which such a comparison can rest (see, for example, Johnson 1994, 2001; Lehmer 1971; Thiessen 1977; Toom 1992a, 1992b). However, there are important problems in using this corpus of sites for present purposes.

Interpreting a date depends on understanding the archaeological context from which the dated material was recovered, and especially on evaluating the relationship between the event of interest and the event being dated. This is particularly important in the case of sites occupied for long periods of time, where a date on one kind of material (for example, a house or palisade post) may pertain to the site's construction while a date on another kind of material (for example, burned corn) may pertain to an episode at some unknown point in the site's post-construction occupation. In sites occupied for periods of time shorter than the error margin on a radiocarbon date, this distinction may not be important, but it is crucial for sites occupied for longer periods of time, particularly because Plains archaeologists often use single averaged dates to assess the age of whole sites. Two exceptionally well-documented cases of violence in the Middle Missouri region highlight this issue.

When Did the Crow Creek Massacre Occur?

The Crow Creek site (Gregg and Zimmerman 1986; Kivett and Jensen 1976; Willey 1990; Zimmerman and Bradley 1993) is a large Initial Coalescent town in south-central South Dakota whose chronology illustrates the difficulties that can arise in linking radiocarbon dates to specific research problems. As noted above, excavations at Crow Creek have revealed undoubted evidence for the massacre and mutilation of roughly 500 people and the destruction of their homes by fire. The occupants of the Crow Creek site were clearly either members of, or descended from, groups who migrated into the Middle Missouri region from the Central Plains after the drought of the late 1200s. A radiocarbon date of 630±50 RCYBP (calibrated one-sigma range: 1299–1327 [p = .39], 1346–1375 [p = .39], 1375–1393 [p = .23]) on charcoal directly associated with the Crow Creek bone bed is often taken as evidence that the massacre at the site occurred in approximately A.D. 1320 (although the calibrated range makes it clear that this date is only one of several equally possible ones). This would then imply that the community was wiped out within a generation or so of the arrival of Central Plains farmers in South Dakota, and might suggest that at least some of the victims were themselves Central Plains migrants.

However, the age of the charcoal excavated from the bone bed has no necessary connection to the specific timing of the massacre: the age tells us about the death of the wood that produced the charcoal, not about the death of the villagers with whom the charcoal was found. The destruction of the Crow Creek village by fire after the attack would have provided innumerable sources of burned material that could have found its way into the ditch with the bodies of the massacre victims. It is more likely that this date pertains to some phase of the *construction* rather than to the *destruction* of some part of the community, as does a second radiocarbon date of 560±75 (calibrated one-sigma range: 1305–1355 [p = .51], 1360–1365 [p = .04], 1386–1427 [p = .44]) obtained from a house post recovered during the initial investigation of the site. Taken together, these two dates are consistent with an occupation of the site spanning most of the fourteenth century. In addition, a suite of tree-ring dates (a dating technique that has been questioned on the Plains, see Caldwell and Snyder 1982) clusters in the early 1400s and shows a hiatus during the later 1400s; two dates in the early 1500s suggest a later occupation just prior to the contact period (Weakly 1971).

In fact, the archaeology of the Crow Creek site shows patterns consistent with an Initial Coalescent occupation of at least this duration, and possibly longer. The site contains at least 50 houses and two, or possibly three, fortification lines, but these were not all built at the same time. The inner, and older, of the two northern fortification lines truncates one excavated house and appears to truncate two other unexcavated house pits (Kivett and Jensen 1976:Figures 1 and 6), implying that the initial settlement of the site by Central Plains groups was undefended and that the inner ditch and palisade were built after this house was abandoned.

Long use of the houses at the site is also indicated by large numbers of trash-filled indoor pits, intersecting storage pits (suggesting that the locations of older pits had been forgotten), and extensive evidence for either interior remodeling and repair of structures or reuse of house pits (Kivett and Jensen 1976:Figures 3 through 7). In addition, some of the houses were built in pits that were dug into existing midden, implying an extended period of occupation and garbage disposal prior to their construction, and the inner fortification ditch accumulated at least a meter of midden, presumably prior to the construction of the outer fortification line (Kivett and Jensen 1976:11, 15). Test excavations outside of house depressions in several areas of the site revealed midden deposits a meter or more thick (Kivett and Jensen 1976:26–29). Finally, the site shows clear evidence of post-burning, and thus post-massacre, occupation, including pits intruding into the burned houses and, in one case, as much as 30 to 40 cm of midden above a burned house (Kivett and Jensen 1976:20).

All of this evidence implies a long and complex occupation history that is difficult to accommodate to an initial site settlement during the early part of the influx of Central Plains groups around A.D. 1300 and the destruction and abandonment of the site by the mid-1300s. However, the range of radiocarbon dates from Crow Creek, as well as the tree-ring dates on the site (Weakly 1971) fit well with these data. The aggregate chronological information on the site suggests a chronology that is consistent with the complexity of the site's archaeologically visible occupation history, with the radiocarbon dates suggesting that the site was likely founded during the early to middle 1300s and the tree-ring dates implying that occupation persisted well into the 1400s, and perhaps as late as the early 1500s. Post-burning occupation of the site implies that the massacre took place somewhere in the middle of this span of time, but none of the available chronometric data tell us exactly when.

Violence Prior to A.D. 1300: The Fay Tolton Site

Crow Creek is thus a site whose complexity and probable long occupation history make it extremely important to consider the exact relevance of any given piece of chronological information to any given specific research problem. A second site in the study area, Fay Tolton (Wood 1976), though, illustrates a simpler situation.

Fay Tolton is an Initial Middle Missouri Tradition town of at least 33 earthlodges on a promontory above the Missouri River floodplain in central South Dakota (Wood 1976). Wood (1976:42) reports four radiocarbon dates, three of them on fragments of charred willow baskets (885±50 B.P., 920±60 B.P., and 850±170 B.P.) and one on a house post (860±150 B.P.). Johnson (1994:481) subsequently dated five charred chokecherry seeds at 865±60 B.P. Although some of these dates have fairly large standard errors, they are clearly comfortably close to one another. The archaeology of the site is consistent with a brief occupation; unlike Crow Creek, Fay Tolton shows no evidence of house remodeling, truncation of houses by pits or other features, reorganization of the layout of the settlement, or of extensive trash deposits. Like many Initial Middle Missouri communities (Toom 1992a; and see below), Fay Tolton thus seems to have been occupied briefly, as implied both by the pattern in the archaeological data and by the narrow range of the radiocarbon dates from both construction and subsequent occupation.

The site is defended by a ditch across the narrow neck of the promontory (limited excavation failed to identify a palisade) and, as at Crow Creek, osteological evidence indicates that this defense failed at least once. Human burials are almost unknown in Middle Missouri Tradition sites, perhaps because the inhabitants of those sites, like their Mandan and Hidatsa descendants, exposed their dead on scaffolds instead of interring them. However, excavations in two houses at Fay Tolton recovered five bodies. In one house, a decapitated young man was found stuffed into an empty storage pit. In the second, an older adult male was found seated in a storage pit with his head and shoulders above the rim of the pit and the vertebral column of a bison laid across his chest, with the ends of the column resting on the floor of the house. He was facing directly towards an alcove adjacent to the entrance to the house. This alcove contained the skeletons of two teenage girls and an eight- or nine-year-old child sprawled on the floor amidst a remarkably intact array of household debris, including the willow storage baskets from which the dates noted above derive, and at least one whole pot. Cut marks and extensive necrosis on the skull of the child (Holliman and Owsley 1994) indicate that she or he had been scalped but not killed several weeks before the attack in which the child was finally murdered.

In contrast to the complex pattern at Crow Creek, the Fay Tolton data suggest a fairly close relationship between the radiocarbon dates and the attack on the town. The construction date (on the house post) and the dates on the baskets and seeds correspond closely, implying that the baskets were made, and the seeds were gathered, at roughly the same time that the town was built. There is no good evidence that the town was occupied for very long, and the absence of evidence for any post-massacre occupation implies that it was abandoned after the attack.

Occupation Span and Radiocarbon Dating in the Middle Missouri Region: Choosing Sites for Analysis

The contrast between the Crow Creek and Fay Tolton sites makes it clear that there is a great range of variation in the ways in which horticultural communities along the Missouri River were occupied, and that this range of variation has important implications for interpretations of the radiocarbon ages of those sites. Research in the region (Johnson 1994; Lehmer 1971; Thiessen 1977; Toom 1992b) has focused more on working out overall regional culture history than on addressing the chronological details of the occupation at any individual site. With this goal in mind, such work typically averages together all of the acceptable dates from any given site as a means of sorting those sites in time. This approach has served its purpose well, but it is less well-suited to an analysis like that presented here. Averaging dates on a site like Fay Tolton should provide a fairly accurate estimate of the timing of the site's construction, occupation, and catastrophic abandonment, while averaging together dates from a site like Crow Creek places the site generally in time but cannot be used to estimate the date of any specific event in the site's occupation.

Lacking chronometric data gathered to assess when specific events in complex sites occurred (such as the construction of the fortification lines at Crow Creek), this analysis relies primarily on average dates from sites whose archaeology is consistent with a brief occupation. Length of occupation is assessed using Toom's (1992a:85–87) criteria of multiple occupations, house rebuilding, and house superposition as well as intersections among pits (Toom's criterion of surface-visible middens is dropped because this variable can be strongly affected by geomorphic processes.[2])

Table 3.1 thus expands Toom's data, first, by considering all of the dated sites in the region listed by Johnson (1994) for which excavation data could be found, second, by dropping the information on surface-visible midden (which, like midden depth, is strongly affected by geomorphic factors that have little to do with occupation span) and, third, by adding information on intersections among pits or between pits and other features (for example, hearths or house entrances). The sites in this table are strikingly, although not perfectly, dichotomous, tending to show either all of the indicators of relatively long occupation or none of them. The clarity of this pattern suggests that certain locations along the Missouri River were occupied for much longer periods of time than others. Although, as Toom and Johnson (1994) both note, the typical pattern of occupation overall appears to be one in which villages were occupied briefly, there are clearly some villages that were substantially more permanent than others. While this has implications for many aspects of the ways of life these sites document, it is important here because it helps to distinguish sites whose average dates can usefully be compared to the Moon Lake drought sequence from sites whose dates must be considered very carefully before they can be used for such a comparison.

Table 3.1 provides a basis for selecting sites for analysis here. Johnson (1994) provides the most complete list and analysis of radiocarbon dates for the Middle Missouri region.[3] This analysis screens Johnson's data in two ways. First, it divides the sites in Table 3.1 into those showing two or fewer indicators of long-term occupation and those showing three or more such indicators, and assumes that sites in the second group (for example, Crow Creek) require particular attention to ensure that the available dates are relevant here, while sites in the first group do not require such attention. Note that this eliminates the problems with the "uncertain" entry under the "intersecting pits" variable for the Stony Point site in Table 3.1, as this site falls into the first of these groups regardless of this entry.[4]

Second, this analysis re-computes some of Johnson's site averages. Johnson excluded all dates with standard errors over 100 years, even when these dates were statistically identical to dates with smaller error margins and there were no reasons to suppose they were inaccurate. Because averaging dates both pools the mean values and reduces the overall error margins, excluding these latter dates is arguable, and the dates used here were re-averaged to incorporate them.

A total of six sites (Pretty Head, Sommers, Cattle Oiler, Crow Creek, Mitchell, and Demery) show evidence of relatively long-term occupation. Of these six, I exclude four (Pretty Head, Cattle Oiler, Crow Creek, and Sommers) because their occupational histories are too complex for the available dates to be useful here, or because their dates are problematic (see Johnson's [1994] extended discussion). The dates from the remaining sites (Mitchell and Demery), though, provide useful information, and I include Johnson's (1994) overall site dates, keeping in mind their limited use for dating specific events, as discussed above. I include mean dates on individual structures from these sites as well.

Table 3.1. Summary of Evidence for Duration of Occupation in Radiocarbon-Dated Middle Missouri Sites

Site	Multiple occupations?	Houses rebuilt?	Houses superimposed?	Intersecting features?	Reference
Antelope Dreamer	no	no	no	no	Toom 1990, 1992a
Jiggs Thompson	no	some?	no	yes	Caldwell and Jensen 1969
Langdeau	no	some?	no	yes	Caldwell and Jensen 1969
Pretty Head B	yes	minor	no	no	Caldwell and Jensen 1969
Sommers	yes	yes	yes	yes	Steinacher 1990
Cattle Oiler	yes	yes	yes	yes	Moerman and Jones 1966
Eagle Feather	no	no	no	no	Toom 1992a
Stony Point	no	no	no	uncertain	Toom 1992a
Ketchen	no	no	no	no	Johnson 1979
Durkin	no	no	no	no	Johnson 1979
Crow Creek (IMM)	yes	yes	no	yes	Kivett and Jensen 1976
Shermer	no	yes	yes	yes	Sperry 1968
Mitchell	yes	yes	yes	yes	Alex 1981
Fay Tolton	no	no	no	no	Wood 1976
La Roche C	no[a]	no	no	no	Hoffman 1968
Cross Ranch	no	some	no	no	Calabrese 1972
Fire Heart Creek	yes	some	no	no	Lehmer 1966
Demery	yes	yes	yes	yes	Woolworth and Wood 1964
Hosterman	no	no	no	no	Miller 1964
Molstad	no	no	no	no	Hoffman 1967
Arzberger	no	yes	no	yes	Spaulding 1956
Huff	no	no	yes	yes	Wood 1967
Paul Brave	no	some	no	no	Wood and Woolworth 1964
Crow Creek (IC)	yes	yes	yes	yes	Kivett and Jensen 1976
Whistling Elk	no	no	no	no	Steinacher 1983; Toom and Kvamme 2002

Note: In the entries for the Crow Creek Site, "IC" Refers to Initial Coalescent and "IMM" Refers to Initial Middle Missouri.

a. Area C of the locality designated as the La Roche "site" was occupied only once; the locality as a whole was occupied more than once (Hoffman 1968).

Table 3.2. Radiocarbon and Calibrated Calendar Ages for Fortified and Unfortified Sites in the Middle Missouri Region

Site	Fortified/Defensible	^{14}C Date	1–Sigma Cal. Age
Fay Tolton	yes	885±30	1068–1083 (.15) 1124–1137 (.12) 1157–1214 (.73)
Jake White Bull	yes	730±50	1225–1226 (.02) 1242–1300 (.94) 1373–1377 (.04)
Jiggs Thompson	yes	770±60	1224–1228 (.03) 1241–1299 (.97)
Antelope Dreamer	no/defensible	740±25 (all dates)	1265–1288 (1.00)
Antelope Dreamer	no/defensible	705±30 (maize only)	1278–1299 (.96) 1374–1376 (.04)
Whistling Elk	yes	640±40	1298–1322 (.38) 1350–1390 (.62)
Huff	yes	450±50	1427–1466 (1.00)
Arzberger	yes	420±40	1437–1485 (1.00)
Molstad	yes	365±45	1447–1520 (.69) 1589–1624 (.31)
Mitchell	yes	910±20 (overall age)	1042–1092 (.65) 1119–1140 (.27) 1154–1162 (.09)
Mitchell	yes	890±30 (house 4 only)	1058–1087 (.30) 1122–1138 (.17) 1156–1193 (.42) 1198–1209 (.11)
Paul Brave	no	885±70	1040–1099 (.38) 1116–1141 (.16) 1152–1218 (.46)
Langdeau	no	870±40	1060–1086 (.18) 1122–1138 (.11) 1156–1221 (.70)
Stony Point	no	775±40	1224–1231 (.14) 1239–1280 (.86)
Ketchen	no	780±35	1224–1230 (.14) 1240–1278 (.86)
Eagle Feather	no	760±40	1224–1228 (.05) 1241–1286 (.95)
Fire Heart Creek	no	720±80	1221–1311 (.77) 1354–1387 (.23)
Durkin	no	650±40	1295–1319 (.39) 1352–1389 (.61)
La Roche C	no?	570±55	1306–1355 (.60) 1387–1417 (.40)

continued

Site	Fortified/Defensible	^{14}C Date	1–Sigma Cal. Age
Cross Ranch	no	610±30	1304–1329 (.44)
			1343–1367 (.39)
			1385–1395 (.18)
La Roche A and B	no	330±20	1516–1530 (.15)
			1547–1598 (.64)
			1617–1634 (.21)
Demery	no	520±30 (overall)	1405–1431 (1.00)
Demery	no	540±40 (house only)	1329–1343 (.25)
			1395–1430 (.75)

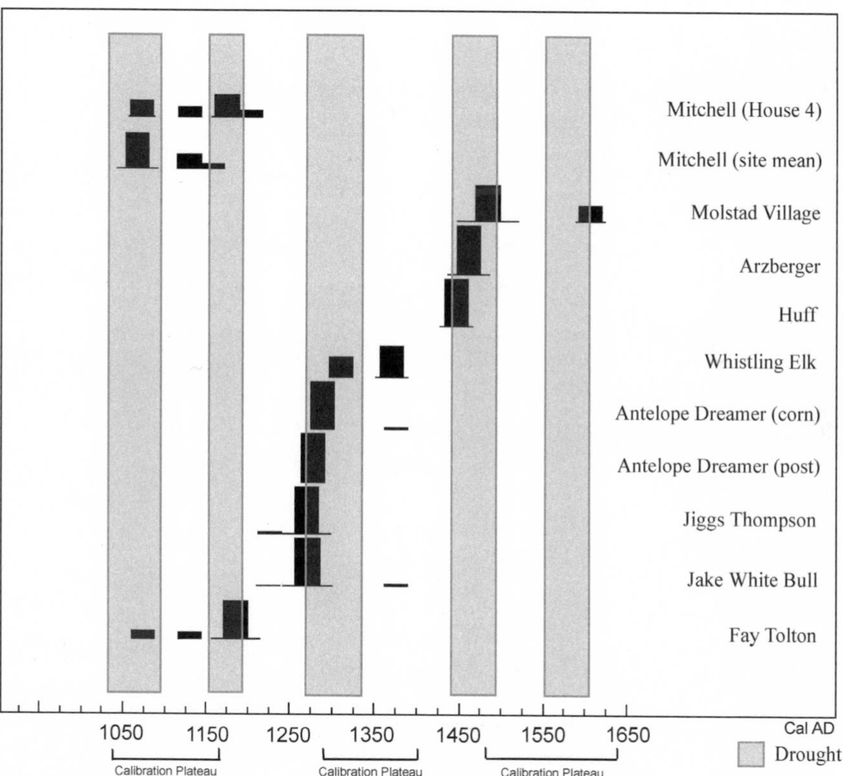

Figure 3.2. Calibrated one-sigma age ranges of mean radiocarbon dates for fortified sites in Table 3.2. The horizontal lines for each site indicate the calibrated calendar age interval(s) for the site's radiocarbon age; the height of the vertical bar indicates the relative probability of each calibrated interval within the one-sigma range.

Finally, as Toom (1992a, 1992b) and Johnson (1994) discuss, there are two series of dates on the Antelope Dreamer site, one (slightly older) series run on the outer rings of burned house posts and one (slightly younger) series run on carbonized maize recovered from the floor of a burned house. Johnson (1994) averages these together to date the site as a whole. However, it is possible to interpret these series as representing distinct aspects of the occupation of this site, with the house post dates pertaining to its construction and the corn dates to its apparently sudden abandonment. Although no skeletons were found when the site was tested, the burning of the structures with much, if not all, of their contents intact strongly implies that the site was attacked and destroyed. This, then, implies that the age of the corn provides a close estimate of the date of the attack. This chapter includes the mean of the corn dates and the mean of the charcoal dates separately.

Drought, Warfare, and Radiocarbon Dates in the Middle Missouri Region

Table 3.2 lists the radiocarbon ages for the subset of sites in Table 3.1 that pass the criteria discussed in the preceding section, and these ages provide the basis for an analysis of the relation between evidence of violence and drought intervals. Figure 3.1 illustrates the locations of the sites in Table 3.2. Evidence for violence takes two forms.

First, several sites in the sample show evidence of having been attacked. This is most obvious at Fay Tolton, but the combination of burned houses and intact floor assemblages at Antelope Dreamer and Whistling Elk (Steinacher 1983; Toom 1990) suggest that these sites may also have been destroyed in raids. A similar pattern at Mitchell (Alex 1981) suggests that raiders may have penetrated the community at least once in its history. At Whistling Elk, the fragments of a whole pot that had been filled with flaked stone tools, along with a second concentration of tools that may have been contained in a bag or basket, were recovered from the floor of one of the houses, suggesting the site occupation ended abruptly and perhaps catastrophically (Steinacher 1983).

Second, many sites in the Middle Missouri region are fortified, and the presence of fortifications suggests the threat of violence even in sites where it is not possible to document an actual attack. Conversely, the absence of direct evidence of violence or of fortifications suggests that a site was occupied during more peaceful times. Information on fortifications derives from published site reports and from data compiled by Winham et al. (1994).

Drought and War? The Chronology of Fortifications and Attacks

Figure 3.2 arrays the calibrated age ranges for the nine fortified sites in Table 3.2 against the periods of drought indicated in the Moon Lake sediment sequence. I include the Antelope Dreamer site, which is not fortified but is located in a remote and highly defensible location and which, as noted below, appears to have been attacked. Plateaus in the calibration curve have clearly blurred the chronological position of some of these sites (particularly Fay Tolton, Whistling Elk, and Molstad Village) but even so, this figure shows a striking co-occurrence of droughts and fortifications. This is clearest for Antelope Dreamer, Huff, and Arzberger, whose age ranges fall entirely or almost entirely within drought intervals. Fay Tolton, Jiggs Thompson, Jake White Bull, and Molstad Village fall predominantly within drought intervals. While the Mitchell site shows evidence of a complex occupational history, and dates from it need to be considered cautiously, it appears to fit with the pattern of other fortified sites: both the overall mean site date and the mean date on House 4 imply that the site was probably built during the drought of either the late eleventh or late twelfth century.

The three sites with dated attacks include Fay Tolton, whose mean date is a good approximation to the date of its destruction because of its brief occupation. In addition, Antelope Dreamer and Whistling Elk have dates on burned corn recovered from the floors of houses that, like those at Fay Tolton, burned with their contents intact. Although these sites lack osteological evidence of violence, it is likely that these dates mark successful attacks as well. Of these three, Whistling Elk may fall either into a drought or a non-drought interval; its dates are ambiguous (although Steinacher [1983] suggests that its ceramic assemblage is consistent with the earlier part of its age range). However, the calibrated age ranges for the other two sites fall predominantly into drought intervals, with the dates on burned corn from Antelope Dreamer showing this pattern most clearly.

Overall, then, while the pattern is not perfect, the available data suggest that fortifications were built and villages were attacked in the Middle Missouri region during periods when farming was likely to have been unproductive because of drought. Other aspects of the archaeology of a number of sites are also consistent with this. The direct evidence for subsistence stress in the victims of the Crow Creek massacre fits this pattern very clearly, although, as discussed above, it is not clear exactly when this massacre occurred. The presence of open and empty cache pits containing the bodies of victims at Fay Tolton and in burned houses at Crow Creek, Antelope Dreamer, and Whistling Elk (Kivett and Jensen 1976:Plate 10b; Steinacher 1983; Toom 1990) also suggests that food may have been in short supply when these structures were destroyed. While food storage pits can be empty for more than one reason, the presence of empty pits in both of the excavated houses at Fay Tolton suggests either that the food they once held had been used up prior to the attack or that the attackers emptied them before placing bodies in them. The possibility that one of the victims found in a pit may have been placed in the pit alive and held down inside it is perhaps more consistent with the former possibility than the latter.

Furthermore, one common response of subsistence horticulturalists to drought is to rely more extensively on wild plant foods, and there are data from the Middle Missouri region that are consistent with such a shift in periods of conflict. For example, although field notes from the excavation of the Fay Tolton site in 1957 record the presence of maize in charred seed samples, laboratory analysis of the surviving samples overwhelmingly identified wild species of seeds, with no maize present (Grantham 1976), suggesting that cultigens may have been in short supply. More systematic sampling for floral remains is rare in the region, but Nepstad-Thornberry (1998) summarizes the results of detailed analyses of five sites, two of which (Mitchell and Antelope Dreamer) are either fortified or defensible, and three of which (Brewster, Chan-Ya-Ta, and Phipps) are not. Toom (1992a) summarizes similar data for a sixth site, Travis 1, which also shows no evidence of fortification. While differences among these sites may reflect other factors, such as geographic differences in diet and the strategies used by analysts to sample material at the different sites, both of the fortified/defensible sites show higher frequencies of wild than domesticated seeds, while all of the unfortified sites show the opposite pattern. Data like these hint at the possibility that dietary differences may have existed, although more intensive analysis and comparison will be required to rigorously assess this possibility.

Rain and Peace? The Chronology of Unfortified Sites

If drought precipitated warfare in the Middle Missouri region, it is reasonable to infer that non-drought periods were likely to have been peaceful. Figure 3.3 plots calibrated age ranges against Fritz et al.'s (2000) drought intervals for the ten unfortified sites in Table 3.2, showing three patterns. First, three of these sites (Paul Brave, Langdeau, and La Roche A) appear to have been built during drought intervals. Second, as at Whistling Elk, dates on three other sites (La Roche C, Cross Ranch, and possibly Durkin) span drought and non-drought periods; they are ambiguous. However, in the other five cases, the calibrated age ranges fall predominantly into non-drought intervals, particularly the apparently drought-free period in the early to middle 1200s. This is as true for the one unfortified site that shows some evidence of longer-term occupation (Demery) as it is of the sites whose occupation span is not a problem. During

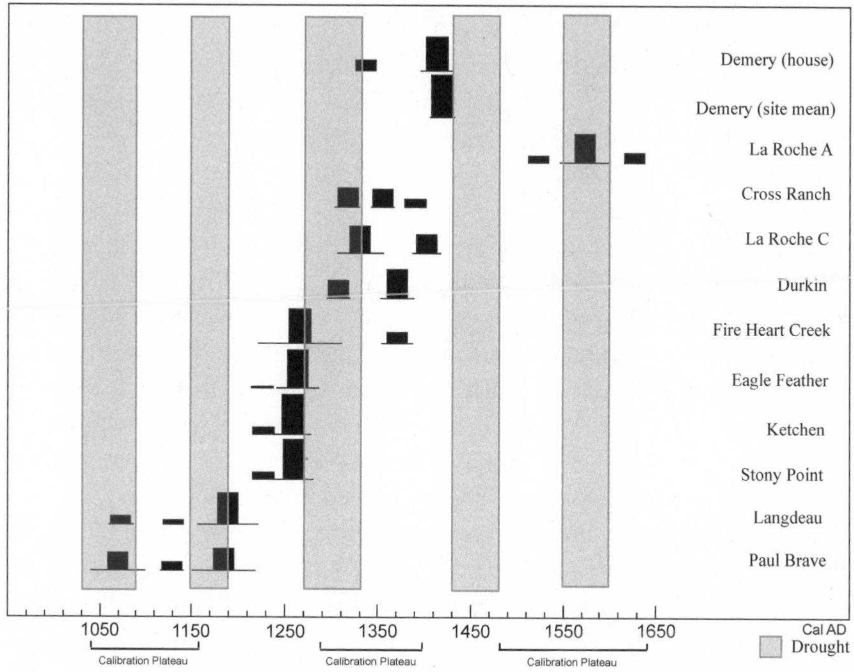

Figure 3.3 Calibrated one-sigma age ranges of mean radiocarbon dates for unfortified sites in Table 3.2. The horizontal lines for each site indicate the calibrated calendar age interval(s) for the site's radiocarbon age; the height of the vertical bar indicates the relative probability of each calibrated interval within the one-sigma range.

non-drought intervals, northern Plains farmers seem rarely to have built towns with ditch and palisade defenses.

More generally, there is an interesting distinction between the sites in Table 3.1 with longer occupation histories and the sample of sites as a whole. While the overall data set in Table 3.1 includes a roughly equal number of fortified and unfortified sites, among sites with long occupations, the ratio of fortified to unfortified sites is six to one. One obvious explanation for this is that the occupation of these sites spanned both drought and non-drought intervals, or, at least, periods of war and peace, with fortifications built in times of war. The construction of a palisade at Crow Creek after the community was established and the extensive midden accumulated in fortification ditches (and at Sommers [Steinacher 1990]) are consistent with this possibility. Some localities on the regional landscape thus probably retained highly visible reminders of past conflict, even during periods of peace.

Contradictory Sites and Calibration Plateaus

Overall, fortified and/or attacked sites date from drought intervals, and unfortified sites date from non-drought periods. There are certainly both discrepant and ambiguous cases, though, and these merit discussion.

The most discrepant sites are Langdeau and Paul Brave, both unfortified communities that appear most likely to have been built during a drought period in either the eleventh or twelfth centuries, and La Roche A, with a moderately high likelihood of having been built during the drought of the late 1500s. Warfare is only one possible response to deprivation caused by drought (or by population/resource imbalances in general, see Read and LeBlanc 2003), and the first two of these cases might suggest that earlier populations in the Middle Missouri region turned to violence in times of stress less often than later populations. Lower populations, less severe droughts, or lesser reliance on horticulture during earlier periods, for example, might have buffered human groups against problems. The incursion of Caddoan speakers to the region after A.D. 1300 might also have produced more permanently hostile relations between well-defined social groups, perhaps making conflict rather than cooperation more likely. The La Roche case, though, clearly does not fit this argument. However, geographic differences in the chances of being raided resulting from changes in the social context of violence may explain the absence of fortifications at this site, as noted below.

Discrepant and ambiguous cases also consistently fall wholly or in part on plateaus in the radiocarbon calibration curve (Stuiver et al. [1998] provide the calibration curves that document these plateaus). Such plateaus represent intervals that radiocarbon can identify but cannot resolve in detail, and their existence introduces an additional degree of ambiguity to the dates on these sites, making it difficult to draw conclusions from them with any confidence. For example, Cross Ranch, La Roche C, and Durkin (all unfortified sites) and Whistling Elk (a fortified site) all fall on the plateau dating from A.D. 1290 to A.D. 1400. Although, as noted above, the ceramic assemblage from Whistling Elk suggests that it dates to the earlier rather than the later part of its range, none of these sites can be placed into drought or non-drought intervals with any confidence solely on the basis of their radiocarbon dates. The calibrated age ranges of Paul Brave, Langdeau, and La Roche A also fall substantially or completely on calibration plateaus.

The pattern of fortification in the mid- to late 1200s, just before this plateau, highlights this problem. Three sites (Stony Point, Ketchen, and Eagle Feather) date fairly confidently to the mid-1200s, a non-drought period, and one site (Fire Heart Creek) may also date to this interval. Three other sites (Antelope Dreamer, Jiggs Thompson, and Jake White Bull) date almost certainly to the

Table 3.3. Johnson's (2001) Chronology of Primary Subdivisions of the Middle Missouri and Coalescent Traditions, A.D. 1000–1650

Tradition	Subdivision/Variant	Age
Coalescent	Extended	A.D. 1400/1450–1650
	Initial	A.D. 1300–1500
Middle Missouri	Terminal	A.D. 1400–1500
	Extended	A.D. 1200–1400
	Initial	A.D. 1000–1300

late 1200s, a period of drought. Despite the small difference in age between these two groups of sites (the mid-points of the mean dates of the earlier sites [770±20 B.P.] and later sites [740±25 B.P.] differ by only 30 years), they show an exceptionally clear pattern: all of the sites dating to the drought of the late 1200s are fortified or defensible, and all of the sites dating before this drought are not. The 1400s—another non-plateau period—show a similar pattern, with the unfortified Demery site most likely constructed in the non-drought interval of the early 1400s and the fortified Arzberger, Huff, and (probably) Molstad Village sites apparently constructed during the drought of the later 1400s.

Interestingly, despite its absence of fortifications, excavations at Demery revealed a combination of burned houses and intact floor assemblages that suggests a successful attack (Woolworth and Wood 1964). The dates used here for Demery pertain to the site's construction, not to its destruction, and are clearly consistent with its establishment during a drought-free period in the early 1400s. However, Demery shows indications of longer-term occupation, and it is possible that this occupation extended into the drought of the late 1400s. If so, it is conceivable that it was destroyed in a raid, although the available data obviously cannot assess this possibility with any certainty.

Not Just Climate: Fortified Sites in Time and Space

The data considered so far suggest that the environmental causes of war in the Middle Missouri region remained fairly constant for some 650 years, from A.D. 1000 to A.D. 1650. However, the social context in which human groups decided whom to fight changed significantly over this period. Prior to A.D. 1300, the region appears to have been populated by the ancestors of the closely related Mandan and Hidatsa, both Siouan-speaking groups. After A.D. 1300, the region witnessed an incursion of Caddoan-speaking groups, the ancestors of the Arikara and probably the Pawnee, from the Central Plains. Although there is debate over whether warfare prior to the eighteenth century was between or within these groups (Bamforth 1994; Lehmer 1971; Toom 1992b; Zimmerman and Bradley 1993), there is no doubt that they were hostile towards one another when Europeans first encountered them. In contrast, while Lehmer (1971) suggested that there may have been more than one migration of Siouan-speaking farmers into the Missouri Trench prior to A.D. 1300, such migrations clearly must have been by very closely related Siouan groups. Warfare prior to the fourteenth century Caddoan incursion, then, must have been either among closely related horticultural communities or between these communities and groups outside of the Middle Missouri region.

The temporal patterns of violence identified above pertain to both of these linguistic groups, and include sites representing all of the major cultural historical units defined in the Middle Missouri region for the period at issue here. Considering spatial patterns of violence adds an important dimension to this discussion. Many sites in the Middle Missouri region lack radiocarbon or tree-ring dates, but can be dated generally and linked to either the Siouan or the Caddoan groups on the basis of house form, ceramics, and other kinds of archaeological evidence. For the period from A.D. 1000 to A.D. 1650, archaeologists working in the Dakotas have identified two distinct occupations corresponding to the two major linguistic groups in the region: the Middle Missouri Tradition, linked to the ancestors of the Mandan/Hidatsa, and the Coalescent Tradition, linked to the ancestors of the Arikara. Subdivisions of these, based particularly on ceramic differences, are also widely recognized. Table 3.3 summarizes the currently accepted chronology of these finer subdivisions, based on Johnson's (2001) chronological synthesis (also see Johnson 1998; Toom 1992a, 1992b; Winham and Calabrese 1998; Winham et al. 1994).

The constructs listed in Table 3.3 provide imprecise control over time, both because of the length of the periods of time they include and because some periods that were initially seen as sequential (particularly Initial and Extended Coalescent; cf. Lehmer 1971) now appear to overlap significantly in time. However, they provide at least a rough means of examining the spatial distribution of fortified and unfortified sites before and after A.D. 1300. Extended Middle Missouri sites (A.D. 1200–1400) span this date and are therefore excluded here. However, the distributions of Initial Middle Missouri (A.D. 1000–1300), Initial Coalescent (A.D. 1300–1500), Terminal Middle Missouri (A.D. 1400–1500), and Extended Coalescent (A.D. 1400/1450–1650) sites are interesting. Figures 3.4 through 3.7 show the distribution of fortified and unfortified sites in each of these groups, drawing on Lehmer's (1971) site distribution maps and Winham et al.'s (1994) compendium of site descriptions to identify site locations and fortifications.

Roughly half of Initial Middle Missouri sites, including Fay Tolton, are fortified, and fortified sites of this period are scattered throughout Initial Middle

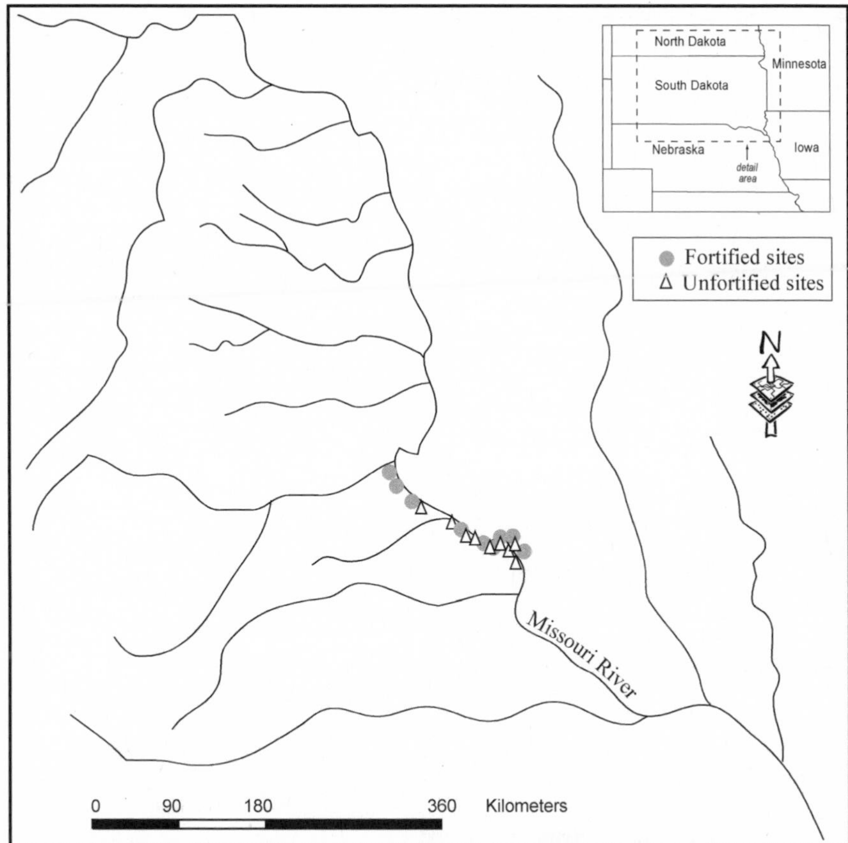

Figure 3.4. Distribution of fortified and unfortified Initial Middle Missouri sites in the Middle Missouri region.

Missouri territory (Figure 3.4). Initial Middle Missouri sites overlap in time with Initial Coalescent sites, and it is possible that some of these sites were fortified against Initial Coalescent groups. However, the data from Fay Tolton leave no doubt that Initial Middle Missouri sites were fortified prior to the 1300s. With this in mind, the distribution of fortified sites suggests that Initial Middle Missouri communities could be endangered regardless of their location, although the association of undefended Initial Middle Missouri sites with non-drought intervals suggests that dangerous conditions were episodic. If all Middle Missouri Tradition groups were closely related to one another, the warfare evident at Fay Tolton and elsewhere is likely to have been within rather than between ethnic or linguistic groups.

About half of Initial Coalescent sites are fortified, but fortified sites of this period are found almost entirely on the east bank of the river, with unfortified

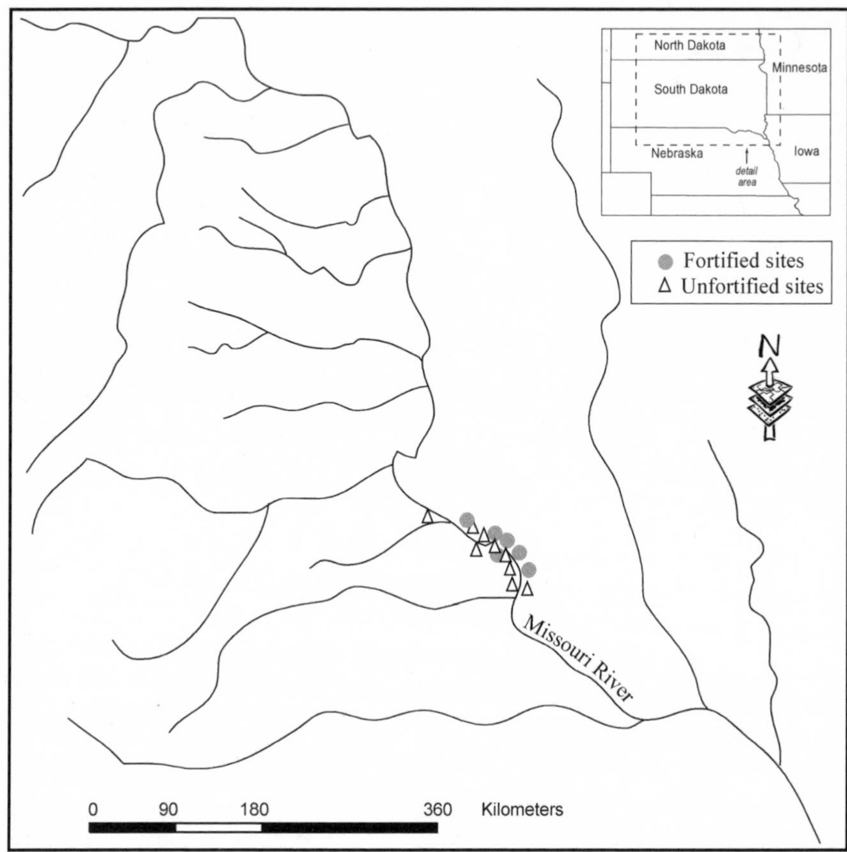

Figure 3.5. Distribution of fortified and unfortified Initial Coalescent sites in the Middle Missouri region.

sites scattered on the west bank (Figure 3.5). This contrast could indicate that danger tended to come from the east, with the river itself serving as protection for communities on the west bank. It could also imply that sites on the two banks were built at different times, but too few Initial Coalescent sites are dated to test this possibility. With Middle Missouri communities in the region as well, though, warfare between these groups seems likely. Initial Coalescent groups on the east bank may also have been in danger from Middle Missouri Tradition groups on the James River to the east, as well as from similar groups in northwestern Iowa.

In contrast, Terminal Middle Missouri sites were almost always fortified, suggesting a level of danger that required fortifications in essentially every case, regardless of specific site ages or locations (Figure 3.6). This pattern is particularly striking because Terminal Middle Missouri sites are extremely large—Huff,

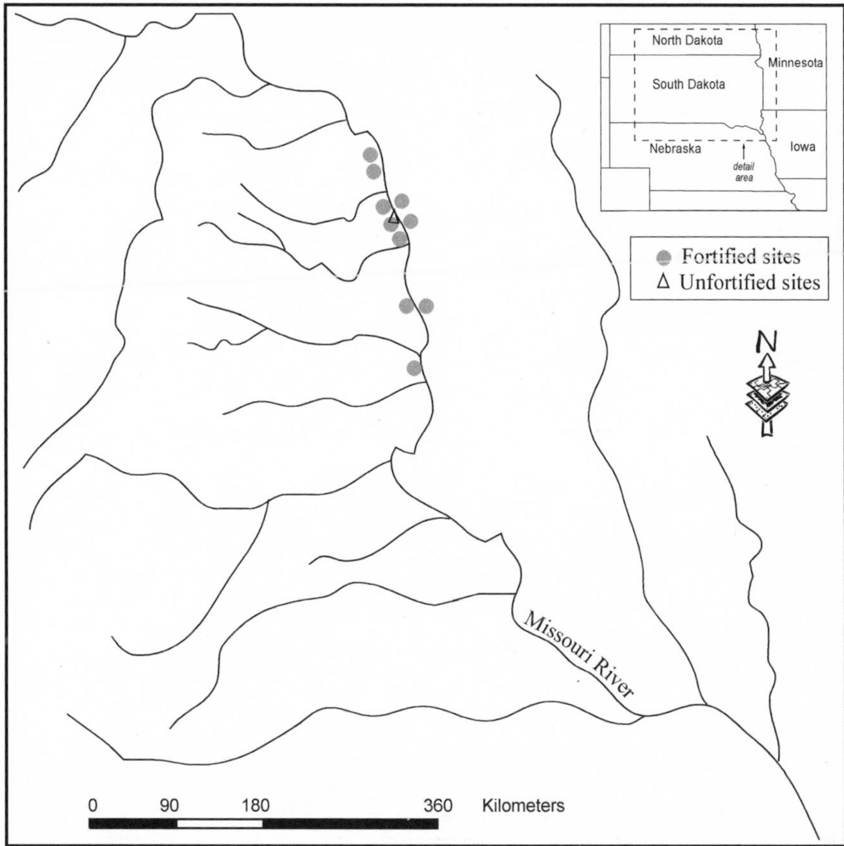

Figure 3.6. Distribution of fortified and unfortified Terminal Middle Missouri sites in the Middle Missouri region.

for example, contains 90 houses and probably housed as many as 1,000 people (Wood 1967)—and must therefore have been formidable targets. Finally, the typically small and scattered Extended Coalescent sites (like the La Roche site and Molstad Village) are fortified primarily in the northern and southern portions of their distribution (Figure 3.7).

The southern Extended Coalescent sites may have been endangered by one or more of the Siouan-speaking groups referred to archaeologically as the Oneota; Oneota occupation is evident in northwestern Iowa and adjacent areas beginning in the fourteenth century (Henning 1998; Ritterbush 2002). Certainly, the post-contact Omaha and Ponca of eastern Nebraska, who are clearly descended from the Oneota, have specific traditions indicating that they raided the Arikara along the Missouri River in southern South Dakota when they first arrived on the Plains (Fletcher and La Flesche 1972:74–75). The northern communities were

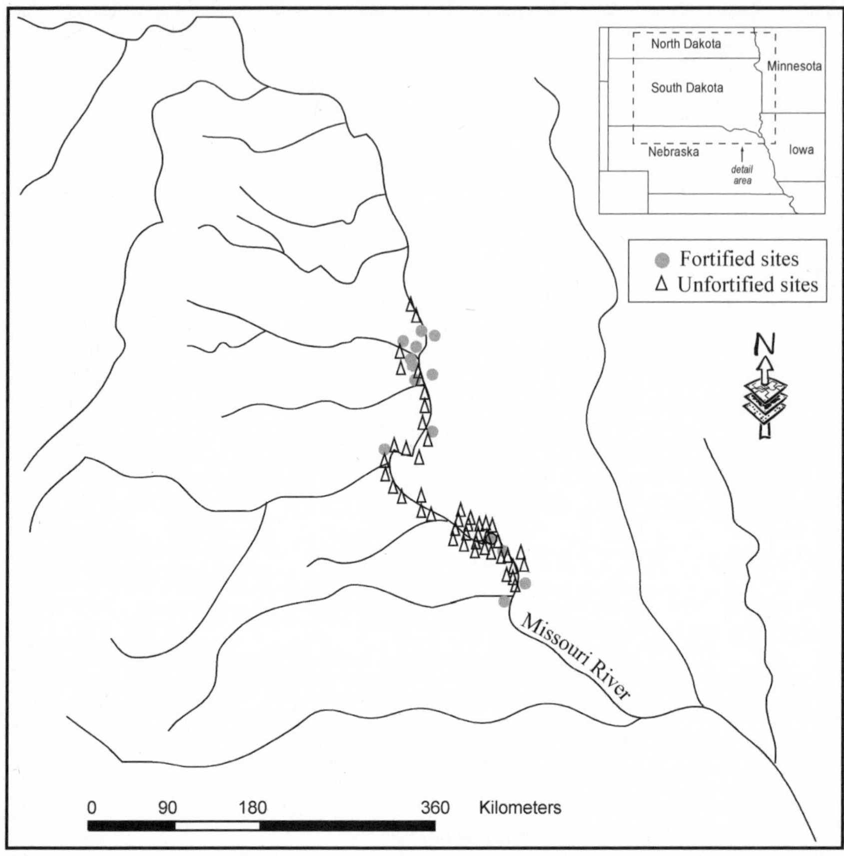

Figure 3.7. Distribution of fortified and unfortified Extended Coalescent sites in the Middle Missouri region.

likely defended against their Terminal Middle Missouri neighbors, although the presence of fortified sites on the northeastern edge of the region that may have been occupied by the ancestors of the post-contact Dakota (Michlovic and Schneider 1993), who ravaged the Middle Missouri towns in the eighteenth and nineteenth centuries, suggest another potential enemy. Regardless, the northern Extended Coalescent communities appear to have had good reasons for building their palisades: 7.66 percent (39 of 509) of individuals buried in Extended Coalescent and later cemeteries in this northern area show marks of scalping, compared to only 0.01 percent (2 of 242) of individuals buried in similar cemeteries in the central part of South Dakota (Owsley 1994). Perhaps significantly, the unfortified La Roche A community is located just south of this latter region.

Lehmer (1971) noted most of these patterns many years ago. However, they have important implications for this analysis, because they document, albeit tentatively, significant shifts in the social context of violence. It is reasonable to infer that early horticultural groups like the one that occupied the Fay Tolton site were endangered by neighboring members of their own social, cultural, and, probably, linguistic group. The social unit making choices about who to fight appears to have been the residential unit, with decisions presumably made at the community/village level. In contrast, by the latest period considered here, we might infer that violence developed between larger social groups rather than within them. Certainly, the scale of violence evident in the massacre at Crow Creek suggests a band of attackers large enough to require cooperation among a number of communities, as does the sophistication of the bastioned fortifications characteristic of Initial Coalescent and Terminal Middle Missouri sites. Alternatively, the ubiquity of fortifications in Terminal Middle Missouri sites might suggest the existence of conflict among these communities as well as with Extended Coalescent groups to the south or other groups to the east, although generally good relations among the Siouan groups after contact are inconsistent with the first of these possibilities.

Conclusions: Human History, Environmental History, and the Course of War

This analysis has documented a strong relation between climatic deterioration and warfare in the Middle Missouri region: although important issues remain to be definitively settled, it seems clear that sites showing evidence of community-level violence date disproportionately to periods of drought. Furthermore, evidence of malnutrition in the massacre victims at the Crow Creek site and a possibly greater reliance on wild plant foods in fortified than in unfortified sites suggest a causal relation between drought and war. Farmers in the Middle Missouri region seem often to have responded to subsistence stress induced by prolonged drought by raiding their neighbors.

However, other evidence considered here also highlights essential aspects of warfare in the Dakotas that climate does not explain: droughts may have led to warfare among farmers there, but social forces appear to have influenced or determined who those farmers went to war against. Prior to the migration of Central Plains (probably Caddoan-speaking) groups into the region around A.D. 1300, fortifications appear to have been scattered throughout the region, suggesting that, during droughts, individual communities sometimes attacked each other. If this is so, these attacks appear to have been carried out against culturally/linguistically related (Siouan-speaking Initial and Extended Middle Missouri) groups, implying a social order in which individual communities formed both decision-making units and, perhaps, units of social group (most likely kin group) identification.

This may have changed with the appearance of Caddoan (Initial Coalescent) groups from the Central Plains in the fourteenth century, although this is not certain. The apparent absence of drought in the region for most of the 1300s suggests that warfare should have been rare at that time. However, whether this is correct or not, by the 1500s Siouan and Caddoan groups show very different geographic distributions of fortifications: the former virtually always lived in large and heavily fortified towns while the latter generally lived in more numerous smaller communities which were fortified mainly at the northern and southern ends of their distribution. Caddoan (ancestral Arikara) groups were presumably endangered in the north by their Siouan (ancestral Mandan and, perhaps, Hidatsa) neighbors and, as noted earlier, possibly by ancestral Dakota groups to the northeast. In the south, the ancestral Arikara probably defended themselves against other Siouan-speaking Oneota groups.

That is, these data suggest a shift over time from a perception that culturally related neighbors could be potential enemies to a perception that culturally distinct "others" could be potential enemies. The exact social and ideological processes that produced these changes are unclear, and the differences in community size and the distribution of fortifications between Terminal Middle Missouri and Extended Coalescent occupations suggest that these processes may have operated differently in different social groups; it is possible that the large Terminal Middle Missouri towns and the social mechanisms needed to integrate them developed as a response to a greater danger of war in more northern areas. Regardless of this problem, though, the Middle Missouri case clearly illustrates a dynamic interaction between a constant environmental context and cause of war and a changing social or cultural setting in which decisions were made about who to go to war against.

We need more detailed work on Middle Missouri regional culture history, climatic change, and intercommunity relations to sort these patterns out more clearly. At minimum, it is essential to continue to refine the radiocarbon chronology for the region, to address the details of occupation history and construction sequence at sites like Crow Creek in more detail, and to seek out other lines of chronological evidence to reduce the imprecision inherent in radiocarbon dating. Dendrochronology holds a largely untapped promise for archaeology on the northern Plains, and it is particularly unfortunate that, after an early interest in it, it has languished for so long. Coupling an increasingly detailed body of chronological data with comprehensive information on environmental conditions and on the social development of horticultural communities in the Middle Missouri region will continue to illuminate the development of warfare there, and this information will have important implications for anthropological perspectives on warfare in general.

Acknowledgments

I wrote this initially in response to Rachel Kluender's invitation to participate in a symposium at the 2001 SAA meetings entitled "Peopling a No-Man's Land: Anthropological and Archaeological Approaches to Pre-State Conflict." Sarah Pfannkuche made this chapter possible by providing references to the new literature on Northern Plains paleoclimate. I also appreciate comments from Stan Ahler and Larry Zimmerman. Finally, many discussions with Curtis Nepstad-Thornberry and Mark Mitchell have helped me to focus and refine the data and interpretations I present here. Christine Ward and Curtis ably produced the illustrations.

Notes

1. Although it is clear that all three of these lakes show similar drought sequences (Fritz et al. 2000), these data must be considered carefully. One of the three (Rice Lake) is in north-central North Dakota, at the extreme northern end of the region examined here. Of the three, it is least likely to measure climatic patterns throughout the region. Furthermore, the climatic sequences from all three localities are dated by radiocarbon, and the specific dates anchoring the time period of interest here vary significantly from sequence to sequence (Fritz et al. 2000:Table 2). Only a single date anchors the critical part of the sequences from Rice Lake and one of the other lakes (Coldwater Lake) and the Coldwater Lake date (620±60 B.P.) falls directly on a plateau in the radiocarbon calibration curve, which reduces its precision. In contrast, the sequence from Moon Lake, in southeastern North Dakota, has three dates in the period from A.D. 900 to A.D. 1600, and none of these fall on plateaus.

2. Johnson (1994) makes a similar case for sites of all ages throughout the region considering ceramic evidence of occupation during more than one period of time, evidence of house rebuilding, and midden depth. The present analysis draws more heavily on Toom's approach for two reasons. First, Johnson's (1994) discussion indicates that ceramics are not strongly time-sensitive for several long periods of occupation in the Middle Missouri region, implying that sites could be occupied for long periods without showing evidence of this in ceramic style. Second, midden depth can be seriously impacted by erosion and modern land use, and is in any event unevenly discussed in published site reports.

3. Since completing his 1994 synthesis, Johnson has dated additional sites and has integrated these dates into a newer version of his synthesis (Johnson 2001). Unfortunately, this newer synthesis was not available when the present analysis was completed, and this chapter relies on the 1994 data.

4. The exception to this is the Pretty Head site. Pretty Head shows evidence for two occupations thought to be close to one another in time, but neither of these appears to have been very long (Caldwell and Jensen 1969). However, it has produced three radiocarbon dates, two (one from each of the occupations) indicating an age in the fourteenth or fifteenth century and one (from the stratigraphically lower occupation) indicating an age in the eleventh or twelfth century (Johnson 1994). With no reason to infer the chronological depth of occupation these dates imply and no basis for choosing among them, it is not possible at present to reliably assess the age of this site, and I do not consider it further here.

References

Alex, R. 1981. The Village Cultures of the Lower James River Valley, South Dakota. Unpublished Ph.D. dissertation, Department of Anthropology, University of Wisconsin, Madison.

Bamforth, D. 1994. Indigenous People, Indigenous Violence: Pre-Contact Genocidal Warfare on the North American Great Plains. *Man* 29:95–115.

Blakeslee, D. 1994. A Reassessment of Some Radiocarbon Dates from the Central Plains. *Plains Anthropologist* 39:203–210.

Bovee, D., and D. Owsley. 1994. Evidence of Warfare at the Heerwald Site. In *Skeletal Biology on the Great Plains,* edited by D. Owsley and R. Jantz, 355–362. Washington, D.C.: Smithsonian Institution Press.

Brooks, R. 1994. Warfare on the Southern Plains. In *Skeletal Biology on the Great Plains,* edited by D. Owsley and R. Jantz, 317–324. Washington, D.C.: Smithsonian Institution Press.

Bryson, R., D. Baerreis, and W. Wendland. 1970. The Character of Late-Glacial and Post-Glacial Climatic Changes. In *Pleistocene and Recent Environments of the Great Plains*, edited by W. Dort and J. Jones, 53–74. Lawrence: University of Kansas Press.

Calabrese, F. 1972. *Cross Ranch: A Study of Variability in a Stable Cultural Tradition*. Plains Anthropologist Memoir No. 9.

Caldwell, W., and R. Jensen. 1969. *The Grand Detour Phase*. Smithsonian Institution River Basin Surveys Publications in Salvage Archaeology, No. 13.

Caldwell, W., and L. Snyder. 1982. Dendrochronology in Plains Prehistory: An Assessment. *Plains Anthropologist* 27:33–40.

Cleaveland, M., and D. Duvick. 1992. Iowa Climate Reconstructed from Tree-rings, 1640–1982. *Water Resources Research* 28:2607–2615.

Duvick, S., and T. Blasing. 1981. A Dendroclimatic Reconstruction of Annual Precipitation Amounts in Iowa cince 1680. *Water Resources Research* 17:1183–1189.

Fletcher, A., and F. La Flesche. 1972. *The Omaha Tribe*. Lincoln: University of Nebraska Press.

Fritz, S. E. Ito, Z. Yu, K. Laird, and D. Engstrom. 2000. Hydrologic Variation in the Northern Great Plains During the Last Two Millennia. *Quaternary Research* 53:175–184.

Grantham, L. 1976. Carbonized Seeds. In *Fay Tolton and the Initial Middle Missouri Variant,* edited by W. R. Wood, 26. Missouri Archaeological Society Research Series No.13.

Gregg, J., and L. Zimmerman. 1986. Malnutrition in Fourteenth Century South Dakota: Osteopathological Manifestations. *North American Archaeologist* 7:191–214.

Grissino-Mayer, H. 1996. A 2129–tear Reconstruction of Precipitation for Northwestern New Mexico, USA. In *Tree-Rings, Environment, and Humanity,* edited by J. Dean, D. Meko, and T. Sweetnam, 191–204. Tucson, AZ: Radiocarbon.

Henning, D. 1998. The Oneota Tradition. In *Archaeology on the Great Plains,* edited by W. R. Wood, 345–414. Lawrence: University Press of Kansas.

Hoffman, J. J. 1967. *Molstad Village*. Smithsonian Institution River Basin Surveys Publications in Salvage Archaeology No. 4.

———. 1968. *The La Roche Site*. Smithsonian Institution River Basin Surveys Publications in Salvage Archaeology No. 11.

Holliman, S., and D. Owsley. 1994. Osteology of the Fay Tolton Site: Implications for Warfare During the Initial Middle Missouri Variant. In *Skeletal Biology on the Great Plains*, edited by D. Owsley and R. Jantz, 345–354. Washington, D.C.: Smithsonian Institution Press.

Johnson, A. M. 1979. Extended Middle Missouri Components in the Big Bend Region, South Dakota. *Special Publications of the South Dakota Archaeological Society*. No. 1.

Johnson, C. 1994. *A Chronology of Middle Missouri Plains Village Sites*. Department of Anthropology, National Museum of Natural History, Smithsonian Institution, Washington, D.C.

———. 1998. The Coalescent Tradition. In *Archaeology on the Great Plains,* edited by W. R. Wood, 308–344. Lawrence: University Press of Kansas.

———. 2001. *A Chronology of Middle Missouri Plains Village Sites*. Paleocultural Research Group Research Contribution No. 39, Flagstaff, AZ.

Jones, T., G. Brown, L. Raab, J. McVickar, W. Spaulding, D. Kennett, A. York, and P. Walker. 1999. Environmental Imperatives Reconsidered: Demographic Crises in Western North America During the Medieval Climatic Anomaly. *Current Anthropology* 40:137–170.

Kivett, M., and R. Jensen. 1976. *Archaeological Investigations at the Crow Creek Site (39BF11)*. Nebraska Historical Society Publications in Anthropology No. 7.

Laird, K., S. Fritz, and B. Cummings. 1998. A Diatom-based Reconstruction of Drought Intensity, Duration, and Frequency from Moon Lake, North Dakota: A Sub-decadal Record of the Past 2300 years. *Journal of Paleolimnology* 19:161–179.

Lehmer, D. 1966. *The Fire Heart Creek Site*. Smithsonian Institution River Basin Surveys Publications in Salvage Archaeology 1.

———. 1971. *Introduction to Middle Missouri Archaeology*. National Park Service Anthropological Papers No. 1.

Lintz, C. 1986. *Architectural and Community Variability Within the Antelope Creek Phase of the Texas Panhandle*. Oklahoma Archaeological Survey, Studies in Oklahoma's Past No. 14.

Michlovic, M. G., and F. E. Schneider. 1993. The Shea Site: A Prehistoric Fortified Village on the Northeastern Plains. *Plains Anthropologist* 38:117–137.

Miller, C. 1964. *The Hosterman Site (32PO7), Oahe Reservoir Area, Potter County, South Dakota*. Smithsonian Institution Bureau of American Ethnology Bulletin 189, No. 35.

Moerman, D., and D. Jones. 1966. Investigations at the Cattle Oiler Site, 39ST224, Big Bend Reservoir, South Dakota. Manuscript on file at the National Park Service, Midwest Archeological Center, Lincoln, NE.

Nepstad-Thornberry, C. 1998. Prehistoric Plant Utilization and the Initial Middle Missouri Tradition. Unpublished Master's thesis, Department of Anthropology, Iowa State University, Ames.

O'Shea, J., and P. Bridges. 1989. The Sargent Site Ossuary (25CU28), Custer County, Nebraska. *Plains Anthropologist* 34:7–21.

Owsley, D. 1994. Warfare in Coalescent Tradition Populations of the Northern Plains. In *Skeletal Biology on the Great Plains,* edited by D. Owsley and R. Jantz, 333–344. Washington, D.C.: Smithsonian Institution Press.

Read, D., and S. LeBlanc. 2003. Population Growth, Carrying Capacity, and Conflict. *Current Anthropology* 44:59–85.

Ritterbush, L. 2002. Leary Site Revisited: Oneota and Central Plains Tradition Occupation Along the Lower Missouri. *Plains Anthropologist* 47:251–264.

Roper, D. 1995. Spatial Dynamics and Historical Process in the Central Plains Tradition. *Plains Anthropologist* 40:203–221.

Spaulding, A. 1956. *The Arzberger Site, Hughes County, South Dakota*. Occasional Contributions from the Museum of Anthropology of the University of Michigan No. 16.

Sperry, J. 1968. The Shermer Site (32EM10). *Plains Anthropologist Memoir* No. 5.

Stahle, D., and M. Cleaveland. 1988. Texas Drought History Reconstructed and Analyzed from 1698 to 1980. *Journal of Climate* 1:59–74.

Stahle, D., M. Cleaveland, and J. G. Hehr. 1985. A 450-year Drought Reconstruction for Arkansas, United States. *Nature* 316:530–532.

Stahle, D., E. Cook, M. Cleaveland, M. Therrell, D. Meko, H. Grissino-Mayer, E. Watson, and B. Luckman. 2000. Tree-ring Data Document Sixteenth Century Megadrought over North America. *EOS* 81:124–125.

Steinacher, T. 1983. *Archaeological Investigations at the Whistling Elk Site (39HU242), 1978–1979*. Division of Archaeological Research, Department of Anthropology, University of Nebraska, Lincoln.

———. 1990. Settlement and Ceramic Variability at the Sommers Site (39ST56), Stanley County, South Dakota. Unpublished Ph.D. dissertation, Department of Anthropology, University of Oklahoma.

Stockton, C., and D. Meko. 1983. Drought Recurrence in the Great Plains as Reconstructed from Long-term Tree-ring Records. *Journal of the Climate and Applied Meteorology* 22:17–29.

Stuiver, M., P. Reimer, E. Bard, J. Beck, G. Burr, K. Hughen, B. Kromer, F. McCormac, J. Plicht, and M. Spurk. 1998. INTCAL98 Radiocarbon Age Calibration, 24,000–0 cal BP. *Radiocarbon* 40:1041–1083.

Thiessen, T. 1977. A Tentative Radiocarbon Chronology for the Middle Missouri Tradition. In *Trends in Middle Missouri Prehistory*, edited by W. R. Wood, 59–82. Plains Anthropologist Memoir No. 13.

Tiffany, J. 1983. An Overview of the Middle Missouri Tradition. In *Prairie Archaeology*, edited by G. Gibbon, 87–108. University of Minnesota Publications in Anthropology No. 3. Minneapolis.

Toom, D. 1990. *Archaeological Test Excavations at Eight Sites in the Lake Sharpe Project Area of Hughes, Lyman, and Stanley Counties, South Dakota 1987*. Western Cultural Resource Management, Boulder, CO.

———. 1992a. Climate and Sedentism in the Middle Missouri Subarea of the Plains. Unpublished Ph.D. dissertation, Department of Anthropology, University of Colorado, Boulder.

———. 1992b. Radiocarbon Dating of the Western Initial Middle Missouri Variant: Some New Dates and a Critical Review of Old Dates. *Plains Anthropologist* 37:115–128.

Toom, D., and K. Kvamme. 2002. The "Big House" at Whistling Elk Village (39HU242): Geophysical Findings and Archaeological Truths. *Plains Anthropologist* 47:5–16.

Weakly, H. 1965. Recurrence of Drought in the Great Plains During the Last 700 years. *Agricultural Engineering*, February: 85.

———. 1971. *Tree-Ring Dating and Archaeology in South Dakota*. Plains Anthropologist Memoir 8.

Wedel, W. 1986. *Central Plains Prehistory*. Lincoln: University of Nebraska Press.

Wendland, W. 1978. Holocene Man in North America: The Ecological Setting and Climatic Background. *Plains Anthropologist* 23:273–287.

Wendland, W., and R. Bryson. 1974. Dating Climatic Episodes of the Holocene. *Quaternary Research* 4:9–24.

Willey, P. 1990. *Prehistoric Warfare on the Great Plains*. New York: Garland Press.

Winham, R., and F. Calabrese. 1998. The Middle Missouri Tradition. In *Archaeology on the Great Plains,* edited by W. R. Wood, 269–307. Lawrence: University Press of Kansas.

Winham, R. P., W. R. Wood, and L. A. Hannus. 1994. *Village Sites of the Middle Missouri Subarea AD 1000 to AD 1887*. National Landmark Theme Study, Archaeology Laboratory, Augustana College, Sioux Falls, SD.

Wood, W. R. 1967. *An Interpretation of Mandan Culture History*. Smithsonian Institution Bureau of American Ethnology Bulletin 198, No. 39.

———. 1976. *Fay Tolton and the Middle Missouri Variant*. Missouri Archaeological Society Research Series No. 13.

Wood, W. R., and A. Woolworth. 1964. *The Paul Brave Site (32SI4), Oahe Reservoir, South Dakota*. Smithsonian Institution Bureau of American Ethnology Bulletin 189, No. 33.

Woodhouse, C., and P. Brown. 2001. Tree-ring Evidence for Great Plains Drought. *Tree-Ring Research* 57:89–103.

Woodhouse, C., and J. Overpeck. 1998. 2000 Years of Drought Variability in the Central United States. *Bulletin of the American Meteorological Society* 79:2693–2714.

Woolworth, A., and W. R. Wood. 1964. *The Demery Site (32CO1), Oahe Reservoir, South Dakota*. Smithsonian Institution Bureau of American Ethnology Bulletin 189, No. 34.

Zimmerman, L., and L. Bradley. 1993. The Crow Creek Massacre: Initial Coalescent Warfare and Speculation About the Genesis of Extended Coalescent. In *Prehistory and Human Ecology of the Western Prairies and Northern Plains,* edited by J. Tiffany, 215–227. Plains Anthropologist Memoir No. 27.

4

The Transformation of Mississippian Warfare

Four Case Studies from the Mid-South

DAVID H. DYE

Through the accounts of the sixteenth-century Spanish and French expeditions to the Southeastern Woodlands of North America, we catch a fleeting glimpse of chiefly polities at war. Fortified towns dotted the landscape in some regions, such as the Tennessee and Mississippi Valleys, while in other areas such as the Caddo region, they were noticeably absent (Perttula 1992:139). Scalping and dismemberment are mentioned, while some narratives hint at warfare iconography. The objectives of success in warfare seem to have been primarily political, revolving around legitimizing dominance and authority, resolving chiefly grievances, and expanding and consolidating one's polity (Dye 2002:130). These remarkable ethnohistoric descriptions provide only tantalizing hints and must be used in conjunction with archaeological evidence. Unfortunately, the majority of Mississippian chiefdoms were devastated by social and political disruptions brought about by European contact, altering the nature of warfare and ushering in new political orders.

Archaeological evidence demonstrates that the Mississippian chiefdoms encountered by the French and Spanish expeditions had undergone a six-hundred-year transformation that gave rise to a distinctive style of warfare. Group selective pressures had eliminated those societies that could not compete in this arena. As is the case with chiefly societies in many parts of the world, leaders who could effectively mobilize and coordinate warriors, negotiate alliances, and successfully defend their territory could displace or incorporate less militarily organized polities (Carneiro 1967; Johnson and Earle 2000:259), thereby establishing regional or local order through forceful incorporation (Carneiro 1981).

Numerous transformations in Mississippian warfare took place over time, resulting from technological changes, historical circumstances, natural forces, social change, and ideological orientations. These factors brought about competition for essential and valuable resources, both tangible and intangible (Lambert 2002:228; Milner 1999). For example, changes in paleoclimate and its effects on the potential food reserves of Mississippian societies would have affected patterns of warfare as chiefdoms emerged and collapsed based on the abilities of local leaders to provide for their populations in time of resources stress (Anderson 2001; Anderson et al. 1995). Human agency—revenge, status rivalry, and political struggles—also fostered a hostile political world.

Mississippian warfare had its origins well into prehistory. Archaeological evidence documents an ancient pattern of guerilla-style ambushes, raids, and skirmishes carried out by relatively small groups of people using bows and arrows and war clubs against neighboring polities. Ethnohistoric accounts suggest that such raids were organized to penetrate an enemy's territory and to return with minimal losses. Raiders executed their tasks swiftly, conducting them with total surprise and unremitting violence (Dye 2002:131; Steinen 1992:135). The threat of physical violence from raiding appears to have been endemic over a large area from A.D. 900 to A.D. 1600.

Coupled with this ancient raiding pattern of warfare was perhaps a more formal, organized form of combat that emerged with the development of chiefly warfare. Formal or "national" warfare necessitated the construction of great defensive structures, including palisades, bastions, and moats around towns which were placed in defensible positions, such as bluff tops, river bends, and islands. Battles composed of large forces on land and water were recorded throughout the sixteenth century and attest to the mobilization potential of chiefly militias by Mississippian rulers (DePratter 1983; Eid 1985). These descriptions and depictions of formal battle structure are often discounted as sixteenth century exaggerations and ethnocentrism (Milanich 1996:86; Milner 1999:127–128). However, the accumulation of large forces was well within the organizational abilities of chiefly rulers, as seen in the military capabilities of less centralized polities such as the Iroquois.

A landscape of chiefdoms separated by large buffer zones resulted. The size of most Mississippian polities was usually 40 kilometers across or less (Scarry 1999a:61) and they were separated from one another by lightly occupied and lightly used buffer zones that were usually 20 to 30 kilometers across. Along river valleys or across upland regions the unoccupied areas were greater (Hally 1993). By increasing spatial separation between neighboring polities, the danger and frequency of military attack would have been curtailed or lessened, reducing competition among neighboring polities (Anderson 1990; DeBoer 1988). Hunting and foraging pressure on upland resources also may have been reduced.

At its height, Mississippian warfare was carried out for reasons ranging from material necessities to the emulation of supernatural heroes. Warrior chiefs and priests sought to reduce stress in their polities while achieving a fundamental connection with otherworldly powers through ritual. The accoutrements of ritualized combat are evident in elite burials and indicate the desire by elites to increase their power and efficacy in their political struggles. Mississippian warfare was characterized by a complex organization based on political, economic, and ideological sources of power. How these sources of power were manipulated and employed changed through time and varied from polity to polity based on environmental conditions, specific political histories, and personal chiefly abilities and ambitions.

Mississippian warfare has been the subject of scholarly interest for several decades following Larson's (1972) initial landmark study (Anderson 1994a, 1994b; DePratter 1983; Dickson 1981; Dye 1990, 1995, 2002, 2004a; Gibson 1974; Milner 1995, 1998, 1999, 2000; Milner et al. 1991; Steinen 1992; Van Horne 1993). The archaeological record in the prehistoric Southeast and lower Midwest is replete with evidence for late prehistoric warfare: fortified settlements, skeletal trauma, utilitarian and symbolic weapons, and combat iconography. Most researchers agree that late prehistoric warfare was endemic, widespread, and an integral component of many aspects of daily life (Anderson 2001:165). Current scholarly debate centers on "why warfare was conducted, the extent to which people's lives were affected by it, and the part it played in particular cultural trajectories" (Milner 1999:108).

In this chapter, I take a diachronic and comparative approach to Mississippian warfare, addressing the transformation of warfare from approximately A.D. 800 to A.D. 1600 (Late Woodland through the Mississippian periods) among four Mississippian chiefdoms in the central mid-South of the Eastern North American Woodlands (Figure 4.1). Comparative analysis of intergroup conflict for specific chiefdoms sheds light on their developmental history and regional context, revealing similarities and differences in their political trajectories. The comparison of cultural developments in these four localities highlights the variability from region to region in organizational complexity and change, population distributions, agricultural intensification, prestige goods exchange, craft specialization, and the nature of warfare throughout the Mississippian period (Table 4.1). In each study, differing developmental trajectories are identified, but the common denominator is the major role that warfare played in the development and maintenance of social hierarchy and the power base of ruling elites.

Mississippian warfare grew out of earlier Late Woodland intersocietal conflict. One of the key characteristics of the emergence of Mississippian society is the initial establishment of hierarchically organized societies based on differential access to basic resources (Sussenbach 1993:130–131). Conflict over resources sparked hostile and aggressive actions among chiefly polities, producing well-documented archaeological signatures of violence (Milner 1998,

1999). Intersocietal conflict, subsistence stress, and the emergence of ranking and hierarchical organization fueled the development of Mississippian warfare, transcending earlier Late Woodland forms of conflict. Shifts in settlement organization, defensive structures, patterning of skeletal trauma, and symbolic representations of combat took place in the Late Woodland to Mississippian transition.

The chiefdoms treated here are Etowah in northeastern Georgia, Moundville in west central Alabama, Lubbub Creek in west central Alabama and east central Mississippi, and Shiloh/Koger's Island in western Tennessee and northwestern Alabama. Each of these polities exhibit differing social and historical trajectories and manifest varying power strategies by ruling elites to expand, consolidate, and entrench their political control in order to protect their varying interests and sources of power and authority. In each case study, I examine: 1) the overall political and social trajectory of each chiefdom, 2) skeletal trauma, 3) settlement data and fortifications, 4) war weaponry, both utilitarian and symbolic, and 5) iconography. In each case the archaeological record documents a heightened level of warfare once chiefs begin to mobilize labor and goods for defensive and offensive strategies. Competition over resources, especially social labor, brings about a restructuring of the social and political geography. The transformation of the Mississippian geopolitical world resulted in large part from competition among chiefly elites who sought to expand their influence among neighboring polities. Their ability or inability to be successful resulted in the regional emergence, fluorescence, domination, and collapse of chiefdoms in a complex matrix of political change.

Warfare in the mid-South was a key element in chiefdom political consolidation, maintenance, and, in many instances, demise in the late prehistory of the region, although the political trajectories of each polity differed in basic ways. Chiefs struggled to gain and hold valuable tangible and intangible resources, while defending their polities against neighboring aggressors. The polities under consideration here support the idea that regional warfare was both deadly and violent, as chiefs manipulated staple and finance wealth and ideology to further their political goals.

Pre-Mississippian Warfare

Warfare originates among hunter-gatherers with the rise of social segmentation among lineal descent groups (Kelly 2000). As these social segments seek collective retribution, retaliation, or revenge from any member of the target, enemy social group, this principle of social substitution may result in prolonged blood feuding and over time often becomes institutionalized among mutually hostile, neighboring social groups. In this light, warfare can be defined as armed conflict carried out by a collective or corporate group of kinsmen who employ lethal weapons with deadly force, which results in the deaths of other persons whose killings are envisioned in advance (Kelly 2000:3–5).

Warfare based on social substitution emerged as tribal societies evolved in Eastern North America approximately 6,800 years ago (Anderson 2002). Appreciable archaeological evidence documents the beginnings of violent conflict among mid-southern hunter-gatherer groups (Bridges et al. 2000; Smith 1993a, 1993b, 1995, 1996a, 1996b, 1997). Widespread long-distance exchange, monumental construction, increases in sedentism, territorial marking, and intergroup conflict are well documented at this time (Anderson 2002; Brown and Vierra 1983:165; Dye 1996; Smith 1986:18–27). With increased exploitation of riverine resources, especially shoal environments, populations increased in the richer resource zones. Economies that specialize in the intensive harvesting of narrow spectrum resources often exhibit increased conflict, resulting from efforts to restrict access to critical resources in favored localities through restricted territorial control and management (Dye 1996:157; Walthall 1980:65–67; Winters 1974:xi). Intergroup conflict may have emerged as a result of territorial boundary maintenance (Price and Brown 1985:12) and population growth caused by innovations in subsistence technology (Anderson 2002). This combination of environment and demography may have set the stage for the early appearance of pre-agricultural, hunter-gatherer warfare (Haas 1999:22–23).

A raiding style of warfare resulting in violent death was already established and ritualized in the mid-South and Midwest by the Late Archaic period (ca. 4000–1000 B.C.). Indications of raiding are seen in the pattern of perimortem mutilation or dismemberment due to trophy-taking behaviors and practices, and in mass burials, broken and fractured bones, and embedded spear points (Bridges et al. 2000; Mensforth 2001, 2006; Smith 1993a, 1993b, 1995, 1996a, 1996b, 1997). Although, in general, there is a low but sustained level of mortality from violence at this time from interpersonal disagreements and within group social contests, organized intergroup raiding or warfare by formal kin groups also took place, resulting in the deaths of multiple individuals (Bridges et al. 2000; Mensforth 2001, 2006).

The use of modified human bones as grave accompaniments has its beginnings in the Late Archaic (Jacobi and Hill 2001). Grave accompaniments include skull cups and gorgets, carved fibulae and radius awl/pins, and modified and cut tibia and femur shafts (Smith 1997:257–258). Trophy-taking behavior at such an early archaeological horizon among intensive hunter-gatherers may have been one avenue of prestige enhancement, indicating the "catalytic" role of warfare in the development of incipient social complexity (Smith 1997:257).

Success in warfare may have been one means for acquiring elevated status among Late Archaic populations (Anderson 2002).

Current evidence of warfare during the period 1000 B.C.–A.D. 900 suggests a continued pattern of small-scale raiding among kin groups. The continuation of trophy-taking behavior underscores the symbolic dimension of intergroup conflict. Warfare at this time appears to have been widespread and endemic, but lacking the intensity and organization of centuries to come. The introduction of the bow and arrow as early as A.D. 600 (Blitz 1988:131; Nassaney and Pyle 1999:253) ushered in new patterns of combat characterized by a reorganization of the scale and practice of social conflict. With the adoption of the bow and arrow, emerging forms of political organization and increasing reliance on improved forms of defensive structures set the stage for a transformation in violent conflict.

The Transformation of Mississippian Warfare

The Etowah Chiefdom

Immediately prior to the emergence of the Etowah chiefdom, the Upper Coosa drainage of northeastern Alabama and northwestern Georgia was occupied by four contiguous Late Woodland (A.D. 700–1000) population clusters (Little 1999; Little et al. 1997:157–158).[1] These clusters shared several broad similarities: fortifications with protected parallel-walled entranceways and adjacent ditches, use of the bow and arrow, widespread use of shelled maize cached in underground storage pits, and pottery types associated with adjacent regions found in local assemblages.[2] One of the site clusters, Coker Ford, had sites situated on defensive positions, such as prominent elevations overlooking alluvial plains. Some locales were abandoned, while in other areas polities coalesced into larger groups, creating population clusters separated by buffer zones, areas generally devoid of significant populations. Defense against hostile neighbors was an important concern for these four groups.

Simple chiefdoms first emerged in northern Georgia around A.D. 1000, soon after the intensification of maize agriculture and its use as a storable surplus (Hally 1996; Hally and Langford 1988; Little 1999). The Etowah site's initial rise as a chiefly Mississippian center had modest beginnings from A.D. 1000 to A.D. 1100 (Early Etowah phase), marked by initial construction episodes on the largest mound (Mound A) and evidence of large public buildings and a plaza used in feasting activities. This Early Mississippian occupation was concentrated along the edge of the Etowah River (Figure 4.2). Etowah social groups at this time appear to have been relatively egalitarian.

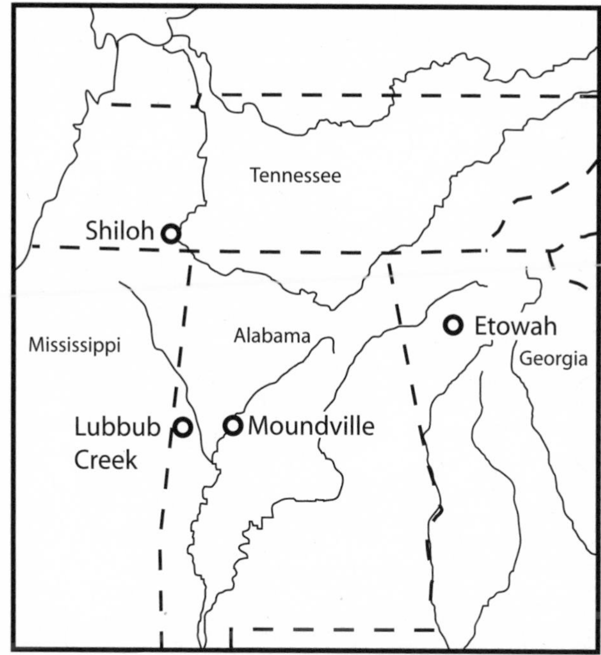

Figure 4.1. The mid-South region, with Mississippian chiefdom centers discussed in the text.

Figure 4.2. Map of Etowah (adapted from King 2003, Figure 5).

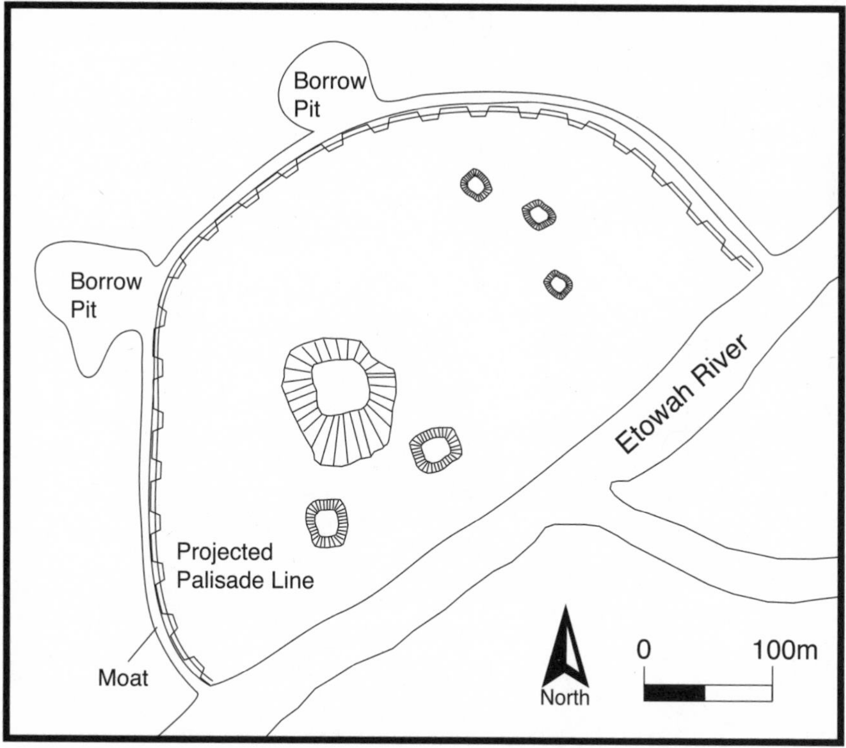

Table 4.1. Summary of Chronological Developments at the Mississippian Chiefdoms Considered in the Text

Date A.D.	General	Etowah	Moundville	Lubbub Creek	Shiloh
1600			Site abandonment; regional population exodus	Site abandonment; regional population exodus	
1550	Contact Period	Site abandonment; regional population exodus			
1500		Capital of tributary simple chiefdom			
1450	Mississippian Post-Climax		Gradual atrophy of centralized control	Fortifications renewed	
1400		Site abandonment			Site abandonment; regional population realignment
1350			Unfortified vacant necropolis		
1300	Mississippian Climax	Fortified capital of regional chiefdom			
1250		Intensive monumental construction	Intensive monumental construction	Unfortified small chiefly center	
1200		Site abandonment; regional population exodus			Short-term fortified capital of regional chiefdom
1150			Fortified capital of regional chiefdom	Fortified independent small chiefly center	
1100	Mississippian Beginnings	Neighboring chiefdoms emerge			
1050					Intensive monumental construction? Maize intensification?
1000		Independent small chiefly center	Maize intensification	Maize intensification	
950	Transition to Mississippian	Maize intensification			
900					

Figure 4.3. Artist's reconstruction of Etowah (rendering by Steven Patricia).

Between A.D. 1100 and A.D. 1200 (Late Etowah phase), mound construction continues on Mound A and begins on Mound B, while the site itself is enlarged, perhaps to accommodate *in situ* population growth. By now, Etowah is one of several small, independent, simple chiefly polities in the region. Around A.D. 1200, the local independent chiefdoms collapsed, resulting in a general population exodus. The Etowah Valley, including the Etowah site, was abandoned between A.D. 1200 and 1250 (Hally and Langford 1988:56; Hally and Rudolph 1986:53–57; King 1991, 1996, 2001:4, 2004:153).

The Etowah site was reoccupied around A.D. 1250 (Middle Mississippian Early Wilbanks phase), marking the time when the area of the site and the pace of mound building increased markedly. Etowah began its rapid rise to political and social greatness (King 2003, 2004) (Figure 4.3). A mortuary mound (Mound C) was created as a repository reserved for Etowah's elites, whose eligibility for burial in the mound was based both on ascribed and achieved ranking principles (Blakely 1995). Many of the early Mound C burials contained few if any grave goods.

After about A.D. 1325 (Late Wilbanks A.D. 1325–1375) a small plaza was built in front of Mound A. Mound construction continued at the site. Some of the later Mound C burials were accompanied by exotic, non-local, military-related items such as shark tooth war clubs (Morse 1998), greenstone celts, monolithic axes, and flint "swords." Ritual combat weapons include copper axes, war clubs mounted with copper and stone-headed celts, flint swords, and monolithic axes.

The burials represent five isolated burial clusters, with one preeminent individual in each group who is accompanied in death by retainers (Blakely 1977:58; Brain and Phillips 1996:169; King 2001:6; Larson 1954:21, 1971, 1993; Waring 1968:93). The preeminent individual in each burial cluster was associated with a copper headed celt or ax. These symbolic or ritual combat artifacts were confined to the highest status individuals, who appear to have held political and ideological offices that were restricted to the elite segment of the polity (Schultz et al. 2001).

Warfare iconography at Etowah was associated with several types of prestige goods. Hightower marine shell gorgets and sheet-copper plates are revealing in their portrayal of dancing figures holding human heads and symbolic combat weaponry. The weapons include flint swords, monolithic axes, and war clubs identical to those found as elite mortuary accompaniments. Headdresses incorporated sheet-copper cutouts in the form of miniature baton-shaped war clubs and arrow points. Scalp symbolism was expressed in sheet-copper gorgets and pendants. The rise of military iconography is associated with political entrenchment (King 2001:6–8). Warfare imagery apparently was an integral component of elite attempts at legitimizing political and social authority through the materialization of a warrior ideology.

As warfare imagery was being portrayed, a formidable fortification with bastions and accompanying ditch was constructed around three sides of the 22 ha site, beginning at and returning to the Etowah River in a deep arc. The palisade wall, believed to have stood about 3.7 m in height, was plastered with clay to prevent its conflagration. The 3-m-deep ditch widened slightly from 7.6 m in width at the bottom to 9.5 m at the top. The builders' skill in earth construction is seen in the flat bottom and almost vertical walls (King 1996:120). The creation of the fortification complex implies a concern for defense that apparently had not existed to the same degree previously (King 2001:7).

There is evidence at Mound C of a destructive event possibly linked to warfare and the abandonment of the site. Marble male and female painted figures had been placed in a log-lined tomb at the base of Mound C's ramp. Statues such as these are believed to represent the mythical founders of ruling lineages (Brown 1976, 2001; Knight 1986; Waring 1968), buried in much the same fashion as members of Etowah's elite ranks. The statues were placed along with the disarticulated (or dismembered) remains of four individuals that had been scattered across the floor, as well as exotic artifacts. The marble figures were found broken, placed one atop the other, as if they had been hurriedly placed in the tomb (King 2001; Larson 1971:65). Shortly after the burial of the statues, the tomb was covered by a thin, midden-like smear of human bone and ritual-related objects which continued down the face of Mound C's ramp. This deposit contained many of the same kinds of elaborate, non-local ritual artifacts recovered from late Mound C burials.

These mortuary events have been interpreted as the hurried burial of Etowah's founding chiefly lineage (Kelly and Larson 1957). The burial of the statues may have taken place under some duress, perhaps the threat of armed conflict, for the burial was followed soon afterwards by the ransacking of the last contents of the Mound C mortuary temple (Brain and Phillips 1996:174–175). The human remains and sacred objects seem to have been tossed from the temple and then trampled as it was being pillaged by invaders (King 2001:8).

Desecrating an enemy's sacred temple was one of the greatest insults an invader could perpetrate against an enemy and was a primary goal of Mississippian military attacks recorded by sixteenth century conquistadors (Anderson 1994b:80, 1999b; DePratter 1983:63; Dye 1990:219, 1994:47; Dye and King 2006). Anderson (1994b:81) notes that attacks on a chiefdom's sacred center could bring about its abandonment and eventual political realignment of the regional population.

Coincident with the destruction of the mortuary shrine, the palisade at Etowah was burned. King believes "the fact that the destruction of the palisade happened prior to the period of abandonment of the site and that it was never rebuilt implies that its destruction was intentional and that the two events are somehow related" (King 2001:7). With the burning of the palisade and the conflagration of the temple, the site was abandoned for one hundred years between A.D. 1375 and A.D. 1475, but this time the Etowah River Valley was not abandoned (Southerlin 1993), suggesting the resident population shifted its political allegiance or affiliation to the regional center of the victor.

After the long hiatus as a political center, the site was reoccupied from A.D. 1475 to A.D. 1550 (Brewster phase). Three additional mounds were constructed during this time. Status was both achieved and ascribed. The highest status individuals were buried adjacent to or within mounds accompanied by exotic and specialized artifacts.

The Etowah site enters the Protohistoric period when Hernando de Soto bivouacked there from August 21 to 30, 1540. The inhabitants reported to the expedition that the province was known as Itaba and was part of a paramountcy, whose regional center was the nearby Little Egypt site. The Etowah site and all of the affiliated towns of northwestern Georgia and northeastern Alabama were abandoned between A.D. 1550 and A.D. 1600, as aboriginal populations migrated down the Coosa drainage. These population movements apparently were spurred by depopulation and associated social disruption brought about by the introduction of European diseases into the interior Southeast. By the early seventeenth century, the Upper Coosa drainage was essentially devoid of aboriginal inhabitants (Smith 1989, 2000).

In summary, Etowah began as a small chiefdom among other similar polities. After two hundred years of political stability, the Etowah valley was abandoned, perhaps becoming a buffer zone between competing regional chiefdoms. The valley was reoccupied after 50 years or so. As Etowah's elite consolidated their political power, the site began its rise to regional prominence after A.D. 1275. Elite entrenchment took place by A.D. 1325, based in part on the exchange of prestige goods, monumental construction projects, erection of a powerful palisade, and excavation of an impressive barrier ditch. Military authority was a vital component of elite political and ideological efficacy. About A.D. 1375, Etowah suffered an attack in which the palisade and temple were destroyed. The site was once again abandoned. After a one-hundred-year hiatus, the population returned to the site. Etowah then became the political capital of Itaba, under the regional center of Coosa, 50 km to the north in the neighboring Coosawattee River Valley (Hudson et al. 1985; King 1999). Etowah was abandoned again in the early seventeenth century for a third and final time as a result of the devastating consequences of European contact.

The Moundville Chiefdom

The Moundville chiefdom, located on Black Warrior River in west central Alabama, underwent a social and political transformation that was fundamentally different from the Etowah regional center.[3] The Moundville polity lacked the series of abandonments as experienced at the Etowah regional center, which resulted in a different configuration of political authority and regional military interaction.

The creation of the Moundville regional center began around A.D. 1020 (terminal Late Woodland) with a series of settlements scattered along the Black Warrior River Valley. Living within small egalitarian communities (Welch 1990:210–212, 1998a:135), the inhabitants relied on wild foods, employing a mobile settlement strategy focused on warm-season floodplain villages and cold-season extractive camps (Welch 1991). As semi-sedentary foragers, they initially lived in small villages, but later coalesced into a few relatively large villages, possibly as a result of intergroup conflict. They continued cultivating small-seeded plants in gardens plots, with maize being incorporated as a minority crop. By A.D. 1100 maize production became intensified (Scarry 1993) and large underground storage pits disappeared from the archaeological record (Mistovich 1988), being replaced by large, aboveground granaries. Skeletal trauma

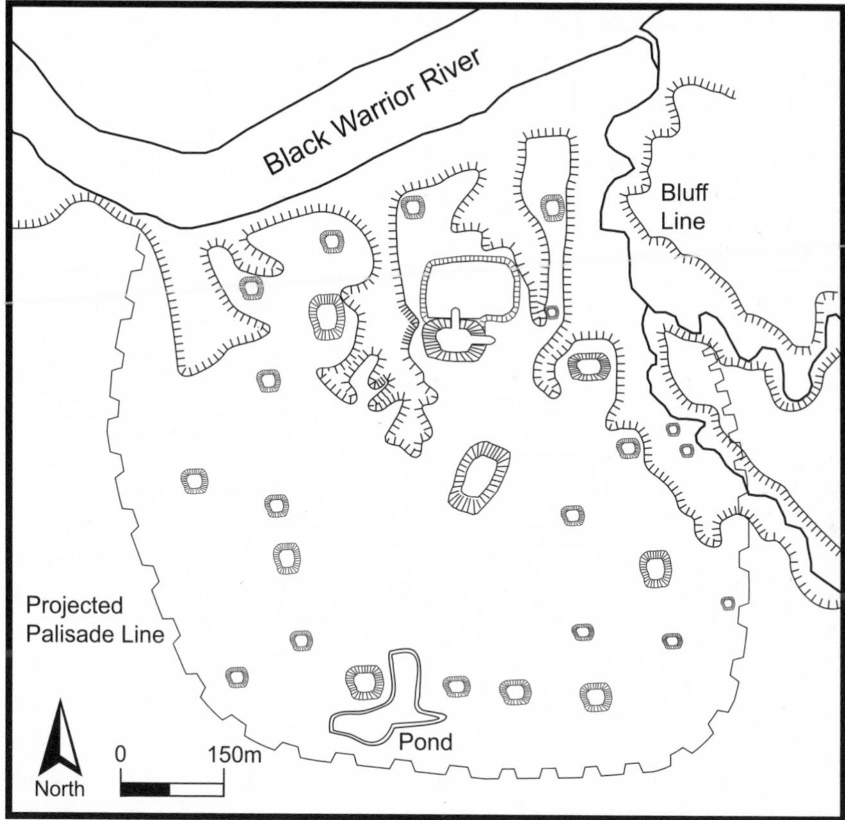

Figure 4.4. Map of Moundville (adapted from Knight and Steponaitis 1998, Figure 1.1).

is unknown from this time, and although fortifications have not been located, the bow and arrow had been introduced. There is little evidence for institutionalized ranking in the Late Woodland period. Few non-local goods have been found at terminal Late Woodland sites, although the local production of crafts, particularly shell beads, intensified (Knight and Steponaitis 1998:11) as community leaders attempted to attract followers.

Between A.D. 1020 and A.D. 1260 (Early Moundville I period) the hallmarks of Mississippian culture appear in the Black Warrior River Valley: chiefdom political organization, platform mounds, quadrilateral wall-trench architecture, aboveground granaries, and shell-tempered ceramics occurring in a variety of new vessel shapes (Figure 4.4). Conspicuous changes are evident in the subsistence economy, settlement organization, and social structure. The subsistence economy witnessed the emergence of a stable agricultural economy. Dependence on maize became more pronounced, increasing to about 40 percent of the average dietary caloric intake. Minor crops included beans, squash, chenopod, maygrass, and sunflower. Beans were an important source of protein.

At the same time, there was an abrupt change in settlement organization. The nucleated terminal Late Woodland communities were reorganized into smaller and more dispersed farming communities. These hamlets now included small truncated mounds, perhaps substructures for elite residences, marking the emergence of small-scale ranked society.

Even at this early date, Moundville was beginning to take on the role of first among equals in the region. Moundville elites engaged in the circulation of raw materials, particularly non-local rocks and minerals. Mound sites served as "central nodes of authority for leaders who employed the ritual of mound building and the accumulation and distribution of exotic goods as key elements of their efforts to expand and consolidate their authority in a competitive setting" (Knight and Steponaitis 1998:13). Shortly after A.D. 1100, Moundville emerged as a center of political and ceremonial activity characterized by initial political centralization and "chronic interregional strife," but regional political consolidation does not seem to have been effectively achieved by this time (Knight and Steponaitis 1998:13). By A.D. 1260 (Late Moundville I) some people aggregated at the Moundville center from the rural population.

Shortly after A.D. 1200 Moundville suddenly became transformed into a major regional center (Figure 4.5). The new paramountcy marked the political consolidation of at least a 40 kilometer segment of the Black Warrior River valley, the layout and construction of all the major mounds, and the establishment of the basic plan of the political center. This fundamental blueprint included the layout and leveling of the central plaza, the positioning of central and peripheral earthen mounds, and construction of a wooden palisade. Social space became ranked as Moundville elites consolidated their emerging power through the placement of mounds, plazas, and other social spaces, including the palisade wall.

The approximately 5 kilometer palisade was initially constructed around A.D. 1200, enclosing Moundville within a rough semicircle terminating at the banks of the Black Warrior River on each end. The palisade contained square tower bastions at intervals of 35–40 meters. They were approximately 4 m wide and 7 meters deep. Only a portion of the palisade has been excavated, but given the palisade's overall length, there may have been as many as 125 bastions along its circumference.

In one recently excavated palisade area two distinct lines of fortification were present (Scarry 1995). The more northerly palisade was built about A.D. 1150–1210. It was rebuilt or altered at least six times, probably over a period of 60 or

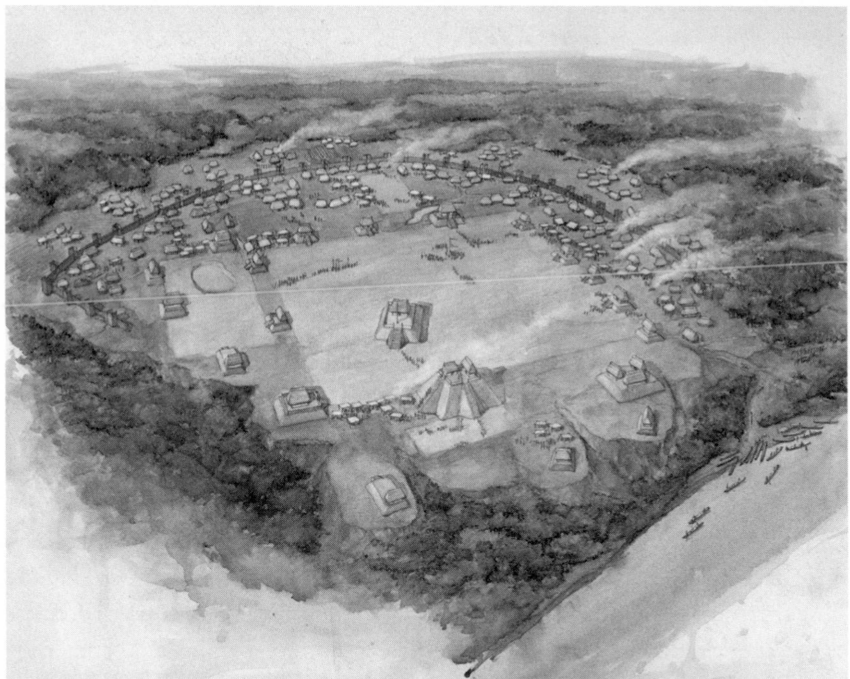

Figure 4.5. Artist's reconstruction of Moundville (rendering by Steven Patricia).

more years. This palisade was later removed and replaced by one slightly to the south about A.D. 1300. This segment was repaired at least once and may have been in place from 20 to 40 years (Scarry 1995). Much of the domestic activity took place within the palisade, indicating that some of the nearby population had moved within the town's defensive walls.

Moundville may have had few if any nearby competitors (Welch 1998a:135). No community within 300 to 400 kilometers of Moundville had a sufficiently large population to have stood alone as an enemy of the populous Moundville polity. Welch (1991:187–188) notes that there is "little evidence for *reciprocal* exchanges between Moundville and other polities." Populations living north, east, or south of Moundville prior to A.D. 1250 either moved into the Moundville communities or moved further away with limited mutual interaction (Paul Welch, personal communication 2004).

The direct political control of Moundville was apparently limited to an area approximately 20 by 50 kilometers (Steponaitis 1983:4) along the Black Warrior River valley. While there is evidence for interaction between Moundville and Mississippian polities outside the Black Warrior River valley in the form of stylistic affinities between pottery types and assemblages, there is little evidence that sites outside the Black Warrior River valley were under Moundville's direct control (McKenzie 1966:38; Scarry 1999b:236; Walthall 1980:228–236).

By A.D. 1260, the entire region had been consolidated into a single polity, with Moundville as the primary center linked to several second-order administrative communities. The power of the paramount chiefs at this time is manifested in the immense amount of labor they mobilized to level the plaza, construct the earthworks, and raise the wooden palisade. The creation and maintenance of the elaborate palisade testifies to the paramounts' concern for military security and the inhabitants' awareness of the need for defense of the site (Bridges et al. 2000:40; Vogel and Allan 1985).

Moundville was once again radically transformed around A.D. 1300, this time from a thriving, fortified regional town to a largely unfortified, vacant ceremonial center with elite residences and an associated necropolis. Moundville's rulers distanced themselves both symbolically and physically from their followers as the paramountcy endeavored to entrench itself. The resident population vacated the center, moving into dispersed farmsteads in the nearby Black Warrior River valley, leaving the elite and their retainers as permanent residents. "The tributary economy was in full swing, as numerous second-order administrative centers mobilized the labor and the agricultural surplus of a farmstead-based population numbering perhaps 10,000 people" (Knight and Steponaitis 1998:20). The palisade ceased to be rebuilt or maintained after this time. Whatever threat had existed in the past, apparently had now dissipated.

One means by which the Moundville paramounts sought to separate themselves from their followers was through the elaboration of chiefly cult symbolism. Burials of paramounts and other elites with iconographically encoded luxury goods and regalia reflect attempts at symbolic separation. Images found in chiefly cult paraphernalia contain references to warfare emphasizing iconographic representations of trophy heads, scalps, and weapons.

The graves of the Moundville nobility were marked by the inclusion of exotics, most commonly marine shell and pearl beads, copper gorgets and pendants, copper-clad wooden ear disks, notched stone palettes, mineral-based pigments, and galena crystals (Knight and Steponaitis 1998:18; Peebles 1974; Peebles and Kus 1977:439; Steponaitis and Knight 2004). At the apex of the hierarchy were adult males who were segregated from the remainder of the population by their artifact associations. Some of the adult males have adult skulls buried with them as grave goods (Peebles and Kus 1977:439), perhaps as trophy skulls. Some are accompanied by infant skeletons and infant skulls, pearl beads, copper-covered shell beads, and copper axes (Peebles and Kus 1977:439). Copper axes were the most prestigious item at Moundville and conferred super-ordinate status on those with access to them (Brain and Phillips 1996:348; Peebles and Kus 1977:439).

Some adult males were taller than other males and exhibited more frequent healed fractures and piercing wounds (Powell 1988:144–145, Table 47, 193–196). Buried with richer funerary accompaniments, they apparently were distinguished warriors and members of an elite who were entitled to sumptuary privileges. Their prowess in warfare may have enhanced their ranked status. Evidence for mound use, skilled crafting, and the display of human skeletal remains, particularly skulls and limb bones, "likely to have been taken in war," is evident between A.D. 1260 and A.D. 1450 (Knight 2004:313)

Exotic objects interpreted as stylized scalps were rendered in sheet copper and carved in stone as pendants, or painted and engraved on pottery (Hudson 1976:251; Wilkins 2001). These symbolic scalps, interred with elite members of Moundville society, underscore the clear association of elite efficacy in warfare with the materialization of their authority. As badges of rank, these ritual regalia signified political positions, ritual offices, and social relationships.

Warfare iconography at Moundville is expressed as elite, symbolic weaponry, and as images of dismemberment in a variety of exotic goods formed from copper, marine shell, flint, slate, and ceramics. Long, flint "swords" were chipped from non-local chert. Axe heads were fashioned from copper, and spatulate celts were manufactured from greenstone for elite use. Monolithic axes were created from single pieces of stone. Ritual regalia were imported in the form of sheet-copper shaped into arrowhead symbol badges. Pottery carried iconographic themes. For example, the second most prevalent iconographic theme in Moundville Hemphill-style engraved art is the war-trophy theme (Gillies 1998:56–62; Knight 1995; Lacefield 1995:42–43). The components of the theme center on dismemberment and include the following motifs: scalp lock, skull, forearm bones, hand-and-eye motifs, serrated or dismembered human heads, and raptor heads and tails.

Lankford (2004) provides a convincing argument that the Moundville war-trophy theme motifs were cosmic symbols, reflecting elements of the widespread mythic understanding of the Above World geography, specifically, a particular location on the Path of Souls. Images of hands, for example, reference the Hand (Orion) constellation that served as a portal into the night sky. The mythic back-story involves one of the Twin Heroes, who had gone to the Above World through a hole in the sky. While there, he cut off the hand of a sky chief and hung it in the sky. Lankford's argument underscores the multiple dimensions of trophy-taking behavior and reminds us that such behavior often is prompted through mythic charters.

By A.D. 1400, Moundville underwent a major transformation. Most of the mounds on the site's southern flank were no longer in use. Further basic structural changes took place again in the years after A.D. 1450 when the Moundville chiefdom collapsed as a centralized political structure. Elite activities centering on skilled crafting and mound use are lost (Vernon J. Knight Jr., personal communication 2004). Nucleated villages reappeared in the Black Warrior Valley. In this time of decline, archaeological evidence suggests increasing independence among the scattered communities of the Black Warrior Valley. Few burials at this time at the Moundville site contained grave goods, and there is no evidence of social inequalities, either within or between sites.

After A.D. 1550, skeletal remains suggest a return to egalitarian status. In general the population was unhealthy, in part a result from introduced European diseases and their social consequences. Local populations suffered from high rates of infant mortality, malnutrition, infection, and degenerative diseases. Elevated occurrences of cribra orbitalia and porotic hyperostosis (Hill 1981) are evident, due to high pathogen load exacerbated by malnutrition (Schoeninger and Schurr 1998).

Most of the secondary mound sites were abandoned by approximately the middle of the sixteenth century, but several mounds at Moundville were still being occupied. The inhabitants of the Black Warrior Valley "seem to have been nucleated in small, independent, egalitarian villages where they led short, unhealthy lives" (Welch 1998a:136).

From November 30 through December 9, 1540, Hernando de Soto encountered the chiefdom of Apafalaya at Moundville (Hudson 1997:257–259). The expedition's chroniclers suggest the polity was a nominally centralized, minimally functioning chiefdom that unified a district of several towns (Hudson et al. 1990:183–191). There may have been a hereditary paramount recognized among the town chiefs, who was perhaps the personification of community unity, but who had no real political power.

All of the mounds at Moundville were abandoned by the end of the sixteenth century during a time of radical reorganization and change (Sheldon 1974). Most of the people in the Black Warrior Valley were living in a few nucleated villages without mounds. There is no evidence for organizational structure above the village level. By now, the Mississippian hierarchy had disappeared, and dependence on maize had dropped significantly.

The Black Warrior villages continued to be occupied until about A.D. 1650 when the valley was finally depopulated due to the external pressures of broadscale conflict and continued devastation brought about by introduced diseases. The Black Warrior River become known in historic times as Potagahatchie, the "river at the boundary," a buffer zone between warring proto-Creeks to the east and Western Muskogean speakers to the west (Knight 1982).

In summary, Moundville had a distinctly different rise to prominence than Etowah. The first phase of fortification building occurred at the beginning of its political centralization and consolidation, about A.D. 1150, when it was protecting itself from nearby neighbors whom it may have been trying to bring under its influence. After active efforts at political consolidation between mutually antagonistic polities, Moundville became a regional paramount center around A.D. 1200. The center began reinforcing its fortifications around A.D. 1300 when it was perhaps defending itself from other aggressors in an attempt to maintain its regional prominence. After A.D. 1300, the palisades fell into disrepair as Moundville became a largely vacant ritual center. Moundville slowly atrophied politically after A.D. 1400, losing much of its regional influence.

The Lubbub Creek Chiefdom

The egalitarian populations that occupied the central Tombigbee Valley from A.D. 600 to A.D. 1000 practiced a generalized hunting, collecting, and gardening economy.[4] Large, riverine base camps were occupied for much of the year with seasonal movements to small transitory camps (Jenkins 1982). One of these base camps was the Lubbub Creek site, destined to become a regional center. Site use is represented by scattered clusters of midden, post molds, burials, and large underground storage pits. Corn became increasingly important, but it remained a minor dietary supplement (Caddell 1981). These Late Woodland populations were "under considerable health stress" (Blitz 1993:44) and subsistence stress resulting from overcrowding that is well documented in the central Tombigbee Valley (Knight and Steponaitis 1998:11). Growth in population and increasing sedentism is signaled by an increase in the number of sites, site size, and midden buildup (Jenkins 1982:110).

The intensification of maize production by the end of the Late Woodland period may have brought about changes in the way subsistence surpluses were stored. At Late Woodland base camps the inhabitants dug large, deep storage pits to hold wild foods such as acorns and nuts (Blitz 1983; Jenkins and Ensor 1981). These underground storage pits would have been useful for concealing food surpluses while community members were absent (DeBoer 1988). By the end of the period, a shift had taken place toward aboveground grain storage.

The introduction of the bow and arrow in the Late Woodland period (Blitz 1988; Ensor 1981) created a dangerous social environment as individual farmsteads became vulnerable to attack. The increased incidence of violence may have resulted from and given rise to the subsistence stress and overcrowding experienced by local populations. In this light, the bow and arrow may have presented new opportunities for resource exploitation or territorial expansion, fostering significant demographic changes (Blitz 1988, 1993:99).

The incidence of warfare was relatively high in the Late Woodland, perhaps exacerbated by the introduction of the bow and arrow and competition over resources. For the first time, there is unambiguous evidence of violent conflict among the Tombigbee populations (Blitz 1993:33). Violent death is seen in single and grouped human burials with embedded arrow points (Hill 1981). Evidence of violent traumatic injury, as indicated by "parry" fractures and embedded projectile points, is present in 24 percent (19 of 78) of the Late Woodland population (Cole et al. 1982; Powell 1988:487–489; Welch 1990:Table 25). At Site 1Pi61, for example, 13 percent of the individuals had embedded points; some of them were buried in mass graves. The way in which some of these individuals were buried has led some researchers to suggest they were captives (Hill 1981). Both sexes exhibit roughly equal mortality rates from violence at this time. Forty-six percent of the males and 36 percent of the females had at least one healed fracture. Twenty-five percent of the population had upper body fractures, presumably due to blows from war clubs. The adoption of the bow also brought about a significant increase in mortality. Site 1Pi61 had a ten percent rise in mortality over earlier Archaic populations as a result of endemic raiding due to the technological superiority of the bow and arrow (Bridges et al. 2000). The bow gave Late Woodland populations the ability to conduct an increasingly lethal style of raiding.

By A.D. 1000, the beginning of the Early Mississippian period, the Lubbub Creek community settlement pattern consisted of a local political center composed of a central ceremonial precinct with a low platform mound, adjacent plaza, and a community habitation area spread out in an arc around the mound. Dispersed small settlements or farmsteads were associated with the center. Settlements comprised a series of clustered populations surrounded by extensive buffer zones devoid of people (based on archaeological surveys). The distribution of local political centers and their clustered pattern suggests a landscape shaped by social and political conditions, especially intergroup warfare (Blitz 1993:45). The economy was based on maize production, gathering, and hunting.

The emergence of the Mississippian political organization and adaptation along the central Tombigbee was a successful social, technological, and economic response to the increasing subsistence stress between A.D. 1000 and A.D. 1200. The basic economic response was a sudden shift from a foraging-gardening strategy to dependence on large-scale field technologies and above-ground storage. The social dimension of the response included the emergence

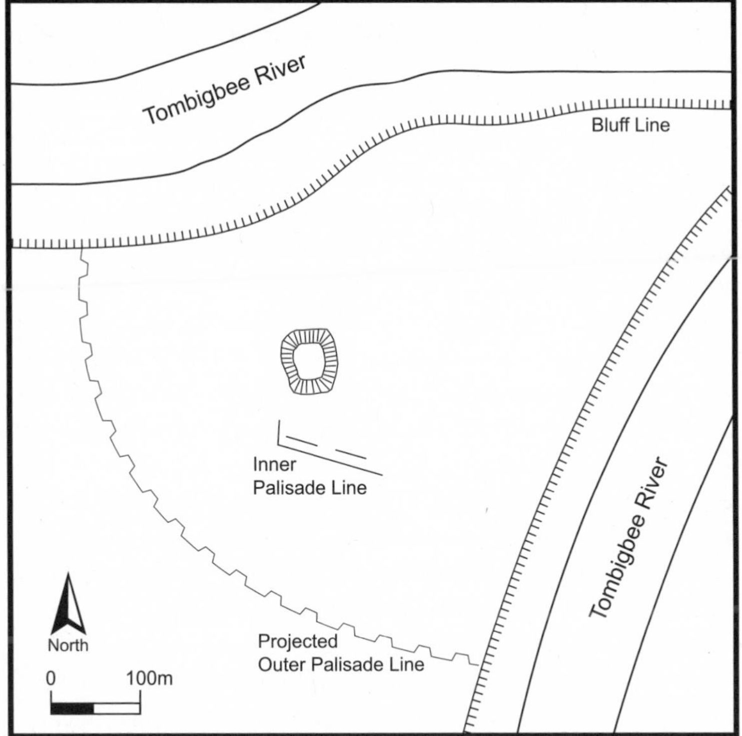

Figure 4.6. Map of Lubbub Creek (adapted from Blitz 1993, Figure 35).

of social ranking, although the reorganization of society began prior to the shift in economics.

The Lubbub Creek community by A.D. 1200 had grown to 8.5 hectares within a 19 hectare area bounded by a bend in the Tombigbee River and a bastioned palisade that formed a defensive barrier across the narrow neck of the river bend (Cole and Albright 1983) (Figure 4.6). The central site precinct was enclosed by an additional set of walls separate from the palisade. The 600-m palisade had as many as 20 rectangular bastions set at 30-m intervals (Bridges et al. 2000:39). The palisade provided limited safety. Evidence of violent traumatic injury as indicated by "parry" fractures or embedded projectile points is present in 18 percent (6 of 33) of the Early Mississippian population (Cole et al. 1982; Powell 1988:487–489; Welch 1990:Table 25).

Maize production rapidly intensified at this time to become a staple after A.D. 1000. The preferred storage method of aboveground granary or corncrib storage placed local farmsteads at security risks because of their visibility, ease of seizure, and association with ruling elites. A rival chief could steal his neighbor's corn supply to feed his population, thereby increasing his own wealth and social standing while at the same time undermining the political efficacy of his enemy.

The storage of corn and the need for its defense at Lubbub Creek suggests that a formal, institutionalized office of war leader existed to protect and defend it. Social ranking based on burial data is evident. War leadership would have constituted a role separate from a civil office based on ritual and communal storage. If so, the civil chief/war chief duality so common in the historical period may have roots deep in prehistory (Blitz 1993:125).

Blitz (1993:179–181) has developed a model to account for the rise of military leadership in Early Mississippian populations. Stimulated by various technological, social, and demographic factors, central Tombigbee populations around A.D. 1000 began to intensify their production of maize beyond low-level gardening, creating logistical problems in a subsistence economy that continued to rely heavily on wild foods. Dispersed farmsteads provided optimal access to natural resources but left families and their maize harvest vulnerable to attack. New cooperative labor patterns were initiated to address these problems: the communal storage of food surpluses at a fortified center was one solution. Meanwhile, formal leadership roles emerged to oversee a cooperative economic and mutual defense organization, resulting in the local-center-farmstead polity. Two potential spheres of political influence were created: management of pooled food surpluses and leadership in war. Food-storage management and leadership in war were sufficient basis for formal, institutionalized chiefly authority in small-scale Mississippian societies such as Lubbub Creek.

Between A.D. 1200 and A.D. 1450 (Middle Mississippi period), fortifications appear to have been abandoned at the Lubbub Creek site. The site area expanded to 11.3 ha with 5 to 18 houses in use at any one time, representing a population of 25–90 people. Despite the abandonment of the palisade, the platform mound and plaza precinct remained the central focus of the community. Several construction stages raised the mound to its maximum height, and two ramps were added. No significant changes occurred in subsistence practices. The frequency of violent death is around 11 percent at Lubbub Creek, equivalent to the earlier Late Woodland Site 1Pi61. Only adults are associated with warfare. Lubbub burials show high mortality from violence, but rarely from embedded arrow points. The palisade at Lubbub may have protected its inhabitants from the bow and arrow, but they were still susceptible to other types of attacks, especially raiders armed with war clubs (Bridges et al. 2000).

Chiefly leadership, possibly war leaders, is suggested by evidence from a burial (Burial 20) interred in a formal, perhaps elite, cemetery. The grave contained the primary interments of two adult males in their mid-thirties, placed one atop the other in an extended position. In association with the bottom male was a repoussé copper plate embossed with a falcon symbol and a dozen sheet-copper arrow-shaped symbol badges, probably used as ritual regalia, and a war club with a greenstone celt (Blitz 1993:102; Bridges et al. 2000:39; Cole et al. 1982:Table 2; Hill 1981). The uppermost male appears to have been a sacrificial victim, based on the presence of a triangular projectile point in the chest cavity. A set of dismembered arms, legs, and feet accompanied the individuals. These limbs, articulated in a manner suggesting interment while fleshed (Hill 1981:278), are interpreted as war trophies (Jenkins 1982).

The non-local copper symbol badge headdress has been interpreted as an indicator of institutionalized chiefly office or rank (Jenkins 1982:130–132; Larson 1959, 1971; Peebles and Kus 1977). The symbolism of the copper-badge headdress suggests that the formal office was reinforced by ideological sanctions (Jenkins 1982:130). Possession of the ritual regalia suggests the individual who possessed it negotiated within a wide exchange-and-information network beyond the local area.

The copper plate depicts a falcon. Brown (1985:140) has identified the falcon and falcon impersonators as important symbols of chiefly authority and of military leadership. The falcon symbolism, strongly identified with warfare in the Southeast (Brown 1985:140; Howard 1968:43–45; Hudson 1976:128–129), together with human "trophies" and evidence of violent death in Burial 20, underscores Jenkins's suggestion that the office was associated with leadership in war. Perhaps this position was the prototype of, or structurally similar to, the role of war chief in the historical Southeast (Blitz 1983:104).

The period from A.D. 1450/1500 to A.D. 1600 marks a time of social stress and accelerated culture change. Interregional conflict is indicated by the renewed fortification of the Lubbub Creek site with a dry moat, or ditch, 230 m in diameter, 4 m wide, and 1.3 m deep. The community and probably its neighbors invested a great of energy in this defensive work (Bridges et al. 2000:39). The construction demarcated a 4.2 ha community, in which the population had declined to between two and seven houses in use at any one time. The use of maize began to decrease as subsistence emphasis returned to an increasing reliance on wild foods.

The De Soto expedition crossed the Tombigbee River north of the Lubbub chiefdom on December 14, 1540, passing through an uninhabited buffer zone (Hudson 1997:259). The central Tombigbee River valley was abandoned by the early seventeenth century as these Western Muskogean populations either moved north to the Upper Tombigbee Valley to join the Chickasaws, or south-westward to the Upper Pearl River Valley to join with or become the Western Choctaws, or in between to join with or become the Chakchiumas (Galloway 1995:Fig. 9.1).

In summary, Lubbub Creek had an early period of local political consolidation which resulted in the construction of the Early Mississippian palisade. The fortification was later abandoned as the Lubbub Creek chiefdom came under the political domination of the nearby Moundville paramountcy. The breakdown of the Lubbub regional political consolidation may be the result of the gradual demise of the Moundville chiefdom. Another palisade went up in the fifteenth century, once again to protect the polity from outside aggressors, perhaps representing the intersocietal competition among neighboring populations.

The Shiloh/Koger's Island Chiefdom

Between A.D. 700 and A.D. 1000, the settlement pattern in the western Middle Tennessee Valley consisted of small, permanent, nucleated riverbank villages or hamlets, from which the inhabitants foraged and practiced floodplain horticulture.[5] Upland rockshelters and open-air sites served as temporary hunting and collecting camps. A shift from dart points to arrow points at this time signals the introduction of the bow and arrow. No fortifications have been observed, but the compact nature of the sites suggests they may have been palisaded. Mass burials have been recorded for several sites, but skeletal analysis has not been conducted to determine causes of death. Status is believed to have been egalitarian. By A.D. 900–1000, large-scale abandonment of the western Middle Tennessee River floodplain (Pickwick Basin) may have taken place as Late Woodland populations filtered southward into upland tributary valleys (Meyer 1995; Walthall 1980).

The abandonment of the Middle Tennessee Valley coincided with the emergence of Early Mississippian settlements downriver at the Shiloh chiefdom (Welch 2001, 2005), and upriver at the Langston chiefdom (Walthall 1980:200–205), resulting in a broad 250 km buffer zone between the two areas (Futato 1998:226; Meyer 1995:40–42; Walthall 1980:196–211). Langston populations fortified their villages and used natural features for defense, such as swamps and bluffs. A buffer zone also emerged between the Shiloh chiefdom and the Link Farm chiefdom 40 km to the north (Dye 2004b).

The Shiloh phase regional center, the Shiloh site, was occupied from approximately A.D. 1050 to A.D. 1400 (Figure 4.7 and 4.8). The population appears to have relocated from a river edge village to the nearby high bluff, where the site was briefly fortified with a bastioned palisade encircling eight mounds. The polity extends some 68 km along the Tennessee River. One island within the polity

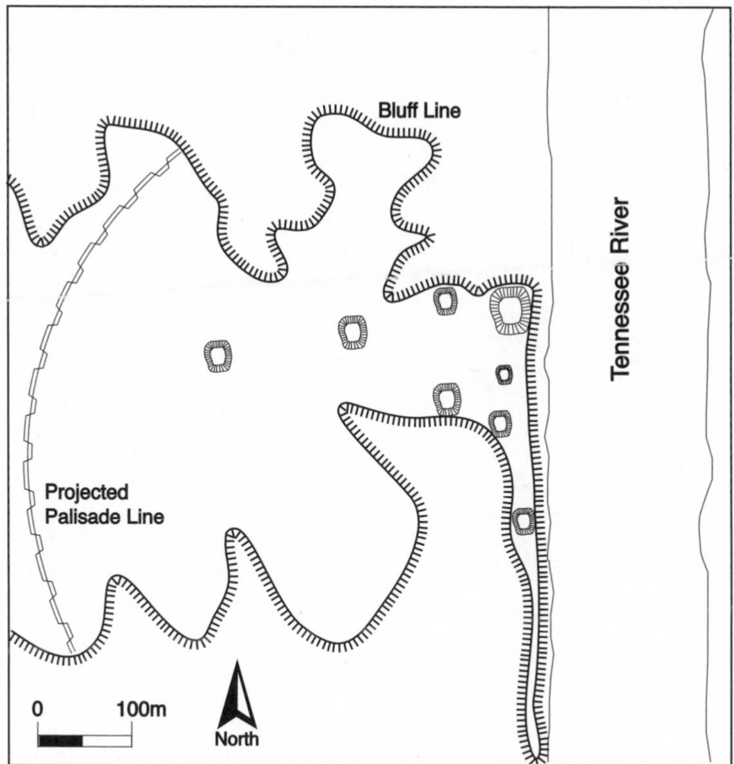

Figure 4.7. Map of Shiloh (adapted from Welch 2001, Figure 20).

was a local political center based on the presence of a platform mound. Upon abandonment of the Shiloh locale, the inhabitants may have moved upstream to the western Middle Tennessee River valley (Koger's Island phase). The area may have been settled by inhabitants of the Shiloh polity, who abandoned their regional center around A.D. 1400 (Welch 2001:291).

These post-Shiloh, Koger's Island phase sites include cemeteries and local centers with substructure mounds on islands, and fall and winter upland hunting camps. Island sites proved to be desirable because of their defensibility and deep deposits of arable soil (Walthall 1980:230). The regional center for the Koger's Island phase may have been Site 1Lu21, located on Seven Mile Island. At a nearby site on Koger's Island, a Mississippian cemetery intruded into a Late Woodland village. A large village may have been located east of the cemetery on the island's upper end (Moore 1915:242; Walthall 1980:232). It is not known if the settlements on the two islands were contemporary or if the settlements represented a population gradually moving upstream from island to island. Seven Mile Island is approximately 20 km upstream from Koger's Island.

Figure 4.8. View of Shiloh (photo by David H. Dye).

Analysis of the Koger's Island and Perry burials indicates the presence of sustained raiding (Bridges 1996; Bridges et al. 2000; Dye and Jacobi 2000; Jacobi and Dye 2001). At the Koger's Island cemetery there is varied and widespread skeletal trauma within the burial population. Almost half (47 percent) of the 109 individuals exhibit some degree of trauma. Of those individuals, almost one-quarter (22 percent) exhibit trauma to the crania in the form of either scalping or depression fractures. Two-thirds of the trauma is found on the upper body as fractures, while one-third (33 percent) is manifested as lower-body fractures. These fractures mirror the trauma that might be expected from hand-to-hand combat. No embedded arrow points were found.

Almost three-quarters (70 percent) of the population appear to have been buried with extra body parts probably obtained through trophy-taking. For example, Burial 15 is a relatively complete skeleton buried in an individual grave as opposed to a mass grave, thus reducing the chance for mixing. This 40- to 44-year-old male had a fractured right rib, right fibula, and left femur. In addition, he had an extra right hand interred as a trophy.

Four of the burials were headless. As these skulls were not found in other contexts, we can assume that they were probably taken by enemies as war trophies. Burial 13, an adult male 35–39 years of age, was not only found headless, but he also lacked forearms and hands. In addition, he had cut marks on at least one of his distal humerii. This patterning conforms to the expected profile of trophy-taking resulting from raiders. Those individuals with the greatest trauma appear to be neither high status nor low status, but middle-status males who regularly participated in a style of warfare that emphasized raiding and the use of handheld weapons employed in close combat.

Four high-status males who have badges of office and items of wealth exhibit no or only slight trauma that was not fatal, as these fractures eventually healed. Nevertheless, warrior symbolism appears to have been important in high-status graves. Burial 20, a preeminent adult male, was buried with several symbolic weapons: greenstone celts, a spatulate celt, copper symbol badge headdress, and raptor regalia.

Perimortem cranial trauma or mutilation in seven mass burials (and one single interment) from the Koger's Island cemetery suggests that these individuals died violently. Two instances of healed cranial injuries inflicted with a celt or axe suggest some individuals survived attacks. Multiple burials generally included adult males, except for one interment that consists of females and children. Skeletal trauma in the mass burials was restricted to adults, and males were more likely to exhibit skeletal trauma than females. The disproportionate number of adult males in the mass graves, and the absence of males older than 50 years from the non-mass grave burials, suggest that a high percentage of males died violently at an early adult age (Bridges 1996:73).

The age and sex ratios of the burials, the numbers of individuals presumably killed at the same time, the lack of postmortem scavenging, and the relatively complete, articulated skeletons suggest the dead were quickly retrieved. The male mass burials at Koger's Island probably represent individuals who died defending their community, while the multiple grave containing females and children more likely was a work party or family group attacked while away from the village.

Mid-sized sites, such as Koger's Island and Perry, with defensive aspects such as island locations, show high mortality from upper-body and cranial fractures caused by various types of war clubs, though rarely from embedded arrow points (Bridges et al. 2000). Warfare appears to have been pervasive in this region based on the recurring nature of these attacks and would have had a large impact on the demography of the population (Bridges 1996).

Sometime after A.D. 1450 Pickwick Basin was once again abandoned and appears to have reverted back to an unpopulated buffer zone. Its abandonment may be related to a general mid-Southern and Midwestern depopulation due in part to climatic deterioration or other causes, which may have "exacerbated a competitive and often hostile political environment that rendered the region less hospitable" (Cobb and Butler 2002:637). The western Middle Tennessee Valley was a buffer zone once again in historic times between mutually hostile and competing Chickasaw groups to the west and Creek settlements to the east.

In summary, the Shiloh chiefdom established its regional center atop a bluff and sometime during its history erected a large palisade that was not rebuilt. The subsequent Koger's Island chiefdom may represent a population that migrated downstream into a former buffer zone and established a short-term residence on several nearby islands. They remained for a short period and then abandoned the area after suffering severe attacks.

Discussion

Fortifications, Abandonments, Buffer Zones, and Enemies

The construction of fortifications at Mississippian political centers signals periods of intense conflict among neighboring polities. Initial efforts at defensive palisades in the Late Woodland mid-South presumably mark a response to early efforts at surplus corn storage, the emergence of institutionalized ranking, and the growth of a warrior ethos. The defense of aboveground corncribs may have proven difficult in the face of bow-and-arrow technology. In response to threats of interpolity raiding and thievery of storable surplus, defensive palisades and the warrior elites who prompted their construction become widespread in terminal Late Woodland and Early Mississippian times.

Between A.D. 900 and A.D. 1000 offensive posturing is evident in areas such as the Upper Coosa drainage of northwest Georgia, where populations responded to aggressive behavior by placing sites in defensible positions, such as prominent elevations. Palisade walls and ditches enclosed settlements to protect the inhabitants from other polities, perhaps their neighbors. Areas that previously had been settled were now abandoned as populations coalesced for protection, creating buffer zones of habitable real estate among polities. Black Warrior River valley populations, likewise, may have moved into a few relatively large villages in response to endemic warfare. The middle Tennessee River valley, the Black Warrior River valley, and the middle Tombigbee River valley populations do not seem to have been fortified at this time, but buffer zones are evident between them in which populations were spread over wide areas, restricting upland buffer zones for hunting and foraging territories.

Early Mississippian populations began to palisade their settlements after granaries were established and efforts were initiated to bring about local political consolidation. The early phases of consolidation and its continued maintenance were based on "the warrior mobilization potential of southeastern chiefdoms" (Milner 1999:120). Although palisades were built to guard staple and wealth finance and to withstand attacks from bow-and-arrow warfare, the political impetus was born in chiefly aggrandizement.

Bastioned palisades were constructed at Moundville, Lubbub Creek, and perhaps Shiloh between A.D. 1000 and A.D. 1200. The first Moundville palisade system was built about A.D. 1200 and repaired or rebuilt some six times within a period of 60 or more years. Moundville's palisade was erected during the final phase of initial centralization and about the time of regional political consolidation, as might have been the case for Lubbub Creek and Shiloh. The building and maintenance of elaborate wooden walls is testimony to the need for military security, but it is also an important indication of the strength and power of leaders who coordinated their construction and almost certainly created the need for monumental fortifications by attacking their neighbors.

Palisades were erected to protect the inhabitants against neighboring aggressors. Ethnohistoric accounts indicate that one's enemies generally were one's neighbors. In the case of Moundville, those neighbors would have been chiefly polities to the west, southwest, southeast, north, and east. The closest neighbors would be central Tombigbee populations 53 km away, and Moundville-like groups to the west and east, and these polities would be the most likely aggressors. The palisade at Lubbub Creek may have been a response to Moundville's own consolidating efforts, considering the short distance between the two polities. Large portions of the western middle Tennessee Valley were abandoned or mostly depopulated at this time, and late in the Early Mississippian period the Etowah Valley was abandoned. People in these areas may have lacked the ability to maintain defense of their settlements in the face of hostile and overt aggression by increasingly powerful and centralized neighbors. One solution to attacks may have been coalescence into one or another of these regional chiefdom spheres.

Strongly fortified sites were a necessity for survival. The Lubbub palisade was abandoned by A.D. 1200, perhaps indicating that regional stability had been imposed by being included in the political orbit of another system, such as the Moundville chiefdom during its phase of political consolidation. The expansion of the complex chiefdom at Moundville appears linked to the disappearance of fortifications at nearby centers such as Lubbub Creek and perhaps the disappearance of polities in other areas (Welch 1990, 1991). The removal, control, or "suppression of potential rivals seems to have been a common strategy by elites in complex Mississippian chiefdoms" (Anderson 1999a:222). At about A.D. 1300 a second and final palisade system with bastions was constructed and repaired at Moundville at least once in a 20–40 year period. The inhabitants of Etowah built a massive bastioned palisade with accompanying ditch around A.D. 1325. The Moundville defensive measures may have been taken as a prophylactic against the Etowah populations to the northeast, the Lubbub Creek chiefdom to the west, middle Tennessee Valley polities to the north, or Gulf Coast groups to the south. The Shiloh polity was abandoned around A.D. 1400 and a series of islands upriver in the Pickwick Basin are inhabited after a 300-year abandonment or light occupation of the area, suggesting that population movement may have been the last recourse to survival in the face of aggressive and belligerent neighbors.

The Etowah regional center's palisade was burned and the site abandoned between A.D. 1375 and A.D. 1475, but the valley retained its population, suggesting that the Etowah site was no longer the principal center and the locale's population had reoriented its allegiance to another polity, perhaps the Coosa paramountcy to the northwest. Etowah was reoccupied between A.D. 1475 and A.D. 1550, but not fortified. The Lubbub Creek Site was fortified again, this time with a palisade wall and a dry moat. This construction activity may correlate with the decline of Moundville as a regional stabilizing influence and the growth of mutually antagonistic polities such as the Alabama River phase populations.

The Koger's Island polity appears to have abandoned the Pickwick Basin about A.D. 1450, thus leaving the western middle Tennessee Valley vacant until the early nineteenth century. This abandonment may have been part of the general, large scale, contemporaneous population movement out of the "vacant quarter" in the fifteenth century as a result of climatic deterioration which "exacerbated a competitive and often hostile political climate" (Cobb and Butler 2002:637). The Koger's Island population may have continued up the Tennessee River and into the Guntersville Basin.

In the Protohistoric (A.D. 1550–1700) period, the Etowah Site was abandoned for a third and final time, and the entire upper Coosa Valley was depopulated about A.D. 1580 due to European disease. The Black Warrior River valley and the middle Tombigbee River valley were both abandoned about A.D. 1650 as surviving populations moved north, south, and west.

While each Mississippian political center followed its own trajectory, they only can be understood in their broader political context. For example, the emergence of each polity is characterized by the fortification of the major towns. Then, they either gradually or suddenly lost their importance or existence, or were abandoned as power waxed and waned from one regional center to another in a context of endemic warfare as elites sought and competed for status and resources. Buffer zones placed some degree of distance between neighboring polities to ensure protection, creating large areas of rich, inhabitable land that was vacant for centuries because of the hostile environment created by chiefs as they sought to establish and lay claim to rights of dominance among one another.

Skeletal Trauma and Weapons

General changes in weaponry and tactics can be traced over time along with their demographic effects. The bow and arrow, for example, created a competitive advantage in intergroup conflict (Blitz 1988:124), restructured the scale and organization of warfare (Nassaney and Pyle 1999:260), and brought about an increase in mortality in the mid-South (Bridges et al. 2000:56).

War clubs are a significant implement of war in the Late Woodland period, as evidenced by the skeletal trauma at Site 1Pi61. Some 25 percent of the population had upper-body fractures, presumably due to blows from war clubs (Bridges et al. 2000:Table 3.1). Greenstone celts as burial accompaniments date to the Middle Woodland, where they conferred elite status on preeminent individuals (Walthall 1980:119). Presumably, they were mounted in wooden handles for use as war clubs. Although greenstone celts in Mississippian times have been interpreted as domestic woodworking tools, hematite stains suggest they may have been used in combat, in addition to woodworking (Wilson 2001:126).

The bow may not have immediately necessitated the construction of fortified communities, but fortifications that arose between A.D. 1000 and A.D. 1200 (Lubbub, Shiloh, Moundville) have specific design layouts that are a direct response to bow warfare: tall, plastered palisade walls, closely spaced bastions (ca. 30 m apart), constricted entrances, and ditches (Blitz 1988; Lafferty 1973; Larson 1972). The plastering of Mississippian palisades and houses may be a response to the use of fire-tipped arrows by massed warriors for greater fire-power based on sixteenth century descriptions and illustrations (DePratter 1983:47).

By Middle Mississippian times, death by violence was approaching 11 percent at middle-sized palisaded sites such as Lubbub Creek (Bridges et al. 2000:44). Handheld weapons such as war clubs proliferated into several forms by this time, ranging from sticks and staffs to swords and hatchets. Simultaneously, warrior symbolism became a central element of elite identity. Flint knives, possibly used for scalping, are often found in elite burials. Long versions of these knives, "swords," are also found in elite graves. Socio-technic weapons made from copper, exotic stone, and copper-covered wood, including clubs, bifaces, maces, axes, celts, knives, and arrow points, became widespread as part of a prestige goods exchange system, and were used for social display, conferring political authority on those who owned and manipulated them (Brown 1996:469–488; Van Horne 1993:75). Elite personages at this time were buried with socio-technic weapons and with human remains in the form of sacrificial victims (infants and adults) and trophies (Hill 1981; Peebles 1971:82; Peebles and Kus 1977:439). By this time more males were dying from violent causes than females in contexts associated with warfare. At Koger's Island, for example, there is a dramatic increase in early male mortality (Bridges 1996; Bridges et al. 2000:57). Males at Moundville display more fractures than females (Powell 1988:194).

The nature of settlement defense is directly related to the types and severity of violent trauma. Small, undefended hamlets, for example, exposed individuals to attack from arrows and consequently have high percentages of individuals with embedded arrow points. Even these percentages may underestimate by one-third the numbers of individuals inflicted with or killed by arrow points (Milner 2005). Mid-sized sites with defensive features such as palisades, or defensive positioning on islands, bluffs, or river bends, on the other hand, have high mortality from upper-body and cranial injuries due to axes and war clubs, but rarely from arrow points. The largest and best-defended sites, which would have been formidable to invaders, were largely secure from warfare except under unusual circumstances such as massive storming tactics (Bridges et al. 2000:60).

Iconography

Warrior identity is closely linked to Mississippian elite status. Southeastern Ceremonial Complex (SECC) art comprises a limited set of beliefs concerning a specific religious cult whose subject matter is the otherworld, especially the celestial stratum of a tiered cosmos that portrays warrior heroes existing in mythic time and their supernatural exploits, rather than the mundane themes of common warfare (Knight et al. 2001:133). The core of the SECC, as manifested in the four case studies discussed here, consists of socio-technic weapons and figural art represented in repoussé sheet-copper plates and engraved marine-shell gorgets.

The elaboration of warrior symbolism was manifest at all four regional centers after their efforts at political consolidation had taken place and during the time they were entrenching their political and social authority. Elaboration of the materialization of ideology took place at each regional center at different times: Etowah (A.D. 1250–1375), Moundville (A.D. 1300–1450), Lubbub Creek (A.D. 1200–1450/1500) and Koger's Island (A.D. 1400–1450). Chiefly warrior cult symbolism was expressed differently at each regional polity, yet some elements are common to all four chiefdoms.

SECC ritual weaponry was affiliated with the warfare-cosmogony complex of Mississippian sacra (Knight 1986:677–678). Warrior cult imagery, including weaponry, death, trophy-taking, and dismemberment are prominent in scenes of combat, beheaded foes, and human sacrifice, documenting the triumphs of archetypal, mythical, otherworldly guardians and heroes in combat against races of giants, supernatural monsters, and the like (Knight et al. 2001:138–139). The combatants are, however, depicted in culturally appropriate attire and accoutrements. The weaponry found in elite burials is the same as that illustrated in the bird-man copper plates and marine-shell gorgets from Etowah. Both artifact genres portray supernatural, mythic heroes, and combined with certain charter myths, may have been used to reinforce elite status through success in mortal combat. Items such as axes, celts, and long bifacial "swords" are brandished by these bird-man figures, representing a mythic model that could be replicated in rituals with chiefly actors using symbolic or socio-technic weaponry (Knight et al. 2001:139).

Perhaps typical of these weaponry forms, ceremonial greenstone artifacts, commonly interred with adult males (Peebles and Kus 1977), were manufactured and controlled by the Moundville elite, while utilitarian celts were not under elite control (Wilson 2001:126). Copper artifacts may have been curated and controlled by the Etowah elite (Brain and Phillips 1996), and Dover swords may have passed through the hands of the Shiloh elites, terminating in the exchange network at Etowah and Moundville. At each chiefdom, sheet-copper symbol badges in the form of arrow points or war clubs, the two primary instruments of war, marked the highest ranked individuals. In addition, these superordinate burials are accompanied by what seem to be retainers and iconography depicting raptor imagery. The clear association of military regalia, raptor imagery, and retainer burials with elite status seems to denote a distinct political office associated with warfare (Peebles 1971; Peebles and Kus 1977; Scarry 1992, 1996, 1999b). Retainer burials, as part of the mortuary and mourning program, may have been conducted to dedicate the soul of an enemy to the deceased male elite in order "to serve as his servant while traveling the Spirit Trail" (Hall 2000:250). The burial of ritual paraphernalia and regalia seems to have taken place at the end of a polity's period of consolidation or, in some cases, at the end of the polity's existence as an autonomous entity.

Symbolic objects, such as sheet-copper symbol badges, are ideal signifiers of political position and social relationships. Ceremonial burial of warfare paraphernalia, ritual regalia, and retainer burials conveyed important messages about the nature and source of chiefly leadership and their mythic charters.

Conclusions

The causes and transformation of Mississippian warfare centered on the political ambitions of chiefs to consolidate political authority within their polity as well as to establish external relationships with neighbors through alliances, tribute, or incorporation. The initial rise of tribal societies around 5,000–6,000 years ago may have brought about the first emergence of warfare based on kin-based raiding (Anderson 2001). Although many examples of skeletal trauma undoubtedly resulted from interpersonal violence, organized raiding may have occurred periodically. Tribal warfare is based on the organized means of violence carried out by small, informal, and temporary kin militia groups working under weak chains of command with rudimentary powers of dispersion (Reyna 1994:40–43). Key evidence for intergroup conflict, such as embedded dart points and trophy-taking, existed as early as 6,000 years ago. Skeletal trauma in the form of perimortem mutilation associated with trophy-taking and mass burial of individuals with embedded projectile points and broken bones and fractures is evident some 3,000–4,000 years ago. Modified human bone as grave accompaniments is evidence of the prestige conferred by trophy-taking in raids. The establishment of buffer zones and territoriality at this time may well have resulted from competition over scarce resources.

By A.D. 1, a continued emphasis on trophy-taking is evident. Greenstone celts as high-status burial accompaniments signal the use of war clubs in organized forms of violence. By A.D. 600, bow-and-arrow technology became a major force in reshaping the nature of warfare and brought about high mortality rates and traumatic injuries (Bridges et al. 2000:59). Embedded arrow points and upper-body trauma signal the appearance of a more intense warfare pattern based on bow-and-arrow technology coupled with war clubs. In some areas of the mid-South, warfare at A.D. 900 is evident in large-scale demographic shifts: populations abandoned some areas and moved into others, buffer zones between polities became evident, and raiding escalated into more organized forms of warfare, necessitating fortified settlements. Mass graves serve to underscore the lethality of an energized raiding pattern, perhaps on a larger scale than previous intergroup violence.

By A.D. 1000, warfare-related mortality increased, especially at vulnerable, undefended, small or mid-sized sites. As male militias became the predominant form of combat organization, greater male mortality became the norm, perhaps creating a significant disruption in demographic balance. Variation in the causes of death is correlated with site size and degree of site defense. An increase in upper-body and cranial fractures, especially at larger or better-defended sites, signals the rise of war clubs in hand-to-hand combat and an increase in the taking of scalps as trophies. With the advent of fortifications, there came an increasing standardization and sophistication in military strategy and tactics (Bridges et al. 2000:61; Dye 2002).

By approximately A.D. 1200, the stage was set for an organized and violent style of warfare instituted and carried out by chiefly elites who competed with one another for the furtherance of their political agendas, including alleviating resource stress and exercising influence in their geopolitical realm. Prowess in warfare enhanced their ranked status (Brown 1976; Gibson 1974; Knight 1986). Bow-and-arrow technology, fortified settlements, and war clubs, coupled with the organizational capacity of chiefly elites who had the authority and power to wield and coordinate sizable armed forces, meant that chiefs who consolidated their own local river valley chiefdoms could muster lethal force against neighboring regional polities. The abilities of warrior chiefs to influence adjacent polities and extract resources through tribute had the potential to lead to ever larger polities, resulting in increasingly complex political formations, including paramount chiefdoms (Hudson et al. 1985).

In the four case studies presented here, the political trajectories of each chiefdom differ in fundamental ways, but each chiefdom shows varying attempts at chiefly strategies geared for success and survival. Etowah, Moundville, Lubbub Creek, and Shiloh were each fortified with bastioned palisades and surrounded by buffer zones of 50–200 km. These buffer zones remained viable but hazardous areas as long as powerful chiefs controlled populations within the political sphere of mutually antagonistic chiefdoms. Etowah, Moundville, Lubbub Creek, and Koger's Island each participated in an iconography that emphasized ferocity in warfare and ideologically sanctioned military leadership that associated high status with hypertrophic, symbolic weapons of war.

The chiefdoms differed in the degree of skeletal trauma their populations suffered. Moundville's populations enjoyed relative security behind their palisade walls, while small centers such as Lubbub Creek and Koger's Island were subjected to lethal intergroup conflict. Population aggregation also differed with respect to the four polities. Etowah witnessed rising and falling population fluctuations, while Moundville saw a general population movement into the main center and back out again. The Koger's Island chiefdom was short-lived within the middle Tennessee Valley and demonstrates the lethality of occupying a buffer zone between competing hostile societies. In sum, individual chiefdoms were the products of the regional histories in which they existed (King 2001:1).

The transformation of Mississippian warfare was the result of chiefly strategies for success and survival. Chiefs appropriated iconographic warfare imagery to help consolidate their political power. For example, the scalp lock became part of elite regalia in the form of the bellows-shaped apron on the Etowah copper plates and as pendants used by the Lubbub Creek, Moundville, and Koger's Island elite. Chiefs mobilized labor and goods for both defensive fortifications and offensive military attacks.

The growth of the Mississippian military organization was based in large part on the hierarchical structure and formal institutions of ranking (Dye 2002). The basic units may have been composed of kin groups within a chain of command that began with the chief. These chiefly militias (Reyna 1994:44) allowed chiefs and their war councils to marshal forces composed of able-bodied males from the chiefdom population and to deploy them with devastating and deadly effect against their enemies. While most aggression seems to have been directed at one's neighbors, the capability of moving several hundred warriors over great distances can be attested in the historic eyewitness accounts of Iroquois war parties.

The ultimate intent of chiefly aggression was military efforts marshaled to achieve political consolidation within the local area. In order to accomplish political agendas, such as relieving resource stress through consolidation, chiefs amassed wealth to mobilize a warrior militia through ceremonial feasting, presentation of honors, and war rituals. The rise of prominent leaders and their destructive force is clearly marked in the archaeological record by signs of a violent world, reflected by defensive features, demographic shifts, skeletal trauma, and symbolic combat weaponry.

While these four chiefdoms followed their unique trajectories, they also show similarities. Each chiefdom exhibits some degree of institutionalized hierarchy, access to social labor, defensive posturing, and symbolic combat weaponry. With the introduction of the bow and arrow, coupled with a more centralized political organization, ruling elites sought ways to relieve resource stress and amass the wealth necessary to mobilize social labor for building defensive structures and deploying offensive forces. Hierarchical forms of organization provided one means for elites to effectively coordinate and manipulate chiefly militias for defense and offense. While root causes of intersocietal conflict may stem from demographic and environmental conditions, symbolic combat weaponry and a heroic martial ideology signals the use of mythic warrior sagas to charter justifications for aggressive actions.

Acknowledgments

This chapter benefited greatly from the generous and thoughtful comments of David G. Anderson, John H. Blitz, Adam King, Vernon J. Knight Jr., Keith J. Little, Vincas P. Steponaitis, and Paul D. Welch. Their suggestions are appreciated. Any errors in fact or interpretation are mine. I especially would like to thank Robert W. Dye for his help with Figures 4.1, 4.2, 4.4, 4.6, and 4.7 and Steven Patricia for his permission to use his magnificent Etowah and Moundville renderings. Lastly, I would like to thank Elizabeth Arkush and Mark Allen for their invitation to participate in this volume.

Notes

1. The case study presented on warfare in the Upper Coosa drainage and the Etowah Chiefdom is based on recent archaeological analysis and synthesis of the Upper Coosa drainage in northwestern Georgia and northeastern Alabama by Jeffrey P. Brain and Philip Phillips (1996), Adam King (1991, 1996, 1999, 2001, 2003, 2004), and Keith J. Little (1999).

2. Little (1999:52) interprets the minority pottery types as representing cooperative interactions among neighboring groups, but the evidence may indicate the movement of women captured during times of conflict.

3. The discussion of the Moundville chiefdom is based primarily on recent syntheses of archaeological research by Vernon J. Knight Jr., Vincas P. Steponaitis, and colleagues (Knight 2004; Knight and Steponaitis 1998; Steponaitis and Knight 2004).

4. Sites in the Lubbub Creek locale were excavated by a team of archaeologists under the direction of Christopher S. Peebles as part of the U.S. Army Corps of Engineers Tennessee-Tombigbee Waterway Project in the 1970s and early 1980s. This case study is based primarily on syntheses of those excavations by John H. Blitz (1993), Ned J. Jenkins and Richard A. Krause (1986), and Paul D. Welch (1990).

5. The following discussion of the Shiloh/Koger's Island chiefdoms is based primarily on recent research by Paul D. Welch (1998b, 2001, 2005), unpublished research by David G. Anderson, the research of John A. Walthall (1980), and recent reexaminations of the Koger's Island and Perry site cemeteries by Patricia S. Bridges (1996); Keith P. Jacobi (2005); Patricia S. Bridges, Keith P. Jacobi, and Mary Lucas Powell (2000); David H. Dye and Keith P. Jacobi (2000); Keith P. Jacobi and David H. Dye (2001); and Ben M. Shields (2003).

References

Anderson, D. G. 1990. Stability and Change in Chiefdom Level Societies: An Examination of Mississippian Political Evolution on the South Atlantic Slope. In *Lamar Archaeology: Mississippian Chiefdoms in the Deep South*, edited by M. Williams and G. Shapiro, 187–213. Tuscaloosa: University of Alabama Press.

———. 1994a. Factional Competition and the Political Evolution of Mississippian Chiefdoms in the Southeastern United States. In *Factional Competition and Political Development in the New World*, edited by E. M. Brumfiel and J. W. Fox, 61–76. New York: Cambridge University Press.

———. 1994b. *The Savannah River Chiefdoms: Political Change in the Late Prehistoric Southeast*. Tuscaloosa: University of Alabama Press.

———. 1999a. Examining Chiefdoms in the Southeast: An Application of Multiscalar Analysis. In *Great Towns and Regional Polities in the Prehistoric American Southwest and Southeast,* edited by J. E. Neitzel, 215–241. Albuquerque: University of New Mexico Press.

———. 1999b. Fluctuations Between Simple and Complex Chiefdoms: Cycling in the Late Prehistoric Southeast. In *Political Structure and Change in the Prehistoric South-*

eastern United States, edited by J. F. Scarry, 231–252. Gainesville: University Press of Florida.

———. 2001. Climate and Culture Change in Prehistoric and Early Historic Eastern North America. *Archaeology of Eastern North America* 29:143–186.

———. 2002. The Evolution of Tribal Social Organization in the Southeastern U.S. In *The Archaeology of Tribal Societies*, edited by W. Parkinson, 246–277. Ann Arbor, MI: International Monographs in Prehistory.

Anderson, D. G., D. W. Stahle, and M. K. Cleaveland. 1995. Paleoclimate and the Potential Food Reserves of Mississippian Societies: A Case Study from the Savannah River Valley. *American Antiquity* 60(2):258–286.

Blakely, R. L. 1977. Sociocultural Implications of Demographic Data from Etowah, Georgia. In *Biocultural Adaptation in Prehistoric America*, edited by R. L. Blakely, 45–66. Athens: University of Georgia Press.

———. 1995. Social Organization at Etowah: A Reconstruction of Paleodemographic and Paleonutritional Evidence. *Southeastern Archaeology* 14(1):46–59.

Blitz, J. H. 1983. Pre-Mississippian Communities. In *Prehistoric Agricultural Communities in West-Central Alabama: Excavations in the Lubbub Creek Archaeological Locality*, vol. 1, edited by C. S. Peebles, 128–139. Report submitted to U.S. Army Corps of Engineers, Mobile.

———. 1988. Adoption of the Bow in Prehistoric North America. *North American Archaeologist* 9(2):123–145.

———. 1993. *Ancient Chiefdoms of the Tombigbee*. Tuscaloosa: University of Alabama Press.

Brain, J. P., and P. Phillips. 1996. *Shell Gorgets: Styles of the Late Prehistoric and Protohistoric Southeast*. Cambridge: Peabody Museum Press.

Bridges, P. S. 1996. Warfare and Mortality at Koger's Island, Alabama. *International Journal of Osteology* 93:83–94.

Bridges, P. S., K. P. Jacobi, and M. L. Powell. 2000. Warfare-related Trauma in the Late Prehistory of Alabama. In *Bioarchaeological Studies of Life in the Age of Agriculture: A View from the Southeast*, edited by P. M. Lambert, 35–62. Tuscaloosa: University of Alabama Press.

Brown, J. A. 1976. The Southern Cult Reconsidered. *Midcontinental Journal of Archaeology* 1(2):115–135.

———. 1985. The Mississippian Period. In *Ancient Art of the American Woodland Indians*, edited by D. Brose, J. A. Brown, and D. W. Penny, 92–145. New York: Harry N. Abrams.

———. 1996. *The Spiro Ceremonial Center: The Archaeology of Arkansas Valley Caddoan Culture in Eastern Oklahoma*. 2 vols. Memoirs of the Museum of Anthropology 29. Ann Arbor: University of Michigan.

———. 2001. Human Figures and the Southeastern Ancestor Shrine. In *Fleeting Identities: Perishable Material Culture in Archaeological Research*, edited by P. B. Drooker, 76–93. Occasional Paper No. 28. Center for Archaeological Investigations. Carbondale: University of Southern Illinois.

Brown, J. A., and R. K. Vierra. 1983. What Happened in the Middle Archaic? Introduction to an Ecological Approach to Koster Site Archaeology. In *Archaic Hunters and Gatherers in the American Midwest*, edited by J. L. Phillips and J. A. Brown, 165–195. New York: Academic Press.

Caddell, G. M. 1981. Plant Resources, Archaeological Plant Remains, and Prehistoric Plants-use Patterns in the Central Tombigbee River Valley. In *Prehistoric Agricultural Communities in West-Central Alabama: Excavations in the Lubbub Creek Archaeological Locality*, vol. 4. Office of Archaeological Research, Report of Investigations 14. Tuscaloosa: University of Alabama.

Carneiro, R. L. 1967. *The Evolution of Society: Selections from Herbert Spencer's Principles of Sociology*. Chicago: University of Chicago Press.

———. 1981. The Chiefdom: Precursor to the State. In *The Transition to Statehood in the New World*, edited by G. D. Jones and R. R. Kautz, 37–79. Cambridge: Cambridge University Press.

Cobb, C. R., and B. M. Butler. 2002. The Vacant Quarter Revisited: Late Mississippian Abandonment of the Lower Ohio Valley. *American Antiquity* 67(4):625–641.

Cole, G. G., and C. H. Albright. 1983. Summerville I-II Fortifications. In *Excavations in the Lubbub Creek Archeological Locality*, Vol. 1, edited by C. S. Peebles, 140–196. Report submitted to U.S. Army Corps of Engineers, Mobile.

Cole, G. G., M. C. Hill, and H. B. Ensor. 1982. Appendix 3: Bioarchaeological Comparisons of the Late Miller III and Summerville I Phases in the Gainesville Lake Area. In *Archaeological Investigations in the Gainesville Lake Area of the Tennessee-Tombigbee Waterway*, Vol. 5, edited by N. J. Jenkins, 187–258. Office of Archaeological Research, Report of Investigations 12. Tuscaloosa: University of Alabama.

DeBoer, W. R. 1988. Subterranean Storage and the Organization of Surplus: The View from Eastern North America. *Southeastern Archaeology* 7:1–20.

DePratter, C. B. 1983. Late Prehistoric and Early Historic Chiefdoms in the Southeastern United States. Unpublished Ph.D. dissertation, Department of Anthropology, University of Georgia, Athens.

Dickson, D. B. 1981. The Yanomamo of the Mississippi Valley? Some Reflections on Larson (1972), Gibson (1974), and Mississippian Period Warfare in the Southeastern United States. *American Antiquity* 46(4):909–916.

Dye, D. H. 1990. Warfare in the Sixteenth-century Southeast: The de Soto Expedition in the Interior. In *Columbian Consequences*, Vol. 2, edited by D. H. Thomas, 211–222. Washington, D.C.: Smithsonian Institution Press.

———. 1994. The Art of War in the Sixteenth-century Central Mississippi Valley. In *Perspectives on the Southeast: Linguistics, Archaeology, and Ethnohistory*, edited by P. B. Kwachka, 44–66. Southern Anthropological Society Proceedings, No. 27. Athens: University of Georgia Press.

———. 1995. Feasting with the Enemy: Mississippian Warfare and Prestige-goods Circulation. In *Native American Interactions: Multiscalar Analysis and Interpretations in the Eastern Woodlands*, edited by M. S. Nassaney and K. E. Sassaman, 289–316. Knoxville: University of Tennessee Press.

———. 1996. Riverine Adaptations in the Midsouth. In *Of Caves and Shell Mounds*, edited by K. C. Carstens and P. J. Watson, 140–158. Tuscaloosa: University of Alabama Press.

———. 2002. Warfare in the Protohistoric Southeast, 1500–1700. In *Between Contacts and Colonies: Archaeological Perspectives on the Protohistoric Southeast*, edited by C. B. Wesson and M. A. Rees, 126–141. Tuscaloosa: University of Alabama Press.

———. 2004a. Art, Ritual, and Chiefly Warfare in the Mississippian World. In *Hero, Hawk, and Open Hand: American Indian Art of the Ancient Midwest and South*, edited by R. F. Townsend, 191–205. New Haven: Yale University Press.

———. 2004b. Buffer Zones, Warfare, and Settlement Patterning: Mississippian Polity Spacing in the Tennessee Valley. Paper presented at the 16th Annual Meeting of Current Research in Tennessee Archaeology, Nashville.

Dye, D. H., and K. P. Jacobi. 2000. Raiding and Mortuary Patterning at the Koger's Island Site, Lauderdale County, Alabama. Paper presented at the 57th Annual Meeting of the Southeastern Archaeological Conference, Macon.

Dye, D. H., and A. King. 2006. Desecrating the Sacred Mortuary Shrines: Late Prehistoric Warfare in the Southeast. In *When Peace Fails: Conflict and Violence in Indigenous North America*, edited by R. J. Chacon and R. G. Mendoza. Tucson: University of Arizona Press, in press.

Eid, L. V. 1985. "National" War Among Indians of the Northeastern North America. *Canadian Review of American Studies* 6:125–154.

Ensor, H. B. 1981. Classification and Synthesis of the Gainesville Lake Area Lithic Materials: Chronology, Technology and Use. In *Archaeological Investigations in the Gainesville Lake Area of the Tennessee-Tombigbee Waterway*, Vol. 3, edited by N. J. Jenkins, 187–258. Office of Archaeological Research, Report of Investigations 13. Tuscaloosa: University of Alabama.

Futato, E. M. 1998. Ceramic Complexes of the Tennessee River Drainage. *Journal of Alabama Archaeology* 44(1–2):208–241.

Galloway, P. K. 1995. *The Choctaw Genesis: 1500–1700*. Lincoln: University of Nebraska Press.

Gibson, J. L. 1974. Aboriginal Warfare in the Protohistoric Southeast: An Alternative Perspective. *American Antiquity* 39(1):130–133.

Gillies, J. L. 1998. A Preliminary Study of Moundville Hemphill Representational Engraved Ceramic Art Style. Unpublished Master's thesis, Department of Anthropology, University of Alabama, Tuscaloosa.

Haas, J. 1999. The Origins of War and Ethnic Violence. In *Ancient Warfare: Archaeological Perspectives*, edited by J. Carman and A. Harding, 11–24. Phoenix Mill, UK: Sutton Publishing Ltd.

Hall, R. L. 2000. Sacrificed Foursomes and Green Corn Ceremonialism. In *Mounds, Modoc, and Mesoamerica: Papers in Honor of Melvin L. Fowler*, edited by S. R. Ahler, 245–253. Scientific Papers 28. Springfield: Illinois State Museum.

Hally, D. J. 1993. The Territorial Size of Mississippian Chiefdoms. In *Archaeology of Eastern North America: Papers in Honor of Stephen Williams*, edited by J. B. Stoltman, 143–168. Jackson: Mississippi Department of Archives and History.

———. 1996. Platform Mound Construction and the Instability of Mississippian Chiefdoms. In *Political Structure and Change in the Prehistoric Southeastern United States*, edited by J. F. Scarry, 92–127. Gainesville: University Press of Florida.

Hally, D. J., and J. B. Langford Jr. 1988. *Mississippi Period Archaeology of the Georgia Valley and Ridge Province*. Laboratory of Archaeology Series, Report 25. Athens: University of Georgia.

Hally, D. J., and J. L. Rudolph. 1986. *Mississippian Period Archaeology of the Georgia Piedmont*. Laboratory of Archaeology Series, Report 24. Athens: University of Georgia.

Hill, M. C. 1981. Analysis, Synthesis, and Interpretation of the Skeletal Material Excavated for the Gainesville Section of the Tennessee-Tombigbee Waterway. In *Archaeological Investigations in the Gainesville Lake Area of the Tennessee-Tombigbee Waterway*, Vol. 4, edited by N. J. Jenkins, 187–258. Office of Archaeological Research, Report of Investigations 14. Tuscaloosa: University of Alabama.

Howard, J. H. 1968. *The Southeastern Ceremonial Complex and Its Interpretation*. Memoir 6. Columbus: Missouri Archaeological Society.

Hudson, C. 1976. *The Southeastern Indians*. Knoxville: University of Tennessee Press.

———. 1997. *Knights of Spain, Warriors of the Sun: Hernando de Soto and the South's Ancient Chiefdoms*. Athens: University of Georgia Press.

Hudson, C., C. C. DePratter, and M. T. Smith. 1990. The Hernando de Soto Expedition: From Mabila to the Mississippi River. In *Towns and Temples along the Mississippi*, edited by D. H. Dye and C. A. Cox, 181–207. Tuscaloosa: University of Alabama Press.

Hudson, C., M. T. Smith, D. J. Hally, R. R. Polhemus, and C. C. DePratter. 1985. Coosa: A Chiefdom in the Sixteenth Century Southeastern United States. *American Antiquity* 50(4):723–737.

Jacobi, K. P. 2006. Disabling the Dead: Human Trophy Taking in the Prehistoric Southeast. In *The Taking and Displaying of Human Trophies by Amerindians*, 2 vols., edited by R. J. Chacon and D. H. Dye. New York: Springer-Kluwer, in press.

Jacobi, K. P., and D. H. Dye. 2001. Headless in Alabama: Raiding and Mortuary Patterning at the Perry Site and Koger's Island. Paper presented at the 58th Annual Meeting of the Southeastern Archaeological Conference, Chattanooga.

Jacobi, K. P., and M. C. Hill. 2001. Prehistoric treatment of the Dead: Bone Handling in the Southeastern United States (abstract). *American Journal of Physical Anthropology Supplement* 32:85.

Jenkins, N. J. 1982. Archaeology of the Gainesville Lake Area: Synthesis. In *Archaeological Investigations in the Gainesville Lake Area of the Tennessee-Tombigbee Waterway*, Vol. 5, edited by N. J. Jenkins. Office of Archaeological Research, Report of Investigations 12. Tuscaloosa: University of Alabama.

Jenkins, N. J., and H. B. Ensor. 1981. The Gainesville Lake Area Excavations. In *Archaeological Investigations in the Gainesville Lake Area of the Tennessee-Tombigbee Waterway*, Vol. 11, edited by N. J. Jenkins, 187–258. Office of Archaeological Research, Report of Investigations 11. Tuscaloosa: University of Alabama.

Jenkins, N. J., and R. A. Krause. 1986. *The Tombigbee Watershed in Southeastern Prehistory*. Tuscaloosa: University of Alabama Press.

Johnson, A. W., and T. Earle. 2000. *The Evolution of Human Societies: From Foraging Group to Agrarian State.* 2nd ed. Stanford: Stanford University Press.

Kelly, A. R., and L. H. Larson Jr. 1957. Explorations at the Etowah Indian Mounds near Cartersville, Georgia: Seasons 1954, 1955, 1956. *Archaeology* 10(1):39–48.

Kelly, R. C. 2000. *Warless Societies and the Origin of War*. Ann Arbor: University of Michigan.

King, A. 1991. Excavations at Mound B, Etowah: 1954–1958. Unpublished Master's thesis, Department of Anthropology, University of Georgia, Athens.

———. 1996. Tracing Organizational Change in Mississippian Chiefdoms of the Etowah River Valley, Georgia. Unpublished Ph.D. dissertation, Department of Anthropology, Pennsylvania State University, University Park.

———. 1999. DeSoto's Itaba and the Nature of Sixteenth Century Paramount Chiefdoms. *Southeastern Archaeology* 18(2):110–123.

———. 2001. Long-term Histories of Mississippian Centers: The Developmental Sequence of Etowah and its Comparison to Moundville and Cahokia. *Southeastern Archaeology* 20(1):1–17.

———. 2003. *Etowah: The Political History of a Chiefdom Capital.* Tuscaloosa: University of Alabama Press.

———. 2004. Power and the Sacred: Mound C and the Etowah Chiefdom. In *Hero, Hawk, and Open Hand: American Indian Art of the Ancient Midwest and South*, edited by R. F. Townsend, 151–156. New Haven: Yale University Press.

Knight, V. J., Jr. 1982. Document and Literature Review. In *Phase I Archaeological Reconnaissance of the Oliver Lock and Dam Project Area, Tuscaloosa, Alabama*, edited by L. S. Alexander, 27–102. Report of Investigations 33. Office of Archaeological Research. Tuscaloosa: University of Alabama.

———. 1986. The Institutional Organization of Mississippian Religion. *American Antiquity* 51(4):675–687.

———. 1995. An Assessment of Moundville Engraved "Cult" Designs from Potsherds. Paper presented at the 52nd Annual Meeting of Southeastern Archaeological Conference, Knoxville.

———. 2004. Characterizing Elite Midden Deposits at Moundville. *American Antiquity* 69:304–321.

Knight, V. J., Jr., and V. P. Steponaitis. 1998. A New History of Moundville. In *Archaeology of the Moundville Chiefdom,* edited by V. J. Knight Jr. and V. P. Steponaitis, 1–25. Washington, D.C.: Smithsonian Institution Press.

Knight, V. J., Jr., J. A. Brown, and G. E. Lankford. 2001. On the Subject Matter of Southeastern Ceremonial Complex Art. *Southeastern Archaeology* 20(2):129–141.

Lacefield, H. L. 1995. A Preliminary Study of Moundville Engraved Pottery. Unpublished Master's thesis, Department of Anthropology, University of Alabama, Tuscaloosa.

Lafferty, R. H. 1973. An Analysis of Prehistoric Southeastern Fortifications. Unpublished Master's thesis, Department of Anthropology, Southern Illinois University, Carbondale.

Lambert, P. M. 2002. The Archaeology of War: A North American Perspective. *Journal of Archaeological Research* 10(3):207–241.

Lankford, G. E. 2004. World on a String: Some Cosmological Components of the Southeastern Ceremonial Complex. In *Hero, Hawk, and Open Hand: American Indian Art of the Ancient Midwest and South*, edited by R. F. Townsend, 207–217. New Haven: Yale University Press.

Larson, L. H., Jr. 1954. Georgia Historical Commission Excavations at the Etowah Site Summer 1954. *Early Georgia* 1(3):18–22.

———. 1959. A Mississippian Headdress from Etowah, Georgia. *American Antiquity* 25(1):109–112.

———. 1971. Archaeological Implications of Social Stratification at the Etowah Site, Georgia. In *Approaches to the Social Dimension of Mortuary Practices*, edited by J. A. Brown, 58–67. Society for American Archaeology, Memoir 25.

———. 1972. Functional Considerations of Warfare in the Southeast during the Mississippi Period. *American Antiquity* 37(3):383–392.

———. 1993. An Examination of the Significance of a Tortoise-shell Pin from the Etowah Site. In *Archaeology of Eastern North America, Papers in Honor of Stephen Williams,* edited by J. B. Stoltman, 169–185. Archaeological Report 25. Jackson: Mississippi Department of Archives and History.

Little, K. J. 1999. The Role of Late Woodland Interactions in the Emergence of Etowah. *Southeastern Archaeology* 18(1):45–56.

Little, K. J., H. O. Holstein, C. E. Hill, and P. Jones. 1997. *Archaeological Investigations of the Dry Creek Site*. Archaeological Resource Laboratory Research Series 2. Jacksonville: Jacksonville State University.

McKenzie, D. H. 1966. A Summary of the Moundville Phase. *Journal of Alabama Archaeology* 12(1):1–58.

Mensforth, R. P. 2001. Warfare and Trophy Taking in the Archaic Period. In *Archaic Transitions in Ohio and Kentucky Prehistory,* edited by O. H. Prufer, S. E. Pedde, and R. S. Meindl, 110–138. Kent: Kent State University Press.

———. 2006. Human Trophy Taking in Eastern North America During the Archaic Period: Its Relationship to Warfare and Social Complexity. In *The Taking and Displaying of Human Trophies by Amerindians*, 2 vols., edited by R. J. Chacon and D. H. Dye. New York: Springer-Kluwer, in press.

Meyer, C. C. 1995. *Cultural Resources in the Pickwick Reservoir*. Report of Investigations No. 75. Division of Archaeology, Alabama Museum of Natural History, Moundville: University of Alabama.

Milanich, J. 1996. *The Timucua*. Oxford: Blackwell.

Milner, G. R. 1995. An Osteological Perspective on Prehistoric Warfare. In *Regional Approaches to Mortuary Analysis*, edited by L. A. Beck, 221–244. New York: Plenum Press.

———. 1998. Archaeological Evidence for Prehistoric and Early Historic Intergroup Conflict in Eastern North America. In *Deciphering Anasazi Violence; With Regional Comparisons to Mesoamerica and Woodland Cultures*, edited by P. Y. Bullock, 69–91. Santa Fe, NM: HRM.

———. 1999. Warfare in Prehistoric and Early Historic Eastern North America. *Journal of Archaeological Research* 7(2):105–151.

———. 2000. Palisaded Settlements in Prehistoric Eastern North America. In *City Walls: The Urban Enceinte in Global Perspective*, edited by J. D. Tracy, 46–70. New York: Cambridge University Press.

———. 2005. Nineteenth-century Arrow Wounds and Perceptions of Prehistoric Warfare. *American Antiquity* 70(1):144–156.

Milner, G. R., V. G. Smith, and E. Anderson. 1991. Warfare in Late Prehistoric West-Central Illinois. *American Antiquity* 56(4):581–603.

Mistovich, T. S., 1988. Early Mississippian in the Black Warrior Valley: The Pace of Transition. *Southeastern Archaeology* 7(1):21–38.

Moore, C. B., 1915. Aboriginal Sites on Tennessee River. *Journal of the Academy of Natural Sciences of Philadelphia* 16:171–422.

Morse, D. F., 1998. A Shark Tooth Club from Arkansas. *Arkansas Archeological Society, Field Notes* 282:5–6.

Nassaney, M. S., and K. Pyle. 1999. The Adoption of the Bow and Arrow in Eastern North America: A View from Central Arkansas. *American Antiquity* 64(2):243–263.

Peebles, C. S. 1971. Moundville and Surrounding Sites: Some Structural Considerations of Mortuary Practices II. In *Approaches to the Social Dimensions of Mortuary Practices*, edited by J. A. Brown, 68–91. Society for American Archaeology, Memoir 25.

———. 1974. Moundville: The Organization of a Prehistoric Community and Culture. Unpublished Ph.D. dissertation, Department of Anthropology, University of California, Santa Barbara.

Peebles, C. S., and S. Kus. 1977. Some Archaeological Correlates of Ranked Societies. *American Antiquity* 42(3):421–448.

Perttula, T. K. 1992. *"The Caddo Nation": Archaeological and Ethnohistoric Perspectives*. Austin: University of Texas Press.

Powell, M. L. 1988. *Status and Health in Prehistory: A Case Study of the Moundville Chiefdom*. Washington, D.C.: Smithsonian Institution Press.

Price, T. D., and J. A. Brown. 1985. Aspects of Hunter-gatherer Complexity. In *Prehistoric Hunter-Gatherers: The Emergence of Cultural Complexity*, edited by T. D. Price and J. A. Brown, 3–20. New York: Academic Press.

Reyna, S. P. 1994. A Mode of Domination Approach to Organized Violence. In *Studying War: Anthropological Perspectives*, edited by S. P. Reyna and R. E. Downs, 29–65. New York: Gordon and Breach.

Scarry, C. M. 1993. Agricultural Risk and the Development of the Moundville Chiefdom. In *Foraging and Farming in the Eastern Woodlands*, edited by C. M. Scarry, 157–181. Gainesville: University Press of Florida.

———. 1995. *Excavations on the Northwest Riverbank at Moundville: Investigations of a Moundville I Residential Area*. Report of Investigations No. 72. Office of Archaeological Services. Tuscaloosa: University of Alabama.

Scarry, J. F. 1992. Political Offices and Political Structure: Ethnohistoric and Archaeological Perspectives on the Native Lords of Apalachee. In *Lords of the Southeast: Social Inequality and the Native Elites of Southeastern North America,* edited by A. W. Barker and T. R. Pauketat, 163–183. Archaeological Papers of the American Anthropological Association No. 3. Washington, D.C.: American Anthropological Association.

———. 1996. Stability and Change in the Apalachee Chiefdom: Centralization, Decentralization, and Social Reproduction. In *Political Structure and Change in the Prehistoric Southeastern United States*, edited by J. F. Scarry, 192–227. Gainesville: University Press of Florida.

———. 1999a. How Great were the Southeastern Polities? In *Great Towns and Regional Polities in the Prehistoric American Southwest and Southeast*, edited by J. E. Neitzel, 59–74. Albuquerque: University of New Mexico Press.

———. 1999b. Elite Identities in Apalachee Province: The Construction of Identity and Cultural Change in a Mississippian Society. In *Material Symbols: Culture and Economy in Prehistory*, edited by J. Robb, 342–361. Occasional Paper 26. Center for Archaeological Investigations. Carbondale: Southern Illinois University.

Schoeninger, M. J., and M. R. Schurr. 1998. Human Subsistence at Moundville: The Stable-isotope Data. In *Archaeology of the Moundville Chiefdom*, edited by V. J. Knight Jr. and V. P. Steponaitis, 120–132. Washington, D.C.: Smithsonian Institution Press.

Schultz, T. C., D. H. Dye, and C. Walker. 2001. The Ritual Accouterments of Warfare at Etowah. Paper presented at the 66th Annual Meeting of the Society for American Archaeology, New Orleans.

Sheldon, C. T., Jr. 1974. *The Mississippian-Historic Transition in Central Alabama*. Ph.D. dissertation, University of Oregon, University Microfilms, Ann Arbor.

Shields, B. M. 2003. An Analysis of the Archaic Human Burials at the Mulberry Creek (1CT27) Shell Mound, Colbert County, Alabama. Unpublished Master's thesis, Department of Anthropology, University of Alabama, Tuscaloosa.

Smith, B. D. 1986. The Archaeology of the Southeastern United States: From Dalton to De Soto, 10,500–500 B.P. *Advances in World Archaeology* 5:1–92.

Smith, M. O. 1993a. Intergroup Violence Among Prehistoric Hunter/Gatherers from the Kentucky Lake Reservoir. *American Journal of Physical Anthropology Supplement* 16:183–184.

———. 1993b. A Probable Case of Decapitation at the Late Archaic Robinson Site (40SM4), Smith County, Tennessee. *Tennessee Anthropologist* 18(2):1131–1142.

———. 1995. Scalping in the Archaic Period: Evidence from the Western Tennessee Valley. *Southeastern Archaeology* 14(1):60–68.

———. 1996a. Biocultural Inquiry into Archaic Period Populations of the Southeast: Trauma and Occupational Stress, In *Archaeology of the Mid-Holocene Southeast,* edited by K. E. Sassaman and D. G. Anderson, 134–154. Gainesville: University Press of Florida.

———. 1996b. Parry Fractures and Female-directed Interpersonal Violence: Implications from the Late Archaic Period of West Tennessee. *International Journal of Osteoarchaeology* 6:84–91.

———. 1997. Osteological Indications of Warfare in the Archaic Period of the Western Tennessee Valley. In *Troubled Times: Violence and Warfare in the Past*, edited by D. L. Martin and D. W. Frayer, 241–265. New York: Gordon and Breach.

Smith, M. T. 1989. Aboriginal Population Movements in the Early Historic Period Interior Southeast. In *Powhatan's Mantle: Indians of the Colonial Southeast*, edited by P. H. Wood, G. A. Waselkov, and M. T. Hatley, 135–149. Lincoln: University of Nebraska Press.

———. 2000. *Coosa: The Rise and Fall of a Southeastern Mississippian Chiefdom*. Gainesville: University Press of Florida.

Southerlin, B. G. 1993. Mississippian Settlement Patterns in the Etowah River Valley near Cartersville, Bartow County, Georgia. Unpublished Master's thesis, Department of Anthropology, University of Georgia, Athens.

Steinen, K. T. 1992. Ambushes, Raids, and Palisades: Mississippian Warfare in the Interior Southeast. *Southeastern Archaeology* 11(2):132–139.

Steponaitis, V. P. 1983. *Ceramics, Chronology, and Community Patterns: An Archaeological Study at Moundville*. New York: Academic Press.

Steponaitis, V. P., and V. J. Knight Jr. 2004. Moundville Art in Historical and Social Context. In *Hero, Hawk, and Open Hand: American Indian Art of the Ancient Midwest and South*, edited by R. F. Townsend, 167–181. New Haven: Yale University Press.

Sussenbach, T. 1993. Agricultural Intensification and Mississippian Developments in the Confluence Region of the Mississippi River Valley. Unpublished Ph.D. dissertation, Department of Anthropology, University of Illinois, Urbana-Champaign.

Van Horne, W. W. 1993. The Warclub: Weapon and Symbol in Southeastern Indian Societies. Unpublished Ph.D. dissertation, Department of Anthropology, University of Georgia, Athens.

Vogel, J. O., and J. Allan. 1985. Mississippian Fortifications at Moundville. *Archaeology* 38:62–63.

Walthall, J. A. 1980. *Prehistoric Indians of the Southeast: Archaeology of Alabama and the Middle South*. Tuscaloosa: University of Alabama Press.

Waring, A. J. 1968. The Southern Cult and Muskhogean Ceremonial: General Considerations. In *The Waring Papers: The Collected Papers of Antonio J. Waring, Jr.*, edited by S. Williams, 30–69. Papers of the Peabody Museum of American Archaeology and Ethnology 50. Cambridge: Harvard University.

Welch, P. D. 1990. Mississippian Emergence in West-Central Alabama. In *The Mississippian Emergence*, edited by B. D. Smith, 197–225. Washington, D.C.: Smithsonian Institution Press.

———. 1991. *Moundville's Economy*. Tuscaloosa: University of Alabama Press.

———. 1998a. Outlying Sites Within the Moundville Chiefdom. In *Archaeology of the Moundville Chiefdom*, edited by V. J. Knight Jr. and V. P. Steponaitis, 133–166. Washington, D.C.: Smithsonian Institution Press.

———. 1998b. Middle Woodland and Mississippian Occupations of the Savannah Site in Tennessee. *Southeastern Archaeology* 17(1):79–92.

———. 2001. *Archaeology at Shiloh Indian Mounds, 1899–1999*. Report submitted to Southeastern Archeological Center. Tallahassee: National Park Service.

———. 2005. *Archaeology at Shiloh Indian Mounds, 1899–1999*. Tuscaloosa: University of Alabama Press.

Wilkins, K. S. 2001. Oblong Copper Gorgets from Moundville. *Journal of Alabama Archaeology* 47(1):69–74.

Wilson, G. D. 2001. Crafting Control and the Control of Crafts: Rethinking the Moundville Greenstone Industry. *Southeastern Archaeology* 20(2):118–128.

Winters, H. D. 1974. Introduction to the New Edition. In *Indian Knoll* by W. S. Webb, v–xxvii. Knoxville: University of Tennessee Press.

5

Prehistoric Warfare in Palau

JOLIE LISTON AND H. DAVID TUGGLE

Introduction

It is said in the Palau Islands of southwestern Micronesia that there was great lawlessness in the archaic time, when beings were half-human and half-fish.[1] Then the demi-god Chuab created political institutions to promote order (Parmentier 1987:138–139; Tellei et al. 2004:15). These institutions took the form of eight village councils that formed a peaceful political federation. But the federation dissolved over an affront to the dignity and respect of Chuab's ranked hierarchy by the violation of a food distribution convention. Ruchel (messenger gods) then "came to Belau with the declared intention of increasing proper behavior by imposing new laws" (Parmentier 1987:154) but failed to establish a stable political structure. So Uchelianged, the high god, destroyed the inhabitants of Palau by a great flood and began a new era. The goddess Milad gave birth to four children (villages) in the four largest areas of Palau, but interaction among the new villages was still entwined with the institutions of Chuab, and conflict has always persisted.

There is no Western time frame in these traditions, but they tell us that from the Palauan perspective, there has always been some form of political structure that promoted alliances on one hand, and enmity and war on the other. This is further indicated in Palauan traditions that move from myth to history. As Parmentier (1987:90) notes: "the subject of warfare dominates [Palauan] historical traditions as recorded in stories, chants, songs, proverbial expressions, and pictorial carvings." The "pictorial carvings" are the carved and painted beams of a village structure known as the *bai* (Figure 5.2).[2] The bai functioned as men's houses and as meetinghouses of a village's ruling council, and the artwork expressed the village or region's legends and history, including specific battles (Figure 5.3) that were perceived to have elevated the social status of the village (Telmetang 1993).

Ethnographically, warfare was thus an institutionalized component of traditional Palauan culture—one of the expressions of the ethos of Palauan competition (Hezel 1983; McKnight 1960). Archaeological evidence suggests that war and competition were in fact a part of the ancient fabric of this society. The

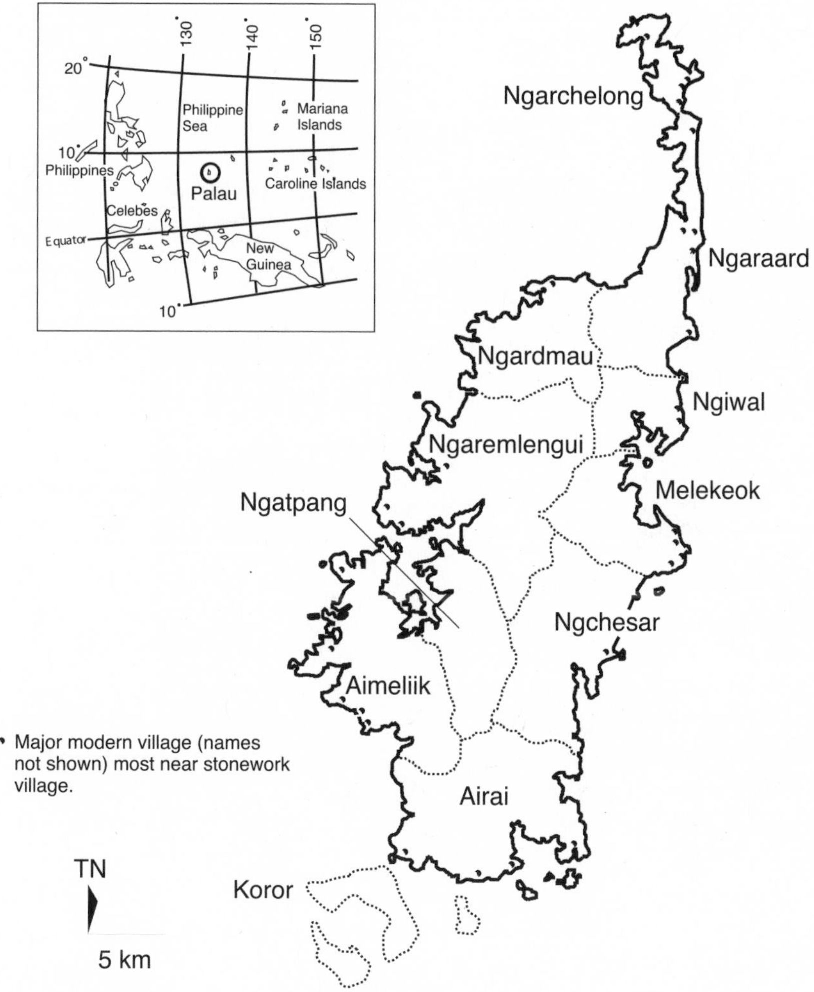

Figure 5.1. The Pacific and the Islands of Palau. On the main island of Babeldaob the political districts and major modern villages are shown, most of which are near or incorporate earlier stonework villages of the same name.

present chapter employs archaeological, ethnographic, and historical information in an analysis of the nature of Palauan warfare and its transformations. Too little is known about early Palauan archaeology to be able to address the origins of this institution in more than the most general terms of incipient competition, and thus the "cause of war" is not a topic of the chapter. The chapter presents Palauan warfare in the form of a model of long-term patterns of conflict and defense related to settlement and subsistence.

Figure 5.2. One of three *bai* (meeting houses) that once stood on the Bai Melekeong stone platform in the center of Melekeok village.

Figure 5.3. Two traditional war scenes from a *bai* decoration; redrawn from paintings on the *bai* of Airai; each scene shows an attack by boat against a stone platform at a coastal edge. In the bottom scene the front of a *bai* is shown on the far left.

Island Description

This research centers on Babeldaob,[3] the largest of the some 300 islands in the Palau archipelago (see Figure 5.1) that spreads along a 150 kilometer north-south arc in the Western Carolines of Micronesia. Babeldaob, volcanic in origin, is 45 km long and ranges from 0.3 km to 13 km wide. Its area of 333 km^2 makes up about three-fourths of the total land area of the entire chain.

The interior uplands of Babeldaob, with a maximum elevation of 242 m, are formed by three low mountain systems that generally split the island along its north-south axis. The central mountain area, the Rael Kedam, is heavily eroded with numerous steep-sided valleys and associated ridges. A lowland zone of gently rolling hills circles the base of the upland mountain and ridge system. In limited places, mostly on the northeast coast, there are thin strips of bottomlands defined by beaches or swamp forest. Thick mangrove forests encircle much of Babeldaob. A shallow lagoon of some 1200 km^2 separates the island from the surrounding barrier reef.

Palau has a hot maritime tropical rainy climate with annual rainfall ranging from 300 cm to 400 cm. Intensive weathering of the basalt-andesite breccias has resulted in the formation of clay soils, over 70 percent of which are lateritic. These are deep but infertile soils, severely leached and highly acidic (Corwin et al. 1956). Vegetation is composed of roughly equal areas of savanna and mixed-tropical forest, and small sections of swamp forest.

A Model of Palauan Warfare and its Transformations

Recent intensive archaeological investigations, combined with ethnographic and historical data, provide substantial evidence concerning the nature of warfare in two of the three major chronological periods of Palau's history.[4] For simplicity these periods are referred to as the Settlement and Expansion Era, the Terrace Era, and the Stonework Era. There is little evidence of warfare during the initial period of settlement and population expansion (possibly from around 1500 B.C. until about 600 B.C.), but the situation is quite different for the two subsequent periods.

Around 600 B.C., the beginning of the Terrace Era, a change in settlement pattern occurred that indicates a significant concern with warfare and defense. At that time, villages of earth platforms began to be developed on ridgelines and other elevated inland areas, with associated construction of massive earthworks sculpted from the hills surrounding the settlements (Figures 5.4, 5.5, 5.6, 5.7). These earthworks are the famous terraces of Palau (see, for example, Morgan 1988; Osborne 1966), which are interpreted here as a combination of functional defenses and symbolic expressions of power. At the peak of the terrace development in the first millennium A.D., the terrace complexes formed

Figure 5.4. The Ngerkelalk complex in Aimeliik dominates the surrounding heavily modified landscape. The high point of the complex is a circular crown (with a single tree on its top), which has an erosion-filled ditch completely surrounding its base.

Figure 5.5. The steep step-terraces leading to the crown at Roisingang, Ngaraard, which is capped by a knob that overlies a probable chiefly burial or burials. A deep trench extends along the base of the most evident terrace facing; the facing is c. 3 m high.

Figure 5.6. The small crown is in the center of a vast set of terraces in Aimeliik.

Figure 5.7. The Ngermelkii crown and great ditch (center of the photo) in Ngatpang are part a complex of expansive earthworks that surround the major bay on the west side of the island.

Figure 5.8. A coastal entrance to the stonework village of Ngerbau in Ngarchelong showing the stone euatel, in this case a defensive embankment. Passengers from boats docking in this area had to be permitted passage through the Euatel Era Ngerbau, at the beginning of the path into Ngerbau.

defensive boundaries for large, independent competing polities composed of groups of villages.

A second major settlement change occurred around A.D. 1000, the beginning of the Stonework Era.[5] The terrace complexes and ridgeline villages were abandoned, villages were resettled close to the coast, and village architecture changed from earth platforms with early stone architecture to massive stone construction (Figure 5.8). Warfare at this time involved larger, but less centralized polities, and shifted from defense of the polity's boundaries to defense of individual villages. This is the pattern that was in place at the time of European contact, and thus is the basis for the ethnographic descriptions of Palau and the recording of traditional warfare and related political organization.[6]

These sequential settlement and warfare systems of the model are not proposed as monolithic entities. The periods are hundreds of years long and certainly had local variations in time and space, and cycles of development and change within them. However, the fact that Palauan archaeology is barely out of its infancy means that the intensive research necessary for understanding these details remains to be carried out. Among other things, the information on contemporaneity of settlement within eras is extremely limited. Thus, the model that is presented here is necessarily general. However, the two contrasting patterns of political organization and warfare had long persistence, and as such provide a framework for future intensive archaeological and ethnographic investigation.

Ethnographic and Historical Data

The first known European contact with Palau was in the mid-1500s, but visits to this isolated island chain were intermittent for two centuries. Limited contact in the late 1600s produced the first descriptions of ethnographic value, but detailed accounts of the islands were not written until the late 1700s.

Two items of particular note were recorded about Palau at this time. First, Palauans did not engage in long-distance navigation, and so were not a part of the vast trading network of the western Caroline Islands. The second is that societies in Palau appeared to be engaged in constant warfare (Keate 1788). The nineteenth century German ethnographer Kubary summarized the role of war in Palauan culture: "War has a different sense here than it has in other places. It is a political institution, a traditional custom, and a means of raising tribute" (Kubary 1873:32).

Political Organization: Background to Warfare

For ethnographic Palau, the village was the primary political unit and the focus of warfare. Villages, adjacent to the coast, were organized concentrations of residences, adjacent burial platforms, and meeting houses built on stone foundations, connected by extensive networks of stone paths (Figure 5.9).

The villages were located close to their irrigated lowland swamp taro fields and controlled specific areas of the adjacent lagoon and reef. Each village had its own ruling council that was ideally composed of ten chiefs, the senior-ranking male titleholders from each of the village's ten kin groups.[7] At the same time, the council's ten chiefs were divided into two groups, which were themselves ranked (one headed by the highest ranking chief, the other by the second highest ranking); this was a reflection of Palauan dualism that runs through all the culture's social, political, and spatial organization. Decisions were made by council deliberation, and the highest-ranking chief could not act unilaterally (Force 1960:142). At the same time (as described by Force 1960:40):

> . . . the council of chiefs incorporated the competition and rivalry which was characteristic of village organization in general. The faction headed by the number-two-ranking chief was always interested in wrestling any power possible from the faction headed by the number-one-ranking chief.

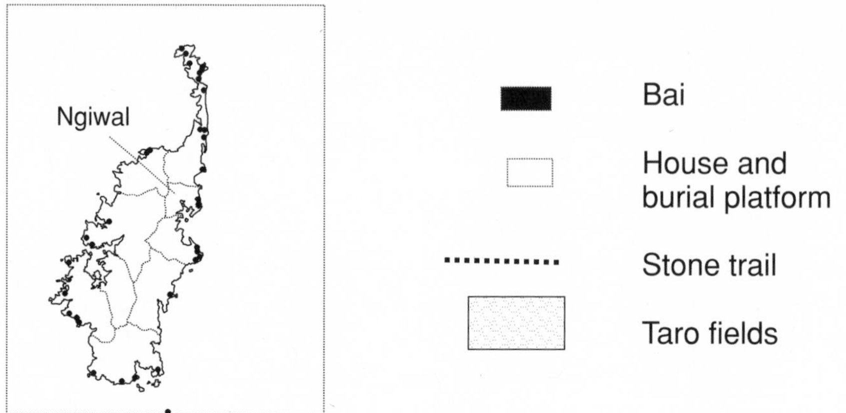

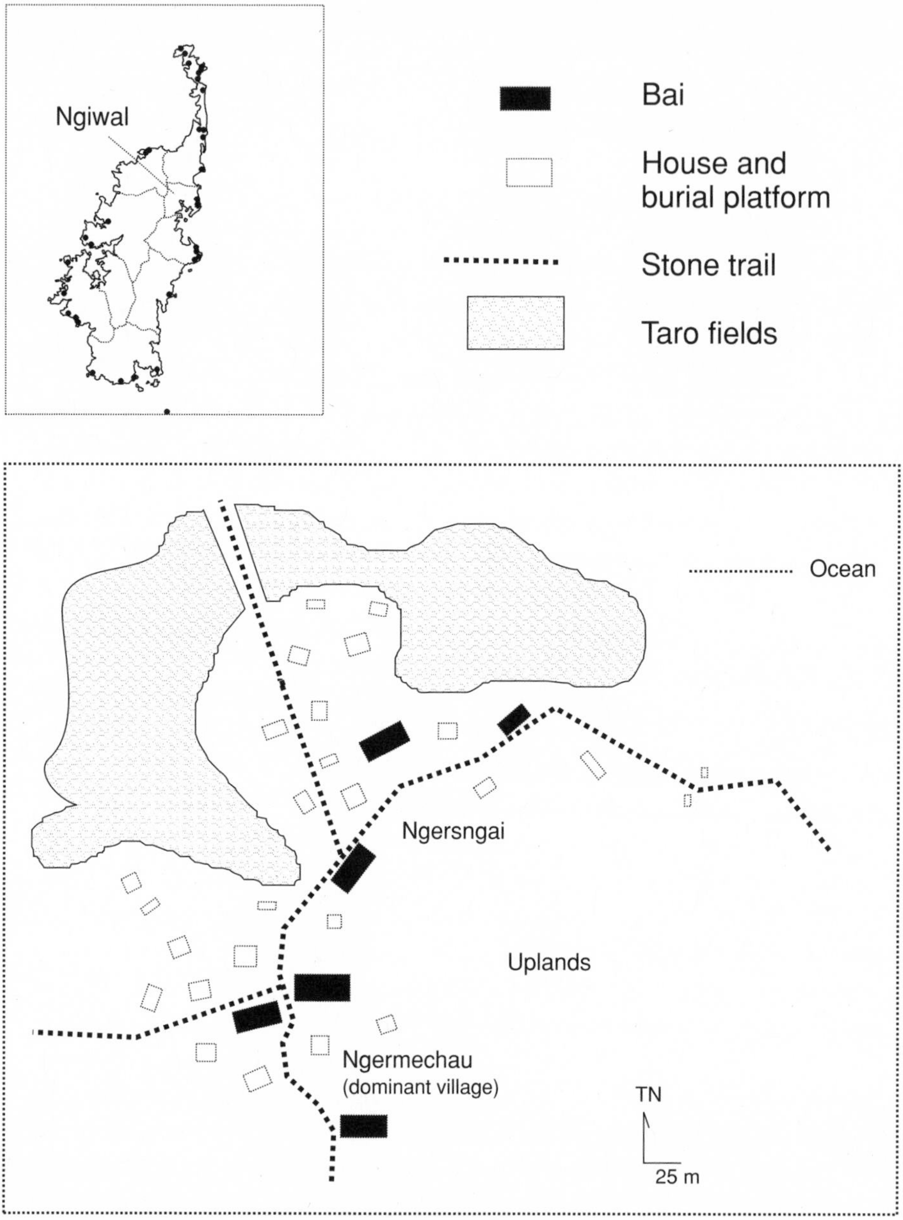

Figure 5.9. Two stonework villages in Ngiwal.

> In many cases it is possible to trace the ascent of the number two [kin group] on the council to the number one position.

Seen in this are the two elements that are critical to understanding Palauan warfare: an extremity rigid ideal social structure overlying a fluid system of internal change driven by competition (compare Force 1960; Hezel 1983; McCutcheon 1981; McKnight 1960).

Villages were part of two larger political associations, called districts and federations (Parmentier 1987:55).[8] Districts, as described by Parmentier (1987:61),

> . . . consist of dependent villages affiliated with a dominant capital village . . . [but] member villages are fully distinct entities with titleholders, houses, and clubs that are not merely subservient to the corresponding institutions at the capital. Furthermore, villages in the district maintain political relationships of various sorts with villages in other districts, ties that do not necessarily pass through the capital.

Each district (see Figure 5.1), generally bounded by natural features, was a group of villages forming a semi-independent subsistence and economic region, but functioning with a low level of political integration. There was no district council of chiefs; rather district authority was exercised by the council of the capital village itself, in turn dependent upon cooperation of the councils of the member villages (Parmentier 1987:64). The districts had some long-term continuity as far as their general boundaries were concerned (a function of geography),[9] but there was significant change over time in composition, in the specific village that served as capital, and in the name of the district (Parmentier 1987:61). These changes were largely a function of success and failure in village warfare, within or between districts.

The limited integration of the district is emphasized by the fact that villages maintained political relationships with villages in other districts, became allies to form subdistricts, changed district membership, and formed federations that cross-cut districts. Federations were

> . . . networks of shifting alliances among villages from several districts . . . [and they] were the product of military expansion of a powerful village, the temporary solidarity of villages allied against a common enemy, or the result of kinship and marriage ties shared by local representatives of high-ranking house affiliation networks (Parmentier 1987:65).

Traditional Warfare

The aspiration of each political unit was power and associated prestige; warfare was a dominant means to establish and maintain this. Through conquest, the victor could acquire new territory, destroy a village, and establish tribute relationships, all steps to becoming a more powerful village or district. Oral histories and historical accounts record incessant and structured warfare, as shifting, unstable alliances of villages, districts, and federations changed composition, organization, and function.

There were two types of warfare (Parmentier 1987:79). The first was raiding for the purpose of killing an individual from another village and taking the head. This was related to the prestige of a high-ranking chief, who organized the raiding party. If the raid was successful it was also a means of solidifying village alliances as the head trophy was then taken to other villages for a special ceremony.

The other form of warfare was for village power and prestige, and involved a full attack on another village. Victory could come after a quick skirmish and capitulation or a more prolonged siege. Battles took place on land and at sea. The primary weapon was a long (1.5–3.5 m) bamboo spear with a barbed hardwood tip. Also used were darts, hardwood swords (30 cm), wooden clubs, rayfish spines, daggers, and possibly blowguns (Hijikata 1993:48; Keate 1788).

A vanquished village might simply acknowledge its subservient position, or attackers might burn the village, destroy gardens, and kill many of the inhabitants (Parmentier 1987:79). Success in this type of warfare was one means of becoming a district capital, acquiring prestige items, or creating a tribute relationship. The victor collected the spoils of war, including canoes, provisions lying close to shore, or prize possessions of the highest chief. Victory dances were held, and prisoners were put to death, the heads of the higher ranked ones displayed on bamboo supports or placed on an offering stone. Villagers not slaughtered or taken as tribute might flee to resettle with an allied village or relative. Much of Palauan oral history focuses on the migration accounts of these defeated villagers. Where a conquered village was not demolished, its inhabitants were forced into a tribute relationship with the victors. Tribute took the form of slaves serving as concubines and laborers, or material goods such as food or valuables. In cases where villages were defeated and overrun, the men's bai was often dismantled and moved to the victor's village, or in some instances, the entire village architecture was relocated, sometimes split up among the villages of the conquering district, and the land absorbed and resettled by the captors. Such village warfare could take place within a district or across district lines. These wars could involve the temporary federations, which in some cases were formed by tribute (or "enslaved") villages to overthrow the dominant village (Parmentier 1987:85).

It is important to emphasize that these generalizations, involving references to land acquisition and population resettlement, do not refer to a social system of increasing complexity, centralization, or integration (compare Hezel 1981:66–74; Parmentier 1987:64–65; Vidich 1949). A number of leveling mechanisms were at work. Power was diluted by the structure of the ranked kin groups, by the ideology and practice of competition that allowed ranked position change (whether among kin groups within a village or between villages), and by the fact that it was prestige through symbolic recognition that was ultimately more important than physical domination. This also has to be seen against the geography of the large island of Babeldaob, whose rugged terrain militated against a central place of authority and physical control of villages along its extensive coastline and interior valleys. Regardless of the number or extent of alliances, the Palauan traditions and ethnographic summaries always refer to villages as "autonomous," and the districts and federations as loose and fluid.

This is well illustrated by the events of the contact period. In the late 1700s there were two competing federations in Palau. The capital of one was on Koror and the other was in the district of Ngatelngal (now called Melekeok) on Babeldaob. The high chief of the Koror federation enlisted the aid of armed English seamen and in a few skirmishes quickly gained recognition from the rival chiefs (Keate 1788). However, this was not the beginning of a "kingdom" of any sort: it was not followed with a new structure or organization to take advantage of the new situation, and thus had no permanence (Hezel 1983:73; Vidich 1949). It took another hundred years, 1883, before traditional warfare was largely brought to an end, when a formal peace agreement between Koror and Melekeok was worked out by a British captain (Hezel 1983:280).

Settlement and Expansion Era (1500–600 B.C.)

Radiocarbon dates from definite cultural context suggest that early settlement occurred around 1500 B.C., although paleoenvironmental evidence suggests settlement was somewhat earlier (Athens and Ward 2004; Liston et al. 1998).[10] This remains a major issue in Palauan archaeology. Early settlements on the coast had an abundance of marine resources available from the lagoon, reef, and the open ocean. Cultivation of dryland taro (*Colocasia esculenta*) and the giant swamp taro (*Crytosperma chamissonis*) supplemented these resources. However, suitable areas for swamp taro were very limited, and it is probable that coastal settlements remained small.

By roughly 1300 B.C. the pollen record shows a dramatic rise in savanna indicators that suggests the practice of swidden agriculture in the lowlands. Due to the infertile lateritic soils, the settlers must have frequently relocated in the lowland zone and up the river valleys in order to access previously unexploited areas. It is probable that raiding and defense did not play a large role in the socioeconomic system of the initially small colonizing population.

The Terrace Era (600 B.C.–A.D. 1000): Settlement Pattern and Warfare

By about 600 B.C. there is evidence that construction of monumental architecture was underway in the form of earthen terrace complexes cut from ridges and hills. Construction and use of these earthworks continued until about the beginning of the eleventh century A.D.[11] Villages of this period were located in the lower ridge zones of the uplands and in the lowlands hills. The settlement pattern of villages and terraces of this era indicates small, fortified polities. Evidence for fortification lies in the morphology of the terrace complexes, while the relative distribution of the earthworks and villages argues for multi-village organization.

Villages and Monumental Architecture

Settlements from this time period were located either on long, narrow ridgelines or on low hillsides. They are archaeologically defined by some combination of earth platforms, rudimentary stone architecture, and dense artifact scatters.[12] Earth platforms, many spanning the width of the narrow ridgelines, are interspersed along the length of the ridges; many have step-terraces on the slopes below them. These earth platforms were foundations for wooden structures; larger platforms supported several structures. There is rudimentary stonework associated with the earthen platforms, including single-course pavings, paths, rough facings, and edging along the high points of various earthworks. There are no oral traditions concerning any of the specific village sites of this era. Palauans questioned today about these locations are surprised to learn there had once been settlements there.

Although the existence of the ridgeline villages has only been recently recognized, the associated monumental earthen terraces have long been known. However, the extent of terrace distribution has been underestimated. Many terraces are in savannah and stand out in sharp relief (see Figure 5.4), but numerous other terrace complexes are hidden under forest cover, unidentified until recent surveys were carried out. The sculpted landscapes cover as much as 20 percent of the island of Babeldaob. Determining the age and function of the

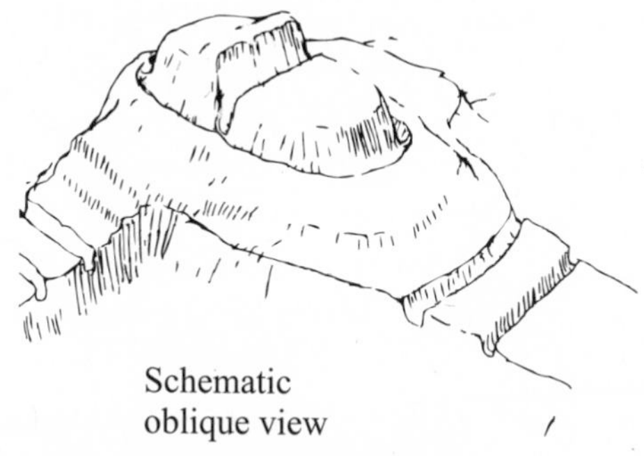

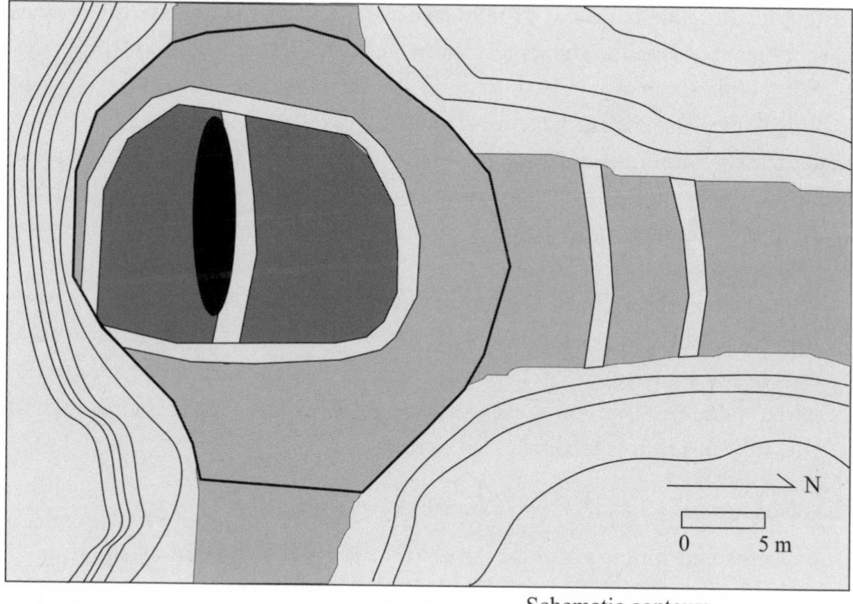

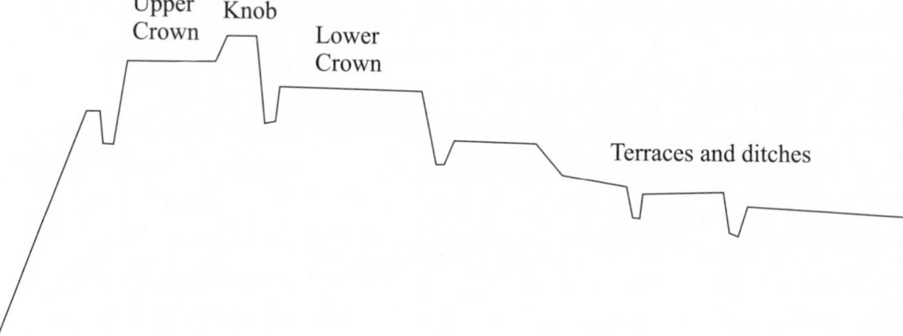

Figure 5.10. Drawing of terrace and crown with defensive features, Kuei Terrace Set, Ngiwal.

earthworks falls almost exclusively into the archaeological realm[13] because they were not in use at the time of European contact, and they figure only rarely in Palauan traditions.

Palau's earthworks, created by a combination of sculpting and cut-and-fill techniques, have three basic features that are found in isolation or as part of larger complexes: (1) step-terraces in a great variety of forms; (2) a high point that has been termed a "crown," [14] and (3) ditches (Figure 5.10, and see Figure 5.6). Step-terraces are the chief component of the complexes. Often following natural land contours, the steps come in a variety of forms and cover large areas of hill and ridge slope. At the highest point of many terrace complexes the hilltop has been cut or mounded to form the crown (Phear 2004; Tuggle 2005), a steep-sided and flat-topped structure.[15] There are at least 100 crowns throughout Babeldaob. The largest known crown is Ngerulmud Hill, approximately 15,000 m^2 in area (Liston et al. 1998), but most are small, in the range of 200–600 m^2. The crowns have nearly vertical sides and rise from 3 m to 10 m above the surrounding landscape. Some crowns have surface features, including stone pavements and earth knobs or berms as high as three meters. Subsurface features including pits and postholes have been found in some of the few that have been excavated (Liston 2005; Phear 2004).

Almost every crown has a ditch, up to five meters deep,[16] dug around its base; in some cases there is a combination of ditch and cliff face. Ridgelines leading to crowns often have ditches cut across them, and adjacent crowns have ditches between them. In some complexes, ditches are also found at the base of each of a series of step-terraces leading up to a crown.

Terrace Complexes as Defensive Features

The origins and functions of the great terraces were forgotten by the time of recorded history.[17] In fact, today's older Palauan generation grew up thinking that the terraces were either natural features or created by the biblical flood. The positioning of the step-terraces as a part of village clusters suggests some were used as dryland agricultural fields, and probably had their origin in this function.[18] There is also evidence that terraces were used for burial, habitation, and for ceremonial structures. However, evidence for such activities is found on only a small percentage of the terraces, and in some cases appears to be late period re-use. It is argued here that that the monumental terrace complexes, elaborated well beyond any commonplace purpose, were constructed for reasons related to warfare and competition. They served as both physical and symbolic defense. The crowns were constructed as militarily defensive positions, and the complexes of crowns and terraces were symbolic expressions of power.

The sheer angle and height of the crowns' sides, their isolated and elevated position on the landscape, and the deep ditches strategically placed to impede access to the top (see Figures 5.5, 5.6, 5.10) indicate that they functioned as fortified lookouts, outposts, and places of brief refuge (compare Keeley's "fortified refuges," 1996:58).

Geographically, the majority of crowns are positioned to provide a commanding view over great expanses of the island. Additionally, many that are separated by great distances have a clear line of sight between them, and in this capacity they could serve as sentry posts for guarding the immediate area, or for alerting distant allies. Oral traditions (relating to a later era, but with possible application to the period of terraces) tell of the allied village relationship between Oikull and Melekeok; sentries on outposts located on high points of the two villages gave warning of impending attacks by using smoke signals (Tellei et al. 2004:74).

Lower crowns within step-terrace systems could have served as lookout positions for those engaged in activities in the surrounding area. In this capacity they could also have allowed small work groups to take refuge against raiding parties.

Archaeological evidence from the few ditches that have been excavated further indicates defensive use. Post holes (and one burned post base) located along the inner margins of the ditches ringing several crowns indicate the presence of palisades. The trench as a defensive device continued to be used in the later Stonework Era, as described in a section below.

Settlement Pattern, Political Organization, and Warfare

Although they could have done so, Palauan societies never became hilltop chiefdoms *sensu stricto* (Earle 1997), but they became something equivalent, where the ridges and hilltops were used as a defensive perimeter for each cluster of agricultural terraces, dispersed non-terraced dryland fields, villages, and associated sites (Figure 5.11). The major terrace complexes, with the crowns and ditches incorporated into them as defended positions, are strategically located to control access into a village cluster by land (and in some cases from the ocean), and to provide long-distance surveillance from high lookout positions. This defensive system was related to dispersed resources and relatively scattered habitation complexes, but was feasible because the polities were relatively small. There are also buffer zones between these complexes, as would be expected at this level of warfare (compare LeBlanc 1999:224).

The nature of a polity's defense from sea attack at this time is uncertain, but it could have involved construction of stone features, such as barricades near places of village access. Such barricades are associated with the late period of warfare but except by reference in oral histories, their origins are undated. There

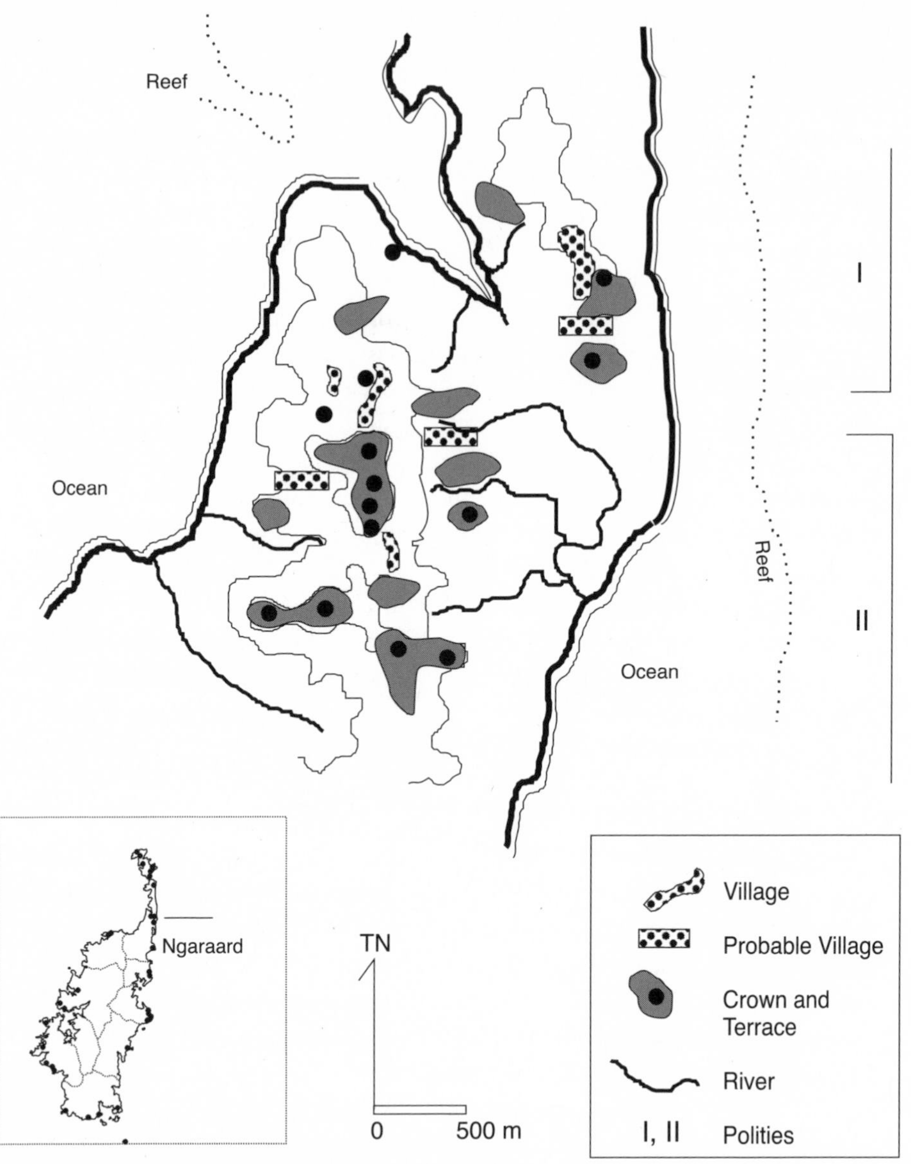

Figure 5.11. Drawing of Terrace Era settlement, Ngaraard.

are some villages at the coast during this time, but they are located where cliffs form natural barriers. An example of one such site cluster is the polity in Ngatpang, which is found spread along the inner margin of a deep bay. The narrow entrance to the bay is guarded by high hills rising from the waterline. Defensive measures did not require the site cluster to be located further inland, as it was protected from attack by the bay's guarded entrance.

The settlement pattern is one of small, fortified polities.[19] The nature of these polities is uncertain, and may have ranged from loose alliances and federations (the contact-period ethnographic pattern) to more centralized chiefdoms. The possibility of centralized political structure is suggested by the extent of the terrace complexes and by indications of complex burials of high-ranking individuals in some of the crowns (Tuggle 2005), by the extent and size of the earthworks, and by the labor force implied by the earthworks. If this was the case, it is a pattern that is significantly different from that of the following Stonework Era. The effort devoted to the defensive complexes also indicates that the scale of warfare (or at least the threat of attack) was also substantially greater in this period than later.

Terrace Complexes and Power

Fortifications have symbolic importance as well as military uses, as Keeley (1996:57) states:

> At the most prosaic level, they symbolize their owner's military sophistication, military power, and determination to hold occupied territory. More abstractly, they demarcate the boundary between defenders and attackers. . . . In chiefdoms and states, fortifications symbolize the importance and manifest the power of a leader.

It is argued here that a major defensive element of the Palauan terrace complexes was the *appearance of power*. The functional elements of defense are evident, but equally important the scale and volume of terrace and crown construction symbolized the ability of the polity (that is, its high chief or ruling council) to mobilize human effort and to obtain divine support. Additionally, as proposed for *late* structures in the Mariana Islands (Hunter-Anderson 1989:45), it is suggested that Palauan terraces functioned as territorial markers to legitimize corporate claims of land and other resources. These symbols dominating the landscape mirrored the associated polities' prestige level as they defined its political boundaries and created defensible terrain.

Stonework Era (A.D. 1000–1800): Settlement Pattern and Warfare

Paleoenvironmental and geomorphological evidence indicates that during the Terrace Era the coastal flats and bottomlands of the island pro-graded significantly, mangrove expanded, and a large expanse of swampland developed. Due in part to erosion during massive terrace construction and use, the accumulation of silt in the still waters of the lagoon provided an ideal location for swamp and mangrove species. Other coastal areas accumulated calcareous beach sands and this pro-graded due to their position relative to channels in the reef and island headlands. This eventually opened up the lowland areas for settlement shift by allowing an agricultural emphasis on swamp and irrigated taro cultivation. The move into this zone began around A.D. 1000. This shift was not simply a population resettlement, but a transformation of Palauan society. Construction and use of the great terrace complexes generally ended, and there were major changes in village organization, architecture, and defense.

Compact clusters of habitation and cultivation areas marked the settlement pattern. District polity boundaries, as ethnographically known, do not have identifiable physical markers (equivalent to the terraces and defended crowns), nor is there a regional defense pattern such as the one that previously existed with the large terrace complexes. However, this does not mean that warfare and defense disappeared. In fact, the archaeological and ethnographic data indicate that this was an era of intensive conflict. But the pattern of conflict and defense had changed, and individual villages became the focus of attack and defense.

Villages

The settlements in use at the time of significant European contact in the late 1700s were characterized by elaborate stone architecture (Figure 5.12, and see Figure 5.8) and became known in Palau as "traditional villages." Their histories figure prominently in Palauan oral traditions. These villages had their origin in the settlement change beginning in A.D. 1000.

The main components of stonework villages were various types of stone platforms—burial platforms (*olbed* and *odesongel*),[20] bai foundations, cooking platforms, and resting platforms (*iliud*). These platforms were constructed of several courses of basalt cobbles and boulders around an earth core. Other stone features include bathing places, docks, boathouses, shrines, wells, and stone paths. Stone monoliths were found at the entrances to villages and on platforms; some of these are backrests, some are carved faces,[21] and others are markers commemorating historic occasions. Most stone villages were constructed on small, low step-terraces, with each household unit on its own terrace. Associated with the

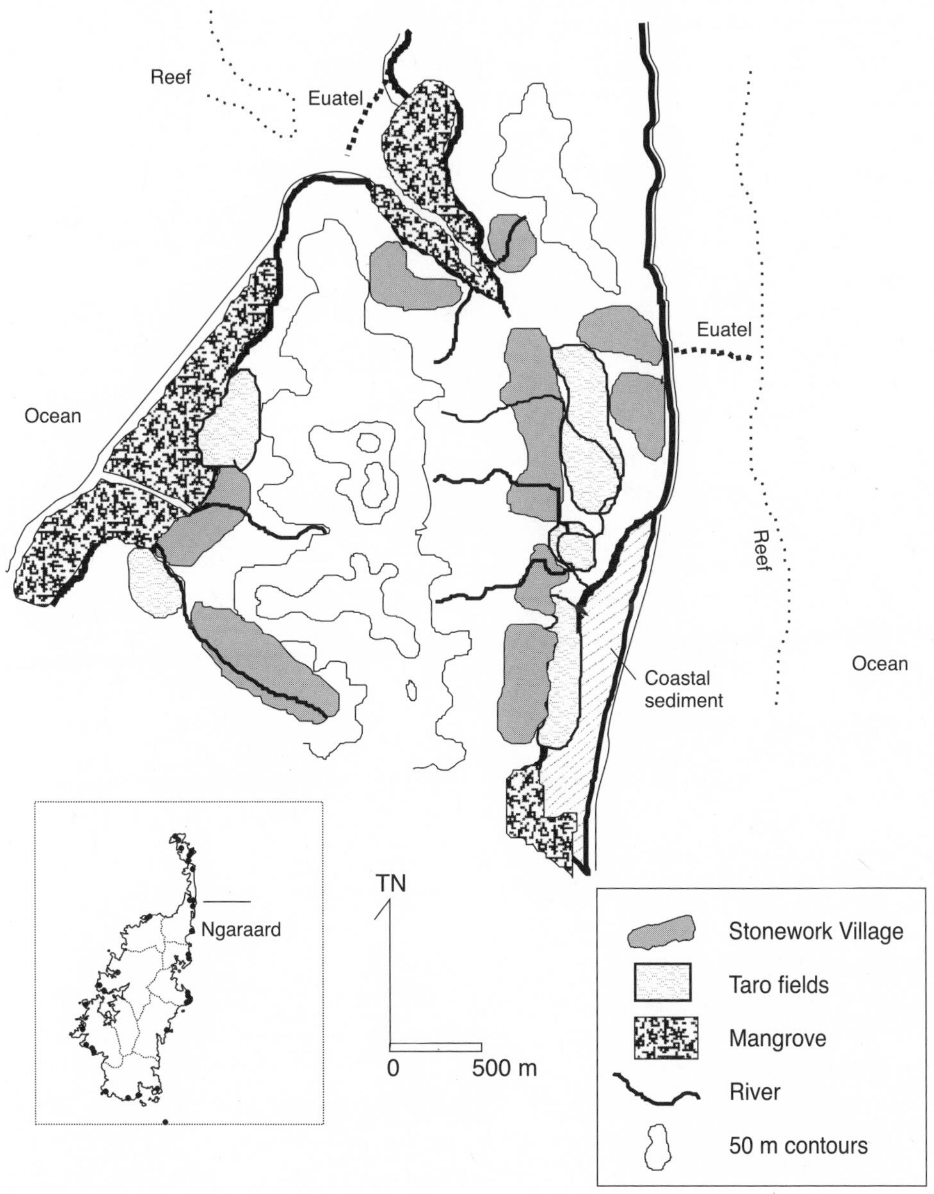

Figure 5.12. Drawing of Stonework Era settlement, Ngaraard, showing transformation from Terrace Era.

settlement and architectural changes were also major shifts in ceramic styles and technology and in the character of lithic assemblages. Ceramic vessels of the Stonework Era in Ngaraard are generally much larger than those of the preceding period with a number of correlated structural features such as thickness and neck form. This may have been related to changes in communal cooking patterns as well as to more extensive use for transport of food and liquids, related to tribute and trade. Lithics are much more common in the earlier, upland villages than in villages of the later period, possibly associated with more intensive bird hunting of the earlier time.[22]

As described in the ethnographic section above, Palau had an elaborate hierarchical system within villages and among villages. Within villages, this hierarchy was materially expressed by variations in size, location, and design of the stonework architecture. Between villages, the expression of status and power in the ranking was through settlement size, relative location, and constituent features. The structures ethnographically identified as the men's meeting house, the bai, have an archaeologically recognized form that allows intra- and inter-village comparisons. Differences in magnitude and elaboration of the bai, and the placement of burial platforms in relation to the bai were key expressions of social status. There was also socially important variation in the quality, elaboration, and size of other community stone features.

Village Defensive Features

As in the previous era, the positioning of defensive features in relation to habitation and agricultural fields reveals the geographic focus of warfare and defense—in this case, the individual village.

The young men's bai were located at entrances to villages where the main paths from surrounding villages met. Young warriors continuously occupied these, ready to confront enemy raiders. Bai that were at the coast also had war canoes immediately adjacent, allowing warriors to meet a seaborne enemy on the water, as far from the village as possible. Villages also had a variety of defensive stone walls, causeways, and platforms (all known as *euatel*, the word for stonework fortification; Figures 5.8, 5.13). Some village entrances had tall walls on either side of a path leading into the village. In some cases, the ancient earthworks that were strategically positioned in relation to the new settlements continued to be used for defensive purposes, primarily as lookout and signal positions. The location of villages at the coast made them more vulnerable to sea attacks than an inland position, but there were a number of defenses related to this. The majority of villages of the Stonework Era were situated so as to be screened from view by mangrove swamps and could only be approached from the ocean by narrow channels cut through the mangrove (see Figure 5.12).

Figure 5.13. An *euatel*, a defensive stone wall (under the mangrove), blocks entry from the lagoon into the channel leading to a stonework village in eastern Ngaraard. This is Cheldeklel a Dirrengulbai Euatel.

Today some of these channels are as much as 2.5 km in length. Villages not sheltered by mangrove swamp—primarily those on the northeast coast—were often barricaded from the lagoon by alluvial swamps that supported irrigated taro fields. Here, the only passages through were stone paths guarded by an entrance of high walls. Massive stonewalls were laid along the coastal edge of some villages. Defensive causeways (*beriber*) were built from the reef to the shoreline with only one opening, easily guarded. These causeways are made of coral and basalt, with some as long as 600 meters and up to five meters wide. Barriers across channels were constructed (see Figure 5.13). Not defenses purely by archaeological imagination, these various features are described as such in the early historical accounts. For example, the village of Pelileu was recorded in the 1700s as defended by a 3.0–3.6 m high stone wall, with a foot bank behind it from which to stand and throw spears (Keate 1788). An earth berm served as a protective wall for the village of Medorm (Osborne 1966:178–179).

A number of historical accounts and oral histories mention battles using ditches, some of which were newly constructed for this purpose, or in other cases, were the ancient ditches of the Terrace Era. For example, trenches are prominent in the story of a battle between two Ngchesar villages (Tellei et al. 2004:65):

> Trenches called *klaidebangel* were dug and lined with spears with their points pointing up, and then covered. On the day of the battle, the villagers of Ngerkesou baited the men of Ngemingel by holding a festive dance at the other side of the trenches. The men of Ngemingel were offended by this behavior since they felt that an inferior village should not hold a festive dance in their sight. The men of the village rushed to attack them whereupon some of them fell into the trenches and were killed.

The story of a battle at Roisersuul between the villagers of Ngersuul and Ngeremlengui includes the following (Tellei et al. 2004:147–148):[23] "The warriors from Ngeremlengui, whooping their war cries, ran forward to intercept the warriors from Ngersuul and immediately fell into the trench. They were set upon by the warriors of Ngersuul and were beaten or speared to death."

Places of refuge (or asylum) play a prominent part in ethnographic accounts of Palauan warfare. These areas were understood by all parties to be havens from attack.[24] Places of refuge included stones, platforms, hilltops, or specific sides of a natural or constructed feature; they are considered sacred sites whose oral tradition often commemorates an important battle, and people today can point out many of them. For example, oral historical accounts tell of a causeway (*beriber*) in Airai that also served as a partition for places of refuge, where those who were on their group's side of the wall were considered in safe territory.

Settlement Pattern and Defense

The subsistence base of the Stonework Era was wet taro, cultivated in swamp and irrigation complexes. Compact villages were located adjacent to the taro fields, and with this shift from dispersed dryland fields and scattered settlement, defenses became commensurately concentrated. This can be seen as rings of defense.

Within a village, the chiefs' bai and the platforms of the higher ranking kin groups were in the center of the village only reached after passing the warrior bai and the various close-in village entrances. Outside of this area of defense were obstructions to the village approach in the form of lagoon barriers, mangrove, and swamps. In addition, a dominant village also relied upon adjacent satellite villages for protection. In most of these cases the villages in these clusters were contiguous. Boundaries were known by the villagers themselves, but would be imperceptible to outsiders.

This defensive patterning resulted in clusters of villages and agricultural areas spread across the district landscape. In the ideal, the capital of the district would also have a ring of protection. The capital village would be found in the district's center where its subordinate villages could block access and protect the capital. However, this ideal was seldom achieved. Subordinate villages would take any opportunity to turn on the dominant one and take over its position as capital. Defense at this scale was seldom effective.

As in the previous era, there were extensive uninhabited areas between large settlement areas or polities that served as buffer zones.

War and Power

During this period, the construction of massive stone architecture, rather than monumental terrace complexes, was the primary expression of Palauan sociopolitical competition. The construction of stonework architecture required a large labor investment. Labor was part of the spoils of war, since captured warriors were used to reconstruct platforms relocated from their conquered villages. But the most important material expression of a village's power was the size and number of a village council's bai. Though almost all villages had several bai, it was the number of wooden structures built on the village councils' bai—as archaeologically recognizable by the number of outlines of the structures in the stone paving—that was of significance. The size of these structures—recognizable by the number of support stones below where the door would have been—was an indicator of a council's power. The majority of villages had one structure with four doors on the bai platform. Some had two structure outlines and fewer still three outlines; many bai had six doors but some had eight. Power was manifested not only in the size, elaboration, or relative placement of the stone features but in its construction as tribute. Those of high status, whether individual chiefs or entire villages, never built their own structures. Power was represented by the ability to either conscript laborers for construction projects or by the possession of enough "valuables" to pay for the construction. Both forms of tribute were acquired through warfare. Valuables, the most significant of which were ranked money beads, were garnered through traditional social events (inheritance, having children, building a house), as spoils of war or the terms of settlement, or as payment for a form of protection insurance, to be left free from harassment. They signified political rank and social power as in turn, the money was then used to pay for another's assistance in particular battles or to help fend off attack. Valuables were part of the institutionalized perpetuation of warfare.

Long-term Transformations: Ngaraard and Ngiwal

Following are two regional cases of the model presented here of the long-term evolution of warfare and defense. Ngaraard and Ngiwal are contiguous states representing traditional districts; they provide two different manifestations of the Palauan settlement pattern within a context of interpolity strife.

Ngaraard

Ngaraard forms the neck of the island, broad in the south and tapering to about one kilometer wide as it stretches north (see Figure 5.1). Splitting the length of the state is a high, jungle-covered ridge system broken by steep drainages and low saddles. On the western side are large mangrove thickets bordering a narrow strip of lowland that rises abruptly to the ridge system. On the eastern coast is a wide expanse of marshy wetlands fronted by a sandy shoreline and a few mangrove swamps. These wetlands are continually planted in taro, which, combined with marine resources, is the traditional subsistence base of the population. The width of the mangrove swamps and extensive coastal flats are geologically recent developments, occurring within the span of Palauan occupation.

The transformation of the cultural landscape in Ngaraard is shown in Figures 5.11 and 5.12.

Terrace Era

A vast terrace complex extends virtually the length of the high ridge complex from the south of the state to just past Klebeang Channel, roughly 5.5 km. Additional, dispersed terrace complexes are found north to the border with Ngarchelong state. The complexes include comparatively low, deep step-terraces, and a series of terraces, whose steps are separated by deep ditches, leading up to small crowns. Ditches are found around the base of most of the crowns, between adjacent crowns, and cut across long finger ridges that culminate in crowns. The Ngaraard terrace system is such a prominent feature of the landscape that it can be seen from the northern tip to close to the southern end of the island, as well as from the ocean on both sides of the island.

Within the Ngaraard system there are villages on ridges between crowns; the ridges were reworked to create a flattened length interspersed with earth platforms separated by wide gullies, and occasionally capped by back-sloping step-terraces. Other villages are on gentle slopes, some with low step-terraces. The three ridges and a broad eroded slope investigated thus far contain dense pottery and lithic scatters, early architectural features in the form of pavings, edgings, and alignments, and numerous pit features. Back-sloping terraces and the wide gullies found separating the earth platforms in habitation sites were used for dryland agriculture. Separating the habitation areas (located on the ridges) are crown and ditch fortifications whose slopes were used for burial and ceremonial activities. The archaeological pattern identified here undoubtedly developed over a significant period of time, and in its most complex form probably represents a single polity.

The relatively small villages were built in high, open areas that afforded a view of either coastline below. Due to the narrow width and high elevation of the island, the polity's villages were not enclosed with defensive terrace complexes, rather these complexes are found on the northern and southern borders, with additional crowns serving as lookout posts and signal towers incorporated into the village areas.

An enormous labor investment was made in the construction of these earthworks, and from a distance they are an imposing symbol of power.

Stonework Era

Of Ngaraard's 24 recorded stonework villages, 8 are still populated.[25] Most of these historic villages line the inland side of the taro-producing alluvial swamps. Shallow step-terraces producing dryland crops such as tapioca are interspersed along the slopes between the dense village clusters. A dense cluster of villages that actually forms three historical village complexes lies in the middle of the state while to the north and south are ethnographically recorded powerful clusters that may have been their own polities or subdistricts. Little is known of the stonework villages that are found hidden deep behind mangrove barriers on Ngaraard's southwestern side. However, they were placed in locations with defense obviously in mind, and the few stories that do concern them indicate they were involved in the warfare that was to consolidate the village clusters into today's pattern.

Ngaraard's oral traditions are replete with tales of warfare waged against neighboring and distant districts and between their own villages. Places of refuge are found on the outer edges of the narrow buffer zones at both Ngaraard's current northern and southern borders. To the north, at the border with Ngarchelong, are two deep ditches cut across the narrowest part of the neck; traditions indicate that these ditches were an element of the defense of each state. However, stonework fortifications barricading individual villages were the leading precaution against attack. A 3-m-wide and 500-m-long rock wall blocks the passage down Klebeang Channel into the capital village of Ngebuked (see Figure 5.13). Attached to one end, a warrior bai guards the village entrance.

Remains of at least two causeways built from the eastern shoreline to the reef block off entrances into the lagoon fronting the southern village complex and at the northern point of the central complex. This might indicate a smaller district than the historically recorded one that extended north to the neck of the island.

Ngiwal

Ngiwal, at Ngaraard's southern boundary, has a long strip of sandy coastline terminating on either end at mangrove-fringed bays (see Figure 5.1). Emptying into the southern bay is the Ngerdekuu River that flows the length of the state. Inland of the coast is a thin strip of marshy wetlands and adjacent savanna lowlands rising to a 60-m-high ridge system. The thickly jungled ridges ascend to the imposing Rael Kedam (central mountain spine) that marks the state's western limit. As in Ngaraard, early settlers to Palau faced a far different coastal landscape. The wide expanse of sandy beach is a recent addition due to progradation (Titchenal et. al 1998:20), and the thick mangrove forests were not as abundant at the time of colonization.

Terrace Era

The Ngiwal earthworks are located along the length of the lowland ridge system directly behind the coast and around the southern bay. The terrace complexes are smaller and less structured than those found in Ngaraard. In the main, their components are heavily eroded modest step-terraces, crowns circled by deep ditches, and ridges lined with earth platforms, crowns, and ditches.[26] The earthworks allow for an unobstructed view of the eastern coastline, the southern bay, and a great length of the Rael Kedam. The crowns marking the border of Ngaraard are clearly visible, as are some of those in the interior of adjoining Melekeok state to the south.

Villages, characterized by densely concentrated artifact scatters accompanied by early stone architecture are located on the heavily eroded low-step-terraces of inland-facing wide bowls and hill slopes, and on earthen platforms along the narrow flattened ridge system. Below the steep-sided ridges, some of which have been artificially widened, are broad step-terraces that likely held dryland agricultural fields. Crowns and ditches to ensure security bound the clustered village and cultivation areas.

The crowns served as lookout posts around settlement clusters, as signal towers between themselves, or with their larger neighbors, and as places of refuge to those working in the dryland fields. The few imposing crowns served as boundary markers. However, the comparative small size and simplicity of the Ngiwal earthworks indicate that this was one of the minor polities of Babeldaob, and may well have been incorporated into more powerful ones at various times.

Stonework Era

Ngiwal contains 15 stonework villages, of which 3 are still occupied. As in Ngaraard, the stone villages are found adjacent to the inland side of the alluvial flats. Those close to the coast are constructed on gentle slopes fronting the lowland ridge system while those found along the Ngeredekuu River valley and the edge of the bay are on finger ridges at slightly higher elevations. The former villages are screened by expanses of wetland taro gardens and latter behind a thick mangrove forest. Earthworks from the earlier era back both the coastal and river valley settlements, affording some protection from an assault from the rear. The complex's step-terraces lie abandoned although historic records indicate that they were cultivated in the first half of the twentieth century.

A stonework village said to be long abandoned, Ngis, is one of the few villages in Palau with three bai outlines; the center one containing four doors on either side, thus indicating it was a powerful and wealthy village (Olsudong et al. 2001). Despite this, oral histories relate how Ngiwal was always subordinate to a dominant district, be it Ngaraard to the north or Melekeok to the south. In fact, little reference is made to Ngiwal in eighteenth century records (Parmentier 1987:62).

Comparison of Ngiwal and Ngaraard

Ngiwal and Ngaraard are quite different geographically, which is clearly reflected in their settlement patterns. The narrow neck of the island where Ngaraard is located provides little opportunity to form a border of crowned terraces around village clusters. Instead, villages were incorporated into the massive earthworks. In the broader expanse of Ngiwal, crowns ring a group of villages and their associated agricultural areas. The clustering of villages into separate polities during the Stonework Era is more distinct in Ngaraard than in Ngiwal. Ngaraard's far larger expanse of coastline suitable for crops of the Stonework Era is the obvious cause of this. Stone villages line the entire bottomlands of Ngiwal's coast with few breaks.

The Ngaraard terraces are larger and more visually impressive than those found in Ngiwal, and there is more complexity in their architectural features. This indicates that during the Terrace Era, Ngaraard probably had much more powerful polities. Of note is the line of high defensive crowns that block the southern boundary of the Ngaraard region, a dramatic symbol of strength for the people of the adjacent Ngiwal polities.

As in the Terrace Era, the defenses of Ngiwal villages during the Stonework Era show less elaboration than the defenses of Ngaraard. Paths leading into the villages are guarded by young men's bai, or high stonewalls are found at the coastal and side entrances, but the walls are less elaborate than those found in Ngaraard, and there are no significant stonework defenses in the mangrove channels.

Ethnographic accounts indicate in ancient times Ngiwal was far more powerful than Ngaraard, but after many battles Ngaraard became the more dominant of the two. The archaeology suggests that this was not a true historical succession, but is a traditional explanation for their recent hierarchical relationship

Discussion and Conclusion

The model of changing settlement pattern and defense proposed here is directly related to the nature of the agricultural base and to changes in the Palauan landscape. The coastline of Palau at the time of original settlement was quite different from that of today. It lacked extensive alluvial flats, swamplands, and mangrove forests. Little is known of the early settlements that existed there three thousand years ago or more, but there certainly was very limited coastal area for village location and for wetland cultivation.

The early era of Palauan prehistory is very poorly known, but a model of population growth, pressure on the limited coastal agricultural base, and commensurate competition between villages can be postulated, with the hope that early coastal villages can be found and excavated. Based on recent archaeological research, the development of the subsequent Terrace Era settlement is beginning to emerge. This was a period of upland villages composed of earthen platforms, with associated massive terrace complexes. This began a few centuries B.C. as an expansion and intensification of dry-land cultivation through construction of small agricultural terraces on lower ridges and the movement of villages from the coasts to areas near the fields, followed by increasing attention to boundary definition and its defense. This concern for territory eventually resulted in the large-scale terraces, the associated complex architectural defenses of crowns and ditches, and the creation of a cultural landscape that was a symbol of power. At the height of the development of these earthworks, they formed extensive systems that are interpreted as boundaries of small polities. The size of some of the earthworks and the labor they would have required, and the possibility that some of the crowns contain elaborate burials of powerful individuals, suggest a more centralized control political authority than existed at the time of European contact. If, however, the core elements of traditional Palauan social organization existed at this time, these polities were based on some form of village alliance equivalent to later districts or federations, but if so they had a stabilizing element that was subsequently lost.

The shift around A.D. 1000 to coastal settlement and the construction of stonework villages was made possible by coastal sedimentation and associated expanded wetlands and mangrove forests. Large areas were then available for various forms of intensive wetland taro cultivation. Paleoenvironmental and archaeological research indicates the coastal sedimentation was at least in part anthropogenic,[27] the result of erosion and alluviation from the large-scale terrace construction and earth moving. When this new resource began to be exploited for its high productivity, the upland dry cultivation terraces were abandoned, and again, villages were moved near the areas of primary agriculture, in this case the wet lowlands.

The timing of the coastal wetland agricultural intensification and the associated process of village movement are unknown in detail, the answers to these problems dependent on future research. Whatever the nature of this process, the implications for Palauan culture were significant. There were changes in defense, architecture, political symbolism, degree of political centralization, and polity size.

Unlike the upland situation, where habitation and fields were relatively dispersed, the coastal villages and associated irrigation fields were compact. The complex of the compact village and wet taro fields allowed defenses to be delimited to the village itself. The development of the mangrove forests augmented this process, improving the defensibility of many of the coastal locales. However, the causal relationship between social organization and defense remains uncertain. The fact that defense could be at the village level does not mean it had to be. If a more centralized authority existed in the preceding period, the concentrated villages involved diminution and eventually collapse of the central authority, and the ultimate development of the ethnographic pattern of autonomous villages. The districts and federations that formed during the Stonework Era were too loose to be able to mobilize defense of common territory, constituting another pressure to constrict defense to local villages.

The great terraces, their agricultural areas abandoned, also lost their practical value as defensive positions, being too far removed from the villages, and with this also lost their symbolic value and their identities as boundaries, and were eventually forgotten. The visual symbols of power shifted, like the defenses, to the individual village, and the expression of Palauan village competition and power became the massive stone architecture and the number and size of the bai. The locations of many of the stonework villages were swampy, alluvial coastal areas, so the shift to elaborate stone architecture in village construction probably began with the functional adaptation to this environment.

Another consequence of the shift probably occurred in the size of polities and in the scale of warfare. Although probably more centralized, the Terrace Era polities were spatially smaller than the Stonework Era districts, the main unit of alliance above the village level. The complete pattern of Terrace Era polities is unknown (due to the absence of information about terrace and crown distribution in many areas of Babeldaob), but the current information suggests that in the area of each of the later traditional districts (see Figure 5.1) there probably had been several Terrace Era polities. At the same time, warfare in the Terrace Era may also have been on a larger scale than that of later times, given the greater attention to physical measures of defense and the labor invested in them.

Palau offers a case of a political system that had two systems of warfare, neither of which led to state-level complexity or kingship organization. It is possible that the Terrace Era political structure may have had such a trajectory, but if so, the shift in subsistence emphasis cut this short, as villages moved to the intensified irrigated fields at the coast and became the main units of political organization. Whether or not the Terrace Era model of political organization is correct, it is clear that during the subsequent Stonework Era, warfare functioned as a leveling mechanism, one of the several aspects of Palauan culture that maintained segmented power, rather than leading to consolidation of power. This results from the fact that warfare was institutionalized within a larger framework of competition and the ideology of power, that is, ranked and competitive kinship units, and ranked and competitive villages. The size and terrain of the island of Babeldaob may also have served as a limiting factor.

Finally, Palau's isolation from the rest of Micronesia resulted in little contact during its pre-Contact history, and as such it is probable that interaction with other cultures had no significant effect on Palauan cultural patterns and change, including those of warfare.

The archaeological research of the last six years has vastly expanded the information available about Palau's prehistory. A broad picture is emerging that makes it clear that warfare was a prominent element of its cultural history, and that there were significant differences in the history of warfare. However, there is a great deal of analysis yet to be carried out, numerous propositions to be tested by future research, and an enormous amount of fieldwork remaining for future archaeologists. Some of the obvious problems that need to be addressed include the nature of early settlement, the pattern of population growth (including the question of when it reached equilibrium), the detailed structure of terrace-era political organization, the size and organization of Terrace Era polities (which could have had an additional level of organization unrecognized archaeologically), variations in time and place of the patterns of settlement and warfare, and the role of external contact in Palau's cultural history. This discussion of warfare in Palau is presented to help direct future research and for comparison with other areas in the cross-cultural investigation of warfare.

Acknowledgments

This chapter is based largely on field research carried out by International Archaeological Research Institute, Inc. for the U.S. Army Corps of Engineers, Pacific Ocean Division, as part of the historic preservation actions associated with the construction of the Compact Road, Republic of Palau, from 1996 through 2003. Various reports for this project are referenced in the text, but much of the final three years' work and a general synthesis are in the writing stage, identified as Liston (2005). All photographs and drawings in the chapter are by the authors.

For the opportunity to carry out this work we are very grateful to the U.S. Army Corps of Engineers, to the Division of Cultural Affairs of the Republic of Palau, and to the people of Palau.

Notes

1. Palau is also spelled Belau.

2. The traditional artwork has carried over to the Palauan storyboard, but the storyboard is a twentieth century development.

3. The Rock Islands, south of Babeldaob, certainly played a part in Babeldaob's prehistoric warfare, but that is a complicated problem not addressed here.

4. Building the chronology of Palau is a complex process that is not addressed in this chapter. The chronology used here for the pre-Contact period is based on more than 200 radiocarbon dates from the island of Babeldaob, and is presented in a generalized manner. The dates and chronological arguments are presented in Liston (1999, 2005).

5. In Palauan history and ethnography, the settlements of this time are commonly called "traditional villages," but the present chapter uses the term "stonework villages" to distinguish them from the earlier settlements that are not identified in Palauan traditions.

6. Detailed cases of village and regional warfare of the late stonework village era are recorded in history and oral tradition in several sources, including McKnight (1960), Parmentier (1987), and Tellei et al. (2004). The application of these histories to the present warfare model requires too detailed a presentation to include in this chapter, but will be found in Liston (2005).

7. This group is termed *kebliil*, which is frequently translated "clan," but this carries inappropriate connotations for the Palauan kin group. For the complexities and intricacies of Palauan kinship and social structure see Force (1960), Force and Force (1972), McKnight (1960), Parmentier (1987), Smith (1983), and Palau Society of Historians (1998).

8. There were additional village political associations not pertinent to the present discussion (see Parmentier 1987:55)

9. In fact, the traditional districts are the basis for the modern political states in Palau.

10. The early settlement date is based on very limited evidence. This is a complicated problem (also see Clark 2005; Fitzpatrick 2003; Phear et al. 2003), and significant early coastal sites on Babeldaob have yet to be found. The problems of settlement date and population growth are discussed in Liston (2005).

11. Small, low step-terraces are used today as foundations for stone platforms and houses in stonework villages or for agricultural fields. The abandoned monumental terraces are generally found further inland.

12. Artifacts, including ceramic types, are described in detail in Liston (1999, 2005).

13. Terrace construction chronology is based, where possible, on the radiocarbon dating of features associated with construction surfaces. Multiple construction periods and deeply buried deposits make it difficult to recognize such associations, but this has been facilitated by the use of mechanical equipment and exposures of extensive profiles.

14. The term "crown" is derived from the supposed resemblance to a hat (Osborne 1966:148). Crowns are also found as isolated features on a ridgeline or bluff, and also within large terrace systems.

15. There are crowns that appear to have rounded tops, but this is caused by slope failure.

16. Alluvium has filled the ditches so that their original depth was not recognized until recent mechanical trenching.

17. There are oral histories about a few crowns concerning their construction by deities, but none of these traditions refer to function.

18. There is no evidence that any of the terraces were irrigated. Irrigation was developed in the alluvial bottomlands.

19. This is one of the most important areas of future research in Palauan archaeology. The model presented here is considered a "best fit" for the existing data, but archaeological knowledge of the villages of the Terrace Era is very limited.

20. *Olbed* and *odesongel* are not used as foundations for houses; rather the titleholder's house is adjacent to the platform, which served as a burial place for high-ranking members of the kin group.

21. Hijikata (1995) believes the stone heads were originally associated with the terrace complexes, but were moved to villages during relatively recent times.

22. Artifacts and artifact change, including ceramic types, are described in detail in Liston (1999, 2005) The analysis of function is ongoing.

23. Archaeological survey of this area indicates that there are six defensive trenches that bisect the ridgeline leading to Roisersuul.

24. There are numerous other examples of the concept of asylum in Micronesia and Polynesia (see, for example, Kelly 1986).

25. In the early twentieth century for administrative purposes most villages were relocated close to newly constructed roads. The "new" villages are generally near their stonework counterparts and the names of the villages remained the same.

26. A ca. 100-m-long ditch, the largest yet located in Palau, is found between a complex of low step-terraces leading to a broad crown.

27. Changes in sea level and climate may also have been factors. This change in coastal landform is being investigated from a number of different perspectives.

References

Athens, J. S., and J. V. Ward. 2004. *Historic Preservation Investigations for the Compact Road, Babeldaob Island, Republic of Palau. Volume IV: The Holocene Paleoenvironment of Palau.* International Archaeological Research Institute, Inc., Honolulu. The U.S. Army Corps of Engineers, Pacific Ocean Division, Fort Shafter, Hawai'i.

Clark, G. 2005. A 3,000-year Culture Sequence from Palau, Western Micronesia. *Asian Perspectives.*

Corwin, G., C. L. Rogers, and P. O. Elmquist. 1956. *Military Geology of Palau Islands, Caroline Islands.* Headquarters U.S. Army Forces Far East, Intelligence Division, Office of the Engineer.

Earle, T. 1997. *How Chiefs Come to Power: The Political Economy in Prehistory.* Palo Alto: Stanford University Press.

Fitzpatrick, S. M. 2003. Early Human Burials in the Western Pacific: Evidence for a *circa* 3000-year-old Occupation on Palau. *Antiquity* 77(298):719–731.

Force, R. 1960. *Leadership and Cultural Change in Palau.* Fieldiana: Anthropology No. 50, Chicago: Chicago Natural History Museum.

Force, R., and M. Force. 1972. *Just One House: A Description and Analysis of Kinship in the Palau Islands.* B. P. Bishop Museum Bulletin No. 235. Honolulu: Bishop Museum Press.

Hezel, F. X. 1983. *The First Taint of Civilization: A History of the Caroline and Marshall Islands in Pre-Colonial Days, 1521–1885.* Honolulu: University of Hawaii Press.

Hijikata, H. 1993. *Collective Works of Hijikata Hisakatsu. Society and Life in Palau, Volume 1.* Translated and edited by Hisashi Endo. The Sasakawa Peace Foundation, Tokyo. Originally published in 1940, Kagaku Nanyo.

———. 1995. *Collective Works of Hijikata Hisakatsu: Gods and Religion in Palau, Volume 2*. Translated and edited by Hisashi Endo. The Sasakawa Peace Foundation, Tokyo. Originally published in 1940, Kagaku Nanyo.

Hunter-Anderson, R. 1989. *Archaeological Investigations in the Small Boat Harbor Project Area, Agat, Guam*. International Archaeological Research Institute, Inc., Honolulu. The U.S. Army Corps of Engineers District, Pacific Ocean Division, Fort Shafter, Hawai'i.

Keate, G. 1788. *An Account of the Pelew Islands, Situated in the Western Part of the Pacific Ocean, Composed from the Journals and Communications of Captain Henry Wilson, and Some of His Officers, Who, in August 1783, Were There Shipwrecked, in the Antelope, a Packet Belonging to the Honourable East India Company*. London: G. Nicol.

Keeley, L. H. 1996. *War Before Civilization: The Myth of the Peaceful Savage*. New York: Oxford University Press.

Kelly, M. 1986. Report 11: The Concept of Asylum. In *The Natural and Cultural History of Honaunau, Kona, Hawaii*, edited by E. H. Bryan and K. P. Emory, 137–150. Department of Anthropology, Bishop Museum, Honolulu.

Kubary, J. 1873. Die Palau Inseln in der Sudsee. *Journal des Museum Godeffroy* I: 181–238, Teiband 1–3. (Translation by anonymous). Friederichsen, Hamburg.

LeBlanc, S. A. 1999. *Prehistoric Warfare in the American Southwest*. Salt Lake City: University of Utah Press.

Liston, J. (Series General Editor) 1999. *Historic Preservation Investigations for the Compact Road, Babeldaob Island, Republic of Palau. Volume V-VIII*. International Archaeological Research Institute, Inc., Honolulu. The U.S. Army Corps of Engineers, Pacific Ocean Division, Fort Shafter, Hawai'i.

———. 2005. *Archaeological Monitoring of the Compact Road, Babeldaob Island, Republic of Palau. Volumes IX–XIV*. International Archaeological Research Institute, Inc., Honolulu. The U.S. Army Corps of Engineers, Pacific Ocean Division, Fort Shafter, Hawai'i.

Liston, J., M. W. Kaschko, and D. J. Welch. 1998. *Archaeological Inventory Survey of the Capital Relocation Site, Melekeok, Republic of Palau*. International Archaeological Research Institute, Inc., Honolulu. Architects Hawaii, Inc.

McCutcheon, M. S. 1981. Resource Exploitation and the Tenure of Land and Sea in Palau. Unpublished Ph.D. dissertation, Department of Anthropology, University of Arizona, Tucson.

McKnight, R. K. 1960. Competition in Palau. Unpublished Ph.D. dissertation, Department of Anthropology, Ohio State University, Columbus.

Morgan, W. N. 1988. *Prehistoric Architecture in Micronesia*. Austin: University of Texas Press.

Olsudong, R., C. T. Emesiochel, and E. T. Kloulechad. 2001. *Inventory of Cultural and Historical Sites and Oral History in Ngiwal and Ngchesar States. (Draft) Volume I: Inventory of Cultural Historical Sites*. Division of Cultural Affairs, Historic Preservation Office, Republic of Palau.

Osborne, D. 1966. *The Archaeology of the Palau Islands, an Intensive Survey*. Bernice P. Bishop Museum Bulletin No. 230. Honolulu: Bishop Museum Press.

Palau Society of Historians. 1998. *Traditional Leadership in Palau.* Traditional and Customary Practices, English Series 3. Division of Cultural Affairs, Ministry of Community and Cultural Affairs, Koror, Republic of Palau.

Parmentier, R. J. 1987. *The Sacred Remains: Myth, History, and Polity in Belau.* Chicago: The University of Chicago Press.

Phear, S. 2004. The Monumental Earthworks of Palau. Unpublished Ph.D. dissertation, Department of Archaeology and Natural History, Australian National University, Canberra.

Phear, S., G. Clark, and A. Anderson. 2003. A Radiocarbon Chronology of Palau. In *Pacific Archaeology: Assessments and Prospects,* edited by C. Sand, 255–263. Les Cahiers de l'Archéologie en Nouvelle-Calédonie 15. Nouméa: Musee de Nouvelle-Calédonie.

Smith, D. R. 1983. *Palauan Social Structure*. New Brunswick: Rutgers University Press.

Tellei, J., U. Basilius, and F. K. Rehuher. 2004. *Historic Preservation Investigations for the Compact Road, Babeldaob Island, Republic of Palau. Volume III: Oral History Documentation*. International Archaeological Research Institute, Inc., Honolulu. The U.S. Army Corps of Engineers, Pacific Ocean Division, Fort Shafter, Hawai'i.

Telmetang, M. 1993. *Bai*. Imuul Series No. 1. Belau National Museum, Inc., Koror State, Republic of Palau.

Titchenal, P., R. Drolet, and J. Pantaleo. 1998. *Ngiwal: Archaeological Data Recovery and Monitoring in a Rural Village on Babeldaob in the Republic of Palau.* Garcia and Associates, Honolulu. Draft prepared for Palau Capital Improvements Projects Office, Division of Public Works, Republic of Palau.

Tuggle, H. D. 2005. The Archaeology of the Early Terrace Era in Ngaraard, Babeldaob. In *Historic Preservation Investigations for the Compact Road, Babeldaob Island, Republic of Palau. Volume IX*. International Archaeological Research Institute, Inc., Honolulu. The U.S. Army Corps of Engineers, Pacific Ocean Division, Fort Shafter, Hawai'i.

Vidich, A. 1949. *Political Factionalism in Palau: Its Rise and Development.* CIMA Report No. 23. National Research Council, Pacific Science Board, Washington, D.C.

6

Transformations in Maori Warfare

Toa, Pa, and Pu

MARK W. ALLEN

Tohi

Kia Ora. We understand these things. We are
warriors still. No longer is tohi practiced—
and more's the pity. But the fighting man
performs the rituals in his heart and guts.
When Death sings in his hair and crackles
to his fingertips he becomes fully alive.
Darkness overcomes him and flames rush
before his eyes. We answered the call to arms—
men from Te Arawa and Ngati Porou, men
from Ngati Kahungunu, men from all the iwi,
from Aurpouri and Ngapuhi in the north,
to Ngaitahu in the south. We had our
nicknames—The Gumdiggers, the Penny Divers,
the Cowboys, and the Foreign Legion, later
Ngati Walkabout. As the war raged on,
from Greece to Crete, to North Africa, to Italy,
we all truly belonged to Ngati Walkabout.
And everywhere we fought, the long tongues
of our bayonets, having tasted human flesh,
hungered for more. We fed our bayonets
on German flesh. They rejoiced in the whana
tukutahi, the mad charge, the terror,
the sexual thrust into flesh, the screams.
Tumatauenga glared over our shoulders
yelling, 'Kill them!' until our bayonets were sated,
and the dead lay steaming like a hangi,
when kaitangata was the warrior's just reward.[1]

Alistair Te Ariki Campbell, from *Maori Battalion: A Poetic Sequence* (2001)

Introduction: Long After in a Place Far Away . . .

The Matmata Hills to the northwest of Tatouine in southern Tunisia might not seem like the most obvious place to gain insight on Maori warfare, but archaeologists sometimes find inspiration in strange places. While there for a 2001 CIEE seminar on Carthage, our SUV caravan wound its way through rugged hill country that has been fought over many times in the past, as attested by many *ksar*, or walled storage facilities. During this trip, my thoughts frequently turned from Berbers and Star Wars film locations to the Maori soldiers who fought in this area in World War Two. In particular, I hoped to catch a glimpse of a dominating height above the Tebaga Gap known as Point 209. The lower slopes of this hill were dubbed Hikurangi (Tail of the Sky) by the soldiers of the Maori Battalion who took Point 209 with great distinction during the last stages of the North African campaign (Cody 1956; Gardiner 1992:111–117; Kippenberger 1949:276–293; Rolf 2001:184–188).

At about 5 p.m. on March 26, 1943, the Maori Battalion (the New Zealand 28th) was once more part of one of the British Eighth Army's famed "left hook" attacks. It was designed to run around the formidable German defenses of the Mareth Line during the push for Tunis from the south. The Maoris were riding on top of Crusader tanks on the east flank of the task force, when a dreaded 88mm gun emplaced on Point 209 opened up and knocked out several Sherman tanks. Elements of the 28th Battalion dismounted and charged the hill to deal with this threat. Only three Maori platoons were arrayed against a battalion of the 443rd Panzer Grenadier Regiment, strongly dug in.

Second Lieutenant Te Moananui-a-Kiwa Ngarimu, a highly ranked member of the Ngati Porou tribe of the East Cape of New Zealand's North Island, led an assault on Hikurangi, personally knocking out two machine gun nests. The fighting over the heights raged on through the night with the two sides separated by as little as 20 m. The Germans counterattacked Ngarimu's sector several times during the night, and he was wounded at least twice. Ngarimu rallied his men each time and regained any lost ground. In one such action, the lieutenant drove off an attack by urging his men to throw rocks at the Germans after they ran out of grenades. But at dawn, he was finally cut down in a hail of gunfire while attacking the summit once more. Later, on March 27th, under cover of artillery, a Maori Battalion captain led a successful charge to the summit of 209, encouraged by others on Hikurangi who performed defiant *hakas* (challenging posture dances and chants). The defense collapsed with over 200 Germans taken prisoner. The 443rd's casualties were very, very heavy. New Zealand Brigadier General Kippenberger (1949:289) described a scene with, "dead and mangled Germans everywhere, more than I had seen in a small area since the Somme in

1916." Twenty-two Maori were killed in the battle, and 77 were wounded. Lieutenant Ngarimu was posthumously awarded the Victoria Cross medal.

I was introduced to Maori participation in the Second World War 11 years before the Tunisian trip. I spent an afternoon in the house of Canon Wi Huata of the *iwi* (tribe) Ngati Kahungunu in Hastings, New Zealand. I was there to talk with him about my dissertation research on prehistoric Maori fortifications (*pa*) in the province of Hawke's Bay since he was an acknowledged *kaumatua* (elder) for the area. Canon Huatu was the padre of the 28th Battalion from the defense of Crete to the invasion of Italy.[2] While our talk first focused on my proposed work and his suggestions (which proved instrumental in the completion of my dissertation research with great assistance from the local Maori community), we moved on to the Battalion and his recent trip to Germany as part of a New Zealand television documentary. He described his meeting with Manfred Rommel, the son of the Desert Fox. He told me stories about the Battalion during the war. It was a truly memorable afternoon, and one that has ever after influenced my research on Maori warfare.

Maori soldiers in the First and Second World Wars fought with modern weapons and tactics as part of traditional Allied units. Yet, they went to war as Maori. They employed traditional tactics and concepts in their approach to war, and to peace afterwards. They intimidated even the vaunted Afrika Korps with their approach to war, their expertise with captured weapons, and their fierce haka. After the war, Maori traditions were followed to seek closure, as described in a book on the 28th Battalion by Wira Gardiner (1992:186–188):

> In May 1972, a contingent of veterans was invited to Germany to attend a reunion of the Afrika Korps . . . twenty-six men led by Ruihi Pene, of Te Arawa, accompanied as in war by their padre, Canon Wi Huata, left New Zealand to attend the ceremony, held in the city of Mainz . . . Rangi Tutaki, of Porongahau, Central Hawke's Bay, described the journey as an opportunity to involve themselves in the Maori custom of 'kawe mate.' That is, the taking of the memory of their fallen comrades to Germany, there to tangi (mourn) for them and to share mutual sorrow with their former enemies. In a letter to the editor in the Hawke's Bay Herald Tribune, he described that the basis for reconciliation between the Maori and German soldier would be the mutual exchange of condolences. Once this had occurred then it could truly be said that matters had been settled. 'Kua ea': a satisfactory resolution had taken place.

All armies are capable of producing soldiers with the bravery and selflessness of Second Lieutenant Ngarimu. But through action in Crete, North Africa, and Italy (including the famous assault on Monte Cassino) members of the Maori

Battalion consistently engaged in such feats. It was plain to the military experts of the day that this was a unique Allied unit, one that incorporated traditional Maori concepts into its *esprit de corps*. Ngarimu was an *ariki* (chief) or *rangatira* (elite). When he charged Hikurangi, he did so strengthened by his *whakapapa* (genealogy). Soldiers of the Battalion fought for *utu* (revenge) and to maintain their personal, tribal, and *hapu* (a local kinship group) *mana*. All soldiers fight for their comrades, living and killed, but Maori troops also fought for their ancestors.

The student of war, even the archaeologist, does well to take advantage of a wide variety of sources and inspirations. Most scholars are fortunate enough to never experience war firsthand (at least those born in the second half of the twentieth century). We have much to gain, therefore, by listening to those who did fight. History shows us that traditional Maori warfare did not cease after contact with Europeans and colonization by the British Empire, but continued and changed over the last two centuries to adapt to the challenges of the modern era. Archaeology shows this transformation to be only the last stage in a long process of shifting warfare patterns over the last eight to ten centuries. In New Zealand, the ancestral Polynesian institution of warfare was repeatedly adapted to new scenarios for new aims. This chapter examines the two most dramatic shifts in Maori warfare: the transition from Ancestral Polynesian *toa* (warrior) patterns to Classic Maori pa (fortification) warfare; and second, the adaptations brought about by the introduction of muskets (*pu*) in the early nineteenth century.

The Polynesian Toa and Early Evidence of Warfare in New Zealand

Archaeological and other evidence strongly suggests that New Zealand was the last major Polynesian island group to be colonized around A.D. 800–1200 (Davidson 1984, 2001; Kirch 2000).[3] Likely islands of origin for these colonists include the Marquesan, Cook, and Society groups. These colonists were no doubt somewhat nonplussed when they arrived in Aotearoa (Land of the Long White Cloud). The vast scale of its mountain ranges, waterways, forests, and coastlines combined with a temperate climate would have been unimaginable from the perspective of an inhabitant of a tropical high volcanic island such as Tahiti or one of the Hawaiian Islands. The presence of unusual birds, including the giant flightless moa (Anderson 1989; Duff 1956) would have seemed equally strange, though archaeology indicates that they quickly recovered from their surprise and discovered the joys of meter-long drumsticks.

For Polynesian colonists, this was a land with tremendous opportunities for "elbow room" without any pressure to limit population growth. The key limitation that had to be faced was that New Zealand's wet and sometimes frosty rainforests were not favorable for the transported Polynesian economy that had nearly always worked so well (Kirch 2000). Even the hardy sweet potato, destined to later become a key part of the Maori political economy, was not really practical as a subsistence staple until the later development of elaborate storage facilities which protected tubers from wet and frost. Nevertheless, these restrictions were off-set by low population densities combined with abundant ocean resources and native terrestrial resources such as bracken fern root and, of course, those gigantic moa.

Roger Duff (1956) first identified two distinct phases or periods in New Zealand prehistory: the Moa-Hunter Period and the Classic Maori Period. Jack Golson (1959) followed the evolutionary tradition of North American archaeology and referred to the early period as the Archaic, a terminology which has stuck though not consistently applied as a stage in evolutionary development (Bellwood 1987; Davidson 1984, 1994; Kirch 2000:277; Sutton 1994). Whatever we choose to call it, the first 300–500 years or so of culture history in Aotearoa is concisely described by Kirch (2000:277–278):

> colonizing Polynesians made a rapid transition from a horticultural to hunting and gathering economy. With this new economic base, population size and density in South Island remained relatively small, but sizable multifunction base villages were established at the mouths of river valleys, such as at Shag River Mouth, Wairau Bar, Murdering Beach, Papatowai, and Little Papanui. From these permanent base settlements, some of which covered several hectares, the interior regions were seasonally exploited for moa and other resources (including stone from nephrite and silcrete quarries). The moa, primary targets of this hunting strategy, included about 13 species ranging in size from smallish birds about the size of a brush turkey up to *Dinornis giganteus*, which stood perhaps 3 m tall.

Population size and density were low, and it can be expected that base villages were relocated occasionally. There is no evidence of settlement hierarchy, sociopolitical integration, or formalized leadership from this period. But all was not peaceful during this period, as should come as no surprise to those familiar with Polynesian society where war and the warrior play such a central role.

Evidence of Warfare in Archaic New Zealand

There are two lines of evidence that suggest that New Zealand experienced warfare soon after colonization, if not right from the beginning. The first set of clues includes several finds of traditional Maori weapons that have been argued

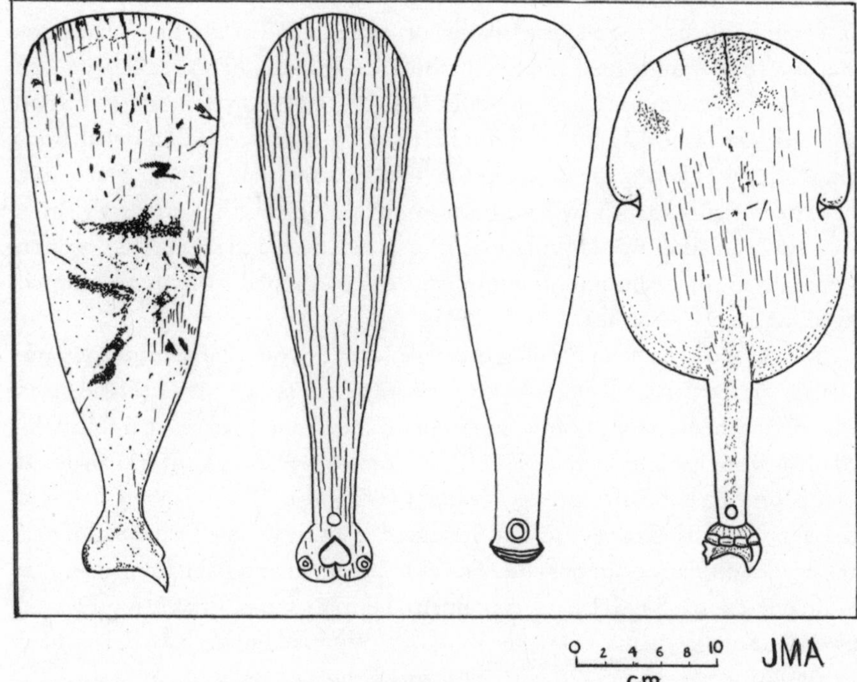

Figure 6.1. From left to right, whalebone club from Vaito'otia, Huahine (redrawn from Sinoto 1979, Figures 12b and 14a); *patu paraoa*, whalebone club (redrawn from Australian Museum 1989, plate 73); *patu onewa*, stone club (redrawn from Australian Museum 1989, plate 72); and *kotiate*, short wooden club (redrawn from Australian Museum 1989, plate 71).

to date back to the Archaic Period. These usually involve forms similar to the *patu* of at least late prehistory: a short war club about a foot in length with a fairly sharp edge made of quality stone, whalebone, or wood (see Figure 6.1). Davidson (1984:100–103, 114) provides references for many of these, and she also notes that in most cases the archaeological context of these are limited to surface collections that are difficult to date. Quite a few of them, however, have been argued to be early based on other diagnostic artifacts from the same basic context. In addition, nearly every museum in New Zealand contains at least a few examples of weapons or possible weapons with unknown provenience that "look early." Without documentation of additional finds from controlled excavations, it is unlikely that their antiquity can be better assessed (though it would be instructive to radiocarbon date some of the wooden forms found in sites with good preservation). However, as Skinner (1931) argued in the 1930s, the New Zealand patu may have been derived from the Society Islands. Over forty years later this position was strongly supported by the discovery on the island of Huahine (one of the Society Islands) of several wooden and four whalebone weapons in a waterlogged site called Vaito'otia (Sinoto 1979, see Figures 12b and 14a) that dates back to about A.D. 800. The common opinion (Bellwood 1978:61; Davidson 1984:101; Emory 1979:202) is that the Huahine whalebone clubs are very likely antecedents to the New Zealand patu.[4] Skinner may well have been right—patu may have been brought along by the very first visitors to New Zealand. It would be curious if such a stylized and specialized weapon (and one so time consuming to produce) was continued without a perceived need for defense or attack.

The second type of archaeological evidence is osteological. Excavations and analyses of Polynesian skeletons have been relatively rare in New Zealand given Maori sentiment, poor preservation in many areas, and preference to bury the dead far from habitation areas. As of 1984, there were fewer than 100 analyzed prehistoric skeletons from New Zealand (Davidson 1984:45), and many of these individuals were very poorly preserved, making detailed paleopathological studies difficult or impossible. For example, the largest single cemetery, at Wairau Bar in the South Island, contained 41 burials, but most were represented by only a few fragments and teeth. Very few additional burials have been added to that list in the past 15–20 years or so given the paucity of recent prehistoric excavations in New Zealand. Nevertheless, a number of the individuals who have been examined do reveal evidence of violent death.

Particularly good evidence comes from a possible massacre at the Washpool Midden site in Palliser Bay on the east coast of the southern North Island. The most clear-cut case of violent death is probably a middle-aged woman who was killed by multiple spear thrusts through the pelvis during the twelfth century (and thus probably within a century or two of first colonization) at Washpool Midden in Palliser Bay (Leach and Leach 1979; Sutton 1979). Leach and Leach (1979:205) state that "the pelvis had several wounds evident, and these are consistent with perforation by a long sharp object such as a spear. One of these was especially severe and passed right through the body of the ischium. The angle of penetration and tunneling of the llamelar bone leaves little doubt that the weapon had been thrust with great force in the genital area."

Analyses of two other adults from the same context at the Washpool Midden site suggests they may well have been violently killed: an estimated 40-year-old man and a 35-year-old woman had their necks broken at the atlas vertebrae (Sutton 1979). A fourth adult had no apparent neck injury, but Leach and Leach (1979:209–210) state that while the bones were very soft and decomposed, "the lower jaw had been forced open with some instrument which had caused considerable damage to the maxillary area and during burial a large rock had been smashed down, thereby imploding the skull." Two of the other individuals in this burial area had the same evidence of something being forced into the mouth: the speared woman and a fifth individual—a young child. Leach and Leach feel that the act of prying open and forcing some object into the mouths of these three people may have taken place during *rigor mortis* (usually within 6–36 hours after death) and may be a death rite rather than evidence of violence. Thus, of a total of five people, we have firm evidence that three of them were violently killed, one had his skull smashed (but perhaps postmortem), and the last was a child whose jaw was forced open apparently after death. This evidence bears all the signs of young and elderly members of a group caught by surprise and killed by raiders. The individuals were all carefully buried later, and grave goods were included, suggesting that they were recovered by their relatives and laid to rest. It is also worth mentioning that Sutton (1979) has documented a wide range of illness, stress, and wear and tear on these people: the adults were people past their prime who had clearly had hard lives. Perhaps the younger adults were away from the Washpool village when the raid took place.

Another small burial area was excavated two km from the Washpool Midden site and nearly adjacent to a fortified site. One adult male and four infants dated to about A.D. 1500 were recovered in a natural cleft. The man had suffered a perimortem crushing fracture to the left humerus and some other injuries, and one of the children died from infection sometime after receiving a sharp fracture above the left eye (Sutton 1979). These people were even more physically stressed than their likely ancestors from Washpool. Periodic violent death seems to have been a part of life in prehistoric Palliser Bay during the Archaic Period.

Another example of early period violence is a man who was killed and eaten at Whangamata on the Coromandel Peninsula (Allo 1972:76). The early date is strongly supported by moa bones from a single individual that were deposited in the same context, as well as other artifacts in the vicinity (Green 1963). The human remains, as well as the other faunal remains, were fragmented and burnt. Interestingly, the human and the moa bones were far less common in the midden than were dog bones. *Kaitangata* (consumption of human flesh) was a key part of Maori warfare by at least the late prehistoric (see Best 2001:64–68; Davidson 1984:137; Vayda 1960:69–72). While it certainly had important symbolic and mana ramifications, it was also a dedicated commissariat practice among *taua* (war parties) that traveled with few provisions.

Houghton completed the most thorough osteological study of prehistoric New Zealand to date. He concluded (1980:138),

> In general, then, fractures and dislocations, deliberate or accidental injury to the skeleton, are uncommon, and interestingly there is scarcely an

> example of the common fracture of some prehistoric communities, the 'parrying fracture,' where the bones of the (usually left) forearm have been broken when attempting to fend off a forceful blow. We don't have enough data to be able to say that evidence of deliberate injury increases with time, into the later prehistoric, as pressure on land and food resources grew, and the evidence of the fortifications is that warfare became endemic.

But Houghton provides only general statements with no sample size for either the numbers of individuals or the number of skeletal elements examined, and his more specific study drew on only a small sample from widely scattered locations (Houghton 1977a). Houghton (1980:138) also mentions injuries such as broken jaws without apparently considering whether they could have resulted from violence. But it is very interesting that he did not identify more than "scarcely" any parry fractures, given the prevalence of shock weapons from late prehistoric and early historic times. Then again, not all casualties of warfare go down fighting.

Despite the limited number of studied skeletons, Davidson (1984:181) concludes that, "the evidence of violent and unpleasant death among the inhabitants of the Washpool in the twelfth century shows that peace was not as universal in early New Zealand as some authorities have suggested." For the few early skeletons studied thus far, it is clear that a fairly large percentage reveal clear, or possibly violent, trauma. Although the data are limited, a more detailed analysis of the available osteological material is certainly desirable, one done in a sensitive manner with Maori oversight.

So what do we have from archaeology so far? We have suggestive evidence of weaponry that may well have been introduced along with the first colonists to New Zealand from the Society Islands. We also have rather qualitative skeletal evidence from an admittedly poor sample that a significant percentage of Archaic Period people were subjected to violence. Certainly, these data need to be reanalyzed and combined with any finds from the past 15 years or so (again, these will be few and would have to be gathered from salvage archaeology reports since burials are now only excavated in the event of construction projects). Alone, these clues of weaponry and limited skeletal evidence might not be entirely convincing, but when they are considered in the context of Polynesian culture, Archaic warfare of at least some scale is hard to question.

The Polynesian Toa

Rarely have archaeology, ethnology, ethnography, linguistics, and physical anthropology worked together as well as they have in the reconstruction of Ancestral Polynesian Society (Kirch 1984, 2000; Kirch and Green 1987). This represents the earliest form of Polynesian culture as it first developed in Western

Polynesia (Fiji, Tonga, Samoa) around 1500 B.C. from its Lapita Culture forebears. Within a few hundred years, this "mother" culture was spread by arguably the most exciting migration story in human history: the exploration and colonization of the most remote Pacific islands, including Hawai'i, Rapanui (Easter Island), and New Zealand. Thanks to decades of interdisciplinary research, we know quite a bit about these people, their material culture, their lifeways, and even their language.

The word toa (warrior) was included in this language, as was ariki (chief). Indeed, warriors have a long history in Polynesia, and they were also key political players. Success in war was one possible avenue for social advancement for those who were not among the highest ranked ariki. Patrick Kirch (1984:195–216) has probably best summarized the role of warriors in Polynesian society, but other descriptions can be found in Goldman (1970) and Sahlins (1958, 1985). Kirch (1984:196) writes,

> The significance of toa, and their ability to challenge the authority of ariki, was bound up with the Polynesian concept of mana. For the ariki, mana 'flowed' from the gods through a series of sacred ancestors. However, since mana was manifest in prowess, power, and especially in an ability to challenge the established order and succeed, it could also be demonstrated in practical action. A chief who was also an accomplished warrior would have greatly enhanced status, for his mana would be unquestioned. Should he suffer defeat, the stigma of low mana would attend him, and his authority and power might well be challenged by another, either from within his group or from outside.

Clearly, toa had been a key part of Polynesian society long before the first canoes touched shore on Aoteoaroa. Almost certainly, there were recognized toa or at least descendants of toa in those first crews. Within this cultural backdrop, the limited evidence of weapons and skeletal trauma speaks louder.

What is less evident, of course, is the nature of early warfare in Archaic Period New Zealand. The key missing ingredient is fortifications. Few of the pa sites that have been dated thus far predate A.D. 1500, though more sites need to be dated to pin down the origin of pa. Nevertheless, we can surmise that Archaic Period warfare consisted of limited raiding or politically motivated attacks by a few individuals. Low population density, difficult terrain, and relatively abundant resources compared to later prehistory would doubtless have minimized direct competition between groups. I thus follow Davidson (1984:181) and argue the earliest conflict in New Zealand was most likely status warfare—war in the context of mana to be gained or lost rather than war to drive away rivals or annex land. Kirch (1984:197) draws on the ethnography of smaller-scale Polynesian societies such as Tongareva to describe this simple form of warfare as including raiding for food, "as well as of avenging insults against one's person or tribe, a means of restoring mana." This "toa warfare" contrasts with the endemic conflict that developed later in New Zealand prehistory.

Pa and Endemic Maori Warfare: The Late Prehistoric Period

By around A.D. 1500, elbow room was much harder to find in New Zealand. There were several reasons for this, including population growth, increased cyclonic activity or other climatic changes, severe deforestation, and numerous extinctions (including the moa). But a technological solution to these increasing problems was evidently one of the key factors in the transformation of Maori warfare during the late prehistoric, usually called the Classic Maori Period. This solution was the development of a sophisticated storage pit technology that enabled horticulture to spread from a very limited role to a key part of the economy in coastal areas of the North Island (where frost is less likely to occur). This section explores how these storage pits transformed the Maori economy and settlement pattern in areas where horticulture was practical, which then led to a much heightened concern with access to key resources (not just good garden lands). This shift in settlement pattern is most obvious in the thousands of pa fortifications that sprang up, mostly after A.D. 1500. Pa are an indication of endemic warfare, as has long been recognized by anthropologists, but they were also the nexus of sociopolitical changes—the development of regional polities including some fairly large and integrated chiefdoms in more favorable areas.

Of Pits and Pa

Based on present evidence, we cannot with certainty determine which came first—the roofed storage pit or the pa (fort). But available radiocarbon dates do indicate that they both originate around the same time, probably around A.D. 1350–1500 (Allen 1994; Davidson 1984:121–127, 1987; Fox 1974, 1976; Schmidt 1996). They were thereafter tied closely together throughout late prehistoric and early historic times in New Zealand. Maori storage pits were elaborate affairs. They were subterranean and covered with pitched roofs. This insulation and protection combined with drainage systems and storage racks kept *kumara* (sweet potato) tubers free from frost and moisture. This technology enabled storage throughout the cold, wet winter for subsistence needs, political expenditures, and perhaps most importantly for spring plantings. Storage pits, along with intensification of gardening practices (Best 1925; Leach 1979) such as improving drainage, windbreaks, and developing warmer and more friable soils enabled a more sedentary settlement pattern in favorable horticultural areas (mainly the coastal parts of the North Island). Kumara was not likely a major staple in most places, but it was an important part of subsistence and was very much a key political commodity accorded much prestige (Firth 1929).

Improved garden lands and pits full of kumara were inviting targets for potential raiders. The need to protect these assets and to control access to favorable locations led to the proliferation of pa fortifications. But this was also a political process, as leaders organized the construction of pa, the most expensive and largest scale economic project undertaken in prehistoric New Zealand (Allen 1994, 1996, 2003; Kirch 2000:283). Pa construction entailed extraordinary labor and capital investment in clearing land, hauling and erecting palisade posts on hilltops, and the excavation of earthworks for defense, living space, and food storage. People agreed to do this work for a very elementary reason: security. In the process, they bound themselves into polities controlled, or at least dominated, by ariki or rangatira (chiefs or elites).

Early European visitors to New Zealand were very impressed by the scale and ingenuity of the Maori pa. Over 6,000 have been recorded throughout New Zealand thus far, mostly along milder coastal areas of the North Island where horticulture was practical. These fortifications range in size from small fortified hamlets to vast earthwork fortresses up to 35 hectares or more in size that would not be completely out of place in Iron Age Europe. Pa were usually sited to take advantage of natural defenses in the form of hilltops, ridgelines, cliffs, swamps, and islands (Figure 6.2). Natural protection was augmented by terraces, escarpments, ditches, banks, and raised fighting stages that served as lookouts and platforms from which to hurl rocks down on attackers. Most pa were surrounded by palisade lines constructed of timber; sometimes three or more of these stockades could surround even very large pa. Entrances to pa were carefully protected by winding pathways that exposed intruders to attack from the flanks and above. The most detailed descriptions of pa can be found in Best (1927), Davidson (1984, 1987), and Fox (1976).

The Evidence for Warfare in the Late Prehistoric

Aside from the vast number of pa sites, there are several other indicators of the intensity of warfare in late prehistoric and very early historic New Zealand. One particularly powerful type of evidence is the rich and detailed Maori oral history and whakapapa (genealogy). These are too numerous to describe here, but perhaps the most useful compilations of this material include Best (1924, 1927, 2001) and Vayda (1960). These are further discussed in the next section of this chapter. A second set of evidence is ethnohistorical accounts. The journal of any

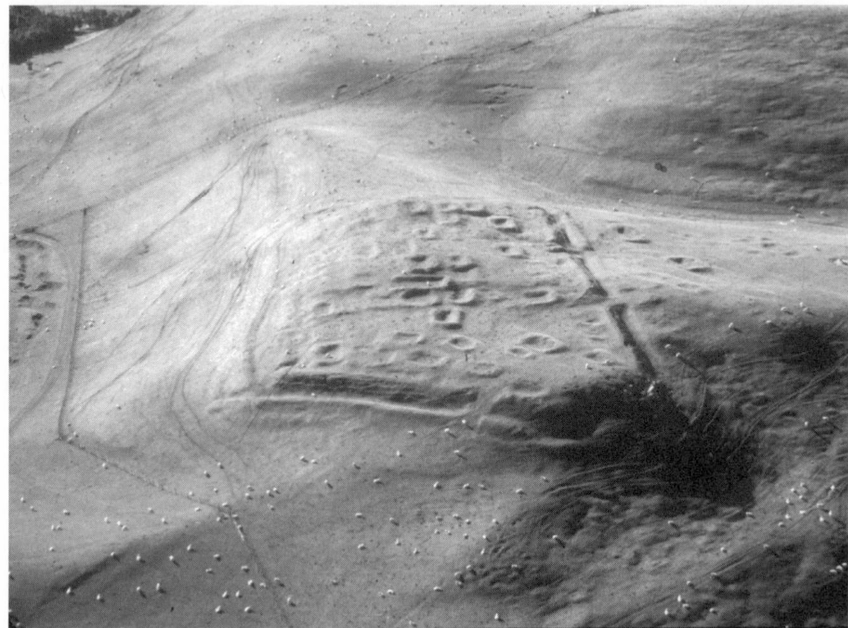

Figure 6.2. Aerial photograph of prehistoric *pa* (V22/86), Hawke's Bay. The site sits on top of a low hill. Ditches and banks were constructed for each of the four sides. Palisade lines existed along the inside edge of the ditches. This particular site functioned mainly as a fortified food store for *kumara* (sweet potatoes) given the large number of raised rim storage pits in the interior, as well as several outside the *pa*.

early visitor (for examples see: Banks 1963; Cook 1961, 1968; Salmond 1991) to New Zealand also makes it clear that warfare was always a possibility, though it did evidently vary in frequency in time and space. Detailed descriptions of Maori warfare are readily found in this literature. Third, there is an abundance of formal weapon types from late prehistoric New Zealand. Hundreds of Maori weapons are curated in most museums in the country, as well as many international institutions. Unfortunately, most of them have questionable context, as they were collected in the nineteenth century (for example, see Furey 1996).

A fourth line of evidence is archaeological and merits some discussion. There are a few cases of clear-cut warfare visible through excavation of human remains and sacked pa sites. Unfortunately, large areal excavations of pa sites are thus far limited. As late as 1984, only 20 or so pa had even been dated (Davidson 1984:192). More than this number have been subjected to areal excavation (that is, more than test pits or trenches), but it is still a very small sample of the total of over 6,000 pa. Without exposure of large blocks, it is very difficult to be able to spot the smoking gun of an attacked pa site. Hence, the historian

Belich (1996:79–80) argues from this scanty negative evidence that "storming a pa must have verged on the impossible. It therefore comes as no surprise that Maori appear to have seldom bothered trying it. . . . few pa show archaeological evidence of sack."

However, of the small sample of large-scale excavations, quite a few sites show conclusive proof that they were indeed attacked. The most obvious is a pa that sat on the shore of Lake Mangakaware in the central North Island (Bellwood 1978, 1987). This waterlogged site has outstanding evidence due to the extent of excavations and excellent preservation. Bellwood (1987:155–156) states,

> The Mangakaware site covered only about 0.2 hectare, but produced excellent evidence for settlement layout, since the bases of the wooden house walls were all preserved, as were the palisades, and also many wooden artifacts thrown into the lake. Massive timber palisades driven up to 3 m in the ground formed the defenses, with a double row on the vulnerable landward side. The pa was entered through a very narrow palisaded passage. . . . quite a number of broken weapons and ornaments were found in this passage, together with human bone and red ochre. Evidently a battle had centered on this spot, and excavations in one area inside the pa revealed clear traces of cannibalism.

The Mangakaware excavation report (Bellwood 1978) provides detail on patu and spear fragments clustered around a shattered and burnt human femur that was covered in red ochre. A hearth inside the pa contained the burnt and fragmented remains of at least one adult. Some of the long bones had been carved (to reduce the mana of the victim?), and a wooden handle and flakes found near the pit were quite likely used for butchering. This fortification was breached and at least one defender eaten—an uncommonly clear example of a sacked fortification.

Excavations at Peketa Pa in the South Island point to another successful sack, given extensive burning and an abundance of *in situ* artifacts (Brailsford 1981:131–136). Likewise, excavations at Waioneke Pa in the Kaipara area of the North Island exposed a broken patu and "just inside the palisade" the shallow graves of two individuals "with severe head wounds" that may indicate "the ultimate fate of the pa" (McKinlay 1971:90). As noted by Davidson (1984:192), this does suggest that the defenders held off the attackers since the bodies were not mutilated. Two other individuals were buried in the unusual context of a pit inside a pa on Motutapu Island, but while no pathologies were noted, they were only excavated partially and the bone was poorly preserved (Houghton 1977b; see also Davidson 1984:56, Figure 42). More poorly documented excavations at Pa Bay on Bank's Peninsula (Thacker 1960), Ongari Point in the Bay of Plenty (Shawcross 1964), Pari Whakatu near Claverly (Scarlett 1960), and at Mapoutahi Pa in Otago (Anderson and Sutton 1973) provide other examples of widespread burning within pa, occasional broken weapons, and likely examples of cannibalism.

In Hawke's Bay, a lake island pa called Roto a Tara is famous for having been attacked several times in the early nineteenth century after European contact, but before the introduction of firearms to the region (Allen 1994; Buchanan 1973; Prentice 1976). Archaeologists who first recorded the site noted the large quantity of human bone that strongly points to casualties inflicted during one or more of these episodes since relatives did not usually bury their dead within their own settlements. There are perhaps hundreds more sites throughout New Zealand that contain surface evidence of human remains. We can only guess at the percentage of pa sites that were sacked, much less that were unsuccessfully attacked. But we do know that it definitely happened.

There are other victims of violence who died outside of pa, such as a young woman from the Coromandel Peninsula who was almost certainly killed by a club stroke to the back of the head, decapitated, and eaten. Her skull and articulated cervical vertebrae were associated with a hearth (Calder and Calder 1977; Houghton 1977a:47, 1980:126–127).

All this is not to say that pa were ineffective military, economic, and political attempts to deal with population and resource stress in late prehistoric New Zealand. Indeed, I have recently argued that the Maori case indicates that archaeologists working in other areas of the world may well have downplayed the effectiveness of fortifications (Allen 2003). In particular, their latent offensive role is usually ignored. Vayda (1960:75) states that "surprises are said to have been the usual cause of the fall of pa. But if the defenders remained within the pa and all attempts at surprising them failed, then the attackers either abandoned the objective or else turned to other measures." Most often, the former was the selected course of action since protracted sieges were beyond the logistical capacity of most attacking taua (war parties). Pa surely fell, mostly from surprises or treachery, but also occasionally they were sacked by direct and overwhelming assault. In most cases, however, defenders could be fairly confident they were safe so long as they were vigilant and had provisions against short sieges.

On the other hand, a significant number of all of the larger-scale pa excavations undertaken thus far in New Zealand reveal sure, likely, or possible evidence of attack and/or cannibalism. This realization ought to end the argument that pa were mostly built as symbolic constructions of Maori cosmology (see below).

Explanations for Maori Warfare in the Late Prehistoric

A key pioneer of the anthropological study of Maori warfare was Andrew Vayda (1960, 1961, 1976), who went to New Zealand on a Fulbright to conduct his Columbia University dissertation research in the late 1950s.[5] The importance of his work spread much further than New Zealand, as numerous citations throughout this volume (or any other works on the anthropology of warfare) show. Vayda became one of the leading anthropologists on both warfare and ecology (particularly among horticulturalists) and is also a recognized expert on the anthropology of the Pacific. Vayda's (1960, 1961) early Maori work focused on the role of ecology in warfare. He did an exhaustive survey of ethnohistory, ethnography, and Maori oral history to compile a treatise on the practice of Maori warfare. Importantly, he also offered up an explanation for the endemic nature of war in prehistoric and early historic New Zealand. Vayda argued that the dense temperate rainforest that covered much of New Zealand made land clearance very difficult. Groups faced with a shortage of garden lands would thus have found it easier to seize new garden areas through force.

Vayda (1976) further developed his model of Maori warfare by positing that it was a process rather than a series of discrete events. Probing raids established which groups were weaker and pointed the way for growing or larger polities to expand. Raids that indicated defensive weakness were an invitation to a more serious attempt at driving out inhabitants. Eventually, enough sustained attacks (or one or more devastating episodes) might well dislodge a group from their lands, which would then be annexed by the aggressors. He emphasized the ecological adaptation of this process as it would encourage populations to move into previously unoccupied areas. Warfare had the overall effect of spreading population into less favorable areas, where losing groups were forced into clearing new gardens.

This ecological model has continued to be the dominant theory in explaining the endemic warfare of New Zealand and the proliferation of fortifications. More recent work has stressed the role of storage pit technology and to a lesser extent the costs of investing in gardening other than initial land clearance (increasing drainage, construction of protective stone walls, preparing soils, and the like). The most comprehensive examples of the ecological argument can be found in Anderson and McGlone (1992) and McGlone et al. (1994). Other summaries are standard in culture histories of New Zealand or the Pacific (Bellwood 1978; Davidson 1979, 1987; Kirch 1984, 2000).

Drawing on the theoretical work on social power by Timothy Earle (1987, 1991, 1997) and Michael Mann (1986), I have also argued that Maori warfare was not just a process of ecological adaptation (Allen 1991, 1992, 1994, 1996, 2003; Liu and Allen 1999). In a regional study of Hawke's Bay on the east coast of the North Island, I utilized the distribution and nature of pa sites to reconstruct the development of chiefdoms and other forms of polities. The distribution of pa in Hawke's Bay clearly shows that leaders in firm control of the most favorable economic areas of the region built the largest and most integrated regional polities (Allen 1994, 1996). While easily cleared land was not as limited as suggested by Vayda (1960, 1976), access to maritime, brackish lagoon, riverine, and forest resources were also key factors in the desirability of land (see Allen 1996 for detailed discussion). Garden productivity was determined more by the number of frosts and the lack of droughts (Hawke's Bay summers are very dry due to rain shadow effect) than by the costs of clearing land. Warfare or the threat of warfare pushed people into chiefdoms to protect productive areas and to lessen the chances of successful attack.

I have argued that the construction of pa was very much a political and economic task organized by ambitious leaders and negotiated with their followers. People weighed the costs of warfare against the extra labor and loss of autonomy that came with life under the sway of more powerful leaders. The New Zealand historian James Belich (1996:87) has since argued that "groups made pa, but pa also helped make groups," but I would emphasize instead that it was chiefs who organized and financed pa, and in the process made polities. This is a crucial distinction, for it recognizes the political role of both pa and warfare. Perhaps because of the dominance of the functionalist ecological model, most New Zealand specialists have not seriously examined pa construction as a political, agent-based process.

There is one other theoretical perspective that has been fairly popular. It sees Maori pa less as functioning in the realm of war or sociopolitical power, but instead as symbols of Maori cosmology. This perspective was first put forward by Mihaljevic (1973). Sutton (1990, 1993) and his colleagues employed this perspective in an intensive and thorough program of survey and excavation centered on the Pouerua chiefdom in Northland. More recently, Barber (1996:876) has argued that fortifications "of the 15th and 16th centuries at least may represent a monumental reaffirmation of and appeal for the extension of a more beneficent and productive order into a now more permanently capricious island world."

There is no doubt that pa were important symbols of group mana and Maori cosmology, just as the house I am currently sitting in is a symbol of Western organization of space and my socioeconomic status relative to other Southern Californians. But in my view, my house functions most importantly, as comedian George Carlin would say, as a shelter for my stuff. People built pa under the organization and capital investment of a chief primarily in an effort to keep from getting killed and to ensure control over local resources and economic investments.

This section has discussed major transitions in Maori warfare that came about sometime after A.D. 1500. The ultimate causes of these changes were population growth and a reduction in at least some important subsistence resources. But the catalyst that directed these transitions was intensification of horticulture through elaborate storage technology, improvements in gardens, and increasing differential value of land and other resources (shellfish beds, freshwater, forests, and productive bracken fern areas). Good resources became scarcer and more coveted, and aspiring leaders took advantage of this change. Warfare was transformed from a mechanism of obtaining or maintaining mana to a means of taking or protecting desirable resources. The most obvious change was the development of defensive warfare: an explosion of fortifications in areas that could support intensive horticulture. Pa made conquest much more difficult, but at the same time enabled ambitious leaders to attract followers through the promise of enhanced security. Pa were important tactically to protect stored food and, of course, people. They could also function strategically to hinder or prevent outsiders from entering particular areas.

Offensive war also developed beyond simple raiding, though to be sure raids continued on the chance of catching people outside of their pa and as a means of testing defensive strength and commitment. But on occasion at least, direct assaults were made on fortifications. This required a change in warfare to include new tactics, organization, logistics, and even technology (such as sapping, employing fire, the use of the *koromahanga* or *rou* [stout ropes with wooden bars to pull down palisades—see Best 1927:158, Figure 43], and scaling ladders). It also probably required overwhelming numbers of warriors (Allen 2003). Sometimes, these storming attempts succeeded. It is likely that such events brought even greater mana to successful ariki. Certainly, they are long remembered in Maori oral history.

Early Historic Maori Warfare: The Devastation Wrought by Pu

The Maori continued to call the shots for quite some time after first European contact. Indeed, Abel Tasman was sent packing in 1542 when one of his boat crews was attacked, dispatched, and eaten by South Island warriors near the national park that now bears his name (an effective way to deal with Europeans who then avoided New Zealand until Cook's first voyage in 1769). European and American presence in Aoteoroa until the 1840s was by the leave of the local Maori groups. Whalers, traders, deserters, and vagabonds were often welcomed into tribes. Sometimes they became true Pakeha Maori (European or foreigner Maori) who functioned as economic, military, religious, or political leaders

(Bentley 1999). Sometimes they made a mistake or wore out their welcome in some other way, and found themselves the main course of a good meal (though some groups did not care for the taste of Pakeha).

Many changes were wrought by the presence of itinerant travelers and more permanent Pakeha residents in Aotearoa. These included new crops (especially the white potato), new animals (pigs, chickens, horses, and cattle), new economic opportunities (whaling, trading flax, prostitution), and of course, new technologies. Metal tools, as always, were highly prized—such as axes for felling trees and tomahawks for felling men. But the most desirable and most devastating addition was the pu, or musket.

The first known significant use of the musket in Maori warfare was in 1807 when a war party of Nga Puhi from Northland attacked the Ngati Whatua of Kaipara on the west coast north of Auckland armed with several guns they had acquired through trading and probably through offering women as prostitutes to visiting Pakeha sailors. Surprisingly, it was the defenders who triumphed despite this new weapon, called pu by the Maori. The Nga Puhi, however, became more determined than ever to obtain more guns and experience in order to extract utu (revenge) against the Ngati Whatua as well as traditional enemies further south in the Auckland and Bay of Plenty regions. From this moment, Maori warfare was irreversibly changed.

This first attack foreshadowed the large-scale and long-distance Musket Wars which started in earnest in 1818. They lasted roughly until the signing of the Treaty of Waitangi with the British Empire in 1840 (though smaller scale conflict continued into the 1870s at least). The Musket Wars became one of the most drastic and tragic arms races to be found anywhere or at any time. It is estimated that 20,000 to 50,000 Maori perished directly due to violence during this period (a loss of perhaps a third or more of the entire Maori population in about 30 years of fighting—see Pool 1977). Much of this history is known from both contemporary Pakeha observers as well as Maori oral history. For the most recent accounts of these wars, see Belich (1996) and Crosby (1999).

The key issue during this new period of Maori warfare was one of access to the new technology: the pu. Groups that had them could essentially run amok on long-distance war expeditions to avenge past wrongs, or just for enjoyment and mana. Time and time again, groups who were attacked for the first time by war parties armed with pu saw with shock their ariki fall from fighting stages—felled by loud bangs and puffs of smoke. In many cases attackers so demoralized entire pa garrisons that they were able to rout and slay nearly all of the inhabitants. This often led to an orgy of cannibalism that could last for several days before they moved on to the next settlement. In Hawke's Bay, one unfortunate hapu nearly decimated by muskets in the 1820s became ever after known as Ngati

Matepu (Descendents of Those Killed by Muskets). Often overlooked, the newly introduced white potato was also vital to the transitions of the Musket Wars, as it permitted the long-distance raids that would have been logistically impossible in prehistoric New Zealand (Belich 1996:159).

The Musket Wars also led to drastic sociopolitical change, as chiefs with guns and white potatoes were able to build larger war parties that could accomplish far more. Successful acquisition of muskets and their use in war led to powerful mana. Perhaps the most famous of these was the Nga Puhi chief Hongi Hika who traveled to England and met King George. As described by Belich (1996:160):

> He made something of a splash in high society, where he 'conducted himself with an air of conscious superiority, and that scrupulous regard to etiquette by which he was generally distinguished.' He studied for a time at Cambridge, attending soirees, assisting Professor Samuel Lee with a Maori-language grammar, and gathering gifts. . . . Hongi spent four months in Sydney on the way home, selling the gifts he had received in England and buying guns with the proceeds. In 1821, he arrived home with as many as 400 or 500 muskets, perhaps the largest single shipment Maori ever acquired. This was a remarkable feat of procurement, and it seems impossible to see Hongi as a passive victim of Europe. . . . The rivals as well as the enemies of northern Nga Puhi trembled, as well they might.

In a particularly cold-blooded maneuver, Hongi sought out rival chiefs in Sydney and told them he was going to kill and eat their people, and then went out and did it. He also bought armor to use against hand-to-hand weapons, which proved very effective in a number of instances. Missionary accounts and Maori histories suggest that his taua inflicted at least several thousand killings over the next six years, until Hongi received his own fatal wound. Many other chiefs throughout New Zealand likewise built their mana through musket raids.

As always, this change in offensive warfare brought about defensive responses. These included moving to more remote areas, according more power to local chiefs to better prepare defenses, forming new alliances, scattering and hiding, and other methods of lowering the threat of attack by musket-armed war parties. The most important response was, of course, for people to secure their own muskets for self-defense or to mount their own attacks. New Zealand in the 1820s and 1830s became the scene of a desperate arms race to procure muskets from Europeans and Americans trying to unload a surplus from the Napoleonic Wars.

But one other key change is quite visible archaeologically—the transformation of pa defenses. The archaeologist Nigel Prickett (2002:20–21), an authority on nineteenth century fortifications in New Zealand, both Maori and Pakeha, notes:

> When Maori first obtained guns in the early . . . 19th century defenders were forced off the high and exposed platforms of the old-style pa to take up positions low in firing trenches. These were traversed or zigzagged to contend with enfilading fire (enemy fire down the length of a position). At the same time pa were shifted from hilltops, with their advantage in hand-to-hand fighting, to level, or near-level ground, which gave defenders a good field of fire. This gave rise to the so-called 'musket pa,' of which there are numerous examples, mostly in the north of the North Island.

Musket pa (Figure 6.3) often dispensed with multiple formidable palisade walls and instead built a single line of stockade shielded by a flax screen in front to conceal the defenders and to stop musket balls. Flanking angles were also frequently added to trenches on two or more corners of the defenses. Sites were also quite a bit smaller to ensure enough firepower to protect the entire perimeter. Also, the excavated earth from trenches was usually placed on the outside of the trench, rather than as a defensive bank behind a ditch. Best (1927:367–413) devotes considerable attention to general design and specific examples of musket pa. Maori pa engineers thus quickly developed effective responses to musket attacks, though the defenders needed to have a few guns of their own as well. An offensive technique developed to counter these formidable defenses was the construction of tall towers near the pa to be attacked. These elevated platforms allowed attackers to fire down into the pa. In other words, the Maori adapted to gun warfare much more rapidly and with a lot less fuss than the professional military forces of the Western World.

Vayda (1976) employed an ecological approach to describe the Musket Wars as a disrupted war process. He argued that the introduction of firearms altered the prehistoric war system which in turn then expanded settlement into marginal areas. In this view, the concept of utu (revenge) was a functional one until it got out of hand because of muskets. Pu (and the white potato) broke down the stalemate of fortifications and enabled every slight or wrong in recent or even distant memory to be summoned up for retribution. Very old perceived wrongs were righted through utu. Of course, this only shifted the revenge and mana imbalance and thus called for further retributions if at all possible. This bloody course ran on unabated until the inevitable point was reached: eventually all surviving groups had secured muskets. For every arms race, there is an inevitable stalemate until the next technological innovation comes along. The New Zealand Musket Wars provide a classic textbook case of this process. Vayda (1976:101) summarizes:

Figure 6.3. Aerial photograph of Waikoukou Pa (V22/9) in Hawke's Bay. This is an example of the modifications to *pa* defenses to accommodate the introduction of muskets in the nineteenth century. Instead of a ditch and bank system, earthwork ramparts are placed on the outside of the defenses to provide cover for the defenders. Note the two lines of ramparts. The *pa* is located on level ground below a ridge in order to create a clear field of fire. Inside the defenses are several terraces and storage pits.

> The magnitude of the perturbations was great enough to affect even deeply ingrained ideas and behavior. By 1830, the value of fighting for revenge was, according to the missionaries' accounts, being questioned by many of the Nga Puhi, who found themselves increasingly beset by death and illness and threatened by their erstwhile victims who now also had guns. . . . Moreover, when all the tribes were equipped with muskets, it soon became apparent that easy victories could no longer be won. Many Maoris turned to Christianity for a new set of values whereby not taking revenge for injuries suffered could, most opportunely, be justified. In the late 1830s and early 1840s, conversion to Christianity was rapid and massive, and firearms were cast aside. The war process, which had operated adaptively in pre-European times but now seemed to produce only death, destruction, and despair, was abandoned.

The ecological system view of prehistoric Maori warfare certainly has limitations (such as ignoring sociopolitical issues or concern with the individual), but it is very clear that muskets did fundamentally and tragically alter the course of war in the early historic period. The ideology of utu combined with unequal access to new, destructive weapons led to horrific slaughter until the scales of war were once again in balance.

Although the second half of the nineteenth century is beyond the scope of this chapter, it must be pointed out that Maori warfare did not cease with the Treaty of Waitangi which brought New Zealand into the British Empire. Beginning in the late 1850s, certain tribes and other groups perceived that their interpretation of the treaty was not the same as the Pakeha's. This led to a series of bloody colonial wars that pitted the British army, together with colonial troops and Maori allies, against "rebel" iwi (tribes), mostly in the North Island (especially the Waikato and Taranaki). There were also still some small-scale intertribal or inter-hapu wars or battles during this period, such as the battle of Pakiaka Bush in Hawke's Bay in 1857 (Allen 1994:375–376). These wars saw the Maori once again adapt to new technology of warfare as they conceived and perfected artillery-proof defenses, earlier than in the American Civil War or other conflicts. Maori fortifications confounded even seasoned and much better-equipped British troops through clever use of bunkers, trenches, deceptive targets intended to draw fire and waste ammunition, and kill zones that directed attacking troops right where defenders wanted them. These wars were in the past called the Maori Wars or the Land Wars, but a consensus is developing to refer to them as the New Zealand Wars (Belich 1986, 1996; Prickett 2002). They are a fascinating development in the continued transformation of Maori warfare into the historic period, as was Maori participation in the First and Second World Wars. As the introduction to this chapter revealed, the Maori way of war did not disappear after contact with the outside world. Indeed, it has kept pace with and accommodated the revolutionary changes in warfare from the nineteenth to the twenty-first centuries.

Discussion and Conclusion

The Maori case is an instructive and rich one for the anthropology of war. The short time span of New Zealand's human past provides an enlightening look at how warfare can evolve out of a colonizing cultural pattern of revenge and status rivalry, to a state of entrenched and endemic war over land and other resources, and then be quickly transformed by the introduction of a destabilizing weapon.

It also provides archaeologists with a reminder as to the effectiveness of fortifications in pre-state level warfare where the means of making war were limited. Without sophisticated missile systems or logistical capabilities, Maori pa were very effective forms of defense (Allen 2003). There are also plenty of data to prove, however, that fortifications were indeed put to the test and sometimes even sacked, probably with great loss of life. While there is no doubt that fortifications are important symbols of groups and their leaders, their expense and problems were tolerated only because they gave people a better chance to keep their land and to stay alive.

The introductory chapter to this volume outlined two common perspectives on the relationship of warfare and society: 1) how factors in the social landscape affect the practice, duration, or intensity of warfare, and 2) how war itself causes its own transformations, directly or indirectly. A study of Maori warfare over the past 1,000 years speaks to both of these issues.

The first perspective is best addressed in the transition from the Polynesian toa pattern of warfare to endemic pa warfare around 500 years ago. As people began to fill the vast New Zealand landscape, and as hunted and gathered resources became more scarce, Maori society changed. Intensification of horticulture, greater reliance on storage, and increased sedentism led to the development of chiefdoms in favored areas, and probably more social integration and social differentiation in all areas. Improved gardens, stored food, and other productive resources were the nexus of these social transformations, but also became highly desirable targets of enemy groups bent on raids, plunder, and seizure of choice areas. Leaders helped to provide security for people and their investments by organizing and constructing pa fortifications. Warfare became endemic; though surely not constant, it was constantly threatened. Vigilant groups in strong pa with dependable allies fared well most of the time, but failure to secure these conditions could lead to catastrophic attacks from neighbors close by or further away. After all, chiefs, who had developed regional polities through the finance and organization of pa, also could opt to increase their mana through offensive military action as well.

The second issue, how war transforms itself and society directly or indirectly, is most easily viewed in the transformations in Maori warfare brought about by the introduction and rapid adoption of the musket a few decades after European contact. One would hope that modern day political and military strategists would take note of this crystal clear example of the possible consequences of an uncontrolled arms race. Indeed, Jared Diamond (2003:M3) recently relied on the New Zealand Musket Wars in a newspaper editorial on weapons proliferation:

> The Musket Wars illustrate the potential instability of a situation in which a potent new technology is unevenly distributed. The wars began when only a few tribes had guns, and they ended when they all had them. If nukes follow a similar course, North Korea's going nuclear could trigger a desperate scramble by other countries to acquire the weapon in self-defense.

But the issue of how war transforms itself can also be looked at in a more subtle way. While all Polynesian societies have similar cultural concepts to maintain mana against insult, affront, or attack, the Maori ideology of utu is unique. This deeply embedded value system evolved in New Zealand under conditions of endemic warfare. It served as an incentive to maintain a strong deterrent that tolerated no transgression whatsoever. A failure to retaliate to any kind of threat or attack was an invitation to more attacks, perhaps even direct assaults aimed at destroying or removing a group. Fierce and assured counterstrikes were the best means to maintain land and to protect a polity. This was in effect a policy of mutually assured revenge.

Utu pervaded Maori society, as can be seen in its hold during the Musket Wars. Only once the costs of war were too great for even the most bellicose leaders could utu be suppressed. Clearly, Maori warfare evolved into a powerful force driven by an ideology of revenge and the maintenance of mana. When Tumatauenga, the God of War, got his hands on muskets, he must have been satisfied with the horrible result. But the concept was not driven from Maori culture for good, as is attested by its reawakening during the bloody Land Wars of the late nineteenth century, as well as the exploits of the Maori Battalion in the Second World War.

Acknowledgments

Above all, I wish to thank the Runanganui o te Ngati Kahungunu and the *kaumatua* of Hawke's Bay who supported my research. Kia Ora. I also gratefully acknowledge the assistance of University of California, Los Angeles, Fulbright New Zealand, the New Zealand Historic Places Trust, and the New Zealand Department of Conservation. The Cal Poly Pomona International Center's funding is gratefully acknowledged, as are the participants in the 2001 Legacy of Ancient Carthage CIEE faculty seminar who tolerated my search for Tunisian World War II battlefields with patience. Liz Arkush provided exceptional editorial assistance and several important suggestions. Jose Alvarez drew Figure 6.1.

Notes

1. A *tohi* is a ritual to prepare young men or boys for success in war or similar endeavors. The poet is linking the bayonet with a traditional Maori weapon: the sword-short spear combination *taiaha*, in which the blade was viewed and often decorated as a defiant tongue that challenged (and tasted) enemies. Tumatauenga is a Maori war deity. *Hangi* are earth ovens. *Kaitangata* is cannibalism—"consumption of people."

2. Interested readers can view a photograph of Canon Huata in a *National Geographic*

article on New Zealand (Jordan 1987:680). Other images of the Canon during the war are available in Gardiner 1992, as is a photograph of Lt. Ngarimu.

3. It is important to note the current debate on New Zealand's first settlement owing to Holdaway's (1996) recent study that suggests that introduced species of rats can be dated to more than two thousand years ago.

4. Davidson (1994) has noted the possibility that the patu form may have been taken back to the Society Islands by return voyagers. Given the early date of the Huahine clubs, this does not seem too likely unless the accepted age of first settlement of New Zealand is pushed back at least several hundred years.

5. Detailed descriptions of traditional Maori warfare are also available in Best (1924, 1927, 2001).

References

Allen, M. W. 1991. New Zealand Archaeology and an Active Maori Involvement. *Anthropology UCLA* 18:70–82.

———. 1992. The Pa of Hawke's Bay: Preliminary Results of Fieldwork. *Archaeology in New Zealand* 35:17–26.

———. 1994. Warfare and Economic Power in Simple Chiefdoms: The Development of Fortified Villages and Polities in Mid-Hawke's Bay, New Zealand. Unpublished Ph.D. dissertation, Department of Anthropology, University of California, Los Angeles.

———. 1996. Pathways to Economic Power in Maori Chiefdoms: Ecology and Warfare in Prehistoric Hawke's Bay. *Research in Economic Anthropology* 17:171–225.

———. 2003. Hillforts and the Cycling of Maori Chiefdoms: Do Good Fences Make Good Neighbors? Manuscript on file, Department of Geography and Anthropology, California State Polytechnic University, Pomona.

Allo, J. 1972. The Whangamata Wharf Site (N49/2): Excavations in a Coromandel Coastal Midden. *Records of the Auckland Institute and Museum* 9:61–79.

Anderson, A. J. 1989. *Prodigious Birds: Moas and Moa-hunting in Prehistoric New Zealand*. Cambridge: Cambridge University Press.

Anderson, A. J., and M. McGlone. 1992. Living on the Edge—Prehistoric Land and People in New Zealand. In *The Naïve Lands: Prehistory and Environmental Change in Australia and the South-West Pacific*, edited by J. Dodson, 199–241. Melbourne: Longman Cheshire.

Anderson, A. J., and D. G. Sutton. 1973. Archaeology of Mapoutahi Pa, Otago. *New Zealand Archaeological Association Newsletter* 16(3):107–118.

Australian Museum. 1989. Taonga Maori: Treasures of the New Zealand Maori People. Sydney: The Australian Museum.

Banks, J. 1963. *The Endeavour Journal of Joseph Banks, 1768–1771*, edited by J. C. Beaglehole, 2 volumes. 2nd ed. Sydney: Halstead Press.

Barber, I. G. 1996. Loss, Change, and Monumental Landscaping: Towards a New Interpretation of the "Classic" Maori emergence. *Current Anthropology* 37:868–880.

Belich, J. 1986. *The New Zealand Wars and the Victorian Interpretation of Racial Conflict.* Auckland: Auckland University Press.

———. 1996. *Making Peoples: A History of the New Zealanders.* Auckland: Allen Lane, Penguin Press.

Bellwood, P. 1978. *Archaeological Research at Lake Mangakaware, Waikato, 1968–1970.* Otago: Otago University Studies in Prehistoric Anthropology No. 12 and New Zealand Archaeological Association Monograph Number 9.

———. 1987. *The Polynesians: Prehistory of an Island People.* Rev. ed. New York: Thames and Hudson.

Bentley, T. 1999. *Pakeha Maori: The Extraordinary Story of the Europeans Who Lived as Maori in Early New Zealand.* Auckland: Penguin Books.

Best, E. 1924. *The Maori* (2 volumes). Wellington: Harry Tombs.

———. 1925. *Maori Agriculture.* New Zealand Dominion Museum Bulletin 9. Wellington: Dominion Museum.

———. 1927. *The Pa Maori.* New Zealand Dominion Museum Bulletin 6. Wellington: Dominion Museum.

———. 2001. *Notes on the Art of War,* edited by J. Evans. Auckland: Reed Books.

Brailsford, B. 1981. *The Tattooed Land: The Southern Frontiers of the Pa Maori.* Wellington: Reed Books.

Buchanan, J.D.H. 1973. *The History and Place Names of Hawke's Bay,* edited by D. R. Simmons. Wellington: Reed Books.

Calder, A., and J. Calder. 1977. A Headache or a Pain in the Neck? A Small-scale Salvage Excavation of a Midden/Burial at Opito Bay, Coromandel. *New Zealand Archaeological Association Newsletter* 20(1):39–40.

Campbell, A. Te Ariki. 2001. *Maori Battalion: A Poetic Sequence.* Wellington: Wai-te-Ata Press.

Cody, J. F. 1956. *28 (Maori) Battalion: Official History of New Zealand in the Second World War 1939–45.* Wellington: War History Branch, Department of Internal Affairs.

Cook, J. 1961. *The Journals of Captain James Cook on His Voyages of Discovery*, Volume 2, edited by J. C. Beaglehole. Cambridge: Cambridge University Press.

———. 1968 [1955]. *The Journals of Captain James Cook on His Voyages of Discovery*, Volume 1, edited by J. C. Beaglehole. Cambridge: Cambridge University Press.

Crosby, R. D. 1999. *The Musket Wars: A History of Inter-Iwi Conflict 1806–45.* Auckland: Reed Books.

Davidson, J. M. 1979. New Zealand. In *The Prehistory of Polynesia*, edited by J. D. Jennings 222–248. Cambridge: Harvard University Press.

———. 1984. *The Prehistory of New Zealand.* Auckland: Longman Paul.

———. 1987. The Paa Maori Revisited. *Journal of the Polynesian Society* 96: 7–26.

———. 1994. The Eastern Polynesian Origins of the New Zealand Archaic. In *The Origins of the First New Zealanders*, edited by D. G. Sutton, 208–219. Auckland: Auckland University Press.

———. 2001. Maori. In *Encyclopedia of Prehistory, volume 3, East Asia and Oceania,* edited by P. N. Peregrine and M. Ember, 222–242. New York: Kluwer Academic and Plenum Publishers.

Diamond, J. 2003. Muskets and Nukes: The Patterns of Proliferation. *Los Angeles Times*, March 16, 2003:M1.

Duff, R. S. 1956. *The Moa-Hunter Period of Maori Culture*. Wellington: Government Printer.

Earle, T. K. 1987. Chiefdoms in Archaeological and Ethnohistorical Perspectives. *Annual Review of Anthropology* 16:279–308.

———. 1991. The Evolution of Chiefdoms. In *Chiefdoms: Power, Economy, and Ideology*, edited by T. K. Earle, 1–15. Cambridge: Cambridge University Press.

———. 1997. *How Chiefs Come to Power: The Political Economy in Prehistory*. Stanford: Stanford University Press.

Emory, K. P. 1979. The Societies. In *The Prehistory of Polynesia,* edited by J. D. Jennings, 200–221. Cambridge: Harvard University Press.

Firth, R. 1929. *Economics of the New Zealand Maori*. London: George Routledge and Sons.

Fox, A. 1974. Prehistoric Maori Storage Pits: Problems in Interpretation. *Journal of the Polynesian Society* 83:141–54.

———. 1976. *Prehistoric Fortifications in the North Island of New Zealand*. New Zealand Archaeological Association Monograph No. 6.

Furey, L. 1996. *Orurangi: The Archaeology and Material Culture of a Hauraki Pa, Auckland*. Bulletin of the Auckland Institute and Museum Number No. 17.

Gardiner, W. 1992. *Te Mura o Te Ahi: The Story of the Maori Battalion*. Auckland: Reed Books.

Goldman, I. 1970. *Ancient Polynesian Society*. Chicago: University of Chicago Press.

Golson, J. 1959. Culture Change in Prehistoric New Zealand. In *Anthropology in the South Seas*, edited by J. D. Freeman and W. R. Geddes, 29–74. New Plymouth: Avery.

Green, R. C. 1963. Summaries of Sites at Opito, Sarah's Gully, and Great Mercury Island. *New Zealand Archaeological Association Newsletter* 6(1):57–69.

Holdaway, R. N. 1996. Arrival of Rats in New Zealand. *Nature* 384:225–226.

Houghton, P. 1977a. *Human Skeletal Material from Excavations in Eastern Coromandel*. Records of the Auckland Institute and Museum 14:45–50.

———. 1977b. *Prehistoric Burials from Recent Excavations on Motutapu Island*. Records of the Auckland Institute and Museum 14:37–43.

———. 1980. *The First New Zealanders*. Auckland: Hodder and Stoughton.

Jordan, R. P. 1987. New Zealand: The Last Utopia? *National Geographic* 171(5):654–681.

Kippenberger, Sir H. 1949. *Infantry Brigadier*. Oxford: Oxford University Press.

Kirch, P. V. 1984. *The Evolution of the Polynesian Chiefdoms*. Cambridge: Cambridge University Press.

———. 2000. *On the Road of the Winds: An Archaeological History of the Pacific Islands Before European Contact*. Berkeley: University of California Press.

Kirch, P. V., and R. C. Green. 1987. History, Phylogeny, and Evolution in Polynesia. *Current Anthropology* 28:431–456.

Leach, B. F., and H. M. Leach. 1979. Burial Positions and Orientations in Palliser Bay. In *Prehistoric Man in Palliser Bay*, edited by B. F. Leach and H. M. Leach, 205–213. Wellington: National Museum of New Zealand Bulletin No. 21.

Leach, H. M. 1979. The Significance of Early Horticulture in Palliser Bay for New Zealand Prehistory. In *Prehistoric Man in Palliser Bay*, edited by B. F. Leach and H. M. Leach, 241–249. Wellington: National Museum of New Zealand Bulletin No. 21.

Liu, J. H., and M. W. Allen. 1999. Evolution of Political Complexity in Maori Hawke's Bay: Archaeological History and Its Challenge to Intergroup Theory in Psychology. *Group Dynamics: Theory, Research, and Practice* 3:64–80.

McGlone, M., A. J. Anderson, and R. N. Holdaway. 1994. An Ecological Approach to the Polynesian Settlement of New Zealand. In *The Origins of the First New Zealanders*, edited by D. G. Sutton, 139–163. Auckland: University of Auckland Press.

McKinlay, J. R. 1971. Waioneke 1968–1969. *New Zealand Archaeological Association Newsletter* 14(3):86–91.

Mann, M. 1986. *The Sources of Social Power*. Cambridge: Cambridge University Press.

Mihaljevic, J. M. 1973. The Prehistoric Polity in New Zealand: An Exercise in Theoretical Paleosociology. Unpublished Master's thesis, Department of Anthropology, University of Auckland.

Pool, D. I. 1977. *The Maori Population of New Zealand 1769–1971*. Auckland: Auckland University Press and Oxford University Press.

Prentice, W. T. 1976. A Maori History of Hawke's Bay. In *History of Hawke's Bay*, edited by J. G. Wilson, 19–109. Dunedin: Reed.

Prickett, N. 2002. *Landscapes of Conflict: A Field Guide to the New Zealand Wars*. Auckland: Random House.

Rolf, D. 2001. *The Bloody Road to Tunis: Destruction of the Axis Forces in North Africa, November 1942–May 1943*. London: Greenhill Books.

Sahlins, M. 1958. *Social Stratification in Polynesia*. Seattle: University of Washington Press.

———. 1985. *Islands of History*. Chicago: University of Chicago Press.

Salmond, A. 1991. *Two Worlds: First Meetings Between Maori and Europeans 1642–1772*. Auckland: Viking, Penguin.

Scarlett, R. J. 1960. Excavations at Pari Whakatau, Claverly. *New Zealand Archaeological Association Newsletter* 4(1):2–7.

Schmidt, M. 1996. The Commencement of *Pa* Construction in New Zealand Prehistory. *Journal of the Polynesian Society* 105:441–451.

Shawcross, W. 1964. Archaeological Investigations at Ongari Point, Katikati, Bay of Plenty: A Report on the First Season of Excavations. *New Zealand Archaeological Association Newsletter* 7(2):79–98.

Sinoto, Y. H. 1979. Excavations on Huahine, French Polynesia. *Pacific Studies* 3(1):1–40.

Skinner, H. D. 1931. On the Patu Family and Its Occurrence Beyond New Zealand. *Journal of the Polynesian Society* 40:183–196.

Sutton, D. G. 1979. The Prehistoric People of Eastern Palliser Bay. In *Prehistoric Man in Palliser Bay*, edited by B. F. Leach and H. M. Leach, 185–203. Wellington: National Museum of New Zealand Bulletin No. 21.

———. 1990. Organization and Ontology: The Origins and Operation of the Northern Maori Chiefdom, New Zealand. *Man* 25:667–692.

———. 1993. (editor). *The Archaeology of the Peripheral Pa at Pouerua, Northland, New Zealand*. Auckland: Auckland University Press.

———. 1994. Conclusion: Origins. In *The Origins of the First New Zealanders,* edited by D. G. Sutton, 243–258. Auckland: Auckland University Press.

Thacker, M. 1960. Excavations at Pa Bay, Bank's Peninsula. *New Zealand Archaeological Association Newsletter* 4(1):8–12.

Vayda, A. P. 1960. *Maori Warfare*. Wellington: Polynesian Society Monograph No. 2.

———. 1961. Expansion and Warfare Among Swidden Agriculturalists. *American Anthropologist* 63:346–358.

———. 1976. *War in Ecological Perspective*. New York: Plenum Press.

7

Slavery and Warfare in African Chiefdoms

CHAPURUKHA M. KUSIMBA

The publication of Lawrence Keeley's *War Before Civilization* in 1996 has spawned a new and vigorous interest in the origins, causes, and consequences of war and violence in society. The arguments presented in the book are bold, detailed, and lucid. Keeley's book was a plea for anthropologists to reject Rousseauian stereotypes of pre-contact peace in pre-colonial non-western societies and come to terms with the increasing amount of evidence for prehistoric warfare from around the globe (Keeley 1996:21, but see Haas 2002:331).[1] A few years earlier, Jonathan Haas and Winfred Creamer had done the unthinkable: they wrote a monograph in which they presented evidence of stress, violence, carnage, and even cannibalism in the American Southwest, a region previously presumed to have been an island of peace (Haas and Creamer 1993). These works made a strong case for including conflict and violence in anthropological attempts to understand the past initially exemplified by Turney-High (1949). Ever since the self-imposed censorship curtain was lifted, there has been a plethora of publications, especially by Southwestern American archaeologists, on warfare and violence (for example, Haas 1990, 2002:336–337; LeBlanc 1999; Lekson 1999, 2002; Rice and LeBlanc 2001; Wilcox and Haas 1994). Topics once considered taboo, like cannibalism, are now being written about and defended (Lambert 2002; LeBlanc 1999; Turner 1999; Turner and Turner 1999; White 1992). Stephen Plog (2003) recently lauded archaeology's attempt to unravel the past in its entirety. He also cautioned about the irresponsibility of debating sensitive topics using titles that might serve to further alienate archaeology from indigenous peoples with whom the discipline already has tenuous relations (for example, Billman et al. 2000; Dongoske et al. 2000; Lambert et al. 2000; Lekson 1999; Preston 1998; Turner 1999). Plog (2003:183) urges us to "explore ways of productively fuse[ing] scientific archaeology and indigenous oral traditions" in order to meaningfully arrive at a solution complementary but not inimical to alternative ways of knowing past human experiences (for example, Mason 2000; Whiteley 2002).

A number of cross-cultural studies have made a strong case that the origins of warfare in society are traceable to ecological and sociopolitical factors (Carneiro

1990; Ember 1982; Ember and Ember 1992, 1995; Ferguson 1984, 1990, 1998; Haas 1990, 2002; Keeley 1996; Kolb and Dixon 2002; Redmond 1994; Webster 1985). Ecological factors, including environmental deterioration, droughts, insect infestations, and epidemic diseases weaken existing social and political superstructures. Sociopolitical factors often involve competition for resources owing to demographic pressure. Foreign intrusion and conquest can disrupt traditionally established and ritually sanctioned ways of dealing with crises and impose new traditions, practices, and policies. The prevalence of warfare in archaeological, historical, and ethnohistorical records suggests that armed conflict is a culturally universal behavior of societal responses to resource scarcity and associated stress. Strategies for avoiding warfare might involve the widening of the interaction sphere beyond political and ecological boundaries to include new reciprocal relations of exchange and alliance building, and/or intensification of production (Cassey 1998; Herlehy 1984; Johnson and Earle 2000; Kusimba 2003; Kusimba and Kusimba 2004). But these do not always work. Studies show that many societies in different regions of the world have used both peaceful and violent means to deal with resource scarcity, but the latter is now fashionably underscored to be the most common way (Brown 1991:347–350; Dikshitar 1944; Keeley 1996:139; Martin and Frayer 1997; McInnis 1969:397; Rice and LeBlanc 2001). Resource scarcity creates an environment of fear, mistrust, and xenophobia, which may elicit violent responses towards foreigners and rivals. Carol and Melvin Ember (1992) showed that non-industrial societies most frequently embroiled in warfare were those that had a history of chronic but unpredictable disasters, including droughts, floods, and insect infestations, among others. Responses to disasters are varied, but underlying them is an ethic of fear that becomes institutionalized, leading to violent and aggressive interactions with strangers and outsiders. Societies ruled by fear may teach the young to be suspicious of strangers (Friedlander 1997; Gay 1993). Children's narratives can often indicate to what degree a society's ethic is based on fear and terror of outsiders. Carol and Melvin Ember (1992:245) hypothesize that "if people have a history of resource problems, their fear of scarcity may spill over into fear of others. In any case, mistrustful adults may be more likely to respond aggressively to the arousal of fears, and therefore socialization for mistrust may lead to war." Lekson (2002) has recently applied this idea to archaeology in the Southwest.

Like the American Southwest, Africa was long considered a garden of peace. More recently, archaeological studies have associated the rapid increase in warfare and devastation of the African cultural landscape, including the collapse of regional economies, to Eurasian slavery (Kusimba 2004). However, historical studies show that Africa's fortunes began to unravel towards the end of the fifteenth century (Curtin 1967, 1984; Sheriff 1987; Thornton 1992; Wilmsen

1989). Around this time, prolonged drought, famine, and disease also raged (Merritt 1975; Watts 1997). Interethnic conflicts and warfare became more common and regularly afflicted Africans. Demand for enslaved African labor not only transformed African demographic structure but also changed the ways in which Africans approached crises (Herlehy 1984; Lovejoy 2000; Ringrose 2001).

In West Africa, two factors were important in the sixteenth century: (1) the European demand for enslaved African labor, and (2) powerful African states' ambitions to extend and preserve their political superiority and independence (Manning 1990; Stahl 2001:190–191). People took extraordinary measures to protect themselves from a crisis never before experienced—that of chattel slavery (Diouf 2003). Alliance building for warfare or defense among neighboring polities became a common political strategy (Cassey 1998; Stahl 2001:196). Rapid settlement shifts to inhospitable and defensible locales like hillsides and mountains provided refuge from slave seekers and warring states (Bah 1976, 2003; Cordell 2003; De Barros 2001; DeCorse 1998, 2001; Diouf 2003; Holl 2002; Soumonni 2003). Investment in local technologies, including textiles and ironworking, declined as people became more dependent on imports. Soumonni (2003:4) shows that the inhospitable lacustrine areas in South Benin were settled as refuges from the slave trade because they were the most secure places to escape the slave hunters during the eighteenth century: "the search for security in a period of violence and fear created by slave raiders and traders forced fleeing populations to seek a decent life in an environment that was then and still largely remains unattractive." T. Mouctar Bah has examined "the various refuge sites and defense mechanisms that enabled several communities to protect themselves against slave raids and to preserve their freedom and identity, in an often hostile environment" (Bah 2003:16). No permanent structures were ever erected during the height of the slave trade except for fortified settlements (Bah 1976).

In this chapter, I explore two related questions. What were the causes of post-sixteenth century warfare in East Africa? Second, what is the relationship between warfare and slave trade in East Africa? I use ethnohistorical data, early European writings, and renderings by historians and archaeologists to propose that the origins of warfare in post-sixteenth century East Africa were closely allied with Eurasian commerce in ivory and enslaved Africans. However, I argue that external economic and sociopolitical factors played a predominant role in defining the nature of relationships, interactions, and conflicts amongst East African peoples (Figure 7.1). My intention here is not to offer an exegesis on slavery. Others before me have done a much better job (for example, Cooper 1977, 1980; Gates 1996; Glassman 1995; Lovejoy 2000; Manning 1990). In-

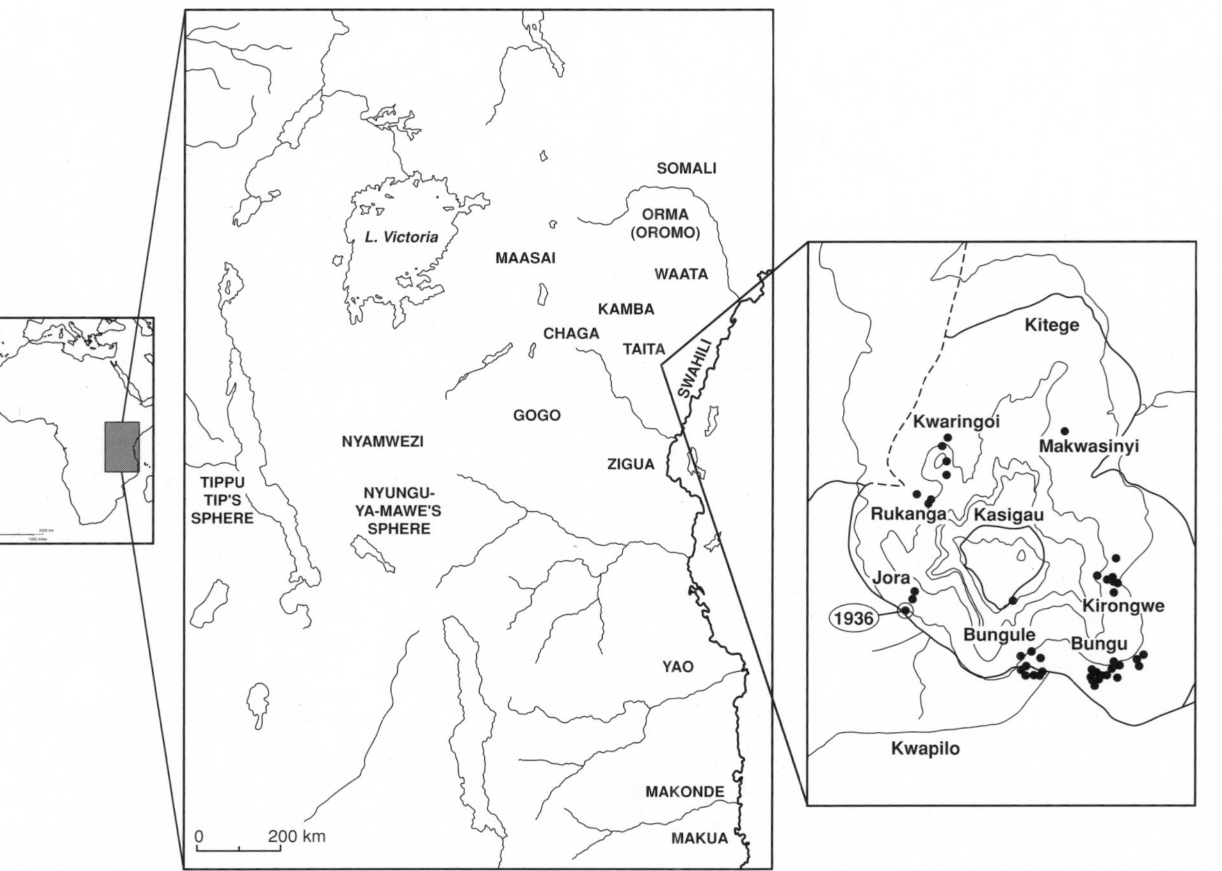

Figure 7.1. Map of East Africa showing sites discussed in the text. Inserted map on the right is of the research area.

stead, I use accounts of slavery and slave trade to show how these two processes could have caused endemic warfare in East Africa. I then discuss the impact of elephant over-hunting on the ecosystem—what I call here the elephant's revenge. I will follow this with an archaeological example of the responses to ivory and slave trade in East Africa by examining three fortified rockshelter refuges in Kasigau, Kenya. Finally, I discuss the implications of these refuges for better understanding post-contact warfare.

Approaching the Slave Trade Through Archaeology

Slave trading was an important aspect of the preindustrial economic systems of the Old World (Frank 1998; Lovejoy 2000; Ringrose 2001). Captured humans were part of the cargo in trade conducted for centuries between trading partners and associates in the Afrasian world, along with other trade items such as ivory, gold, hides and skins, timber, rock crystal, ambergris, and spices, among others. Historians have established that enslaved as well as free Africans were present in Asia at least two millennia before the European conquest and settlement in the Americas (Alpers 1975; Freeman-Grenville 1965; Harris 1971, 1985; Lovejoy 2000; Sheriff 1987).

The role of slavery and the slave trade in the development of social complexity has not yet fully been debated. John Alexander (2001) recently attributed archaeologists' silence to the difficulty in recognizing material evidence for slavery in the record. In his words, there is a "near-impossibility, in the present state of field techniques of recognizing chattel-slavery from material remains unassociated with documentary evidence" (Alexander 2001:56). The suggestion that evidence of the slave trade or slaves is "not likely to be recognized archaeologically" or is "archaeologically unrecognizable" because any such evidence can be interpreted in many different ways is deeply troubling. In other words, should archaeologists not bother to understand slavery and slave trading in Africa because the discipline is methodologically impotent to address historical events for which there is overwhelming historical, oral traditional, and eye-witness evidence? Positions such as these weaken archaeology's authority to address events for which little documentary evidence exists when its leaders shy from discussing historical events of great relevance in shaping modern global relationships. Slavery was a prominent cultural practice and ideology in the Judeo-Christian and Islamic worlds. East African Coastal culture, and especially its Islamic ideologies, ascribed a subservient stigma to slavery, which has long outlived the existence of legal definitions (Benjamin 2002; Glassman 1983). Interestingly, in a recent book devoted to the archaeology of Islam, the author devoted little space to slavery and the slave trade in the evolution of Islamic culture (Insoll 1999). Keeley (1996:85) equally has little to say about the impact of slavery in promoting interethnic violence among "primitive societies" despite the fact that all of his ethnographic data is drawn from the post-contact period. So insignificant is slavery and slave trading in archaeological publications on warfare and the evolution of culture (for example, Haas 2002).

Archaeology can investigate slavery and slave trading as successfully as history, sociology, economics, and cultural geography (for example, Curtin 1984; Lovejoy 2000; Ringrose 2001; Rodney 1969). However, to do so, archaeology initially must develop a systematic methodology for locating and identifying material remains of slavery in the archaeological record (Alexander 2001). This necessitates archaeology forging a disciplinary interdependence while maintaining its explicitly scientific approach.[2]

Slavery and Warfare: Insights from Folklore

A thread that runs through African folklore and the stories that African children were told in the nineteenth and early twentieth century consists of talking animals that outwit people and have their own chiefdoms, states, and kingdoms. Those stories anthropomorphized animals, and we loved every bit of them. However, some stories also consisted of the *kamanani*, who were comprised of cannibals, ogres, little people, half-men, werewolves, goblins, witches and other monsters and dangerous creatures. Looking back at those evenings in our grandparents' house, these strange stories conveyed an underlying message: wild, violent, malevolent creatures ruled the bush. It seemed that the world in which our ancestors lived was relatively unforgiving, one in which one couldn't make too many mistakes. The Malawian proverb runs, "It is the people who make the world; the bush has wounds and scars" (Ilife 1995:1). Indeed, there were numerous stories of wounds and scars endured by those who ventured into forbidden territories. Few returned to tell stories of success. They were mostly stories of encounters and narrow escapes from one-eyed giant monsters hopping on one leg, or half-men, with one long tooth, who were so belligerent they challenged you to a wrestling match. There were stories of beautiful women or handsome warriors who thought they were too good to find brides or bridegrooms among their own people, only to end up marrying ogres disguised as humans. The characters in these stories usually ended up eaten, but on some rare occasions they would be rescued by their despised brother or sister. Those lessons instilled fear, mistrust, and suspicion of the world yonder; most of all, they taught compliance, obedience, teamwork, and cooperation among members of the same group. Many other stories referred to kinsmen who had disappeared without a trace. We later learned they were victims of slave raiders and endemic warfare brought to East Africa by slave seekers.

How may we interpret these narratives in the context of violence and warfare in precolonial African chiefdoms? How is it that these narratives of distrust and fear are contradicted by the relationships that developed between later foreigners and Europeans (for example, Hobley 1929)? Why were relatively few colonial powers able to colonize and "pacify" Africa in a relatively short time? These questions require that we explore the African experience that may have spawned these narratives (for example, Baskerville 1922; Chatelain 1894; Denette 1898; Theal 1882; Werner 1996 [1933]). And indeed, as Whiteley (2002) and Mason (2000) show, similar accounts should be revisited by archaeologists in many areas of the world as well.

Droughts, famines, diseases, wars, slave taking, and slave raiding punctuated sixteenth to nineteenth century East Africa. Narratives of cannibalism, migrations, and peonage are responses to famines, diseases, and other disasters. A cannibal is a human being who customarily eats human flesh; yet in many African narratives relating events of cannibalism, cannibals are seen as non-human. Discussing cannibalism in Zulu tales, Callaway (1885:156) pointed out a long time ago that:

> It is perfectly clear that the cannibals of the Zulu legends are not common men; they are magnified into giants and magicians. Perhaps it might be said that the attributes of the legendary *amazimu* were transferred to the abhorred beings, which, driven by famine, kept up the habit when it was no longer needed. As Ulutuli Dhladhla told the bishop, *amazimu* rebelled against men, forsook them, and liked to eat them, and men drove them away . . . so they were regarded as a distinct nation, for men were game (*izinyamazane*) to them (quoted in Werner 1996 [1933]:172).

The suggestion that cannibals were once human implies that when they took on their habit of devouring human flesh, they ceased to be human. They became brutes that had to be exterminated, and every effort was made to kill them whenever they were sighted. The treatment of witches, suspected witches, and sorcerers should fall into this realm.

The cultural ethic of fearing strangers is deeply rooted in the slaving culture that became a part of the African everyday experience for more than four centuries. Disappearance of members of one's community and raids by slave hunters were carried out in an environment so violent and inhuman that in order for the raider and slave taker to conduct their business, they had to dehumanize others.

Myths and legends told to children contain germs that bear archaeological signatures worth exploring. Indeed, the same institutionalized fear of slavery and its effects that is encoded in children's stories is visible archaeologically in the form of fortifications. Large-scale fortification of settlements and migration to hillside locations began in the sixteenth century in East Africa. Ethnohistorical and archaeological evidence indicate that increasing regionwide insecurity was the primary cause of abandonment of an accessible settlement in favor of a fortified settlement and stockades (Fadiman 1982; Wagner 1949:40). Fortified settlements were widespread in East Africa during the latter part of the eighteenth and nineteenth centuries (Fadiman 1982; Forsbrooke 1960; Gillman 1944; Perham 1979; Scully 1969; Spear 1978; Wagner 1949). These fortifications correspond to three kinds identified by Keeley (1996:57–58). Fortified settlements, refuges, and maroon settlements in East Africa attest to the fear that permeated African society for over 400 years.

Causes of Warfare in East Africa

Political, economic, and ecological factors were responsible for the escalation of violence and armed conflict in post-sixteenth century East Africa. These factors include foreign conquest, the slave trade, droughts, famines, diseases, and elephant over-hunting. I briefly discuss the contributions of each factor to warfare in the region.

Foreign Conquest

The encounter between Africans and Europeans began in the early fifteenth century and changed the course of African history. The Portuguese established their first settlement at Ceuta in 1415, the second at Qsar es Seghir in 1458, and the third at Tangiers in 1471 (DeCorse 1998:221). The year 1488 is significant for African history, as it marked the establishment of what became a permanent European presence in sub-Saharan Africa. During that year, Bartholomew Dias and his crew successfully circumnavigated the Cape of Good Hope in search of a sea route to India around Africa. In 1498, Vasco da Gama ventured on to India, accomplishing the vision of Prince Henry the Navigator (Freeman-Grenville 1973:81). For the next two centuries, the Portuguese and their rivals, the Dutch and English, would vie for economic and political control in the Indian Ocean and the South Seas (Frank 1998; Pearson 1998; Ringrose 2001).

The Portuguese provoked local chiefdoms and states into wars that they won, and took control of the many ports of trade along the African coast (Kusimba 1999; Ringrose 2001:56). At this time, there were several hundred villages, towns, and cities along the length of the East African coast (Kirkman 1964;

Wilson 1978, 1980). These settlements were connected to each other through coastal and hinterland trade (Nicholls 1971). They were linked together by a common language, Kiswahili, which was the *lingua franca* of the region. The residents of the Coast were nominally Muslim, having adopted Islam as a regional religion earlier in ninth century (Horton 1996; Nurse and Spear 1985; Pouwels 2000). Portuguese eyewitness accounts provide testimony about the state of Coastal settlement at the beginning of the sixteenth century (Barbosa 1918).

The Portuguese used four methods to subjugate these coastal polities. First, they offered protection treaties with city-states and polities in exchange for an annual tribute to the King of Portugal. Second, they waged punitive expeditions against uncooperative city-states and polities, forcing them into becoming tribute-paying subjects of the King of Portugal. Third, they organized punitive expeditions against chiefdoms and city-states that defaulted on tribute payment. Finally, they often disguised themselves as pirates and plundered merchant ships on the high seas (Kusimba 1999).

The Portuguese adopted a scorched-earth policy in their wars against natives. Defeated towns were looted and burned, making it expensive to rebuild them. Surviving residents were sent into slavery abroad or enslaved locally (Barbosa 1918:39). Political instability due to Portuguese interference in local politics led to large-scale movements and migrations, and frequent violence between the inhabitants of the coast and the hinterlands (Newitt 1987). Insecurity was a major factor contributing to the decline in interregional trade and economy (Pearson 1998; Ringrose 2001).

Before the Portuguese dominance of the Red Sea and Indian Ocean, all merchant ships complied with the code of trade called *cartaz*. The *cartaz* was a shipping license that prevented unlicensed foreign merchant ships from navigating the waterways without paying taxes to the local port authorities. The *cartaz* also minimized piracy (Pearson 1998; Ringrose 2001:150). After the Portuguese gained control of the major Red Sea and Indian Ocean ports of trade, they imposed their own tax codes. However, the Portuguese were too few to efficiently police the Indian Ocean, and incidences of piracy and robbery on the high seas increased. Reports of insecurity and piracy inevitably discouraged merchants' fleets, particularly from Egypt, Arabia, and China, and gradually led to the severing of direct trade contacts amongst Indian Ocean trading partners. Jain (1990) and Chau (1967) have demonstrated that Arab and Chinese merchants conducted the bulk of the trade in the Indian Ocean between the eleventh and the mid-fifteenth centuries. After the mid-fifteenth century, the Ming dynasty stopped sponsoring overseas trade and concentrated on control of Chinese ports. The Portuguese traditional hatred for Muslim Arabs and

Turks motivated them to favor Indian merchants, especially Gujarati, over other merchants (Naqvi 1972; Pearson 1987). Consequently, Gujarati merchants monopolized Indian Ocean trade and, by the eighteenth century, were the largest financiers of Indian Ocean trade (Das Gupta 1987). Before the Portuguese conquest, the regional and international economy had been based on a traditional person-to-person exchange network in which friendship, brotherhood, alliances, and kinship ties were as important as the trade items themselves. The rules and regulations imposed by the conquerors weakened those traditional networks of commercial interaction and exchange.

Consequences of Slave Trade in East Africa

A number of African chiefdoms and societies traded with the Coast. Some are famously known to have had a monopoly of direct trade with the Coast: the Giriama, Akamba, and Oromo in Kenya and the Nyamwezi, Yao, and Makua in Tanzania and Mozambique (Figure 7.1). In Kenya, regional and interregional trade was carried out among the Akamba, Oromo, Taita, Waata, Giriama and Swahili from earlier times (Mutoro 1998; Robertson 1997). The Waata foragers of Tsavo hunted game such as elephant, rhino, zebra, buffalo, and ostrich, and sold the skins, dried meat, and ivory to Coastal Mijikenda in exchange for palm wine, cloth, grain, and beads. The Oromo pastoralists traded ivory and cattle with Pokomo, Giriama, and Swahili. The Taita agro-pastoralists visited the coast to sell sun-dried vegetables, meat, ivory, and grains in exchange for palm wine, cloth, beads, and hardware. The Taita would travel to Jomvu Market, near Mombasa, to sell ivory and cattle directly to Swahili, Arab, and Indian merchants. The Akamba were trading partners with Giriama, Taita, and Waata. The Akamba would come to Rabai as well as Jomvu, and Giriama traders would travel to Akamba land for ivory and cattle.

These trade relationships were dependent on fictive ties called *undugu wa chale* (blood brotherhoods) in Kiswahili (Herlehy 1984:293–294).[3] Brotherhoods provided opportunities for people who were otherwise strangers, competitors, and potential enemies to enter into fictive ties that legitimized their relationship and partnership beyond the family to the wider community. Membership in the community conferred certain advantages: freedom to exploit resources while enjoying the protection of the whole community. In this sense, brotherhoods served to reduce tensions and suspicions arising from competition for resources while simultaneously providing opportunities for access to technical and sacred knowledge (Herlehy 1984; Kusimba and Kusimba 2004).

Guns, wealth, and increased demand for slaves enabled some groups to shift from a subsistence economy to full-time trading in slaves, and this meant raiding and preying on other communities. The Nyamwezi, Yao, Makua in Tanzania, and

Swahili and Akamba in Kenya were the greatest beneficiaries. Before the eighteenth century, many hinterland groups including the Yao, Nyamwezi, Akamba, and Makua among others had been primarily agriculturists who also hunted and were involved in iron blacksmithing. The rising demand for ivory and slaves in the sixteenth and seventeenth centuries created opportunities for hinterland chiefs and elders to accumulate wealth through monopolization of long-distance trade and manipulation of sociopolitical power (Alpers 1969:405–420). For example, being matrilineal, Yao children traditionally belonged to the mother's lineage, preventing men from gaining political power. However, the ivory/slave-trade boom provided new opportunities to subvert the matrilineal system by enabling ambitious Yao dealers to accumulate slave women and their children. Enslaved women were free of the traditional *lobola*, or bride-wealth obligation, and their children belonged to the father's lineage under the new system. Thus, the Yao participation in the slave trade and acquisition of slave women created a new class of "Big Men," the merchant chiefs, who successfully increased their lineage and social and political power to extend their territorial boundaries. For example, Chief Mataka, whom David Livingstone met, was a slave trader and warrior who waged a series of wars, and conquered, enslaved, and sold many of his neighbors into slavery to the Arabs and Swahili (Alpers 1969:413–414).

The availability of guns and other weapons to slave raiders and dealers was responsible for the wars that devastated chiefdoms in southern Tanzania and northern Mozambique (Alpers 1975:98; Freeman-Grenville 1965; Sheriff 1987:42). Slave raids and warfare arising from the trade were so horrific that some groups killed themselves and their children to avoid enslavement. Others mutilated themselves in order to repel the slave raiders. Margery Perham (1979:214) relates a grim story of the Makonde:

> These were the first people I met who mutilate themselves as a decoration, except for the fairly common elongation of the ear. The women here make a hole in their upper lip and plug it with a piece of wood and stretch it with increasingly large plugs until they call to mind the duck-billed platypus. Their appearance is so horrible that it is depressing to go through their country. They cannot smile at you—they can hardly talk—when drinking water they have to pour down their throats and, their faces have no expression. . . . It is said that it was done at first to make them repulsive so they would not be raided by the slavers.

The transformation of these societies from subsistence agriculture to slave trading led to instability and insecurity. The increased wealth and overseas goods, including firearms, caused some groups like Yao and Makua to expand their territories and wage war against their neighbors.

The slave trade significantly changed the quality of life and relationships among communities. Legitimate trade and exchange declined. Trust amongst former trading partners and neighbors vanished. Large-scale slave raiding minimized interaction among different ethnic groups. The common saying in East Africa is that "those who live on the other side of the hill are cannibals who love to eat children," and I believe the folklore narratives of fear and distrust that I earlier described were shaped by this context. The slave trade was responsible for increased warfare, insecurity, displacement, relocation, and migrations. Famine and disease became daily experiences that crippled the subsistence economies of East African peoples. Depopulation, raiding, fear, and the abandonment of homes are common scenes missionaries and travelers described as they traversed the nineteenth century East African interior. Their accounts bear witness to the devastation wrought by the slave trade and the various responses that African peoples undertook to protect themselves from extermination. Obviously, the slave trade was a prominent economic practice in eighteenth and nineteenth century East Africa.

Livingstone discussed the depopulation caused by slave raiding. Near Lake Nyasa, a Waiyau chief he had stayed with was responsible for supplying Arab caravans with slaves:

> Here the destruction is quite recent . . . they almost depopulated the broad fertile tract, of some three or four miles between the mountain range and the Lake, along which our course lay. It was wearisome to see the skulls and bones scattered about everywhere; one would fain not to notice them, but they are so striking as one trudges along the sultry path, that it cannot be avoided (Livingstone 1880:97–98).

Accounts of explorers and missionaries bear witness to the terrible times East African peoples experienced. Slave raids and warfare caused people to flee their homes, leaving farms unattended. Farming declined, and people gradually lost the ability to feed themselves.

Large-scale and abrupt abandonment of farmsteads, villages, and towns to seek a new, more precarious way of life became the order of events in much of nineteenth century East Africa. Duff MacDonald (1882:76) noted that 4,000 inhabitants of an island in Lake Chirwa, in southern Malawi, were "obliged to live there for protection from slavers." Famine and disease epidemics in the late nineteenth century may have partly been caused by abrupt climate changes in the mid-nineteenth century, but they should also be seen in the light of the changes that weakened pre-existing networks of relationships that took care of resource shortages caused by droughts, insect infestations, and other natural disasters common in Africa. Formerly, when those crises occurred, people moved in with neighbors and affinal relatives until the crisis was over. The demand for slaves destroyed the safety network for interior people in crises (Ambler 1988; Benjamin 2002; Cooper 1977, 1980; Glassman 1983, 1991, 1995; Kraph 1860; Mazrui and Shariff 1994; Mbotela 1934; Merritt 1975:210; Robertson 1997:35; Willis 1993; Ylvisaker 1982).

Slave trade and slavery had a devastating effect on African people, and its repercussions have compromised the economy and stability of African societies up to the present day. But could slavery alone have been responsible for warfare in East Africa? The impact of environmental factors including droughts, famines, and diseases in causing warfare are discussed below.

Droughts, Famines, and Diseases

Climate change affects the balance of culture and nature and makes it difficult to sustain economic, political, and social stability (Fagan 2000). Abrupt climate changes cause people to drastically reorganize their survival strategies. Ecological disasters like droughts, earthquakes, floods, and disease epidemics often force people to respond in various uncharacteristic ways. Historically, these disasters have been blamed for the decline and collapse of many societies. The large-scale decline of urban centers after 500 A.C.E. in India (Dhavalikar 1996), the collapse of the Ethiopian kingdom of Aksum (Butzer 1981), and the devastation reported in thirteenth century American Southwest (Haas and Creamer 1993) have been linked to prolonged droughts (Dhavalikar 1999:8; Haas and Creamer 1993; LeBlanc 1999; Lekson 1999, 2002; Rice and LeBlanc 2001).

East Africa underwent periods of prolonged droughts during the sixteenth century. Rivers, wells, and water holes dried up; crops failed; and water-borne diseases including cholera, typhoid, and even plague were reported. Many previously densely inhabited areas along the coast and in the hinterland suffered population loss, as people migrated to more hospitable areas. For the coastal areas, Kirkman (1964) attributed the abandonment of many cities to climate change and warfare arising from competition over resources. Indeed, historians report that in East Africa, ecological crises such as drought and famine are among the most prominent markers in history. For example, among the Akamba of Kenya, some given names like Mutulungo, "the famine of privately acting," mean that each family struggled alone during this famine; Muvunga, loosely meaning, "rice," comes from small-scale European relief efforts including distribution of rice during this period. Like the Akamba, the Taita peoples of Tsavo recall their history by naming the times of the famine, which, on average, occurred once in five years. Eyewitness accounts and oral traditions show that the Tsavo region experienced severe drought and famine from the 1860s to the 1890s. Droughts and famine were often accompanied by cholera and smallpox. Believed to have started in Maasai country, these diseases rapidly spread to the coast and other regions by caravan traders (Merritt 1975:98). The Taita remember the Mwakisenge famine of 1885–1886 as the worst in their history. All rivers and springs dried up, there were massive die-offs of wildlife, and starving lions and other predators, including slave and food hunters, roamed the Tsavo plains. Fights over food caused many violent feuds resulting in deaths. People reportedly sold or leased their children into slavery in exchange for food. High mortality among children, women, and the elderly occurred. It is reported that even the hyenas could not dispose of the great numbers of bodies. Famine forced people to relocate wherever rumor suggested there would be food. Some Sagalla emigrated to Giriama, leaving their villages vulnerable to attack by slave hunters. The Dabida and Kasigau relocated to Taveta, Chagga, and Pare. Some Kasigau went to the coast and allowed themselves to be enslaved by the Swahili and Arabs in exchange for food. Of the estimated 10,000 Taita people before the Mwakisenge famine, only 1,000 survived. In short, the Mwakisenge famine killed 90 percent of the Taita (Merritt 1975:100–112).

In the past, traditional fictive relationships, like the brotherhoods, allowed East African peoples to temporarily relocate to their neighbors during ecological crises. Nineteenth century crises were different. Slavery and ethnic warfare had weakened traditional networks of alliances to the point where few societies trusted strangers and were willing to take them in. In fact, many took advantage of their neighbors' misfortunes and profited from them. It is said that desperate parents resorted to killing their own children because they could not feed them. Cannibalism was reported in many regions. Droughts, diseases, and famine played major roles in initiating warfare, but still they alone could not have been responsible for the violence that became so characteristic of eighteenth and nineteenth century Africa. In the next section, I discuss the role of elephants as a keystone species in shaping the cultural landscape histories of the region.

The Elephant Curse

The high demand for ivory in Western and Asian markets affected the East African environment less directly. However, its effects on the number and distribution of elephants, and the choices of places for human settlement, were overwhelming. The elephant has an important presence in African culture as image and material, and it is often represented in folklore and art. Its most important effect on humans, however, lies in the fact that it has shaped much of the natural African landscape, rendering it more fit for habitation by human beings. Richard Klein (1980) has speculated that the first significant interaction of elephant and human lineages may have been during the Pliocene, when

Loxodonts and other proboscideans created the first woodland environment where australopithecines are thought to have evolved. Since then, elephants have played a pivotal role in human affairs and an important role in shaping the ecosystem of African environments.

As they forage, elephants create and maintain broad paths through impenetrable bamboo and elephant grass belts, and in forested areas, they keep extensive glades in a permanent state of early succession, not only breaking down trees but also tearing up acres of saplings for their roots (Maugham 1906). They excavate and weed out water holes, and garden interconnected glades and clearings into tangled vegetation. Thus, elephants open up habitats for ground dwelling mammals. Such habitats are more productive, by reason of access to both sun and water, and more ecologically diverse than either deep forest or open grasslands. A major advantage of elephant-maintained environments from a human standpoint is that they are not hospitable to the tsetse fly, the vector of sleeping sickness for humans and trypanosomiasis for cattle, because the tsetse fly requires deep shade for survival. Elephants have opened up much of tropical Africa, particularly lowland areas, for pastoralists and agro-pastoralists.

Many elephant-hunting techniques have been used by African societies. Trapping through the use of pits and snares, seemingly the safest technique, has been limited in application, presumably because of the intelligence of the prey. Hence, traditional elephant hunters often had to rely on attacks on animals that were more or less freely moving and able to defend themselves, although perhaps partially immobilized by vegetation, terrain, or fire-ringing. Such attacks were dangerous and required long periods of training (Schweinfurth 1874:I, 438). They also required weapons with excellent cutting and penetrating qualities.

The introduction of high-quality iron and steel (and after the sixteenth century, guns) made possible the creation of effective elephant-killing weapons. Weapons of stone, bone, and wood were undoubtedly capable of killing elephants. But I do not believe that even the bravest and most skillful individuals would often have chosen to attack an elephant when armed with a spear or knife that might injure an eye or trunk but otherwise would barely penetrate the animal's skin. A heavy iron spear or an arrow with an iron point would offer a far greater likelihood that an elephant could be slowed or incapacitated in the initial attack, and we believe that this was what first made the routine hunting of elephants possible. The gun increased the range at which hunters could kill elephants. It also meant that relatively few specialized hunters could kill many more elephants.

The other prerequisite for large-scale, regular hunting of elephants in East Africa was a motive. This was supplied by the rise of the hinterland-coastal trade in ivory, both for use by local elites and for export. Historical sources make it clear that substantial quantities of ivory were being shipped to West Asia and the Mediterranean and probably to South Asia as well by the twelfth century (Kusimba and Bronson 2004; Pearson 1998; Thorbahn 1979). The trade must already have been in existence during the ninth century, when cities oriented toward overseas commerce first appeared on the Swahili coast.

It is proposed that this early demand for substantial quantities of ivory was the cause of an initial decline in elephant populations in the more accessible parts of the East African interior. Conducted largely by peripatetics like the modern Waata and Okiek (Kusimba 2003) armed with high-quality iron weapons, this early phase of the ivory trade must have caused significant rearrangements of the elephant population. It was evidently not as devastating as the second phase of the eighteenth and nineteenth centuries, marked by the introduction of effective guns and gunpowder. The first-phase hunters, after all, left a good many elephants for the second-phase hunters to kill. But any level of sustained, selective predation is enough to alter the distribution of animal populations, perhaps especially when the animals are as intelligent and as capable of intra-species communication as elephants. Elephants must have become much less common in the areas immediately adjacent to the coast and near the main trade routes to the interior.

The thinning out of local elephant populations would have led to important changes in vegetation. Dense forest cover would have developed in areas with sufficient rainfall and along rivers, and elephant grass and thorn bush in drier savannas. Tsetse flies would have increased in numbers, and with them trypanosomiasis. This, plus the decrease in available forage, would have had a strongly negative effect on the survival not only of humans but also of the domestic ruminants on which the majority of recent East African societies depend.

Guns facilitated the hunting of people for enslavement. They also allowed humans to kill too many elephants, which are major sustainers of tsetse-free grasslands. Numerous other factors, naturally, would also enter into the schistosomiasis-human relationship: local and regional shifts in rainfall quantities and distribution; degree of non-human and human predation on other grazing animals; intensity of swidden cultivation; the deliberate burning of forest and grasslands; non-industrial uses of wood by humans; the availability of tools capable of cutting sod and tilling established grassland; the presence of other effective elephant-killing methods (such as poison), and so forth. However, where guns were used extensively to hunt elephants, they may have played an important and even central role in promoting the spread of schistosomiasis. This may have been far more important, in both environmental and human terms, than the other factors listed.

Numerous epidemics and the area's declining ecological health—both captured in oral traditions and in the archaeological record—should be understood in these terms. Over-hunting of the elephant, a keystone species in the African savanna, had adverse effects on people and wildlife. After all, a large part of the peoples' diet, especially during lean seasons, was derived from wildlife, which in turn depended on the savanna grasslands that were opened and maintained by elephants. The elephant had its revenge when diseases wiped out about 60 percent of the people who had survived enslavement and about 90 percent of the cattle, buffalo, and other large mammals in East Africa by the 1890s. The elephant's victory, however, was to be relatively short-lived. Entering the scene was the colonial and professional white hunter, backed by his Maxim gun and other killing machines. The rest is history. In a final ironic reversal of fortune in the modern era, every conceivable conservation biologist, both amateur and professional, envisions teaching the "primitive" African ways of coexisting with the majestic elephants (Caputo 2002; Kurtis 1999; Patterson 1907).

In the next section, I tackle the vexing problem of archaeological correlates for warfare in African chiefdoms.

Fortified Rockshelters of Kasigau, Southeast Kenya

Mount Kasigau, hereafter Kasigau, is one of the four Taita Hills of southeastern Kenya. This prominent inselberg has continuously been inhabited for over 12,000 years. Some areas were more extensively modified than others. The variations in landforms, environment, and human activities on and around Kasigau have created different types of sites. Many sites were inhabited contemporaneously. These include rockshelters (some with ephemeral occupations, others with more substantial architectural investment); terrace sites with space for both housing and agriculture; and flatland sites both at the base and on top of the mountain. Today, the Kasigau area includes small villages, isolated homesteads (some of which are on terraces), and peripheral pastoral camps. I suspect the same type of subsistence diversity was present in the past as well.

Since beginning archaeological surveys in Kasigau in 2000, our field crew has located more than 40 archaeological and many ethnoarchaeological sites. Over the course of the project, we mapped a variety of sites and extensively excavated at eight rockshelters (Bungule 7, 9, 20, 28, 31, Kirongwe 1, 4, 5), a terrace (Bungule 29B), and an iron smelting site (Kirongwe 7). We also mapped three mortuary sites (Bungule 30, Makwasinyi 1, and Sungululu 1) and extensively studied skulls from two sites (Makwasinyi and Sungululu 1). Previously only three sites described by Robert Soper in the 1960s had been known (Soper 1966). In the following section, I describe excavation results at three rockshelter

Figure 7.2. Line drawing illustrating the fortified site of Bungule 28. Sites such as this were constructed beginning in the seventeenth century.

enclosures, Bungule 28, Bungule 31, and Bungule 20, and discuss their implications for understanding resistance to slavery by hinterland peoples (Figure 7.1, inset).

The Bungule 28 Fortified Rockshelter Enclosure

Bungule 28, hereafter B28, is composed of three large rocks with two overhanging rockshelters. The entrance to the shelter is up a steep slope and over the remains of a wall, which formerly enclosed the site. The wall enclosed the entire entrance to the shelter and was over seven m long at the mouth. The wall must have stood at least two m high in places when the site was still inhabited. There was a doorway to allow animals and people into the site (Figure 7.2).

Table 7.1. Radiocarbon Dates of Bungule 20 and Bungule 28

Lab number	Uncalibrated ages (years BP)	Calibrated ages A.D. (2 sigma)	Site	Site type
ISGS-5231	120±70	1671–1955	Bungule 20	Fortified Rockshelter
ISGS-5230	150±70	1670–1955	Bungule 20	Fortified Rockshelter
A-0218	207±40	1508–1955	Bungule 20	Fortified Rockshelter
ISGS-4873	290±70	1460–1955	Bungule 20	Fortified Rockshelter
ISGS-4874	300±70	1456–1955	Bungule 20	Fortified Rockshelter
ISGS-5232	330±70	1449–1804	Bungule 20	Fortified Rockshelter
ISGS-5233	380±70	1434–1670	Bungule 20	Fortified Rockshelter
ISGS-5229	790±70	1158–1392	Bungule 20	Not fortified
ISGS-5054	170±70	1654–1955	Bungule 28	Fortified Rockshelter
ISGS-5059	180±70	1653–1955	Bungule 28	Fortified Rockshelter
ISGS-5067	180±70	1653–1955	Bungule 28	Fortified Rockshelter
ISGS-5056	240±70	1510–1955	Bungule 28	Fortified Rockshelter

The site is small, only 10-m-long, 6-m-wide, and 1.5-m-high. Loess and rock fall have filled many areas, leaving little standing room. Some areas where the rocks have not spalled are stained with soot, suggesting the shelter had fire hearths. The surface collections made in the enclosure consisted of goat dung and small artifacts, porcupine quills, dik dik (*Madoqua kirkii*) bones, and twine. The shelter has an entrance and exit, allowing air to flow through the site. The view of the surrounding landscape is excellent from the site.

Excavations conducted in the interior of the rockshelter and in a midden at the entrance revealed the contemporaneous use of the enclosure by humans and their livestock. A low wooden wall partitioned spaces for people from those of livestock. The area designated as Area I (A1) yielded a hearth, maize cobs, calabash seeds, two small pink beads, charcoal, bones, shell and seeds, and wooden arrowheads. Twine and some metal pieces were also recovered. The area was kept clean by tossing the refuse outside the shelter entrance. Area 2 (A2) contained large amounts of fossilized animal dung, layered in thick heaps. There were large pieces of wood interspersed in the dung that were mostly likely used to tether the animals. No ash was associated with A2, and while some artifacts including beads, charcoal, bones, and shell were recovered, A2 appears to have primarily been reserved for penning animals.

Excavations at B28 revealed at least three habitation sequences. During the first phase, people exclusively used the shelter. An ostrich eggshell bead recovered in this phase indicated strong links with the pastoral Neolithic peoples identified in nearby B9 and in the Tsavo Park. During the second phase, humans and livestock contemporaneously inhabited the site. Based on uncalibrated radiocarbon dates of 170±70, 180±70, and 240±70 B.P., rockshelter fortification began less than 400 years ago (Table 7.1). During the early twentieth century, the enclosure was used predominately as a goat pen.

The artifacts recovered suggested that B28 was a sub-component of the Kasigau sociopolitical system. There were very few ceramics at the site, suggesting the infrequent use of the rockshelter in meal preparation. The beads recovered throughout the site suggested the existence of trade relationships with the coast. B28 residents had access to agricultural products such as millet, sorghum, maize, and gourds, and hunted to supplement their diet. They also tended animals for milk and meat.

In sum, evidence from B28 suggests that livestock were doubly protected from the outside by the exterior dry stone enclosure and the wooden fence. A great deal of effort was expended to dig strong foundations to secure the walls.

The Bungule 31 Fortified Rockshelter Enclosure

The second site, Bungule 31 (B31), is a rockshelter enclosure located up a steep slope about 500 meters west of B28. Located at the top of an almost vertical 20-m slope, the shelter is formed by one large rock leaning into another, creating a triangular opening. The interior length was 9 m across the front, the maximum interior depth (to the north) was 8 m, and the interior height varied from 1.6 m at the center of the cave to 1.0 m at the doorway in the north and 2.0 m at the highest point in the south (Figure 7.3).

A wall had been constructed across the mouth of the shelter. The entrance was well preserved: three vertical slabs remained in place, and two large Y-shaped wooden posts with cross pieces of wood blocked the doorway. Inside, the northwestern part of the shelter was at a slightly lower elevation and contained a pile of interlocked sticks, which could have been a bed or a partition. As usual, the partitioned area was near the entrance and received light. The southeastern part of the shelter was at a slightly higher elevation and more rocky (although the surface remained even). In the far southeast on top of some boulders and beyond the described shelter limits was a low-ceilinged potential sleeping area. No pottery was recovered on the surface, and the only surface animal remains were a heavily gnawed lesser kudu mandible and a porcupine quill.

In terms of the spatial arrangement of activities in the site, three areas were noted. First, the dry-stone architecture on the exterior of the shelter had collapsed in many areas, and the rocks and wooden posts of the construction were scattered outside and immediately inside the entrance. The wooden posts in this architecture average eight to ten cm in diameter and some of the posts were two to three m in length. The second area was an internal wooden construction located immediately north of the entrance to the shelter that may have

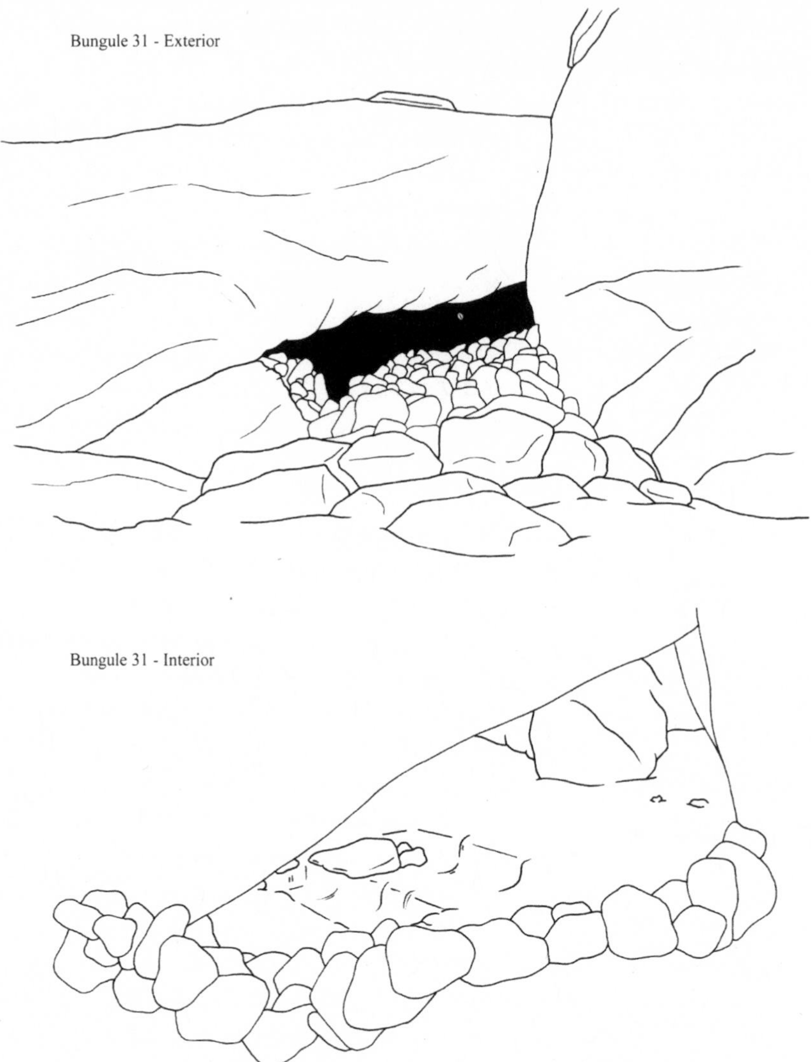

Figure 7.3. Line drawing of Bungule 31.

acted as an organizational feature of the internal space of the shelter. The wood used to build the structure is different from the thick wooden posts used in the dry-stone architecture, averaging two to three cm in diameter. Excavations of B31 provided a great deal of information on the use of space in rockshelter sites. Based on our finds, the shelter was divided into two main areas. First, the eastern higher part of the shelter (as in B28) represents the goat-pen space of the site. Evidence for goat pastoralism, including dung and the burning of dung, are found in the rocky area of the shelter. Second, the western lower/flatter part of the shelter (roughly one-third of the whole) was set aside for people. As in B28, the size of the enclosure could comfortably hold three to five people. The sparseness of the material remains point to the possible intermittent use of the enclosure. Like B28, a great deal of labor, time, and materials were invested in building the enclosure.

The Bungule 20 Fortified Rockshelter Enclosure

The most intact of the Kasigau rockshelter enclosures is Bungule 20 (B20). The enclosure is faced with a large stone wall reaching nearly two m in height (Figures 7.4 and 7.5). The wall is supported by a vertical wooden frame. Erosion of

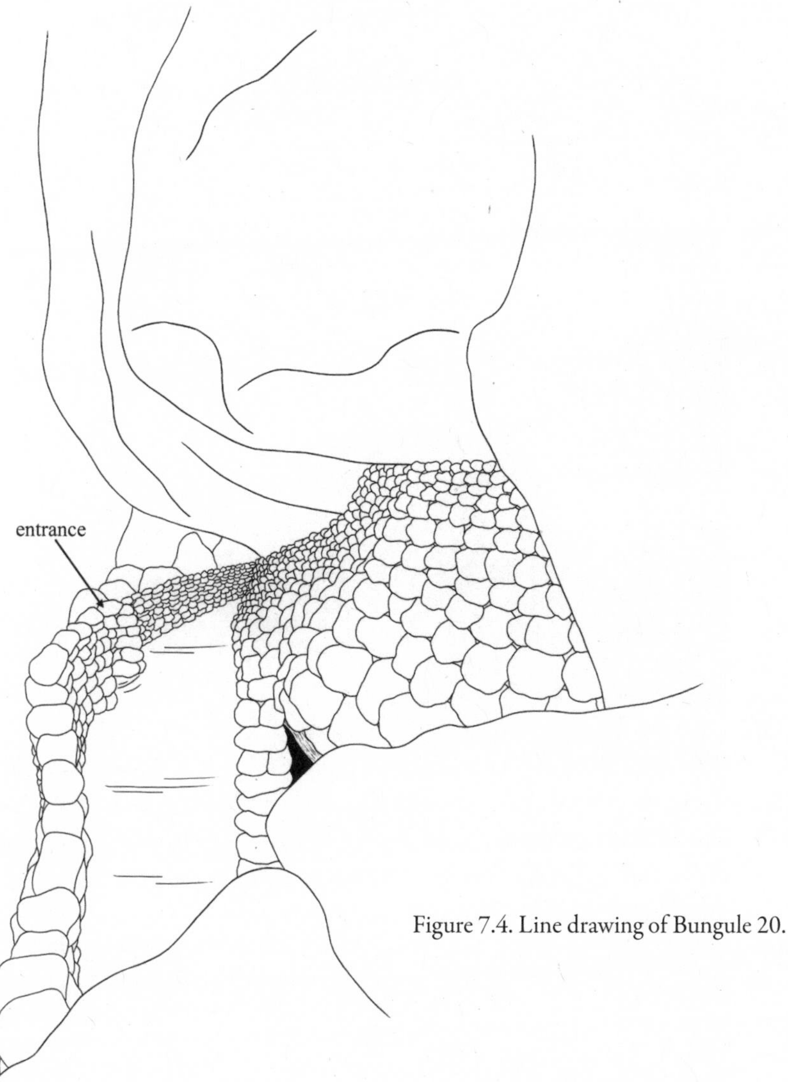

Figure 7.4. Line drawing of Bungule 20.

Figure 7.5. Photograph of Bungule 20.

the terrace and cliff has moved the stone wall, leaving a gap of about one m. The doorway is a tunnel at least 1.5-m long under the wall and is lined with vertical slabs supporting at least four heavy beams which in turn support the meter of rocks above. The doorway emerges into an area protected by a wooden partition, which runs parallel to the wall. This entire front portion of the shelter is littered with cultural debris including ceramics, and was the likely site for human occupation activities. Behind the partition, piles of dessicated dung domi-

Table 7.2. Intensity of Desiccated Dung Deposits at Bungule 20

Dung layer	Location and thickness
E in east strata; Level 12	~112–125 cm, Squares B2 and B3 ~10 cm thick
C in east strata; Level 10 and 11, includes organic	~95–112 cm, Squares B2 and B3; ~10–12 cm thick
D in east strata: Levels 6, 7, 9, 10 (burnt dung)	~59–60 cm, Squares B3 and B4; ~30–35 cm thick
B in east strata; Levels 6, 7, 8, 9 (dense dung)	~59–60 cm, Squares B2 and B3; ~30–32 cm thick

nate the shelter. The dung extended under the front wall to the paths outside and a clear, sheltered area adjacent to the enclosure.

B20 is one of the largest rockshelters in Kasigau, measuring 66 m^2 with a ceiling ranging between .30 and 1.75 m high. As in other enclosures, a partitioned area was constructed to separate people from their animals. Surface finds include an almost-intact bed, a hearth, and pottery sherds. These appear to be modern surface deposits not associated with the primary *in situ* archaeological deposits. Three radiocarbon samples obtained from the vines and wood holding the dry stone wall had uncalibrated radiocarbon ages of 207±40, 290±70, 300±70 B.P., placing the calibrated date of construction of the dry wall some time in the last 400 years at two standard deviations.

Excavations also revealed a detailed process of dry-stone construction, involving a foundation, a wooden frame composed of termite-resistant poles secured with twine before piling on dry stones, which were strengthened by clay mortar. The final structure was strong, impenetrable, and aesthetically pleasing. The wooden enclosure may have served multiple functions.

The dung deposits both in the exterior and interior enclosures reveal the intensity of pen feeding that was carried out at the site. Table 7.2 illustrates the intensity of dung deposits in the outside section east of the shelter.

Archaeological Implications of Fortified Rockshelters

How may we interpret the archaeological data recovered from B28, B31, and B20? Comparatively few archaeological finds were recovered from all of the enclosures, suggesting that they primarily functioned as centers for pen feeding of animals and as refuges for humans. Based on our survey and excavation data, a number of features characterize dry-stone architecture in the Kasigau area. First, all rockshelter enclosures date from the last 400 years B.P., a time when large-scale slavery and slave trading was prevalent in Africa. Rockshelter fortification signaled a departure from the traditional practice of erecting wooden frame enclosures or using open rockshelters as temporary camps. Second, all three sites had an entrance and an exit. The exit was not always easily detectable from outside and appears to have been designed to allow humans to leave the enclosure either undetected or without having to use the main entrance. Third, rockshelter fortification requiring deep foundations, strong wooden frameworks, and mortar suggests the primary motive for their construction was defense.

Several inferences can be drawn from these data. Without doubt Kasigau people had prior experience in dry-stone architecture and used a specific design to build the rockshelter enclosures. Rockshelter fortification required leadership and labor mobilization common among chiefdoms and early states. Based on the radiocarbon dates, all the rockshelters were constructed and used in the mid-eighteenth through the late nineteenth centuries. Human occupation of the shelters ended in the early twentieth century, but they continued to be used as goat pens.[4] These enclosures have comparatively little cultural material, strongly suggesting they were intermittently used as "maroons" or refuges to which people and livestock retreated when they were under siege (Agorsah 1993).

Investment in the construction of fortified rockshelters raises a number of questions. Post-sixteenth-century East Africa was punctuated by the ivory and slave trade. The wars to secure slaves caused widespread unrest, which contributed to the decline and collapse of farming and pastoral chiefdoms and states, leaving people more vulnerable to famine (Kusimba 1999, 2004). Dwindling elephant populations due to over-hunting left the savanna poorly maintained and thus they reverted to woodlands and forests that became hosts to the tsetse fly. People responded to disease by relocating to other areas, primarily the cooler and healthier mountaintops. How may we then interpret the Kasigau fortified rockshelter data?

Historical accounts, oral traditions, location and investment in the rockshelters provide multiple lines of evidence that rockshelter fortification in Kasigau was primarily for defensive purposes. Dry-stone architecture specifically for penning animals is not widely practiced among African pastoralists. Fortifying animal corrals is unnecessary and economically irresponsible. The structural design and internal use of space suggests strategies that took advantage of the landscape to effectively respond to a specific threat. The walls were so thick they would have required considerable effort to break. Such walls were not necessary for the safety of livestock.

I have shown that a number of reasons compelled the people of Kasigau to fortify rockshelters. Oral traditions suggest that when slave-raiding and cattle-rustling intensified in the Tsavo region, people abandoned their settlements in the valleys and plains for the safety of the hill tops, caves, and fortified rockshelters (Kusimba 2004). These oral narratives are bolstered by the fact that many unprotected rockshelters were not used during this period, nor were the villages in the plains and the base of the hills. Tsetse fly infestation in the plains could have contributed to shifting of homesteads to cooler hillside and hilltop residences, as well as defensive considerations.

Before the eighteenth and nineteenth centuries, the Kasigau area was an important trading partner with the Coast. It was located on the caravan route from the Coast into the hinterland. The people of Kasigau were active participants in the trade networks, as suppliers of resources for the traders and their cargo. The evidence from the excavation of three rockshelters B28, B31, and B20 suggest a shifting scenario. All three sites exhibited little evidence for trade except for a few beads, implying little participation in the economic interactions that had been ongoing in earlier periods. This lack of a material connection to trade, coupled with the evidence for defensive sites on the hill, suggests a shift in the nature of relationships between Kasigau and the Coast. Afraid of regular raids from better-armed and numerically superior enemies, the Kasigau people responded by moving up the hillsides and abandoned cattle herding in favor of goat herding.

Discussion and Conclusion

Numerous factors caused warfare in East Africa. I have argued that four centuries of demand for ivory and enslaved people, together with climate change, weakened traditional means of conflict resolution amongst neighboring chiefdoms and states. Alliance systems that existed amongst different ethnic groups were irreparably destroyed. The insecurity wrought by slaving expeditions destroyed agrarian and pastoral systems and made people more prone to crises, creating instability, suspicion, fear, and indigence. Droughts, accompanied by disease epidemics including cholera, typhoid, and famine, further destroyed societies affected by slave raiding. It would be naïve to argue that conflict and warfare did not exist before large-scale slave trade. Conflict was indeed part of the cultural mosaic of East Africa. However, the slave trade changed the conduct of warfare in East Africa—for instance, surrender in combat was very quickly forgotten. Losing a war meant losing your wealth and being enslaved as well. Gone was the style of combat in which "a warrior wishing to surrender lifted his spear above his head and shouted 'Take cattle!'" (Fadiman 1982:46; Keeley 1996:85, citing Huntingford 1953:77–78; Otterbein 1967:352). As a result, skirmishes became bloodier and more ruthless as combatants fought to the death rather than be taken or witness their family taken into slavery. Slavery disrupted previous relations of debt peonage (with rights) transforming it into modern chattel slavery. As the slave trade became more prevalent and people began to associate it with the coast, the relationship between the coast and the hinterland increasingly became strained (Benjamin 2002:305; Glassman 1983, 1995; Willis 1993:52).

The archaeological, ethnographic, historical, and oral accounts discussed here show how slavery and warfare that arose from this political economy disrupted the way of life of African people for more than 400 years, or sixteen generations. Post-sixteenth-century fortified settlements, including hilltops, rockshelters, and cave dwellings; sacred and ritual sites; market centers; trade routes; tombs and graves along trade routes; cemeteries; and residential quarters of both free people and slaves on plantations provide overwhelming material evidence for slavery, slave trade, and warfare. These sites demonstrate that recognizing slave trade through archaeology in East Africa is not only possible, but long overdue. The onus for archaeology now is to develop innovative methodologies for studying these numerous sites. Although as Alexander (2001) reminds us, there are problems of direct association of slave material culture from the free and slaves in Africa, one can go beyond this predicament by utilizing indirect evidence—enslaved peoples' narratives of resistance to domination often have within them coded messages for which there is no corresponding material evidence. Often the slave culture of resistance minimized material possessions, making it difficult for archaeology to identify (for example, Agorsah 1990, 1993; Baker 2001; Orser 1996; Orser and Funari 2001; Singleton 1999, 2001). We need to develop ways of decoding these messages in order to identify them archaeologically. This study shows that there is abundant archaeological data waiting to be carefully studied. Slave plantations, runaway slave settlements along the coast of East Africa, and fortified settlements in the interior should form the basis for the archaeological study of enslaved peoples' resistance to slavery—similar to work done in the United States and the Caribbean. Fortified settlements in the interior can be studied as the record of African peoples' responses to slavery. Coastal households and plantations need to be carefully surveyed, mapped, and excavated to show the nature of relationships between masters and slaves. Here, more overt forms of resistance could be discerned through the careful study of the artifacts associated with ritual, magic, witchcraft, infanticide, sterility, and so forth.

In sum, I have shown that post-sixteenth-century East Africa was a difficult place to live for African peoples. The peoples' narratives carry numerous messages of a changing cultural and ecological landscape. For example, the name adopted for Tsavo means "the place of slaughter" in the Akamba language, suggesting the people's perceptions about the place and especially their relationship to it. The narratives in folklore at this time emphasized conformity, nurtured mistrust and cultivated hatred for the other. I have shown here that archaeologists can mine narratives to explain the intangible past. With a little openness, archaeology's contributions to the debate on slavery trade in Africa are potentially rich.

To conclude, warfare in post-sixteenth-century East Africa was caused by numerous factors that were both naturally and culturally induced. These factors were related in very complex ways. Even the devastation wrought by what we think of as external factors, like natural disasters, has to be understood in terms of the human-made social destabilization which prevented traditional mechanisms from coping with them adequately. Internal factors like attitudes of fear and distrust, which encouraged warfare and hostility, were themselves shaped by an environment of warfare and slave raiding. Factors we think of as subsidiary, like the ivory trade, actually affected the environment and human settlement in dramatic and unforeseen ways. Despite the terrible devastation brought by slavery and the other crises to this era, East Africans showed themselves to be resourceful, resistant, and resilient, as shown by the evidence in the fortified rockshelters. Archaeology has great potential to uncover this history. Along with the sensitive interpretation of survivors' oral narratives and folklore, it can bring to light the stories of those who never wrote histories, and whose perspectives are not included or preferred in traditional academic histories.

Notes

1. Although Keeley makes a powerful argument for the evidence of conflict and organized violence in the past, the interpretation of warfare in the past is still problematic. He mentions three points that I find problematic: a) Primitive societies were and are far more violent than modern state societies in terms of homicide rates; b) The number of people involved in actual warfare is greater in primitive societies than in modern societies; and, c) Straightforward comparisons of homicide rates of modern states and hunter-gatherer groups suggest that homicide and hence organized violence is far greater in non-state as opposed to state level societies.

Since present hunter-gatherer communities are marginalized economically and socially, their loss of agency can be directly correlated with their level of crime. Maybe a better comparison would be to compare homicide rates in high-density or inner-city areas of modern states where similar conditions of marginality apply. Modern homicide rates are also offset by modern medicine and its ability to cure near-fatal wounds. Such techniques were not available and still are not available to hunter-gatherer or rural communities wherein even non-lethal wounds can ultimately cause gangrene or sepsis and turn fatal. Maybe a better test would be to compare hospital records in high-density or inner-city areas for the total number of assault cases that would have been fatal had they not been treated.

The social division of labor is less in hunter-gatherer societies than in state level societies. Hence, more people rely on the same resources (especially in marginal economic zones), leading to violence. The homicide rates must be compared with the overlap of resources and strategies causing strife in modern hunter-gatherer communities.

The other major problem that arises in *War Before Civilization* is that Keeley uses a straightforward comparison between population and number of people affected by warfare. So, the interpretation that in primitive societies (which are smaller), a larger percent of population will be affected by warfare seems confirmed by the statistical data. However, the statistical data might confirm losses and profit but it does not explain the relation between population and number of warring peoples (Rahul Oka, personal communication 2003).

2. A scientific perspective characterized by laws of great generality and scope from which numerically precise predictions can derive is impossible. However, a science characterized by a search for understanding by means of statements of general laws that have undergone the most critical examination in pursuit of better and deeper insights is achievable in the social sciences and humanities (Goldstein and Goldstein 1978:6–8).

3. The blood-brotherhood ceremony involved sacrificing a goat or chicken, then making cuts in the participants' chests and rubbing the meat, usually a liver, into the wounds and exchanging and eating the blood-soaked meat. The participants would then pledge brotherhood, loyalty, and protection of each other and their families. It was believed that misfortune would befall any individual or close members of his family and extended family if that oath was broken (Bakari 1981:167–168).

4. Some rockshelters at lower elevations are being mined for house construction. Some residents have begun using the fossil dung to fertilize their vegetable gardens.

References

Agorsah, K. E. 1990. Archaeology of Maroon Heritage in Jamaica. *Archaeology Jamaica* 2:14–19.

———. 1993. Archaeology and Resistance History in the Caribbean. *African Archaeological Review* 11:175–195.

Alexander, J. 2001. Islam, Archaeology and Slavery in Africa. *World Archaeology* 33(1):44–60.

Alpers, E. A. 1969. Trade, State and Society Among Yao in the Nineteenth Century. *Journal of African History* 10(30):405–420.

———. 1975. *Ivory and Slaves in East and Central Africa.* London: Heinemann Press.

Ambler, C. 1988. *Kenyan Communities in the Age of Imperialism.* New Haven: Yale University Press.

Bah, T. M. 1976. The Impact of Wars on Housing in Pre-Colonial Black Africa. *African Environment* 76:3.

———. 2003. Slave-Raiding and Defensive Systems South of Lake Chad from the Sixteenth to the Nineteenth Century. In *Fighting the Slave Trade: West African Strategies,* edited by A. Diouf, 16–30. Athens: Ohio University Press.

Bakari, M. B. 1981. *Customs of the Swahili People.* Berkeley: University of California Press.

Baker, H. D. 2001. Degrees of Freedom: Slavery in Mid-First Millennium B.C. Babylonia. *World Archaeology* 33:18–26.

Barbosa, D. 1967 [1918]. *The Book of Duarte Barbosa: An Account of the Countries Bordering on the Indian Ocean and Their Inhabitants, Written by Duarte Barbosa and Completed in 1518 A.D.* Milwood, NY: Kraus Reprint.

Baskerville, R. G. 1922. *The King of the Snakes and Other Folklore Stories from Uganda.* London: Sheldon Press.

Benjamin, J. J. 2002. East Africa and the World: The Relationship of Knowledge and Power in the Construction of History, Race, and Identity. Unpublished Ph.D. dissertation, Department of Anthropology, State University of New York.

Billman, B. R., P. M. Lambert, and B. L. Leonard. 2000. Cannibalism, Warfare, and Drought in the Mesa Verde Region During the 12th Century A.D. *American Antiquity* 65:145–178.

Brown, C. 1991. *The Illustrated History of Canada.* Toronto: Lester.

Butzer, K. W. 1981. Rise and Fall of Axum, Ethiopia: A Geo-Archaeological Interpretation. *American Antiquity* 46:471–495.

Callaway, H. 1885. *The Religious System of the Amazulu*. London: The Folklore Society.

Caputo, P. 2002. *The Ghost of Tsavo: Tracking the Mythic Lions of East Africa*. Washington, D.C.: National Geographic Society.

Carneiro, R. 1990. Chiefdom-level Warfare as Exemplified in Fiji and the Cauca Valley. In *The Anthropology of War*, edited by J. Haas, 190–211. New York: Cambridge University Press.

Cassey, J. 1998. The Ecology of Food Production in West Africa. In *Transformations in Africa: Essays on Africa's Later Past*, edited by G. Connah, 48–70. Leicester: Leicester University Press.

Chatelain, H. 1894. *Folk-Tales of Angola*. Boston: G.E. Stechert.

Chau, J. K. 1967. [12th century] *Chu Fan Chi: Chinese and Arab Trade in the Twelfth and Thirteenth Centuries*. Translated by R. Hirth and W. W. Rockhill. St. Petersburg: The Imperial Academy of Sciences.

Cooper, F. 1977. *Plantation Slavery on the East Coast of Africa*. New Haven: Yale University Press.

———. 1980. *From Slaves to Squatters: Plantation Labor and Agriculture in Zanzibar and Coastal Kenya, 1890–1925*. Nairobi: Kenya Literature Bureau.

Cordell, D. D. 2003. The Myth of Inevitability and Invincibility: Resistance to Slavers and the Slave Trade in Central Africa, 1850–1910. In *Fighting the Slave Trade: West African Strategies,* edited by S. A. Diouf, 31–49. Athens: Ohio University Press.

Curtin, P. D. 1984. *Cross-Cultural Trade in World History.* New York: Cambridge University Press.

Curtin, P. D., (editor). 1967. *Africa Remembered: Narratives by West Africans from the Era of the Slave Trade*. Madison: University of Wisconsin Press.

Das Gupta, A. 1987. Introduction II: The Story. In *India and the Indian Ocean*, edited by A. Das Gupta and M. N. Pearson, 25–45. Oxford: Oxford University Press.

De Barros, P. 2001. The Effects of the Slave Trade on the Bassar Iron Working Society of Togo. In *West Africa During the Atlantic Slave Trade: Archaeological Perspectives,* edited by C. DeCorse, 59–80. Leicester: Leicester University Press.

DeCorse, C. R. 1998. The Europeans in West Africa: Culture Contact, Continuity, and Change. In *Transformations in Africa: Essays on Africa's Later Past,* edited by G. Connah, 219–244. Leicester: Leicester University Press.

DeCorse, C. R., (editor). 2001. *West Africa during the Atlantic Slave Trade: Archaeological Perspectives*. Leicester: Leicester University Press.

Denette, R. E. 1898. *Notes on the Folk-lore of the Fjort (French Congo)*. London: Folklore Society.

Dhavalikar, M. K. 1996. Environment: Its Influence on History and Culture in Western India. *Indica* 33(2):81–118.

———. 1999. The Golden Age and After: Perspectives in Historical Archaeology. Presidential Address to the Indian History Congress, Platinum Jubilee (60th) Session. Calicut, India.

Dikshitar, R.V.R. 1944. *War in Ancient India*. New Delhi: Motilal Banarsidass Publication.

Diouf, S. A. 2003. *Fighting the Slave Trade: West African Strategies*. Columbus: Ohio University Press.

Dongoske, K., D. L. Martin, and T. J. Fergusson. 2000. Critique of the Claims of Cannibalism at Cowboy Wash. *American Antiquity* 65:179–190.

Ember, C., and M. Ember. 1992. Resource Unpredictability, Mistrust, and War: A Cross-Cultural Study. *Journal of Conflict Resolution* 36:242–262.

Ember, M. 1982. Statistical Evidence for an Ecological Explanation of Warfare. *American Anthropologist* 84:732–752.

Ember, M., and C. Ember. 1995. Worldwide Cross-Cultural Studies and Their Relevance for Archaeology. *Journal of Archaeological Research* 3:87–111.

Fadiman, J. A. 1982. *An Oral History of Tribal Warfare: The Meru of Mt. Kenya*. Athens: Ohio University Press.

Fagan, B. 2000. *The Little Ice Age: How Climate Made History*. New York: Basic Books.

Ferguson, R. B. 1984. Introduction: Studying War. In *Warfare, Culture, and Environment*, edited by R. B. Ferguson, 1–82. Orlando: Academic Press.

———. 1990. Explaining War. In *The Anthropology of War*, edited by J. Haas, 26–55. New York: Cambridge University Press.

———. 1998. Violence and War in Prehistory. In *Troubled Times: Violence and Warfare in the Past*, edited by D. Martin and D. Frayer, 312–355. War and Society Series. Volume 4. Amsterdam: Gordon and Breach.

Forsbrooke, H. A. 1960. The 'Masai Walls' of Moa: Walled Towns of the Segeju. *Tanganyika Notes and Records* 41:30–37.

Frank, A. G. 1998. *ReOrient: Global Economy in the Asia Age.* Berkeley: University of California Press.

Freeman-Grenville, G.S.P. 1965. *The French at Kilwa Island: An Episode in Eighteenth Century East African History*. Oxford: Clarendon.

———. 1973. *Chronology of African History*. Oxford: Oxford University Press.

Friedlander, S. 1997. *Nazi Germany and the Jews: The Years of Persecution 1933–39*. London: Phoenix Giant.

Gates, H. L., Jr. 1996. *Wonders of the African World*. New York: Knopf.

Gay, P. 1993. *The Cultivation of Hatred: The Bourgeoisie Experience: Victoria to Freud*, vol. 3. New York: W. W. Norton and Company.

Gillman, C. 1944. Annotated List of Ancient and Modern Indigenous Structures in Eastern Africa. *Tanganyika Notes and Records* 17:44–55.

Glassman, J. 1983. The Runaway Slave in Coastal Resistance to Zanzibar: The Case of the Witu Sultanate. Master's thesis, Department of Anthropology, Madison, University of Wisconsin.

———. 1991. The Bondsman's New Clothes: The Contradictory Consciousness of Slave Resistance on the Swahili Coast. *Journal of African History* 32(2):277–312.

———. 1995. *Feasts and Riot: Revelry, Rebellion and Popular Consciousness on the Swahili Coast, 1856–1888*. Portsmouth: Heinemann.

Goldstein, M., and I. F. Goldstein. 1978. *How We Know: An Exploration of the Scientific Process*. New York: Plenum Press.

Haas, J. 1990. Warfare and the Evolution of Tribal Politics in the Prehistoric Southwest. In *The Anthropology of War*, edited by J. Haas, 171–189. New York: Cambridge University Press.

———. 2002. Warfare and the Evolution of Culture. In *Archaeology at the Millennium: A Source Book*, edited by G. M. Feinman and T. D. Price, 329–350. New York: Kluwer Academic Publishers.

Haas, J., and W. Creamer. 1993. *Stress and Warfare Among the Kayenta Anasazi of the Thirteenth Century A.D.* Fieldiana: Anthropology, n.s. 21. Chicago: Field Museum of Natural History.

Harris, J. E. 1971. *The African Presence in Asia: Consequences of the East African Slave Trade*. Evanston: Northwestern University Press.

———. 1985. Malik Ambar: African Regent-Minister in India. In *African Presence in Early Asia*, edited by I Van Sertima and R Rashidi. Journal of African Civilizations 7(1). New Brunswick: Transaction Books.

Herlehy, T. J. 1984. Ties That Bind. *International Journal of African Historical Studies* 17(2):285–308.

Hobley, C. W. 1929. *From Chartered Company to Crown Colony*. London: Frank Cass.

Holl, A.F.C. 2002. *The Land of Houlouf: Genesis of a Chadic Chiefdom (1900 B.C.–1800 A.D.)*. Ann Arbor: University of Michigan Museum of Anthropology.

Horton, M. 1996. *Shanga: A Muslim Trading Community on the East African Coast*. Nairobi: British Institute in Eastern Africa.

Huntingford, G.W.B. 1953. *The Nandi of Kenya: Tribal Control in a Pastoral Society*. London: Routledge and Kegan Paul.

Ilife, J. 1995. *Africa: History of a Continent*. Cambridge: Cambridge University Press.

Insoll, T. 1999. *The Archaeology of Islam*. Boston: Blackwell Publishers.

Jain, V.K. 1990. *Trade and Traders in Western India*. New Delhi: Munshiram Manoharlal Publishers Pvt. Ltd.

Johnson, A. W., and T. K. Earle. 2000. *The Evolution of Human Societies: From Foraging Group to Agrarian State.* 2nd ed. Stanford: Stanford University Press.

Keeley, L. H. 1996. *War Before Civilization: The Myth of the Peaceful Savage.* New York: Oxford University Press.

Kirkman, J. S. 1964. *Men and Monuments on the East African Coast.* London: Lutterworth Press.

Klein, R. G. 1980. Environmental and Ecological Implications of Large Mammals from Upper Pleistocene and Holocene Sites in Southern Africa. *Annals of the South African Museum* 81:223–283.

Kolb, M. J., and B. Dixon. 2002. Landscapes of War: Rules and Conventions of Conflict in Ancient Hawai'i (and Elsewhere). *American Antiquity* 67:514–534.

Kraph, J. L. 1860. *Travels, Researches, and Missionary Labours During an Eighteen Year's Residence in Eastern Africa.* Boston: Ticknor and Fields.

Kurtis, W. 1999. *The Maneaters of Tsavo.* Chicago: Kurtis Productions.

Kusimba, C. M. 1999. *The Rise and Fall of Swahili States.* Walnut Creek, CA: Altamira Press.

———. 2004. Archaeology of Slavery in East Africa. *African Archaeological Review* 21(2): 59–88.

Kusimba, C. M., and B. Bronson. 2004. Iron and Environment in East Africa. *South African Archaeological Bulletin* 71:6–7.

Kusimba, C. M., and S. B. Kusimba. 2004. East Africa. In *African Archaeology: A Critical Introduction,* edited by A. B. Stahl, 394–419. Cambridge: Blackwell.

Kusimba, S. B. 2003. *African Foragers.* Walnut Creek, CA: Altamira Press.

Lambert, P. M. 2002. The Archaeology of War: A North American Perspective. *Journal of Archaeological Research.* 10(3):207–242.

Lambert, P. M., B. L. Leonard, B. R. Billman, R. A. Marlar, M. E. Newman, and K. J. Reinard. 2000. Response to Critique of the Claim of Cannibalism at Cowboy Wash. *American Antiquity* 65:397–406.

LeBlanc, S. A. 1999. *Prehistoric Warfare in the American Southwest.* Salt Lake City: University of Utah Press.

Lekson, S. H. 1999. Chaco Canyon Death Squads. *Archaeology* (May/June):67–73.

———. 2002. War in the Southwest, War in the World. *American Antiquity* 67:607–624.

Livingstone, D. 1880. *Last Journals of David Livingstone in Central Africa From 1865 to His Death.* London: John Murray.

Lovejoy, P. E. 2000. *Transformation in Slavery: A History of Slavery in Africa.* 2nd ed. Cambridge: Cambridge University Press.

MacDonald, D. 1882. *Africana: or, the Heart of Heathen Africa.* Vol. 1. London: London: Simpkin Marshall.

McInnis, E. 1969. *Canada: A Political and Social History.* 3rd ed. Toronto: Holt, Rinehart, and Winston.

Manning, P. 1990. *Slavery and African Life: Occidental, Oriental, and African Slave Trades.* Cambridge: Cambridge University Press.

Martin, D. L., and D. W. Frayer. 1997. *Troubled Times: Violence and Warfare in the Past.* Amsterdam: Gordon and Breach Publishers.

Mason, R. 2000. Archaeology and Native American Oral Traditions. *American Antiquity* 65:239–266.

Maugham, R.C.F. 1906. *Portuguese East Africa: The History, Scenery, and Great Game of Manica and Sofala*. London: John Murray.

Mazrui, A. M., and I. N. Shariff. 1994. *The Swahili: Idiom and Identity of an African People*. Trenton: Africa World Press.

Mbotela, W. J. 1934. *Uhuru Wa Watumwa*. London: Sheldon Press.

Merritt, H. 1975. A History of the Taita of Kenya to 1900. Unpublished Ph.D. dissertation, Department of Anthropology, Indiana University, Bloomington.

Mutoro, H. W. 1998. Precolonial Trading Systems of the East African Interior. In *Transformations in Africa: Essays on Africa's Later Past*, edited by G. Connah, 186–203. Leicester: Leicester University Press.

Naqvi, H. K. 1972. *Urbanization and Urban Centres Under the Great Mughals: 1556–1707*. Vol. 1. Shimla, India: Indian Institute of Advanced Study.

Newitt, M.D.D. 1987. East Africa and the Indian Ocean Trade. In *India and the Indian Ocean*, edited by A. Das Gupta and M. N. Pearson, 201–223. Oxford: Oxford University Press.

Nicholls, C. S. 1971. *The Swahili Coast: Politics, Diplomacy and Trade on the East African Littoral, 1798–1856*. Africana Publishing Co: New York.

Nurse, D. and T. Spear. 1985. *The Swahili: Reconstructing the History and Language of an African Society, 800–1500*. Philadelphia: University of Pennsylvania Press.

Orser, C. E. 1996. *Images of the Recent Past: Readings in Historical Archaeology*. Walnut Creek, CA: Altamira Press.

Orser, C. E., and P.P.A. Funari. 2001. Archaeology and Slave Resistance and Rebellion. *World Archaeology* 33:61–72.

Otterbein, K. 1967. The Evolution of Zulu Warfare. In *Law and Warfare*, edited by P. Bohannan, 351–356. Garden City: Natural History Press.

Patterson, J. H. 1907. *The Man-Eaters of Tsavo and Other East African Adventures*. London: Macmillan.

Pearson, M. N. 1987. Cafilas and Cartazes.In *Essays in Indian Medieval History*, edited by I. S. Chandra. Indian History Congress Golden Jubilee Year Publications Series, vol. 3. New Delhi

———. 1998. *Port Cities and Intruders: The Swahili Coast, India and Portugal in the Early Modern Era*. Baltimore: John Hopkins University Press.

Perham, M. 1979. *East African Journey: Kenya and Tanganyika 1929–30*. London: Faber.

Plog, S. 2003. Social Conflict, Social Structure and Processes of Culture Change. *American Antiquity* 68:182–186.

Pouwels, R. L. 2000. The East African Coast, c. 780–1900 C.E. In *The History of Islam in Africa*, edited by N. Levitzioni and R. L. Pouwels, 251–272. Athens: Ohio University Press.

Preston, D. 1998. Carnivals of the Canyon. *The New Yorker* November 30:76–89.

Redmond, E. M. 1994. *Tribal and Chiefly Warfare in South America*. Ann Arbor: Museum of Anthropology Memoirs No. 28, University of Michigan.

Rice, G. E., and S. A. LeBlanc (editors). 2001. *Deadly Landscapes: Case Studies in Prehistoric Southwestern Warfare*. Salt Lake City: University of Utah Press.

Ringrose, D. R. 2001. *Expansion and Global Interaction, 1200–1700.* New York: Longman.

Robertson, C. 1997. Gender and Trade Relations in Central Kenya in the Late Nineteenth Century. *International Journal of African Historical Studies* 30(1):23–47.

Rodney, W. 1969. Upper Guinea and the Significance of the Origins of Africans Enslaved in the New World. *The Journal of Negro History* 54(4):327–345.

Schweinfurth, G. 1874. *The Heart of Africa: Three years' travels and Adventures in the Unexplored Region of Central Africa from 1868 to 1871*. 2 vols. New York: Harper and Collins.

Scully, R. T. 1969. Fort Sites of East Bukusu, Kenya. *Azania* 4:105–114.

Sheriff, A.M.H. 1987. *Slaves, Spices and Ivory in Zanzibar: Integration of an East African Commercial Empire into the World Economy, 1770–1873.* Athens: Ohio University Press.

Singleton, T. A. 1999. *"I, too, am America": Archaeological Studies of African American Life*. Charlottesville: University Press of Virginia.

———. 2001. Slavery and Spatial Dialectics on Cuban Coffee Plantations. *World Archaeology* 33:98–114.

Soper, R. 1966. Archaeological Sites in Tsavo West National Park. Unpublished manuscript. Nairobi: British Institute in Eastern Africa.

Soumonni, E. 2003. Lacustrine Villages in South Benin as Refuges from the Slave Trade. In *Fighting the Slave Trade: West African Strategies*, edited by A. Diouf, 3–14. Athens: Ohio University Press.

Spear, T. 1978. *The Kaya Complex: A History of the Mijikenda Peoples of the Kenya Coast to 1900.* Nairobi: Kenya Literature Bureau.

Stahl, A. B. 2001. *Making History in Banda: Anthropological Visions of Africa's Past*. Cambridge: Cambridge University Press.

Theal, T. M. 1882. *Kaffir Folklore*. London: Swan Sonneschein.

Thorbahn, P. F. 1979. Precolonial Ivory Trade of East Africa: Reconstruction of a Human-Elephant Ecosystem. Unpublished Ph.D. dissertation, Department of Anthropology, University of Massachusetts, Amherst.

Thornton, J. K. 1992. *Africa and Africans in the Making of the Atlantic World*. Cambridge: Cambridge University Press.

Turner, C. G. 1999. A Reign of Terror: Butchered Human Bones Point to Cannibals in Chaco Canyon. *Discovering Archaeology* 1(3):48–51.

Turner, C. G., and J. A. Turner. 1999. *Man Corn: Cannibalism and Violence in the Prehistoric American Southwest*. Salt Lake City: University of Utah Press.

Turney-High, H. H. 1949. *The Practice of Primitive War, Vol. 1: A Study of Comparative Sociology*. Missoula: The University of Montana Publications in the Social Sciences.

Wagner, G. 1949. *The Bantu of North Kavirondo*. London: Oxford University Press.

Watts, S. 1997. *Epidemics and History: Disease, Power, and Imperialism*. New Haven: Yale University Press.

Webster, D. L. 1985. War and Evolution of the State. *American Antiquity* 40:464–470.

Werner, A. 1996 [1933]. *Africa: Myths and Legends.* London: Senate.

White, T. D. 1992. *Prehistoric Cannibalism at Mancos 5MTUMR-2346.* Princeton: Princeton University Press.

Whiteley, P. M. 2002. Archaeology and Oral Tradition: The Scientific Importance of Dialogue. *American Antiquity* 67:405–415.

Wilcox, D., and J. Haas. 1994. The Scream of the Butterfly: Competition and Conflict in the Prehistoric Southwest. In *Themes in Southwest Prehistory*, edited by G. J. Gummerman, 211–238. Santa Fe: School of American Research Press.

Willis, J. 1993. *Mombasa, the Swahili, and the Making of the Mijikenda.* Oxford: Clarendon Press.

Wilmsen, E. N. 1989. *Land Filled with Flies: A Political Economy of the Kalahari.* Chicago: University of Chicago Press.

Wilson, T. H. 1978. *The Monumental Architecture and Archaeology North of the Tana River.* Nairobi: National Museums of Kenya.

———. 1980. *The Monumental Architecture and Archaeology of the Central and Southern Kenya Coast.* Nairobi: National Museums of Kenya.

Ylvisaker, M. 1982. The Ivory Trade in the Lamu Area. *Paideuma* 28:221–231.

II

Warfare and the Transition to Statehood

8

Warfare and the Development of States in China

ANNE P. UNDERHILL

Warfare and Sociopolitical Change

A long-standing topic in anthropology is the relationship between change in the nature of warfare and change in sociopolitical organization. As noted by Ferguson (1990:47), two topics of research have received considerable attention: warfare as a cause of political centralization and the effects of sociopolitical change on warfare. Because of limited access to relevant publications, archaeological and historical data from East Asia are rarely considered in such debates, while publications tend to emphasize the uniqueness of China, without offering a comparative perspective.

This chapter evaluates material and textual evidence for the causes and consequences of warfare from the Yellow River valley in northern China, beginning with the late prehistoric Longshan period (ca. 2600–1900 B.C.) and ending with the formation of the Qin empire in 221 B.C. Warfare may be defined as "inter-group armed conflict, often with lethal force" (Haas 2001:331). It varies in frequency, intensity, and scale, from occasional raiding with few if any deaths, to formal battles with massive destruction of human life and property (Lambert 2002:209). For discussions of potential material evidence for warfare from earlier prehistoric periods in the Yellow River valley, see Cheng and Zhong (1990), Liu (1996a, 2000), Shao (2000), Underhill (1989, 2002), Underhill et al. (in press), Yang (1992), and Yates (1999). For assessment of other areas in China, see Dematte (1999), Shao (2000), Shelach (1999), Yang (1992), and Yates (1999).

Warfare as a Cause of Social Change

Arguments for warfare as a causal factor in facilitating change in sociopolitical organization tend to emphasize preconditions and material incentives for warfare: environmental and economic stress on populations, and differential access to resources. For instance, such conditions encouraged greater community aggregation and more defensive strategies in the American Southwest, leading to greater tribal integration (Haas 1990). Similarly, Carneiro (1970, 1978, 1990) argues that stress over resources in environmentally or socially circumscribed areas causes conquest warfare in chiefdoms, facilitating the acquisition of greater political power by some individuals, and leading to the development of states.

In other contexts, however, warfare is only one of several factors that facilitate the concentration of political power. Warfare can be an indirect cause of state formation, enhancing stronger leadership and enabling the acquisition of wealth outside kinship networks (Webster 1975). There also is significant variation in the impact of warfare on sociopolitical change in chiefdoms. Earle (1997) shows that the degree of importance of warfare in increasing chiefly power varied in Peru, Denmark, and Hawai'i. Other studies highlight the variation within late prehistoric Europe alone (Chapman 1999; Kristiansen 1999). After states have developed, warfare is just one strategy of elites in physically enforcing their demands (Haas 1982). As discussed below, it is often expected that warfare was an important factor enabling elites to increase their political power during the late prehistoric period in northern China. At present, however, the limited physical evidence for warfare does not support this argument. Rather, warfare increased in frequency, intensity, and scale after states developed. It also is clear that the relationship between leadership in warfare and high sociopolitical status became more pronounced over time during the early Bronze Age.

Research in other areas of the world has shown that as organizational complexity increases, the nature of warfare changes. The frequency, intensity, and scale of warfare tend to be greater in centralized societies, and the importance of capturing land or resources becomes more pronounced as the need for surplus increases (Haas 2001:336, 340). The changes in material evidence for warfare reflect these changing aims. For example, after the rise of the Olmec polity in Mesoamerica, a professional military developed, and specialized weapons began to be produced for the first time, while fortifications increased (Hassig 1992:15, 17, 32). Below I describe how an integral part of the growth of states in China was an increase in the frequency, intensity, and scale of warfare. Improvements in military technology were both a cause and an effect of increasingly powerful states. Many innovations in weapons technology were made possible by state resources. At the same time, in ancient China as well as other areas (Haas 2001:339), people were painfully aware of the increased costs of war that accompanied the growing power of states.

The Causes of Warfare

The most difficult task is to understand the factors that cause warfare. Stress over economic resources is commonly regarded as a major cause of warfare (Haas 2001). This can involve essential resources for survival, or simply resources perceived as valuable. In some areas, leaders may have deliberately exacerbated resource stress by promoting an atmosphere of fear (Lekson 2002:618). In more than one part of Mesoamerica, a major cause of warfare after states developed may have been protection of trade routes, given an uneven distribution of resources (Hassig 1992). For ancient China, economic factors do not fully explain the prevalence of warfare. It appears that both essential and prestigious materials were contested in several periods. Another causal factor was family honor, with respect to past, present, and future generations.

We are far from understanding the range of variation in cultural responses to stress over economic resources—which may or may not result in warfare. There can be diverse responses, even in similar culture areas (Milner 1999; Vayda 1976). Also, the roles of related causal factors need to be identified (Webster 1993:419). Archaeological research can help identify and explain a range of causal factors and responses to warfare, as well as peaceful alternatives for dealing with challenging conditions such as resource stress. I believe that this kind of research is more productive than endlessly debating whether intersocietal violence is an inherent part of human nature (see Haas 1999:13; Otterbein 2000:801).

Perceptions of the Enemy

The archaeological and historical records are good resources for evaluating variation in other aspects of warfare. One aspect that deserves further attention is the degree to which enemies are conceptualized as inferior "others." An important pattern noted by Keeley (1996; see Carman and Harding 1999:5), is that people who believe humans in other communities are outsiders feel justified in using more lethal warfare. Warfare always involves outsiders to some extent, but as more than one example in the modern era shows, there are different perceived degrees of "outsiders." At a minimum, warfare involves different political communities, or "groups whose members possess and recognize a high level of common interest and who are prepared to defend their interests, or augment them, through the use of violence" (Webster 1993:418). This process is even more pronounced when communities regard others as having a different, and inferior, culture—whether defined in terms of belief systems, language, economic practices, physical features, or other factors. In more than one period, people in ancient China believed they had ideological justification for waging war against inferior outsiders.

At present there is far more information about the nature of warfare during the literate early Bronze Age of China than for the prehistoric period. Material evidence for warfare has not been investigated to a great extent, such as human skeletal remains indicating violent death and settlement areas with traces of burning and raiding (for example, Haas 2001:332; Lambert 2002). Nevertheless, there is evidence for an increase in the scale and complexity of defensive features at settlements from the late prehistoric to the early historic periods. As noted for North America (Lambert 2002:229), warfare during the early Bronze Age of China became increasingly lethal, made possible in part by substantial innovations in weapons technology. Another important pattern evident from graves and historical records is a strong relationship between conduct in warfare and degree of personal political power. An essential part of this process, as in prehistoric Europe (Chapman 1999; Kristiansen 1999) and the early historic period in the Caribbean (Whitehead 1990), is elite rituals involving warfare.

The Longshan Period of Northern China

The Longshan period (ca. 2600–1900 B.C.) of the Yellow River (Huang He) valley is important for understanding the rise of early states in China. It is clear that there were multi-community polities with settlement hierarchies and emerging social stratification (Dematte 1999; Liu 1996a, 1996b, 2000; Liu and Chen 2001; Shao 2000; Underhill 2002; Underhill et al. 2002; Underhill et al. in press). Current material evidence is insufficient to conclude that any states developed during this period, although such evidence may eventually be found. Many scholars expect that a key characteristic of early states is strong military power, given paleographic evidence for the development of the Chinese character for state (*guo*), incorporating the image of a weapon (see Chang 1983:365; Dematte 1999:143). Chen (1997) proposes that warfare is a key process in the development of states and that the process should occur relatively quickly. In this case, then, there should be evidence for intense warfare during the Longshan period preceding the initial emergence of states in one or more regions. The physical evidence to support this important argument, however, has not been found to date.

One convincing kind of evidence for some form of warfare during the Longshan period is a marked increase in defensive, walled sites in more than one area of the central and lower Yellow River valley (see Dematte 1999; Liu 2000; Underhill 1994; Underhill et al. in press). While only two undisputed walled sites are described in publications from the immediately preceding Yangshao and Dawenkou periods, by the end of the Longshan period there are several enclosures of rammed earth (*hangtu*) in the following areas: southern Shanxi province, northern Henan, north-central Henan near Zhengzhou, northwest Shandong, eastern Henan, central Shandong, and southeastern Shandong/northern Jiangsu. As noted for other areas of the world, a marked increase in fortifications indicates a widespread fear of raiding and protection of key re-

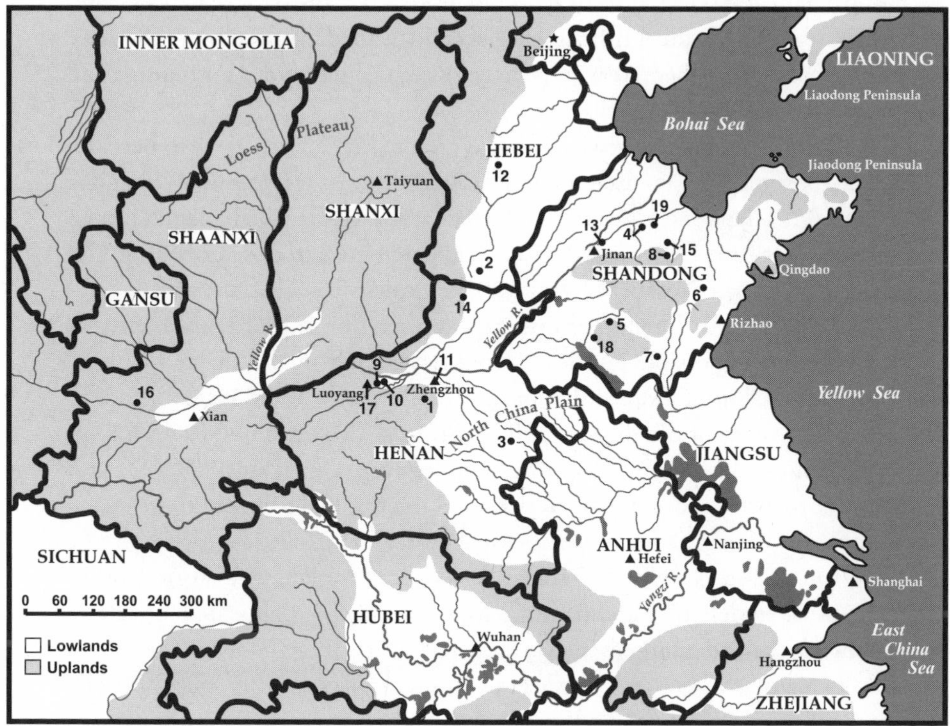

Figure 8.1. Sites from the Longshan, Erlitou, Shang, and Western Zhou Periods mentioned in the text (1 = Guchengzhai, 2 = Jiangou, 3 = Pingliangtai, 4 = Dinggong, 5 = Yinjiacheng, 6 = Chengzi, 7 = Dafanzhuang, 8 = Zhufeng, 9 = Erlitou, 10 = Yanshi, 11 = Zhengzhou, 12 = Taixi, 13 = Daxinzhuang, 14 = Anyang, 15 = Subutun, 16 = Fengchu, 17 = Chengzhou, 18 = Lu, 19 = Qi).

sources (Vencl 1999:67). The impact of warfare on social change, however, is not clear. The majority of settlements from the Longshan period are not walled. It is likely that warfare was not frequent or large in scale (Underhill et al. in press). Also, it appears that the walled enclosures were built at different phases of the Longshan period. Thus, they probably signify variation in the nature and rate of intercommunity competition during the Longshan period. Although information on dating is limited, relatively early enclosures may have been built in eastern Henan and central Shandong (Underhill et al. in press).

There must have been a substantial mobilization of labor to construct these walls, but the effort was not necessarily coordinated by elites at every site. There is substantial variation in the sizes of the enclosed areas (up to 30 ha; Underhill et al. in press). Smaller sites probably were minor regional centers (Underhill 1994; Underhill et al. in press). At a few of these sites, large structures hypothesized as elite residences have been found inside the walls. At several sites, habitation areas outside the walls also have been identified, while at more than one site, it appears that there were some lower ranking households both inside and outside the enclosures.

Additional labor-intensive, defensive architectural features have been reported for some sites. For example, a surrounding moat was found at Dinggong (Figure 8.1; Shandong University 1993), guardhouses at Pingliangtai (Henan Province Institute 1983), and a maze-like, defensive exterior corridor at Guchengzhai (Henan Province Institute 2002; Underhill et al. in press).

At present, it is difficult to interpret the relationship of these construction episodes to possible increases in political power in the affected regions. For late prehistoric Europe, it has been argued that fortifications represent effective management of labor by individuals who also exhibited leadership in warfare and mobilization of labor through feasting (Chapman 1999:103). It is plausible that this process characterizes the larger walled sites, but there are no clear physical traces of warfare at any walled site. There is little evidence for the Longshan period as a whole (Table 8.1). As noted for late prehistoric Greece, the increase in defensive architectural features also could indicate more effort to control access to resources such as land, people, and craft goods (Kokkinidou and Nikolaidou 1999:96). In order to consider this possibility, there must be systematic comparisons of craft goods in walled sites versus sites without walls within the same settlement system.

It is important to investigate geographic variation in the nature and rate of change in warfare during the Longshan period. In some regions of northern China, where defensive walls were rare or non-existent, other patterns may indicate greater concern with defense and control of resources. In southeastern Shandong, for instance, systematic, regional survey reveals the development of a distinct settlement hierarchy during the Longshan period and a marked nucleation of population, likely representing greater concern with defense and control of resources (Underhill et al. 2002). More systematic, regional surveys could identify different kinds of settlement patterns indicating concern with defense during the Longshan period. Focusing on the distribution of all Longshan settlements across the physical landscape, rather than walled sites alone, would help identify conditions of environmental or social circumscription as possible contributing factors to warfare.

The absence of walled enclosures in several regions, however, should not be taken as proof that warfare was absent; there could have been other defensive features such as wooden palisades, as found in eastern North America. There, palisades could range from screens (smaller posts, not requiring special labor management) to walls (bigger posts, requiring some kind of labor management)

Table 8.1. Changes in Warfare from the Late Prehistoric Period to the Qin Empire in Northern China

Nature of Warfare	Status of Soldiers	Fortifications	Weapons
Qin empire (221–206 B.C.)			
First empire (short-lived), other states conquered temporarily	Forced conscription of citizens into military service; many ranks evident from terracotta soldiers in the emperor's tomb; could increase rank by showing heads of victims	More sections of previous walls connected, and other additions, forming the Great Wall	More innovation in weaponry: iron more available for weapons, such as swords
Eastern Zhou: Warring States (ca. 481–221 B.C.)			
Only 7, but larger, states left; constant battles, bigger scale, larger armies, longer battles and wars; former etiquette in battle dropped; treatises on military strategy written	Few nobles in the military, many more low-ranking people were professional soldiers, states began forced military conscription	Many more built such as watch stations, forts, large defensive walls along state boundaries	Great innovation in weaponry: iron used for many forms, grappling hook for fighting on boats, new methods for sieges
Eastern Zhou: Spring and Autumn (ca. 770–481 B.C.)			
Several small states, constant battles to gain territory; rules of etiquette in battle—men should kill those of the same rank only	Officers are still nobles of high lineages and status; concern if the enemy used proper ritual behavior	More built such as watchtowers, walls around states; but more battles in open areas	Nobles on chariots used convex bows, infantry used lances (*mao* spears)
Western Zhou (ca. 1046–770 B.C.)			
State established by conquest, larger army; administrative areas unstable, frequent warfare; later efforts to expand state	Textual data and graves indicate high status and political power for military officers; inscriptions on bronze vessels describe battles	Some walled centers identified	New forms of weapons include shorter bronze dagger-axe; more chariots

continued

Table 8.1.—*Continued*

Nature of Warfare	Status of Soldiers	Fortifications	Weapons
Late Shang (ca. 1200–1046 B.C.)			
Warfare is frequent to get land, labor, sacrificial victims; unstable state borders evident from oracle bone inscriptions; some longer border wars	Oracle bones indicate king and one consort (Fu Hao) were military commanders; high status graves for military officers; large infantry, kin mobilized by lineage leaders	Unknown for the late Shang period at Anyang	Increase in quantities of bronze and jade weapons in elite graves; appearance of bronze helmets, leather shields and armor, chariots for battle
Early-Middle Shang (ca. 1600–1200 B.C.)			
increase in intensity, scale, frequency likely; possible structure for storage of weapons at Yanshi	Bronze weapon forms in elite graves	Yanshi (190.0 ha), Zhengzhou (317.9 ha), and other walled enclosures much larger; more effort to protect resources	First appearance of bronze projectile points (*zu*)
Erlitou/Xia (ca. 1900–1500 B.C.)			
increase in intensity, scale, frequency likely during this early state period; no written records	Labor-intensive jade weapon forms in elite graves; warfare more linked to elite status	unknown at the Erlitou site	Specialized weapon forms appear, in bronze and jade (*ge* dagger-axe, *yue* battle-axe)
Longshan (ca. 2600–1900 B.C.)			
Skeletal data suggest sporadic raiding	Labor-intensive, symbolic jade weapons link warfare to status	Great increase in walled enclosures at sites in several areas, varying in size, largest over 300 ha	Multi-functional, potential tool-weapons of stone, bone; 1 specialized weapon form (*zhang* blade) emerges

(Milner 1999:119–120). There has been little effort so far to identify other defensive locations, such as settlements on steep hilltops as in late prehistoric and early historic Europe (Hill and Wileman 2002).

At present there are few direct, physical traces of warfare at Longshan sites, although the situation could change as more skeletal remains and settlement areas are carefully examined. One site has graphic evidence for intercommunity violence, and others should be identifiable. At the Jiangou (or Chien-kou) site in southeastern Hebei, archaeologists discovered a few disarticulated skeletons in a well (representing males and females of all ages). Notably, two skulls—identified as belonging to females—reveal traces of scalping with a stone knife after the victims had died, while four other skulls, of which two were identified as male have traces of hacking with an axe (Chang 1986; Chen 2000:12; Underhill 1989:221; Yan 1982:38–39). The excavators propose that skullcaps were used as drinking cups, a custom also known in historic period Fiji, involving victorious chiefs (Carneiro 1990:204). Since the Jiangou site dates to the middle Longshan period (Yan 1982), it is possible that the intensity of warfare had increased since the early Longshan period in southeastern Hebei.

As in late prehistoric Europe (Chapman 1999), a wide range of Longshan stone and bone tools could have been effective weapons. Habitation contexts should have abundant evidence for such tools. My attempts to tabulate potential weapons from Longshan site reports have yielded mixed results, since stone or bone tools at Neolithic sites have not been a focus of research until recently. Another problem is inconsistency in describing forms of stone tools from site to site. My earlier study shows numerous projectile points at habitation sites from the Longshan period, and an increase over time at two sites (Underhill 1989). Systematic collection and analysis of chipped stone, ground stone, bone, and shell artifacts from Neolithic sites are required before adequate assessments of potential weapons (or "tool-weapons," Chapman 1999) can be made.

It appears that mourners placed small quantities of both actual and symbolic weapons in burials during the Longshan period. It is difficult to distinguish these two kinds of weapons from reports, but symbolic weapons seem to be more common. Burials at four sites (Table 8.2) have yielded possible weapon forms made from either common stone or jade. There is little information about identification of sex from skeletal remains, but some of the potential weapons in graves are linked to males (see Changwei Area 1980; Institute of Archaeology 1988; Linyi Group 1975; Shandong University 1990).

The fact that some of these symbolic weapons are made of the prestigious and labor-intensive material jade suggests an emerging ideology linking warfare, relatively high status for males, and ritual during the Longshan period. As discussed below, this trend becomes intensified during the early Bronze Age.

Table 8.2. Tool-Weapons in Adult Graves from the Longshan Period (ca. 2600–1900 B.C.) in Northern China

Type of Tool-Weapon	Dafanzhuang	Sanlihe	Chengzi	Yinjiacheng
Stone *zao* chisel		2 graves (male), 1 each		
Stone *chan* shovel	1 grave (unknown sex), 1 item			
Stone *zu* projectile point	1 grave (unknown sex), 4 items		1 grave (male), 1 item	
Stone *dao* knife			1 grave (unknown sex), 1 item	
Jade *dao* knife				1 grave (male), 1 item
Stone *yue* battle-axe				3 graves (1 male, 2 unknown sex), 1 item in each

Note: Dafanzhuang site: Shandong, 26 graves total. Sanlihe site: Shandong, 98 graves total. Chengzi site: Shandong, 54 graves total. Yinjiacheng site: Shandong, 65 graves total.

At the site of Yinjiacheng, there is a jade form described as a *dao* knife in the grave of a male (Shandong University 1990). Another high-ranking Longshan burial at Zhufeng in north-central Shandong contains a jade form described as a *yue* battle-axe (Shandong Province Institute 1990). The late Neolithic tools described as *yue* battle-axes vary in form but have broad, curved blades. The function is presumed on the basis of similarity to the more distinct bronze *yue* from the early historic period (discussed below). It appears that none of these jade items shows any traces of use. Stone *yue*, however, could have been used for more than one purpose.

There are additional symbolic weapons of jade and other fine stones with no evidence of actual use in warfare from Longshan period sites, but little is known of their context. These include long, thin *dao* knives and fine *yazhang* blades (see Childs-Johnson 1988; Underhill 2002; Wu 1995). The unusual *yazhang* form probably had a more limited function than the *yue* form discussed above. Therefore it may represent the first specialized form of weapon, although it probably was only symbolic in nature. There is more than one *yazhang* blade with no information on context from the early Longshan period site of Dafanzhuang (see Underhill 2002). The collection of Longshan items in the Department of Anthropology at The Field Museum includes an adze-shaped object (Figure 8.2) and a *yazhang* blade (Figure 8.3). I hypothesize that the finest of these items such as the *yazhang* blades were exchanged between elites in commemoration of defensive alliances, a general pattern of behavior evident from the early Bronze Age, as discussed below. Other symbolic jade weapons also could have circulated within polities, given by elites to lower-ranking individuals for their service and loyalty.

Currently, the earliest identifiable state dates to after ca. 2000 B.C., during the Erlitou period in the central Yellow River valley (Chang 1986; Liu 1996a; Liu and Chen 2003; see also Underhill et al. in press). As Liu (2000:20) notes, the occurrence of multiple walled sites and other centers in northern and central Henan during the Longshan period probably represents increased intercommunity competition. At present, however, there is insufficient archaeological evidence to conclude that warfare was a key factor in the rise of the Erlitou state. It is likely that some form of warfare existed during the Longshan period in more than one region, but the current physical evidence indicates a picture of occasional raiding rather than conquest warfare. Probably the frequency and intensity of raiding the resources of other communities (including goods and labor) increased in comparison to earlier periods. This process was not only motivated by economic factors. Judging from the symbolic weapons in burials, personal ability in warfare brought prestige. It is clear that a more thorough assessment of the nature and significance of warfare must be done on a regional

Figure 8.2. Longshan Period, jade adze-shaped object (1462.127216) (The Field Museum, Department of Anthropology).

basis in conjunction with evidence for other kinds of social change, including identification of the nature of environmental and economic stresses that may have faced various Longshan communities.

The Early Bronze Age

Little is known about warfare during the four identified phases of the Erlitou period, ca. 1900–1500 B.C. During the early state period, production of both bronze vessels and weapons was mastered (see Bagley 1999; Chang 1986; Underhill 2002). Two skulls with traces of scalping were found in 1990 at an Erlitou period site (Chen 2000:11). Warfare may have increased over time during the early state period, since numerous projectile points and some dismembered human skeletons were found in late (phase IV) contexts at the site of Erlitou

Figure 8.3. Longshan Period, jade *yazhang* blade (1462.127348) (The Field Museum, Department of Anthropology).

(see Liu and Chen 2003:91–92). A possible complicating factor is that such skeletal remains could represent ritual remains of human sacrifice instead.

The only other potential physical evidence for warfare to date is the presence of labor-intensive, symbolic weapons made of jade and bronze in elite graves (Table 8.1). The recently published report for the site of Erlitou (Institute of Archaeology 1999) indicates that five forms of jade weapons were made (*dao* knife, *yazhang* blade, *yue* battle-axe, *ge* dagger-axe, and *chan* shovel). Like their Longshan period counterparts, some of these symbolic weapons were quite large. Large size, in addition to form, probably symbolized the high status of the user (see Childs-Johnson 1995). These jade symbolic weapons also could have been exchanged between elites as gifts in commemoration of military alliances. During the Erlitou period, the *yue* battle-axe and *ge*-dagger-axe were also produced in bronze (Table 8.3). It is possible that these were actually used in warfare, but

Table 8.3. Tool-Weapons and Weapons in Elite Adult Graves from the Erlitou and Shang Periods (Early Bronze Age)

Type of Tool-Weapon and Weapon	Erlitou	Taixi	Guojiazhuang	Fu Hao
Jade *dao* knife	1 grave (unknown sex), 1 item		Grave M160, male, has 2	1
Bronze *dao* knife		1 grave (unknown sex), 1 item	4 graves (unknown sex), 1 each	
Jade *yazhang* blade	3 graves (unknown sex), 1 each			
Bronze *yazhang* blade		1 grave (unknown sex), 1 item		
Jade *yue* battle-axe	1 grave (unknown sex), 1 item		Grave M160, male, has 1	2
Bronze *yue* battle-axe	3 graves (unknown sex), 1 each	1 grave (unknown sex), 1 item	1 grave (unknown sex), 1 item; M160 male has 3	3
Jade *ge* dagger-axe	2 graves (unknown sex), 1 each	1 grave (unknown sex), 1 item	2 graves (unknown sex), 2 each; M160 male, 5 items	39
Bronze *ge* dagger-axe	3 graves (unknown sex), 1 each	5 graves (unknown sex), 1 each	31 graves (unknown sex), 1–5 each; M160 male has 119	91
Jade *chan* shovel	2 graves (unknown sex), 1 each			
Jade *mao* spearhead				2
Bronze *mao* spearhead			8 graves (unknown sex) 1–6 each; M160 male has 97	
Bronze *ben* adze			2 graves (unknown sex), 1–2 each	
Bronze *zao* chisel		1 grave (unknown sex), 1 item	2 graves (unknown sex), 1 each	
Bronze *zu* projectile point		5 graves (unknown sex), 1–5 in each	8 graves (unknown sex), 1–10 each; M160 male has 906	37 complete ones
Bone *zu* projectile point			2 graves (unknown sex), 9 each	
Jade *ji* dagger-axe				9
Bronze *ji* dagger-axe		1 grave (unknown sex), 1 item		

Note: Erlitou site: Henan, Erlitou period, ca. 1900–1500 B.C., 33 graves total. Taixi site: Hebei, Middle Shang period, ca. 1400–1200 B.C., 64 graves total. Guojiazhuang site: Section of Anyang, Henan, Late Shang period, ca. 1200–1046 B.C., 191 graves total. Fu Hao (female) tomb: Xiaotun, Anyang site, Late Shang period.

no studies of use-wear have been done. Both the bronze *yue* and *ge* dagger-axe appear to have been specialized weapon forms. As shown below, they were even more important during the later Shang period. Given the several forms of symbolic jade weapons and the effort to produce weapons in the new, prestigious material, bronze, it can be concluded that elite status was more tightly linked to conduct in warfare.

Evidence for warfare during the early Shang period in northern China is more abundant. Recent reports for excavations at the site of Yanshi, near Erlitou, have provided valuable information on the early Shang state. The abundant habitation remains here include a large structure that may have been an armory (Underhill et al. in press; Zhao 2001). The linear, windowless room may have held numerous wooden racks for weapons. It calls to mind Han period (206 B.C.–A.D. 220) armories as depicted on rubbings from tombs (see Yang 1992:192–194). This finding is significant for two reasons. First, it suggests that the frequency and scale of warfare had increased. Also, weapons probably were tightly controlled by state officials. The storage structure for weapons was found adjacent to the palace area, within a walled enclosure. This enclosure at Yanshi is 190 ha in size, bigger than most Longshan period enclosures, indicating a concerted effort by state authorities to control access to resources. As Lee (2004:183–184) notes, an effective addition was the later construction of an outer enclosure around an earlier, smaller enclosure. The effort to increase the defensive features at Yanshi evidently stemmed from competition to replace Erlitou as the regional political center.

The inner enclosure at the somewhat later site of Zhengzhou is 317.9 ha in size (Chang 1980:273). In addition, an outer wall has been identified in the south and west (Liu and Chen 2003:93). Again the double enclosure suggests an increased effort by elites to protect their resources. Zhengzhou also has graphic evidence for the control of human resources by state authorities. Archaeologists found a ditch containing numerous fragments of human skulls—sawed in half, possibly ritually sacrificed war captives (see Chang 1980:276; Liu and Chen 2003:95). It appears that the custom of scalping deceased victims increased during the Shang period, judging from the presence of a few skulls with cut marks at Zhengzhou. The significance of the custom in the early Bronze Age is not clear, since texts rarely mention it (Chen 2000:11).

Other relatively early Shang period sites have been found in northern China. Some of these sites may represent communities controlled by the Shang at centers such as Zhengzhou, while others probably represent other small states (Underhill and Fang 2004). Nevertheless there was a similar elite ideology over a wide area. At the Taixi site (Hebei Province Institute 1985), elite graves contain several forms of bronze weapons—the *dao* knife, *yazhang* blade, *yue* battle-axe, *ge* dagger-axe, *zao* chisel, *zu* projectile point, and *ji* dagger-axe, as well as the jade *ge* dagger-axe (Table 8.3). There was an increased effort to symbolize elite status by including bronze weapon forms in graves (Figure 8.4). The Field Museum has a bronze *ge* dagger-axe collected at the Shang period site of Daxinzhuang in Shandong.

The oracle-bone inscriptions found at the late Shang site of Anyang (ca. 1200–1046 B.C.) provide the first written evidence about warfare and the nature of the state. They reveal that frequent warfare enabled state authorities to gain resources such as agricultural land, human labor, goods, and victims to offer as sacrifices to the royal ancestors. Several inscriptions mention unstable borders with neighboring *fang* territories, and the need to acquire more land for agricultural production to support the large dependent population of administrators and key crafts people (Bagley 1999; Chang 1980; Keightley 1999; Yates 1999). Relations with the various *fang* territories fluctuated and were a constant source of concern. The Shang kings were able to successfully control some of these territories, while they were required to engage in long-term wars with others (Yates 1999:14). Some *fang* territories probably contained specific raw materials desired by the Shang authorities; for instance, it is likely that areas containing copper and tin sources (possibly southern Shanxi) were often contested (Chang 1980:257–258). The recent discovery of a walled enclosure dating to the initial establishment of Anyang during the middle Shang period indicates an early concern with defense at the settlement (see Anyang Team 2003).

Inscriptions also indicate that the Shang elites regarded the people inhabiting the *fang* territories as "non-Shang," or cultural outsiders. Some of these people evidently were herders from northern areas who competed to use lands for grazing instead of farming (Chang 1980:256). The inscriptions often mention difficulties in controlling the Qiang people, inhabitants of an area between western Henan and Shaanxi, who may have been sheepherders. The scale of the battles involved is suggested by one inscription mentioning that 300 Qiang victims were offered as a single sacrifice to the Shang royal ancestors (Chang 1980:194, 249).

Categorization of people as outsiders during the Shang period would have included criteria of lineage relations in addition to lifestyle, and probably also language. The Shang oracle-bone inscriptions clearly indicate the presence of ranked lineages and that leaders could only come from high-ranking lineages. Kings frequently sought guidance from their powerful ancestors and were obligated to periodically offer gifts to sustain them—human sacrifices, food, and drink (Keightley 1999, 2000; Underhill 2002). Ideology and lineage honor were significant motivational forces for leaders to engage in warfare. These factors probably also inspired the soldiers who seem to have been lower ranking

Figure 8.4. Bronze *ge* dagger-axe (2307.235925) (The Field Museum, Department of Anthropology).

lineage members. The oracle-bone inscriptions indicate that lineages during the late Shang period were both social and military units (Chang 1980; Yates 1997:81).

There is textual and material evidence that leadership in warfare was directly linked to political status during the late Shang period. As Yates (1999:8–9) points out, warfare was a key component of the political-religious system during the late Shang period. The oracle-bone inscriptions make it clear that the king was directly involved in initiating and leading battles. Many inscriptions describe the king asking the gods and royal ancestors of his highest-ranking lineage whether specific campaigns would be successful. The king's sons, the heads of their own minor lineages, also had the right to wage war (Keightley 1999:270–271). Notably, the inscriptions state that one of King Wu Ding's wives, called Fu Hao, was a distinguished military commander in her own right. She is credited with helping to expand the late Shang state (Chang 1980; Yates 1999:13). Keightley (1999:284) suggests that attacks were initiated relatively quickly by the king, and before each battle he sought approval from the gods and ancestors. It is evident that the king could effectively mobilize the populace for battle and for other kinds of labor (Chang 1980; Keightley 1999:280; Yates 1999).

The inscriptions also mention several ranks of military personnel. It is difficult to interpret the exact nature of terms for military officers such as *duo ma* (many horses), but it is feasible to suggest (Yates 1999:13–14) that these individuals were high-ranking charioteers. Also, the term for "many artisans" could have referred to officials who managed production of bronze weapons for the state. Officials led their lower ranking lineage members, who formed the infantry, into battle. It is estimated that the average size of an infantry unit was 3,000 soldiers (Keightley 1999:284; Yates 1999:13).

There is considerable archaeological evidence that leadership in warfare was directly linked to political and social status. A wide variety of jade and bronze weapons have been found in cemeteries in the Anyang area (Table 8.3), including new forms of weapons made from these prestigious materials. At Guojiazhuang, likely a cemetery for a descent group branch, new weapons include the *mao* spearhead (bronze), *ben* adze (bronze), and *zu* projectile point (bronze). One grave, M160, stands out with respect to both quantity and quality of items. The excavators conclude that the deceased individual was a high-ranking military officer, judging from inscriptions on bronze vessels (Institute of Archaeology 1998). They also identify an important new trend in burial goods: the weapons in these late Shang period graves are made of relatively soft, poor-quality bronze. Burying items with the dead that were cheaper to produce was no doubt instigated in part by economic factors (discussed further in Underhill 2002).

Graves located in the core of the royal area at Anyang also have significant quantities of weapons. Like grave M160, the unlooted tomb of the consort Fu Hao contains numerous weapons, in this case relatively large quantities of *ge* dagger-axes (both bronze and jade), as well as bronze projectile points (see Institute of Archaeology 1980; Underhill 2002). The tombs in the royal cemetery area of Xibeigang, looted long ago, probably once contained large quantities of weapons. In one tomb (M1004), archaeologists still found more than 100 bronze helmets, about 360 bronze *ge* dagger-axes, 36 bronze spearheads, leather armor and shields, and chariot fittings (Bagley 1999:185). The jade *ge* dagger-axe at The Field Museum (Figure 8.5) is very similar to those from excavated late Shang contexts.

As evident from the elite tombs in the Anyang area, there was more than one kind of innovation in military technology during the late Shang period. The presence of leather shields and armor, as well as bronze helmets, indicates more prolonged, lethal warfare. Yang (1992:45) describes several innovations and explains how the shape of the *ge* dagger-axe was improved to make it more le-

Figure 8.5. Jade *ge* dagger-axe (1689.182828) (The Field Museum, Department of Anthropology).

Figure 8.6. Bronze *yue* axe from Subutun, Shandong, Late Shang Period (adapted from Yang 1992, Figure 59).

thal. The introduction of the chariot also must have had a significant impact on warfare, although the specific impact has been debated. There is no evidence of either the wheel or horses in northern China until the late Shang period; it appears these were imported from the northern steppes (Bagley 1999:206–207). Chariots may have been effective for observation of terrain, command of soldiers, and display of military might by officers during battle, rather than serving as combat units (Bagley 1999:206; Keightley 1999:285). Cheng (1960:208–209), however, argues that chariots were crucial factors in combat, holding a driver in the center, archer on the right, and soldier with dagger-axe on the left.

An especially important form of weapon during the Shang period was the bronze *yue* battle-axe. These large, imposing weapons are relatively rare and have been found in several sites in northern China dating to both the middle and late Shang periods (Cheng and Zhong 1990; Yang and Yang 1986). Axes of this kind were recovered from the graves of M160 at Guojiazhuang and Fu Hao. A famous example from the late Shang period site of Subutun in Shandong (Figure 8.6) demonstrates the power that these axes must have had in the eyes of the Shang and their neighbors. As noted by Yates (1999:18), this form clearly was reserved for high social and military status, possibly because it was suitable for beheading sacrificial victims, physical traces of which are numerous at Anyang (Bagley 1999:193). I propose that these bronze axes were gifts by Shang elites to local elites in other areas in commemoration of military alliances and to reward loyalty to the state. There is textual evidence that this kind of elite activity took place during the Western Zhou and later periods.

The Western Zhou and Later Periods

The onset of the Western Zhou dynasty marked a new era in the nature of warfare. There is abundant textual evidence that the formation of the Western Zhou state ca. 1045 or 1046 B.C. (see Qiu and Cai 2001; Shaughnessy 1999; Yates 1999) was accomplished by conquest. During the late Shang period, the Western Zhou polity was often in conflict with the Shang king. Eventually the Zhou were able to conquer the Shang, with the aid of allies who also had been targets of the Shang, such as the Qiang people (Chang 1980:249; Shaughnessy 1999:302). Texts thought to have been written at least partially during this period mention that King Wen began campaigns against the Shang that were completed by his son, King Wu, after his death. The final conquest is said to have involved 45,000 troops and 300 chariots (Shaughnessy 1999:307–309).

The core area of the new state was the Wei River valley in modern Shaanxi province. Shaughnessy (1999:311–312, 320) explains that in order to administer this new, large territory the Zhou king sent his sons and other kinsmen to control different areas. They set up some capitals of subsidiary, dependent states further east at Chengzhou (modern Luoyang, Henan) and at two places in modern Shandong province, Lu (modern Qufu) and Qi (modern Zibo). It appears that many capitals were surrounded by earthen walls, such as the early Western Zhou period site of Fengchu in Shaanxi (Hsu and Linduff 1988:291; Needham et al. 1994). The fortification of these administrative centers indicates that control over subject states was tenuous. Like their Shang predecessors, a frequent problem of the Western Zhou kings was maintaining control of the different state territories—a problem that would eventually have fatal consequences. In the later years of the dynasty, the kings attempted to expand the state territory, often encountering major defeats. The texts consistently describe the enemy in each area as a different kind of people, such as the eastern and southern Yi peoples, perhaps from areas such as northwestern Jiangsu, eastern Henan, and southern Shandong (Shaughnessy 1999:323–324).

The early Western Zhou kings deliberately adopted ritual practices of the Shang, at least in part to help legitimize their rule (Rawson 1999). It appears that they also sought divine guidance before an attack. In one instance, commanders interpreted a comet as a sign that a battle should proceed. After a terrible defeat, the bronze vessel inscription noted that "the heavens were greatly obscured" (Shaughnessy 1999:322). The Western Zhou kings also expanded ritual practices that highlighted the elite social, political, and ideological standing of military officers. Bronze vessels for sacrificial offerings to royal ancestors continued to be made in state workshops, but now they had a new role. The production of individual bronze vessels was commissioned by Western Zhou officials to commemorate military victories. Details of battles were often provided, as well as gratitude to the king and certain high-ranking ancestors (Shaughnessy 1999:318–319).

These vessels also were used by military officials in specific rituals. As related by Shaughnessy (1999:320), one inscription describes a libation rite in the Zhou ancestral temple. The participants were invited by the king after a military victory by an official named Yu. The inscription relates how Yu was asked to present his trophies of war (perhaps heads) before an offering was made to the royal ancestors. Then the guests were served a fermented beverage described as "wine" (see Underhill 2002), and all the participants made toasts in celebration. The inscription includes a list of men taken captive (including local leaders), as well as captured animals and chariots. Yu was requested to present the booty for display and for registration by the state authorities.

Textual data also make it clear that Western Zhou elites exchanged military goods as gifts. Chariots were especially valued gifts; they were given to nobles by the king (Rawson 1999:395, 397). Chariot fittings and weapons were exchanged as well; bronze *yue* axes continued to be especially important for displaying high military status (Yates 1999:17–18). One inscription states that the king awarded a lord a black, carved dagger-axe (presumably a *ge*, probably of fine stone) for military service to the state; other axe-men vassals are mentioned as well (Shaughnessy 1999:318). It is possible that this kind of elite exchange system took place earlier during the Shang period, although we lack relevant textual information. The high status of military personnel is also evident from graves containing bronze weapons, chariots, horses, and lower ranking soldiers (Hsu and Linduff 1988; Rawson 1999:395–396).

There has been some debate whether superior military technology enabled the Western Zhou to defeat the Shang. Hsu and Linduff (1988:87–88) conclude that the advantage was mainly a larger infantry who fought on foot and who were well protected with armor. One new weapon in this period was a short bronze dagger-axe shaped like a willow leaf, possibly a result of increased contact with peoples from the northeastern steppes (Yates 1999:19). Another important innovation was the bronze sword (*jian*; Figure 8.7; Yang 1992:82). This example from The Field Museum could date to either the Western or early Eastern Zhou period.

In 770 B.C., the Western Zhou were defeated in battle, ending the monopoly of power in northern China for several hundred years. Several small states subsequently vied for power during the Eastern Zhou period (770–221 B.C.), fighting hundreds of battles over territory. Warfare continued to be a key component of state religious systems in northern China during the first part of the Eastern Zhou period, to 481 B.C., known as the Spring and Autumn period (Yates 1999:8–9). As the frequency and intensity of warfare increased, so did the depth of the ideological motivation of the participants. As Lewis (1990:36) explains, serving the state in battle was a religious duty—to bring honor and glory to both the ancestors and the extant lineage, while bringing prestige to the high ranking individuals in leadership roles. Texts from the period mention numerous cases in which insulting the enemy and invoking a sense of shame on another lineage spurred intense battles (Lewis 1990:37–41).

It was essential to follow proper ritual procedure before, during, and after battles during the Spring and Autumn period. During battles men were to kill only those of similar rank. Commanders continued to seek divine assistance in battle. If they were successful, they offered the left ears of the defeated as sacrificial offerings

Figure 8.7. Zhou Period, bronze *jian* sword (1114.116755) (The Field Museum, Department of Anthropology).

(Yates 1999:20–21). The composition of the army was essentially the same; the infantry consisted of low-ranking men, led into battle by their lineage leaders (Lewis 1990). Chariots continued to be used in battle, and rather than focusing on scaling city walls, more battles took place in open terrain (Lewis 1990; Yates 1999).

The later, or Warring States phase (ca. 481–221 B.C.), of the Eastern Zhou period ushered in dramatic changes in warfare. Both the abundant textual and archaeological data make it clear that ritual no longer played a significant role in warfare. The sole aim was total destruction of the enemy and preservation of the state (Yates 1999:25). Military treatises were written, the most famous of which is the *Sunzi* (*The Art of War*), outlining military strategies with the goal of achieving victory by any means, especially deception (see Gawlikowski and Loewe 1993; Lewis 1990; Needham et al. 1994). Individual battles and wars lasted longer. Scenes of battles were even depicted on bronze vessels (see Cheng and Zhong 1990:68–69).

In addition, there were dramatic changes in social organization. As state territories grew, the role of lineages in military organization declined. Professional soldiers and officers went to battle, rather than lineage leaders and their sons (Yates 1999:21–22). Infantry units were larger, coming from a wider population in the state territory, including villages, allowing low-ranking men to enhance their social standing by success in warfare (Lewis 1990:67, 77). Some of the previous practices of rewarding military service, however, were retained. Rulers presented generals they hired for particular battles with a bronze axe to symbolize their conferred rights and privileges (Yates 1999:26).

The increase in frequency, intensity, and scale of warfare motivated more construction of defensive structures, especially in border areas. Many new watchtowers and walls around sections of state borders were constructed, while some walls built during the preceding Spring and Autumn period were joined together (Lewis 1999:629). The more widespread availability of iron made it possible to produce large quantities of weapons, in both old and new forms. Lewis (1999:622) describes how new weapons were produced, such as a grappling hook (*gou ju*) to prevent enemy boats from fleeing, and the deadly accurate cross-bow. Yang (1992:95) argues instead that the cross-bow was first invented during the Spring and Autumn period, probably in the southern state of Chu. New forms of ladders were made to scale city walls as well. New forms of body armor were invented during the Warring States period, first using lacquered leather plates, and later, metal (see Dien 2000).

The constant state of warfare and the culture of violence during the Eastern Zhou period took a toll on the populace. From texts it appears that elites engaged in rituals honoring violence, some involving animals, since hunting was regarded as a form of warfare (Lewis 1990:153–154, 157). Some voices of dissent emerged during this tumultuous period. The pacifist Mencius wrote that leaders ought to be able to avoid war and regarded warfare as evil in most circumstances (Lewis 1990:129).

In 221 B.C., the Qin defeated the other states and the Qin empire emerged. It appears that several factors contributed to their impressive, but short-lived, victory. Prior to the decisive battle, the Qin state had required its citizens to engage in military service. Individuals could increase their rank by displaying the heads of the enemy, regardless of whether battles were won or lost (Yates 1999:27). Historians debate whether superior technology was responsible for the military success of the Qin. Yates (1999:29) concludes that an efficient military organization (including control over troops and efficient transport of supplies) was more important than the greater availability of iron weapons. The hundreds of terracotta soldiers from the first emperor's tomb, showing different hairstyles and clothing by rank, provide a glimpse of this complex organizational structure (Archaeological Team 1987; Qian et al. 1982), as well as the initial construction of the Great Wall.

Conclusions

Archaeological and textual data from northern China provide valuable information on the relation between change in sociopolitical organization and change in warfare. During the Longshan period, there was a dramatic increase in the establishment of settlements surrounded by earthen walls. This pattern suggests that defense was a greater concern in comparison to earlier periods. Further archaeological fieldwork in individual regions is necessary to investigate the rise and fall of polities during each phase of the Longshan period. This research must assess the nature of interactions between all settlements in specific regions, not just those with earthen walls. Only then can we begin to investigate possible sources of economic or social stress that people may have attempted to resolve by violence.

There is little physical evidence for warfare during the Longshan period, although systematic investigations of skeletal remains and settlement areas on a regional basis could change this in the future. Nevertheless, the production of labor-intensive, symbolic jade weapons during the Longshan period indicates the emergence of an important link between high status and warfare that becomes more pronounced over time in northern China. It suggests that the causes of warfare could have included not only economic factors but also a desire to bring honor to lineage members, as seen in later periods. At present, the hypothesis that warfare was a major causal factor for the initial emergence of states in northern China is not supported by the archaeological data.

There is abundant archaeological, and especially textual, evidence to trace changes in warfare as state organization evolved. The more powerful states became, the larger the role that warfare played. Oracle-bone inscriptions and archaeological remains from the late Shang period show that warfare was common, large in scale, and strongly supported by the state. Lineage units were also military units, and high ranking individuals also were leaders in battle.

Evidently warfare during the late Shang period was partially caused by economic factors, since, for example, the inscriptions mention the need to acquire new agricultural lands. It appears, however, that other, non-economic, causal factors also were important, especially ideological justification and lineage honor. Kings engaged in battle, and a common goal was to capture humans to offer as sacrifices to the royal ancestors. Here we find another trend that intensifies in later periods—viewing at least some of the enemy as outsiders, since the Qiang people usually were offered as human sacrifices.

State support spurred the production of several new forms of specialized weapons during the Erlitou and Shang periods, especially of bronze. Their prevalence in elite burials indicates that skill in warfare was linked to political and social status—for both men and women. The large bronze axes may have been exchanged between elites in commemoration of military alliances, judging from descriptions of such behavior in later periods. The introduction of the horse and chariot during the late Shang period facilitated success in warfare and also created a new symbol of elite status.

It is clear that after the Shang period, new states were established by conquest. During the Western Zhou period, warfare continued to be a key activity of the state. Leadership in warfare was essential for political leaders, who also seem to have been lineage heads. Inscribed bronze vessels commemorated victories and were exchanged between elites, along with other goods such as chariots and jades. There were further innovations in weapons technology, including new forms of bronze dagger-axes and the introduction of the sword.

During the first (Spring and Autumn) part of the Eastern Zhou period, warfare was constant, as a number of relatively small states vied for supremacy. More than ever before, wars took place to defend the honor of lineage members, both past and present. A deeply embedded system linking social status, political leadership, and state ritual with warfare motivated military leaders. At this time, evidently, the enemy did not consist entirely of cultural outsiders. It seems there was a more narrow conception of outsider, as defined by the lack of lineage ties. Some people defined as the enemy would have had similar social and ritual practices, but no doubt those in more distant areas would have been regarded as culturally inferior. Yet it appears these same peoples were allies in later wars.

Significant changes in the organization of warfare took place in the Warring States period that followed. Ritual protocol was no longer a concern, and ordinary citizens could distinguish themselves in battle, since soldiers were drawn from the wider populace. At the same time, state support and interpolity competition spurred the development of new and more lethal weapons. A new material, iron, made it possible to produce large quantities of weapons. Probably more than one factor enabled the Qin to establish an empire: superior military organization, a large infantry (including conscripts), and widely available iron tools.

The Chinese data are valuable for assessing ancient warfare from a comparative perspective. More archaeological fieldwork is needed to find support for the possibility that economic stress caused increased warfare during the late Neolithic, Longshan period. As commonly expected for chiefdoms in other areas of the world, there may have been perceived shortages of resources (either basic or prestige goods) in contexts of social or environmental circumscription. More frequent raiding may have been a conscious strategy on the part of elites to acquire both honor and resources, given the presence of ritual objects symbolic of warfare in some graves. The limited evidence for the Neolithic period as a whole is similar to the prehistoric period of North America, in that there was increasingly lethal warfare. It is likely that another pattern, as seen for prehistoric Europe and the early historic Caribbean, is the development of elite rituals about warfare. Evidence that warfare was a key factor in the initial emergence of states remains to be found.

After states developed in northern China, as seen in more than one part of Mesoamerica, the power of the state increased in conjunction with the importance, frequency, and ferocity of warfare. Here also, military and political leadership were intertwined, and there was increasing professionalism in the military. Another common trend is that more battles and the prestige of warfare motivated technological innovation, eventually setting off an "arms race."

A pattern that seems more prevalent for ancient China than for other areas is the importance of lineage honor in motivating warfare—the perceived need to honor past and present consanguineal kin with meritorious conduct in battle. A related pattern that is evident from more than one early historic period in China is the perception of the enemy as outsiders. In each cultural tradition, of course, the definition of outsiders would vary. In northern China, cultural outsiders, in part, would have been those who had different ritual practices and who came from different lineages. By the Eastern Zhou period, it appears that people had a narrower definition of exactly who was an outsider—probably with respect to genealogical, social, and political relations. Ironically, however, historic texts also show that outsiders who were considered enemies in one period could be regarded as allies in the next. As seen in more recent human history across the globe, perceived differences between people can fluctuate widely, making the difference between peace and war.

Lui 2004, which describes more recently reported walled sites from the Longshan period, became available after this chapter went to press.

Acknowledgments

I am grateful to Elizabeth Arkush and Mark Allen for their insightful comments on the draft of this chapter. Jill Seagard, Department of Anthropology, The Field Museum, prepared Figures 8.1 and 8.6. She also scanned the photographs of the items from the anthropology department collections in The Field Museum for Figures 8.2–8.5 and 8.7.

References

Anyang Team, Institute of Archaeology, CASS. 2003. Henan Anyang Shi Huanbei Shang Cheng de Ji Cang Yu Shi Jue (Test Excavations and Preliminary Conclusions Regarding the Shang City at Huanbei in Anyang City, Henan). *Kaogu* 5:3–16.

Archaeological Team, Pit of the Terracotta Figures at Qin Shi Huang Mausoleum and the Museum of Qin Terracotta Figures. 1987. *Terra-cotta Warriors and Horses at the Tomb of Qin Shi Huang, the First Emperor of China*. 4th ed. Beijing: Wenwu Press.

Bagley, R. 1999. Shang Archaeology. In *The Cambridge History of Ancient China*, edited by M. Loewe and E. Shaughnessy, 124–231. Cambridge: Cambridge University Press.

Carman, J., and A. Harding. 1999. Introduction. In *Ancient Warfare: Archaeological Perspectives*, edited by J. Carman and A. Harding, 1–9. London: Sutton Publishing Ltd.

Carneiro, R. 1970. A Theory of the Origin of the State. *Science* 169:733–738.

———. 1978. Political Expansion as an Expression of the Principle of Competitive Exclusion. In *Origins of the State*, edited by R. Cohen and E. Service, 205–223. Philadelphia: Institute for the Study of Human Issues.

———. 1990. Chiefdom-level Warfare as Exemplified in Fiji and the Cauca Valley. In *The Anthropology of War*, edited by J. Haas, 190–211. New York: Cambridge University Press.

Chang, K. 1980. *Shang Civilization*. New Haven: Yale University Press.

———. 1983. *Art, Myth and Ritual*. Cambridge: Harvard University Press.

———. 1986. *The Archaeology of Ancient China*. 4th ed. New Haven: Yale University Press.

Changwei Area Archaeological Group and Museum of Zhucheng County. 1980. Zhucheng

Chengzi Yizhi Fajue Baogao (Excavation Report for the Site of Chengzi at Zhucheng, Shandong). *Kaogu Xuebao* 3:329–385.

Chapman, J. 1999. The Origins of Warfare in the Prehistory of Central and Eastern Europe. In *Ancient Warfare: Archaeological Perspectives*, edited by J. Carman and A. Harding, 101–142. London: Sutton Publishing Ltd.

Chen, X. 1997. Qintong Shidai yu Yuqi Shidai-Zailun Zhongguo Wenming de Qiyuan (Bronze Age and Jade Age: A Further Study of the Origin of Chinese Civilization). In *Kaogu Qiuzhi ji*, edited by Institute of Archaeology, CASS 29–42. Beijing: China Social Sciences Press.

———. 2000. Zhongguo Gudai de Botoupi Fengsu ji Qita (The Practice of Scalping in Ancient China). *Wenwu* 1:48–55.

Cheng, D., and Z. Shao-yi. 1990. *Zhongguo Gudai Bingqi Tuji* (A Pictorial Collection of Ancient Chinese Weapons). Beijing: The Chinese People's Liberation Army Publishing House.

Cheng, T. 1960. *Archaeology in China. Volume II. Shang China*. Cambridge: W. Heffer and Sons Ltd.

Childs-Johnson, E. 1988. *Ritual and Power: Jades of Ancient China*. New York: China Institute in America.

———. 1995. Symbolic Jades of the Erlitou Period: A Xia Royal Tradition. *Archives of Asian Art* 48:64–91.

Dematte, P. 1999. Longshan-era Urbanism: The Role of Cities in Predynastic China. *Asian Perspectives* 38:119–153.

Dien, A. 2000. Armor in China Before the Tang Dynasty. *Journal of East Asian Archaeology* 2–4:23–59.

Earle, T. 1997. *How Chiefs Come to Power*. Stanford: Stanford University Press.

Ferguson, R. B. 1990. Explaining War. In *The Anthropology of War*, edited by J. Haas, 26–55. New York: Cambridge University Press.

Gawlikowski, K., and M. Loewe. 1993. Sun Tzu Ping Fa [The Art of War]. In *Early Chinese Texts. A Bibliographical Guide*, edited by M. Loewe, 446–455. Berkeley: The Society for the Study of Early China and the Institute of East Asian Studies, University of California.

Haas, J. 1982. T*he Evolution of the Prehistoric State*. New York: Columbia University Press.

———. 1990. Warfare and the Evolution of Tribal Polities in the Prehistoric Southwest. In *The Anthropology of War*, edited by J. Haas, 171–189. New York: Cambridge University Press.

———. 1999. The Origins of War and Ethnic Violence. In *Ancient Warfare: Archaeological Perspectives*, edited by J. Carman and A. Harding, 11–24. London: Sutton Publishing Ltd.

———. 2001. Warfare and the Evolution of Culture. In *Archaeology at the Millennium: A Sourcebook*, edited by G. Feinman and D. Price, 329–350. New York: Kluwer Academic/Plenum Publishers.

Hassig, R. 1992. *War and Society in Ancient Mesoamerica*. Berkeley: University of California Press.

Hebei Province Institute of Archaeology. 1985. *Gaocheng Taixi Shang dai Yizhi* (The Shang Site of Taixi at Gaocheng). Beijing: Wenwu Press.

Henan Province Institute of Archaeology and the Xinmi City Yanhuang History and Culture Research Association. 2002. Henan Xinmi shi Guchengzhai Longshan Wenhua Chengzhi Fajue Jianbao (Short Report of the City Site of the Longshan Culture at Guchengzhai at Xinmi city, Henan). *Huaxia Kaogu* 2:53–82.

Henan Province Institute of Archaeology and the Zhoukou District Cultural Relics Institute. 1983. Henan Huaiyang Pingliangtai Longshan Wenhua Chengzhi Shijue Jianbao (Short Report of the Test Excavations at the Longshan Culture City Site of Pingliangtai at Huaiyang, Henan). *Wenwu* 3:21–36.

Hill, P., and J. Wileman. 2002. *Landscapes of War. The Archaeology of Aggression and Defense*. London: Tempest Publishing, Ltd.

Hsu, C., and K. Linduff. 1988. *Western Chou Civilization*. New Haven: Yale University Press.

Institute of Archaeology, CASS. 1980. *Yinxu Fuhao Mu* (The Tomb of Fuhao at Yinxu). Beijing: Wenwu Press.

———. 1988. *Jiaoxian Sanlihe* (The Sanlihe Site at Jiaoxian). Beijing: Wenwu Press.

———. 1998. *Anyang Yinxu Guojiazhuang Shang Dai Muzang* (Shang Period Burials from Guojiazhuang at Yinxu, Anyang). Beijing: The Encyclopedia of China Publishing House.

———. 1999. *Yanshi Erlitou 1959 nian-1978 nian Kaogu Fajue Baogao* (The Erlitou Site in Yanshi. Excavations in 1959–1978). Beijing: The Encyclopedia of China Press.

Keeley, L. 1996. *War Before Civilization: The Myth of the Peaceful Savage*. New York: Oxford University Press.

Keightley, D. 1999. The Shang: China's First Historical Dynasty. In *The Cambridge History of Ancient China*, edited by M. Loewe and E. Shaughnessy, 232–291. Cambridge: Cambridge University Press.

———. 2000. *The Ancestral Landscape: Time, Space, and Community in Late Shang China (ca. 1200–1045 B.C.)*. China Research Monograph 53. Berkeley: Institute of East Asian Studies, University of California.

Kokkinidou, D., and M. Nikolaidou. 1999. Neolithic Enclosures in Greek Macedonia: Violent and Non-violent Aspects of Territorial Demarcation. In *Ancient Warfare: Archaeological Perspectives*, edited by J. Carman and A. Harding, 89–99. London: Sutton Publishing Ltd.

Kristiansen, K. 1999. The Emergence of Warrior Aristocracies in Later European Prehistory and Their Long-term History. In *Ancient Warfare: Archaeological Perspectives*, edited by J. Carman and A. Harding, 175–189. London: Sutton Publishing Ltd.

Lambert, P. 2002. The Archaeology of War: A North American Perspective. *Journal of Archaeological Research* 19(3):207–241.

Lee, Y. 2004. Control Strategies and Polity Competition in the Lower Yi-Luo Valley, North China. *Journal of Anthropological Archaeology* 23:172–195.

Lekson, S. H. 2002. War in the Southwest, War in the World. *American Antiquity* 67(4): 607–624.

Lewis, M. 1990. *Sanctioned Violence in Early China*. Albany: State University of New York Press.

———. 1999. *Warring States Political History*. In *The Cambridge History of Ancient China*, edited by M. Loewe and E. Shaughnessy, 587–650. Cambridge: Cambridge University Press.

Linyi Group to Protect Cultural Relics. 1975. Shandong Linyi Dafanzhuang Xinshiqi Shidai Muzang de Fajue (Excavation of Neolithic Burials at Dafanzhuang, Linyi, Shandong). *Kaogu* 1:13–22, 6.

Liu, Li. 1996a. Settlement Patterns, Chiefdom Variability, and the Development of Early States in North China. *Journal of Anthropological Archaeology* 15(3):237–288.

———. 1996b. Mortuary Ritual and Social Hierarchy in the Longshan Culture. *Early China* 21:1–46.

———. 2000. The Development and Decline of Social Complexity in North China: Some Environmental and Social Factors. In *Indo-Pacific Prehistory: The Melaka Papers. Volume 4*, edited by P. Bellwood, D. Bowdery, J. Allen, E. Bacus, and G. Summerhayes 14–34. Canberra: Australian National University.

———. 2004. *The Chinese Neolithic*. Cambridge: Cambridge University Press.

Liu, L., and C. Xingcan. 2001. Settlement Archaeology and the Study of Social Complexity in China. *The Review of Archaeology* 22(2):4–22.

———. 2003. *State Formation in Early China*. London: Gerald Duckworth and Co., Ltd.

Milner, G. 1999. Warfare in Prehistoric and Early Historic Eastern North America. *Journal of Archaeological Research* 7(2):105–151.

Needham, J., R. Yates, K. Gawlikowski, E. McEwen, and W. Ling. 1994. *Science and Civilisation in China. Volume 5. Chemistry and Chemical Technology. Part VI. Military Technology: Missiles and Sieges*. Cambridge: Cambridge University Press.

Otterbein, K. 2000. A History of Research on Warfare in Anthropology. *American Anthropologist* 101(4):794–805.

Qian, H., H. Chen, and S. Ru. 1982. *Out of China's Earth*. New York: Harry N. Abrams, Inc. Publishers.

Qiu, S., and L. Cai. 2001. Xia Shang Zhou Duandai Gongcheng Zhong de Tanshisi Niandai Kuangjia (A C14 Chronological Framework for the Xia-Shang-Zhou Chronology Project). *Kaogu* 1:90–100.

Rawson, J. 1999. Western Zhou Archaeology. In *The Cambridge History of Ancient China*, edited by M. Loewe and E. Shaughnessy, 352–449. Cambridge: Cambridge University Press.

Shandong Province Institute of Archaeology. 1990. Shandong Linqu Zhufeng Longshan Wenhua Muzang (Burials of the Longshan Culture at Zhufeng, Shandong). *Kaogu* 7:587–594.

Shandong University, Department of History, Archaeology Specialty. 1990. *Sishui Yinjiacheng* (Excavation Report of the Yinjiacheng Site at Sishui). Beijing: Wenwu Press.

———. 1993. Shandong Zouping Dinggong Yizhi Disi, Wu Ci Fajue Jianbao (Short Report on the Fourth and Fifth Excavation of the Dinggong Site at Zouping, Shandong). *Kaogu* 4:295–299.

Shao, W., 2000. The Longshan Period and Incipient Chinese Civilization. *Journal of East Asian Archaeology* 2(1–2):195–226.

Shaughnessy, E. 1999. Western Zhou History. In *The Cambridge History of Ancient China*, edited by M. Loewe and E. Shaughnessy, 292–351. Cambridge: Cambridge University Press.

Shelach, G. 1999. *Leadership Strategies, Economic Activity, and Interregional Interaction. Social Complexity in Northeast China*. New York: Kluwer Academic/Plenum Publishers.

Underhill, A. 1989. Warfare During the Chinese Neolithic Period: A Review of the Evidence. In *Cultures in Conflict: Current Archaeological Perspectives*, edited by D. Tkaczuk and B. Vivian, 229–240. Calgary: Archaeological Association, University of Calgary.

———. 1994. Variation in Settlements During the Longshan Period of Northern China. *Asian Perspectives* 33:197–228.

———. 2002. *Craft Production and Social Change in Northern China*. New York: Kluwer Academic/Plenum Press.

Underhill, A., and H. Fang. 2004. Early State Economic Systems in China. In *The Economies of Chiefdoms and States*, edited by G. Feinman and L. Nicholas, 119–132. Salt Lake City: University of Utah Press.

Underhill, A., H. Fang, and F. Luan. In press. Development of Regional Polities in Northern China. *Journal of Archaeological Research*.

Underhill, A., G. Feinman, L. Nicholas, G. Bennett, H. Fang, F. Luan, H. Yu, F. Cai. 2002. Regional Survey and the Development of Complex Societies in Southeastern Shandong, China. *Antiquity* 76:745–755.

Vayda, A. 1976. *War in Ecological Perspective: Persistence, Change, and Adaptive Processes in Three Oceanian Societies*. New York: Plenum Press.

Vencl, S. 1999. Stone Age Warfare. In *Ancient Warfare: Archaeological Perspectives*, edited by J. Carman and A. Harding, 57–72. London: Sutton Publishing Ltd.

Webster, D. 1975. Warfare and the Evolution of the State: A Reconsideration. *American Antiquity* 40:464–470.

———. 1993. The Study of Maya Warfare: What it Tells us About the Maya and What it Tells us About Maya Archaeology. In *Lowland Maya Civilization in the Eighth Century A.D.*, edited by J. Sabloff and J. Henderson, 415–444. Washington, D.C.: Dumbarton Oaks Research Library and Collection.

Whitehead, N. 1990. The Snake Warriors—Sons of the Tiger's Teeth: A Descriptive Analysis of Carib Warfare ca. 1500–1820. In *The Anthropology of War*, edited by J. Haas, 126–170. New York: Cambridge University Press.

Wu, H. 1995. *Monumentality in Early Chinese Art and Architecture*. Stanford: Stanford University Press.

Yan, W. 1982. Jiangou de Tougai Bei he Botoupi Fengsu (Skull Cap Cups from Jiangou and the Custom of Scalping). *Kaogu Yu Wenwu* 2:38–41.

Yang, H. 1992. *Weapons in Ancient China*. Beijing: Science Press.

Yang, X., and B. Yang. 1986. Shang Dai de Qingtong Yue (Bronze Yue from the Shang Period). In *Zhongguo Kaoguxue Yanjiu—Xia Nai Xiansheng Kaogu Wushi Nian Jin-*

ian Lunwen Ji (Archaeological Research in China. Essays in Commemoration of Fifty Years of Mr. Xia Nai in Archaeology), edited by Archaeological Research in China Editorial Committee, 128–138. Beijing: Wenwu Press.

Yates, R. 1997. The City-State in Ancient China. In *The Archaeology of City-States*, edited by T. Charlton and D. Nichols, 71–90. Washington, D.C.: Smithsonian Press.

———. 1999. Early China. In *War and Society in the Ancient and Medieval Worlds. Asia, The Mediterranean, Europe, and Mesoamerica*, edited by K. Raaflaub and N. Rosenstein, 7–45. Cambridge: Harvard University Press.

Zhao, Q. 2001. Yanshi Shang Cheng Jianzhu Xie Lun (Discussion of the Raised Architectural Features at the Shang City of Yanshi). *Huaxia Kaogu* 2:34–52.

9

Collapse, Conflict, Conquest

The Transformation of Warfare in the Late Prehispanic Andean Highlands

ELIZABETH N. ARKUSH

As warfare comes to the forefront of archaeological investigation, a new wealth of data can be applied to anthropological models that include warfare. What these data illuminate first of all is the complexity, contingency, and unpredictability of the trajectories of warring societies—the difficulty of reconciling real-life sequences with the necessarily simplified worlds of our theoretical models. In addition, the sheer variety of ways in which warfare may be integrated into other aspects of society is striking. Despite its violent and destructive nature, war as a social institution is generative, defining and maintaining groups and group identities, structuring and justifying political hierarchy, and supplying a rich source of images and narratives to be interwoven with belief and expressed in material culture.

The Andean region is an excellent place to study these contrasts, because warfare profoundly affected its prehistory, but in very different ways at different times. This chapter traces the role of warfare in the Andean highlands over the latter part of the archaeological sequence from approximately A.D. 600 (the beginning of the Middle Horizon) to the time of the Spanish conquest in 1532.[1] It focuses in particular on the evidence for warfare; on the relationship between warfare and centralized political leadership and polity expansion; and on the representation of warlike or violent themes, in particular the role of militarism in elite legitimization.

Political Leadership and Polity Expansion

Two contrasting models of conquest and political fragmentation have emerged from the anthropological and archaeological literature on warfare (see Introduction, this volume; Allen 2003). On the one hand, beginning with Carneiro's landmark article (1970), anthropologists have argued that warfare was a key causal factor in the development of sociopolitical hierarchies and large-scale, centralized polities (Carneiro 1970, 1981, 1990; Earle 1997; Ferguson 1984; Redmond 1994; Webster 1975). This view is supported by the fact that conquest warfare clearly played an important role in the rise of many state societies (see, for instance, Redmond and Spencer, this volume; Underhill, this volume; LeBlanc, this volume).

However, paradoxically, chronic warfare can also fragment regions and make further political consolidation nearly impossible. This point has not been theoretically developed except by Allen (2003), but it is implied by theoretical models such as chiefly cycling (Anderson 1994; Wright 1984), and the evidence for it is abundant. It is clear from ethnographic studies that in many regions, intense warfare is or was practiced without corresponding political consolidation. Indeed, the very ethnographic studies that created anthropological perceptions of non-state warfare were, almost by definition, of fragmented, decentralized societies unable or uninterested in forming larger stable polities (for example, Chagnon 1968; Meggitt 1977; Vayda 1960). Archaeologists have also documented many past landscapes fragmented by warfare, such as the mosaics of autonomous villages protected by defensive location or light fortifications in parts of the Eastern Woodlands of North America (Milner 1999), or the clusters of allied defensive sites in New Zealand (Allen 1994, 1996, 2003) and the American Southwest (LeBlanc 1999; Rice and LeBlanc 2001; Wilcox and Haas 1994). Such archaeological studies demonstrate that societies may engage in warfare for long periods of time without consolidating into larger political units.

The differences in these two outcomes trace to fundamental variation between the practice of raiding warfare and true conquest—that is, the takeover of people, not just territories. But what causes some sociopolitical groups to raid and others to conquer? How do some regions with intermittent or chronic warfare develop polities powerful enough to forge states and empires from conquest, while others do not? These divergent outcomes pose a challenge for including warfare as a causal factor in models of social change.

Representations of Warfare, Violence, and Power

Much of the evidence for war that archaeologists draw upon is not in fact the direct result of violent conflict (burned settlements, skeletal trauma) or people's immediate response to it (fortifications, defensive settlement location) but a second-order body of material culture that alludes to and represents warfare. Depictions of warriors, public sacrifices and other violent displays, curated human trophies, weapons crafted more for show than for use, warriors' graves—these representations provide less information about the frequency and intensity of war itself than they do about the place it held in cosmology and ritual, in elite propaganda, in gender roles, and in social group identities. For instance, beautifully crafted display weapons from Mississippian contexts (see Dye, this volume) signaled status at the highest levels. Mythic narratives of combat and subjugation provided parallels for earthly war-leaders to emphasize their divine qualities. As such, the warfare conducted by rival chiefs in the Mississippian area should be considered not just a distinctive pattern of warfare practice on the ground (involving, for instance, the sacking of important ceremonial structures), but also a body of beliefs, elite justifications, and representations of power that revolved around warfare.

On the other hand, warfare was not always linked closely to elite legitimization, and many contexts of warring societies lack these sorts of representations. Such cases do not mean that beliefs about warfare were not present, but they suggest that they were not heavily drawn upon for propagandistic purposes. For instance, Earle (1991, 1997:187–188) traces a transition in Wessex, from the Bronze Age "Age of Stonehenge," characterized by monumental construction and elaborate elite barrow-graves full of warrior-related items, to the late Bronze Age or Early Iron Age, when these patterns ceased with the rise of hill forts and smaller, more fragmented societies. Leaders, while less powerful, were surely present in the later period, but they were intentionally deemphasized. While warfare was practiced in both types of societies, its relationship to political hierarchy was different.

These contrasts in the ideological uses of warfare illuminate a basic tension between warfare as a field of individual endeavor and elite achievement, and warfare as a crucible of group solidarity. These two opposed messages or morals can both be drawn from warfare, and may be emphasized in material culture at different times, even in the same region. Meanwhile, the dramatic, destructive nature of group violence guarantees that whatever messages people choose to frame about warfare, whether they justify political hierarchy or stress group identity, will be potent and highly charged.

As this review illustrates, warfare in the Andean highlands varied in intensity and scale over time (Table 9.1). It gave rise to both conquest states and small, fragmented, raiding polities—as implied at the most basic level by the traditional archaeological breakdown of the Andean sequence into horizons, integration or conquest periods, and intermediate periods, periods of fragmentation and regional development. In addition, the importance of warfare in elite power ideology changed markedly throughout the sequence. These contrasts are particularly striking because they occurred over time in the same environment and among the same peoples, relying on essentially the same subsistence and military technologies. Thus, we are left with only a small number of possible explanations for the changing role of warfare in the Andean highlands.

Table 9.1. Culture Chronology and Warfare Patterns in the Later Andean Highlands

Date A.D.	Period	General	Andean highlands: Northern		Central	Cuzco region	Titicaca Basin	Moquegua	Far southern
1550 1500 1450	**Late Horizon (LH)**	Inca conquest and consolidation	Inca empire. Prolonged conflict on northern frontier		Inca empire	**Inca**	Inca empire	Inca empire	Inca empire
1400 1350 1300 1250 1200 1150 1100 1050 1000	**Late Intermediate Period (LIP)**	Fragmented regional polities. Pervasive evidence of warfare; military basis of political leadership; little militaristic iconography.	Greater centralization, intensified warfare Regional cultures. Some evidence of warfare	Marca Huamachuco	Nucleation and intensified warfare Regional cultures. Warfare.	**Early Inca**: gradual consolidation, limited warfare	Intense warfare Regional cultures	Intensified warfare Some warfare	Evidence of warfare Dispersed regional cultures
950 900 850 800 750 700 650 600	**Middle Horizon (MH)**	Elaborate militaristic displays at state centers. Some evidence of violence, conquest, and/or resistance in provinces.	Some Wari centers; widespread Wari interaction / influence	Marca Huamachuco	**Wari**	Wari presence in Lucre and Huaro Valleys	**Tiwanaku**	Tiwanaku and Wari centers	Tiwanaku interaction / influence

The First Highland States: The Middle Horizon (A.D. 600–1000)

The Middle Horizon (MH) is a period defined by the rise of two contemporary, centralized states in the Andean highlands, Wari and Tiwanaku. Both of these states developed an urban capital replete with civic and ceremonial architecture, a well-integrated heartland, a number of centers or colonies far from the heartland under direct political control, and a much wider sphere of exchange and cultural or ideological influence. While Andeanists actively debate the extent to which these states used military coercion to consolidate power, the evidence reviewed here suggests that warfare was indeed involved in their expansion. In addition, both Wari and Tiwanaku produced violent or militaristic displays that suggest that violence was a central theme in belief and was related to elite power, at least conceptually. The two states shared a similar religious iconography centered on the same principal deity. This iconography included war-related images such as armed figures and severed trophy heads. Finally, the relationship between Wari and Tiwanaku probably included warfare or the threat of warfare at least occasionally. Their political spheres overlapped at one point, in the Moquegua valley; evidence from that region is discussed at the end of this section.

Wari

Wari is located in the Ayacucho Valley of the central Peruvian highlands (Figure 9.1), where an earlier pattern of clustered but unfortified sites existed. The site of Wari itself is located on a hill spur, and its location may have been chosen for defensive or strategic reasons, considering the disadvantages of the place—above all, that it lacks a water source. Thus, competition may have existed between the settlements or settlement clusters of the valley prior to their domination by Wari. At the beginning of the MH, Wari became an urbanized center encompassing up to 15 km^2 of occupation, with large-scale residential areas, a precinct of ceremonial architecture, elite burials, and possible palaces (Schreiber 2001). While Wari's surroundings were largely depopulated, some subsidiary centers are fortified (Pérez 1999), suggesting that Wari's control and protection of the valley was maintained partly through military domination. This interpretation is supported by evidence from skeletal remains. At the site of Conchopata, a nearby settlement involved in ceramic manufacture and ceremony, Tung (2003) has found that cranial trauma increased dramatically with the rise of the Wari empire, jumping from 8 percent of all adults in the previous period to 25 percent during the Middle Horizon. These individuals might have been involved in conflict over Wari's control of its immediate surroundings, or they may have been conscripted for military duty further away in one of Wari's expansionistic campaigns.

Figure 9.1. Middle Horizon sites and place names mentioned in the text.

But in general, the Wari heartland does not show much evidence of warfare itself. There is, however, evidence about war's role in ideology and ceremony. For instance, an important ceremonial structure at Conchopata contained a cache of six burned trophy heads—skulls with post-mortem perforations on the forehead, enabling them to be strung with a cord and carried or displayed (Ochatoma and Cabrera 1999:226).[2] Trophy head-taking was already a very old tradition in the Andes, and one that had been celebrated in iconography for centuries (Cordy-Collins 1992, 2001; Tello 1918; Verano 1995). Ethnographic analogy for this widespread practice (Divale 1973; Keeley 1996:99–103), and ethnohistoric accounts of Inca trophy head-taking, suggest that trophy heads such as the ones at Conchopata were taken from enemies captured or killed in war. Andean trophy heads were often carefully prepared and cached in locations associated with ritual, and the skulls from Conchopata are no exception, suggesting that they held ideological significance.

Wari iconography is also indicative of the importance of violence in Wari ideology. Trophy heads are quite common in Wari art, as well as other military themes. For instance, ceramics from Conchopata portray warriors carrying shields and armed with bows and arrows or axes (Ochatoma and Cabrera 1999, 2002). Drawing on the distinctions between depicted warriors in face paint, arms, dress, and shield motifs, Ochatoma and Cabrera (1999:234–235, 2002:240–243) posit that Wari had professional warriors with a military hierarchy.

Very soon after Wari consolidated control over the Ayacucho valley, it embarked on a program of imperial expansion. Wari or Wari-related ceramics are present in low densities over much of the northern and central Peruvian highlands and the southern and central coast, but direct Wari control is best demonstrated by the construction of numerous administrative centers in Wari's distinctive architectural style. At around A.D. 600–700, these widely scattered centers appear across a vast expanse of the Andean highlands (Schreiber 1992:96–112, 2001:83–85; Williams 2001). Most Wari provincial centers are sited strategically to control views of the surrounding terrain, passes, and important routes (see Schreiber 1992:99–107). Nevertheless, most are not in easily defensible locations and very few are effectively fortified,[3] suggesting that their builders did not consider local groups to be particularly threatening. Many interstitial regions were apparently left untouched by Wari. The result was a very long, narrow empire—really, an archipelago of controlled nodes—extending over 1,300 km along the axis of the Andes.

Here I review a few examples of Wari provincial interactions in the best-studied areas to evaluate the idea that Wari expansion was accomplished through conquest warfare, or accompanied by violent resistance.

Pikillacta, in the Lucre Basin of the southern Cuzco Valley (McEwan 1987, 1989, 1991, 1996), is an example of a Wari center that was clearly designed to dominate its valley and withstand a military threat from outside. Pikillacta is a large walled complex, two km^2 in area, supported by a suite of regional sites strategically positioned to control each of the five passes into the Lucre Basin. Massive walls were built across the main southern and southeastern valleys leading into the basin, including the monumental Rumicolca wall blocking access from the south. Several subsidiary sites are on hills or hillsides. In addition, Pikillacta itself may have housed warriors. One walled sector of Pikillacta consists of many neat rows of small domestic structures, accessed by tightly controlled internal routes. McEwan considers the rigid layout and limited access to this residential area to imply an organized labor group, perhaps a military garrison (McEwan 1991:117). As at Wari and Conchopata, decapitated skulls are found cached at Pikillacta and may be related to violent conflict (Bauer and Bauer 1984; Verano 1995:202).[4] The level of investment in defense at Pikillacta and its satellites is unusual among Wari provincial centers. Pikillacta is one of the closest Wari highland centers to the contemporaneous state of Tiwanaku, so its defenses, especially the Rumicolca wall to the south, may have been intended to thwart an attack from Tiwanaku quarters (Schreiber 1992).

In the Huamachuco area in the northern highlands, the evidence points to initial, possibly peaceful cooperation between local inhabitants and Wari settlers, followed by violent resistance and a Wari retreat (McCown 1945; J. Topic 1991; T. Topic 1991; Topic and Topic 1983, 2000). The Huamachuco area was dominated by the monumental, nucleated, mesa-top center of Marca Huamachuco before, during, and after the Wari presence in the region. Marca Huamachuco itself is a highly defensible site, with walls (formed by the backs of long, double-storied galleries of residential units) blocking off access routes to the mesa top. The first indication of Wari activity in the area came early in the MH, when construction began on Viracochapampa, an ambitious Wari center four-to-five km southeast from Marca Huamachuco. While Viracochapampa was strategically situated on a route of travel (J. Topic 1991:162), the site was on low-lying ground and not particularly defensible. The construction effort probably required the conscription of local Huamachuco laborers, though not in onerous numbers (J. Topic 1991). The non-defensive location of Viracochapampa and the probable use of local labor point to an initially friendly relationship between Wari settlers and Marca Huamachuco. Meanwhile, there is also evidence of interaction at the site of Cerro Amaru, a possible shrine or elite area affiliated with Marca Huamachuco, which includes Wari-related storerooms and Wari artifacts. But the relationship was soon cut short; Viracochapampa's construction was abandoned before it was finished, and the site was never occupied (Topic and Topic 1983).

Although the Topics, the primary researchers in the area, do not view the Wari-Huamachuco relationship as conflictive, destruction episodes in the region may be linked to Viracochapampa's premature abandonment. Large portions of Cerro Sazon, a site that may have housed Wari workers and planners during the construction of Viracochapampa (J. Topic 1991), were burned at some point in the Middle Horizon. At Cerro Amaru, the Wari-related storerooms and a mausoleum containing Wari pottery and other imports were also burned in the MH (J. Topic 1991; Topic and Topic 1983). One building at Viracochapampa was burned after construction (J. Topic 1991:162). Meanwhile, Marca

Huamachuco continued to flourish and build monumental architecture during and after Wari's departure from the area (J. Topic 1991). Here, violent conflict appears to have played a role in Wari defeat, not expansion.

Some of the best evidence for the impact of Wari expansion on provincial populations comes from the study of human skeletal remains. The Majes valley in Arequipa shows Wari contact, and there is a possible Wari administrative site in the coastal stretches of the valley (Malpass 2001). Here, Tung's (2003) study of 143 individuals from the sites of La Real and Beringa revealed a very high incidence of healed cranial fractures in the MH, with nearly one-third of all adults affected. La Real in particular provides good evidence of severe, sustained warfare. Sex-based differences in trauma frequency were nearly statistically significant at La Real (41 percent of males and 19 percent of females; $p = 0.056$), though not at Beringa (Tung 2003:209). The wounds at La Real are predominantly on the left or middle sides of the skull, indicating that they were sustained in face-to-face combat with a right-handed opponent (Tung 2003). Many La Real males had multiple, healed head wounds; one man had survived a total of six wounds on the frontal and parietal bones. Five trophy heads were also found at La Real, and trophy heads are portrayed in art at the site. While it is not certain that the injured individuals from these sites were resisting Wari dominance, the combination of a Wari presence and high rates of trauma is suggestive. On the other hand, Kellner (2002) finds a decrease in the rate of cranial trauma from 13 percent to 6 percent in the Nazca valleys with the advent of Wari control in the MH. More such bioarchaeological studies are needed to clarify the nature of Wari interaction with local peoples.

There is also evidence of conflict and disruption from regions just outside the orbit of Wari's direct political control—conflict that may have been caused indirectly by Wari's expansion (Schreiber 1992:271–275). At the beginning of the MH, the coastal Lima polity collapsed. At the same time, the Moche state contracted dramatically, abandoning its capital in the Moche Valley and centers to the south and shifting far to the north. Meanwhile, great wall systems along the northern margins and the necks of the Santa and Viru valleys were in use (Topic and Topic 1987; Willey 1953; Wilson 1988). In the sierra above these valleys, small, autonomous groups built fortified settlements in the MH (T. Topic 1991). Middle Horizon fortified sites are evident farther north as well, in the Cajamarca area (Julien 1988). The causes of these disruptions are somewhat unclear, but it is possible that chain reactions of expansion and population displacement were sparking warfare and fortification on the fringes of the Wari sphere.

Thus, while there is still much to be investigated, Wari does seem to have engaged in violent conflict with other populations, and military conquest is the most plausible explanation for Wari's control over parts of the northern and central highlands. Military themes were also a major component of Wari iconography, suggesting that warrior personae and trophy-taking played important roles in Wari ideology.

Tiwanaku

Tiwanaku is located south of Lake Titicaca in the high-altitude intermontane plain, or *altiplano*, of northwestern Bolivia. The urban center of Tiwanaku reached its apogee around A.D. 800, when it encompassed a core of ceremonial edifices faced in Tiwanaku's spectacular stonemasonry, walled neighborhoods or compounds of elite residences and artisan communities, and an extensive residential sprawl six km^2 in size (Janusek 1999; Kolata 1993; Stanish 2001). Tiwanaku is located on flat ground and is unfortified, like nearly all of its probable colonies. Around A.D. 600, Tiwanaku began to expand, exerting direct control over the southern Titicaca Basin, and establishing colonies or enclaves far to the east, west, and south of the center.

Indirect evidence for Tiwanaku militarism comes from the extensive and ubiquitous production of projectile points in the urban center. Giesso (2003:382) finds that these points, which would be more suitable for warfare than hunting because of their brittleness, are highly standardized, and concludes from the pattern of production debris and finished points that Tiwanaku residents produced points as taxation for state needs—presumably, for military campaigns.

However, much of the evidence for warfare in Tiwanaku's heartland is symbolic or iconographic. For instance, the most famous carved stone sculpture at Tiwanaku, the Gateway of the Sun, depicts a central deity holding what Kolata (2003:200) identifies as an atlatl in one hand and a sling in the other. As in Wari, armed figures and trophy heads are major themes in Tiwanaku iconography, not only in ceramics but on the impressive stone monoliths that formed the foci of ceremonial courts and plazas (Kolata 2003). Blom and colleagues (2003:444) note that skulls made into drinking vessels and polished from long use have been found at Tiwanaku, and a weaving tool made from a human tibia comes from a nearby satellite. The use to which these trophies were put suggests that they were taken in warfare.

A dramatic illustration of the ceremonial importance of violence comes from human remains deposited in several separate events at the Akapana, a massive, terraced, artificial pyramid in Tiwanaku's ceremonial core. The lowest terrace and the pyramid base yielded the partially dismembered remains of at least 21 individuals, including several isolated skulls, in association with smashed pottery and camelid body parts (Blom et al. 2003; Manzanilla and Woodward 1990). Several of the human remains were violently hacked apart at or near the time of death; afterwards, carnivore tooth-marks and weathering testify that they were left in the open to be observed for some time (Blom et al. 2003:439). The victims were mostly male (Blom et al. 2003:444). One body is associated with a large offering of smashed polychrome pots that recurrently depict human trophy heads (Alconini 1995). These remains are best interpreted as sacrifices of real or symbolic captive warriors in a public location of great ceremonial importance.

One intriguing and culturally distinctive aspect of Tiwanaku warfare may have been the capture of the *huacas* or sacred idols of rival centers, as recorded later for the Inca period—an act perhaps conceptually equivalent to the taking of a head from a defeated opponent. *Huaca* capture is directly indicated by the Arapa monolith. This elaborately carved, 5.75-m-tall stela from Arapa on the northern shores of Lake Titicaca was broken in two, and the lower portion taken to Tiwanaku, over 200 km away, where it was found in an elite residential context (Chávez 1975): a symbolic act of violent appropriation of a powerful and probably sacred symbol. The walls of the sunken court or Kalasasaya at Tiwanaku incorporate dozens of stone tenon heads in diverse materials and styles, some of which stylistically belong to an earlier period. Kolata (1993:142, 249) and others have interpreted these stone heads as the captured *huacas* of enemy groups. In short, the symbolism of violent domination was elaborately developed at Tiwanaku. Public displays included or alluded to symbols of violence, conquest, and trophy-taking, indicating that these elements were an integral part of Tiwanaku idioms of power.

Outside of the heartland, Tiwanaku pursued a strategy of expansion that gave it a foothold in diverse ecological zones. Its colonies or affiliated settlements[5] are found to the east in Cochabamba in lowland Bolivia and to the west in the coastal valleys of Moquegua and Azapa, where they were apparently organized for intensive agricultural production of lowland crops, supported in some cases by Tiwanaku ceremonial installations and the dissemination of fine exports. A Tiwanaku presence is also evident far to the south in the mineral-rich San Pedro de Atacama oasis of Chile. In almost every case, Tiwanaku-affiliated provincial settlements are unfortified; exceptions are found in the Arequipa valley, where sites with Tiwanaku materials are strategically located on hilltops, and at least three have defensive walls (Cardona 2002:78–87). Crania from MH cemeteries at San Pedro de Atacama show moderate levels of trauma (Torres-Rouff et al. 2005 find a 12 percent incidence of healed cranial trauma from a sample of 92; but see Neves et al. 1999 and Nuñez 1992). At this point, compelling evidence for Tiwanaku militarism in the provinces is lacking.

Scholars such as Janusek (2004) and Goldstein (2005) view Tiwanaku's relationship to other peoples as incorporative rather than coercive. In this view, voluntary affiliation to Tiwanaku brought benefits for provincial participants, such as an association with a prestigious ideology, access to valued imports, and participation in Tiwanaku rituals and feasts. If this view is correct, Tiwanaku provides an alternative model of state expansion from that of the conquest state largely supported by Wari.

Wari and Tiwanaku in the Moquegua Valley

Wari and Tiwanaku both had colonies in the Moquegua coastal valley. Several scholars have investigated these sites, producing a detailed body of research. On the whole, the evidence points to a relationship of avoidance, indirect competition, perceived hostility, and perhaps violence.

First appearing at the beginning of the MH around A.D. 600, Tiwanaku's presence in the middle Moquegua valley included Omo, an administrative and ceremonial center with a Tiwanaku-style platform mound, and by the ninth century, Chen Chen, a large habitation center with a huge associated cemetery, as well as numerous small hamlets near agricultural fields and canals (Goldstein 1989). There are two strongly fortified hilltop sites on the west side of the middle valley (Moseley 1989:248–249; Moseley et al. 1991:135–136), and the settlements at Omo are located on potentially defensible bluff-tops; other Tiwanaku sites in the Moquegua valley are low-lying and undefended, suggesting a relatively low military threat from native inhabitants or from Wari colonists.

Wari moved into the mostly uninhabited upper valley at around the same time or shortly after (Williams 2001), building the fortified, highly defensible center of Cerro Baúl. Baúl is located on a mesa 600 m above the valley floor, with only one narrow path leading to the top; several stone walls along the path further restrict access (Moseley et al. 1991). Other Wari sites in the upper drainage are on hillsides and are often walled, notably Cerro Mejia, the hill adjacent to Cerro Baúl, which controls access to Baúl as well as its main water canal, and is protected with multiple walls (Moseley et al. 1991). Wari people in Moquegua clearly perceived a threat of hostilities.

Indeed, the Wari presence in Moquegua could not have been welcome to Tiwanaku-affiliated populations. The water taken to irrigate crops for Cerro Baúl and its supporting settlements reduced the water available to the Tiwanaku centers downstream, and perhaps caused the eventual abandonment of much of Chen Chen's agricultural system (Williams 2002). Meanwhile, artifacts from both Wari and Tiwanaku-affiliated sites in the Moquegua valley indicate remarkably little interaction between these cultures, especially in times of low water supply (Owen and Goldstein 2001; Williams 2002). There is a nearly perfect spatial segregation of Tiwanaku and Wari settlements into the middle and upper valley sectors, separated by an apparent buffer zone (Owen and Goldstein 2001). However, more direct evidence for violent conflict in Moquegua is lacking at this point. While there was considerable obsidian point manufacture and retouching on Cerro Baúl, Isla and others (Isla 2002; Isla et al. 1998) believe these points may have been intended for ritual use rather than warfare, since they were found in contexts that do not appear to be military stockpiles. Meanwhile, Blom's skeletal analysis of burials from the Tiwanaku site of Chen Chen revealed a low incidence of overall trauma and few cranial fractures, comprising only about five percent of the male population in Chen Chen—a rate comparable to that from the Tiwanaku heartland itself (Blom 2003; Isla et al. 1998). Any initial violence indicated by Cerro Baúl's defenses may have given way to a stalemate characterized by avoidance and indirect competition rather than outright warfare. This picture of scrupulous avoidance and probable hostility at the sole place where Tiwanaku and Wari came into close contact contrasts perplexingly with the shared religious iconography of the two great Middle Horizon polities.

Finally, around A.D. 950, towards the end of the MH, Tiwanaku-related Tumilaca settlements appear in the upper valley, alongside, contemporaneous with, and presumably allied with Cerro Baúl (Williams and Nash 2002). Tiwanaku and Tiwanaku-related ceramics appear in ceremonial contexts atop Cerro Baúl at this time, suggesting interaction and possibly détente.

Collapse

This development was soon followed by the collapse of both Wari and Tiwanaku in the eleventh century A.D., and the abandonment of most of their provincial centers. In some places, abandonment was accompanied by violent attack.

The confrontation in Moquegua was succeeded around A.D. 1000 by the abandonment and intentional destruction of Omo, Chen Chen, and several other Tiwanaku-affiliated sites (Moseley et al. 1991). The architecture was razed and occupation areas churned by large, closely spaced pits that broke through floors and overturned foundations, leaving a thoroughly destroyed wasteland.[6] The ceremonial platform structure at Omo had its walls toppled and many worked stone blocks smashed. The culprit may have been Wari aggression or a local revolt (Moseley et al. 1991)—perhaps the Tumilaca people friendly with Cerro Baúl. Cerro Baúl itself was abandoned some time in the eleventh century, at the same time as Wari's collapse. While several of the structures at Cerro Baúl (including temples) were burned at this time, Williams and Nash (2002) believe that closing ceremonies were responsible, rather than an attack.

In the Wari heartland, Wari itself was abandoned and the population of the area dropped dramatically (Schreiber 2001). At Conchopata, some tombs appear to have been disturbed in the subsequent epoch, leading Ochatoma and Cabrera (1999:240) to suggest Conchopata's abandonment was violent. Possible destruction events associated with Viracochapampa's abandonment have been noted above. McEwan (1996) notes that Pikillacta was abruptly abandoned in the middle of major new construction sometime between A.D. 800 and A.D. 1000. Careful preparations for Pikillacta's abandonment were made—entrances were sealed, structures intentionally filled, and offerings possibly removed—but a massive burning episode just after abandonment suggests the site was sacked by hostile groups (McEwan 1996). Sudden abandonment and burning is also noted at a Wari site in the Huaro valley (Glowacki 2002:275). On the other hand, Schreiber (1992) sees a gradual and orderly abandonment of the Wari center of Jincamocco in the Carhuarazo Valley.

Tiwanaku was not abandoned until ca. A.D. 1150, but monumental construction ceased around A.D. 1000 (Janusek 2004). In the late eleventh century a rich palace complex at the Putuni platform in the city was abruptly abandoned (leaving large quantities of alcoholic beverages and meat behind) and deliberately burned (Couture and Sampeck 2003:262), suggesting violent upheaval.

In sum, the MH should not be considered a time of rampant warfare, but it is clear that military strategies and violent symbols were central to its evolution. Wari control appears to have been achieved through conquest in at least some colonies. The case for Tiwanaku's militarism is less clear, although the Wari defenses at Pikillacta and Cerro Baúl, its centers closest to Tiwanaku territory, suggest Tiwanaku posed a military threat. While actual combat may have been sporadic, confined to periods of expansion and local resistance or the suppression of uprisings, themes of militarism, combat, and violent subjugation were important to elite ideology in the MH for both polities, and particularly for Tiwanaku state ceremony. The extent of conquest versus voluntary incorporation needs more study; but both Tiwanaku and Wari presented themselves as conquerors to their constituencies.

Warfare and Fragmentation: The Late Intermediate Period (ca. A.D. 1000–1450)

The period just prior to Inca expansion was remembered by native informants as the time of *auca runa* or warriors (Guaman Poma 1980:I:52 [1613]), an era of fragmented local polities engaged in constant warfare. These memories have been broadly substantiated archaeologically. In the Andean highlands, the Late Intermediate period, or LIP, is seen as a dark age of political fragmentation, intense conflict, and flattened social hierarchies after the collapse of Wari and Tiwanaku (Julien 1993; Matos 1999; Parsons and Hastings 1988). With the exception of the expansive Chimu state on the northern coast of Peru, the Andes in the LIP were broken into relatively small regional polities. Defensive settlement patterns are common in the highlands at this time, suggesting that warfare was pervasive (Figure 9.2).

Other major social changes occurred in the LIP. In comparison to earlier and later settlements, even the largest LIP highland centers have little in the way of civic/ceremonial architecture, elaborate elite residences, or finely crafted items, suggesting a flattening of the social hierarchy and a decreased reliance on ideology to legitimize leaders. The elaborate warlike iconography of preceding periods largely disappeared in many parts of the Andean highlands, to be replaced with primarily abstract designs. This iconographic shift suggests major ideological as well as political upheaval.

Archaeological Evidence for Warfare

One of the most striking changes during the LIP, particularly in the highlands, is the shift to defensively located sites and the building of hilltop forts and refuges, known in both Quechua and Aymara as *pukaras*. While the general outlines of this pattern have been recognized for some time, particularly for the south-central Andes (Parsons and Hastings 1988), a review that includes more recent survey projects makes clear just how widespread this defensive settlement pattern was (Figure 9.2). There is also a small but growing body of bioarchaeological evidence for violent conflict.

The Northern Sierra

The evidence for warfare in the Ecuadorean highlands is plagued with chronological problems; the sequence lacks a distinct MH because the direct influence of Wari did not extend this far north, and since Inca pottery is rare in the far northern empire, it can be difficult to distinguish between Inca period and earlier sites. The first significant evidence for warfare is found in the Integration Period (ca. A.D. 500–1460): hilltop sites, sometimes fortified; plentiful stone or bronze mace heads, axes, and other weapons (Bravomalo E. 1992; Ogburn 2001:161). Pukaras are plentiful in northern Ecuador and have traditionally been interpreted as Inca sites, but many were probably originally constructed by indigenous inhabitants and reutilized by the Incas in their northward expansion (for instance, those northeast of Quito [Bray 1991, 1992] and on the northern side of the Pambamarca complex [Connell et al. 2003]). Some lowland sites in southern Ecuador near Saraguro were abandoned in the late LIP (A.D. 1200–1460) in favor of hilltop locations, suggesting an increased concern with defense (Ogburn 2001).

In the northern Peruvian sierra in the Cajamarca area, the early LIP is characterized by hilltop settlements lightly fortified with walls and ditches (Julien 1988, 1993). The Cajamarca area became more politically centralized around

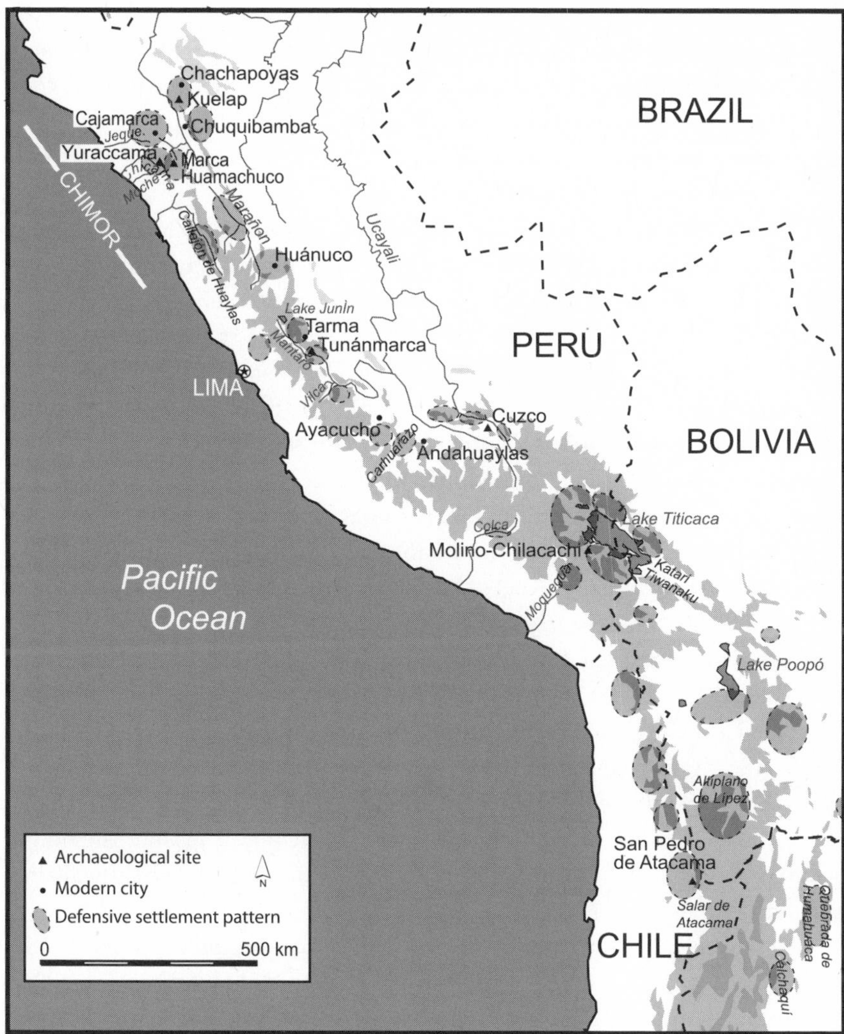

Figure 9.2. Late Intermediate period sites in the text.

A.D. 1200–1532, developing three large centers with elite architecture and fine ceramics (Julien 1993). In Huamachuco to the south, occupation continued at the highly defensible Marca Huamachuco, as well as several other hilltop sites (Topic and Topic 1987). To the west of Cajamarca and Huamachuco, long walls supplemented with hilltop stations were built in the middle and upper Chicama and Jequetepeque valleys and the upper Moche watershed; these may have protected Chimor against highland invasions (Julien 1988:198; Schaedel 1985:452; Topic and Topic 1987). The high Chicama watershed had a two-tiered settlement hierarchy of larger centers and smaller satellites (Krzanowski

1977, 1983, 1985); prominent among the centers is the densely occupied Yuraccama complex of 11 sites on a large ridge, connected by roads and defended by high, continuous habitation or terrace walls (Krzanowski 1977). This site complex is quite large for its context, with 300–400 houses,[7] but as is so common in the Andes, most of the Yuraccama sites have no close source of water and would have been unable to withstand prolonged sieges.

Fortified hilltop sites of varying sizes are pervasive further south. They appear in the Callejón de Huaylas in the twelfth to thirteenth centuries (Ponte 2000:243–244) and are found to the east in the upper reaches of the Marañon (Wassilowsky 1999), where walled hilltop outposts are strategically placed to protect unfortified villages within their view (Mantha 2004). Settlements of the Huánuco area further south are not usually fortified, but typically occupy defensible ridgetop locations (Morris and Thompson 1985).

Warfare affected the eastern slopes of the northern Andes as well. The Chachapoyas region was noted in Inca histories for its fierce warriors, and many LIP Chachapoyas sites are defensibly located or fortified (Schjellerup 1992, 1997). The most famous is Kueláp,[8] a hilltop, walled settlement about 25 km southwest of the modern-day town of Chachapoyas. Kueláp is protected by a cliff and two monumental stone-walled terraces—the walls, of finely cut limestone blocks, are 10–20 m high—as well as a defensive tower or bastion which contained a cache of 2,500 sling stones and broken stone axe-heads (Narváez 1987). The site is accessed by narrow defiles that enter the terraces and slope up to their tops, where the residential area is located. With about 400 circular houses, Kueláp is one of the largest known Chachapoya sites, but the houses are arrayed with little evidence of planning and do not include a clearly distinct elite area.

Bioarchaeological evidence from the Chachapoyas region supports the idea that violence was prevalent. Schjellerup and colleagues (Jakobsen et al. 1986–1987; Schjellerup 1997:222) found high rates (22 percent)[9] of cranial fractures on skulls from several Chachapoya sites east of Chuquibamba, as well as two (unsuccessful) cases of trepanation to cure victims of mace-wounds. The victims of violence were mostly male. (Stone mace-heads are found in many LIP Chachapoya sites near Chuquibamba; Schjellerup 1997:222). Nystrom and Verano's (2003) analysis of the remains of 97 individuals from Kueláp found a comparable rate (16 percent) of craniofacial trauma, but no significant difference in trauma rates between sexes or among ages.

The Central Sierra

Some of the best data available on the LIP comes from surveys in the central sierra in the provinces of Junín, Huancavelica, and Ayacucho, where extensive fortification and high rates of trauma[10] point to intense warfare. Parsons and colleagues (Parsons et al. 1997, 2000) document how the peoples of the Tarma drainage south of Lake Junín built a dispersed pattern of ridge-crest walled settlements in the LIP, particularly in the hilly pasturage zone. Walls are paired with external ditches, and sometimes incorporate parapets or towers on the outer face. The sites cluster into four large groups, each with one or two large settlements and a number of smaller ones (Parsons et al. 1997); however, the largest centers are still quite small at around 150 houses, and the decentralized political landscape suggests raiding for stores and livestock, rather than conquest.

Immediately to the south, members of the Upper Mantaro Archaeological Research Project (Earle 1997; Earle et al. 1980; Hastorf et al. 1989) examined the territory associated with the Wanka people. Here, in the late MH and early LIP (A.D. 800–1300), settlements moved to ridges, and some were fortified. But by around A.D. 1300, the population started to rise steeply and people nucleated into a handful of very large, mesa-top sites around the northern end of the Mantaro Basin. These centers are fortified with one or two enclosure walls and few gates. The largest Wanka center, Tunánmarca, contains about 3,800 houses for an estimated population size of over 10,000, and is one of the largest sites known for the LIP in the central Andes as a whole. Nevertheless, like many other LIP sierra sites, it and other Wanka centers display little evidence of planning or central organization. Circular houses are clustered tightly together, often forming self-contained units around small walled patios, linked by a maze of alleys rather than central streets. Tunánmarca has a central plaza, but public or ceremonial architecture is lacking. Elite compounds are distinguished by finer masonry, more house structures, and somewhat greater quantities of prestige goods, but these differences are minimal: "A Wanka elite was apparently not a distinctive class" (Earle 1997:61). Mesa-top centers such as Tunánmarca were tied to smaller satellite sites in the vicinity through exchange and shared ceramic styles (Costin 1986; LeBlanc 1981). While the presence of satellite sites implies a political hierarchy, it is worth noting that they are still often defensibly located and are usually found within a five km radius from the nucleated centers, so the centers do not appear to have controlled any substantial territory. However, the transition from the early to late LIP in the Mantaro Valley shows how defensive pressures resulted in extreme population nucleation and a degree of political consolidation, even in the apparent absence of a powerful elite.

Central highland conflict bled onto the western slopes of the Andes. West of the Mantaro-Junín area, in the upper reaches of the Chillón valley, the LIP settlement pattern is one of small, walled habitation sites high on hillsides and far from resources, including water (Farfán 1995; Silva 1992).

Lavallee and Julien's (1973) study of the Asto territory to the south, between the Mantaro and Vilca rivers, documents a defensive settlement pattern that may correspond to a single polity, on a much more modest scale than the Upper Mantaro centers. Asto settlements are defensible or lightly fortified, located on ridgetops with commanding views. They are spaced one to five km apart, so that every site is visible from at least one neighbor, potentially allowing sites to signal for aid in times of danger (Lavallee and Julien 1973:28). These sites are considerably smaller than those of the Upper Mantaro, on the order of 120 houses, with one large site—possibly a capital—of about 850 houses. While lacking evidence for planning, Asto sites do show some internal organization: often a central plaza on the peak or saddle separates two habitation zones, which may represent the two moieties of the settlement (Lavallee and Julien 1973:49). Mace-heads and bola stones[11] were found in excavated houses. Asto inhabitants were concerned to protect goods from raiding, invariably locating corrals inside the defensive walls, and placing rock-lined storage pits inside the higher, better-protected structures. Nevertheless, no site contains cisterns and the closest water sources are 45 minutes' to an hour's walk away. As the authors note, "This absence of water must have strongly limited the defensive capacity of the villages . . . in this epoch, military operations, though doubtless frequent and brutal, simply involved sacking and pillaging" (Lavallee and Julien 1973:59, my translation).

To the south of modern-day Ayacucho and to the east towards Andahuaylas, the pattern of defensible and fortified sites continues (Meddens 1999; Valdez and Vivanco 1994; Vivanco 1999). Sites contain unplanned agglutinated collections of up to 700 houses (Vivanco 1999), as well as small plazas and corrals. They are situated for visibility and defensibility, and some are strongly fortified. Defensive, as well as some fortified, sites continue into the Carhuarazo Valley, where, after A.D. 1200, a settlement hierarchy emerges with two dominant towns surrounded by lesser settlements (Schreiber 1987, 1993).

Cuzco and its environs form an important exception to the overall pattern of LIP fragmentation and warfare, and will be treated in the next section.

The Titicaca Basin and Western Valleys

Contact-period accounts describe large, unified, pre-Inca kingdoms in the Lake Titicaca area consolidated through conquest warfare and led by hereditary warlords. From the viewpoint of archaeology, warfare was clearly prevalent in the Titicaca Basin, as attested by plentiful pukaras, with the largest on the order of 500 to 1,000 houses. However, these hill forts are so numerous they contradict the textual accounts of stable regional control.

There are numerous fortified sites densely packing the hills of the northern and northwestern Titicaca Basin, in the area attributed to the Colla; most date

Figure 9.3. Cerro C'acjro, a *pukara* (hilltop fort) in the northern Lake Titicaca basin. A triple wall defends this approach.

to the late LIP, after about A.D. 1300 (Arkush 2005). While the area cannot be considered politically unified, patterns of site placement and intervisibility suggest that many fortified sites relied on systems of allies for defense. Pukaras vary greatly in size and defensibility: some were intensively occupied by nucleated populations with over 400 houses, while others were rarely used refuges. Defenses consist of concentric fieldstone walls (Figure 9.3), up to five-m-high and four-m-thick; many walls have parapets remaining, and gates may be baffled or staggered to prevent direct entry. Stone mace-heads, projectile points, and piles of sling stones are common. Central streets at a handful of nucleated centers indicate planning in their layout, but possibly elite residences are not distinguishable except by size, and there is little civic or ceremonial architecture, aside from tombs.

A similar settlement pattern is found just to the south, in the Lupaca area (Hyslop 1976). Stanish and colleagues' survey (1997) demonstrated that the largest of the Lupaca pukaras were evenly spaced along the hills near the lake, suggesting the existence of several independent centers in the LIP (Frye 1997). Small storage structures and many storage vessels (de la Vega 1990) might have protected harvested crops from raiders or supplied forts for a possible siege. But defenses, however effective, did not obviate actual violence; 15 percent of the 44 adult crania from an LIP funerary cave at Molino-Chilacachi in the Lupaca area had frontal or parietal fractures, including several healed injuries (de la Vega et al. 2002).

The far northern and eastern parts of the Titicaca Basin, though less well studied, have numerous pukaras, densely occupying hilltops (Bennett 1950, 1993; Neira 1967; Tapia 1978), and defensive settlement patterns continue down the eastern slopes of the Andes northeast of Lake Titicaca in Sandia and Carabaya (Tapia 1985). Fortification in the southeastern basin is more limited, with one refuge fort (with bola stones) in the Tiwanaku valley (Albarracín-Jordan and Matthews 1992:279), two in the Katari valley (Janusek and Kolata 2003:155), and one lightly fortified hilltop on the Taraco peninsula (Bandy 2001:233). Here, where Tiwanaku was centered, a massive population emigration after the collapse (Bandy 2001) may have eased the pressure of competition.

West of the Titicaca Basin there is more evidence of warfare. In the upper Colca valley, rather than living in walled hilltop settlements, people built refuge hill forts within close range of the largest settlements (Wernke 2003:252–260), suggesting that warfare was somewhat less intense than in the Titicaca Basin. In the upper Moquegua valley, a transition can be charted from post-Wari Tumilaca settlements from the early LIP (A.D. 1000–1200), which are characterized by some defensive walls or site locations, to the intensified warfare of the succeeding Estuquiña period in the late LIP (after A.D. 1200), in which settlements are located on hilltops and often heavily fortified with walls and ditches at routes of access (Moseley 1989; Owen 1995; Stanish 1992). Throwing or sling stones have been found on several Estuquiña period sites, including a cache of 23 stones inside a defensive wall (Stanish 1992); nevertheless, strategic points, such as canal intakes, are not protected, and all fortified Moquegua sites lack internal water sources. Moseley (1989:251) infers that this fortification pattern was a response to intermittent raiding, but not siege warfare or prolonged campaigns. The Tumilaca-Estuquiña transition also suggests that here, it was not until the late LIP that violent clashes became severe.

The Far Southern Andes

Warfare was clearly present in the LIP in southern Bolivia and northern Chile and Argentina, though populations tended to be smaller and polities less centralized throughout the sequence. Pukaras dot the hills of the southern *altiplano* of Bolivia south of Lake Poopó (Arellano 1992; Lecoq 1997; Nielsen 2002), and pukaras or defensive settlement patterns are found further east in the lowlands as well (Albarracín-Jordán 2003; Lecoq and Céspedes 1997). Warfare in this region appears to date to the late LIP: Nielsen (2002) reports that in the Altiplano de Lípez around A.D. 1275–1300, there was a transition from low-lying sites to permanently occupied pukaras of up to 100 houses, armed with sling stones and projectile points. These small-scale societies would have presumably practiced raids, ambushes, and massacres.

This rather late chronology of warfare is repeated in the Quebrada de Humahuaca in extreme northern Argentina (Nielsen 2001). In the first part of the LIP (A.D. 900–1200), settlements began to move from lowland positions to higher and occasionally defensible locations. Structures became more tightly packed and access routes more labyrinthine. Mace heads first appear in this time period, and towards the end of it, trophy heads and decapitated individuals are found for the first time (Nielsen 2001:195, 197). But warfare reached its maximum intensity in the second half of the LIP (A.D. 1200–1430), when many settlements were abandoned, and the rest clustered more closely in defensible locations with good visibility; some were partly fortified. Wooden bows have been found from this period, and trophy heads, decapitated bodies, and skeletal traumas reach a peak (Nielsen 2001:214, 241). While there is still only limited evidence for social differentiation, arms in tombs and rock art scenes showing elaborately garbed warriors in conflict may indicate a link between social status and a warrior identity. Likewise, in the nearby valley of Calchaquí, the later part of the LIP saw movement to higher, fortified sites simultaneous with a population increase (DeMarrais 1997, 2001). The small-scale societies of northwest Argentina, while they never developed great social stratification or political consolidation, were moving gradually in that direction in the LIP, and that movement seems closely related to intensified warfare.

Finally, conflict and fortification was pervasive to the west, in the upper coastal valleys and western highlands of southern Peru and northern Chile, from the border to the Salar de Atacama (Llagostera and Costa 1999; Nuñez and Dillehay 1978; Santoro et al. 2004). Skeletal trauma at San Pedro de Atacama reached a height in the LIP, with 29 percent of 144 skulls bearing healed wounds, including many crania with multiple injuries (Torres-Rouff et al. 2005). There is no significant difference in injury rates between the sexes, which may suggest that violence was not confined to organized battles of male soldiers, but included the ambushes and raids characteristic of small-scale societies.

Summary

It is clear that warfare in the LIP was extremely widespread, and much more intense than in the MH (or indeed, any other period). LIP people felt unsafe enough to move to hilltop locations, often far from water, and expend considerable labor on massive stone fortifications. However, warfare was directed at local enemies; the proliferation of forts and the small settlement hierarchies reflect the absence of centralized political structures that could have directed violence towards external enemies. Despite the defensive pressure to nucleate, sites with more than 400 houses are quite rare, indicating relatively small social units and the absence of administrative and economic institutions needed to provision urban sites. Where settlement hierarchies exist, subsidiary sites are commonly fortified and defensible, implying that any protection offered by the larger centers was limited. The lack of internal water sources at many sites does not suggest that these forts were unsophisticated, but rather that LIP populations relied on their relationships with allies and the military incapacity of their foes, instead of on building and supplying impregnable citadels for long sieges. Thus, while there is a diversity of settlement sizes and social organization in the Andean highlands of the LIP, it is easy to believe that most warfare consisted of raiding, harassment, and extermination, rather than the establishment of stable political control over the losers.

Where archaeologists have been able to construct fine-grained chronologies, warfare appears to have escalated in the latter part of the LIP, after about A.D. 1200–1300. After this threshold, fortification first appeared in the northern Titicaca Basin, in the extreme southern highlands of Bolivia and Argentina, and the Callejón de Huaylas of north-central Peru; in other areas such as the Upper Mantaro Basin and the upper Moquegua Valley, warfare had existed before, but intensified after that point. Explanations of warfare in the LIP must thus account for both its initial appearance and its later intensification. In addition, political centralization did increase during the LIP in some areas (Julien 1993:266), such as the Cajamarca area, the Upper Mantaro, the Carhuarazo Valley, and above all, the Cuzco Valley (see below). This shift towards centralization may have been related to the increasing pressure of warfare in the late LIP.

Warfare and Political Leadership: Insights from Ethnohistory

In addition to archaeological evidence about warfare in the LIP, information about this pre-Inca period can be gleaned from the chronicles, early Colonial Spanish accounts that distilled the memories and oral histories of native informants. One theme that appears so commonly in the chronicles that it seems hard to dispute is the specifically military basis for political leadership among the pre-Inca Andean cultures. The local leaders of the Andean highlands, including the early Incas, are consistently described as *sinchis* or war leaders. The cleric Pedro Sarmiento de Gamboa explains the term *sinchi* in detail, and his passage bears repeating here despite its length.

> [Before the Incas,] all the people were uncivilized and dispersed, and lived in general liberty, each one being master only of his own house and fields . . . And, as there arose quarrels between them, they arranged a certain kind of militia for their defense, in this way. When those of one village knew

> that those of other places were coming to make war on them, they got one of their own people, or even a stranger to their land, who was a valiant man of war. And often such a man would come forth voluntarily to protect them and wage war for them against their enemies. And they would follow this man and obey him and fulfill his orders during the war. But once it was finished, he stayed a private man as before, like the rest of the people; and neither before nor after would they give him tribute, nor any kind of tax. In that time and even today they call such a one *sinchi*, which means "valiant." (Sarmiento 1988:46 [1572:Ch. 8])

This description of a *temporary* war leader resembles the sort of tribal or Big Man organization Redmond (1994) and Carneiro (1998:23) document for essentially acephalous, raiding groups like the Yanomamö and other tribes of northern South America. Other chroniclers give similar versions of pre-Inca temporary war leaders (for example, Mercado de Peñalosa 1885:58 [1586]). For instance, the early chronicler Cieza de León states:

> Before the Incas ruled them . . . they built fortresses called *pucaras* in the mountains, from which they would go to battle with one another, howling in strange tongues, [fighting] over farmland or for other reasons, and they would kill many people, taking the spoils to be found and the women of the vanquished, with which they climbed triumphantly back again to their mountaintop fortresses. . . . All lived in disorderly savagery, because for certain they say that they had no lords then, aside from the captains who led them in war. (Cieza de León 1984:v.2:6 [1550:II.iv], cited and translated by Parsons et al. 2000:50)

While such descriptions cannot be taken completely at face value, they are suggestive of impermanent leadership and raiding rather than conquest warfare; in Cieza's portrayal, warriors raid spoils and women, and then retreat to their fortresses without establishing territorial control over their enemies.

However, there are also reports of institutionalized, hereditary leaders emerging in some regions, particularly around Lake Titicaca (Betanzos 1996:93 [1551–1557:I.xx]; Cieza de León 1984:274, 279 [1550:I.c, cii], 1985:15, 22, 110, 121 [II.vi, viii, xxxvii, xli]; Cobo 1979:96–97, 139–140 [1653:12.1, 12.13]). Their route to power is invariably said to be conquest, as in this account by Hernando de Santillán (1968:104 [1563:ch. 4]):

> Before they [the Incas] began to rule there was neither order nor law; before, each valley or province had its *curaca* [lord], and each valley waged war with its neighbor, and because of this there was neither commerce nor communication between them; and each valley had a language distinct

> from the next; they waged battles against each other, and the custom was for those who gained the victory and subjugated the others to make the subjects grow for them maize and coca and *ají*, and give them livestock and the other things they had, in acknowledgement. And so by fortune there were some particular curacas who subjugated valleys and provinces. . . .

Chroniclers such as Santillán narrate the genesis of these leaders in evolutionary terms similar to Carneiro's conquest model: conquering lords emerge from a landscape of local *sinchis* with limited and impermanent power. Such accounts point to a certain fluidity in the pre-Inca Andes, in which some societies were located close to the transition between raiding and conquest warfare, and between temporary and institutionalized leadership.

A particularly informative study in this regard is D'Altroy's (1994:174) examination of *sinchi* leadership in the Upper Mantaro drainage on the basis of information collected in the course of Toledo's 1570 visita (Toledo 1940). In interviews, local Wanka informants stated that ideally, *sinchi* leaders were selected by consensus, and had power only in wartime. However, in practice, informants claimed, *sinchis* encouraged warfare for their own interests, held onto power in peaceful interludes, and passed power on to sons. The main reasons cited for warfare were competition over lands, stored food, herds, and women. Lands would be expropriated from their former owners and divided among the victors, an outcome associated with raiding rather than conquest. Indeed, one Wanka informant explicitly stated that wars might be caused when a community grew in population, increasing its need for farmland and spoils (Hastorf 1993:98)—a picture of population pressure and resource scarcity familiar from materialist explanations for warfare. Nevertheless, the statements of Wanka informants also make it clear that wars were pursued for the disproportionate benefit of the *sinchis*. The military basis of *sinchi* leadership may have encouraged *sinchis* to promote warfare and perpetuate hostilities in order to retain power and justify their preferred status, a scenario similar to that documented among New Guinea Big Men (Feil 1987; Sillitoe 1978). In the Wanka area, home to some of the largest nucleated centers of the LIP, war leaders may have been moving towards ascribed, institutionalized power.

Representations of Violence in the LIP

Even while the chronicles suggest that leaders of the highland Andes in the LIP based their status on war leadership, the normal indicators of a link between warfare and elite legitimization—warlike iconography,[12] special militaristic grave goods, large scale public sacrifices, and so on—are generally lacking in the LIP highlands. For instance, trophy-head iconography, so central to earlier traditions, became much rarer in the LIP, and the representation of armed deities all but disappeared. Such displays that do refer to warfare are indirect and do not seem designed to justify a social or political hierarchy. For instance, weapons are often found in graves or tombs of this period in the Titicaca Basin (for example, de la Vega et al. 2002), but they are utilitarian, not prestige objects, and since graves typically contain multiple individuals, they are not associated with any particular warrior or leader. As another example, in the central and southern Andes in the LIP, defenses are frequently associated with *chullpas* or aboveground tomb structures housing the remains of multiple individuals. Chullpas line defensive walls or guard the edges of hilltop sites in areas as far-flung as the Junín (Parsons et al. 2000), the Upper Moquegua (Moseley 1989:245), the Colca Valley (Wernke 2003), and the far southern altiplano of Bolivia (Nielsen 2004). Moseley (1989) terms this pattern a possible "symbolic defense"—not just walls, but powerful ancestors protected communities from hostile incursions. If so, warfare and defense were presented in material culture at this time as collective tasks (Earle 2001; Nielsen 2004), rather than as arenas for the display of a leader's preeminence.

Imperial Conquest: The Late Horizon (ca. A.D. 1450–1532)

The Late Horizon, or LH, is defined as the period of Inca conquest, and as such, it was shaped by expansionistic warfare and the violent suppression of rebellions.[13] The study of Inca warfare benefits not only from archaeology, but also from a wealth of textual evidence: chroniclers' versions of the Inca histories of imperial conquest, and accounts by the Spanish conquistadors who faced the Inca armies firsthand. Several scholars have drawn together excellent syntheses of these sources (Bram 1941; Cisneros and Lumbreras 1980; D'Altroy 1992, 2002; Hemming 1970; Murra 1986; Quiroga I. 1962; Rawls 1979; Rostworowski 1999:65–97; Rowe 1946; Urteaga 1919–1920). Archaeology adds to the textual accounts (for syntheses, see D'Altroy 1992, 2002; Hyslop 1990; Rawls 1979). Because these overviews are readily available, I treat Inca warfare in a streamlined fashion, focusing on the importance of warfare in the formation of the Inca state and imperial expansion, and the role of warfare in Inca ideology and legitimization.

The Origins of the Inca State: The Cuzco Heartland in the LIP

Recent surveys in the birthplace of the Inca state have confirmed that the Cuzco Valley and some neighboring areas formed a significant exception to the overall pattern of LIP fragmentation and warfare (Bauer 1992, 2004; Bauer and Covey 2002; Dwyer 1971; Hefferman 1996). During the LIP, the Cuzco Valley (Figure 9.4) saw urbanization at Cuzco surrounded by much smaller satellites, as well as ambitious irrigation works and terraces, suggesting a restructuring of agricultural production to supply the needs of the emerging state. Cuzco and its surrounding settlements were undefended, as were settlements in some neighboring regions in the LIP, in particular the Paruro area just to the south (Bauer 1992). The Limatambo area west of Cuzco to the Apurimac River also has no LIP fortification and only moderately defensive locations (Hefferman 1996).[14] Bauer and Covey (2002) posit that these areas were incorporated peacefully by the emerging Inca state. On the other hand, the LIP defensive settlement pattern reappears along the Urubamba River valley, beyond in Vilcabamba (Covey 2003; Lee 2000), and northwest of Cuzco towards Machu Picchu (Kendall 1985; Rawls 1979:109–111). Southeast of Cuzco in the Lucre Basin, the inheritors of Wari Pikillacta built settlements with little fortification in the LIP, but protected themselves from Inca attack with a buffer zone and the massive fortified center of Tipón (Bauer and Covey 2002). To the north and northeast of Cuzco near Pisac, local polities built nucleated hilltop centers in the first part of the LIP, and then moved to lower, undefended settlements as they came under Inca control (Bauer and Covey 2002; Covey 2003). The single exception is Pukara Pantillijlla, a previously independent hilltop site that became a secondary Inca administrative center after about A.D. 1300, growing greatly in size and housing Inca-style rectangular civic architecture (Covey 2003). This development is particularly interesting because it clearly signals the conquest and incorporation of a previously independent polity.

Thus, during the LIP, while much of the rest of the highlands was involved in intense warfare without great political consolidation, the early Incas developed a well-integrated, unified valley anchored at the urban center of LIP Cuzco. The non-defensive settlement pattern of Cuzco and its immediate environs suggests that this consolidation was achieved either without warfare or too rapidly to result in fortification. The early Incas then proceeded to gain control of regions just outside of the Cuzco Valley, in Paruro, Limatambo, and the Urubamba Valley, through a mixture of strategies involving conquest, marriage alliances, and peaceful incorporation (Bauer and Covey 2002; Covey 2003).

Imperial Conquest and Hostile Frontiers

Perhaps because of the preceding period of consolidation, the Incas had little trouble in subduing the same heavily fortified highland groups that had been largely unable or unwilling to conquer each other in the LIP. Textual evidence leaves little doubt that this subjugation was accomplished largely through military conquest. Inca strengths consisted mainly in manpower and logistics rather than training, technology, or mobility. By the Contact period, Inca armies numbered in the tens to hundreds of thousands, a scale of warfare manpower that

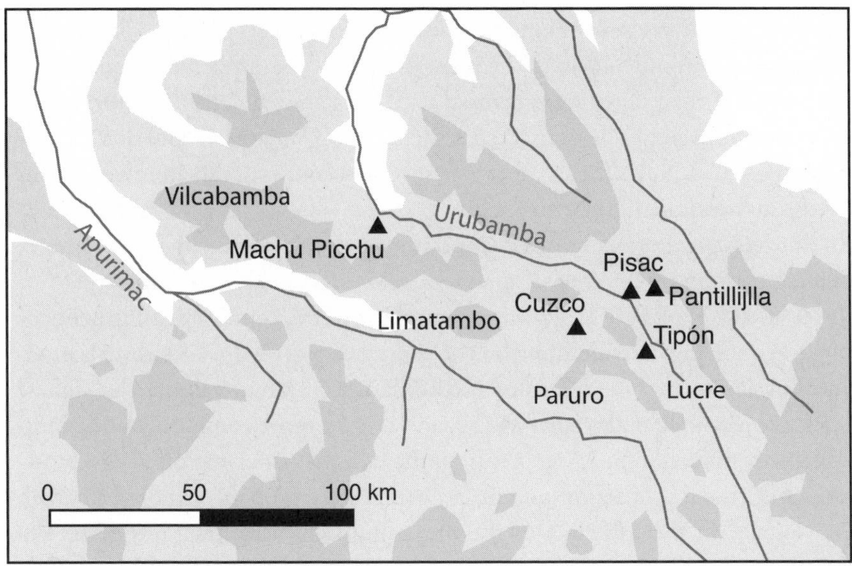

Figure 9.4. The Cuzco area in the Late Intermediate period.

was completely new to the Andes. They were supported by continuous investment in an impressive system of roads and storehouses that grew as the empire did (D'Altroy 1992, 2002; Hyslop 1984). This logistical system enabled the Incas to concentrate large armies at a single point and set prolonged sieges where necessary, strategies that had clearly been beyond the military capabilities of LIP highland societies. On the other hand, Inca armies were made up of ordinary male subjects who were conscripted as part of their rotating labor service and had little military training. The Incas also had no technological advantage; they used the same weapons and tactics as their foes (Rawls 1979:130–132; Urteaga 1919–1920), and their forts conformed by and large to the Andean canon (see below). Their large armies, their quantities of auxiliaries, and the slow pace of llamas must have severely reduced mobility (D'Altroy 1992, 2002), giving enemies ample time to learn of the Inca army's approach.

Nevertheless, imperial conquest proceeded relatively rapidly, with one conquest providing wealth and manpower for the next. Most foes were weakly centralized polities, who, through centuries of infighting, had developed deep enmities with their nearby neighbors. Their leaders could not manage to muster or coordinate large enough forces to effectively resist the Inca invasion. In addition, they could be manipulated by allying with one against the other, thus subduing the latter more easily and winning the loyalty of the former (Bram 1941:52–53). This pattern of divide and conquer is repeatedly mentioned in the chronicles and must have been one of the keys to Inca success. As the Inca empire expanded, its treatment of new subjects swayed others towards submission. Groups that surrendered without resistance could be expected to be treated leniently, and their elites were favored with gifts and enhanced authority, but resisting groups might be massacred or deported (Caillavet 1985:411; D'Altroy 2002:207–208). Nevertheless, there are several accounts of rebellions, and their violent suppression, in the chronicles.

Archaeological evidence of violent trauma possibly caused by Inca conquest is emerging from recent skeletal analyses. Preliminary analysis by Murphy (Murphy et al. 2003) of Late Horizon mummies from the cemetery of Puruchuco-Huaquerones, just outside Lima on the central coast (Figure 9.5), reveals moderate but significant rates of healed and perimortem cranial trauma. The highest incidence is among males aged 25–50, and it is far more common among individuals considered to be lower status on the basis of associated offerings. However, under the *pax Inca*, most Andean peoples were probably exposed to much less violence in the LH than in the preceding LIP. Very low rates of cranial trauma are found in both Verano's reanalysis (2003) of burials from Machu Picchu and Torres-Rouff and colleagues' (2005) study of LH remains from San Pedro de Atacama.

Destruction episodes can also document the violence of Inca conquest. For instance, at Los Amarillos in the Quebrada de Humahuaca in northwest Argentina, a native pukara's platform compound with rich elite tombs was destroyed and burned at the transition to Inca control (Nielsen and Walker 1999). A similar transformation occurred at Pukara de Turi in northern Chile, where the Incas took over a native fort and destroyed older ceremonial buildings in order to construct Inca architecture in the highest part of the site (Gallardo et al. 1995). Like the appropriation of the Arapa monolith by Tiwanaku several centuries before, these episodes illustrate the significance of ritual destruction in warfare: not only settlements and defenses were targeted, but ceremonial structures.

A third form of archaeological evidence of Inca militarism comes from Inca forts. Unlike the societies of the LIP, the Inca state had little in the way of fortification except in border zones. Settlements in the empire's interior were unfortified, even provincial centers known to have housed thousands of soldiers (D'Altroy 2002:210). The capital itself was not fortified, though it had the fortress refuge of Sacsayhuaman. The lack of fortification in the Inca empire speaks to the rapidity of conquest and the relative strength of the Inca regime. It also resulted from the fact that the inhabitants of LIP fortified or hilltop sites were resettled to lower land after Inca conquest (for example, Earle et al. 1980; Hyslop 1976; Lavallee and Julien 1973; Stanish et al. 1997). Hyslop (1990:149) notes the military significance of the fact that these previously dispersed, fortified populations moved into low-lying towns on roads, with Inca or local ad-

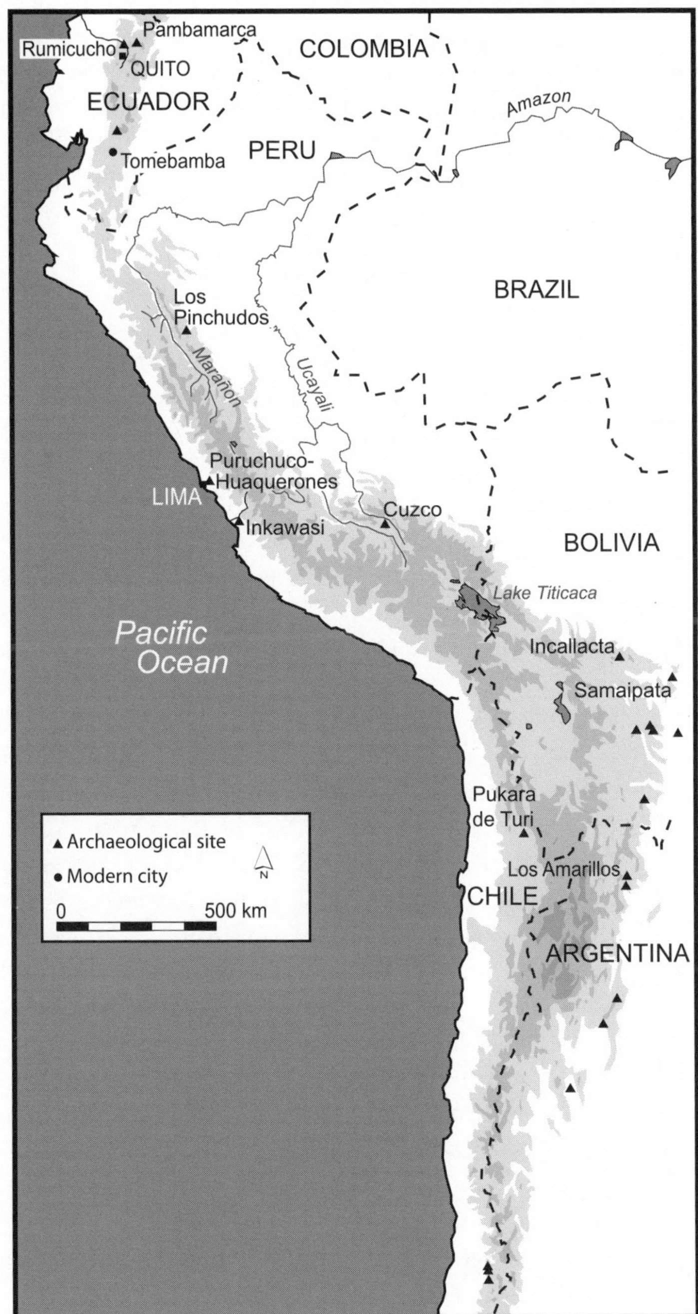

Figure 9.5. Late Horizon sites mentioned in the text and major Inca forts.

ministrators within reach, easily controllable, countable, and taxable by the state apparatus. Some people were forcibly moved away from their homelands, or loyal populations were resettled to a newly conquered area to keep an eye on potentially rebellious natives—and some went to staff Inca forts (Caillavet 1985; Espinoza 1975; Raffino et al. 1991).

Inca forts are primarily military garrisons in border zones. Border forts do not make a continuous chain, but are clustered in areas where the Incas had particular difficulty with hostile native populations, especially in Ecuador near Quito, and to a lesser extent in eastern Bolivia (see D'Altroy 2002; Hyslop 1990; Raffino and Stehberg 1999). These forts often appear in groups, where each fort could be quickly supported by reinforcements (D'Altroy 2002; Rawls 1979). The empire's southern and southeastern frontiers in Chile and Argentina were slightly and inconsistently fortified, often incorporating forts originally constructed in the late LIP by local peoples (D'Altroy 2002; Gallardo et al. 1995; Hyslop 1990; Nielsen 2001; Planella and Stehberg 1997; Raffino and Stehberg 1999; Stehberg 1995). In Bolivia, a greater density of Inca forts on the eastern frontier faced hostile tribes of the tropical forest; indeed, some were overrun by Guaraní groups (Chiriguanos) shortly before the arrival of the Spaniards (Alconini 2004; Hyslop 1990; Lee 1992; Nordenskiöld 1917; Pärssinen and Siirriäinen 1998).

Many highly defensible forts pack the hills of northern Ecuador (Almeida 1999; Bray 1991, 2005; Oberem 1969; Plaza Schuller 1976, 1980), reflecting the prolonged Inca campaign against the bellicose peoples of the northern frontier and the difficulty of controlling an area so distant from Cuzco. Again, some Ecuadorean hill forts may actually have been built by local populations and reused by the Incas (Plaza Schuller 1980), but two clusters seem to trace the slow progress of the Inca campaign: one north of Tomebamba (Cuenca), and one north of Quito stretching into Guayllabamba. Forts also extend into the forests of the western slopes of the Andes (Lippi 1998). Inca pukaras north of Quito include small, lightly occupied hilltop outposts, but also large forts equipped for permanent settlement, such as the Pucara de Rumicucho (Almeida 1999) and Pambamarca (Hyslop 1990; Oberem 1969; Plaza Schuller 1980), a remarkable complex of 14 walled installations on a single mountain, some linked to each other by trenches. Sling stones, bola stones, and mace heads have been found at these and other Inca forts in Ecuador. While large-scale garrisons like Pambamarca housed forces that could launch attacks, they also clearly demonstrate that here, the Incas anticipated threats requiring serious defenses.

While Inca fortifications used the same architectural techniques as those of LIP populations—concentric walls or wall-ditch complexes, baffled gates and non-aligned gates, parapets with sling-stone piles—the density, design, and defensibility of Inca forts varied from region to region, depending on function, the level of threat, and local architectural tradition (Hyslop 1990:189). The lack of a standard plan suggests that Inca fort building was expedient rather than formalized. Often there are few structures inside; armies could camp inside and local populations could take temporary refuge, but they were not permanently staffed with large garrisons. Many Inca forts have large plazas and ritual spaces, which can compromise the defensibility of the sites, and some have evidence of other functions, such as feasting (for example, Alconini 2004), that imply that interaction with local populations was not always hostile.

Warfare and Elite Legitimization

Inca material culture does not reflect an individualizing cult of the emperor, nor does it directly represent warfare. Violent themes such as trophy heads are generally absent from Inca iconography, and there is little archaeological evidence of militaristic displays such as trophies and the sacrifice of war captives.

Documentary evidence tells a different story, however. Ethnohistoric descriptions make it clear that warfare was frequently celebrated and memorialized in public Inca rituals. The Incas arranged triumphal processions in Cuzco after important victories; war captives were displayed in these processions, and the victory celebrations might sometimes involve their sacrifice (for example, Betanzos 1996:94–95 [1551–1557: Pt.1, Ch. 20]; Sarmiento 1988:105 [1572: Ch. 37]). Staged ritual battles commemorated important military victories (Duviols 1997). For instance, nobles from the two moieties of Cuzco battled at the funeral ceremonies of Pachacuti Inca, "representing the wars the lord had in his life" (Betanzos 1996:136), and Topa Inca's victories in Quito were commemorated with a staged battle in which captive warriors from the campaign were placed in the fortress of Sacsayhuaman and vanquished by Inca soldiers armed with gold and silver weapons (Santa Cruz Pachacuti 1993:192–193). Although trophies are not commonly found in LH sites, trophies were said to be taken from the bodies of prominent enemy leaders—heads were displayed on pikes, triumphal cups were made of their skulls, drums of their skin, and flutes of their shin-bones (Ogburn 2004; Rowe 1946:179). These trophies were primarily intended for public display, as proofs of Inca military dominance, rather than for personal prestige. For instance, drums made of the skin of defeated elites would be played in battle and in festivals (Ogburn 2004). Warfare was also alluded to in more restricted environments, such as the *llasahuasi* in Cuzco, a structure housing the severed head of a Titicaca Basin lord and the captured regalia of his generals (Betanzos 1996:94–95 [1551–1557: Pt.1, Ch. 20]; Sarmiento 1988:105 [1572: Ch. 37]), or in dramas performed at court, which often related to military deeds (Bram 1941:78). In sum, these ethnohistoric sources reveal an otherwise invisible realm of displays and performances that referenced warfare in the LH. Such performances may have existed in previous periods without leaving much material trace (with exceptions such as the sacrificial remains from the Akapana at Tiwanaku).

Indeed, the chronicles make clear that the Inca emperors' legitimacy was achieved through victory in war. Cieza de Leon remarks on posterity's contempt for Incas who were "remiss, cowardly, given to vices and loving idleness without enlarging the empire" (1984:28 [1550:2.11]). In Inca histories, the earliest Inca kings are described as *sinchis*, local war leaders raiding for booty and glory (even though, as we have seen from archaeological evidence, warfare afflicted their area less than others in the highlands). The empire's origins were traced to the mythic Inca conquest over the Chancas to the west by Pachacuti, first of the great Inca conquerors; indeed, Pachacuti only obtained the throne by demonstrating his worthiness in this victory (Duviols 1997). These histories are valuable not as literal records of what happened, but as records of the worldview of Cuzco elites at the time of the Spanish conquest. Although Inca rulers as individual fighters may not have accomplished much on the battlefield,[15] the language of the chronicles makes it clear that victories were attributed to them personally, and the importance of warfare and military conquest in the chronicles speaks to the central role of militarism in Inca elite ideology.

Nevertheless, one must bear in mind that these oral histories were the birthright of a small, select Cuzco nobility. Inca material culture did not broadcast themes of violence and military domination to a wide audience in the same way that Middle Horizon material culture did. Militaristic propaganda seems rather to have been disseminated in public performances and in the telling of history, acts less amenable to archaeological investigation.

Discussion and Conclusions

This span of Andean prehistory witnessed two episodes of political consolidation and expansion, separated by a collapse, a hiatus of political fragmentation, and gradual, very uneven regrouping. In all periods, warfare seems to have been closely related to these political processes.

Warfare was related to polity expansion in the Middle Horizon, at least in the case of Wari. It is possible that Tiwanaku achieved widespread political power through relationships that were largely incorporative rather than coercive. Violence accompanied collapse as well as expansion, with destruction episodes at several Wari and Tiwanaku centers at the time of their abandonment. In the hiatus period of the Late Intermediate period, endemic warfare afflicted much of the Andean highlands, altered settlement patterns dramatically, and must have had a great impact on peoples' daily lives. Some political consolidation occurred unevenly in the most populous parts of the highlands, but it was not on a large scale, and it may have occurred through confederation and defensive nucleation rather than conquest. Finally, the Incas have always been seen as a conquest empire, because of the importance laid on conquest in Inca narratives of their own origins and expansion. Yet recent research in the Cuzco heartland suggests that in its earliest stages, Inca state emergence proceeded relatively peacefully; only later did conquest warfare become the engine of the Incas' explosive growth. The Andean sequence thus illustrates, not only the difference between raiding and conquest warfare, but the multi-linearity of trajectories of warfare and peace.

In addition, the *idea* of warfare played a varied role. At some times, warfare and combat formed a central theme in craft and ceremony, celebrated and manipulated as a source of elite power; at others, it lost its attraction as an idiom, despite its prevalence in practice. The fading of violence in ceremony and material culture after the collapse of the Middle Horizon states is especially intriguing, and demonstrates vividly that the romance of war may rise or fall at different times from warfare itself. In this portion of the Andean sequence, violent displays and representations appear more closely related to the needs of the political hierarchy than to warfare's actual impact on people's lives. This sequence is a cautionary tale for archaeologists against relying on iconography as evidence of warfare's presence or absence.

The evidence considered here also makes clear the relative difficulty of detecting warfare in horizon or political integration periods. In general, because conquest is a rapid process decided in a few military encounters, rather than constituting repeated battles over an extended period, in the absence of textual evidence it is much more difficult to detect conquest warfare archaeologically than the sort of chronic, non-conquest warfare that afflicted the LIP.

It would be premature at this point to attempt a single coherent explanation for why Andean warfare accompanied both political expansion through conquest and extreme fragmentation. However, I would like to highlight the two main explanatory frameworks that emerge naturally from this discussion and that most Andean archaeologists would favor. They are not mutually exclusive.

The traditional archaeological approach to Andean prehistory has been one in which endogenous processes of population growth and political development shaped outcomes. In this framework, developments are largely seen as contingent on previous history within a region. For example, the classic explanation for the warfare and breakdown of social networks in the LIP is that it was the result of the collapse of the MH states that had unified much of the highlands. This framework forms a natural fit with the concept that expansionistic conquest warfare first requires a certain degree of political and economic organization. The rise of Andean militaristic states was powered by their success in reaching a level of organization that enabled them to field large armies of foot-soldiers on extended expeditions. When this organization faltered, the provinces under their sway quickly broke away, sometimes with destructive acts. Without such political and economic organization, the local leaders who followed found it quite difficult to extend their power geographically, especially against rival populations protected by the hilltop forts so common in the Andean highlands. The Cuzco Valley was an exception—a place where people achieved consolidation and centralization fairly early, without much fortification or chronic warfare. After the Incas arrived at a critical mass of well-integrated heartland, they had a key advantage in numbers and logistical capability that allowed them to expand rapidly and conquer a vast empire. This approach, while surely correct in some ways, does not adequately explain why political organization sufficient for conquest and expansion was achieved in some times and places and not others.

An alternative explanatory framework that has increasingly attracted attention in Andean archaeology is that environmental stresses played a key role in shaping social outcomes. The Andean productive environment is sensitive to climate change, and major transformations in the archaeological sequence fit well in some respects with environmental explanations. Ice cores from the Quelccaya glacier and sediment cores from Lake Huiñamarca indicate an extended period of severe drought in the south-central highlands during the LIP (Abbott et al. 1997; Thompson et al. 1985). This drought has been proposed as a probable cause for the collapse of Tiwanaku (Binford et al. 1997; Kolata 2000; Ortloff and Kolata 1993). It could explain conflict in the LIP as well; harsh environmental conditions would be conducive to conflict, while hindering political consolidation and conquest. The escalation of conflict in several regions in the late LIP may also be related to worsening climate (Nielsen 2001, 2002; Seltzer and Hastorf 1990). Many other questions are not fully explained by the environmental approach—why militarism is more clearly marked for Wari expansion than for Tiwanaku, for instance, or why the Middle Horizon polities remained stable during earlier times of drought (Stanish 2003:223).

Nevertheless, to consider the possible effects of environmental conditions on the course of warfare in the Andean area is to give an added dimension to the distinction between raiding warfare and conquest warfare. When times are bad, warring groups should have no desire to conquer more mouths to feed—rather, they should wish to drive out enemies and expand onto their land, or raid their stores and livestock to alleviate short-term shortages. Only when times are good should populations produce enough surplus to make them attractive candidates for conquest and annexation. Ideally, periods of raiding war, conquest war, and relative peace in the Andes could be tested against fine-grained reconstructions of local climate change, as Bamforth (this volume) does for the North American Great Plains. More research must be done, both paleoclimatic and archaeological, to evaluate this possibility. Despite many unanswered questions, the Andean area, with its great diversity of societies and its long history of warfare, promises to be fertile ground for examining the varied forms of warfare, its diverse role in representation, and its complex effects on the human societies of the past.

Acknowledgments

I am grateful to the many colleagues who helped me track down sources for this chapter, including Axel Nielsen, Tiffiny Tung, Deborah Blom, Bruce Owen, John Topic, John Verano, Ken Nystrom, Melissa Murphy, Christina Torres-Rouff, and Tamara Bray. My own research in the Titicaca Basin was made possible by the National Science Foundation, University of California, Los Angeles, and Peru's Instituto Nacional de Cultura. I also thank Mark Allen, Aimee Plourde, and the anonymous reviewers, who gave me helpful comments on an earlier draft.

Notes

1. I restrict this discussion to later periods because they best illustrate the contrasts I seek to examine. I also include coastal areas only when they bear directly upon developments in the highlands.

2. Disembodied skulls have also been found at Wari itself, placed in pits below residential floors (Brewster-Wray 1983 cited in Verano 1995:201). One intact example was found wrapped in cloth fastened with copper pins. Whether these were trophies, sacrifice victims, or revered ancestor relics is uncertain.

3. Wari provincial centers are normally designed as a single unit enclosed by a thick, high wall, tightly restricting access, and their internally subdivided architectural pattern of grids of walled patio compounds would have made these sites a challenge to penetrate militarily. However, they do not fit the classic Andean pattern of fortification using concentric walls on high ground. For instance, Viracochapampa is walled and has only two entrances, but it is located on flat ground. While Viracochapampa and similar sites could certainly have been defended, significant compromises to their defensibility were made by the demands of the Wari architectural canon.

4. Bauer and Bauer (1987) report a cache of ten bodiless skulls without grave goods. The lack of mandibles, cut marks or trauma suggests the skulls were secondary burials, and it is not clear whether they were trophies or revered relics (Bauer and Bauer 1987; McEwan 1991:109).

5. In Moquegua, there is good evidence from domestic architecture, mortuary patterns, and ceramics that these settlements actually were composed of highland colonists (Goldstein 1989; Goldstein and Owen 2001), and osteological studies in Moquegua and Azapa confirm the highland connection (Blom et al. 1998; Rothhammer and Santoro 2001). A Tiwanaku presence in Cochabamba is evidenced by pottery, but settlement patterns there changed little from the preceding period and actual colonies may not have been established (Higueras 2001).

6. Notably, destruction focused on residential and monumental areas, rather than on cemeteries, which would have been the logical target for looters.

7. House counts, rather than site areas in hectares, are given here as a more consistent basis for population comparison between different regions investigated by different archaeological projects.

8. Kueláp was occupied some time after A.D. 800 until the Late Horizon, but like most Chachapoya sites, has not been precisely dated; burnt roof thatch may signal a destruction episode at the time of the Inca conquest (Narváez 1987).

9. This statistic must be treated with care as it concatenates material from sites of both the LIP and Inca periods.

10. Verano (2002), examining Hrdlicka's (1914) sample of 212 crania from sites in Peru's central highlands, finds extraordinarily high rates of trauma: 55.7 percent for men, 31.6 percent for women, and 26.9 percent for juveniles. Unfortunately this sample is not well-dated and may range from the MH through the LH. It does demonstrate that violence occurred against women and children as well as men, implying "conflicts involving whole villages, rather than organized warfare by men alone" (Verano 2002:232). Verano suggests a connection to ritual battles, but the pattern could also be explained by ambushes, massacres, and sniping characteristic of decentralized societies (see Milner 1999).

11. The bola or *ayllu* was a cord attached to several stone or bronze weights by means of a medial groove or a hole, thrown in both warfare and hunting (Urteaga 1919–1920:305, 309).

12. An exception is petroglyphs depicting combat; for example, see Romero (1996).

13. Since the Late Horizon is defined as the period of Inca control, it starts several decades earlier in some places than others; A.D. 1450 is an average date.

14. It is notable, however, that Hefferman's survey did find stone mace heads, so war was not completely absent.

15. D'Altroy (2002:215) gives some cases from the chronicles of Inca commanders engaging in battle. The mummy of Pachacuti, which was found by the Spaniards, was said to have had a battle scar on its head (Rostworowski 1999:33). When Inca rulers did fight, they were carried on a litter, and probably played a more symbolic than lethal role in battle. The Inca's or his royal delegate's main function on campaign was not to lead troops but to negotiate terms with enemy leaders (Bram 1941:50–51).

References

Abbott, M. B., M. W. Binford, M. Brenner, and K. Kelts. 1997. A 3500 ^{14}C yr High-Resolution Record of Water-Level Changes in Lake Titicaca, Bolivia-Peru. *Quaternary Research* (47):169–180.

Albarracín-Jordan, J., and J. E. Matthews. 1992. *Prehispanic and Early Colonial Settlement Patterns in the Lower Tiwanaku Valley, Bolivia*. La Paz, Bolivia: Producciones CIMA.

Alconini, S. 1995. *Rito, Simbolo e Historia en la Pirámide de Akapana, Tiwanaku: Un Análisis de Cerámica Ceremonial Prehispánica*. La Paz, Bolivia: Editorial Acción.

———. 2004. The Southeastern Inka Frontier Against the Chiriguanos: Structure and Dynamics of the Inca Imperial Borderlands. *Latin American Antiquity* 15(4):389–418.

Allen, M. W. 1994. Warfare and Economic Power in Simple Chiefdoms: The Development of Fortified Villages and Polities in Mid-Hawke's Bay, New Zealand. Unpublished Ph.D. dissertation, Department of Anthropology, University of California, Los Angeles.

———. 1996. Pathways to Economic Power in Maori Chiefdoms: Ecology and Warfare in Prehistoric Hawke's Bay. *Research in Economic Anthropology* (17):171–225.

———. 2003. Hillforts and the Cycling of Maori Chiefdoms: Do Good Fences Make Good Neighbors? Manuscript on file, Department of Geography and Anthropology, California State Polytechnic University, Pomona.

Almeida Reyes, E. 1999. *Estudios Arqueologicos en el Pucara de Rumicucho (II Etapa)*. Quito: Museos del Banco Central de Ecuador.

Anderson, D. G. 1994. *The Savannah River Chiefdoms: Political Change in the Late Prehistoric Southeast*. Tuscaloosa: University of Alabama Press.

Arellano, A. J. 1992. El Desarollo Cultural Prehispánico en el Altiplano y Valles Interandinos de Bolivia. In *Prehistoria Sudamericana: Nuevas perspectivas*, edited by B. J. Meggers, 309–325. Santiago: Taraxcum.

Arkush, E. 2005. Colla Fortified Sites: Warfare and Regional Power in the Late Prehispanic Titicaca Basin, Peru. Unpublished Ph.D. dissertation, Department of Anthropology, University of California, Los Angeles.

Bandy, M. 2001. Population and History in the Ancient Titicaca Basin. Unpublished Ph.D. dissertation, Department of Anthropology, University of California, Los Angeles.

Bauer, B. 1992. *The Development of the Inca State*. Austin: University of Texas Press.

———. 2004. *Ancient Cuzco*. Austin: University of Texas Press.

Bauer, B. S., and R. A. Covey. 2002. Processes of State Formation in the Inca Heartland (Cuzco, Peru). *American Anthropologist* 104(3):846–865.

Bauer, T. W., and B. S. Bauer. 1987. Selected Aspects of Skulls Found by the Pikillacta Archaeological Project 1982. Appendix 2. In *The Middle Horizon in the Valley of Cuzco, Peru: The Impact of the Wari Occupation of Pikillacta in the Lucre Basin*, by G. F. McEwan, 190–196. BAR International Series 372. Oxford: British Archaeological Reports.

Bennett, W. C. 1933. Archaeological Hikes in the Andes. *Natural History* 33(2):163–174.

———. 1950. Cultural Unity and Disunity in the Titicaca Basin. *American Antiquity* 16(2):89–98.

Betanzos, J. de. 1996 [1551–1557]. *Narrative of the Incas*, translated by R. Hamilton. Austin: University of Texas Press.

Binford, M. W., A. L. Kolata, M. Brenner, J. W. Janusek, M. T. Seddon, M. Abbott, and J. H. Curtis. 1997. Climate Variation and the Rise and Fall of an Andean Civilization. *Quaternary Research* 47:235–248.

Blom, D. 2003. Health and Variation in Moquegua's Tiwanaku Settlements. Paper presented at the 68th annual Society for American Archaeology Meetings, Milwaukee.

Blom, D. E., B. Hallgrímsson, L. Keng, M. C. Lozada Cerna, and J. E. Buikstra. 1998. Tiwanaku "Colonization": Bioarchaeological Implications for Migration in the Moquegua Valley, Peru. *World Archaeology* 30(2):238–261.

Blom, D. E., J. W. Janusek, and J. E. Buikstra. 2003. A Reevaluation of Human Remains from Tiwanaku. In *Tiwanaku and its Hinterland: Archaeology and Paleoecology of an Andean Civilization*, edited by A. L. Kolata. Urban and Rural Archaeology 2:435–446. Washington, D.C.: Smithsonian Institution Press.

Bram, J. 1941. *An Analysis of Inca Militarism*. New York: J. J. Augustin.

Bravomalo de Espinosa, A. 1992. *Ecuador Ancestral*. Quito: Artes Gráficas Señal.

Bray, T. 1991. Inca Imperialism on the Northern Frontier. Unpublished Ph.D. dissertation, Department of Anthropology, State University of New York, Binghamton.

———. 1992. Archaeological Survey in Northern Highland Ecuador: Inka Imperialism and Pais Caranqui. *World Archaeology* 24(2):218–233.

———. 2005. Pucaras, Personnel, and Imperial Practice: A Comparative Look at Inca Fortress Installations around the Empire. Manuscript on file, Department of Anthropology, Wayne State University, Detroit.

Brewster-Wray, C. C. 1983. Spatial Patterning and the Function of a Huari Architectural Compound. In *Investigations of the Andean Past*, edited by D. Sandweiss. Ithaca: Cornell University Press.

Caillavet, C. 1985. La Adaptación de la Dominación Incaica a las Sociedades Autóctonas de la Frontera Septentrional del Imperio: (Territorio Otavalo-Ecuador). *Revista Andina* 3(2):403–423.

Cardona Rosas, A. 2002. *Arqueología de Arequipa: De Sus Albores a los Incas*. Arequipa, Peru: Magazine Impresores.

Carneiro, R. L. 1970. A Theory of the Origin of the State. *Science* (169):733–738.

———. 1981. The Chiefdom: Precursor of the State. In *The Transition to Statehood in the New World*, edited by G. D. Jones and R. R. Kautz, 37–79. Cambridge: Cambridge University Press.

———. 1990. Chiefdom Level Warfare as Exemplified in Fiji and the Cauca Valley. In *The Anthropology of Warfare*, edited by J. Haas, 190–211. Cambridge: Cambridge University Press.

———. 1998. What Happened at the Flashpoint? Conjectures on Chiefdom Formation at the Very Moment of Conception. In *Chiefdoms and Chieftaincy in the Americas,* edited by E. M. Redmond, 18–42. Gainesville: University Press of Florida.

Chagnon, N. A. 1968. Yanomamö Social Organization and Warfare. In *War: The Anthropology of Armed Conflict and Aggression*, edited by M. Fried, M. Harris, and R. Murphy, 85–91. Garden City, NY: Natural History Press.

Chávez, S. 1975. The Arapa and Thunderbolt Stela: A Case of Stylistic Identity with Implications for Pucara Influence in the Area of Tiahuanaco. *Ñawpa Pacha* (13):3–25.

Cieza de León, P. 1984 [1550]. *La Crónica del Perú*, edited by M. Ballesteros. Madrid: Historia 16.

———. 1985 [1550]. *El Señorío de los Incas*, edited by M. Ballesteros. Madrid: Historia 16.

Cisneros Velarde, L., and L. Guillermo Lumbreras. 1980. *Historia General del Ejercito Peruano*. Lima: Comision Permanente de la Historia del Ejercito del Peru.

Cobo, B. 1979 [1653]. *History of the Inca Empire [Historia del Nuevo Mundo, Bks. 11–12]*, translated by R. Hamilton. Austin: University of Texas Press.

Connell, S. V., C. Gifford, A. L. González, and M. Carpenter. 2003. Hard Times in Ecuador: Inka Troubles at Pambamarca. *Antiquity* 77(295). http://antiquity.ac.uk/ProjGall/Connell/Connell.html

Cordy-Collins, A. K. 1992. Archaism or Tradition? The Decapitation Theme in Cupisnique and Moche Iconography. *Latin American Antiquity* 3(3):206–220.

———. 2001. Decapitation in Cupisnique and Early Moche Societies. In *Ritual Sacrifice in Ancient Peru*, edited by E. P. Benson and A. G. Cook, 21–33. Austin: University of Texas Press.

Costin, C. 1986. From Chiefdom to Empire State: Ceramic Economy among the Pre-Hispanic Wanka of Highland Peru. Unpublished Ph.D. dissertation, Department of Anthropology, University of California, Los Angeles.

Couture, N. C., and K. Sampeck. 2003. Putuni: A History of Palace Architecture in Tiwanaku. In *Tiwanaku and its Hinterland. Archaeology and Paleoecology of an Andean Civilization*, edited by A. L. Kolata. Urban and Rural Archaeology 2:226–263. Washington, D.C.: Smithsonian Institution Press.

Covey, R. A. 2003. A Processual Study of Inka State Formation. *Journal of Anthropological Archaeology* 22:333–357.

D'Altroy, T. N. 1992. *Provincial Power in the Inka Empire*. Washington, D.C.: Smithsonian Institution Press.

———. 1994. Factions and Political Development in the Central Andes. In *Factional Competition and Political Development in the New World*, edited by E. Brumfiel and J. Fox, 171–188. Cambridge: Cambridge University Press.

———. 2002. *The Incas*. Malden, Mass.: Blackwell.

de la Vega, E. 1990. Estudio Arqueologico de Pucaras o Poblados Amuralladas de Cumbre en Territorio Lupaqa: El Caso de Pucara-Juli. Tesis Bachiller, Universidad Catolica Santa Maria.

de la Vega M., E., K. L. Frye, and C. Chávez J. 2002. La Cueva Funeraria de Molino-Chilacachi (Acora), Puno. *Gaceta Arqueológica Andina* 26:121–137.

DeMarrais, E. 1997. Materialization, Ideology, and Power: The Development of Centralized Authority among the Pre-Hispanic Polities of the Valle Calchaquí, Argentina. Unpublished Ph.D. dissertation, Department of Anthropology, University of California, Los Angeles.

———. 2001. La Arqueología del Norte del Valle Calchaqui. In *Historia Argentina Prehispánica*, edited by E. Berberián and A. Nielsen, 1:289–346. Córdoba, Argentina: Editorial Brujas.

Divale, W. T. 1973. *Warfare in Primitive Societies: A Bibliography*. Santa Barbara, CA: American Bibliographical Center, Clio Press.

Duviols, P. 1997. Del Discurso Discrito Colonial al Discurso Prehispánico: Hacia el Sistema Sociocosmológico Inca de Oposición y Complementaridad. *Bulletin de l'Institut Francais d'Études Andines* 26(3).

Dwyer, E. B. 1971. The Early Inca Occupation of the Valley of Cuzco, Peru. Unpublished Ph.D. dissertation, Department of Anthropology, University of California, Berkeley.

Earle, T. K. 1991. Property Rights and the Evolution of Chiefdoms. In *Chiefdoms: Power, Economy and Ideology*, edited by T. K. Earle, 71–99. Cambridge: Cambridge University Press.

———. 1997. *How Chiefs Come to Power: The Political Economy in Prehistory*. Stanford: Stanford University Press.

———. 2001. Institutionalization of Chiefdoms: Why Landscapes are Built. In *From Leaders to Rulers*, edited by J. Haas, 105–124. New York: Kluwer Academic/Plenum Publishers.

Earle, T. K., T. N. D'Altroy, C. J. LeBlanc, C. A. Hastorf, and T. L. Levine. 1980. Changing Settlement Patterns in the Upper Mantaro Valley, Peru. *Journal of New World Archaeology* 4:1–49.

Espinoza Soriano, W. 1975. Los Mitmas Huayacuntu en Quito o Guarniciones para la Represion Armada, Siglos XV y XVI. *Revista del Museo Nacional, Lima* (41):351–394.

Farfán Lovatón, C. 1995. Asentamientos Prehispánicos de la Cuenca Alta del Chillón. *Gaceta Arqueological Andina* (24):31–61.

Feil, D. K. 1987. *The Evolution of Highland Papua New Guinea Societies*. Cambridge: Cambridge University Press.

Ferguson, R. B. 1984. Introduction: Studying War. In *Warfare, Culture, and Environment*, edited by B. R. Ferguson, 1–81. Orlando: Academic Press.

Frye, K. L. 1997. Political Centralization in the Altiplano Period in the Southwestern Titicaca Basin (Appendix 2). In *Archaeological Survey in the Juli-Desaguadero Region of Lake Titicaca Basin, Southern Peru*, edited by C. Stanish, 129–141. Chicago: Field Museum of Natural History.

Gallardo I., F. Mauricio Uribe R., and P. Ayala R. 1995. Arquitectura Inka y Poder en el Pukara de Turi, Norte de Chile. *Gaceta Arqueological Andina* (24):151–171.

Giesso, M. 2003. Stone Tool Production in the Tiwanaku Heartland. In *Tiwanaku and its Hinterland: Archaeology and Paleoecology of an Andean Civilization*, edited by A. L. Kolata, Urban and Rural Archaeology 2:363–383. Washington, D.C.: Smithsonian Institution Press.

Glowacki, M. 2002. The Huaro Archaeological Site Complex: Rethinking the Huari Occupation of Cuzco. In *Andean Archaeology*, edited by W. Isbell and H. Silverman, 267–285. New York: Plenum.

Goldstein, P. 1989. Omo: a Tiwanaku Provincial Center in Moquegua, Peru. Unpublished Ph.D. dissertation, Department of Anthropology, University of Chicago.

———. 2005. *Andean Diaspora: The Tiwanaku Colonies and the Origins of South American Empire*. Gainesville: University Press of Florida.

Goldstein, P., and B. Owen. 2001. Tiwanaku en Moquegua: Las Colonias Altiplánicas. In *Huari y Tiwanaku: Modelos y Evidencias*, Segunda Parte, 139–168. Lima: Pontificia Universidad Católica del Perú.

Guaman Poma de Ayala, F. 1980 [1613]. *El Primer Nueva Cronica y Buen Gobierno*. Mexico City: Siglo Ventiuno.

Hastorf, C. A. 1993. *Agriculture and the Onset of Political Inequality before the Inka*. Cambridge: Cambridge University Press.

Hastorf, C. A., E. Sandefur, T. K. Earle, H. E. Wright, L. LeCount, and G. Russell. 1989. Settlement Archaeology in the Jauja Region of Peru: Evidence from the Early Intermediate Period through the Late Intermediate Period: A Report on the 1986 Field Season. *Andean Past* 2:81–129.

Hefferman, K. 1996. *Limatambo: Archaeology, History and the Regional Societies of Inca Cusco*. Oxford: British Archaeological Reports.

Hemming, J. 1970. *The Conquest of the Incas*. New York: Harcourt Brace and Co.

Higueras, A. 2001. El Periodo Intermedio (Horizonte Medio) en los Valles de Cochabamba: Una Perspectiva del Análisis de Asentamientos Humanos y Uso de Tierras. In *Huaru y Tiwanaku: Modelos y Evidencias*, segunda parte, edited by P. Kaulicke and W. H. Isbell, 625–646. Lima: Boletin del PUCP 5.

Hrdlicka, A. 1914. Archaeological Exploration in Peru. *Smithsonian Miscellaneous Collections* 63: 47–53.

Hyslop, J. 1976. An Archaeological Investigation of the Lupaqa Kingdom and its Origins. Unpublished Ph.D. dissertation, Department of Anthropology, Columbia University.

———. 1984. *The Inka Road System*. New York: Academic Press.

———. 1990. *Inka Settlement Planning*. Austin: University of Texas Press.

Isla C., J. 2002. Investigaciones Arqueológicas en Cerro Baúl. *Gaceta Arqueológica Andina* 26:87–120.

Isla C., J., P. R. Williams, L. Medina, and D. Blom. 1998. The Nature of Wari Militarism at Cerro Baul. Paper presented at the 63rd annual meeting of the Society of American Archaeology, Seattle, Washington.

Jakobsen, J., J. B. Jorgensen, L. K. Jorgensen, and I. Schjellerup. 1986–1987. "Cazadores de Cabezas" en Sitios pre-Inca de Chachapoyas, Amazonas. *Revista del Museo Nacional* 48:139–186.

Janusek, J. W. 1999. Craft and Local Power: Embedded Specialization in Tiwanaku Cities. *Latin American Antiquity* 10(2):107–131.

———. 2004. Tiwanaku and Its Precursors: Recent Research and Emerging Perspectives. *Journal of Archaeological Research* 12(2):121–183.

Janusek, J. W., and A. L. Kolata. 2003. Pre-Hispanic Rural History in the Katari Valley. In *Tiwanaku and its Hinterland. Archaeology and Paleoecology of an Andean Civilization*, edited by A. L. Kolata. Urban and Rural Archaeology 2:129–171. Washington, D.C.: Smithsonian Institution Press.

Julien, D. 1988. Ancient Cuismancu: Settlement and Cultural Dynamics in the Cajamarca

Region of the North Highlands of Peru, 200 B.C.–A.D. 1532. Unpublished Ph.D. dissertation, Department of Anthropology, University of Texas, Austin.

———. 1993. Late Pre-Inkaic Ethnic Groups in Highland Peru: An Archaeological-Ethnohistorical Model of the Political Geography of the Cajamarca Region. *Latin American Antiquity* 4:246–273.

Keeley, L. H. 1996. *War Before Civilization*. New York: Oxford University Press.

Kellner, C. M. 2002. Coping with Stress: Bioarchaeological Analyses of Nasca Health During the Early Intermediate Period and Early Middle Horizon. Unpublished Ph.D. dissertation, Department of Anthropology, University of California, Santa Barbara.

Kendall, A. 1985. *Aspects of Inca Architecture—Description, Function, and Chronology*. Oxford: BAR International Series no. 242.

Kolata, A. 1993. *The Tiwanaku: Portrait of an Andean Civilization*. Cambridge, MA: Blackwell.

———. 2000. Environmental Thresholds and the "Natural History" of an Andean Civilization. In *Environmental Disaster and the Archaeology of Human Response*, edited by G. Bawden and R. M. Reycraft, 163–178. Albuquerque: Maxwell Museum of Anthropology, University of New Mexico.

———. 2003. Tiwanaku Ceremonial Architecture and Urban Organization. In *Tiwanaku and its Hinterland: Archaeology and Paleoecology of an Andean Civilization*, edited by A. L. Kolata, Urban and Rural Archaeology 2:175–201. Washington, D.C.: Smithsonian Institution Press.

Krzanowski, A. 1977. Yuraccama, the Settlement Complex in the Alto Chicama Region (Northern Peru). In *Polish Contributions in New World Archaeology*, edited by J. Kozlowski, 29–58. Krakow: Zakland Narodwy im Osolinskich.

———. 1983. *The Cultural Chronology of the Northern Andes of Peru (the Huamachuco-Quiruvilca-Otuzco Region)*. Warsaw: Sociedad Polaca de Estudios Latinoamericanos, Comisión Andina, Documentos de Trabajo No. 1.

———. 1985. *Implicaciones Demográficas del Patron de Asentamiento Prehispánico en los Andes*. El caso del valle Alto Chicama, Perú. 71:79–96.

Lavallee, D., and M. Julien. 1973. *Les Etablissements Asto a l'Epoque Préhispanique*. Lima.

LeBlanc, C. J. 1981. Late Prehispanic Huanca Settlement Patterns in the Yanamarca Valley, Peru. Unpublished Ph.D. dissertation, Department of Anthropology, University of California, Los Angeles.

LeBlanc, S. A. 1999. *Prehistoric Warfare in the American Southwest*. Salt Lake City: University of Utah Press.

Lecoq, P. 1997. Patrón de Asentamiento, Estilos Cerámicos y Grupos Etnicos: El Ejemplo de la Region Intersalar en Bolivia. In *Saberes y Memorias en los Andes: In Memoriam Thierry Saignes*, edited by T. Bouysse-Cassagne, 59–89. Paris/Lima: IHEAL-IFEA.

Lecoq, P., and R. Céspedes. 1997. Panorama Archéologique des Zones Méridionales de Bolivie (Sud-est de Potosí). *Bulletin de l'Institut Francais d'Études Andines* 26(1):21–61.

Lee, V. R. 1992. *Investigations in Bolivia*. Wilson, WY: Copyright V. R. Lee.

———. 2000. *Forgotten Vilcabamba: Final Stronghold of the Incas*. Wilson, WY: Copyright V. R. Lee.

Lippi, R. 1998. *Una Exploración Arqueológica del Pichincha Occidental, Ecuador*. Quito: Museo Jacinto Jijon y Caamaño.

Llagostera M., A., and M. Costa J. 1999. Patrones de Asentamiento en la Epoca Agroalfarera de San Pedro de Atacama (Norte de Chile). *Estudios Atacameños* 11:30–34.

Malpass, M. A. 2001. Sonay: Un Centro Wari Celular Ortogonal en el Valle de Camana, Peru. In *Huari y Tiwanaku: Modelos vs Evidencias, Segunda Parte*, edited by P. Kaulicke and W. H. Isbell, 51–68. Boletín de Arqueología PUCP no. 5. Lima: Pontificia Universidad Católica del Perú.

Mantha, A. 2004. *Rapayán: Une Culture Tardive du Haut Marañón dans les Andes Centrales du Pérou*. Montreal: Université de Montréal.

Manzanilla, L., and E. Woodward. 1990. Restos Humanos Asociados a la Pirámide de Akapana (Tiwanaku, Bolivia). *Latin American Antiquity* 1(2): 133–149.

Matos Mendieta, R. 1999. The "Señorios" in the Sierra and the Central Coast. In *The Inca World: The Development of Pre-Columbian Peru, A.D. 1000–1534*, edited by L. L. Minelli, 37–48. Norman: University of Oklahoma Press.

McCown, T. D. 1945. *Pre-Incaic Huamachuco: Survey and Excavation in the Region of Huamachuco and Cajabamba*. Berkeley: University of California Press.

McEwan, G. 1987. *The Middle Horizon in the Valley of Cuzco, Peru: The Impact of the Wari Occupation in the Lucre Basin*. BAR International Series 372. Oxford: British Archaeological Reports.

———. 1989. The Wari Empire in the Southern Peruvian Highlands: A View from the Provinces. In *The Nature of Wari: A Reappraisal of the Middle Horizon Period in Peru*, edited by R. M. Czwarno, F. M. Meddens, and A. Morgan, 53–71.

———. 1991. Investigations at the Pikillacta Site: A Provincial Huari Center in the Valley of Cuzco. In *Huari Administrative Structure: Prehistoric Monumental Architecture and State Government*, edited by W. H. Isbell and G. F. McEwan, 93–119. Washington, D.C.: Dumbarton Oaks.

———. 1996. Archaeological Investigations at Pikillacta, a Wari Site in Peru. *Journal of Field Archaeology* 23:169–186.

Meddens, F. 1999. La Secuencia Cultural de la Cuenca de Chicha - Soras. In *XII Congreso Peruano del Hombre y la Cultura Andina*, edited by I. Pérez, W. Aguilar S., and M. Purizaga V., 2:200–210. Ayacucho: Universidad Nacional San Cristóbal de Huamanga.

Meggitt, M. 1977. *Blood Is Their Argument*. Palo Alto, CA: Mayfield.

Mercado De Peñalosa, Don P. 1885 [1586]. Relación de la Provincia de los Pacajes. In *Relaciónes Geográficas de Indias: Peru*, edited by M. Jiménez de la Espada, v. 2: 51–64. Madrid: Ministerio de Fomento, Tip. de M. G. Hernández.

Milner, G. E. 1999. Warfare in Prehistoric and Early Historic Eastern North America. *Journal of Archaeological Research* 7(2):105–151.

Morris, C., and D. Thompson. 1985. *Huánuco Pampa: An Inca City and its Hinterland*. London: Thames and Hudson.

Moseley, M. 1989. Fortificaciones Prehispánicas y Evolución de Tácticas Militares en el Valle de Moquegua. In *Trabajos Arqueológicos en Moquegua, Perú*, edited by L. K. Watanabe, M.E. Moseley, and F. Cabieses, 1:237–252. Lima: Programa Contisuyo del Museo Peruano de Ciencias de la Salud y Southern Peru Copper Corporation.

Moseley, M., G. Feinman, P. Goldstein, and L. Wantanabe. 1991. Colonies and Conquest: Tiahuanaco and Huari in Moquegua. In *Huari Administrative Structure: Prehistoric Monumental Architecture and State Government*, edited by W. H. Isbell and G. F. McEwan, 93–120. Washington, D.C.: Dumbarton Oaks.

Murphy, M., G. Cock, and E. Goyacochea. 2003. *Preliminary Report on the Relationship Between Status and Health at the Inca Cemetery of Puruchuco-Huaquerones, Peru*. Institute of Andean Studies, 43rd Annual Meeting, Berkeley.

Murra, J. V. 1986. The Expansion of the Inka State: Armies, War, and Rebellions. In *Anthropological History of Andean Polities*, edited by J. V. Murra, N. Wachtel, and J. Revel, 49–58. Cambridge: Cambridge University Press.

Narváez Vargas, L. A. 1987. Kuelap: Una Ciudad Fortificada en los Andes Nor-Orientales de Amazonas, Peru. In *Arquitectura y Arqueología: Pasado y Futuro de la Construcción en el Perú*, edited by V. Rangel F., 115–142. Chiclayo: Universidad de Chiclayo.

Neira Avedaño, M. 1967. Informe Preliminar de las Investigaciones Arqueológicas en el Departamento de Puno. *Anales del Insituto de Estudios Socio Económicos* 1(1). Puno.

Neves, W. A., A. M. Barros, and M. A. Costa. 1999. Incidence and Distribution of Postcranial Fractures in the Prehistoric Population of San Pedro de Atacama, Northern Chile. *American Journal of Physical Anthropology* 109:253–258.

Nielsen, A. E. 2001. Evolución Social en Quebrada de Humahuaca (A.D. 700–1536). In *Historia Argentina Prehispánica*, edited by E. Berberián and A. Nielsen 1:171–264. Córdoba, Argentina: Editorial Brujas.

———. 2002. Asentamientos, Conflicto y Cambio Social en el Altiplano de Lípez (Potosí). *Revista Española de Antropología Americana* (32):179–205.

———. 2004. Warfare and Social History in the South Andes A.D. 1200–1450. Paper presented at the 69th SAA Meetings, Montreal.

Nielsen, A. E., and W. H. Walker. 1999. Conquista Ritual y Dominación Política en el Tawantinsuyu: El Caso de Los Amarillos (Jujuy, Argentina). In *Sed non Satiata: Teoría Social en la Arqueología Latinoamericana Contemporánea*, edited by A. Zarankin and F. Acuto, 153–169. Buenos Aires: Ediciones del Tridente.

Nordenskiöld, E. 1917. The Guarani Invasion of the Inca Empire in the Sixteenth Century: An Historical Indian Migration. *Geographical Review* 9:103–121.

Nuñez, L. 1992. *Cultura y Conflicto en los Oasis de San Pedro de Atacama*. Santiago: Editorial Universitária.

Nuñez, L., and T. Dillehay. 1978. *Movilidad Giratoria, Armonía Social y Desarollo en los Andes Meridionales: Patrones de Trafico e Interacción Económica*. Antofagasta, Chile: Universidad del Norte.

Nystrom, K. C., and J. W. Verano. 2003. Warriors of the Clouds? Inference and Interpretation of Trauma from Chachapoya, Peru. Paper presented at the 73rd American Association of Physical Anthropology Meetings, Tempe, AZ.

Oberem, U. 1969. La Fortaleza de Montaña de Quitaloma. *Boletín de la Academia Nacional de Historia* 114:196–204. Quito.

Ochatoma Paravicino, J., and M. Cabrera Romano. 1999. Descubrimiento del Area Ceremonial en Conchopata, Huari. In *XII Congreso Peruano del Hombre y la Cultura An-*

dina, edited by I. Pérez C., W. Aguilar S., and M. Purizaga V., 2:212–244. Ayacucho, Peru: Universidad Nacional San Cristóbal de Huamanga.

———. 2002. Religious Ideology and Military Organization in the Iconography of a D-shaped Ceremonial Precinct at Conchopata. In *Andean Archaeology II*, edited by H. Silverman and W. H. Isbell, 225–247. New York: Kluwer/Plenum.

Ogburn, D. 2001. The Inca Occupation and Forced Resettlement in Saraguro, Ecuador. Unpublished Ph.D. dissertation, Department of Anthropology, University of California, Berkeley.

———. 2004. Human Trophies in the Late Prehispanic Andes: Display, Propaganda and Reinforcement of Power Among the Incas and Other Societies. Paper presented at the 69th annual SAA conference, Montreal.

Ortloff, C., and A. Kolata. 1993. Climate and Collapse: Agroecological Perspectives on the Decline of the Tiwanaku State. *Journal of Archaeological Science* 20:195–221.

Owen, B. 1995. Warfare and Engineering, Ostentation and Status in the Late Intermediate Period Osmore Drainage. Paper presented at the 60th annual SAA conference, Minneapolis.

Owen, B., and P. Goldstein. 2001. Tiwanaku en Moquegua: Interacciones Regionales y Colapso. In *Huari y Tiwanaku: Modelos y Evidencias, Segunda Parte,* edited by P. Kaulicke and W. Isbell, 169–188. PUCP Boletín de Arqueología no. 5. Lima: Pontificia Universidad Católica del Perú.

Parsons, J. R., and C. M. Hastings. 1988. The Late Intermediate Period. In *Peruvian Prehistory*, edited by R. W. Keatinge, 190–229. Cambridge: Cambridge University Press.

Parsons, J. R., C. M. Hastings, and R. Matos M. 1997. Rebuilding the State in Highland Peru: Herder-cultivator Interaction During the Late Intermediate Period in the Tarama-Chinchaycocha Region. *Latin American Antiquity* 8(4):317–341.

———. 2000. *Prehispanic Settlement Patterns in the Upper Mantaro and Tarma Drainages, Junín, Peru*. Ann Arbor: Museum of Anthropology, University of Michigan.

Pärssinen, M. H., and A. Siirriäinen. 1998. Cuzcotoro and the Inka Fortification System in Chuquisaca, Bolivia. *Baessler-Archiv (Neue Folge)* 46(1):135–164.

Pérez Calderón, I. 1999. Investigaciones en la Periferia del Complejo Huari. In *XII Congreso Peruano del Hombre y la Cultura Andina*, edited by I. Pérez C., W. Aguilar S., and M. Purizaga V., 2:246–270. Ayacucho, Peru: Universidad Nacional San Cristóbal de Huamanga.

Planella, M. T., and R. Stehberg. 1997. Intervención Inka en un Territorio de la Cultura Local Aconcagua de la Zona Centro-Sur de Chile. *Tawantinsuyu* 3:58–78.

Plaza Schuller, F. 1976. *La Incursión Inca en el Septentrional Andino Ecuatoriano*. Otavalo: Instituto Otavaleño de Antropología.

———. 1980. *El Complejo de Fortalezas de Pambamarca*. Otavalo, Ecuador: Instituto Otavaleno de Antropologia.

Ponte R., V. M. 2000. Transformación Social y Política en el Callejon de Huaylas, Siglos III-X D. C. In *Huari y Tiwanaku: Modelos vs. Evidencias,* edited by P. Kaulicke and W. Isbell, 219–251. PUCP Boletín de Arqueología no. 4. Lima: Pontificia Universidad Católica del Perú.

Quiroga Ibarrola, C. A. 1962. Ensayo Monografico de la Organizacion del Ejercito y Armas Empleadas por los Soldados del Tawantinsuyo y por los Conquistadores Espanoles. In *Actas y Trabajos de II Congreso Nacional de Historia del Peru*, 2: 358–416. Lima: Centro de Estudios Historico-Militares de Peru.

Raffino, R., A. Nielsen, and R. Alvis. 1991. El Dominio Inca en dos Secciones del Kollasuyu: Aullagas y Vallegrande. *El Imperio Inca, Comechingonia* 9(2):99–153.

Raffino, R., and R. Stehberg. 1999. Tawantinsuyu: The Frontiers of the Inca Empire. In *Archaeology in Latin America*, edited by G. G. Politis and B. Alberti, 167–181. London: Routledge.

Rawls, J. M. 1979. An Analysis of Prehispanic Andean Warfare. Unpublished Ph.D. dissertation, Department of Anthropology, University of California, Los Angeles.

Redmond, E. A. 1994. External Warfare and the Internal Politics of Northern South American Tribes and Chiefdoms. In *Factional Competition and Political Development in the New World*, edited by E. M. Brumfiel and J. W. Fox, 44–54. Cambridge: Cambridge University Press.

Rice, G. E., and S. A. LeBlanc, (editors). 2001. *Deadly Landscapes: Case Studies in Prehistoric Southwestern Warfare*. Salt Lake City: University of Utah Press.

Romero G., A. 1996. Enfrentamientos Rituales en la Cultura Arica: Interpretación de un Icono Rupestre. *Chungará* 28(1–2):115–132.

Rostworowski de Diez Canseco, M. 1999. *History of the Inca Realm*. Cambridge: Cambridge University Press.

Rothhammer, F., and C. M. Santoro. 2001. El Desarrollo Cultural en el Valle de Azapa, Extremo Norte de Chile y su Vinculación con los Desplazimientos Poblaciones Altiplanicos. *Latin American Antiquity* 12(1):59–66.

Rowe, J. H. 1946. Inca Culture at the Time of the Spanish Conquest. In *The Andean Civilizations (Handbook of South American Indians, v. 2)*, edited by J. Steward, 183–330. Washington, D.C.: Smithsonian Institution Press.

Santa Cruz Pachacuti Yamqui Salcamayhua, J. de. 1993 [1613]. *Relación de Antigüedades Deste Reyno del Pirú*. Lima: Institut Francais d'Etudes Andines.

Santillán, H. de. 1968 [1563]. Relacion del Origen, Descendencia, Politica y Gobierno de los Incas. In *Crónicas Peruanas de Interés Indigena*, edited by F. Esteve Barba, 97–149. Madrid: Ediciones Atlas. Biblioteca de Autores Españoles v. 209.

Santoro, C. M., Á. Romero Guevara, V. G. Standen, and A. Torres. 2004. Continuidad y Cambio en las Comunidades Locales, Períodos Intermedio Tardío y Tardío, Valles Occidentales del Area Centro Sur Andina. *Chungará* 36(supl.):235–247.

Sarmiento de Gamboa, P. 1988 [1572]. *Historia de los Incas*. Madrid: Miraguano / Polifemo.

Schaedel, R. P. 1985. Coast-highland Interrelationships and Ethnic Groups in Northern Peru (500 B.C.–A.D. 1980). In *Andean Ecology and Civilization: An Interdisciplinary Perspective on Andean Ecological Complementarity*, edited by S. Masuda, I. Shimada, and C. Morris, 443–473. Tokyo: University of Tokyo Press.

Schjellerup, I. 1992. Patrones de Asentamiento en las Faldas Orientales de los Andes de la Region de Chachapoyas. In *Estudions de Arqueología Peruana*, edited by D. Bonavia, 355–364. Lima: Fomciencias.

———. 1997. *Incas and Spaniards in the Conquest of the Chachapoyas: Archaeological and Ethnohistorical Research in the Northeastern Andes of Peru.* Copenhagen: The National Museum of Denmark.

Schreiber, K. J. 1987. From State to Empire; the Expansion of Wari Outside the Ayacucho Basin. In *The Origins and Development of the Andean State*, edited by J. Haas, S. Pozorski, and T. Pozorski, 91–96. Cambridge: Cambridge University Press.

———. 1992. *Wari Imperialism in Middle Horizon Peru.* Ann Arbor, MI: Museum of Anthropology, University of Michigan.

———. 1993. The Inca Occupation of the Province of Lucanas. In *Provincial Inca*, edited by M. A. Malpass, 77–116. Iowa City: University of Iowa Press.

———. 2001. The Wari Empire of Middle Horizon Peru: The Epistemological Challenge of Documenting an Empire Without Documentary Evidence. In *Empires: Perspectives from Archaeology and History*, edited by S. E. Alcock, T. N. D'Altroy, K. D. Morrison, and C. M. Sinopoli, 70–92. New York: Cambridge University Press.

Seltzer, G. O., and C. A. Hastorf. 1990. Climatic Change and its Effect on Agriculture in the Central Peruvian Andes. *Journal of Field Archaeology* 17(4):397–414.

Sillitoe, P. 1978. Big Men and War in New Guinea. *Man* 13(2):252–271.

Silva Sifuentes, J. E. 1992. Patrones de Asentamiento en el Valle de Chillón. In *Estudions de Arqueología Peruana*, edited by D. Bonavia, 393–403. Lima: Fomciencias.

Stanish, C. 1992. *Ancient Andean Political Economy.* Austin: University of Texas Press.

———. 2001. The Origin of State Societies in South America. *Annual Review of Anthropology* (30):41–64.

———. 2003. *Ancient Titicaca: The Evolution of Complex Society in Southern Peru and Northern Bolivia.* Berkeley: University of California Press.

Stanish, C., E. de la Vega, L. Steadman, C. Chavez, K. L. Frye, L. Onofre, M. T. Seddon, and P. Calisaya. 1997. *Archaeological Survey in the Juli-Desaguadero Region of the Lake Titicaca Basin, Southern Peru.* Chicago: Field Museum of Natural History.

Stehberg, R. 1995. *Instalaciones Incaicos en el Norte y Centro Semiárido de Chile.* Santiago, Chile: Direccion de Bibliotecas, Archivos y Museos.

Tapia Pineda, F. 1978. *Contribuciónes al Estudio de la Cultura Precolombina en el Altiplano Peruano.* La Paz, Bolivia: Instituto Nacional de Arqueología.

———. 1985. *Contribución a la Investigación Arqueológica en los Valles de Sandia y Carabaya, en el Departamento de Puno—Peru.* Puno, Peru: Grupo de Arte Utaraya.

Tello, J. C. 1918. *El Uso de las Cabezas Humanas Artificialmente Momificadas y su Representación en el Antiguo Arte Peruano.* Lima: Ernesto R. Villaran.

Thompson, L. G., E. Mosley-Thompson, J. F. Bolzan, and B. R. Koci. 1985. A 1500-year Record of Tropical Precipitation in Ice Cores from the Quelccaya Ice Cap, Peru. *Science* 229:971–973.

Toledo, F. de. 1940 [1570]. Información Hecha por Orden de Don Francisco de Toledo en su Visita de las Provincias del Perú. In *Don Francisco de Toledo, Supremo Organizador del Peru, Su Vida, Su Obra [1515–1582]*, edited by R. Levillier, 2:14–37. Buenos Aires: Espasa-Calpe.

Topic, J. R. 1991. Huari and Huamachuco. In *Huari Administrative Structure: Prehistoric*

Monumental Architecture and State Government, edited by W. H. Isbell and G. F. McEwan, 141–164. Washington, D.C.: Dumbarton Oaks.

Topic, J. R., and T. L. Topic. 1983. El Horizonte Medio en Huamachuco. *Revista del Museo Nacional*(47):13–52.

———. 1987. The Archaeological Investigation of Andean Militarism: Some Cautionary Observations. In *The Origins and Development of the Andean State*, edited by J. Haas, S. Pozorski, and T. Pozorski, 47–55. Cambridge: Cambridge University Press.

———. 2000. Hacia la Comprensión del Fenómeno Huari: Una Perspective Norteña. In *Huari y Tiwanaku: Modelos vs. Evidencias*, edited by P. Kaulicke and W. H. Isbell, 181–217. Boletín de Arqueología PUCP no. 4. Lima: Pontificia Universidad Católica del Perú.

Topic, T. L. 1991. The Middle Horizon in Northern Peru. In *Huari Administrative Structure: Prehistoric Monumental Architecture and State Government*, edited by W. H. Isbell and G. F. McEwan, 233–246. Washington, D.C.: Dumbarton Oaks.

Torres-Rouff, C., M. A. Costa-Junquiera, and A. Llagostera. 2005. Violence in Times of Change: The Late Intermediate Period in San Pedro de Atacama. *Chungará* 37(1):75–83.

Tung, T. 2003. The Health Impact of Wari Imperialism: A Bioarchaeological Assessment of Communities in the Core and Periphery. Unpublished Ph.D. dissertation, Department of Anthropology, University of North Carolina, Chapel Hill.

Urteaga, H. H. 1919–1920. El Ejercito Incaico. *Boletin de la Sociedad Geografica de Lima* 35–36:283–331.

Valdez, L. M., and C. Vivanco. 1994. Arqueología de la Cuenca del Qaracha, Ayacucho, Peru. *Latin American Antiquity* 5(2):144–157.

Vayda, A. P. 1960. *Maori Warfare*. Wellington, New Zealand: A. H. and A. P. Reed.

Verano, J. W. 1995. Where do They Rest? The Treatment of Human Offerings and Trophies in Ancient Peru. In *Tombs for the Living: Andean Mortuary Practices*, edited by T. D. Dillehay, 189–227. Washington, D.C.: Dumbarton Oaks.

———. 2002. Trepanation in Prehistoric South America: Geographic and Temporal Trends over 2,000 Years. In *Trepanstion: Discovery, History, Theory*, edited by R. Arnott, S. Finger, and C.U.M. Smith, 223–236. Lisse, Netherlands: Swets and Zeitlinger.

———. 2003. Human Skeletal Remains from Machu Picchu. In *The 1912 Yale Peruvian Scientific Expedition collections from Machu Picchu: Human and Animal Remains*, edited by R. L. Burger and L. C. Salazar, 65–117. New Haven: Yale University Publications in Anthropology.

Vivanco P., C. 1999. Raqaraqaypata y Ñawpallaqta, dos Poblados de la Epoca Chanka el el Area Sur de Ayacucho. In *XII Congreso Peruano del Hombre y la Cultura Andina*, edited by I. Pérez, W. Aguilar S., and M. Purizaga V., 2: 271–286. Ayacucho: Universidad Nacional San Cristóbal de Huamanga.

Wassilowsky, A. H. 1999. Investigaciones Arqueológicas en la Cuanca Sur del Río Yanamayo, Callejon de Conchucos (1995–1997). In *XII Congreso Peruano del Hombre y la Cultura Andina*, edited by I. Pérez, W. Aguilar S., and M. Purizaga V., 2:54–83. Ayacucho: Universidad Nacional San Cristóbal de Huamanga, Ayacucho.

Webster, D. 1975. Warfare and the Evolution of the State: A Reconsideration. *American Antiquity* 40:464–470.

Wernke, S. A. 2003. An Archaeo-History of Andean Community and Landscape: The Late Prehispanic and Early Colonial Colca Valley, Peru. Unpublished Ph.D. dissertation, Department of Anthropology, University of Wisconsin, Madison.

Wilcox, D. R., and J. Haas. 1994. The Scream of the Butterfly: Competition and Conflict in the Prehistoric Southwest. In *Themes in Southwestern Prehistory*, edited by G. J. Gumerman, 211–238. Santa Fe: School of American Research Press.

Willey, G. R. 1953. *Prehistoric Settlement Patterns in the Virú Valley, Perú*. Washington, D.C.: U.S. Govt. Print. Office, Smithsonian Institution 155.

Williams, P. R. 2001. Cerro Baúl: A Wari Center on the Tiwanaku Frontier. *Latin American Antiquity* 12(1):67–83.

———. 2002. Rethinking Disaster-induced Collapse in the Demise of the Andean Highland States: Wari and Tiwanaku. *World Archaeology* 33(3):361–374.

Williams, P. R., and D. Nash. 2002. Imperial Interaction in the Andes: Wari and Tiwanaku at Cerro Baúl. In *Andean Archaeology*, edited by W. Isbell and H. Silverman, 243–265. New York: Plenum.

Wilson, D. J. 1988. *Prehispanic Settlement Patterns in the Lower Santa Valley, Peru: A Regional Perspective on the Origins and Development of Complex North Coast Society*. Washington, D.C.: Smithsonian Institution Press.

Wright, H. T. 1984. Pre-state Political Formations. In *On the Evolution of Complex Societies: Essays in Honor of Harry Hoijer*, edited by T. Earle, 41–77. Malibu: Undena Publications.

10

From Raiding to Conquest

Warfare Strategies and Early State Development in Oaxaca, Mexico

ELSA M. REDMOND AND CHARLES S. SPENCER

As Westerners we have been taught that warfare is evil, a last resort when diplomacy fails. This attitude has blinded us to the fact that in Mesoamerica, warfare was as much a creator as a destroyer.

Marcus 1992:442.

The hilltop site of Monte Albán at the center of the Oaxaca Valley in the southern highlands of Mexico was first occupied at 500 B.C., the beginning of the Early Monte Albán I phase (500–300 B.C.). Monte Albán became the capital of the early Zapotec state, one of the first state-level polities to emerge in Mesoamerica. The earliest archaeological evidence of the Zapotec state can be detected during the Late Monte Albán I phase (300–100 B.C.), when a regional settlement hierarchy of four levels appeared in the Oaxaca Valley, as well as the earliest palace and multiroom temple, both associated with key institutions of the Zapotec state (Flannery 1983a:132–136; Kowalewski et al. 1989:125–138; Marcus and Flannery 1996:162–164; Spencer and Redmond 2001a:221–223).

The idea that warfare may have played a role in Monte Albán's founding and emergence as a state capital can be traced back to 1946, when Alfonso Caso proposed that the carved stone inscriptions on Building J, located in Monte Albán's plaza in the Monte Albán II phase (100 B.C.–A.D. 200), referred to the conquest of towns or places by Monte Albán (Caso 1947:27–28). The possibility that warfare also occurred during the founding Monte Albán I period (500–100 B.C.) was strengthened in 1962 when Michael Coe interpreted the carved stone depictions called *danzantes* on the façade and steps of Building L as slain and mutilated captives:

> The distorted pose of the limbs, the open mouth and closed eyes indicate that these are corpses, undoubtedly chiefs or kings slain by the earliest rulers of Monte Albán. In many individuals the genitals are clearly delineated, usually the stigma laid on captives in Mesoamerica where nudity was considered scandalous. Furthermore, there are cases of sexual mutilation depicted on some *danzantes*, blood streaming in flowery patterns from the

severed part. To corroborate such violence, one *danzante* is nothing more than a severed head. (Coe 1962:95–96)

We can now present a comprehensive examination of the warfare strategies of the rival polities that existed in the region prior to the establishment of Monte Albán, and during the critical Monte Albán I period of state formation, using regional survey data as well as the findings of archaeological investigations that have been carried out at Monte Albán and at sites from the three arms of the Oaxaca Valley (Blanton 1978; Kowalewski et al. 1989; Marcus and Flannery 1996; Spencer and Redmond 2001a). Moreover, survey and excavations in some of the places outside the Oaxaca Valley that may have been recorded on Building J as places conquered by Monte Albán have recovered evidence of military campaigns by the valley Zapotec against non-Zapotec polities beginning at the onset of the Late Monte Albán I phase (ca. 300 B.C.) (Redmond 1983; Spencer 1982; Spencer and Redmond 1997, 2001b). Because the Monte Albán state is recognized as a primary state, one that emerged in a pristine context of interacting pre-state societies, our examination of early Zapotec warfare strategies prior to and during the Monte Albán I period can contribute to the larger discussion of the role played by raiding, interpolity conquest, and territorial expansion in the very process of state formation (Algaze 1993; Carneiro 1970; Service 1975; Spencer and Redmond 2004a; Wright 1977, 1986).

Zapotec Warfare Strategies in the Sixteenth Century

A starting point for investigating early Zapotec warfare strategies is the sixteenth- and seventeenth-century ethnohistoric literature about the Zapotec, from which much information about warfare in the Late Postclassic period can be culled (see also Marcus 1992:388–391; Redmond 1983:26–29; Whitecotton 1977:139–142). The following synthesis is drawn from the writings of Fray Juan de Córdova (1942 [1578]) and Fray Francisco de Burgoa (1934a, 1934b [1674]), and the *Relaciones Geográficas* compiled for Zapotec towns by Spanish officials in 1579–1581 and 1609 (Gómez de Orozco 1928; Paso y Troncoso 1905). Of course, many hundreds of years separate the sixteenth-century Zapotec from their early forebears who founded the Monte Albán state. We are also aware that the Dominican friars and Spanish officials who wrote these accounts of Zapotec culture held many preconceptions regarding native Indian practices, including warfare. Despite these limitations, this information about Zapotec warfare strategies in the Late Postclassic period can be brought to bear upon and evaluated against earlier instances of Zapotec warfare that must be reconstructed from archaeological and epigraphic evidence.

The sixteenth-century Zapotec pursued warfare with an all-out intensity expressed as *viva quien vence* (may he live who vanquishes) (Espíndola 1905:117 [1580]). Most Zapotec towns were characterized as being in a state of perpetual warfare with neighboring towns and polities. So dominant was the Zapotec nation that its rulers had expanded beyond its borders and entered regions inhabited by the Mixe, Chatino, and Chontal, as well as the coastal regions to the south and north, wounding, killing, and defeating until they commanded the fertile plains of Tehuantepec (Burgoa 1934a:412 [1674]). The motivations for pursuing warfare included revenge, boundary disputes, and the taking of captives for use as slaves and sacrificial victims (Burgoa 1934b:10 [1674]; Espíndola 1905:127 [1580]; Ximénez Ortiz 1905:18 [1579]).[1] Warfare was also conducted in order to subjugate towns and regions and exact tribute from these conquered places (Burgoa 1934b:341 [1674]; Córdova 1942:88 [1578]; Villegas 1928:129 [1580]).

Preparations for war involved logistical considerations and ritual divinations and sacrifices. Fighting forces were mobilized and trained, trenches and fortifications were readied, and military equipment and war provisions were garnered. Spies gathered information about enemy movements and stratagems (Burgoa 1934b:265, 345 [1674]; Córdova 1942:33, 186 [1578]; Espíndola 1905:140 [1580]). Zapotec rulers did not carry out military campaigns unless the ritual divinations and sacrifices performed in the temple by specialized priests before carved-stone images of divine beings brought auspicious responses. The supreme being, *Bezalao*, and his solicitor in war, *Cozichacozee*, were portrayed in carved-stone images and painted depictions as armed anthropomorphic figures with fierce expressions. These supernatural beings infused warriors with the strength and courage needed to achieve success in war (Espíndola 1905:139 [1580]; Santamaría and Canseco 1905:34 [1579]; Villegas 1928:127 [1580]; Zárate 1905:198–199 [1581]).

Zapotec fighting forces were organized into squadrons of warriors, led by military captains. Sometimes a Zapotec ruler went to war, but generally he appointed a military commander to go in his stead. These military leaders and distinguished warriors led the vanguard. There were separate titles for novices, general warriors, and distinguished warriors. There was also a clear distinction between how military leaders, other members of the ruling elite, and commoners dressed and armed themselves for war. Military leaders wore quilted cotton armor, *piaga xilla quelayè*, and helmets decorated with polished stone ornaments or feathers of many colors. The majority of fighting men were commoners who wore only their loincloths. They painted their faces and bodies with various pigments in order to look fierce in the eyes of their opponents. The designs they painted on their faces included jaguar markings. Warriors who were singled out for their bravery wore a special hair-knot, *quìchayy*, on the crown of their heads as a badge of courage. Some warriors wore the skins of deer, jaguars, and other felines, which may have been the costumes of certain warrior orders (Asensio 1905:102 [1580]; Burgoa 1934a:412 [1674], Burgoa 1934b:341 [1674]; Córdova 1942:38, 45, 183, 211, 285, 292, 308, 316, 409 [1578]; Espíndola 1905:140 [1580]; Villegas 1928:129 [1580]; Ximénez Ortiz 1905:18 [1579]).

When fighting forces went to war, *quelayè*, they carried their idols alongside the hollowed-log drum in the middle of their formations and sang. Zapotec forces also carried a large obsidian dagger, greater in length than a man's lower arm,[2] and adorned with green feathers (Córdova 1942:53 [1578]; Ximénez Ortiz 1905:17–18 [1579]).

Zapotec warfare strategies ranged from ambushes to open battles. The Zapotec campaign against Aztec armies in Tehuantepec was an ambush or surprise attack, carried out by an allied fighting force that divided into two wings in order to surround the enemy and attack at the right moment.[3] The Zapotec force prepared for the arrival of unsuspecting enemy forces by taking a defensible hilltop, often fortifying it with concentric walls of stone slabs and boulders, and provisioning it with food and water. Spies brought information concerning the enemy's position. At the appropriate moment and under the cover of darkness, the allied troops descended silently upon the enemy camp and attacked from different directions (Burgoa 1934b:342 [1674]; Marcus 1983a:316). The troops used war signals to communicate with one another during the mêlée. Zapotec warriors engaged in face-to-face combat, wielding wooden broadswords, *yagaquèça pitànco*, studded with flint and obsidian blades, lances, clubs, bows and arrows, and round shields made of strong, woven cane that were sometimes decorated with feathers. Some of the arrowpoints and lance tips were treated with poison. In theory, combat lasted until the enemy was defeated; according to the *Relación de Tecuicuilco*, a town in the Zapotec Sierra, each attack lasted only a short while because the combatants fought hand to hand, and the outcome was soon decided (Burgoa 1934b:342, 345 [1674]; Córdova 1942:252, 277 [1578]; Espíndola 1905:128 [1580]; Gutiérrez 1905:316 [1609]; Villegas 1928:128–129 [1580]).

Fighting forces would also march into enemy territory in overwhelming numbers, and confront the enemy in open battle, *quelatìlla*. In some instances Zapotec troops proceeded to attack communities, *a fuego y sangre*, by setting them on fire with firebrands and massacring any inhabitants who resisted. This is the sort of attack suffered by Miahuatlán in 1539, when warriors from neighboring Tetiquipa and their allies invaded and burned Miahuatlán, killing more than 10,000 inhabitants (Burgoa 1934b:189, 328 [1674]; Córdova 1942:37, 53 [1578]; Gutiérrez 1905:291–292, 314 [1609]). By whistling and hollering in battle, Zapotec warriors were incited to commit acts of bravery and achieve victory (Córdova 1942:29, 380 [1578]). In the aftermath of an attack, the victors plundered the dead and dying enemies and seized their weapons. Widespread looting ensued (Burgoa 1934b:342 [1674]; Espíndola 1905:133 [1580]).

The post-war rituals began on the battlefield when the first captive taken was sacrificed to the presiding idol and his body discarded. The remaining male and female captives were taken to the victors' town; according to the *Relación de Miahuatlán*, a male captive would be bound by his genitals with his bowstring and led by his captors to an uncertain fate as a slave or sacrificial victim. Any slave who tried to escape would be cut into bits (Espíndola 1905:128 [1580]). The war party's ritual obligations to *Bezalao* and his solicitor for war were met at a feast celebrated later in the year when a captive was taken to the temple to be sacrificed by a staff of priests. The victim's chest was opened from nipple to nipple with a stone dagger and his heart was removed and placed on a stone altar before stone idols. Burgoa (1934b:10 [1674]) described the practice of pressing the victim's heart to the idols' lips. The stone figures were bathed in the victim's blood. With these offerings to the idols, the priests also sought strength and courage from the supreme supernatural forces to enable warriors to succeed in future wars (Córdova 1942:368 [1578]; Espíndola 1905:127–128, 133, 138–139 [1580]; Ximénez Ortiz 1905:18 [1579]; Zárate 1905:198 [1581]). The victim's body was then quartered, cooked (by stewing or roasting), and eaten (Gutiérrez 1905:292 [1609]; Ximénez Ortiz 1905:18 [1579]).

In this way, Zapotec military campaigns succeeded in advancing through enemy territory, conquering enemy towns and expanding the Zapotec state's borders. Special garrison troops were assigned to guard defeated towns, which became way stations for Zapotec troops. In order to ensure the allegiance of the newly subjugated populations and to defend the frontier from external threats, the Zapotec established fortified garrisons in the conquered regions, manned by Zapotec military captains and garrison troops under the authority of a frontier-region administrator. The administrator of a frontier region was a member of the ruling elite or a distinguished military captain; in two cases recorded by Burgoa, the administrator of a frontier region was a close relative of the Zapotec ruler (Burgoa 1934a:412 [1674], 1934b:10–11, 235–236, 242, 265, 272, 328, 330, 341 [1674]; Córdova 1942:20, 211, 348 [1578]).

Conquered towns became tributary to the Zapotec state. Subject populations supplied food, equipment, and manpower to Zapotec forts in the region. Tribute (*chiña*, *quelachiña*) in food, resources, products, manpower, and sacrificial victims was sent to the Zapotec rulers in the Oaxaca Valley (Burgoa 1934b:236, 240 [1674]; Córdova 1942:33, 412 [1578]). The inhabitants of conquered regions experienced a reign of terror; terms meaning "to treat tyrannically" can be found in the Zapotec language (Córdova 1942:403 [1578]). Any disobedience was countered with punitive torture—by cutting the victim(s) into pieces and allowing their screams to be heard—and executions. The victims' bones and skulls were used to construct a bulwark or skull rack, *yàgabetoo*, for public display, intended as a symbol of conquest and a terror tactic in frontier regions (Burgoa 1934b:11–12, 342 [1674]; Marcus and Flannery 1996:206; Whitecotton and Whitecotton 1993:394).

Some wars resulted in truces and peace treaties, which occasionally were marked by marriage alliances between sons and daughters of the opposing rulers. Other times, Zapotec emissaries were dispatched into enemy territory to announce the Zapotec ruler's designs for expanding into the region and to propose that the enemy avoid mounting any opposition. This alternative to warfare was predicated on the threat of military action (Burgoa 1934a:394 [1674], 1934b:343–345 [1674]; Córdova 1942:153, 411 [1578]).

The conditions of chronic warfare in which the Zapotec reportedly existed had consequences for all sectors of society. Men were always armed and ready to fight, and spent long periods of time away from home serving as warriors on military campaigns. Consequently, planting and other seasonal agricultural tasks were sometimes disrupted (Canseco 1905:146 [1580]; Espíndola 1905:117, 128, 141 [1580]). In times of war, the inhabitants of Mitla and its satellite villages at the eastern end of the Oaxaca Valley sought refuge at one of four fortified hilltops.[4] Similarly, a hilltop fort manned by distinguished military captains and warriors defended the northern border of the Oaxaca Valley at Huitzo, or *Huijazoo*, the Zapotec term for military watchtower (Burgoa 1934b:11 [1674]). The fort at Huitzo guarded two natural passes into the Oaxaca Valley from the north. The Zapotec rulers at Zaachila established a stronghold on a ridgetop southeast of Quiané that rises from the valley floor like the peak of a sombrero (Canseco 1905:153 [1580]; Mata 1905:195 [1580]).

Zapotec rulers bestowed awards and privileges on warriors who distinguished themselves in warfare; in addition to the hair-knot worn by brave warriors, certain prizes were earned through war. Through brave deeds there was always the possibility not only of being promoted to higher positions within the military, but also of becoming lesser nobility, regardless of one's social position at birth. Indeed, the town of Amatlán, whose Zapotec name, *Quiatila*, meant battleground,[5] was said to have been established by a captain called *Cosichaguela* (night warrior); it was probably as a reward for a brave deed that *Cosichaguela* obtained his title and claim to *Quiatila*, where a lineage of 24 chiefs succeeded him. In this way Zapotec rulers maintained a daring military force, eager to carry out their expansionist policies (Burgoa 1934b:236 [1674]; Córdova 1942:246, 390, 409 [1578]; Gutiérrez 1905:314, 316 [1609]; Villegas 1928:129 [1580]).

Warring Polities in the Rosario Phase (700–500 B.C.)

During the Rosario phase, independent chiefly polities existed in the Oaxaca Valley, represented by settlement clusters in each of the three arms and subregions of the valley (Blanton et al. 1993:66–69) (Figure 10.1). The northern Etla subregion was the most populated, with an estimated population of 2,000 persons, while the eastern Tlacolula and southern Ocotlán-Zimatlán subregions are each estimated to have had about half that population (Marcus and Flannery 1996:125–126). The Etla arm is also the only subregion to exhibit a positive relationship between agricultural productivity and Rosario phase occupation area (Spencer and Redmond 2001a:212). San José Mogote extended over 60–65 ha and was the first-order center for some 18–23 lower-order villages in the Etla subregion. Yegüih was the first-order center for a cluster of 10–12 villages in the eastern Tlacolula subregion, and San Martín Tilcajete dominated a cluster of 10–12 villages in the southern Ocotlán-Zimatlán subregion (Marcus and Flannery 1996:125–126) (Figure 10.2). Our program of mapping and surface collecting at the first-order center of El Mogote (SMT-11a) near San Martín Tilcajete in the southern Ocotlán-Zimatlán subregion revealed a 25-ha occupation during the Rosario phase, making this paramount center less than half the size of San José Mogote.

At the juncture of the three subregions lay an uninhabited area of over 80 km^2 that Marcus and Flannery (1996:124–125) have proposed may have served as a buffer zone between these rival polities (Figure 10.1). Another sign of hostilities on the regional scale is the relatively high frequencies of burned-clay daub recovered on the surface at Rosario phase settlements, resulting from the widespread burning of wattle-and-daub structures; the percentage of sites with burned daub for the Rosario phase was sevaen times greater than the percentage for sites of all phases in the valley (Kowalewski et al.1989:70). Raiding is characteristic of the intensive warfare waged by chiefly polities such as these, usually in pursuit of land, resources, and captives, but also to avenge hostilities suffered in the past. Like the allied attack against Miahuatlán in 1539, chiefly war parties launch surprise raids on enemy villages, sometimes setting them on fire to rout the inhabitants. After killing and seizing captives, a target village is often looted and sometimes intentionally destroyed by fire (Redmond 1994:53–55). While the Tlacolula polity centered at Yegüih awaits investigation, our excavations in the central precinct with mounds at El Mogote in the Ocotlán-Zimaltán sub-

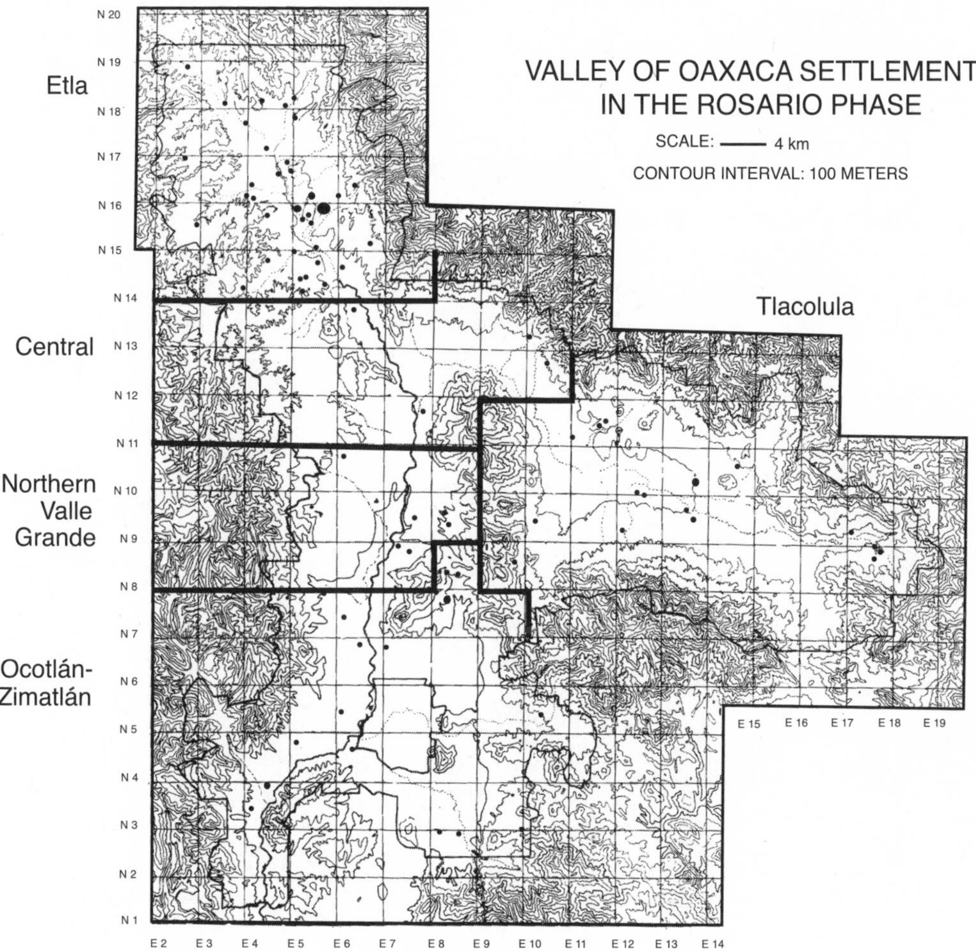

Figure 10.1 Rosario phase (700–500 B.C.) settlements in the Oaxaca Valley, with the boundaries of the subregions indicated (redrawn from Blanton et al. 1993, figure 3.7).

region have not revealed evidence of such attacks during the Rosario phase. Clearer evidence of intervillage raiding has been recovered from the Etla polity centered at San José Mogote, which seems to have been involved in launching raids against enemy settlements and withstanding counter-raids.

At San José Mogote, impressive stone-block-faced platforms were built during the Rosario phase on top of a 15-m-tall modified hill, called Mound 1 by excavators Kent Flannery and Joyce Marcus (1996:126–129). One platform (Structure 19) oriented eight degrees west of north supported another lime-plastered adobe platform (Structure 28), on which stood a rectangular wattle-

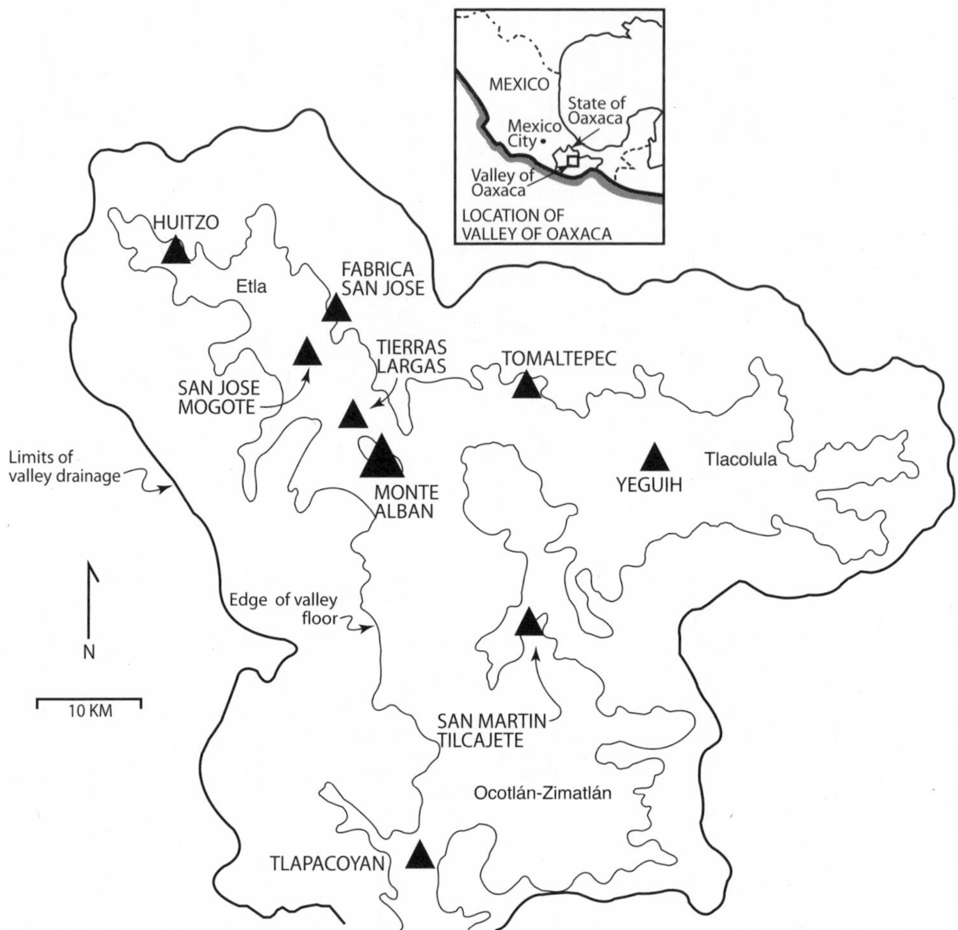

Figure 10.2. The Oaxaca Valley, with the locations of the archaeological sites mentioned in the text (inset adapted from Flannery 1986, figure 3.1).

and-daub temple associated with commemorative offerings and ritual bloodletting instruments. Alongside Structure 19 another stone-faced platform was built with the recessed ground plan of a temple oriented to the cardinal directions. At the threshold of the narrow corridor between the two platforms lay a carved-stone slab, Monument 3 (Figure 10.3), depicting:

> a naked man sprawled awkwardly on his back, mouth open and eyes closed. A complex scroll motif shows us where his chest had been opened to remove his heart during sacrifice. A ribbon-like stream of blood extends from this scroll to the border of the monument, ending in two motifs

> that wrap around the edge of the slab. These two motifs, each made of a circle and a triangle, are stylized drops of blood. (Marcus and Flannery 1996:129–130)

The sacrificed individual's name, "1 Earthquake," taken from the 260-day ritual calendar, is inscribed between his feet and constitutes a sign of his elite status (Marcus 1991:28). Another indication of his elite status is his angled forehead, which may represent the tabular deformation of the skull practiced by Mesoamerican elites (Marcus and Flannery 1996:105–106). Recently, Flannery and Marcus have presented two conventional radiocarbon dates of 630±40 B.C. and 560±40 B.C. obtained from charcoal in hearths overlying this carved stone, which postdate the carved stone beneath and perhaps also the raid or battle during which the named elite individual was seized and later sacrificed (Flannery and Marcus 2003:11802–11803).

The Zapotec practice of returning home from war with captives to be sacrificed in the temple must have existed at this time. This possibility is supported not only by the sacrificed individual depicted on Monument 3, which victorious celebrants would have trodden upon when ascending Mound 1, but also

Figure 10.3. Monument 3 at San José Mogote depicts a sacrificed captive whose heart has been removed, causing streams of blood to flow from his chest. Inscribed between his feet is the ritual calendar day name, "1 Earthquake." Stylized drops of blood issue over the edge of the stone. Monument 3 measures 1.45 m in length (redrawn from Marcus and Flannery 1996, figure 173).

by the adult skeletons recovered by Flannery and Marcus under the wall of an elite residential sanctuary atop Mound 1 at San José Mogote, and under the retaining wall of a temple platform at the village site of Huitzo at the northern end of the Etla subregion (Figure 10.2) (Marcus and Flannery 1996:131).[6] The burial treatment of these likely sacrificed individuals, who lacked ornaments and offerings of any kind, contrasts with the tombs of deceased members of the elite residential compound on Mound 1 at San José Mogote, whose elite status was further indicated by the tabular deformation of their skulls, their personal ornaments, and their funerary offerings. Among the funerary offerings accompanying the elite individual buried in chambered Tomb 10 were 11 small obsidian dart points embedded in a deposit of red ocher. Nearby lay other artifacts associated with Zapotec warfare: a bloodletting instrument of the sort that might have been used in pre-war divinatory rituals, and pottery whistles in the shape of a feline and a bird that were perforated in order to be worn as pendants and that emitted a high-pitched whistle, akin perhaps to the whistles blown in war (Córdova 1942:380 [1578]; Marcus 1998:282; Marcus and Flannery 1996:133). The elite individual buried in Tomb 10 might well have been a distinguished warrior or military leader who was laid to rest with his weapons and other accoutrements.

The Etla polity centered at San José Mogote was also the target of counter-raids during the Rosario phase. Probably in response to heightened warfare in the Etla subregion, one village in Mazaltepec established itself on a piedmont spur more than 50 m above the valley floor overlooking a natural route from the Etla subregion northwest to the Nochixtlán Valley, and may have built defensive walls along its gradual eastern slope at this time (Elam 1989:394; Marcus and Flannery 1996:124). It was during one such attack that the wattle-and-daub temple atop the Structure 28 platform at San José Mogote was set on fire deliberately, a blaze so intense that it turned the perishable temple's daub plaster into vitrified cinders (Marcus and Flannery 1996:128).[7] San José Mogote's ruling elite evidently withstood the attack that culminated in the destruction of their temple, and continued to occupy Mound 1 throughout the Rosario phase. By contrast, the largest Rosario-phase structure exposed at the nearby village site of Fábrica San José (Figure 10.2), burned to the ground at the time of the village's abandonment, in what excavator Robert Drennan characterized as "a group action occurring in a short period of time" (Drennan 1976:118, 142; Marcus and Flannery 1996:134).

Internecine Raiding in the Early Monte Albán I Phase (500–300 B.C.)

After 500 B.C., the largest settlement in the Oaxaca Valley shifted from San José Mogote in the middle of the Etla subregion, to a 400-m-tall mountain known as Monte Albán that rises at the center of the Valley of Oaxaca (Figure 10.4). The settlement established on the highest point of Monte Albán violated the empty no-man's-land that had existed here during the Rosario phase. The mountaintop center was situated four km from the nearest water source (Blanton et al. 1999:49). At the same time that Monte Albán was first settled, with a core occupation of 69 ha around the Main Plaza (Figure 10.5), where several public buildings were constructed, the paramount center of San José Mogote was largely abandoned. Not only did construction cease atop Mound 1, but also the surrounding 40 ha were abandoned, as were many villages in the Etla subregion (Blanton 1978:35; Marcus and Flannery 1996:139). The earliest public buildings constructed at Monte Albán were oriented to the cardinal directions, much like the orientations of the Rosario phase platforms atop Mound 1 at San José Mogote (Acosta 1965:814; Marcus and Flannery 1996:126, 129). The center founded at Monte Albán, most likely by the Etla polity, was more centrally located with respect to the three major branches of the valley. Also accompanying the establishment of Monte Albán, was a proliferation of 38 Monte Albán Early I phase villages around its base, constituting a shift in the demographic center of gravity from Etla to the valley's center (Marcus and Flannery 1996:144). A new regional political landscape was created with the establishment of Monte Albán, which served as the first-order center for both the Etla subregion and the Central Valley area during the Early Monte Albán I phase (Spencer and Redmond 2001a:203–205).

The Oaxaca Valley's other two subregions, by contrast, showed no evidence of abrupt settlement relocations in the Early Monte Albán I phase. The centers of Yegüih and San Martín Tilcajete grew larger and probably continued to serve as the first-order centers of the Tlacolula and Ocotlán-Zimatlán subregions, respectively (Marcus and Flannery 1996:163). The paramount center of El Mogote at Tilcajete doubled in size to extend over an area of 52.8 ha in the Early Monte Albán I phase. Our investigations here have determined that El Mogote's 2.2-ha plaza was constructed at this time, with two mounds in its center and mound platforms arranged around its four sides and at an orientation of 17 degrees east of magnetic north, which differed from the alignment of public architecture at Monte Albán (Figure 10.6). Moreover, El Mogote's ceramic assemblage consisted largely of locally made gray and plain wares; few were the creamware types so common at Monte Albán (Caso et al. 1967:44–46; Feinman 1982:188–191; Kowalewski et al. 1978:170–177). These architectural and

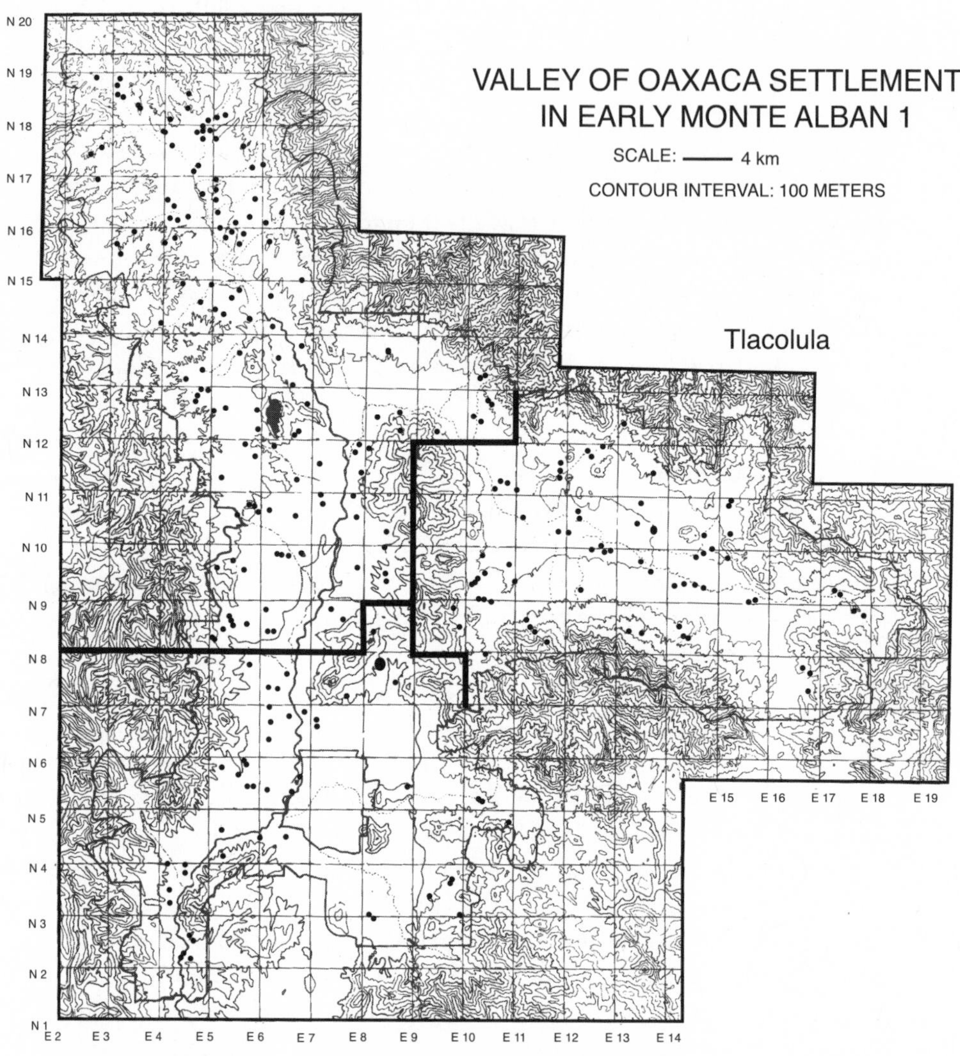

Figure 10.4. Early Monte Albán I phase (500–300 B.C.) settlements in the Oaxaca Valley, with the boundaries of the subregions indicated (redrawn from Blanton et al. 1993, figure 3.9).

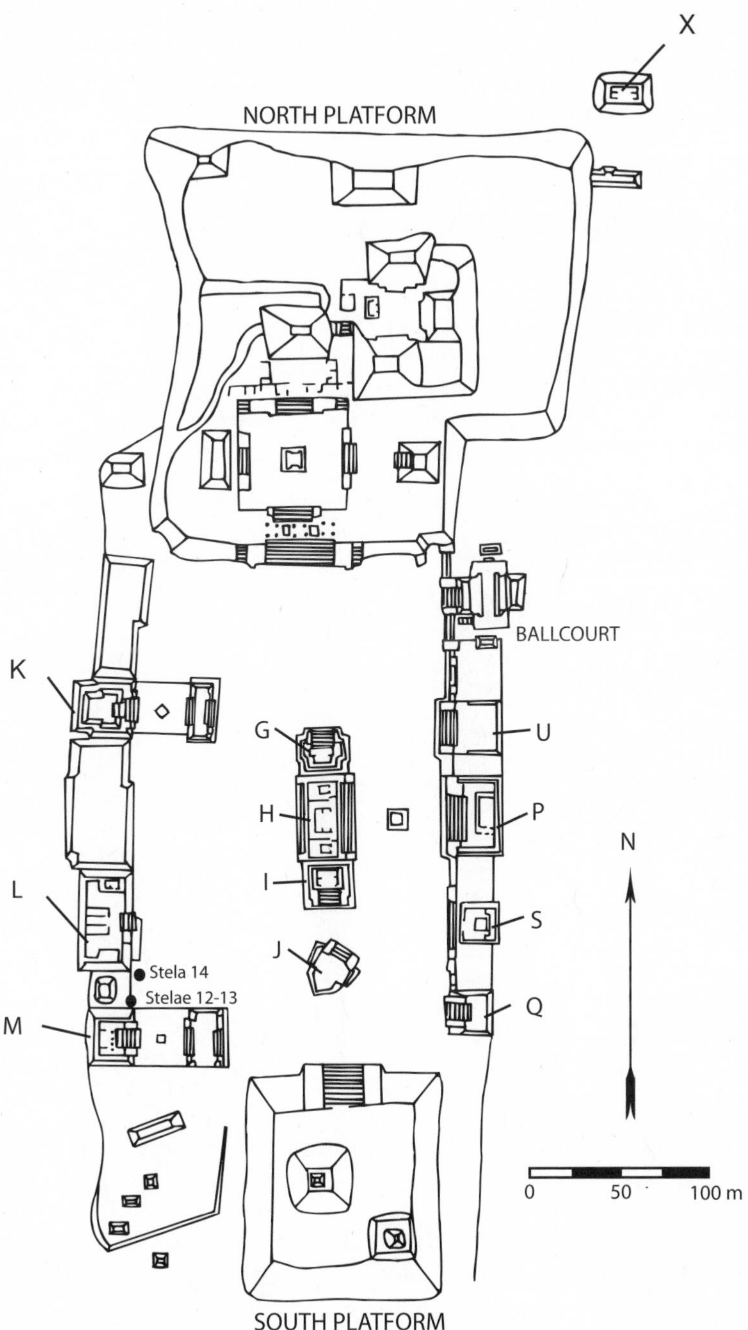

Figure 10.5. Plan of Monte Albán's Main Plaza with major buildings designated (adapted from Marcus 1980:54; and Flannery 1983b, figure 4.12).

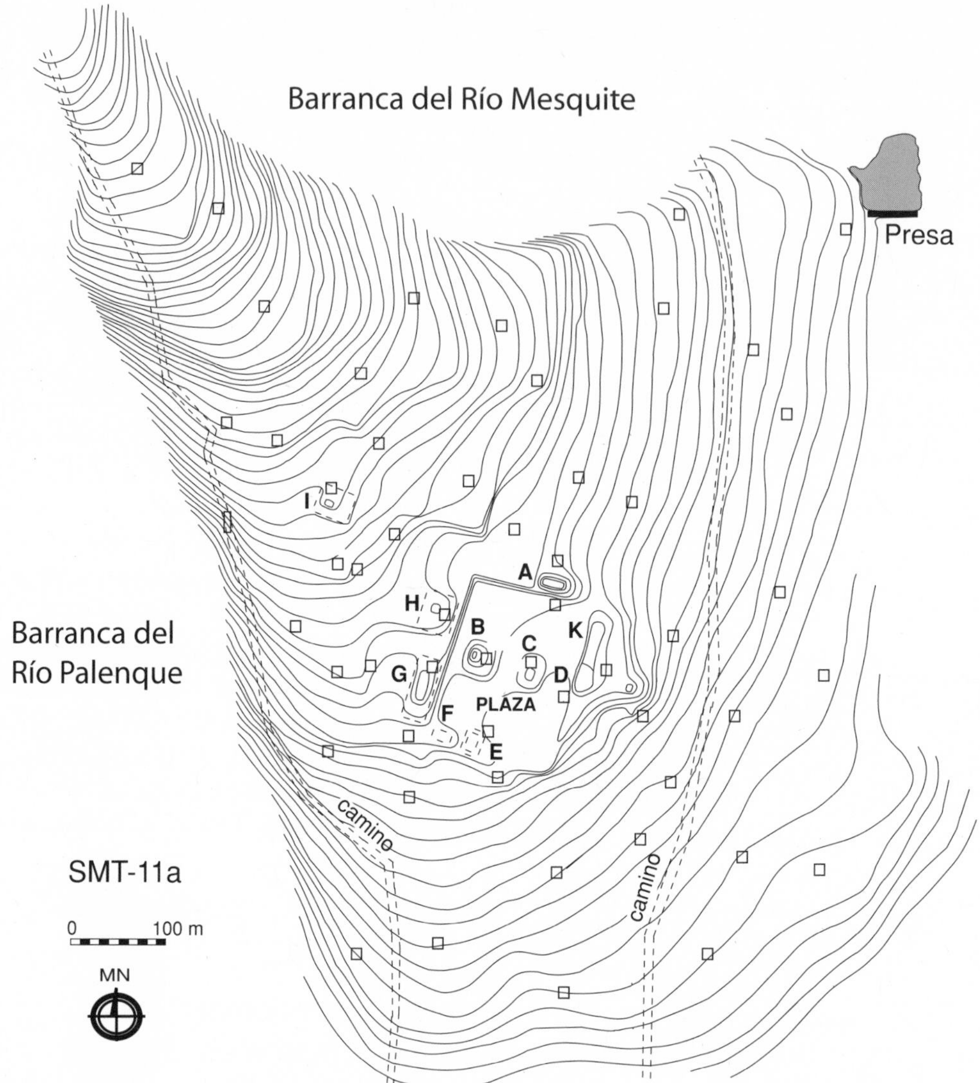

Figure 10.6. Site map of El Mogote (SMT-11a), showing its plaza, major mounds, and surface collection blocks.

ceramic differences support the proposition that the Tilcajete polity retained its autonomy throughout the Early Monte Albán I phase.

On the Main Plaza at Monte Albán, the region's preeminent center, three stone-block platforms were constructed during the Early Monte Albán I phase; they are buried within later mound constructions, and hence incompletely known. Jorge Acosta, who along with Alfonso Caso and Ignacio Bernal conducted the excavations that exposed these early public buildings at Monte Albán, claimed that "we cannot speak of a site plan, but the buildings evidently are oriented to the four cardinal points" (Acosta 1965:814). One platform covered with serpent motifs modeled in stucco lay at the plaza's northern edge. A 6-m-tall platform with flat-backed, rubble-masonry columns flanking a stairway and surfaces painted red lay under Building K on the northwest side of the plaza.

The best known platform built on the Main Plaza during the Early Monte Albán I phase lay within Building L on the southwest side of the plaza (Caso 1947:7; Marcus 1974:89–90) (Figure 10.5). This was a 7-m-tall platform built with monolithic stone blocks and a central stairway. The stairway and top of the platform were faced with stucco. Extending south of Building L's stairway were four rows of carved stone slabs set into a vertical wall; other carved stone slabs formed the risers of the monolithic steps at the base of the stairway (Scott 1978a:30–35). Each stone slab, or *danzante*, depicts a single male, stripped naked, often mutilated, and slain. In all, over 300 such depictions of what are generally recognized as slain captives were displayed on the eastern façade of Building L, in what we can only speculate may have been a symmetrical arrangement of more than four rows of figures on the south and north sides of the stairway (Figure 10.7). Many of the carved stones from Building L's façade were reused in later buildings constructed on the Main Plaza. Nevertheless, a sample of 210 of the stones that are over 50 percent complete (Scott 1978b) can be used not only to describe the fate of captives seized in warfare during Monte Albán's founding period, but also to reconstruct certain aspects of the internecine raids waged by Monte Albán's war parties.

Building L's *danzantes* imply that Monte Albán's war parties fought against all-male fighting forces and that when victorious, they returned to Monte Albán with male captives. Aside from the dozen depictions of bearded and slightly humpbacked individuals that represent old men (Caso 1947:17; Scott 1978a:47), the majority of the *danzantes* represent men of fighting age. Furthermore, the distinction in dress and arms between warriors from the two strata of Zapotec society described in the sixteenth-century *Relaciones* is borne out in the sample of *danzantes* figures. A ranked military organization existed, wherein chiefs, military leaders, and other members of the chiefly elite who were seized in war, stripped naked, and brought to Monte Albán—literally or metaphorically—could still be identified by certain insignia. Their elite status was conveyed by their cranial deformation, helmet or headdress, earspool, earplug, face-paint, mask, necklace, bracelet, and footwear (Figures 10.7–10.9). Those individuals wearing hair-knots and nose-plugs may have earned them for brave deeds (Redmond 1983:27, 111). The individuals with the most insignia are portrayed at large scale and displayed on the bottom row of the southern

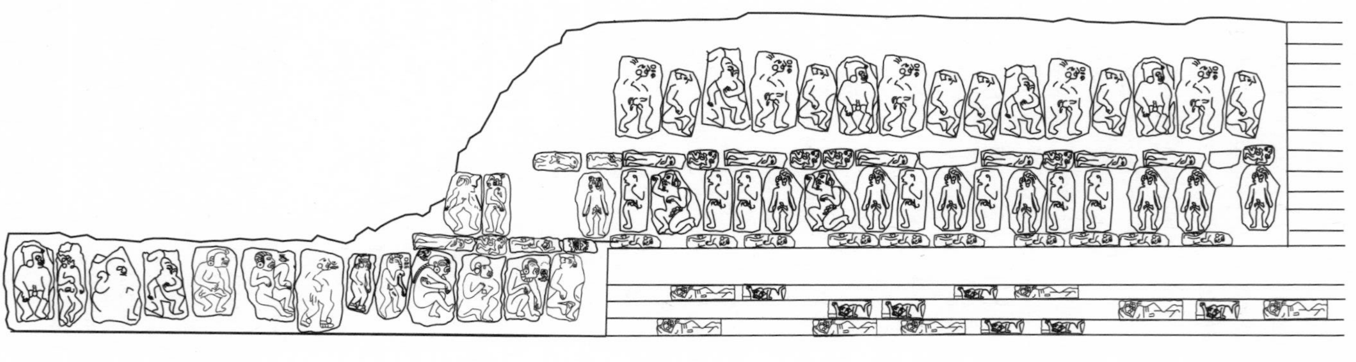

Figure 10.7. A reconstruction of Building L's eastern façade south of the Early Monte Albán I platform's staircase. Only some of the bottom four rows of carved-stone depictions of slain captives are in their original position (adapted from Scott 1978a, figure 18; and Marcus and Flannery 1996:173).

wall (Figures 10.7–10.8). Some of these elite captives are accompanied by a hieroglyphic caption that lists their personal name and mentions that they were seized in war (Marcus 1992:394). By far the majority of the captives depicted on Building L's eastern façade, of course, lacked these elite accoutrements, and we can suggest they were among the multitude of commoners who served as warriors in times of war and wound up as captives (Figure 10.7). In Marcus's words, "the majority of the *danzantes* probably portray lesser villagemen taken in raids and skirmishes" (Marcus 1976:126–127).

The array of headgear and hairstyles worn by many of the captives portrayed on Building L probably reflect the diverse enemy settlements raided by Monte Albán's war parties. In spite of their heterogeneity, Marcus, who has studied the figurines from San José Mogote and other Formative period sites in the Oaxaca Valley (Marcus 1998), maintains that the headgear, hairstyles, and ornaments worn by the *danzantes* conform to Zapotec standards of dress. Moreover, the use of personal names on the hieroglyphic captions that accompany 46 *danzantes* on Building L—similar to the named victim, "1 Earthquake" depicted on Monument 3 at San José Mogote during the previous Rosario phase—further supports the proposition that the captives rendered on Building L were all Zapotec and not foreigners (Marcus 1976:127; Marcus and Flannery 1996:154). The stones bearing named captives commemorated the victorious raid that culminated with the seizure and sacrifice of these distinguished members of the opposing side (Flannery and Marcus 2003:11802).

There is little information on the Building L stones about the war tactics and the weapons used in these internecine raids launched by Monte Albán against other Zapotec settlements. The occurrence of the *atlatl* (spear-thrower) fingerboard and of spears or darts on some of the hieroglyphic captions (Caso 1947:14, fig. 25; Marcus 1992:394) indicates not only that *atlatls* were used in warfare in the Early Monte Albán I phase, but also that the very term for war or battle might have been "hurling spears."[8] Another implement depicted on two of the *danzantes* stones is the stingray spine, which was used in bloodletting rituals (Caso 1947:16, fig. 27; Marcus and Flannery 1996:15).

Some information relating to war tactics appears on the earliest Zapotec hieroglyphic texts that are directly associated with Building L, which refer to the actions by Monte Albán's military leaders that resulted in the gallery of slain captives. One reading of the fragmentary texts on Stelae 12–13, 14, 15, and 17 is that they relate the military victory or seizure of certain individuals by a member of the jaguar lineage. Collectively, the texts record Monte Albán's seizure of an individual on a particular day and year. Stelae 14, 15, and 17, which have glyphs that also appear on certain *danzantes* (for example, D-22, D-55, S-10, J-80, and D-104), may further relate the fate of the individuals defeated or

Figure 10.8. At ground level along the southernmost extension of the Danzantes gallery, Danzante 57 displays a mutilated, slain captive whose hair-knot, shoulder-length headdress, earspool and accompanying hieroglyphic text identify him and commemorate his seizure and sacrifice at Monte Albán. Danzante 57 measures 1.27 m tall and .76 m wide (Scott 1978b).

seized in war (Caso 1947:12–14; Marcus 1983b:93–95; Marcus and Flannery 1996:159–161).

By contrast, Building L's eastern façade is rich in information about the fate of the captives. Defeated in battle and seized, the captives were clearly stripped of their weapons, armor, and clothes. They were bound with rope and brought to Monte Albán; a half-dozen *danzantes* have ropes or tied knots at their neck or at their waists. The rope around the neck and the tied knot or multiple knots were persistent Zapotec symbols of a captive's status (Figure 10.9a) (Caso 1947:16, fig. 26; Scott 1978a:61).[9] In line with this interpretation are later Classic-period carved stone images from Monte Albán's South Platform of an armed warrior holding a rope, and of unarmed captives with their arms bound behind their backs with such ropes—one captive having a knot tied at his neck (Marcus 1992:400). Additional representations of bound captives can be found on certain Monte Albán I ceramic effigy vessels with modeled human heads and appliquéd naked torsos and limbs that Caso (1947:8; see also Caso et al. 1967:150) considered to be similar and broadly contemporaneous with the *danzantes*.[10] Of the half-dozen vessels portraying modeled human figures in supine or prone positions with faces turned up, three depict modeled and incised ropes around their necks (Caso 1947:lám. IV; Caso et al. 1967:fig. 87; Scott 1978a:22, fig. 11a). There is no clear indication of where the stripped and bound captives were taken and held, although the hieroglyphic captions on several of Building L's *danzantes* include the glyph for house or temple (Caso 1947:15; Scott 1978a:55, 57). Perhaps some of the accompanying hieroglyphic captions may refer to individuals "seized in war," who were then "sacrificed in the temple."

Once the captives were brought to Monte Albán, whether or not they were eventually taken to a temple as the *Relaciones* reported and the above hieroglyphic evidence may convey, the Building L stones record the captives' final treatment. In keeping with the *Relación de Miahuatlán*, which described a captive being bound by his genitals with his bowstring and led by his captors to an uncertain fate, at least 72 of the *danzantes* exhibit the effects of genital mutilation, with blood flowing from the severed male organ (Figures 10.8, 10.9). The body position of many of the *danzantes* reveals what probably happened next. Some 158 of the *danzantes* are shown lying sprawled on their backs, the position their bodies assumed immediately after they were sacrificed (Marcus 1992:393–394, figs. 11.15, 11.27–11.28). Thirteen of the *danzantes* are shown with an elliptical shape on their upper chests that may represent the incision performed with a stone dagger in order to remove the heart (Caso 1947:16; Scott 1978a:55–56) (Figure 10.9). All the captives bearing this sacrificial incision on their upper chests are in this supine, postmortem position, some with their arms twisted awkwardly. Finally, three *danzantes* consist only of severed

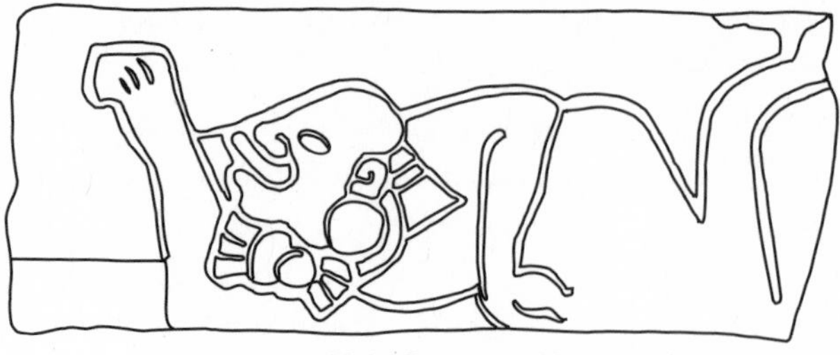

10.9a. Danzante 42

10.9b. Danzante N-19

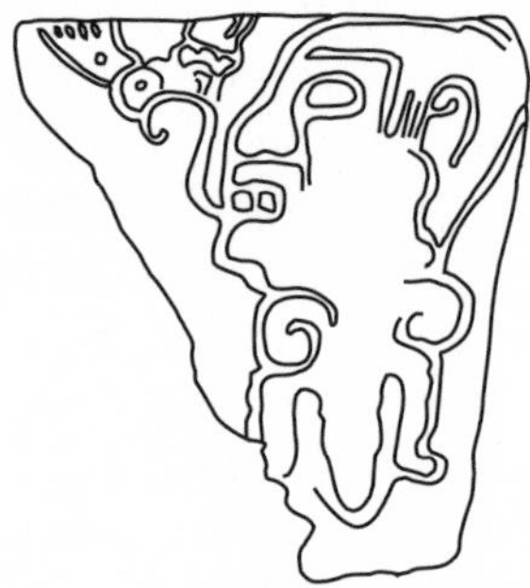

10.9c. Danzante J-112

Figure 10.9. *Top*: On the third riser of Building L's monolithic stairway is Danzante 42, whose cranial deformation, nose-plug, and earspool attest to his elite status. His nudity, prone position, and the rope and tied knot at his neck record his treatment as a captive at Monte Albán (redrawn from Caso 1947, figure 28). Danzante 42 measures .88 m long by .34 m wide (Scott 1978b). *Center*: Danzante N-19 was reset into the western façade of the North Platform long after it had been carved and displayed on Building L's Danzantes gallery to record a stripped captive still exhibiting his cranial deformation, headgear, and earspool, whose sexual organ and heart were excised. Danzante N-19 measures .57 m by .49 m (redrawn from Scott 1978b). *Bottom*: Danzante J-112 is one of three *danzantes* that represent severed heads. The decapitated individual's speech scroll emits compound signs that appear also on the hieroglyphic captions of other *danzantes*. Re-set in Building J, Danzante J-112 measures .50 m tall by .40 m wide (Scott 1978b) (redrawn from Caso 1947, figure 32).

heads, from which flow scrolls of blood. The hieroglyphic captions that accompany two of the severed heads are the same compound sign (Caso 1947: fig. 21s), elements of which may also issue from the speech scroll on the third example (Figure 10.9). The taking of an enemy's head and the erection of skull racks are reported in the ethnohistoric accounts of Zapotec warfare. Moreover, unadorned, inverted heads appear in the hieroglyphic text of Stela 17, one of the early, carved-stone inscriptions associated with Building L (Caso 1947:12, 31, fig. 15; Marcus 1983b:95).

All in all, Building L's eastern façade must have been an impressive symbolic display of Monte Albán's military victories. Marcus has drawn attention to the value of this display of slain captives as military propaganda, wherein the triumphant raids being commemorated were used by Monte Albán's founding rulers to influence their followers and legitimize their authority (Marcus 1992:10–11, 433–434). It is in the context of Monte Albán's founding period, when the polity centered at Monte Albán did not control the entire Valley of Oaxaca, that Marcus attributes the *danzantes*' special significance:

> It is noteworthy that the 310 or more danzantes which appear during Monte Albán I constitute 80% of the total monument record from the site. In other words, it was during the initial occupation of Monte Albán that the effort devoted to carving monumental figures was the greatest. This early effort probably coincides with the time when the rulers of Monte Albán would have felt the greatest need to legitimize their power and sanctify their position. Perhaps by creating a large gallery of prisoners, they were able to convince both their enemies and their own population of their power, although it was not yet institutionalized or completely effective. (Marcus 1974:90)

What the effects of the internecine raids launched by Monte Albán's forces in the early Monte Albán I phase may have been for some of the likely targets are just beginning to be understood. Our excavations at the Tilcajete center of El Mogote have focused on the northern and eastern sides of the plaza, where we have exposed the topmost floors of public buildings and residences on mound platforms A and K, and the plaza floor itself (Figure 10.6). All these floors showed clear evidence of having been burned at the time of the plaza's abandonment, resulting, we think, from an attack against the El Mogote center with the use of fire to drive out its inhabitants. Amid the burned deposits that consisted of charcoal, burned earth, and burned adobe, we recovered a few sherds of type G.12 from a combed-bottom bowl; this type was introduced to the region's ceramic assemblages at the interface between the Early Monte Albán I and Late Monte Albán I phases (Caso et al. 1967:25–26; Marcus and Flannery 1996:144;

Spencer and Redmond 2003:36). A radiocarbon sample (Beta-147541) taken from charcoal fragments littering the burned plaza surface at the southeastern base of Mound A yielded a conventional radiocarbon date of 330±40 B.C., which helps to approximate the timing of the attack and the subsequent abandonment of the El Mogote plaza at the end of the Early Monte Albán I phase (Spencer and Redmond 2003:37).

Interregional Conquest Warfare in the Late Monte Albán I (300–100 B.C.) and Monte Albán II (100 B.C.–A.D. 200) Phases

Monte Albán and the Oaxaca Valley

In the succeeding Late Monte Albán I phase (300–100 B.C.), Monte Albán's occupation extended over nearly all of Monte Albán proper and the adjoining hilltop of El Gallo was first settled, amounting to a resident population that has been estimated at 17,000 persons, a figure that is more than three times the population estimated for the previous phase (Blanton 1978:44; Blanton et al. 1999:53). Monte Albán presided over a regional site-size hierarchy of four levels (Marcus and Flannery 1996: fig. 180). Some 155 lower-order, valley-floor settlements were concentrated within 10 km of Monte Albán (Figure 10.10) (Marcus and Flannery 1996:164).

For all its size and apical position in the regional settlement hierarchy, however, Monte Albán did not control the entire Oaxaca Valley. While the Etla-Central Valley subregion continued to be dominated by Monte Albán, the Tlacolula and Ocotlán-Zimatlán subregions probably remained independent (Feinman 1998:128–129; Marcus and Flannery 1996:163–165; Spencer and Redmond 2001a:206–217). Moreover, Spencer's phase-by-phase analysis of covariance (ANCOVA) of valley-floor sites' membership in these subregions (in terms of the degree of correspondence between the subregion's agricultural productivity and archaeological population levels) suggested that the Late Monte Albán I phase may have witnessed increasing competition between the polities in the Oaxaca Valley's subregions (Spencer and Redmond 2001a:215–216, fig. 19). It was also in the Late Monte Albán I phase that defensive fortifications were erected at Monte Albán. Not only was a large earthen and stone defensive wall constructed across the most gradual, and hence vulnerable, northern and northwestern slopes of Monte Albán, delineating 3 km of the center's perimeter (Figure 10.11), but two smaller walls were also constructed at the southernmost tip of Monte Albán, again to deny easy access up a gradual slope (Blanton 1978:52–54; Elam 1989:396; Marcus and Flannery 1996:150–151). Other settlements in the Oaxaca Valley fortified themselves as well during the Late

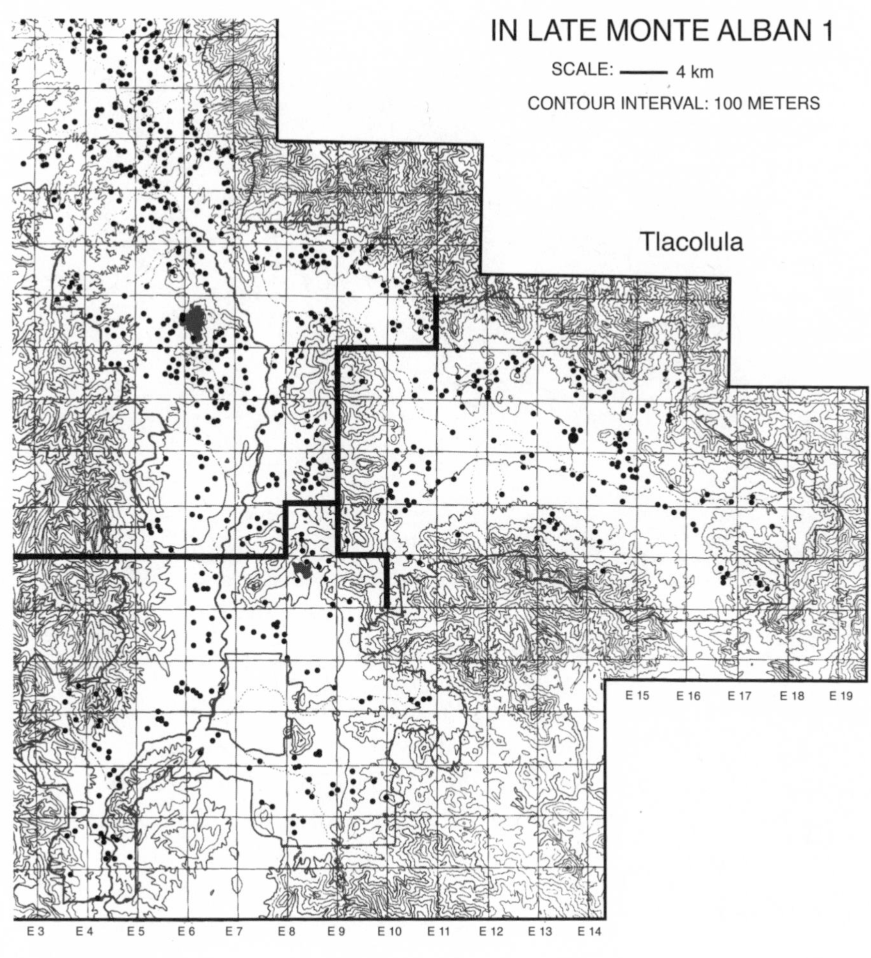

Figure 10.10. Late Monte Albán I phase (300–100 B.C.) settlements in the Oaxaca Valley, with the boundaries of the subregions indicated (redrawn from Blanton et al. 1993, figure 3.12.)

Figure 10.11. View of a segment of Monte Albán's principal defensive wall, which reaches 20 m in width and 9 m in height in places.

Monte Albán I phase; in what Elam (1989:404) characterized as "the first major buildup of defensible sites," 12 settlements assumed defensible hilltop positions and at least 5 featured defensive fortifications. Although the buildup of defensible and fortified settlements was heaviest in the Etla-Central Valley subregion, defensible and fortified sites appeared in the Tlacolula and Ocotlán-Zimatlán subregions as well. Robert Reynolds's decision-tree for the locations of sites in the Etla subregion demonstrated that defense was a major factor in determining site locations at this time and led him to suggest that the concentration of settlements around Monte Albán was motivated in part by the need to have a ready supply of fighting men living nearby (Reynolds 1999:17–18).

At San Martín Tilcajete, the first-order center of the Ocotlán-Zimatlán subregion, the inhabitants of El Mogote, which seems to have come under attack at the end of the Early Monte Albán I phase, built a new plaza at El Palenque (SMT-11b), a more defensible location some 800 m to the west, across a barranca, and 30 m higher in elevation, enclosed by stone walls along the site's gradual southern slope (Figure 10.12). Our excavations have revealed that the El Palenque plaza was built at the onset of the Late Monte Albán I phase. The earliest radiocarbon date from El Palenque was obtained from a chunk of charcoal (Beta-147540) that we recovered from the masonry foundations of Structure 7 in Area I on the plaza's prominent northwest corner (Figure 10.12); it yielded the conventional radiocarbon date of 350±80 B.C. The new Late Monte Albán

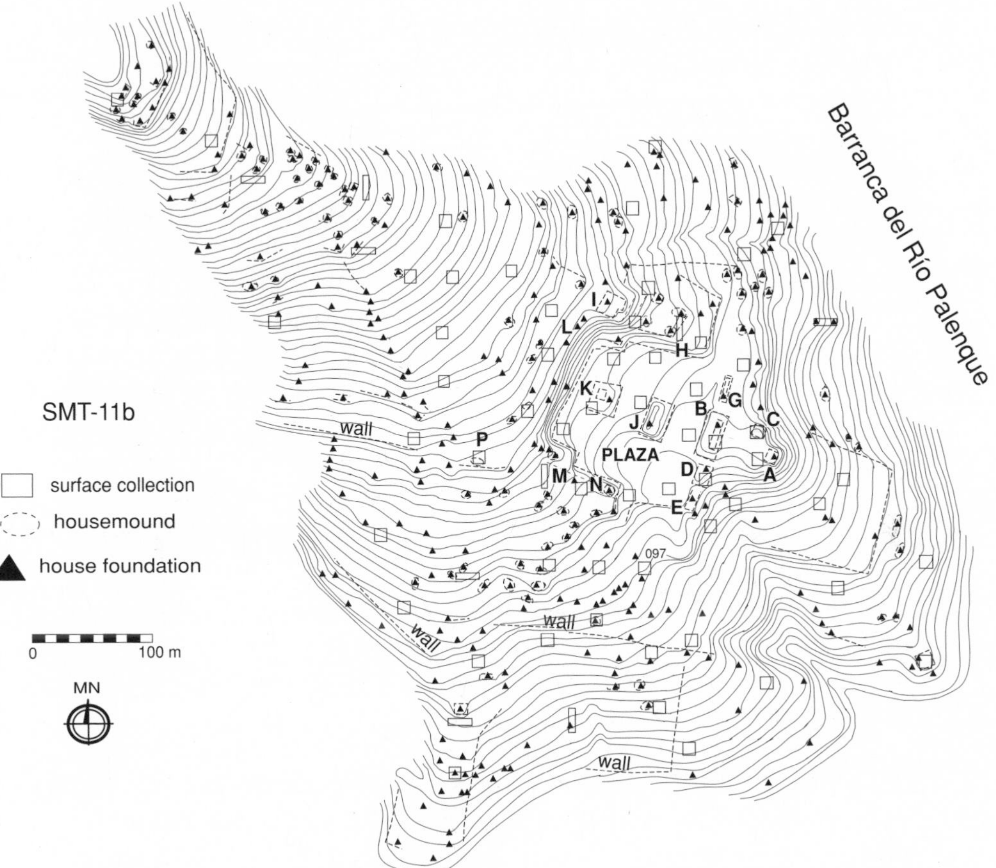

Figure 10.12. Site map of El Palenque (SMT-11b), showing its plaza, major mounds, house mounds with stone foundations, and stone walls evident on the surface, and our surface collections.

I phase plaza at El Palenque, although slightly smaller in area at 1.6 ha than the earlier 2.2 ha plaza at El Mogote, has the same orientation and arrangement of mound platforms (see Figure 10.6). The duplication of El Mogote's plaza layout in this new, defensible location suggests that the inhabitants of El Mogote withstood the attack, but that it prompted them to rebuild their center uphill, behind defensive walls.

The Late Monte Albán I occupation at El Palenque grew to extend over 71.5 ha, representing a 35.4 percent increase over the Early Monte Albán I occupation at El Mogote. Moreover, our excavations have exposed the well-preserved remains of several public buildings that flanked El Palenque's plaza on its northern and eastern sides in the Monte Albán Late I phase. Area I's Structure 7 would have presided over the plaza on its northern side. This 850 m^2 residential compound was made up of eight rooms facing into a patio, two paved courtyards flanked by structures and platforms, and additional structures; it probably served as the local ruler's palace (Spencer and Redmond 2004b). On the plaza's eastern side, we have exposed the remains of a distinct multiroom temple on top of Mound G (Spencer and Redmond 2001a:fig. 18). The appearance of these building types, which Flannery and Marcus (1976:206, 217–219; see also Flannery 1983a:132–136; Marcus and Flannery 1996:178–191) have associated with distinct sociopolitical institutions of the Zapotec state, signal the appearance of state institutions in the Late Monte Albán I phase (Spencer and Redmond 2001a:221–223). Another institution that might have arisen at this time was a full-time military, charged with overseeing the polity's defense and waging war at a moment's notice. One line of evidence to support such a proposition comes from a surface collection (EP-097) located some 50 m south of El Palenque's plaza, which produced a ceramic figurine fragment of a helmeted, chin-strapped male figure wearing a nose-plug, a fringed collar, and what appear to be the folds of a costume or cotton armor (Figure 10.13). The helmet has two protuberances that may represent the eyes of an animal, in keeping with the Zapotec practice of designating felines and other predators as the patrons of military orders.

El Palenque's ceramic assemblage had abundant type G.12 combed-bottom bowls and other Late Monte Albán I diagnostic gray ceramics, but only trace amounts of the thin-walled burnished creamwares that are known to have been produced in the vicinity of Monte Albán (Caso et al. 1967:46–47; Feinman 1982:188–191), suggesting the limited exchange between the Etla/Central and the Ocotlán/Zimatlán subregions. This possibility is supported by the relatively small amount of obsidian present in our lithic assemblages at El Palenque. We suspect that Monte Albán, which probably controlled access to the obsidian imported to the Oaxaca Valley from sources in Central Mexico, prevented the flow of imported obsidian from reaching this first-order center of an autonomous polity in the Ocotlán/Zimatlán subregion. Spencer's analysis of covariance of productive potential and archaeological population estimated for the Oaxaca Valley's three subregions during the Rosario, Early Monte Albán I, and Late Monte Albán I phases revealed that the effects of subregional membership increased in the Late Monte Albán I phase, during which time competition between the subregions must have intensified (Spencer and Redmond 2001a:215–217).

Monte Albán's involvement in hostilities at this time is evident on the household level. Marcus Winter's excavations of a residential terrace on Monte Al-

Figure 10.13. A male ceramic figurine recovered from surface collection (EP-097) at El Palenque (SMT-11b) wears the headdress, noseplug, fringed collar, and dress or armor that may be attributed to a military order. Figurine fragment measures 3.6 cm tall.

bán's northern slope uncovered a tomb in the patio of a residence (Tomb 176) pertaining to the Late Monte Albán I phase, whose principal occupant was an adult male. The tomb's fill included a stingray spine, a ceramic spouted vessel whose modeled exterior portrayed a reclining, bound captive (dubbed a *danzante*), and five fragments of worked long bones of which one was identified as the cut and incised distal end of an adult human's femur (Winter 2002:72, fig.7.4; Winter et al. 1995:60–72). Similar effigy vessels have been recovered in other high-status Late Monte Albán I phase residential and tomb contexts at Monte Albán (Caso 1947:8, lám. IV-V, VII; Caso et al. 1967:150, fig. 87), attesting to the symbolic role of bound captives in sacrificial and funerary rituals.

We know very little about the public buildings constructed on Monte Albán's plaza in the Late Monte Albán I phase, precisely the time period when our investigations at Tilcajete have brought to light the architectural ground plans and artifactual evidence of certain Zapotec state institutions. Yet Monte Albán's position at the top of a four-level site-size hierarchy and its construction of defensive fortifications with gate-like features for regulating the entry and exit of pedestrian traffic are just some of the signs we do have of its emergence as the capital of a state in the Late Monte Albán I phase (Blanton 1978:52; Marcus and Flannery 1996:158–165). This was a period at Monte Albán that Marcus and Flannery have characterized as a time of "spectacular demographic and militaristic expansion" (Marcus and Flannery 1996:165).

The starting point for our investigation of Monte Albán's militaristic expansion during the Late Monte Albán I phase was one of the many public buildings constructed on the Main Plaza in the subsequent Monte Albán II phase (100 B.C.–A.D. 200). This was the pentagonal Building J (Figure 10.5), whose idiosyncratic orientation of 39 degrees east of magnetic north and cross-cutting tunnel have brought it much attention by archaeoastronomers (Aveni and Linsley 1972). Actually, Caso reported that the fill of Building J's original construction contained Monte Albán I ceramics and raised the possibility that Building J was erected prior to the end of the Late Monte Albán I phase and the outset of the Monte Albán II phase (Caso 1938:11, 1947:20; Fahmel Beyer 1991:100–101). Of special interest to us were the 51 carved stones displayed originally on the rear walls of Building J, which Caso (1947:27–28) had identified as records of places conquered by Monte Albán. Each stone is a record of conquest that lists the sign for "hill" or "place," and below it the upside-down human head of a conquered ruler or leader, wearing a distinctive headdress or helmet—one that sometimes includes a hair-knot at the crown of the head, face painting and other insignia, but with eyes that are closed or lifeless (Figure 10.14a).[11] Above the sign for place is a single glyph or the compound glyphs that name the particular place, whose conquest is further alluded to by the accompanying bundle of darts, grasping hand (Figure 10.14a), or the finger-grip of a spear-thrower (Figure 10.14b) (Caso 1947:21–28; Marcus 1992:395–400). In 1976, Joyce Marcus compared the conquered place signs on Building J to places in Oaxaca that had been recorded in a sixteenth-century Aztec tribute roll, and identified four matching toponyms, all of which referred to places outside the Oaxaca Valley (Marcus 1976:130–131; Marcus 1992:176, 396). With some 50 military conquests inscribed on its walls, Building J could be considered a building erected by Monte Albán's rulers to commemorate their military conquests and to define their territorial expansion into neighboring regions (Marcus 1992:175–176, 400). While all the Building J conquest inscriptions bear the constant "hill" or "place" glyph and the variable toponym, not all depict the inverted head of a defeated ruler. When compared to the many portrayals of defeated enemies on Building L, the conquest inscriptions seem to emphasize the conquest of named territory rather than of specific

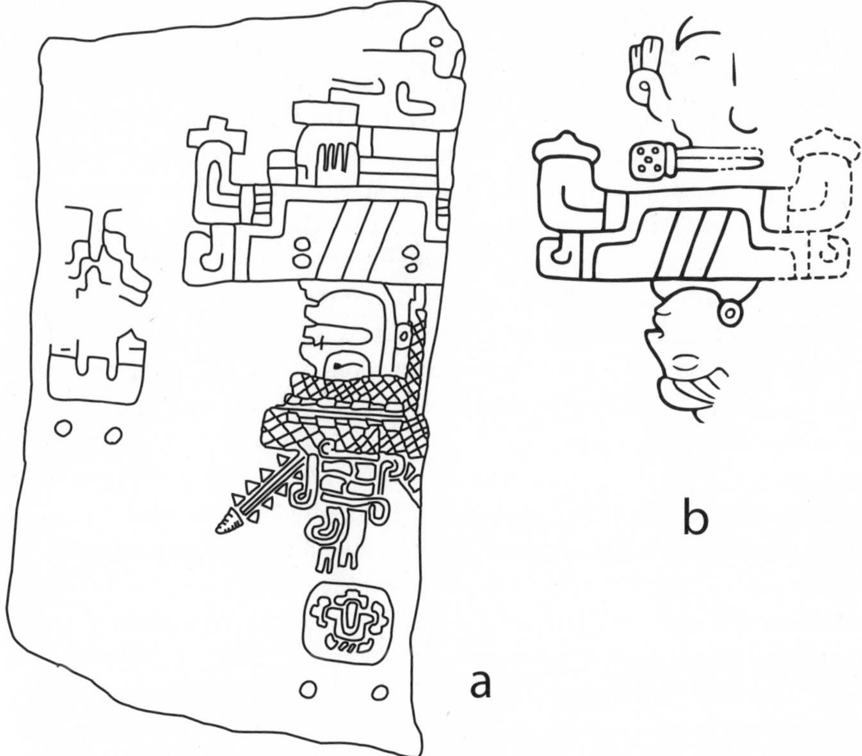

Figure 10.14a. Building J conquest slab Lápida 106. The inscription includes a glyphic text with additional calendrical and noncalendrical information about the military conquest of this "hill" or "place," whose ruler is shown upside-down, wearing a woven headdress with a stingray spine inserted into the brim that is distinctive of this region conquered by Monte Albán (redrawn from Caso 1947, figure 50-A).
Figure 10.14b. Building J conquest slab Lápida 47 records Monte Albán's conquest of Cuicatlán, the "Place of Song" (redrawn from Marcus and Flannery 1996, figure 234).

rulers. According to Marcus, one of the conquered places inscribed as the "Place of Song" on Lápida 47 (Figure 10.14b) was the Cuicatlán Cañada.

Monte Albán and the Cuicatlán Cañada

The Cuicatlán Cañada is a narrow tropical canyon some 50 km north of the Oaxaca Valley that was inhabited by Cuicatec speakers in prehispanic times (Figure 10.15). Watered by the Río Grande and its tributaries, much of the Cañada's alluvium is used to cultivate tropical fruits, including the native *chicozapote* (*Achras zapota*), black *zapote* (*Diospyros digyna*), and *ciruela* (*Spondias purpurea*). We carried out regional survey and excavations here in 1977–1978, in part to evaluate the hypothesis of a Zapotec conquest of this region at about the time of the construction of Building J at Monte Albán, that is, during the Late Monte Albán I (300–100 B.C.) or Monte Albán II (100 B.C.–A.D. 200) phases. Because the evidence of Monte Albán's hypothesized conquest of regions like the Cuicatlán Cañada seemed to be concurrent with Monte Albán's emergence as the capital of a state, the model that we developed for assessing the effects of the hypothesized conquest considered not only the targeted region's transformation into a frontier tributary region, but also the consequences of such an interregional campaign of conquests for the expansionist Zapotec polity itself (for a related discussion about the frontier regions of later, expanding polities in Mesoamerica, see Connell and Silverstein, chapter 11, this volume). We drew upon the sixteenth- and seventeenth-century descriptions of Zapotec military campaigns and territorial expansion in the late prehispanic period, as well as upon other cases of military expansionism (Lattimore 1962; Morris 1972).

Our regional survey of the 35-km-long Cuicatlán Cañada revealed a major disruption in the region's settlement pattern in the Late Formative period Lomas phase (300 B.C.–A.D. 200), corresponding in time to the beginning of the Late Monte Albán I phase (Spencer and Redmond 2001b:198). All 12 of the Cañada's Middle Formative period Perdido phase (750–300 B.C.) communities that had been located on high alluvial terraces were abandoned, including the village site of Llano Perdido (Cs 25) near modern-day Santiago Dominguillo, where we carried out horizontal excavations (Figure 10.16). This 2.25 ha community, which we determined consisted of several large residential compounds, was evidently burned to the ground at the time of its abandonment. Our excavations recovered densities of burned daub and adobe fragments that were five times greater than Drennan (1976) recovered at the contemporaneous Rosario phase village of Fábrica San José mentioned earlier; such densities justify our interpretation that Llano Perdido was destroyed by burning just before its abandonment (Spencer 1982:217–218). A radiocarbon sample (Beta-143347) from a carbonized postmold at Llano Perdido yielded a conventional radiocarbon date of 420±90 B.C. for the abandonment (Spencer and Redmond 2001b:189–191). Furthermore, we encountered the body of a 20–30-year-old female lying on a house floor, along with fragments of a young child's skull (Wilkinson 1997:614), both of whom we think were killed and covered by the collapsing adobe-brick walls of the house during the village's conflagration. This evidence of widespread burning and violence at Llano Perdido brings to mind Burgoa's characterization of Zapotec wars of conquest *a fuego y sangre* (Burgoa 1934b:189, 328, 341 [1674]), which involved encircling and setting fire to the targeted communities and massacring any inhabitants who resisted.

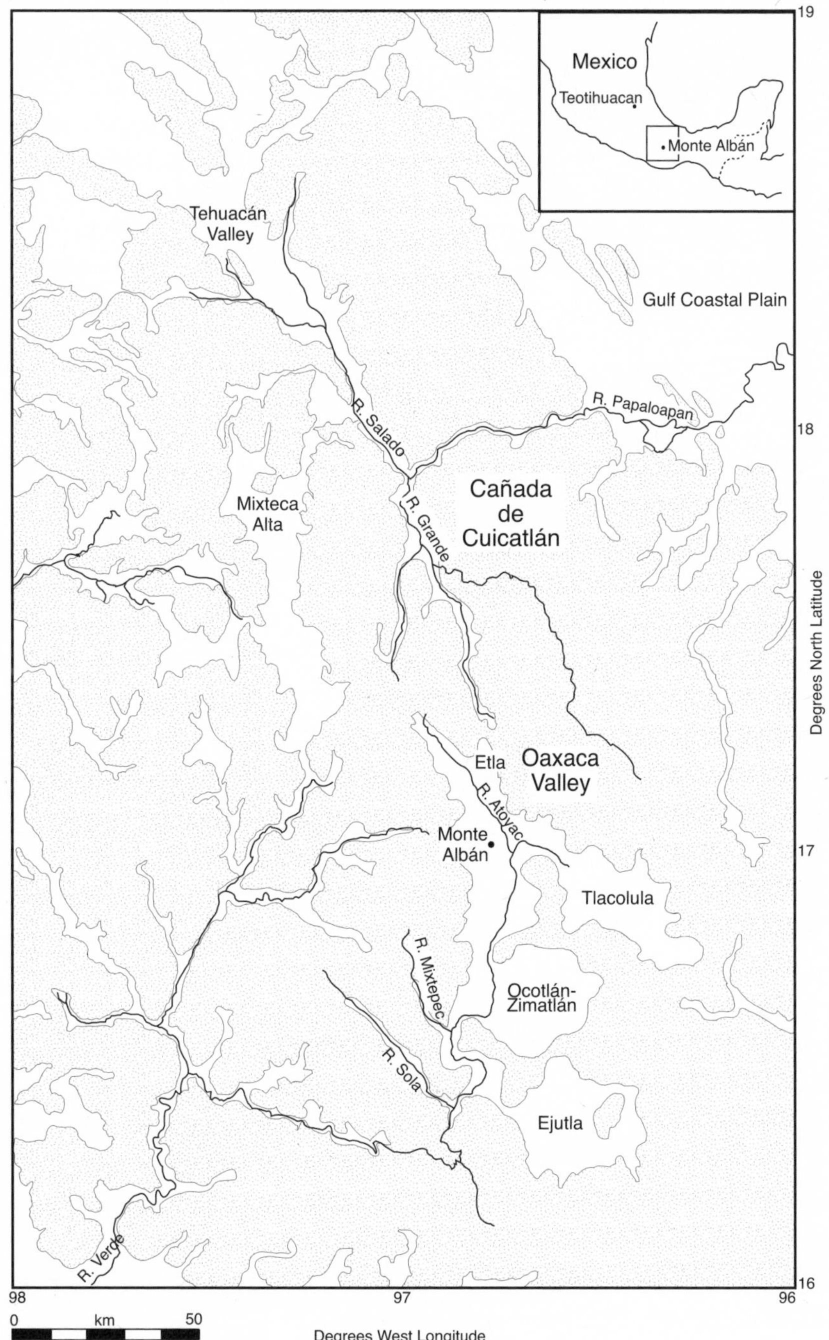

Figure 10.15. The Cuicatlán Cañada is a natural corridor that links the Oaxaca Valley and the Tehuacán Valley.

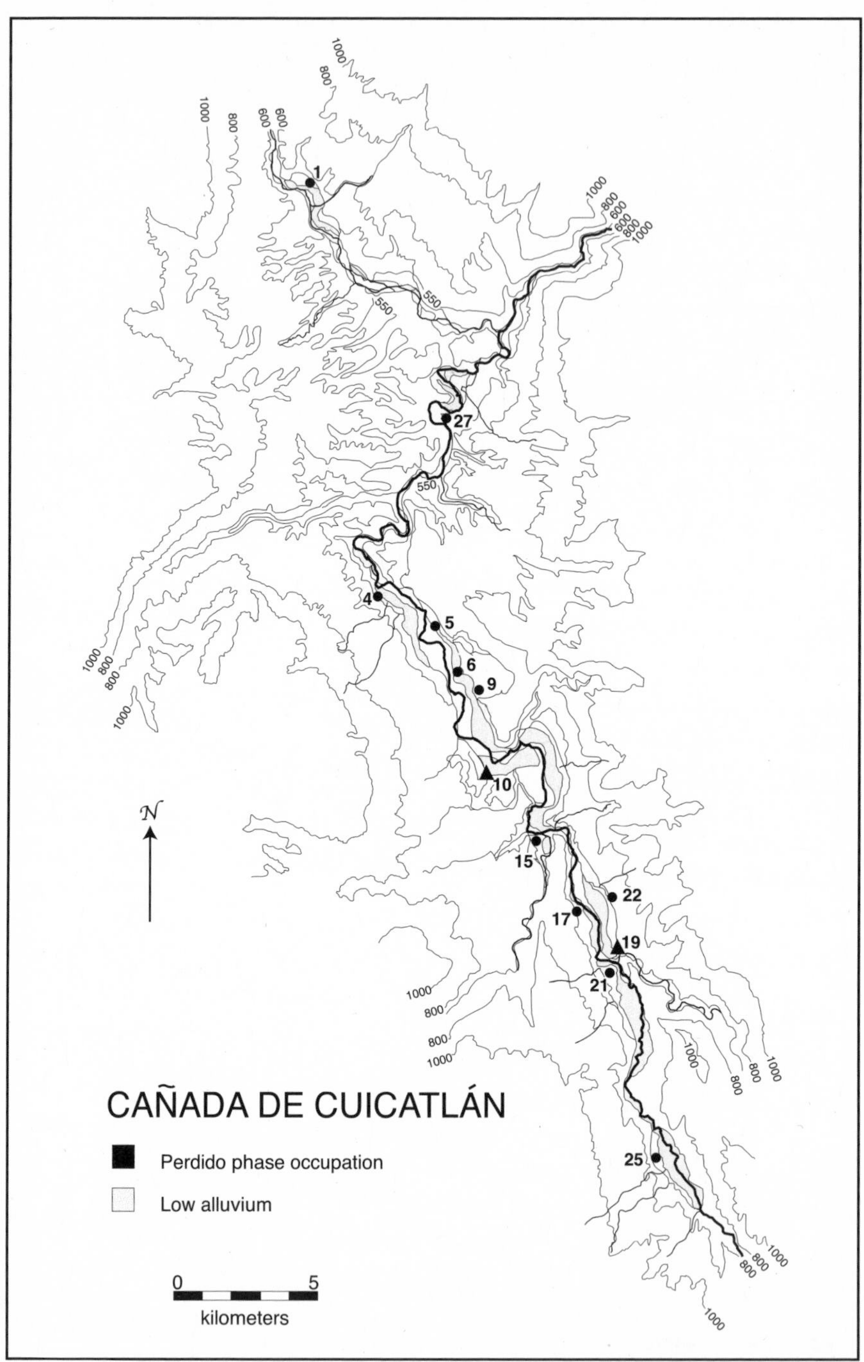

Figure 10.16. Settlements in the Cuicatlán Cañada of the Middle Formative Perdido phase (750–300 B.C.). Sites indicated by a triangle are larger than 5 ha in area; sites indicated by a circle are less than 5 ha in area.

Following the attack and destruction of Llano Perdido, a new settlement was established on the adjacent hill known as Loma de La Coyotera, in a settlement shift repeated throughout the Cuicatlán Cañada in the Lomas phase (300 B.C.–A.D. 200) (Figure 10.17). The hilltop settlement extended over 3 ha, only slightly larger than the earlier village. But the pattern of residence switched from the large compounds of the Perdido phase to life in individual houses on residential terraces (Spencer and Redmond 1997:507). The earliest midden deposits recovered above bedrock and associated with one of these residences contained sherds of the G.12 combed-bottom bowl type that we have noted is highly diagnostic of the Late Monte Albán I phase in the Oaxaca Valley. These midden deposits, chock-full of carbonized *coyol* palm nuts (*Acrocomia mexicana*), black *zapote*, and *ciruela* seeds (Spencer 1982:Table 5.5), have recently been assigned a conventional radiocarbon date (Beta-143349) of 220±70 B.C., corresponding to the early Lomas phase or Late Monte Albán I phase (Spencer and Redmond 2001b:193–195).

The most striking developments in the region's Lomas phase settlement pattern occurred at the northern end of the Cañada, marked by the mountain ridge at the junction of the Río Grande with the Río Salado (Figure 10.17). Only the narrow pass used by the Mexican railroad allows natural access into and out of the region. The single 1.5 ha Perdido phase village here at Santiago Quiotepec was succeeded by a 44-ha complex of 7 Lomas phase settlements, the largest being the site of Paso de Quiotepec (Cs3), which spanned the pass and featured over 200 residences, defensive walls, and a plaza dominated by a 75-m-long ballcourt (1.8 times the length of Monte Albán's ballcourt) (Figure 10.18). Directly south of the pass and major ford across the Río Grande lay a vast plaza, some 200 m on a side, delimited by long 6-m-tall mounds (Cs26) (Figure 10.19). Any traveler entering the Quiotepec area from the north would have transited the pass, forded the river, and crossed this plaza to a pair of staircases at its southeast corner. In the absence of residential architecture here, this plaza, which extended over half of the precious little low alluvium, probably oversaw any traffic into and out of the region (Redmond 1983:97–99).

East of the pass, a fortress (Cs2) stood on the highest point of the mountain ridge, reached by a steep ascent and guarded by defensive walls (Figure 10.20). Two large plazas with impressive mound platforms occupied the highest terrace of Cerro de Quiotepec; a 65-m-long ballcourt lay on the adjacent terrace, retained by a 12-m-tall cut masonry and mortar walls. This site features not only some looted Monte Albán-style tombs that Eduardo Pareyón had salvaged here in 1957 (Pareyón 1960:101–102), which we revisited, but also most of our surface collections in this fortified ceremonial precinct contained distinctive painted and incised Lomas-phase ceramics stylistically similar to creamwares

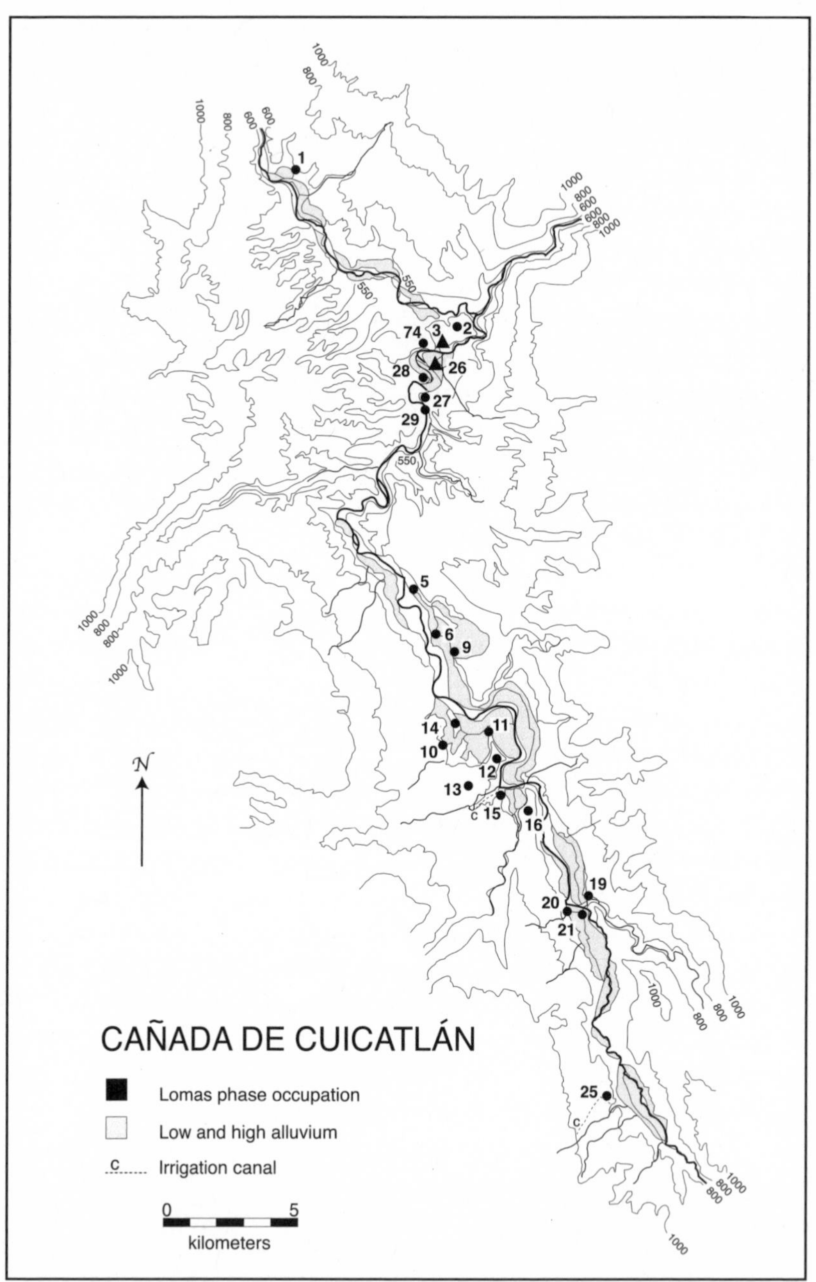

Figure 10.17. Settlements in the Cuicatlán Cañada of the Late Formative Lomas phase (300 B.C.–A.D. 200). Sites indicated by a triangle are larger than 5 ha in area; sites indicated by a circle are less than 5 ha in area. The Río Salado, which flows from the Tehuacán Valley south and past the site of Tecomavaca (Cs1), joins the Río Grande, which flows north the length of the Cuicatlán Cañada, just north and east of Quiotepec (directly east below the ridge occupied by the Cs2 fortress).

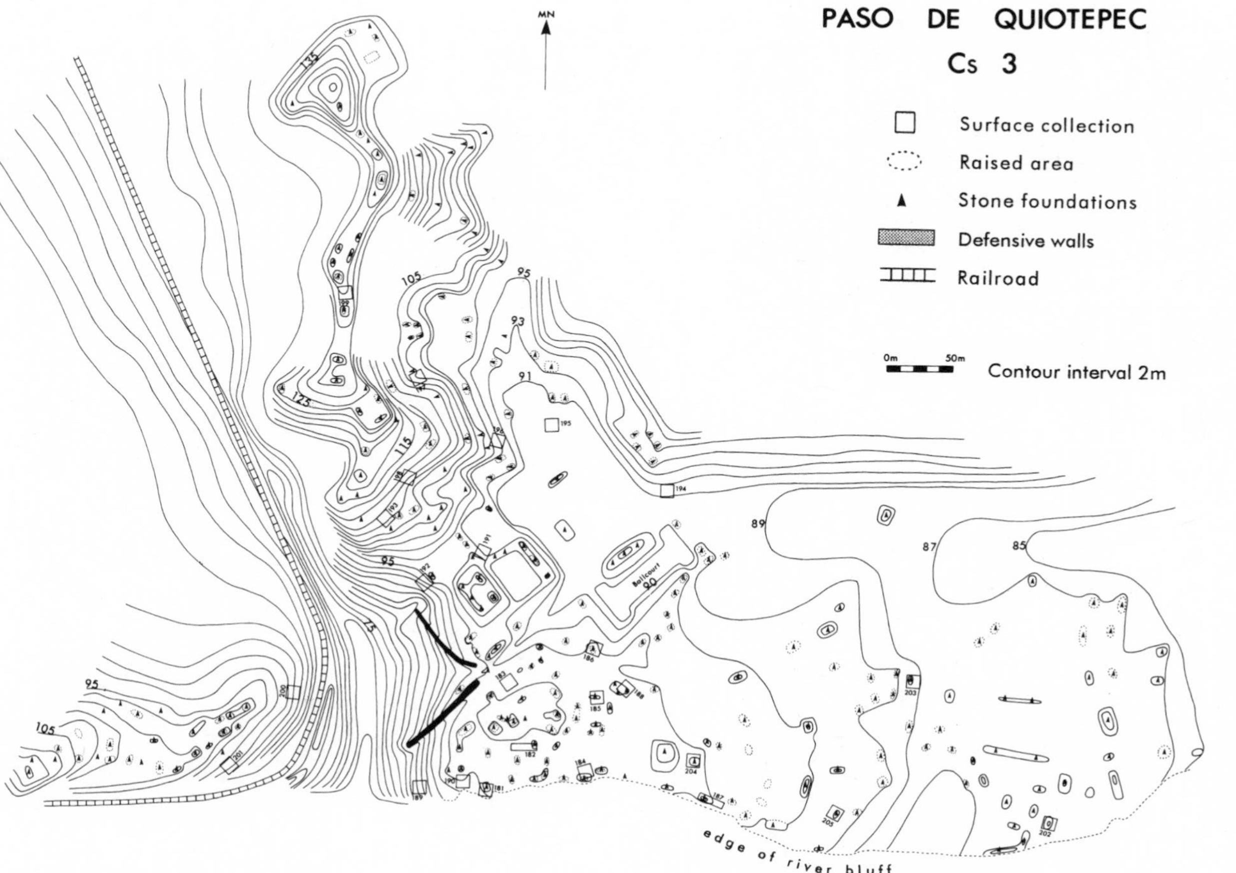

Figure 10.18. Site map of Paso de Quiotepec (Cs3), which extends across the natural pass through the Quiotepec mountain ridge, over an area of 14.67 ha, making it the largest Lomas-phase settlement in the Cuicatlán Cañada.

Figure 10.19. Aerial view of the natural pass through the Quiotepec mountain ridge, the ford on the Río Grande, and the vast plaza delimited by tree-topped mounds at Campo del Panteón (Cs26) on the Quiotepec alluvium, facing north.

of the Monte Albán II phase (100 B.C.–A.D. 200) in the Oaxaca Valley (Redmond 1983:120; Redmond and Harbottle 1983:204). In the process of mapping the mound platform along the southern edge of Cerro de Quiotepec's main plaza, we recovered a chunk of wood charcoal from an exposed profile of mound fill at the mound's western end (Figure 10.20). Although this radiocarbon sample (Beta-147535) was recovered on survey and not through excavation, we considered that its context in the construction fill of the mound and its association with nearby surface collection Cs2-161 merited submitting it for radiocarbon analysis, which produced a conventional radiocarbon date of A.D. 40±70 (Spencer and Redmond 2001b:197–198). This range corresponds to the latter half of the Lomas phase in the Cañada and to the Monte Albán II phase in the Oaxaca Valley. Beta-147535's association with surface collections at Cs2 that yielded Monte Albán II-style ceramics—and the presence of these ceramics at the six other Lomas phase settlements at Quiotepec—further support the proposition that the unprecedented complex of seven settlements at the Cañada's northern boundary at Quiotepec were built in the latter half of the Lomas phase, coeval with the Monte Albán II phase in the Oaxaca Valley (Spencer and Redmond 1997:609). Finally, our regional survey determined that the fortified settlements at Quiotepec, including a lookout-post (Cs74) west of the pass and three additional terraced settlements south of the plaza opposite the pass (Cs27, Cs28, and Cs29), marked the northern boundary of the distribution of Monte Albán-style ceramics; some seven km to the north, site Cs1 featured only the Palo Blanco phase ceramics of the Tehuacán Valley (Redmond 1983:86–87). Zapotec military control of the Quiotepec frontier seems to have been established later in the Lomas phase, well after communities like Llano Perdido were attacked and burned around 300 B.C., at the onset of the Lomas phase or the Late Monte Albán I phase in the Oaxaca Valley. We will elaborate on the timing of the Valley Zapotec's territorial expansion over a distance greater than 100 km to the northern boundary of the Cañada in the concluding section.

In the southern Cañada at Loma de La Coyotera (Cs25), we recovered evidence of a new political economy in the Lomas phase. An irrigation facility was built to channel water from a tributary *barranca* over a series of gullies by means of a dozen stone aqueducts and onto the high alluvial terrace where the village of Llano Perdido had been located (Spencer 1982:222–225). Since the midden deposits at the hilltop community contained huge quantities of tropical fruit and nut remains, in much higher densities than was the case in the midden deposits at the earlier Llano Perdido village, the newly irrigated high alluvium was probably intended for the stepped-up production of *coyol* palm, black *zapote*, and *ciruela*, in order to meet the tribute exacted by the conquering Zapotec from the Oaxaca Valley, where such lowland products cannot be grown (Spencer 1982:228–229). Evidence of a new political order came from Loma de La Coyotera's single public plaza, where the test excavation we placed directly in front of the principal 3-m-tall mound encountered rows of human skulls, more than 61 in all, of adult males, females, and a few subadults, along with the carbonized remains of a wooden post and a small sample of Lomas phase ceramics. We have interpreted this Feature 8 as the remains of a toppled-over skull rack (Spencer and Redmond 1997:520–524); the occurrence of a hyoid bone and of many intact mandibles led Wilkinson (1997:618–619) to suggest that some skulls had been placed on the rack in a fleshy condition at different points in time. The skull rack that was constructed in the small plaza at Loma de La Coyotera in the Lomas phase is reminiscent of the sixteenth-century valley Zapotec's practice of erecting skull racks in order to terrorize the local inhabitants following a conquest (Burgoa 1934b:11–12, 342 [1674]). We have obtained a conventional radiocarbon date from Feature 8's carbonized postmold (Beta-143344) of 10±100 B.C., which dates its construction to the latter part of the Lomas phase, coeval with the Monte Albán II phase in the Oaxaca Valley (Spencer and Redmond 2001b:197). The political allegiance of those responsible for setting up the skull rack at Loma de La Coyotera was clarified by the discovery of an artifact on the surface of the same small plaza. This was the paw from a

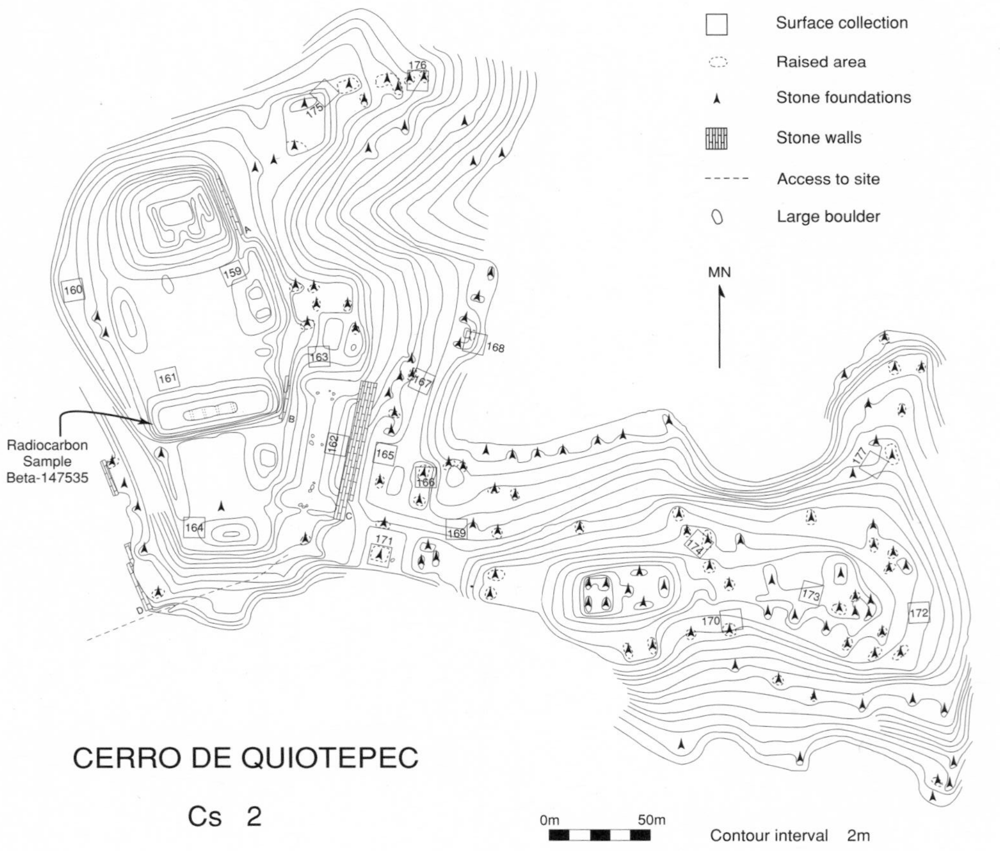

Figure 10.20. Map of Cerro de Quiotepec (Cs2), showing the location of the charcoal sample obtained from a mound on the main plaza that was submitted for radiocarbon dating (Beta-147535).

large, hollow ceramic jaguar statue or urn, similar to the magnificent ceramic jaguar figures recovered from Monte Albán and other Monte Albán II phase sites in the Oaxaca Valley (Spencer and Redmond 2000:168–171). Because Monte Albán's ancient name may have been "Hill of the Jaguar" (Caso et al. 1967:84; Marcus 1976:131), and there are references to Zapotec warrior orders under the patronage of the jaguar (Burgoa 1934a:412 [1674]; Villegas 1928:129 [1580]), this jaguar paw highlights the imposition of a new Zapotec imperial ideology at Lomas phase communities in the Cuicatlán Cañada.[12]

Monte Albán's Other Hinterland Regions

Other regions that show discontinuities in settlement pattern and in the distribution of Monte Albán II ceramics are Ejutla, Miahuatlán, and the Sola Valley (Figure 10.15). Feinman and Nicholas's survey of the Ejutla Valley and excavations at the Ejutla center led them to propose that this region 40–75 km south of Monte Albán along the Atoyac River's route to the Pacific Coast was controlled by the valley Zapotec in the Monte Albán II phase, in part to produce and supply Monte Albán with shell ornaments from Pacific Coast gastropods and pelecypods (Feinman and Nicholas 1990:231–233, 1993:108–113). Thirty km farther to the south in the Miahuatlán Valley, surveys by Donald Brockington (1973) and Charles Markman (1981) have shown similar evidence of Zapotec domination during the Monte Albán II phase in this natural corridor to the Pacific Coast that is known for its natural springs, where pot irrigation and canal irrigation have long been practiced (Brockington 1973:5, 8; Markman 1981:1, 5, 60–61, 71, 80). The Miahuatlán center of El Gueche grew in size and architectural complexity in the Monte Albán II phase, and served as the administrative center for the region (Markman 1981:21–22, 83). Miahuatlán is probably the place referred to as "Canal of the Maize Tassels" on Lápida 43 on Building J (Marcus 1976:129; Marcus and Flannery 1996:198).

Andrew Balkansky's survey of the Sola Valley, also along a natural route from the Oaxaca Valley some 75 km southwest to the Pacific Coast, revealed a series of defensible sites that were established in the Late Monte Albán I phase to guard the *camino real* to the coast. By the succeeding Monte Albán II phase, the Sola Valley showed signs similar to those reported for Ejutla and Miahuatlán of its tributary relationship to Monte Albán (Balkansky 1998:465–466, 2002:37–50).

On the Pacific Coast itself, there are some intriguing archaeological indicators of hostilities coinciding with evidence of a possible valley Zapotec installation in the Tututepec region, where the foothills of the Southern Sierra Madre, south of the Atoyac River's junction with the Río Verde, drop precipitously onto the coastal plain. DeCicco and Brockington's (1956) initial survey of the coast and Arthur Joyce and Andrew Workinger's recent survey, mapping, and excavation projects in the lower Río Verde and Río San Francisco (Joyce 1991; Joyce et al. 1998) have highlighted certain Monte Albán I and II phase (Minizundo and Miniyua phases, respectively, in the lower Río Verde Valley ceramic chronology) sites perched on spurs. On the highest residential terrace at Cerro de la Cruz, Joyce's horizontal excavations of a residential compound exposed the remains of 48 adults lying on the topmost floor of Structure 1 and the eastern edge of the adjacent patio, whose hearth yielded a conventional radiocarbon date of 120±80 B.C., corresponding to the Late Monte Albán I phase (Joyce 1991:132; Joyce et al. 1998:71). Many of these adult individuals lay stacked atop or across one another, and all of them lacked funerary offerings. The skewed mortality distribution and the absence of funerary accompaniments differ from burial populations of this time period, including the sub-floor burials with offerings recovered on another residential terrace at Cerro La Cruz. While Joyce et al. (1998:65–66) have interpreted the Structure 1 remains as the result of a specialized, communal funerary practice, these remains have also been interpreted as the victims of a massacre (Balkansky 2001:560). Overlooking the Río San Francisco from a spur to the northeast is the terraced site of San Francisco de Arriba, whose mound platforms, retaining walls, and abundance of Monte Albán II incised *crema* ceramics[13] distinguished San Francisco de Arriba from other Monte Albán I and II phase sites in DeCicco and Brockington's survey of the region (DeCicco and Brockington 1956:51–52, 55, 59). The results of Andrew Workinger's recent mapping and excavation project at San Francisco de Arriba are helping to assess the possibility that San Francisco de Arriba may have functioned as a Zapotec outpost that was established in the Tututepec region at a distance of 140 km from Monte Albán, following the attack and possible massacre at villages such as Cerro de la Cruz.[14] Based on a series of test pits and trenches he excavated at San Francisco de Arriba (1997–1999), Workinger (2002) reports a major reduction in the San Francisco Arriba's size and mound construction in the Early Terminal Formative period Miniyua phase (150 B.C.–A.D. 100), when "the importation of Valley of Oaxaca ceramics all but ends with the beginning of the Terminal Formative period, a time when the coast appears to have been cut off from the highlands perhaps due to heightened conflicts there" (Workinger 2002:230, 255, 387–388). The succeeding Late Terminal Formative period Chacahua phase (A.D. 100–250) was a time of significant construction of buildings on the platforms bordering the main plaza[15] and on the highest point of the northernmost Ridgeline 2 that marks the site's northern limit (Workinger 2002:107, 146, 232). Workinger (2002:233, 236–237, 321–322) mentions other characteristics in San Francisco de Arriba's architecture and occupation that distinguish it from contemporaneous sites in the region. Tututepec is still known as "Hill of the Birds" by the region's inhabitants, and has been identified as the place rendered on Building J's Lápida 57 by the depiction of a bird perched on a bundle of darts (DeCicco and Brockington 1956:61; Marcus 1992:176).

On the basis of these findings in regions to the north, south, and southwest of the Oaxaca Valley, we can extend the territorial limits of Monte Albán's military expansion and political domination over 100 km to the north to Quiotepec, and 140 km to the southwest to Tututepec by the Monte Albán II phase. In view of the forty other as yet unidentified places recorded on Building J, we can entertain the possibility that at its peak in the Monte Albán II phase, Monte Albán's empire may have spanned over 20,000 km^2 of foreign territory (Marcus and Flannery 1996:206).

Intravalley Conquests and Consolidation in the Monte Albán II phase (100 B.C.–A.D. 200)

Following Monte Albán's conquests of regions to the north, south, and southwest of the Oaxaca Valley and coinciding with the establishment of Zapotec military outposts and tributary centers over a vast territory, a number of developments were taking place at Monte Albán and in the Oaxaca Valley. The Main Plaza was leveled and plastered in the Monte Albán II phase (100 B.C.–A.D. 200), and numerous platforms were built on all four sides and along its centerline to support an array of public buildings (Figure 10.5). Among the diverse buildings erected on the Main Plaza were the commemorative Building J, the ballcourt, the royal palace, and many multiroom temples, which reflected the many different sociopolitical institutions of the early Zapotec state's administration (Flannery and Marcus 1976:221). Moreover, the large anthropomorphic ceramic urns of distinguished military leaders and warriors recovered in Monte Albán II phase tombs and caches may be an indicator that Monte Albán's administration boasted a full-time body of military specialists and warriors (Bernal 1965:801; Caso and Bernal 1952:116, 336; Redmond 1983:171–176).

Not only did Monte Albán preside over a four-level site-size hierarchy, but also by now it had become the administrative center for the entire Oaxaca Valley (Flannery and Marcus 1983:82; Marcus and Flannery 1996:174). Secondary administrative centers emerged in the Etla, Tlacolula, and Ocotlán-Zimatlán subregions. The Etla center of San José Mogote, which had been all-but-abandoned since the founding of Monte Albán, grew to over 60–70 ha and featured a plaza that in its size and configuration of public buildings replicated Monte Albán's Main Plaza (Marcus and Flannery 1996:178–180). The construction of temples resumed on top of Mound 1, with two-room temples like those at Monte Albán, whose features and artifacts can be associated with the burning of incense, ritual bloodletting, and other sacrifices performed by specialized priests (Marcus and Flannery 1996:185–186).

At Monte Albán, human sacrifice was evidently being practiced both inside temples and in more public settings. In the innermost room of the well-preserved two-room temple within Mound X (Figure 10.5), a stone offering box that was painted red abutted the temple's rear wall and a roughly hewn, triangular stone painted red and two ceramic basins were still embedded in the stucco floor. Fragments of an anthropomorphic ceramic urn lay on the floor. A cache (Offering 1) consisting of a carved jade figure of a human with crossed arms, seashells, and a yellow-green disk lay in the nucleus of a column. In the temple's fill lay fragments of sculptured stone bas-reliefs, one of which depicted a human skull (Acosta 1974:73–76; Caso 1935:14–15, 1965:900). These features recovered inside the temple "probably relate to the placement of offerings or incense burners, the washing of sacrificial items, or the collection of blood from sacrificed birds, dogs, infants, or prisoners" (Marcus and Flannery 1996:182). More direct evidence of human sacrifice was recovered alongside the sunken adoratory in the Main Plaza between Mounds H and P (Figure 10.5). The skeletons of five individuals, the majority young adults, rested on the sunken stone pavement east of the adoratory, bedecked with multiple jade-bead necklaces, ear ornaments in the shape of flowers, masks, and pectorals, and also with necklaces of pearls, conchs, and gastropods. One individual was outfitted with a magnificent bat mask consisting of 25 pieces of dark green jade with eyes and teeth of inlaid mother-of-pearl (Acosta 1974:76–77, 82; Caso 1965:900–902). The treatment and final disposition of these multiple individuals, who can best be interpreted as sacrificial victims, recall the Zapotec practice of sacrificing war captives to *Bezalao* and his lieutenant, *Cozichacozee*, to ensure continued success in warfare (Espíndola 1905:139 [1580]; Santamaría and Canseco 1905:34 [1579]; Zárate 1905:198 [1581]). Among the Monte Albán II ceramics recovered alongside two of these victims were fragments of some familiar painted and incised creamware bowls with hollow supports (Acosta 1974:77).

Our investigations at San Martín Tilcajete have documented the incorporation of the previously autonomous Ocotlán-Zimatlán subregion into the Monte Albán polity. Our horizontal excavations of various structures flanking the plaza of the Late Monte Albán I phase site at El Palenque revealed that this community suffered a conflagration at the time of its abandonment. The local ruler's palace, Structure 7, which stood on the highest northern terrace overlooking the plaza (Figure 10.12) was burned to the ground, as evidenced by the burned floors, carbonized roof beams resting in a corridor, and the widespread occurrence of burned adobes and daub. Ceramic vessels and grinding stones were found resting on floors, attesting to the sudden abandonment. Of the three radiocarbon dates we have obtained from these burned deposits, the latest radiocarbon date (Beta-143355) comes from charcoal in an ashy deposit associated with burned adobes and reconstructible vessels directly above the Structure 7's patio surface, which yielded a conventional radiocarbon date of 20±60 B.C. (Spencer and Redmond 2004b). At the multiroom temple atop Mound G on the east side of El Palenque's plaza, Structure 16 (Figure 10.12), a similar burned deposit on its northwestern apron (Beta-143353) produced a conventional radiocarbon date of 30±70 B.C. (Spencer and Redmond 2003). Our excavations of a residence away from the plaza to the southwest in Area P (Figure 10.12) exposed vessels and grinding stones lying by the kitchen's fire-boxes, a sign of its similarly hasty abandonment. We can state with some confidence that the attack, destruction by fire, and abrupt abandonment of El Palenque in the first century B.C., corresponding to the very early years of the Monte Albán II phase, was community-wide.

Settlement then shifted from El Palenque onto Cerro Tilcajete (SMT-23), a 300-m-tall mountain ridge that separates the Ocotlán subregion from the Central Valley proper. Our program of mapping and surface collecting Cerro Tilcajete and Christina Elson's three seasons of horizontal excavations at this hilltop center (Elson 2003) have revealed the very different community that was established here following the abandonment of El Palenque. The terraced hilltop site extended over an area of 24.5 ha and was littered with painted, incised Monte Albán II phase creamware ceramics like those we recovered at the frontier outposts at Quiotepec and that DeCicco and Brockington reported from Tututepec. Cerro Tilcajete's public sector was evidently Plaza II, a small plaza measuring 30-by-40 m with mounds on three sides that overlooked a saddle in the ridge (Figure 10.21). Elson's excavations on top of the largest mound (Mound A) on the northern side of this plaza exposed an elite residence (Structure 1). A radiocarbon sample taken from the mound fill below the foundations of Structure 1 (Beta-143356) produced a conventional radiocarbon date of A.D. 80±70 (Elson 2003:110), corresponding to the Monte Albán II phase. East of the plaza, atop Mound B, Elson exposed the foundations of a two-room temple (Structure 2). These Monte Albán II phase buildings had orientations of 22 degrees east of magnetic north, deviating from the orientation of public architecture at the previous centers of the Tilcajete polity (Elson 2003:104, 109–110, 122–123).

In the process of mapping the hilltop site, we discovered a road that climbed up the northern slope of Cerro Tilcajete from the Central Valley floor, and continued southward along the steeper western slope to reach the saddle in the ridge (Figure 10.21). After crossing the saddle, which was delimited by several

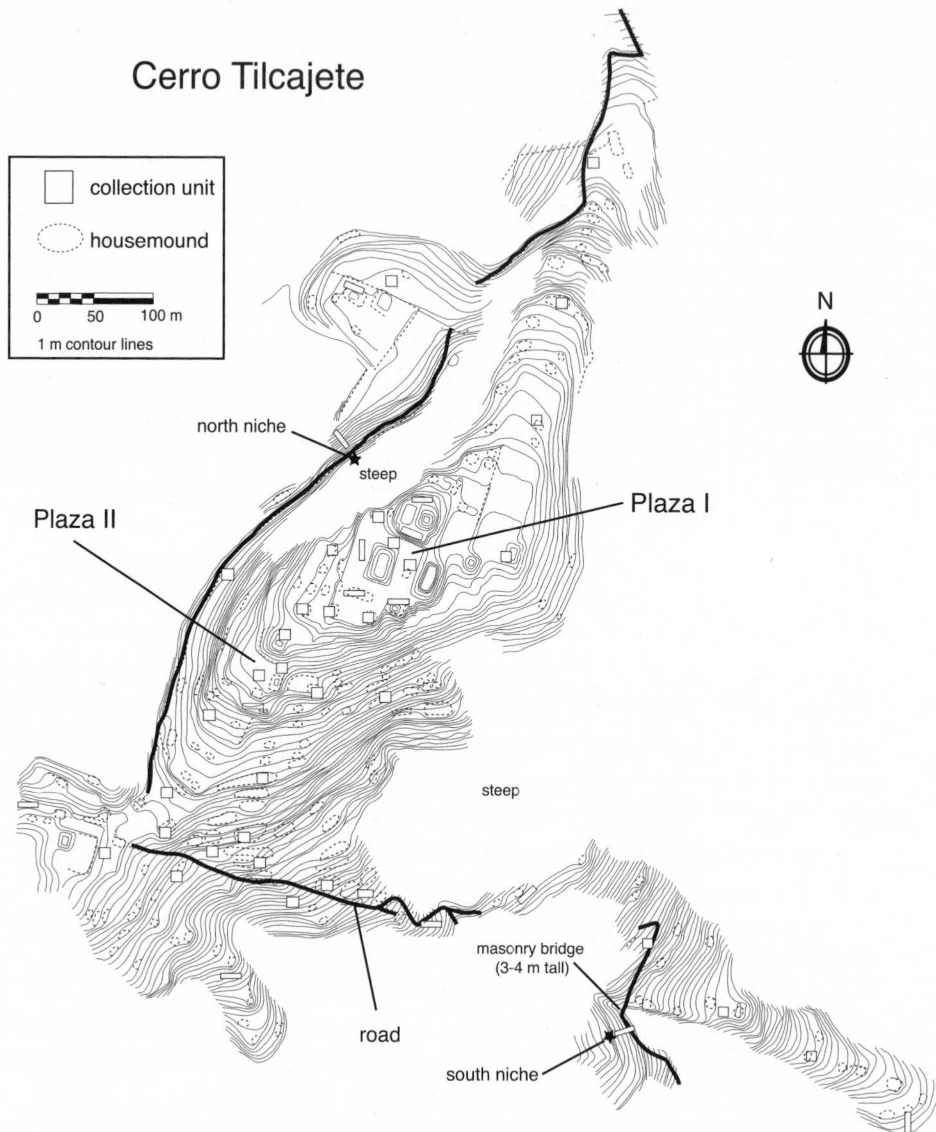

Figure 10.21. Site map of Cerro Tilcajete (SMT-23), showing the plazas, major mounds, terraces with house mounds and stone foundations, and the ancient road, and the locations of our surface collections (Elson 2003: fig. 29).

mound platforms associated with Monte Albán II phase ceramics, the road headed down the southeastward slope of the site toward the Tilcajete alluvium. The discovery of two roadside niches carved into the hillside and associated with Monte Albán II phase ceramics enabled us to link the road with the Monte Albán II phase settlement.

The settlement shift to Cerro Tilcajete, in direct line of sight of Monte Albán, and the reduction in site size and in public architecture contrast with the trajectory of settlement growth and public architecture in the Tilcajete area during the previous Early and Late Monte Albán I phases. The imposition of the road and the abundance of Monte Albán II painted and incised creamware ceramics further signaled the integration of the polity long centered at Tilcajete into the Monte Albán state in the early years of the Monte Albán II phase, some two hundred years after the conquest of the Cuicatlán Cañada and other regions outside the Oaxaca Valley.

Conclusion

Our review of Zapotec warfare began in the Rosario phase (700–500 B.C.) with the intervillage raiding between rival chiefly polities in the Etla, Tlacolula, and Ocotlán-Zimatlán branches of the Oaxaca Valley, and ended with the military subjugation by the Etla-Central Valley polity at Monte Albán of its rivals in the Oaxaca Valley early in the Monte Albán II phase (100 B.C.–A.D. 200). Two hundred years before Monte Albán achieved control over the entire Oaxaca Valley, however, its fighting forces had embarked on the conquest of regions outside the Valley, which offered little resistance and much tribute. Moreover, we have seen that Monte Albán underwent an administrative transformation and became the capital of a bureaucratic state in the Late Monte Albán I phase (300–100 B.C.). Therefore, we wish to consider first the consequences that the internecine raiding of the Rosario and Early Monte Albán I phases would have had on the polities involved, but especially for the polity that established itself at Monte Albán. Then we will outline the implications of Monte Albán's interregional campaigns of conquest in the Late Monte Albán I phase for the emergence of the early Zapotec state and for the consolidation of Monte Albán's authority over the entire Oaxaca Valley.

The Consequences of Internecine Raiding

Separated by more than 80 km^2 of no-man's-land, the chiefly polities that had emerged in the three branches of the Oaxaca Valley in the Rosario phase were nonetheless engaged in internecine raiding. These intervillage raids seem to have involved surprise attacks with the use of fire to drive the inhabitants out of their houses and destroy their temples. Captives were taken as booty, including targeted members of the chiefly elite such as "1 Earthquake," the individual depicted on Monument 3 at San José Mogote (Figure 10.3), whose angled forehead and inscribed name reflected his high status. Captives such as "1 Earthquake" were stripped naked, sacrificed at their captors' temple, and their bodies discarded, reflecting their transformed status as "non-persons" in the eyes of their captors (Peebles and Kus 1977:439; Redmond 1994:116). It is in the context of such raiding that the valley Zapotec developed writing, the earliest known carved-stone inscription in Mesoamerica being the record and display of "1 Earthquake's" sacrifice at San José Mogote (Flannery and Marcus 2003:11802–11803; Marcus 1992:36–38). Such inscribed stone monuments promoted the Etla polity's political agenda as its paramount leaders sought to maintain the allegiance of village chiefs and to mobilize raiding parties on short notice. As Marcus (1992:15–16) has outlined, writing would become a major political tool wielded by Mesoamerican rulers to record important events and to legitimize their position.

Another consequence of the endemic warfare being waged among the rival Rosario phase polities was the founding of Monte Albán in the Early Monte Albán I phase (500–300 B.C.). The establishment of this large center on the mountain that rises at the junction of the valley's three branches represented a dramatic choice of settlement location in a previously unoccupied area that was defensible but removed from sources of water and arable alluvium. While various hypotheses have been proposed for the founding of Monte Albán (Blanton 1976; Sanders and Nichols 1988), the one we favor proposes that Monte Albán was established by a confederacy led by the Etla polity centered at San José Mogote in alliance with villages in the Central Valley (Marcus and Flannery 1996:154). Monte Albán as the administrative center of a military confederacy best accounts for the abandonment of the regional center of San José Mogote at this time, and for the choice of settlement location on a defensible mountaintop that was centrally situated with respect to all three branches of the Oaxaca Valley. Risky though it was, the tactical decision to establish Monte Albán withstood the test of time and precipitated a shift in the demographic center of gravity from the Etla branch to the valley's center, surrounding the hilltop city (Marcus and Flannery 1996:144).

Monte Albán would prove to be the center where not only many internecine raids against valley-floor villages would be planned, launched, and celebrated, but also where the decision to wage conquest warfare at great distances from Monte Albán would eventually be made. We think that one reason for Monte Albán's decision to adopt this novel warfare strategy was the resistance its forces met with from the Tilcajete polity in the Ocotlán-Zimatlán subregion (and perhaps also from the Yegüih polity in the Tlacolula subregion). The Tilcajete polity managed to resist Monte Albán's attacks throughout the Early and Late Monte Albán I phases by a series of coordinated actions, which included the nucleation of population around a central plaza, a shift in settlement to a more defensible location, the construction of defensive walls, and the adoption of certain state-level institutions in the Late Monte Albán I phase (Spencer and Redmond 2003). Faced with such resistance from valley-floor polities, Monte Albán set its sights on less formidable polities in regions outside the Oaxaca Valley.

The Consequences of Monte Albán's Interregional Conquests

The decision to pursue a campaign of conquests against outlying regions at the onset of the Late Monte Albán I phase (ca. 300 B.C.) transformed the way the Monte Albán polity pursued warfare, and helped transform Monte Albán into the capital of a state. Military campaigns were waged by Monte Albán's forces against communities in strategic regions to the north, south, and southwest that, while they could be considered easy targets, were still a two-day march or more from Monte Albán. A large, well-trained, and hierarchical military organization would have been necessary to carry out these extended military campaigns and to establish hilltop outposts and garrisons, fortifications, way stations, and other wartime facilities (Redmond 1983:171–176). Moreover, once the valley Zapotec forces conquered and pacified such outlying regions, they would have been subsumed as tributary provinces under Monte Albán's territorial control. In the Cuicatlán Cañada, Zapotec military control was concentrated at the region's northern boundary at Quiotepec to defend the territory controlled by Monte Albán and to regulate the flow of traffic in and out of this frontier region. Communities in the Cañada's central and southern alluvial fans were probably administered by Zapotec overlords and charged with supplying food and manpower to the frontier and producing large quantities of tropical fruits and palm nuts as tribute. The administration of as many as 50 conquered places would have placed considerable demands on Monte Albán's administration in order to maintain hegemony over them and enforce the collection of tribute from them.

It is in the context of Monte Albán's decision to pursue the territorial conquest of outlying regions that the early Zapotec state emerged. In contrast to pre-state polities, state administrations are both centralized and internally specialized; states are capable of integrating much larger territories because they can delegate authority to specialized administrators who are dispatched to locations far from the state capital to carry out specialized components of the state's central administration, with minimal risk of insurrection (Spencer 1982:7–10; Wright 1977:383). One of us (Spencer 1998) has proposed a mathematical model to account for the limits on territory size that can be effectively administered by pre-state polities that lack internally specialized administrations, and has demonstrated how a successful attempt to increase territory size through military expansion will require that the polity pursuing such a strategy develop both the capacity to delegate partial authority as well as an internally specialized administration. In view of the potential political and economic benefits to be gained through the successful pursuit of territorial conquest, the model would expect the emergence of the state to be accompanied by military expansionism and considerable enlargement of the emerging state's territory through the development of delegated decision-making to specialized administrators in outlying regions and state outposts (Spencer 1998:14–17). Accordingly, we propose that Monte Albán's pursuit of conquest warfare outside the Oaxaca Valley would have demanded the adoption of an internally specialized administration and the delegation of partial authority to specialized military leaders, *copayóhopije*, manning frontier outposts and Zapotec administrators, *Hueni chiña*, overseeing the newly subjugated regions (Córdova 1942:10, 20 [1578]). At the same time, the successful conquest of outlying regions and the exaction of tribute brought additional resources into Monte Albán's coffers that would help to fund this administrative transformation and more (Webster 1975:468–469).

Accompanying Monte Albán's imperial expansion and incorporation of foreign regions during the Late Monte Albán I phase was Monte Albán's unrivaled growth in population, military organization, and resources. Monte Albán drew upon these resources and manpower early in the Monte Albán II phase to consolidate its authority over the Ocotlán-Zimatlán and Tlacolula polities in the Oaxaca Valley, which had been resisting Monte Albán's previous expansionist designs against them. The center of the Tilcajete polity was subdued militarily by the early years of the Monte Albán II phase and a secondary center was strategically established on the mountain ridge between the Central Valley and the Ocotlán sub-valley, traversed by a road that linked these two subregions of the Monte Albán state (Figure 10.21). Other secondary centers were established in the Tlacolula and Etla-Central subregions with abundant architectural and ceramic affiliations attesting to their successful integration into the valley-wide Monte Albán state. Not surprisingly, Spencer's analysis of covariance of the productive potential and archaeological population estimated for the Oaxaca Valley's three subregions, revealed a consequent drop in intersubregional competition following the region's political unification (Spencer and Redmond 2001a:223–224). Reynolds's decision-tree for the location of Monte Albán II phase sites in the Etla subregion also reflected this reduction in conflict (Reynolds 1999:20).

We can conclude from our examination of Zapotec warfare strategies that Mesoamerica's earliest writing in stone and first hilltop city probably resulted directly from conditions of intensified raiding among rival polities in the Oaxaca Valley during the Rosario and Early Monte Albán I phases. This internecine raiding only escalated with the founding and subsequent growth of the Monte

Albán polity. Monte Albán's decision to pursue a campaign of conquests against outlying regions launched a new form of expansionist warfare at a distance, involving the territorial incorporation of other polities. This conquest strategy initiated the process of primary state formation, and transformed Monte Albán into the capital of one of Mesoamerica's first state polities—and perhaps the earliest (Spencer and Redmond 2004a).

We think the Zapotec case can help to refine existing models of the role played by warfare and territorial expansion in the emergence of the primary state. While imperial expansion has long been considered a key force in the subsequent growth of early states, the Zapotec case underscores the central causal role of military expansion very early in the process of state formation. Zapotec forces at Monte Albán embarked on a campaign of military conquests at the onset of the Monte Albán Late I phase (ca. 300 B.C.), the phase in which the evidence of Zapotec state institutions first appears. Moreover, there are three related aspects of Monte Albán's campaigns of military conquest that should be highlighted, beginning with the early timing and the unexpected nature of military expansion, whereby regions outside the Oaxaca Valley were conquered several hundred years before Monte Albán dominated the entire valley. The asymmetric, noncontiguous expansion of the Monte Albán polity may appear to run counter to expected notions of complex societies expanding from the political core out toward an ever farther periphery. Yet the Zapotec case illustrates the tactical decision by Monte Albán's rulers to target smaller polities in outlying regions and seize their territory, labor, and resources, before waging conquest warfare against rival neighboring polities in the valley. Related to the decision to pursue a campaign of military conquests at a distance was the concomitant development of an internally specialized administration at Monte Albán, one having the capacity to delegate authority to military commanders and frontier administrators stationed at considerable distances from the capital. The process of primary state formation we have examined certainly draws attention to the creative forces unleashed by warfare, especially warfare waged at a distance.

Acknowledgments

Our ongoing investigations at San Martín Tilcajete have received the financial support of the following institutions: the National Science Foundation (SBR-9303129), the Foundation for the Advancement of Mesoamerican Studies, Inc., the Heinz Family Foundation (Latin American Archaeology Program), the National Geographic Society (Committee for Research and Exploration), the University of Michigan Museum of Anthropology, and the American Museum of Natural History. Mari Carmen Serra Puche and Joaquín García-Bárcena served in turn as president of the Consejo de Arqueología that granted permission for the Tilcajete fieldwork, and we thank Eduardo Lópex Calzada, director of the Centro INAH, Nelly Robles, Marcus Winter, and Raúl Matadamas of the Centro INAH Oaxaca for their help and support. We thank Joyce Marcus for her insightful comments on an earlier draft of this chapter, and Christina Elson for preparing Figures 10.3, 10.5–10.7, 10.9, 10.12, and 10.21.

Notes

1. Ximénez Ortiz's remark that the town of Iztepexi fought with neighboring towns without any cause or reason, more than anything for exercise, is an example of the Spaniards' preconceptions regarding indigenous warfare.

2. One Zapotec unit of measurement was the length of one's lower arm, from the wrist to the elbow (Marcus and Flannery 1996:21).

3. This campaign against the Aztec was masterminded by the Zapotec, who were recognized as "devious, master diplomats, skilled at dissimulation" (Flannery 1983c:319; Gay 1990:96–100 [1881]).

4. Feinman and Nicholas's intensive survey of the Mitla Fortress in 1998 revealed the hilltop's 52.9 ha of occupation in the Postclassic period, and determined that the site's principal public buildings (nos. 70 and 71) and 5-m-tall stone defensive walls were built in the Postclassic period. The majority of the projectile points recovered lay downslope of the defensive walls (Feinman and Nicholas 2004:47–48, 124).

5. Gutiérrez (1905:314 [1609]) recorded Amatlán's name in Zapotec as *Quiatila,* which we have noted is the word for battle or war (Córdova 1942:53 [1578]), and its Spanish translation as "tierra de peleas o disensión."

6. Corroborating the practice of dismembering, cooking, and eating the bodies of sacrificed victims reported in the sixteenth-century *Relaciones* is a recently reported Rosario-phase roasting pit (Feature 47) excavated at San José Mogote. Feature 47 measured 1.31 m in diameter and its fill of rocks and ash contained roasted human bones, including part of a cranium. Directly associated with a conventional radiocarbon date of 690±40 B.C., this large outdoor roasting pit on the outskirts of San José Mogote was likely intended for the public feast celebrated by the victorious war party (Flannery and Marcus 2005:60, 228).

7. A fallen, carbonized roof beam from St. 28's destroyed temple has yielded a conventional radiocarbon date of 600±60 B.C. (Flannery and Marcus 2003:11802).

8. Certain New World Indians refer to war by this very action verb (Redmond 1998:68).

9. Panamanian chiefdoms marked the new status of the captives they seized in war by branding their faces with tattoos and knocking out one of their incisors (Redmond 1994:47, 102).

10. Two of these modeled ceramic renderings of naked, sprawling humans seem to be female (Caso 1947:lám. V; Caso et al. 1967:fig. 89), which raises the possibility that the Zapotec seized female captives as well.

11. The distinctive headdresses, face-painting styles, and other insignia "may have been characteristic of a particular town, region, or ethnic group" (Marcus 1992:397).

12. Another fragment of a hollow ceramic jaguar paw was recovered in a surface collection placed in the plaza area of the Lomas phase hilltop site of Cuba Libra in the central Cañada (Redmond 1983:130, Plate 34).

13. DeCicco and Brockington (1956:55) noted an element of San Francisco Arriba's ceramic assemblage that did not occur elsewhere in their survey area: "Hay sin embargo, una importante variante y es que la cerámica crema de San Francisco Arriba no aparece en las otras localidades. Esta cerámica crema encaja perfectamente en la clasificación de Monte Albán." The fact that John Paddock, a noted authority of Oaxaca ceramics, assisted them in their ceramic classification of this assemblage lends even more weight to this assertion (DeCicco and Brockington 1956:59).

14. Raul Matadamas's recent work at the contemporaneous site of Bocana La Copalita near Huatulco has contributed another example of a mass interment lacking funerary offerings, which may represent the victims of another attack on a coastal village (Matadamas 1998:179, 207). The possibility that this stretch of coast became tributary to the valley Zapotec in the Late Monte Albán I-II phases is supported by the presence of graphite-and-red painted pottery from this coastal area at Monte Albán (Joyce 1993:73–74).

15. The Early Terminal Formative (150 B.C.–A.D. 100) *crema* sherd that was determined by means of neutron activation analysis to have been imported from the Oaxaca Valley was recovered in the Monte Albán II phase or Late Terminal Formative Chacahua phase (A.D. 100–250) fill of Operation F, lot 1, level 5 excavated in Platform 1 on the north side of the main plaza at San Francisco de Arriba (Workinger 2002:185, 355; Workinger, personal communication 2004).

References

Acosta, J. R. 1965. Preclassic and Classic Architecture of Oaxaca. In *Archaeology of Southern Mesoamerica, Part Two. Handbook of Middle American Indians Vol. 3*, edited by G. R. Willey, 814–836. Austin: University of Texas Press.

———. 1974. XIV Temporada de Exploraciones en la Zona Arqueológica de Monte Albán 1945–1946. *Cultura y Sociedad* año I, t.I(2):69–82.

Algaze, G. 1993. Expansionary Dynamics of Some Early Pristine States. *American Anthropologist* 95:304–333.

Asensio, G. 1905. Relación de Macuilsúchil y su Partido (1580). In *Papeles de Nueva España: Segunda Serie, Geografía y Estadística*. Tomo IV, edited by F. del Paso y Troncoso, 100–108. Madrid: Est. Tipográfico "Sucesores de Rivadeneyra."

Aveni, A. F., and R. E. Linsley. 1972. Mound J, Monte Albán: Possible Astronomical Orientation. *American Antiquity* 37(4):528–531.

Balkansky, A. K. 1998. Origin and Collapse of Complex Societies in Oaxaca (Mexico): Evaluating the Era from 1965 to the Present. *Journal of World Prehistory* 12(4):451–493.

———. 2001. On Emerging Patterns in Oaxaca Archaeology. *Current Anthropology* 42(4):559–561.

———. 2002. *The Sola Valley and the Monte Albán State: A Study of Zapotec Imperial Expansion*. Ann Arbor: University of Michigan Museum of Anthropology, Memoir 36.

Bernal, I. 1965. Archaeological Synthesis of Oaxaca. In *Archaeology of Southern Mesoamerica, Part Two. Handbook of Middle American Indians Vol. 3*, edited by G. R. Willey, 788–813. Austin: University of Texas Press.

Blanton, R. E. 1976. The Origins of Monte Albán. In *Cultural Change and Continuity: Essays in Honor of James Bennett Griffin*, edited by C. Cleland, 223–232. New York: Academic Press.

———. 1978. *Monte Albán: Settlement Patterns at the Ancient Zapotec Capital*. New York: Academic Press.

Blanton, R. E., G. M. Feinman, S. A. Kowalewski, and L. M. Nicholas. 1999. *Ancient Oaxaca*. Cambridge: Cambridge University Press.

Blanton, R. E., S. A. Kowalewski, G. M. Feinman, and L. Finsten (editors). 1993. *Ancient Mesoamerica: A Comparison of Change in Three Regions*. Cambridge: Cambridge University Press.

Brockington, D. L. 1973. *Archaeological Investigations at Miahuatlán, Oaxaca*. Nashville: Vanderbilt University Publications in Anthropology 7.

Burgoa, Fray F. de. 1934a. *Geográfica Descripción* (1674).Tomo I. Publicaciones del Archivo General de la Nación 25. México, D.F.: Talleres Gráficos de la Nación.

———. 1934b. *Geográfica Descripción (1674)*.Tomo II. Publicaciones del Archivo General de la Nación 26. México, D.F.: Talleres Gráficos de la Nación.

Canseco, A. de. 1905. Relación de Tlacolula y Mitla (1580). In *Papeles de Nueva España: Segunda Serie, Geografía y Estadística*. Tomo IV, edited by F. del Paso y Troncoso, 144–154. Madrid: Est. Tipográfico "Sucesores de Rivadeneyra."

Carneiro, R. L. 1970. A Theory of the Origin of the State. *Science* 169:733–738.

Caso, A. 1935. *Las Exploraciones en Monte Albán: Temporada 1934–1935*. Instituto Panamericano de Geografía e Historia, Publicación 18. México.

———. 1938. *Exploraciones en Oaxaca. Quinta y Sexta Temporadas 1936–1937*. Instituto Panamericano de Geografía e Historia, Publicación 34. México.

———. 1947. Calendario y Escritura de las Antiguas Culturas de Monte Albán. In *Obras Completas de Miguel Othón de Mendizábal*, vol. 1. México.

———. 1965. Lapidary Work, Goldwork, and Copperwork from Oaxaca. In *Archaeology of Southern Mesoamerica, Part Two. Handbook of Middle American Indians Vol. 3*, edited by G. R. Willey, 896–930. Austin: University of Texas Press.

Caso, A., and I. Bernal. 1952. *Urnas de Oaxaca*. Memorias del Instituto Nacional de Antropología e Historia 2. México.

Caso, A., I. Bernal, and J. R. Acosta. 1967. *La Cerámica de Monte Albán*. Memorias del Instituto Nacional de Antropología e Historia 13. México.

Coe, M. D. 1962. *Mexico*. New York: Praeger.

Córdova, Fray J. de. 1942. *Vocabulario en Lengua Zapoteca* (1578). México: Pedro Charte y Antonio Ricardo. Reprinted in Biblioteca Lingüística Mexicana I. México, D.F.: Secretaría de Educación Pública.

DeCicco, G., and D. Brockington. 1956. Reconocimiento Arqueológico en el Suroeste de Oaxaca. Dirección de Monumentos Pre-Hispánicos. *Informes* 6. Instituto Nacional de Antropología e Historia. México.

Drennan, R. D. 1976. *Fábrica San José and Middle Formative Society in the Valley of Oaxaca*. Ann Arbor: University of Michigan Museum of Anthropology, Memoir 8.

Elam, J. M. 1989. Defensible and Fortified Sites. In *Monte Albán's Hinterland, Part II: Prehispanic Settlement Patterns in Tlacolula, Etla, and Ocotlán, the Valley of Oaxaca, Mexico*, by S. A. Kowalewski, G. M. Feinman, L. Finsten, R. E. Blanton, and L. M. Nicholas, 385–407. Ann Arbor: University of Michigan Museum of Anthropology, Memoir 23.

Elson, C. M. 2003. Elites at Cerro Tilcajete: A Secondary Center in the Valley of Oaxaca, Mexico. Unpublished Ph.D. dissertation, Department of Anthropology, University of Michigan, Ann Arbor.

Espíndola, N. de. 1905. Relación de Chichicapa y su Partido (1580). In *Papeles de Nueva España: Segunda Serie, Geografía y Estadística*. Tomo IV, edited by F. del Paso y Troncoso, 115–143. Madrid: Est. Tipográfico "Sucesores de Rivadeneyra."

Fahmel Beyer, B. 1991. *La Arquitectura de Monte Albán*. México, D.F.: Universidad Nacional Autónoma de México.

Feinman, G. M. 1982. Patterns of Ceramic Production and Distribution, Periods Early I through V. In *Monte Albán's Hinterland, Part I: The Prehispanic Settlement Patterns of the Central and Southern Parts of the Valley of Oaxaca, Mexico*, by R. E. Blanton, S. A. Kowalewski, G. M. Feinman, and J. Appel, 181–206. Ann Arbor: University of Michigan Museum of Anthropology, Memoir 15.

———. 1998. Scale and Social Organization: Perspectives on the Ancient State. In *Archaic States*, edited by G. M. Feinman and J. Marcus, 95–133. Santa Fe: School of American Research Press.

Feinman, G. M., and L. M. Nicholas. 1990. At the Margins of the Monte Albán State: Settlement Patterns in the Ejutla Valley, Oaxaca, Mexico. *Latin American Antiquity* 1(3):216–246.

———. 1993. Shell-ornament Production in Ejutla: Implications for Highland-Coastal Interaction in Ancient Oaxaca. *Ancient Mesoamerica* 4(1):103–119.

———. 2004. *Hilltop Terrace Sites of Oaxaca, Mexico: Intensive Surface Survey at Guirún, El Palmillo, and the Mitla Fortress*. Fieldiana: Anthropology n.s., no. 37. Chicago: Field Museum of Natural History.

Flannery, K. V. 1983a. The Legacy of the Early Urban Period: An Ethnohistoric Approach to Monte Albán's Temples, Residences, and Royal Tombs. In *The Cloud People: Divergent Evolution of the Zapotec and Mixtec Civilizations*, edited by K. V. Flannery and J. Marcus, 132–136. New York: Academic Press.

———. 1983b. The Development of Monte Albán's Main Plaza in Period II. In *The Cloud People: Divergent Evolution of the Zapotec and Mixtec Civilizations*, edited by K. V. Flannery and J. Marcus, 102–104. New York: Academic Press.

———. 1983c. Zapotec Warfare: Archaeological Evidence for the Battles of Huitzo and Guiengola. In *The Cloud People: Divergent Evolution of the Zapotec and Mixtec Civilizations*, edited by K. V. Flannery and J. Marcus, 318–319. New York: Academic Press.

———. 1986. *Guilá Naquitz: Archaic Foraging and Early Agriculture in Oaxaca, México*. Orlando: Academic Press.

Flannery, K. V., and J. Marcus. 1976. Evolution of the Public Building in Formative Oaxaca. In *Cultural Change and Continuity: Essays in Honor of James Bennett Griffin*, edited by C. Cleland, 205–221. New York: Academic Press.

———. 1983. The Origins of the State in Oaxaca: Editors' Introduction. In *The Cloud People: Divergent Evolution of the Zapotec and Mixtec Civilizations*, edited by K. V. Flannery and J. Marcus, 79–83. New York: Academic Press.

———. 2003. The Origin of War: New ^{14}C Dates from Ancient Mexico. *Proceedings of The National Academy of Sciences* 100(20):11801–11805.

———. 2005. *Excavations at San José Mogote 1: The Household Archaeology*. University of Michigan Museum of Anthropology, Memoir 40. Ann Arbor.

Gay, J. A. 1990. *Historia de Oaxaca* (1881). México: Editorial Porrúa, S.A.

Gómez de Orozco, F. (editor). 1928. Relación de los Pueblos de Tecuicuilco, Atepeq, Zoquiapa, Xaltianguez by Francisco de Villegas (1580). *Revista Mexicana de Estudios Históricos*. Tomo Segundo:121–132.

Gutiérrez, E. 1905. Descripción del Partido de Miahuatlán (1609). In *Papeles de Nueva España: Segunda Serie, Geografía y Estadística*. Tomo IV, edited by F. del Paso y Troncoso, 289–319. Madrid: Est. Tipográfico "Sucesores de Rivadeneyra."

Joyce, A. A. 1991. Formative Period Social Change in the Lower Río Verde Valley, Oaxaca, Mexico. *Latin American Antiquity* 2(2):126–150.

———. 1993. Interregional Interaction and Social Development on the Oaxaca Coast. *Ancient Mesoamerica* 4(1):67–84.

Joyce, A. A., M. Winter, and R. G. Mueller. 1998. *Arqueología de la Costa de Oaxaca: Asentamientos del Período Formativo en el Valle del Río Verde Inferior*. Estudios de Antropología e Historia 40. Centro INAH Oaxaca, México.

Kowalewski, S. A., G. M. Feinman, L. Finsten, R. E. Blanton, and L. M. Nicholas. 1989. *Monte Albán's Hinterland, Part II: Prehispanic Settlement Patterns in Tlacolula, Etla, and Ocotlán, the Valley of Oaxaca, Mexico*. University of Michigan Museum of Anthropology, Memoir 23. Ann Arbor.

Kowalewski, S. A., C. Spencer, and E. Redmond. 1978. Appendix II: Description of Ceramic Categories. In *Monte Albán: Settlement Patterns at the Ancient Zapotec Capital*, by R. E. Blanton, 167–193. New York: Academic Press.

Lattimore, O. 1962. *Studies in Frontier History 1928–1958*. London: Oxford University Press.

Marcus, J. 1974. The Iconography of Power Among the Classic Maya. *World Archaeology* 6(1):83–94.

———. 1976. The Iconography of Militarism at Monte Albán and Neighboring Sites in the Valley of Oaxaca. In *The Origins of Religious Art and Iconography in Preclassic Mesoamerica*, edited by H. B. Nicholson, 123–139. Los Angeles: University of California at Los Angeles, Latin American Center.

———. 1980. Zapotec Writing. *Scientific American* 242:50–64.

———. 1983a. Aztec Military Campaigns Against the Zapotecs: The Documentary Evidence. In *The Cloud People: Divergent Evolution of the Zapotec and Mixtec Civilizations*, edited by K. V. Flannery and J. Marcus, 314–318. New York: Academic Press.

———. 1983b. Zapotec Writing and Calendrics. In *The Cloud People: Divergent Evolution of the Zapotec and Mixtec Civilizations*, edited by K. V. Flannery and J. Marcus, 91–96. New York: Academic Press.

———. 1991. First Dates. *Natural History* 4:26–29.

———. 1992. *Mesoamerican Writing Systems: Propaganda, Myth, and History in Four Ancient Civilizations*. Princeton: Princeton University Press.

———. 1998. *Women's Ritual in Formative Oaxaca: Figurine-making, Divination, Death and the Ancestors*. University of Michigan Museum of Anthropology, Memoir 33. Ann Arbor.

Marcus, J., and K. V. Flannery. 1996. *Zapotec Civilization: How Urban Society Evolved in Mexico's Oaxaca Valley*. London: Thames and Hudson.

Markman, C. W. 1981. *Prehispanic Settlement Dynamics in Central Oaxaca, Mexico: A View from the Miahuatlán Valley*. Vanderbilt University Publications in Anthropology 26. Nashville.

Mata, Fray J. de. 1905. Relación de Teozapotlan (1580). In *Papeles de Nueva España: Segunda Serie, Geografía y Estadística*. Tomo IV, edited by F. del Paso y Troncoso, 190–195. Madrid: Est. Tipográfico "Sucesores de Rivadeneyra."

Matadamas Díaz, R. 1998. Informe Técnico del Proyecto Arqueológico Bocana del Río Copalita, Huatulco, Oaxaca. Primera Fase de la Primera Temporada, de Enero a Abril de 1998. Centro INAH Oaxaca, Mexico.

Morris, C. 1972. State Settlements in Tawantisuyu: A Strategy of Compulsory Urbanism. In *Contemporary Archaeology*, edited by M. P. Leone, 393–401. Carbondale: Southern Illinois University Press.

Pareyón, E. 1960. Exploraciones Arqueológicas en la Ciudad Vieja de Quiotepec, Oaxaca. *Revista Mexicana de Estudios Antropológicos* 16:97–104.

Paso y Troncoso, F. del, (editor). 1905. Relaciones Geográficas de la Diócesis de Oaxaca. *Papeles de Nueva España: Segunda Serie, Geográfia y Estadística*. Tomo IV. Madrid: Est. Tipográfico "Sucesores de Rivadeneyra."

Peebles, C. S., and S. M. Kus. 1977. Some Archaeological Correlates of Ranked Societies. *American Antiquity* 42(3):421–448.

Redmond, E. M. 1983. *A Fuego y Sangre: Early Zapotec Imperialism in the Cuicatlán Cañada, Oaxaca*. University of Michigan Museum of Anthropology, Memoir 16. Ann Arbor.

———. 1994. *Tribal and Chiefly Warfare in South America*. University of Michigan Museum of Anthropology, Memoir 28. Ann Arbor.

———. 1998. In War and Peace: Alternative Paths to Centralized Leadership. In *Chiefdoms and Chieftaincy in the Americas*, edited by E. M. Redmond, 68–103. Gainesville: University Press of Florida.

Redmond, E. M., and G. Harbottle. 1983. Appendix I. Neutron-Activation Analysis of Ceramics from the Valley of Oaxaca and the Cuicatlán Cañada. In *A Fuego y Sangre: Early Zapotec Imperialism in the Cuicatlán Cañada, Oaxaca*, by E. M. Redmond, 185–205. University of Michigan Museum of Anthropology, Memoir 16. Ann Arbor.

Reynolds, R. G. 1999. The Impact of Raiding on Settlement Patterns in the Northern Valley of Oaxaca: An Approach Using Decision Trees. In *Dynamics in Human and Primate Societies*, edited by T. Kohler and G. J. Gumerman, 1–23. New York: Oxford University Press.

Sanders, W. T., and D. L. Nichols. 1988. Ecological Theory and Cultural Evolution in the Valley of Oaxaca. *Current Anthropology* 29 (1):33–80.

Santamaría, B. de, and J. de Canseco. 1905. Relación de Nexapa (1580). In *Papeles de Nueva España: Segunda Serie, Geográfia y Estadística*. Tomo IV, edited by F. del Paso y Troncoso, 29–44. Madrid: Est. Tipográfico "Sucesores de Rivadeneyra."

Scott, J. F. 1978a. *The Danzantes of Monte Albán, Part I: Text*. Studies in Pre-Columbian Art and Archaeology 19. Washington, D.C.: Dumbarton Oaks.

———. 1978b. *The Danzantes of Monte Albán, Part II: Catalogue*. Studies in Pre-Columbian Art and Archaeology 19. Washington, D.C.: Dumbarton Oaks.

Service, E. R. 1975. *Origins of the State and Civilization: The Process of Cultural Evolution*. New York: W. W. Norton and Co.

Spencer, C. S. 1982. *The Cuicatlán Cañada and Monte Albán: A Study of Primary State Formation*. New York: Academic Press.

———. 1998. A Mathematical Model of Primary State Formation. *Cultural Dynamics* 10(1):5–20.

Spencer, C. S., and E. M. Redmond. 1997. *Archaeology of the Cañada de Cuicatlán, Oaxaca*. American Museum of Natural History, Anthropological Papers, No. 80. New York.

———. 2000. Lightning and Jaguars: Iconography, Ideology, and Politics in Formative Cuicatlán, Oaxaca. In *Cultural Evolution: Contemporary Viewpoints*, edited by G. M. Feinman and L. Manzanilla, 145–175. New York: Kluwer Academic/Plenum Publishers.

———. 2001a. Multilevel Selection and Political Evolution in the Valley of Oaxaca, 500–100 B.C. *Journal of Anthropological Archaeology* 20: 195–229.

———. 2001b. The Chronology of Conquest: Implications of New Radiocarbon Analyses from the Cañada de Cuicatlán, Oaxaca. *Latin American Antiquity* 12(2):182–202.

———. 2003. Militarism, Resistance, and Early State Development in Oaxaca, Mexico. *Social Evolution and History* 1(2):26–72.

———. 2004a. Primary State Formation in Mesoamerica. *Annual Review of Anthropology* 33:173–199.

———. 2004b. A Late Monte Albán I Phase (300–100 B.C.) Palace in the Valley of Oaxaca. *Latin American Antiquity* 15(4):441–455.

Villegas, F. de. 1928. Relación de los Pueblos de Tecuicuilco, Atepeq, Coquiapa y Xaltianguez (1580). In *Revista Mexicana de Estudios Históricos*, Tomo Segundo:121–132. Editorial Cultura. México.

Webster, D. 1975. Warfare and the Evolution of the State: A Reconsideration. *American Antiquity* 40(4):464–470.

Whitecotton, J. W. 1977. *The Zapotecs: Princes, Priests, and Peasants*. Norman: University of Oklahoma Press.

Whitecotton, J. W., and J. B. Whitecotton. 1993. *Vocabulario Zapoteco-Castellano*. Vanderbilt University Publications in Anthropology No. 45. Nashville.

Wilkinson, R. G. 1997. Appendix B. Human Skeletal Remains from La Coyotera. In *Archaeology of the Cañada de Cuicatlán, Oaxaca*, by C. S. Spencer and E. M. Redmond, 614–620. American Museum of Natural History, Anthropological Papers, No. 80. New York.

Winter, M. 2002. Monte Albán: Mortuary Practices as Domestic Ritual and Their Relation to Community Religion. In *Domestic Ritual in Ancient Mesoamerica*, edited by P. P. Plunket, 67–82. The Cotsen Institute of Archaeology Monograph 46. University of California, Los Angeles.

Winter, M., C. L. Martínez L., W. O. Autry Jr., R. G. Wilkinson, and P. A. Juárez. 1995. *Entierros Humanos de Monte Albán: Dos Estudios. Proyecto Especial Monte Albán 1992–1994* Contribución No. 7. Centro INAH Oaxaca.

Workinger, A. G. 2002. Coastal/Highland Interaction in Prehispanic Oaxaca, Mexico: The Perspective from San Francisco de Arriba. Unpublished Ph.D. dissertation, Department of Anthropology, Vanderbilt University, Nashville, Tennessee.

Wright, H. T. 1977. Recent Research on the Origin of the State. *Annual Review of Anthropology* 6:379–397.

———. 1986. The Evolution of Civilizations. In *American Archaeology Past and Future: A Celebration of the Society for American Archaeology 1935–1985*, edited by D. J. Meltzer, D. D. Fowler, and J. A. Sabloff, 323–365. Washington, D.C.: Smithsonian Institution Press.

Ximénez Ortiz, J. 1905. Relación de Iztepexi (1579). In *Papeles de Nueva España: Segunda Serie, Geográfia y Estadística*. Tomo IV, edited by F. del Paso y Troncoso, 9–23. Madrid: Est. Tipográfico "Sucesores de Rivadeneyra."

Zárate, B. de. 1905. Relación de Guaxilotitlán (1581). In *Papeles de Nueva España: Segunda Serie, Geográfia y Estadística*. Tomo IV, edited by F. del Paso y Troncoso, 196–205. Madrid: Est. Tipográfico "Sucesores de Rivadeneyra."

11

From Laos to Mesoamerica

Battlegrounds between Superpowers

SAMUEL V. CONNELL AND JAY E. SILVERSTEIN

We are Mesoamerican archaeologists working in the central highlands of Laos. Per hectare, this border area is the most heavily bombed country ever. Our daily commute, via helicopter, takes us to sites of downed aircraft and forgotten skirmishes along the Ho Chi Minh trail. While the vistas are stunning, the sheer quantity of bomb craters covering the countryside is mind-boggling. It seems incongruous to be sitting in a tent in the Salavan Province of Laos drafting a paper on Pre-Columbian warfare, yet the basic political forces that have brought us here in search of missing U.S. military personnel as part of the Central Identification Lab's mission to recover and identify soldiers and pilots lost during U.S. wars have operated and continue to operate in all complex societies. States exist in opposition to other states and interstate competition is a hallmark of social complexity from archaic states to modern civilization. The hill country of Laos was transformed into an international battleground in the 1960s because the United States perceived a threat to its strategic interests, as did China and the Soviet Union. Although Southeast Asia became a battlefield for world superiority, the superpowers did not hold exclusive military authority in this region. Instead, local power struggles and even tribal and ethnic affinities or enmities played out with various factions struggling to broker regional political power through alliances with superpowers.

Dissecting this macabre dance of great states and lesser polities reveals one of the great paradoxes of archaeology. War is one of the most conspicuous of behaviors, involving great tragedy, political drama, significant administrative and organizational direction, and requiring the focused application of economic and human resources yet, in the archaeological record, warfare remains elusive (see Kolb and Dixon 2002; Vencl 1984; Webster 2000). Archaeologists working in the Maya area have, with the exception of a few fortification studies (Webster 1976; Wolley Schwarz 1993), destruction events (Friedel 1999), and the rare embattled city (Demarest et al. 1997), relied on ethnohistory in the analysis of war. What we know of Maya warfare comes largely from history carved upon stelae and lintels. Our best evidence for Central Mexican warfare comes almost exclusively from Colonial period documents and prehispanic codices (for example, Hassig 1988; see Silverstein 2000). Some exceptional archaeological studies have used extensive settlement data, destruction events, rapid abandonment, monument construction, and fortification construction as indirect evidence of warfare or militarism (Plunket and Uruñuela 1994; Sanders et al. 1979:146–149; Redmond and Spencer, this volume); however, despite endemic militarism we still have only a few examples with direct archaeological evidence of warfare in Mesoamerica.

Numerous reasons have been given to explain this paradox. Many warfare events are of short duration, making only limited impact in the archaeological record (Vencl 1984), and battlefields, generally unmarked and far from the normal loci of archaeological investigations, remain unexplored. However, the *raison d'être* for the warfare paradox fails to adequately explain the paucity of war-related data once the ubiquity of militarism is acknowledged (Webster 1993). Evidence of war extends beyond battlefields into realms where more enduring political, economic, and strategic behaviors are visible in the archaeological record, if read within the appropriate theoretical construct. We suggest that the study of war in complex societies requires the use of models of interstate competition based on the relations of not only the largest and most complex super-states, but of all of the players on the political landscape—those caught in between. If we were to study the Vietnam War archaeologically, would we excavate in Washington, D.C., or Honolulu? What conclusions would we draw from the monuments available to us? Would a scar of black marble set into the Mall in Washington, D.C., ever help us understand the magnitude of the conflict that so marred the Laotian countryside or that deposited enough American material resources in foreign lands that it created an entire scrap industry?

If war is to be approached archaeologically, it must include a view from the peripheries, the places that lie between the superpowers. In the case of Southeast Asia, correlating data collected from these client-state-contested political zones with the core-generated history, we could more fully interpret the dynamics of a war that lasted more than a decade and involved millions of people. Laos is a peripheral area scarred for centuries by wars between Khmers, Siamese, and Chinese, and most recently by war ostensibly waged between modern superstates. The great Mesoamerican superpowers had their Laos' and Vietnam's as well, places caught between long-term hostilities. In this chapter we examine two Pre-Columbian examples. Our first example comes from an area in contemporary western Belize, one of many frontiers during the struggle between the two paramount Maya cities of Tikal and Calakmul. The second case comes from Northern Guerrero, Mexico, where smaller city-states were caught between the Aztec and Tarascan empires.

Research presented here illustrates the need to draw data from the peoples who are generally given little notice in a science that, in spite of various calls for an increasing emphasis on hinterlands and boundaries, consistently uses political core-biased perspectives. During the American war, as the Vietnamese refer to it, rarely do we consider the role of the Montagnarde or Hmong people, or the numerous other factions who had so much at stake. Often archaeologists focus on the act of warfare as presented in the history of core polities without studying the context of warfare as it was played out on the frontiers. In order to refine studies of warfare in Mesoamerica, we feel that there is a need to define a theoretical construct for warfare as a part of the complex web of interactions that take place between states. Toward this end, we use ideas coming from political geography, which explicitly uses a spatial perspective, as opposed to purely an historical perspective on political change, to assess interactions between states along their frontiers, including warfare. By modeling the spatial dynamics of how warfare takes place, we may be able to reassess specific locations that were possible focal points for conflict between polities. Our examples focus on peripheral areas where larger centers would likely collide, usually at an important nexus of communication and transportation through which valuable resources would pass. Beyond this, local political motive and action are also considered within the larger geopolitical interaction sphere. Local polities, whose status might vary widely from political pawn or puppet state to shrewd self-serving political ally, often played a crucial role in determining the specific form and outcome of Mesoamerican warfare.

The Spaces Between

> We must recognize the truth that the struggles for existence between societies have been instrumental to their evolution. Neither the consolidation and reconsolidation of small groups into large ones; nor the organization of such compound and doubly-compound groups; nor the concomitant developments of those aids to a higher life which civilization has brought; would have been possible without inter-tribal and inter-national conflicts. (Spencer 1882:241)

Although Spencer's brand of social Darwinism has long been discarded, warfare is part of the natural evolution of societies. As the scale and complexity of polities increase, they invariably come in conflict with foreign groups. We use the term *polity* because it is a generalizing or all-inclusive term of political organization. Political geographers like to use the analogy of a *container* to describe polities (Taylor 1993, 1995). Their formation is generally considered a social-caging process manifested in the growth of focused, inescapably intense, centralized social relations (Mann 1984, 1986). This formulation of politico-spatial organization, or polity making, is seen as:

> involving the attempt to make coincident the functional organization of space into dynamic systems of human interaction and formal organization of space into precisely bounded administrative areas: to create a sense of societal identity with a particular territory based upon the community-forming tendencies of geographical proximity, functional interdependence, and a homogeneity of attitudes and values. (Soja 1971:15)

Political containers have *spatially distinct sets of social relations*. They exist on any scale, ranging from small regional centers nested within larger expansionist empires up to the modern superpower. There are basic underlying patterns in the way polities interact; in other words, they have familiar sets of relations in opposition to other polities, no matter the scale of the polity. These interrelationships generally take on three forms: cooperation, competition, and conflict (Soja 1971). Cooperation is the legitimization of authority through social integration and interaction that creates and then maintains institutions. Competition is the struggle over control and allocation of resources, which is essentially ownership of scarce resources. Lastly, conflict generally evolves from the need to maintain order and to enforce authority. Warfare is the heightened state of conflict between polities, often growing out of the inability to maintain order within competitive relationships along the peripheral boundaries of the container (compare against von Clausewitz 1968).

The Edge of the Container: Frontiers of Competition and Conflict

Our analytical framework is guided by the idea that polities are bounded mosaics of goal networks that have an inward focus defined by a periphery and core (Mann 1986). Like political geographers, archaeologists have long acknowledged the importance of the relationship between the core and periphery in the development of social complexity (Renfrew and Shennan 1982; Schortman and Urban 1992; Wallerstein 1974; Wolf 1982). Recently, scholars have begun a new focus on the dynamics of frontiers and the active role that frontiers play in the larger negotiations for power (Chase-Dunn and Hall 1997; Stark 1998). It is along these dynamic frontiers or boundaries that we would expect to see political interrelations most magnified, especially conflict and competition between polities. Frontiers are created, maintained, disputed, crossed, and changed in similar fashions, with similar degrees of vigilance, regardless of the scale of the polity. Here, along these fluid and always changing frontiers, interregional and local interactions are intensified and vast resources are spent. However, because frontiers are usually located in peripheries, and not at cores, the interests of peripheral polities are not identical with those of the cores. The dialectic between larger interregional interests and nested local interests creates a dynamism along frontiers.

If we can identify these boundaries, we have at our archaeological fingertips an invaluable laboratory for studying critical interactions between polities. The expectation is that evidence for warfare in these in-between zones will be subtle. In fact, the only evidence we may be able to identify that represents a large-scale conflict between larger polities may be in the form of localized warfare, ancillary to larger competitions, that is an extension of a larger overall conflict. Perhaps we will find archaeological evidence in the form of battles fought between smaller polities as they compete for the affection and business of larger political cores (super-states). Imagine if you were in the midst of conflict/warfare waged between larger polities over your own land and the rights to legitimately own and work that land. Local interests/competitions become interwoven within interregional competitions. The following examples from Mesoamerica demonstrate the value in making interpretations about larger political dynamics involving warfare within a context of local competitions for interregional favor.

The Maya Case

Warfare between Super-States: First Tier Conflict between Tikal and Calakmul

> I have long believed that the evidence for Maya warfare, comprehensively examined within the context of robust anthropological models, has great potential for investigating sociopolitical and socioeconomic structures and dynamic processes. Maya warfare is a particularly important subject because evidence for it may be recovered using both epigraphic/iconographic and traditional archaeological approaches. (Webster 1993:415)

There are many players in this story of war, so let us start with a moment in time. In April 562 Wak Chan K'awiil, the leader of Tikal, was defeated in a star-war by Caracol ruler Yajaw Te' K'inich II as part of an all-out assault by Caracol's ally, the ruling family of Calakmul, which was Tikal's major enemy. This reference was pieced together by diligent epigraphers working out a sketchy history detailed on a badly eroded altar found under a logging trail inside a ballcourt at Caracol (Chase and Chase 1987; Martin and Grube 2000). It was hailed as an explanation for the demise of both Tikal and its ally Naranjo, and the accompanying growth of Caracol and Calakmul during what had come to be known at Tikal as the Middle Classic hiatus (A.D. 550–650).

Despite remarkable progress translating Maya texts, there is still contentious debate over the nature of what these statements of victorious warfare connote, especially in terms of understanding the dynamics of Maya regional political organization and the role played by warfare. Were these centers organized as city-states or large super-states capable of carrying out sustained campaigns of war? Were Wak Chan K'awiil and Yajaw Te' K'inich II competing in a ritual ball game or sending armies into battle? Scholars have been outspoken about the importance of viewing Maya text as propaganda and the need to support assertions using material evidence. Can these and other potentially important statements regarding warfare be substantiated using archaeological data from survey and excavations in the Maya area?

As mentioned above, most of the previous studies of the ancient Maya have documented evidence for warfare in the epigraphy painted on ceramic vessels (Reents-Budet 1994; Schele and Miller 1986) and frescoes like the Bonampak murals or carved on monuments such as stelae (Schele and Freidel 1990) or staircases (Demarest 1998). The iconography portrays and the epigraphy talks of wars, victories, and military alliances, but in the Maya area it has been exceedingly difficult archaeologically to document warfare on the ground. Yet, in increasingly more frequent cases, archaeologists have made fortuitous discoveries of berm and ditch walls, such as at Becan in Campeche (Webster 1976) or Tikal (Puleston and Callendar 1967; compare against Webster et al. 2004), or embattlements constructed during periods of prolonged warfare, such as at Dos Pilas (Demarest 1998; Sharer 1994:218–232), Calakmul, Mayapan, Ek Balam (Webster 1993), and Chunchucmil (Dahlin 2000). In a specific test of the epigraphic record, however, research at Caracol has not been able to recover material evidence of warfare, although it is implied by the written record that Caracol came to dominate the Petén region through ruthless assaults on neighboring polities before being overrun by its rivals in A.D. 680 (Chase and Chase 1987; Martin and Grube 2000).

The paucity of evidence may be caused by warfare being limited to highly orchestrated battles among the elite subculture (Demarest 1978). Medieval European, feudal Japanese, and ancient Hawai'ian warfare (Kolb and Dixon 2002) are three examples of warfare in its ritualized form that left few traces in the archaeological record. However, Webster (1993) points out that highly conventionalized warfare does not mean that large-scale destruction and slaughter is avoided. We might be seeing a range of warfare types in the Maya sphere. Chase and Chase (1998) have identified at least four types of hieroglyphic notations for warfare in Classic Maya texts: 1) capture events; 2) destruction events, *hubi*, which are more symbolic than substantive, involving desecration of important state icons or buildings; 3) axe-events involving decapitation; and 4) star-wars, which are major military undertakings. Demarest (1978) suggests that among the Maya there were two forms of warfare. One type was determined by situational ethics and took place on the upper elite level with common understandings of its conventions. The other types of warfare were more unlimited or open because there were fewer shared understandings among peoples. It took place between regions that possibly spoke different dialects. This type of warfare, perhaps like the aforementioned star-war, would have profound effects on entire regions.

Since Proskouriakoff (1960) originally posited that the names of regional centers were carved on monuments as emblem glyphs, models based on the epigraphy have suggested that Maya political organization was centralized around a few regional centers. According to Marcus (1976), the Maya of lowland Mesoamerica were made up of a few (probably four or five) macro-regional archaic states that dominated a hierarchy of secondary and tertiary centers, each in turn administering to progressively smaller regions. Recently, Martin and Grube (1995, 2000) have amassed new data promoting an idea of Maya super-states dominating vast areas of Mesoamerica. The model is bolstered by evidence that Calakmul in Campeche, Mexico, is actually the enigmatic Site Q, which has been identified as the power behind many disruptive insurgencies, especially those of Caracol over Tikal and Naranjo described above (Chase and Chase 1987; Houston 1987; Martin and Grube 1995, 2000). Two paramount cities (Tikal and Calakmul) are assumed to have formed vast hegemonies characterized by an effective duality of economic and ideological control that may have differed less than previously thought from the historically documented Aztec model (see Berdan et al. 1996; Hassig 1985; Hodge and Smith 1994). Tikal and Calakmul apparently controlled complex networks of alliances with trading partners in an effort to dominate the Maya landscape, and warfare was waged between their respective allies to promulgate and maintain regional strangleholds on areas with important natural resources and valuable communication and transportation routes. Remarkable new evidence for warfare between superpowers unearthed at Dos Pilas depicts texts on a battle-torn staircase relating to the events surrounding the war between Tikal and Calakmul, and between their subsidiaries. Apparently Dos Pilas was "a pawn caught in a much larger battle" (Demarest quoted in John Noble Wilford, "Maya Carvings Tell of Two Superpowers," *New York Times* September 19, 2002).

Dos Pilas is a wonderful example of warfare in-between, but is it an exceptional case or is it the norm for other areas of study? The reason Maya warfare has been so hard to find in the archaeological record may be because little emphasis is placed on working out the kinds of evidence available in these in-between zones. This chapter analyzes in brief detail the culture history and archaeological evidence available from an area located along the frontier between the territories of the Maya mega-polities, Tikal and Calakmul. It is our contention that conventional large-scale warfare (the aforementioned star-wars) would be perhaps most visible in the archaeological record along the boundaries between these regional super-states and their respective allies. If Maya mega-polities did in fact exist during the Late Classic, then their conflicts/competitions played an important role in shaping local social histories of Maya landscapes caught in-between, and we should be able to interpret the effects of this warfare.

Caracol and Naranjo: Second Tier Conflict and Those Caught In-Between

Recent interpretations have suggested that the cities of Naranjo and Caracol were competitors and often violent enemies caught within a larger competition between Tikal and Calakmul for control over the southeastern part of the Maya region, including most of central and southern Belize (Figures 11.1 and 11.2) (Martin and Grube 2000). The history is long and varied, but the overall pat-

Figure 11.1. Mesoamerica, showing the Maya sites of Tikal, Caracol, and Calakmul, the Aztec capital of Tenochtitlan, and the Tarascan capital of Tzintzuntzan.

Table 11.1. Chronology of the Tikal-Calakmul Conflict, Showing Different Regional Levels

Macroregional Level (1st and 2nd tiers)	Temporal Period (A.D.)	Control over the Upper Belize River Valley (UBRV) (3rd Tier)	Temporal Name in UBRV (Lecount et al. 2002)
Tikal/Naranjo	~300–562	Buenavista	Ak'ab
Calakmul/Caracol	562–680	Both	Samal
Tikal/Naranjo	680–798	Satellite Xunantunich	Hats' Chaak
Caracol	798–~1000	Autonomous Xunantunich?	Tsak'

tern is one of either Naranjo under the aegis of Tikal, or Caracol under auspices of Calakmul, having control over and/or strongly influencing the southeastern Maya area.

First, a quick review of culture history and chronological phases will provide background. It is best to show this in a simplified flow chart of the history primarily taken from the most recent well-documented book by Martin and Grube (2000) (Table 11.1). Based on generally accepted epigraphy, there is a Tikal/Naranjo period that lasts from the start of the Classic period to around A.D. 562. This is followed by unprecedented growth of Caracol for 120 years during the first half of the Late Classic period (A.D. 562–680, Samal phase). Then during the late Late Classic (A.D. 680–798, Hats' Chaak phase) Caracol experiences a hiatus while Naranjo and Tikal fluoresce to new heights. Lastly, once again, Caracol experiences a revival beginning in A.D. 798 and continuing up through a good portion of the Terminal Classic (A.D. 798–900/1000). The conflict apparently went on for centuries as war was waged back and forth affecting the southeastern Maya area. Much has been written about both second-order sites; the following is a brief synopsis.

The city of Naranjo, located between the Yaxha Lake region and the Belize/Guatemala border (Figure 11.2), plays a critical role in models of Maya regional organization. Although it remains practically untouched by archaeologists, investigators have managed to prepare survey maps and document over 40 monuments at Naranjo (Graham 1978; Graham and Von Euw 1975; Proskouriakoff 1961; Schele and Freidel 1990; Sharer 1994). Based on the readings of inscriptions, the city figured heavily in regional sociopolitics during the Late Classic period, including wars with Caracol in the early A.D. 600s (Chase and Chase 1987) and marriage alliances with Dos Pilas and Tikal in the late A.D. 600s (Demarest 1998; Sharer 1994). The last great leader of Naranjo was Lord Smoking Squirrel, the child of a local Naranjo lord and the daughter of the ruler of Dos Pilas. Until Smoking Squirrel's death in the middle of the eighth century, Naranjo was one of the major players in southeastern Maya regional politics. During

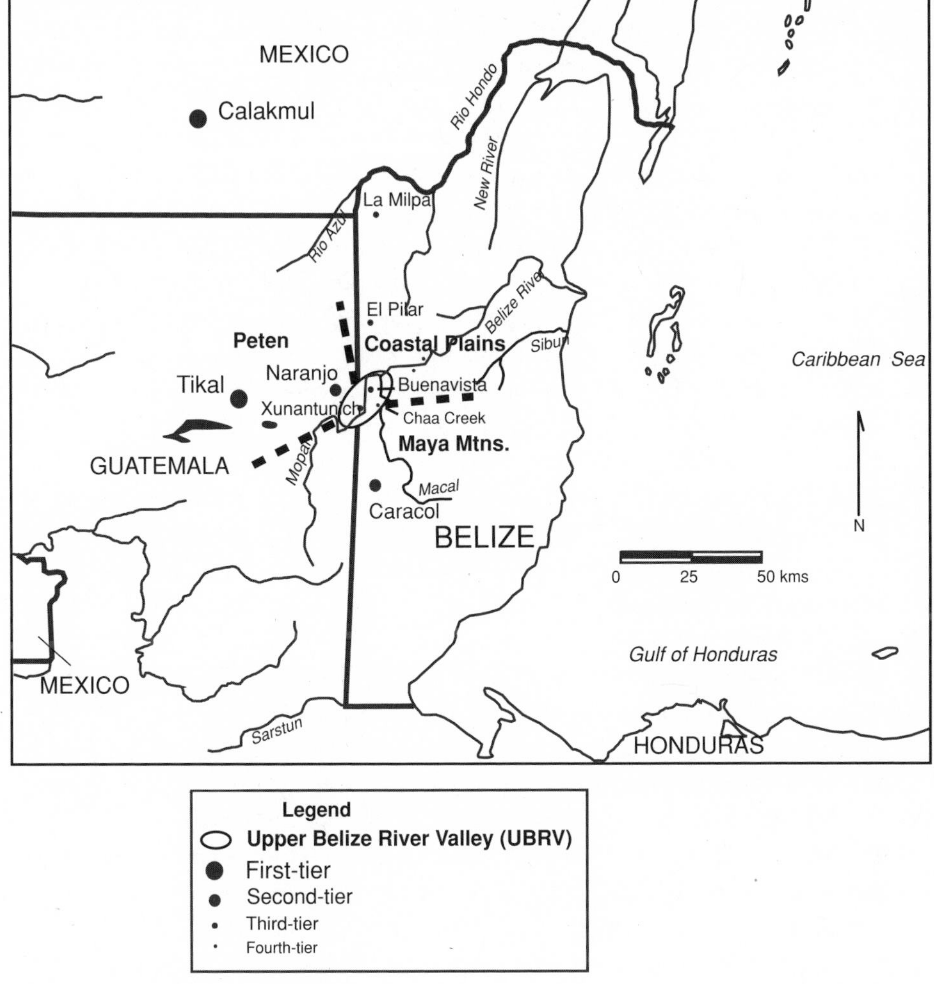

Figure 11.2. The eastern Maya area.

this period the great center of Caracol failed to construct monuments and the power of Tikal was greatly reduced.

The city of Caracol has been continually studied for the last 20 years. Exhaustive survey and excavation by Chase and Chase (1987, 1998) has thoroughly documented the dynastic history and architectural sequences in the city center, as well as an extensive network of raised causeways, *sacbeob*, radiating from the core and stretching for many kilometers in a spoke-like pattern. The *sacbeob* integrate a Caracol epicenter that has been suggested to have held over 100,000 citizens. Caracol's primary temple-pyramid, Ca'ana, is topped by an acropolis that is stylistically equivalent to the main pyramid at Calakmul (the infamous Site Q) in terms of form and perhaps function. As stated above, we know from a translation of a ballcourt marker that Caracol had a hand in the defeats of Naranjo and Tikal, likely under the auspices of Calakmul's might.

The two secondary super-regional centers of Caracol and Naranjo existed within a macro-regional competitive dynamic as second-tier allies of Calakmul and Tikal, respectively. Epigraphers explain that Calakmul enlisted Caracol as an ally along the southern Maya frontier and Tikal entrusted Naranjo to take care of its eastern flank. It appears that the conflict between Caracol and Naranjo concentrated in the area that would cover most of what is today west-central Belize. This frontier region lies at the juncture of three contrasting ecological and geographic zones, all as recognizably distinct in ancient times as they are today (Figure 11.2). The lush tropical upland Petén bajo zone is to the west and northwest, the karstic Vaca Plateau leading to the Maya Mountains lies to the south, and the Belize River valley and Coastal Plains extend to the east and northeast. Generally, the geology of the region consists primarily of underlying limestone and dolomitic formations cross cut by perpendicular fault systems (Cornec 1986; Smith 1998; Wright et al. 1959). The climatic variability and minor geologic differences contribute to a strong diversity in habitats, particularly forest habitats (Beletsky 1999). At the nexus of these geographic zones is the frontier region we are interested in, specifically the upper Belize River valley (UBRV). As we shall see below, the ascension of Naranjo's Lord Smoking Squirrel to power in A.D. 680 roughly parallels dramatic changes taking place in peripheral areas of the southeastern Maya area, in this case specifically the UBRV where the new Naranjo ruler's rise signaled the loss of local power by one city, Buenavista, and the rise to prominence of another, Xunantunich (Ashmore and Leventhal 1993; LeCount 1996; Table 11.1). This concomitant shift in local control over the UBRV is tied to the rise of Naranjo and the fall of Caracol during the Hats' Chaak phase.

Small-Time Cities Representing Big City Interests: Third Tier Conflict on the Frontier

The UBRV region, including Xunantunich, has been extensively studied over the past 40 years. The settlement pattern consists of a series of medium-sized major centers spread across the landscape all within 5–10 km of one another. Dense settlement across the landscape does not concentrate around these centers specifically, but instead focuses on community settlements and their associated smaller minor centers (Ashmore et al. 1994; Connell 2000; Robin 1999; Yaeger 2000). We believe this settlement pattern is a result of being along the important Naranjo/Caracol frontier. Sociopolitical evolution along embattled frontiers is often stunted over time, creating a situation whereby regional integration is segmentary. Locally prominent centers experience a retardation of growth, in terms of the size of architectural constructions and centralized state apparatus. Meanwhile, there is almost an acceleration of hinterland settlement population within these areas during times of peace, although they tend to be more or less wastelands during the actual combative stages of war. The UBRV is the classic case of an apparently rich agricultural area (Birchall and Jenkin 1979) that was so segmented during the Maya era that no one city held sway for longer than a few centuries. These factional competitions were a result, we believe, of continuing efforts within the UBRV to gain access to and curry royal allegiances embedded within the milieu of interregional conflict amongst larger political powers. It is here in the UBRV that Willey et al. (1965) formulated the basis for their Maya model for decentralized political integration depicting city-states vying for power within local regions, and here also, Ball and Taschek (1991) made a case for segmentary states in the Maya area.

This frontier area was not only extensively settled, but the degree of terracing seen in the UBRV rivals what is seen in the dense agricultural systems around Caracol and other major Maya centers (Chase and Chase 1998; Neff 1997, 1998). The Xunantunich Settlement Survey documented extensive settlement and terracing at every community spread across the countryside (Ashmore et al. 1994; Connell 2000; Robin 1999; Yaeger 2000; Yaeger and Connell 1993), including the community of Chaa Creek where Connell's research was carried out. Again, why such a rich agricultural landscape with extensive terracing in such a fragmented political system?

Xunantunich as Frontier City: Fighting for Independence and Power within the UBRV

A string of medium-sized major centers alternated control over the UBRV during the Maya era. Table 11.1 documents the shift in local power and control from the city of Buenavista to the city of Xunantunich during the Late Classic at approximately A.D. 680 (see Figure 11.2). This change in power has been posited to be a result of a shift in the nature of larger political dynamics involving Naranjo and its continued domination of the area (LeCount 1996; LeCount et al. 2002; Yeager 2000). During the Hats' Chaak phase, it is apparent that Xunantunich established local prominence within the valley. Construction activity stopped at the city of Buenavista and expanded at Xunantunich. The final two levels of the impressive Castillo, a 32-m-high central pyramid, were built and new pyramids and palaces were added to the central core of the city (Leventhal 1996, 1997; Leventhal and Ashmore 1994, 1995).

Xunantunich and its immediate hinterland are located along a lazy bend in the Mopan River, and above the best disembarkation point for river-going transport that would have been carrying goods in and out of the Petén region to or from the Belize River and the coast (Figure 11.2). We know that in colonial times, when the British logged the Vaca Plateau area and the Petén, timber was carried by narrow-gauge railway to the bustling border town of Benque Viejo, located just below the ancient city of Xunantunich, and placed into the Mopan for flotation down the river. In prehistory, large amounts of goods would have passed along this same river route and the medium-sized major centers located here would have had significant influence on regional politics. At the base of the ridge below Xunantunich, a little down river from modern day Benque Viejo, the Xunantunich Settlement Survey (Ashmore et al. 1994) documented a series of features along the riverbanks that are indicative of intensive river passage during the Maya era. A monumental staircase leads towards Xunantunich from the banks of the Mopan River, and it appears likely that river-going canoes and rafts were launched and landed from this point.

Tied to the expansion of Xunantunich, a concomitant population explosion took place during the Hats' Chaak phase in the surrounding countryside. Neff (2003) has shown that while 45 percent of all known household mounds were occupied previously, during the Hats' Chaak phase 92 percent of all known structures display activity. This explosion quite possibly may be indicative of a massive influx of people to the region, immigration and population nucleation being two results of extensive and damaging warfare in other regions.

The unprecedented growth continued until the Tsak' phase, also known as the Terminal Classic period. Xunantunich slowly was abandoned and settlement almost completely disappeared from the region. Some evidence does exist for the continued presence of a ruling family at Xunantunich, but likely only a skeletal version. The famous Maya Collapse had come to the UBRV.

Our position herein is that these local UBRV shifts are connected to the much larger regional political shifts explained above. If it can be assumed that, 1) large-scale star-wars were taking place on the interregional level, and 2) the UBRV was along an embattled frontier, then factions within these border zones would have repeatedly seized opportunities to shuffle the deck when changes took place in the upper echelons of royalty. The expectation is that along with these localized shifts in power, there are more tangible pieces of archaeological evidence that point to perhaps violent changes that coincide with shifts in power within the UBRV.

Research in the hinterland community of Chaa Creek turned up intriguing evidence that suggests that competitions for local power embedded within these larger interregional dynamics could be violent. Long-term Maya warfare becomes visible at a small community toppled by a history of conflict. Someone took a torch to this community, destroyed its public buildings, and ultimately murdered some of its members.

The Community of Chaa Creek: Destruction at a Fourth Tier Community

Investigations at the community of Chaa Creek as part of the Xunantunich Archaeological Project (XAP) took place from 1993 to 1997. Research focused on documenting the settlement history of this community located seven km east of Xunantunich (Figure 11.2). The settlement consists of 62 sites which range in size from isolated household mounds and small patio groups to larger platform groups with temple-pyramids up to five m in height. There are four minor centers at Chaa Creek, defined by having platforms and structures over two m high. They are assumed to have housed the local elites and/or been the places where important community activities took place. For example, Stela Group, which contains two badly damaged stelae and a large temple-pyramid on its east side, was the place of ceremony and divination, while another large platform group, Tunchilen Group, was the place for communal gatherings such as feasts. The minor center most pertinent to this discussion of war is Plantain Group, which apparently was the residence of the local elite during the Late Classic period, primarily during the Hats' Chaak phase (see Table 11.1).

Plantain Group

Plantain Group is located on the western end of the middle of the three east-west ridges in the Chaa Creek community (Figure 11.3). The primary feature of this site is a platform two m in height with two long structures, each two to three m high, arranged in an L-shape along the north and east sides of the platform. In 1994, 1995, and 1997, the plaza area was surveyed and excavated extensively. Most of the activity at Plantain Group took place during the Hats' Chaak time period and was tightly connected to Xunantunich, which likely sanctioned subelite activities within the confines of the group. This interpretation is based on the multiple lines of evidence that are covered in the following descriptions.

Most of the artifacts at Plantain Group were recovered from a transition phase special deposit found between the two staircases (between Hats' Kaab and Tsak' phases). A dense amount of utilitarian possessions and valuables were smashed on top of an altar with evidence of heavy burning on its central stone (Figure 11.4). The altar is constructed out of collapse stones presumably gathered from the area. What makes this feature unique is that below the hastily constructed altar, within the sub-platform structure, lay two important crypt interments containing multiple individuals (Figure 11.5). That there are two crypts

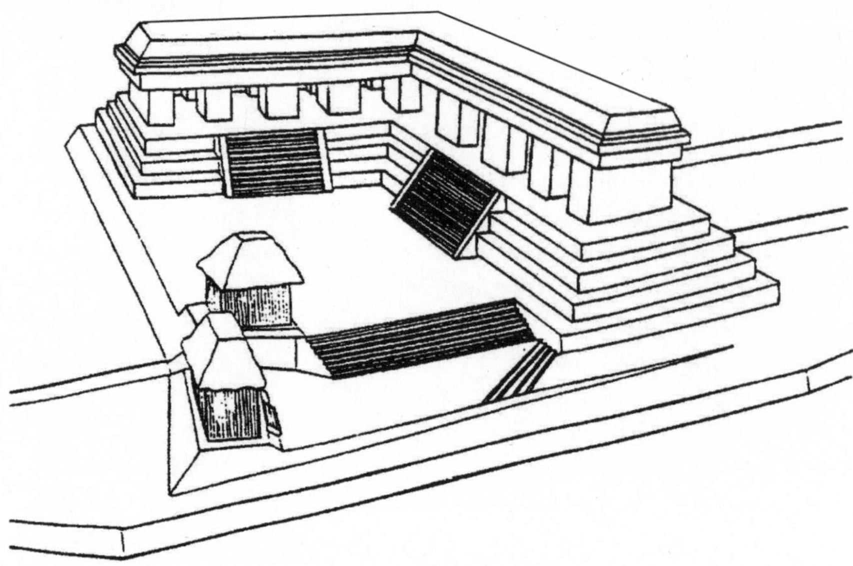

Figure 11.3. Plantain Group at Chaa Creek (drawing by Gregg Cestaro).

was not unexpected, because the whole site was a burial platform with more than 15 crypts laid out in a grid pattern.

However, crypts 95-1 and 95-3 were different. While both contained an intact primary burial in an extended position with the head to the south, each also contained a number of secondary burials placed directly on top of the primary remains (Figure 11.6). These heavily commingled remains are termed secondary deposits because there is no way they could have been placed in as fully fleshed individuals given the space available. In crypt 95-3, dentition and mandibles yield an MNI of five adults and one sub-adult (Adams 1998). In crypt 95-1, two commingled secondary interments display evidence for cranial deformation, a sign of elite status among the Maya. Yet, no significant burial accoutrements were found in any of these crypts, only two small trinkets, a face pendant and a spindle-whorl.

The altar-burial deposit is evidence for a ritual carried out at the site during the beginning of the Terminal Classic time period (A.D. 790–900) marking the termination of the site. This termination coincides with a local abandonment of all settlement at Chaa Creek. The common translation of war/victory glyph is literally "to throw down" or "to cast down," and the archaeological evidence for the ritual smashing of substantial amounts of worldly goods at previously important minor centers, such as Plantain Group, might indicate the end result of local warfare at Chaa Creek. At the Yucatan site of Yaxuna, David Freidel (1999)

Figure 11.4. Termination altar with visible evidence for an intrusive deposit below the plaster floor (crypt 95-1 is visible in the foreground right).

Figure 11.5. Crypts 95-1 above and the exposed 95-3 below. North is to the right.

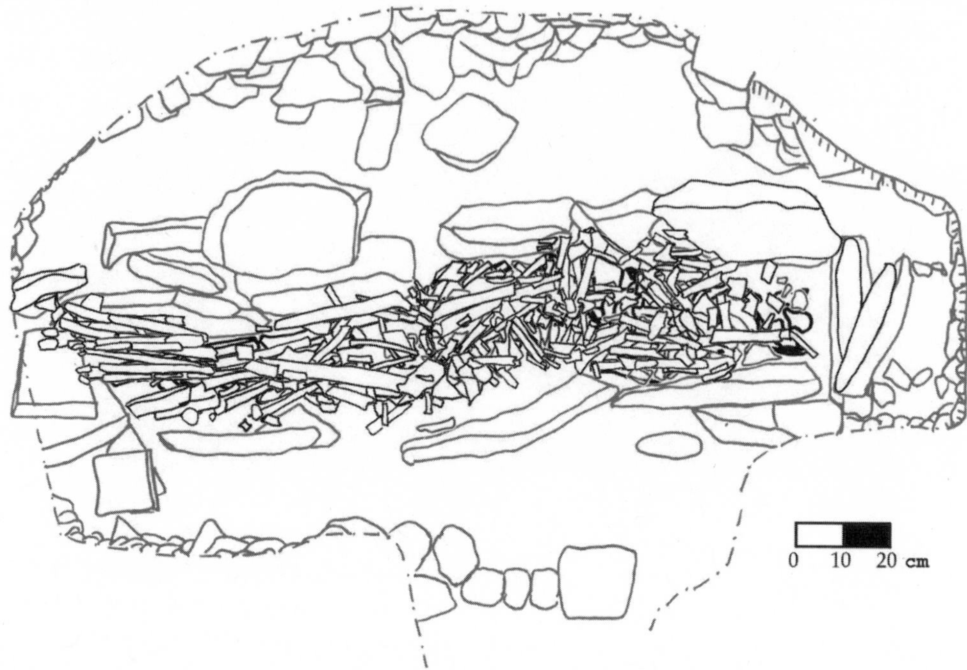

Figure 11.6. Crypt 95-3 commingled remains of six individuals.

has convincingly argued for termination deposits as representative of being on the losing end of warfare, in this case to the nearby political center of Coba. As a final act, the victor selectively negates the power of specific buildings.

Was the termination-altar-burial feature complex at Chaa Creek an act of desecration by a victorious outside group? Rethinking associated evidence suggests the possibility. For example, the tip of a biface was found at Crypt 95-3 within the area containing much of the vertebrae. In addition, the mandibles of the two secondary remains in Crypt 95-1 were found deposited next to the lower limbs. This disarticulation may indicate an act of violence or even sacrifice.

Moving to the architecture at Plantain Group, an unusually large amount of rubble collapse was discovered on and around the front staircase of the platform. It may be interpreted as the remnants of a hastily built wall surrounding the site. At Dos Pilas a series of these walls was constructed to protect the site core from invading polities (Demarest 1998). At Plantain Group, perhaps forces from another political zone overrode Chaa Creek.

Yet there are inconsistencies that point away from warfare with an outside group. Why would enemies take the time to properly bury individuals before ransacking and desecrating a site? The crania of each of the nine burials were placed at the crypt's south end, a signature tradition of the local Belize River area Maya. The remains were then properly covered and an altar was constructed before the termination occurred. Again, this is something that would be peculiar for an outside group to do. This termination deposit was neither a peacetime ritual closing of the site prior to its abandonment, nor was it representative of a star-war or desecration event linked to outside forces. We have come to believe it was an inside job.

By reexamining the local community culture history we come to a better understanding of the events leading up to the site's termination. The bulk of ceremonial and feasting activity at Stela and Tunchilen took place in the Samal phase, and has been argued to represent local community autonomy (Connell 2003). Conversely, Plantain Group displays minimal building activity during the Samal, but in the Hats' Chaak phase Plantain grows in influence while Stela and Tunchilen show little activity. Therefore, on a very basic level we see a replacement of important local lineage activities coinciding with the rise of Plantain Group, likely tied to its strong material connections to Xunantunich royalty. Although there are any number of scenarios that could explain the data gathered from Plantain Group, the contention made here is that local competitors within a potentially lawless frontier zone ransacked Chaa Creek, and that this attack took place at the end of the Hats' Chaak phase following yet another campaign between Caracol and Naranjo that drastically affected the local populace. Plantain Group, with its strong ties to the elites at Xunantunich, was an easy target for local competitors vying for power on the periphery. Defeated, the remnant population of Plantain Group buried their own elites before abandoning the site.

Our example of an active Maya periphery, affected both by interregional politics and homegrown competitive dynamics, portrays a dynamic frontier region consisting of competing and conflicting small-scale cities and communities located within the hypothetical third-tier of Maya regional sociopolitical organization. In the second section of this chapter we leave Maya pseudo-history taking place on a relatively small scale, and enter the realm of more concretely documented historical events taking place on a much more expansive scale in western Mexico along the contested frontier between the Aztec and Tarascan empires. Notwithstanding the temporal, geographical, and scalar differences, the recurring theme of the role of the periphery as a critical zone of action is quite evident.

The Aztec-Tarascan Case: Empires and Clients

Tier 1: When Superpowers Collide

> Year of nine rabbits and 1462 according to our count there was a battle between those of Michuacan and Xiquipilco, which is in the Matlatzinca Valley. (The Codex Telleriano-Ramensis, 1995, Folio 33v)

This seemingly innocuous reference to one of hundreds of minor battles fought during the tenure of the Aztec empire takes on much greater significance when considered in the larger geopolitical context of Postclassic Mexico (Figure 11.7). In Mesoamerica during the mid-fifteenth century A.D., there were two great powers in ascendance: the Aztec empire of central Mexico and Tarascan empire of western Mexico. Between these two powers lay the Matlatzinca Valley, a place where numerous city-states vied for regional dominance and where lords wooed the military support of the great states to the east and west in their quest for regional supremacy and the ability to collect tribute from their neighbors. Even as the lesser rivals of the valley maneuvered for position, the Mexica (Aztecs) and the Michoacanos (Tarascans) became increasingly aware of the strategic threat posed to each from the other.

From this explosive situation comes the second example of the dynamic that existed between super-states and client-states in Mesoamerica. Lesser polities constantly assess their political circumstances and leaders carefully weigh their options in order to preserve or improve their status. In the case of the Matlatzinca Valley, internecine rivalries exploded on the larger geopolitical landscape as factions sought advantageous alliances outside their immediate political sphere.

The skirmish at Xiquipilco suggests that the Tarascans took the initiative in crossing the mountain boundary that separated their land of Michoacan from the Matlatzinca Valley and the Basin of Mexico, home of the Aztec empire that lies just beyond it. At the time of the Tarascan incursion, during the reign of the Aztec Emperor Mocteuczoma Ilhuicamina (ca. A.D. 1440–1468), it is probable that the Aztec empire already held significant influence among the Matlatzinca (Hassig 1988:152). It is also probable that the Tarascan intervention in the Matlatzinca Valley was at the behest of some lord looking to gain an advantageous position in an environment of increased pressure caused by the encroaching empires. Unfortunately, records of the Tarascan empire's conquests are few and limited in scope. Conversely, the circumstances of the Aztec intervention in the Matlatzinca Valley are recorded in explicit detail:

> In Toluca and Matlatzinca, cities that actually belonged to one province, reigned two powerful sovereigns, both valorous men . . . The Toluca ruler had three valiant sons, daring young men who were capable of carrying out

> any great feat . . . The lord of Tenantzinco was governed by a lord Tezozmoctli who had three or four young sons who were also proud of their lineage . . . among these young men from two cities rivalries and envies sprang up and they began to form bands and quarrel with each other . . . the young men of Toluca constantly threatened those of Tenantzinco, swearing to wage war upon them and force them to show their strength.
>
> . . . Tezozmoctli decided to try to stop all this trouble-making before any serious misfortune could happen. Therefore, following the advice of his councilors, he went to Tenochtitlan in person and, appearing before Axayacatl [Aztec emperor ca. A.D. 1468–1481] . . . told how they had become bad neighbors and how they were trying to take other peoples land. (Duran 1994:263)

Axayacatl intervened by demanding tribute from Toluca and Matlatzinca for a new temple. Underlying strategic motives of the Aztec Empire were revealed when Tlacaelel, councilor to many emperors and the power behind the Aztec throne, tried to assuage the anger of Emperor Axayactl after Toluca and Matlatzinca refused to pay the tribute.

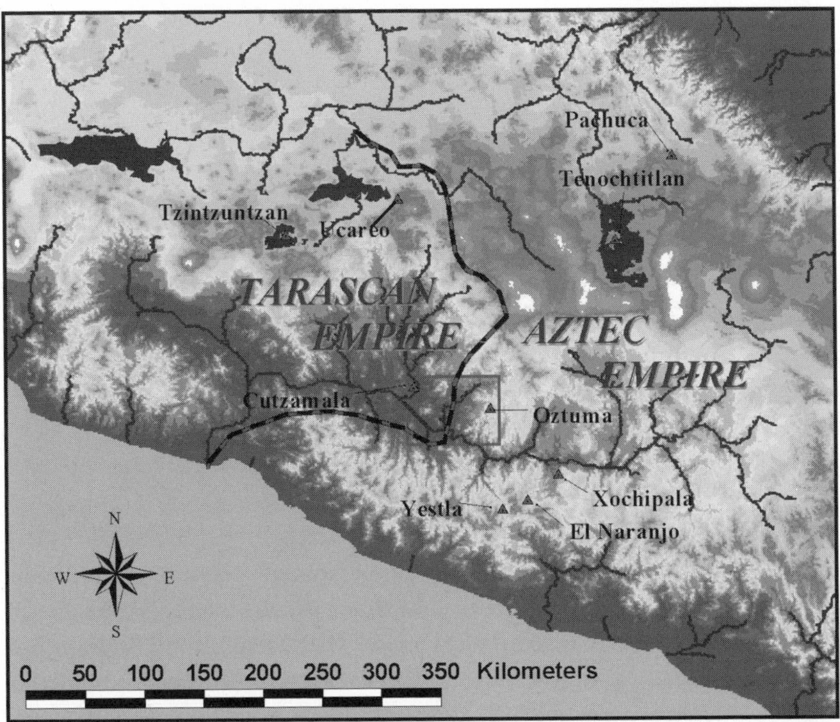

Figure 11.7. Central Mexico in the Late Postclassic.

> My son, do not become so agitated. You must know that since the time of my brother Mocteuczoma I have been convinced that that province should be conquered because I fear that its inhabitants might become allies of the people of Mechoacan, and they could give us an unpleasant surprise some day. See what could happen if we do not subjugate them: they will not obey us or respect us in any way. (Duran 1994:265)

As it turned out, Axayacatl waged a successful campaign and brought the entire Matlatzinca Valley under imperial sway, making the western mountains the frontier between the two empires. Refugees from the Matlatzinca Valley who had been allied with the Tarascans poured into Michoacan, where the Tarascan emperor settled them on new lands. Determined to make the most of their victory in the Matlatzinca Valley, Axayacatl pushed the assault into the Tarascan realm, crossing the mountains with a force of some 24,000 warriors. The Tarascan forces rallied against the invasion, routed the Aztec force, and reportedly killed as many as 20,000 Aztec warriors. This event directed the next several decades of the war. Unable to inflict a decisive military blow across the mountains, the Aztec-Tarascan war turned into a stalemate with both sides fortifying their respective frontiers and maneuvering along the flanks, particularly in the south, in an attempt to gain some advantage.

Tier 2: The Powers between the Empires

From here our focus shifts to the Chontal kingdom of Oztuma located south of that Matlatzinca Valley, along the strategic corridor that follows the Rio Balsas as it winds from the highlands of Mexico down through the Tierra Caliente to the Pacific Ocean (Figure 11.8). Like the Matlatzinca, the Chontal, organized as a handful of independent kingdoms, found themselves in the unenviable position of being in the right place at the wrong time in history. Their fertile valleys and rich mineral resources were secondary to their strategic position along the Aztec-Tarascan frontier. To the west, the Cuitlateca-speaking polities had fallen under the control of the Tarascan empire. The Chontal were faced with a difficult choice. To side with the Mexica was to invite invasion from the west into their vulnerable agricultural lands, yet to reject Aztec sovereignty was equally as dangerous and would surely mean war to the east.

Perhaps encouraged by the weak rule of the Aztec Emperor Tizoc (ca. A.D. 1481–1486) or perhaps by promises of support from the Tarascans, three Chontal city-states, Oztuma, Alahuiztlan, and Teloloapan, banded together and declared independence from the Aztec empire. The Chontal confederation prepared their defenses and, according to their own traditions, repelled numerous Aztec invasions (Silverstein 2000, 2001). With the succession of the Emperor Ahuitzotl (ca. A.D. 1486–1502), the Aztec launched a determined assault. In

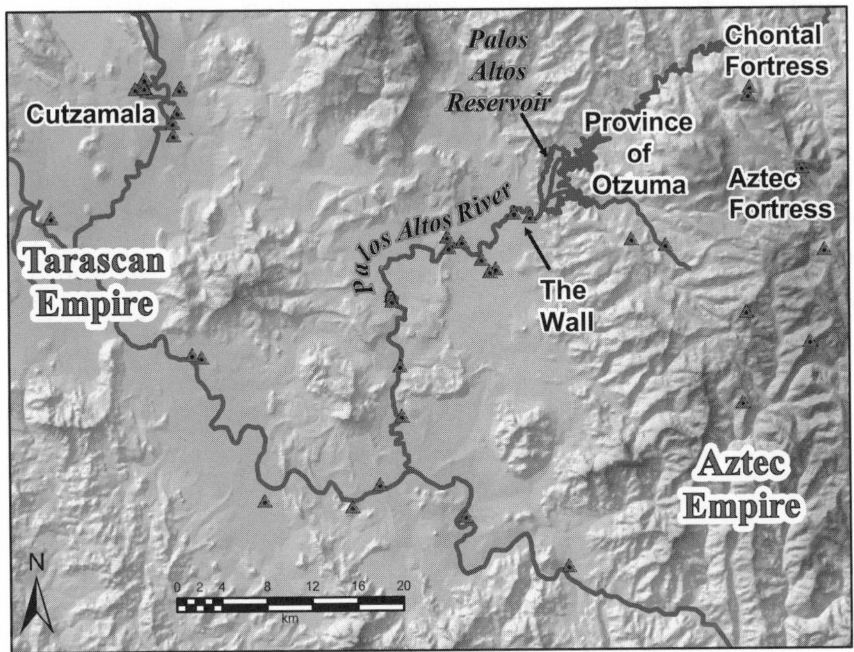

Figure 11.8. The Chontal region.

the end, the Chontal were unable to hold together, and one by one, the members of the confederation fell to the superior Aztec forces. First Teloloapan surrendered and then they aided the empire in crushing Oztuma and Alahuiztlan (Duran 1994; Tezozomoc 1987). Accounts from Tenochtitlan, the heartland of the Aztec empire, state that all of the people of Oztuma and Alahuiztlan were sacrificed; however this is in direct contrast to other sixteenth century documents written in Oztuma. The Chontal admit to heavy losses only after soundly defeating two Aztec invasions. After being defeated by the third Aztec force, the Chontal said that only their king and a few of their leaders were sacrificed. A new king of the Chontal royal lineage took the throne and ruled under Aztec hegemony. Clearly, contrary to Aztec propaganda, the Chontal continued to exist both as a political and ethno-linguistic group after being subjugated.

The Many Facets of the Fortified Frontier: The Ethnohistory and Archaeology of All of the Players

After defeating the Chontal, the Mexica turned their attention to the Tarascan problem. In the town of Cutzamala, some 40 km west of Oztuma, the Tarascan empire had focused its efforts on building a military garrison. The Aztec empire sought to counter this threat with an unprecedented investment in the region, the establishment of a permanent garrison. Ahuitzotl addressed the great lords of the empire:

> O lords, you know that in the war we waged on Teloloapan, Oztoman, and Alahuiztlan, the last two cities were depopulated. All their fruit, cacao, and cotton plantations were deserted, their fields made barren. It would be sad to see those lands lost, left uncultivated and abandoned forever. Therefore, I have decided to send people to settle that country, to benefit by its riches and make it prosper. I have thought about this and, considering how thickly populated those cities once were, I plan to send four hundred men with their families from Tenochtitlan. I also want each of you to send four hundred families so that the total will be one thousand two hundred. From the other provinces should go twenty settlers each, which will make a total of eight hundred. The total will be two thousand, one thousand for each city. (Durán 1994:344)

While ostensibly tempting homesteaders with promises of rich lands and exemption from tribute, the underlying purpose of creating a military garrison against Michoacan remained. A final caveat was given to the settlers as they left, warning them to always be vigilant with armed men because they would be near the frontier with Michoacan, who held the Mexica in mortal hatred (Duran 1994:354).

The narrative histories of the Aztec empire offer little more about Oztuma after the imperial colonization. If these narratives were to be accepted at face value, the Chontal would be presumed eradicated and the Aztec empire in possession of a solidly controlled colonial province. Such an interpretation is consonant with the Codex Mendoza, the main tributary document of the Aztec empire, which lists Oztuma as one of seven imperial military garrisons (Codex Mendoza 1997:folios 17v-18r). Rudolf van Zantwijk's (1967) brilliant reading of the Codex Mendoza makes a compelling case for an economic and kinship link between the garrison and the towns of the empire that supplied the colonists.

However, the most detailed knowledge of the Chontal portion of the Aztec-Tarascan frontier comes from a series of *Relaciónes Geográficas* recorded in Oztuma in 1579 by one Captain Lucas Pinto. Pinto accomplished several things relevant to our understanding of Aztec-Chontal relations. First, his account makes clear that the rumors of the extermination of the Chontal were greatly exaggerated since that people maintained political and cultural integrity well into the Colonial period (Silverstein 2001). Second, Pinto's keen eye for military matters led him to include a detailed description of two fortresses in the Oztuma province, one a massive layered defensive system that housed the Aztec governor and most, if not all, of the Aztec colonists, and the other that of the Chontal and their king. Finally, in reference to a point to be discussed below, Pinto provided

Figure 11.9. The Aztec fortress of Oztuma.

clues about the nature of Chontal-Aztec relations in the aftermath of the Spanish conquest of Mexico.

The reconstruction of the frontier that follows is drawn from ethnohistoric accounts, particularly those of the *Relaciónes Geográficas*, and from archaeological data, as slim as they may be for this little-studied region (RG 1985). The first major archaeological breakthrough came with the discovery and recording of the ruins of the great Aztec fortress of Oztuma in 1939 (Armillas 1942–1944; Figure 11.9). Yet, while this find established the specific location of the Aztec garrison, the fate of the Chontal and their fortress remained a mystery. It was generally thought that the Chontal fortress described in the *Relaciónes Geográficas* had been forsaken or destroyed in the aftermath of the Aztec-Chontal war (Arana 1979; Armillas 1942–1944, 1948, 1951). In 1998, however, the discovery of the Chontal fortress and its correlation with a new set of colonial documents (Jalpa Flores and Ramírez Celestino 1997; Silverstein 2000, 2001) provided the opportunity to create a model of the strategic and operational organization of the frontier.

Relaciónes Geográficas from the Tarascan side of the frontier tell of a force of 10,000 warriors based at the head town of Cutzmala with the primary purpose of capturing the Aztec colony at Oztuma (RG 1987). The Aztec fortress, with its three concentric layers of wall, outlying fortifications, defended causeways, and massive citadel, was therefore a logical response to the Tarascan threat. Even more important was its location on top of a hill that overlooked an important pass and took full advantage of the steep hills that mark the beginning of the Mexican highlands. However, while a strong fortress may guard a single pass, it is vulnerable to being bypassed or cut off, and it is unable to guard multiple resources within a region. It so happens that some 12 km north of the Aztec fortress was the River Alahuiztlan, whose brackish headwaters provided much of the salt for the region. South of Oztuma was the valuable Balsas River, and throughout the hills were minerals including gold, copper, and precious green stones called *chalchahuites*. If the Aztecs were to hold the frontier against their determined foe and exploit these valuable resources, they would require a chain of fortresses spaced so that they could detect any major invasion and communicate it to the Aztec capital, and each fortress could lend support to the other should one be attacked. Yet to spread the few thousand Aztec warriors out over some 40 km of frontier would mean that each small group would be too weak to defend itself against any raid in force or against a rebellion of their Chontal subjects. Instead, the Aztec force stayed together at their fortress at Oztuma, and their Chontal subjects established fortresses and lookouts along the frontier, each within visual communication of the other.

Twelve km northeast of Aztec Oztuma on the modern hill of Ixtepec sits the ruins of the Chontal fortress (Figure 11.10). Ascending Ixtepec, one passes through a series of concentric walls and a stone quarry, arriving at the top of the hill where the remains of a modest temple overlook the Alahuiztlan Valley. In the village of Ixtepec, far below, the descendants of the Chontal people jealously guard a handful of boxes filled with colonial documents dating to the sixteenth century. The earliest of these documents bear the signature of the governor, Don Diego Osorio, son of the Chontal king who ruled Oztuma when Cortez arrived in 1519, and the very man who spoke with Captain Pinto. Other Chontal hilltop fortresses are known to have existed at the city states of Alahuiztlan to the north, Totoltepec to the south, and down to Tetela on the Balsas River. In Totoloapan, east of Oztuma and behind the frontlines, the Aztecs maintained another garrison. Throughout the *Relaciónes Geográficas* are scattered bits of information about the war. In Totoltepec they reported that Tarascan raiders often penetrated their territory at night, and in Oztuma they said that the Tarascans besieged the Aztec fortress at least three times, on the last gaining all but the last layers of defense. The Emperor Mocteuczoma is said to have had daily runners report back to Tenochtitlan on the status of the frontier. The *Relaciónes Geográficas* also states that the Aztec garrison collected whatever they needed from their Chontal subjects, and that materials that could not be found in the province of Oztuma (for example, obsidian) were sent from the heartland of the empire (RG 1985).

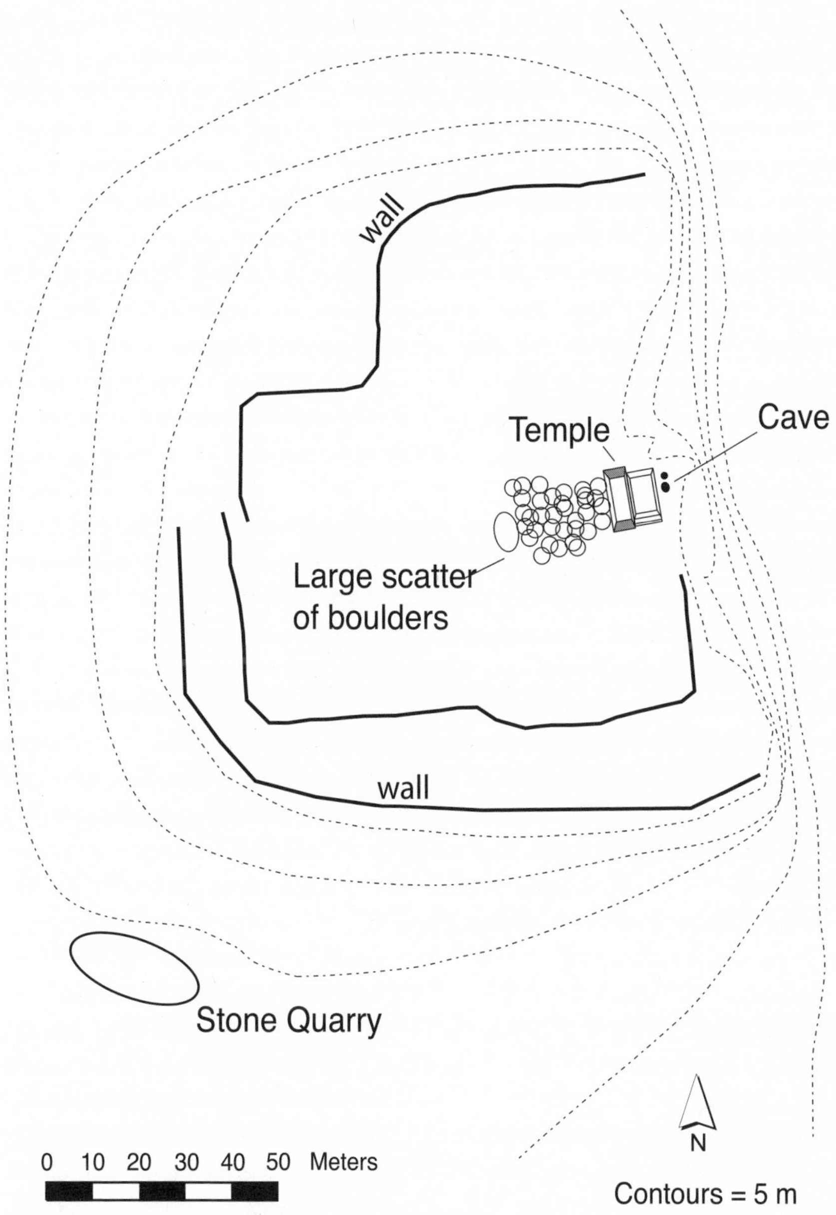

Figure 11.10. The Chontal fortress of Oztuma.

West of Oztuma, coming down from the highlands, were two adjacent valleys formed by the Alahuiztlan River, there called the Palos Altos River as it meanders down to join the Balsas River. These valleys, warm and supplied year-round with water, appear to have held the highest agricultural potential in the region. Yet, by all accounts, they were completely abandoned throughout the early Colonial period and presumably during the Late Postclassic period that preceded it as well. These lands were apparently forfeited during the Aztec-Tarascan war because they were vulnerable to raids and defensively untenable. It seems probable that these lands were worked by the Chontal prior to the war, and that they may have been the deserted cacao and cotton plantations referred to by Ahuitzotl in the passage above when he urged citizens of the empire to colonize Oztuma.

One of these valleys is now covered by the Palos Altos Reservoir, constructed in the 1960s. Archaeological survey data from the Palos Altos Valley (Arana and Cepeda 1966; Castillo Trejo 1967) and the Arcelia region to the west (Silverstein 2000) suggest that the valleys once held vibrant and wealthy communities with numerous small palace complexes and a few small ceremonial centers. What is most curious about this region are the remains of an extensive wall that cuts across a bend in the Palos Altos River, likely built for defensive purposes.

The area that includes the Palos Altos wall was chosen for intensive survey in 1998 during the Proyecto Oztuma-Cutzamala because it was situated directly between the Aztec and Tarascan empires in an area that, judging by the conspicuous absence of towns in colonial sources, appeared to be vacant. At first the wall appeared to the investigation team only as a series of stone mound sites with no associated artifacts (Figure 11.11). As the survey continued a terminus of the wall was found that contained a scatter of sling-stones and obsidian projectiles and blades that suggested a prehispanic battlefield. At this site on the northwestern end of the wall near the Palos Altos River, a clearly defined linear foundation of the wall was visible on the surface. An elderly gentleman from the nearby village of La Montaña informed us that in the 1940s, when he first settled in this region, the wall extended to the town of Palos Altos. Since that time, the rock that made up the wall had been quarried for construction, particularly in the 1960s when it was used to build the massive Palos Altos dam. Once we were made aware of the wall we were able to trace its entire length for a total of 2.8 km, sealing off completely a bend in the Palos Altos River as if to make a large fortified island (Figure 11.12). In the 1940s the wall was said to stand chest high, but parts that still exist suggest that during its use, at least some parts stood two or more m and that it may have had a foss or moat as well. If this wall was defensive in nature, as seems likely from its use of the topography and its orientation, then it was situated in such a way that it would serve to defend both the lower floodplain of

Figure 11.11. The Palos Altos wall.

the Palos Altos River and the upper Palos Altos Valley that was flooded with the construction of the dam.

At this point it is only possible to present potential scenarios of how the presence of this wall relates to the culture history of the no-man's-land between the two empires; however, it seems that its presence in this precise position is more than coincidence. Thus, a likely scenario should include a parsimonious solution to the variables associated with the imperial conflict and the Late Postclassic/Colonial abandonment of the valley floor. One final variable, less secure, is the persistence of the idea in the narrative history of the Aztec empire that the province of Oztuma contained rich agricultural lands. The province of Oztuma, now called the *municipio* General Canuto A Neri, in contrast to the Aztec account, contains only marginal agricultural lands (see quote above) unless those

Figure 11.12. Aerial photograph of the Palos Altos wall.

river valleys that were uninhabited between the Late Postclassic and modern times are considered.

Proposed here is that the prehispanic Chontal province of Oztuma included the two valleys west of the fortified line in the period preceding the imperial confrontation. By the mid-fifteenth century A.D., the Chontal were beginning to feel pressure from the Aztecs, who continuously sought tribute from the provinces on the fringe of their domain. As the century progressed the Chontal began to be pressured from the west, as Tarascan influence escalated any preexisting animosities between the Chontal and their Cuitlateca neighbors. At some point between A.D. 1470–1480, allied with other neighboring Chontal-speaking provinces, Oztuma attempted to create its own power base, either completely independent of either of the threatening empires or in conjunction with the support of one of the empires. In order to do so, the Chontal must have had some confidence in their ability to be perceived as capable of defending themselves from attack from east or west. In this circumstance the Palos Altos wall would have served as a strategic barrier to any incursion from the west, obstructing any army that wished to pass into Chontal territory. However confident the Chontal may have felt, they were wrong. Whether the valley was abandoned after the defeat of the Chontal by the Aztecs, or whether they tried to hold the valley under Aztec auspices, or whether life in the valley became untenable prior to the Aztec-Chontal war, the Chontal eventually lost control of the valley and were forced to retreat up to the hills where they eventually formed part of the fortified Aztec imperial frontier.

The Aftermath

Despite the determined effort by the Tarascan empire to crack the frontier, the Aztec empire held its ground until the Pax España imposed by Cortez was put in place. The Spanish peace, however, did not end the problems for the Aztec settlers at Oztuma. Within 50 years or so, the Chontal were asserting their power, complaining to the Spanish that the Aztecs, now resettled in the valley below their fortress in the town of Acapetlahuaya, were both malicious and illegally trying to take more Chontal land (Jalapa Flores and Ramírez Celestino 1997; Silverstein 2001). Captain Pinto tacitly acknowledged Chontal legitimacy and authority in the region over that of the Nahuatl-speaking Aztecs by paying considerably more attention to the governor of Oztuma than to the lords of Acapetlahuaya. Oztuma, after all, controlled an important salt source that the Spanish wished to exploit to support their mines to the north.

Unfortunately for the Chontal, as the demand for salt diminished and roads became better and modern, Mexico relied less on foot transport and more on beasts and eventually cars, and the mountain home of the Chontal became more and more isolated. The seat of power gradually shifted back to the Nahuatl town of Acapetlahuaya and, as the political and economic fortunes of the Chontal waned, so did their demographics. When the Proyecto Oztuma-Cutzamala arrived in the old colonial town of Oztuma it was completely abandoned. A shepherd boy tossed stones into the old salt wells and explained that the last of the people had left the town for the United States to find work a few years before (Figure 11.13). Another man passing through on his burro directed the team to the town of Ixtepec. In Ixtepec we met Don Lorenzo, who served as a guide up to the old Chontal fortress above his town. At dinner, Don Lorenzo shared salt made from the wells where they still process enough to meet their own needs.

By the late nineteenth century, west of Ixtepec in the no-man's-land valleys that were once fought over by the great Postclassic empires of Mexico, new towns sprang up. It remains a mystery why these lands were not settled in significant numbers prior to this period, but one possible explanation is that the sharp decline in population because of disease and Spanish restrictions and labor demands simply made relocation impossible. The most important of these towns was eventually named Arcelia after Governor Arce of the State of Guerrero and his indigenous love, Celia. With the construction of the Palos Altos Reservoir

Figure 11.13. The abandoned Chontal town of Oztuma.

many towns were resettled down river and the original towns, along with some 23 archaeological sites, were covered by the lake (Castillo Trejo 1967).

Discussion

There is a temptation to say that the destiny of the lands and people of Oztuma and the UBRV was largely determined by two factors; foremost was their geopolitical situation between two competing cities or empires, and second was their situation in the topographical transition zones between the central highlands of Mexico and the Tierra Caliente to the west, in the case of Oztuma, and between the Petén, the Maya mountains, and the Caribbean coast, in the case of the UBRV. The physical geography made both areas vital to larger-scale interests. Oztuma was an ideal place for the Aztec empire to defend its southwestern frontier, and Tarascan pressure necessitated that the Aztecs take advantage of this terrain. The UBRV was located along a vital riverine transportation route that lay equidistant between two competing superpowers. Yet the history, as extrapolated from colonial documents, epigraphy, and the archaeology of the regions, suggests that things were much more complex than is suggested by these macro political and environmental variables.

In the Oztuma example, it is clear from the record, even though much of it was written from the perspective of the Aztec empire, that historic actions were based on the choices made by the Chontal. The creation of a confederation of

Chontal states was a bold and ambitious move, a move not unlike the events and decisions that led to the birth of the Triple Alliance that constituted the Aztec empire. Moreover, although this bid for Chontal autonomy failed, it set up an adversarial relationship with the Mexica that reemerged with some success less than a hundred years later under the Spanish mandate, allowing the Chontal not only to boast of a modicum of success against the mighty Aztec empire, but also to gain some legal standing in land disputes.

Without the assistance of the subjugated Chontal, it is likely that the Aztecs would have had to make a defensive line much closer to the Aztec heartland. If this were the case, the Tarascans would have held a strategic flank on the fortified towns of the southern Matlatzinca Valley. Not only would the Tarascans be in a much better position to strike into the heart of the Aztec empire, but communication to other far-flung southern Aztec-controlled provinces would have been jeopardized with a possible net effect of curtailing Aztec imperialism.

The escalation of the imperial war drew the Chontal into a precarious situation. They were forced to forfeit valuable and rich lands and fortify in the hills in support of the Aztec-fortified colony above Acapetlahuaya. During this period of war, the Chontal must have shifted their economic focus from agriculture to the rich salt, metal, and stone resources available in the mountains and hills. These activities provided a certain level of wealth and status well into the Colonial period, but they eventually faltered with the changing Mexican economy, dooming Chontal Oztuma to become a waning backwater of Mexico.

Most geopolitical maps of the Aztec empire emphasize the internal organization based upon the tributary provinces and the demarcation of boundaries determined by powerful enemy-held territories such as Tlaxcala and Michoacan (Barlow 1949; Berdan et al. 1996; Kelly and Palerm 1952). While there is nothing innately wrong with such images, the observer must also be made aware that such reductionist perspectives can cause cultural myopia, where the frontier begins to look as though it is merely the epiphenomenon created by the force of two metro-poles. When this perspective feeds back into our process of analysis, the role of the occupants of the frontier takes on a secondary status at best. Under such conditions, the idea that the Chontal were their own agents becomes lost and they are seen as mere flotsam on a super-state tide. In reality, even in defeat they made choices that played into the major events of their time. Unlike many of the Matlatzinca who fled to Michoacan, the Chontal chose to honor their promise to the Aztec empire and successfully supported their lords against the Tarascans. Had the Chontal chosen otherwise, the geopolitical organization of Late Postclassic Mexico may have looked very different.

In the Maya example, there was a vast frontier between Naranjo and Caracol that stretched from the Belize River to the lower Petén. In the case of Xunantunich and the rest of the UBRV, frontier dynamics led to the relatively small size of local centers, and critical competitions over control of resources and their transport likely had a tremendous effect on the people living in the surrounding countryside. Frontier zones are generally considered anomalous, in the sense that the impetus for their existence is based upon tension between two political entities. They often develop for political reasons in areas not particularly well suited for large populations. Yet these frontier polities can exhibit significantly more wealth as a result of their strategic political and economic location. Local sub-elites may elevate their status by taking advantage of interregional trade networks and/or manipulating the patronage of important rulers. On the other hand, frontier settlements are more readily affected by events such as warfare, colonization, and/or famine. Such societal changes may significantly alter the social composition of a frontier settlement, but not be noticed at polity capitals where a positive front is portrayed. Xunantunich and its hinterland communities such as Chaa Creek lie at the nexus between three ecologically different and sociopolitically contrasting regions (Figure 11.2). Xunantunich, located on the edge of the Petén along a major river transport route, may have been a gateway leading into and out of the Petén, the Maya mountains, and the coastal regions accessible via the Belize River (Hirth 1978).

Border conditions often rely on a loose and open camaraderie, which can change drastically during times of conflict. In Belize today, the modern border town of Arenal is a fine example of a special arrangement created in a boundary zone. The town has a centrally placed football field upon which local teams play. Half of the field lies within Guatemala and the other half in Belize. This apparent atmosphere of harmony can shift rapidly depending on wider political circumstances or, conversely, local dynamics can affect larger political agendas. For example, tensions between Guatemala and Belize on an international scale recently escalated when a border guard in Arenal (who was not local) shot and killed a drunken border crosser. We should be aware of these types of dynamics in analyzing frontier settlements and how they define political relations.

As archaeologists, we cannot pretend to know the complete machinations behind the processes of competition and conflict between polities. Every incident or event is textured by complex webs of interactions (Mann 1986). For example, while our emphasis has been on sociopolitical, spatial, and economic definitions of frontiers, the role of ideology in the dynamic process should not be neglected. However, many significant interactions of intense competition and conflict along frontiers are about control over resources, primarily those that include a measure of unpredictability in terms of access to and amounts of resources that can be garnered (Ember and Ember 1992; Lekson 2002). A spatial perspective allows us to look at how resources move across the landscape.

In particular, we investigate potentially important nodes of transport and dispersal that, because they are nested within larger-scale interregional competitive dynamics, may display evidence in the material record for conflicts, especially warfare. What are the locations at the edges of containers that are valuable for controlling the passage of goods to the core? Oztuma and Xunantunich were at the nexus of vitally important nodes of resource flow and therefore these polities and their hinterlands, including Chaa Creek's Plantain Group and the Palos Altos River Basin, were both affected by, and affected, large-scale geopolitics and warfare.

Again, as we fly over the pock-marked landscape of Laos and visit villages that have only reconstituted since the end of the Southeast Asian war in the mid-1970s, we consider how the outcome of that war affected these people and how these people affected the outcome of that war. What decisions were made by towns and tribes as they juggled internecine and ethnolinguistic rivalries and alliances, economic resources, possibilities to migrate, loyalty to the king or to the Pathet Lao, and the philosophies of communism and capitalism? How did their decisions feed back into the Cold War period of history? From our own work in the highland border areas between Laos and Vietnam, it is readily apparent that many members of the over 60 ethnic groups in the area were part of what they called village militias during the American war. Allegiances with Americans, ARVN or NVA were highly transitory, with the priority always being placed on local security. Although no one has done a study of the role of village militias during the war, we would expect that militia members were significant players in all operations in the Laotian-Vietnamese border area. Local factions tend to seek out powerful allies as much as superpowers tend to seek out local allies.

In the late 1940s, as the post-World War II world began to sort out the new order, the common goal of independence led many of the Laotian royal princes in different directions. The most famous, Prince Souphanouvang, the Red Prince, a founder of the Pathet Lao and ally of Ho Chi Minh and usual rival of his half-brother, Souvanna Phouma, rose to the office of president with the fall of the French-backed Royal Lao government in 1975. Complex webs of intrigue and family rivalries seem to be a normal part of the dynamic that takes place on frontiers. As we watch the events unfold in the Middle East and ponder the dynamic between the Bin Laden, the Saud, and the Bush families and economic, political, and ideological forces, we cannot assume that the United States, as the superpower, holds all of the cards and is the sole determinant of the course of history. At each level, from nation-states to tribes to families, people from the frontier will strive to follow an agenda that differs from that of the superpower. Because of this dynamic, it is almost assured that even in the most ideal situation, the net outcome of intervention on a frontier will not meet the optimistic expectations inherent in imperial fervor. The variance between imperial ideal, often expressed in core rhetoric, and frontier reality, often expressed in the cost in lives and goods versus gains, may only be fully explained with data that includes a perspective from outside the metro-pole.

References

Adams, B. 1998. Analysis of the Xunantunich Archaeological Project (XAP) Human Skeletal Remains. Unpublished manuscript on file at the University of California, Los Angeles.

Arana, R. M. 1979. Patrones de un Asentamiento Prehispánico en Guerrero. *Vivienda* 4(5):390–409.

Arana, R. M., and G. Cepeda C. 1966. Localización de Sitios Arqueologicos en el Vaso de la Presa de Palos Altos, Guerrero. *Boletín de Instituto Nacional de Antropología e Historia* 26:14–16.

Armillas, P. 1942–1944. Oztuma, Gro., Fortaleza de los Mexicanos en la Frontera de Michoacan. *Revista Mexicana de Estudios Antropológicos* 6:165–175.

———. 1948. Fortalezas Mexicanas. *Cuadernos Americanos* 7(5):143–163.

———. 1951. Mesoamerican Fortifications. *Antiquity* 25(8):77–86.

Ashmore, W., S. V. Connell, J. J. Ehret, C. H. Gifford, L. T. Neff, and J. C. Vandenbosch. 1994. The Xunantunich Settlement Survey. In Xunantunich Archaeological Project: 1994 Field Season, edited by R. Leventhal, 248–288. Manuscript on file, Belmopan and Los Angeles: Xunantunich Archaeological Project.

Ashmore, W., and R. M. Leventhal. 1993. Xunantunich Reconsidered. Paper presented at the Belize Conference at University of North Florida, March 4–6. Jacksonville.

Ball, J. W., and J. T. Taschek. 1991. Late Classic Lowland Maya Political Organization and Central-Place Analysis: New Insights from the Upper Belize Valley. *Ancient Mesoamerica* 2:149–165.

Barlow, R. 1949. *The Extent of the Empire of the Culhua Mexica*. Ibero-Americana 28, Berkeley: University of California Press.

Beletsky, L. 1999. *Belize and Northern Guatemala: The Ecotravellers' Wildlife Guide*. New York: Academic Press.

Berdan, F. F., R. E. Blanton, E. H. Boone, M. G. Hodge, M. E. Smith, and E. Umburger 1996. *Aztec Imperial Strategies*. Washington, D.C.: Dumbarton Oaks Research Library and Collection.

Birchall, C. J., and R. N. Jenkin. 1979. *The Soils of the Belize Valley, Belize*. Supplementary Report No. 15. Surbiton, England: Oversees Development Administration, Land Resources Development Centre.

Castillo Trejo, N. 1967. Trabajos de Rescate Arqueológico en el Area de Embalse de la Presa Palos Altos, Arcelia, Guerrero. *Boletín del I.N.A.H* 12(30):24–29.

Chase, A. F., and D. Z. Chase. 1987. *Investigations at the Classic Maya City of Caracol, Belize: 1985–1987*. San Francisco: Precolumbian Art Research Institute Monograph 3.

———. 1998. Late Classic Maya Political Structure, Polity Size, and Warfare Arenas. In *Anatomia de Una Civilizacion: Aproximaciones Interdisciplinarias a la Cultura Maya*, edited by A. Ciudad Ruiz, Y. Fernandez Marquinez, J. M. Garcia Campillo, J. I. Ponce de Leon, A. Lacadena Garcia-Gallo, L. T. Sanz Castro, 11–29. Madrid: Publicaciones de la S.E.E.M. Number 4.

Chase-Dunn, C. K., and T. D. Hall. 1997. Ecological Degradation and the Evolution of World-Systems. *Journal of World-Systems Research* 3: 403–431.

Codex Telleriano-Ramensis. 1995. *Codex Telleriano-Remensis: Ritual Divination, and History in a Pictorial Aztec Manuscript*, edited by E. Quiñones Keber. Austin: University of Texas Press.

Codex Mendoza. 1997. *The Essential Codex Mendoza*, edited by F. F. Berdan and P. R. Anawalt. Berkeley: University of California Press.

Connell, S. V. 2000. Were They Well-Connected? An Exploration of Ancient Maya Regional Integration from the Middle-Level Perspective of Chaa Creek, Belize. Unpublished Ph.D. dissertation, Department of Anthropology, University of California, Los Angeles.

———. 2003. Making Sense of Variability among Minor Centers: The Ancient Maya of Chaa Creek, Belize. In *Perspectives on Ancient Maya Regional Integration*, edited by G. Iannone and S. V. Connell, 27–41. Los Angeles: Costen Institute of Archaeology Press at UCLA, Monograph 49.

Cornec, J. 1986. *Provisional Geological Map of Belize*. Belmopan, Belize: Geology and Petrology Office, Ministry of Natural Resources.

Dahlin, B. H. 2000. The Barricade and Abandonment of Chunchucmil: Implications for Northern Maya Warfare. *Latin American Antiquity* 11(3):283–298.

Demarest, A. A. 1978. Interregional Warfare and Situational Ethics. In *Codex Wauchope: A Tribute Roll*, edited by M. Giardino, B. Edmundson, and W. Creamer, 101–111. New Orleans: Human Mosaic, Tulane University.

———. 1998. The Vanderbilt Petexbatun Regional Archaeological Project: New Evidence and Interpretations on the Classic Maya Collapse. *Ancient Mesoamerica* 8(2):207–228.

Demarest, A. A., M. O'Mansky, C. Wolley, D. Van Tuerenhout, T. Inomata, J. Palka, and H. Escobedo. 1997. Classic Maya Defensive Systems and Warfare in the Petexbatun Region: Archaeological Evidence and Interpretations. *Ancient Mesoamerica* 8(2):229–253.

Durán, D. 1994. *A History of the Indies of New Spain*. Translated by D. Heyden. Norman: University of Oklahoma Press.

Ember, M., and C. R. Ember. 1992. Resource Unpredictability, Mistrust, and War. *Journal of Conflict Resolution* 36:242–262.

Freidel, D. 1999. Towards an Archaeology of Mayhem: Termination Rituals in Maya Centers. Presented at the 6th Annual UCLA Maya Weekend, University of California, Los Angeles.

Graham, I. 1978. *Corpus of Maya Hieroglyphic Inscriptions*. Papers of the Peabody Museum of Archaeology and Ethnology, Vol. 2, Part 2. Cambridge, MA: Harvard University.

Graham, I., and E. Von Euw. 1975. *Corpus of Maya Hieroglyphic Inscriptions*. Vol. 2, Part 1: Naranjo. Cambridge: Peabody Museum of Archaeology and Ethnology, Harvard University.

Hassig, R. 1985. *Trade, Tribute, and Transportation: The Sixteenth-Century Political Economy of the Valley of Mexico*. Norman: University of Oklahoma Press.

———. 1988. *Aztec Warfare: Imperial Expansion and Political Control*. Norman: University of Oklahoma Press.

Hirth, K. G. 1978. Interregional Trade and the Formation of Prehistoric Gateway Communities. *American Antiquity* 43(1):35–44.

Hodge, M. G., and M. E. Smith (editors). 1994. *Economies and Polities in the Aztec Realm. Studies on Culture and Society*, Volume 6. Albany: Institute for Mesoamerican Studies, The University at Albany.

Houston, S. D. 1987. Notes on Caracol Epigraphy and its Significance. In *Investigations at the Classic Maya City of Caracol, Belize: 1985–1987*, edited by A. Chase and D. Z. Chase, 85–100. San Francisco: Pre-Columbian Art Research Institute Monograph 3.

Jalpa Flores, T., and A. Ramírez Celestino. 1997. *Archivo de Ixtepec de San Simón (Oztuma)*. Estado de Guerrero.

Kelly, I., and A. Palerm. 1952. *The Tajin Totonac: Part 1. History, Subsistence, Shelter and Technology*, No. 13. Washington, D.C.: Smithsonian Institution Institute of Social Anthropology.

Kolb, M. J., and B. Dixon. 2002. Landscapes of War: Rules and Conventions of Conflict in Ancient Hawai'i (and Elsewhere). *American Antiquity* 67(3):514–534.

LeCount, L. J. 1996. Pottery and Power: Feasting, Gifting, and Displaying Wealth among the Late and Terminal Classic Lowland Maya. Unpublished Ph.D. dissertation, Department of Anthropology, University of California, Los Angeles.

LeCount, L. J., J. Yaeger, R. M. Leventhal, and W. Ashmore. 2002. Dating the Rise and Fall of Xunantunich, Belize: A Late and Terminal Classic Lowland Maya Regional Center. *Ancient Mesoamerica* 13(1):41–63.

Lekson, S. H. 2002. War in the Southwest, War in the World. *American Antiquity* 67(4):607–624.

Leventhal, R. M., (editor). 1996. Xunantunich Archaeological Project: 1996 Field Season. Manuscript on file, Belmopan and Los Angeles: Xunantunich Archaeological Project.

———. (editor). 1997. Xunantunich Archaeological Project: 1997 Field Season. Manuscript on file, Belmopan and Los Angeles: Xunantunich Archaeological Project.

Leventhal, R. M., and W. Ashmore (editors). 1994. Xunantunich Archaeological Project: 1994 Field Season. Manuscript on file, Belmopan and Los Angeles: Xunantunich Archaeological Project.

———. (editors). 1995. Xunantunich Archaeological Project: 1995 Field Season. Manuscript on file, Belmopan and Los Angeles: Xunantunich Archaeological Project.

Mann, M. 1984. The Autonomous Power of the State: Its Origins, Mechanisms and Results. *European Archive of Sociology* 25:185–213.

———. 1986. *The Sources of Social Power*. Vol. 1. Cambridge: Cambridge University Press.

Marcus, J. 1976. *Emblem and State in the Classic Maya Lowlands: An Epigraphic Approach to Territorial Organization*. Washington, D.C.: Dumbarton Oaks.

Martin, S., and N. Grube. 1995. Maya Superstates. *Archaeology* 48(6): 41–46.

———. 2000. *Chronicle of the Maya Kings and Queens*. London: Thames and Hudson, Ltd.

Neff, L. T. 1997. Pre-Columbian Agricultural Terraces in the Dos Chombitos Area. In Xunantunich Archaeological Project: 1997 Field Season, edited by R. Leventhal. Manuscript on file, Los Angeles and Belmopan: Xunantunich Archaeological Project.

———. 1998. Precolumbian Lowland Maya Population Dynamics and Intensive Terrace Agriculture in the Xunanatunich Area, Belize, Central America. Paper presented at the 97th Annual Meeting of the American Anthropological Association, Philadelphia, December 2–6.

———. 2003. Demographic Shifts and Agricultural Intensification in the Rise and Fall of Xunantunich. Paper presented at the 68th Society for American Archaeology, Milwaukee, April 13–18.

Plunket, P. and G. Uruñuela. 1994. The Impact of Xochiyaoyotl in Southwestern Puebla. In *Economies and Polities in the Aztec Realm*, edited by M. C. Hodge and M. E. Smith 433–446. Albany: Institute for Mesoamerican Studies.

Proskouriakoff, T. 1960. Historical Implications of a Pattern of Dates at Piedras Negras. *American Antiquity* 25:454–475.

———. 1961. Portraits of Women in Maya Art. In *Essays in Pre-Columbian Art and Archaeology*, edited by S. K. Lothrop 81–99. Cambridge: Harvard University Press.

Puleston, D., and D. W. Callender. 1967. Defensive Earthworks at Tikal. *Expedition* 9(30):40–48.

Reents-Budet, D. (editor). 1994. *Painting the Maya Universe: Royal Ceramics of the Classic Period*. Durham: Duke University Press.

(RG) Relaciones Geográficas. 1985. *Relaciones geográficas del Siglo XVI: Mexico, vols. 6–8*, edited by R. Acuña. Mexico City: Universidad Nacional Autónoma de México.

(RG) Relaciones Geográficas. 1987. *Relaciones geográficas del Siglo XVI: Mexico, vol. 9*, edited by R. Acuña. Mexico City: Universidad Nacional Autónoma de México.

Renfrew, A. C., and S. Shennan (editors). 1982. *Ranking, Resource and Exchange*. Cambridge: Cambridge University Press.

Robin, C. 1999. Towards an Archaeology of Everyday Life: Maya Farmers of Chan Nòohol and Dos Chombitos Cik'in, Belize. Philadelphia: Unpublished Ph.D. dissertation, Department of Anthropology, University of Pennsylvania.

Sanders, W. T., J. R. Parsons, and R. S. Santley. 1979. *The Basin of Mexico: Ecological Processes in the Evolution of a Civilization*. New York: Academic Press.

Schele, L., and D. Freidel. 1990. *A Forest of Kings: The Untold Story of the Ancient Maya*. New York: William Morrow and Co.

Schele, L., and M. E. Miller. 1986. *The Blood of Kings: Dynasty and Ritual in Maya Art*. Fort Worth, TX: Kimbell Art Museum.

Schortman, E. M., and P. A. Urban (editors). 1992. *Resources, Power, and Interregional Interaction*. New York: Plenum Press.

Sharer, R. J. 1994. *The Ancient Maya*. 5th ed. Stanford: Stanford University Press.

Silverstein, J. E. 2000. Imperialism and Conflict on the Aztec-Tarascan Frontier: An Archaeological Study from the Aztec Fortress at Oztuma to the Tarascan Garrison at Cutzmala, Mexico. Unpublished Ph.D. dissertation. Department of Anthropology, Pennsylvania State University, University Park.

———. 2001. Aztec Imperialism at Oztuma, Guerrero: Aztec-Chontal Relations During the Late Postclassic and Early Colonial Periods. *Ancient Mesoamerica* 12(1):31–48.

Smith, J. R. 1998. Geology and Carbonate Hydrogeochemistry of the Lower Mopan and Macal River Valleys, Belize. Unpublished Master's thesis. Department of Geology, University of Pennsylvania, Philadelphia.

Soja, E. 1971. *The Political Organization of Space. Association of American Geographers*, Resource Paper No. 8. Washington, D.C.: Commission of College Geography.

Spencer, H. 1882. *The Principles of Sociology*, Vol. 2. New York: D. Appleton and Company.

Stark, M. (editor). 1998. *The Archaeology of Social Boundaries*. Washington, D.C.: Smithsonian Institution Press.

Taylor, P. J. 1993. *Political Geography: World-Economy, Nation-State and Locality*. London: Longman.

———. 1995. Beyond Containers: Internationality, Interstateness, Interterritoriality. *Progress in Human Geography* 19(1):1–15.

Tezozomoc, D.H.A. 1987. *Crónica Mexicana*. México: Editorial Porrua, S.A.

van Zantwijk, R.A.M. 1967. La Organización de Once Guarniciones Aztecas: Una Nueva Interpretación de Los Folios 17v y 18r del Códice Mendocino. *Journal de la Société des Américanistes* 56(1):149–160.

Vencl, S. L. 1984. War and Warfare in Archaeology. *Journal of Anthropological Archaeology* 3:116–132.

Von Clausewitz, C. 1968. *On War*. London: Penguin Classics.

Wallerstein, I. 1974. *The Modern World-System: Capitalist Agriculture and the Origins of the European World-Economy in the Sixteenth Century*. New York: Academic Press.

Webster, D. 1976. *Defensive Earthenworks at Becán, Campeche, Mexico: Implications for Maya Warfare*. New Orleans: Middle American Research Institute, Publication 41.

———. 1993. The Study of Maya Warfare: What It Tells Us About the Maya and What It Tells Us About Maya Archaeology. In *Lowland Maya Civilization in the Eighth Century A.D.*, edited by J. A. Sabloff and J. S. Henderson, 415–444. Washington, D.C.: Dumbarton Oaks.

———. 2000. The Not So Peaceful Civilization: A Review of Maya War. *Journal of World Prehistory* 14(1):65–119.

Willey, G. R., W. R. Bullard Jr., J. B. Glass, and J. C. Gifford. 1965. *Prehistoric Maya Settlement in the Belize Valley*. Papers of the Peabody Museum of Archaeology and Ethnology, 54. Cambridge, MA: Harvard University.

Wolf, E. R. 1982. *Europe and the People Without History*. Berkeley: University of California Press.

Wolley Schwarz, C.B.V. 1993. Sistema Defensivo de Punta de Chimino, Thesis presented in partial fulfillment of the grade of Licenciada en Arqueologia, Guatemala: Universidad de San Carlos de Guatemala.

Wright, A. C. S., D. H. Romney, R. H. Arbuckle, and V. E. Vail. 1959. *Land Use in British Honduras: Report of the British Honduras Land Use Survey Team*. Colonial Research Publication No. 24. London: Her Majesty's Stationery Office.

Yaeger, J. 2000. Changing Patterns of Social Organization: The Late and Terminal Classic Communities at San Lorenzo, Cayo District, Belize. Unpublished Ph.D. dissertation. Department of Anthropology, University of Pennsylvania, Philadelphia.

Yaeger, J., and S. V. Connell. 1993. Xunantunich Settlement Survey. In Xunantunich Archaeological Project: 1993 Field Season, edited by R. M. Leventhal, 172–201. Manuscript on file, Belmopan and Los Angeles: Xunantunich Archaeological Project.

III

Themes in the Archaeological Study of Warfare

12

Warfare and the Development of Social Complexity

Some Demographic and Environmental Factors

STEVEN A. LEBLANC

The origins of complex societies have long been of interest to anthropologists. Why, after thousands of years of relatively egalitarian societies, did societies with great inequality develop in many places in the world? Why did people give up the broadly egalitarian relations of band and tribal societies for the imbalanced social relations found in chiefdoms and states? This is, of course, one of the fundamental questions of anthropology, and a significant number of different explanations have been proposed.[1]

The purpose here is not to review or critique all the models of the origins of social complexity, but to examine just one aspect—the role warfare has played in these social transformations. This is not to suggest the following process is a single causal explanation, but that considering it in future model building might be valuable. Warfare has certainly been considered an important aspect of the development of social complexity, especially by Carneiro (1970, 1981), but also by Earle (1997), and less specifically by Service (Cohen and Service 1978) and others. Most discussions simply suggest that warfare sometimes played a role without explaining why and under what circumstances it would be a key factor. There are important exceptions including Carneiro (1970, 1981), Earle (1987, 1989, 1997), Haas (1990, 2001), Hayden (1995), and Johnson and Earle (1987) who are more directly concerned with the role of warfare in social complexity, and this chapter is in many ways an extension of these ideas. But, the purpose here is not to review all the ideas and literature surrounding this topic. Instead, the goal is to try to model the role of warfare in some circumstances. This topic pertains to a number of the chapters in this volume, especially those by Liston and Tuggle, Arkush, Redmond and Spencer, Dye, Allen, and Underhill.

There is a logical problem with using warfare to explain complexity. It is becoming increasingly clear that warfare in the human past was virtually ubiquitous, for example, Brown and Stanton (2003), Keeley (1996), LeBlanc (1999, 2003), and Milner (1999). If so, why did it result in increased complexity only occasionally?[2] Although warfare was nearly ubiquitous, this does not mean that warfare explains nothing. On the contrary, if warfare was ubiquitous then all models must include warfare at some level. I hope to show how the interaction of warfare with variables of population dynamics and ecology could give rise to complexity in some cases, but not others. What I propose here involves the existence of buffer zones between polities. Therefore, the model is relevant only when buffer zones were present and of significant size. While I believe such zones were commonly present, there is no reason to believe they were universal in the past. As we build more complex models of the past, such models are unlikely to be universal models, but applicable only when particular circumstances occurred. Any model of how warfare can result in a rise in social complexity should predict a number of stages and consequences that are observable with archaeological and historical data (or both in combination). These models can be framed in terms of spatial and ecological parameters that should enhance their ability to be tested against actual data. I outline such a model and look at a few examples. However, the real test of the model must be done by the experts in particular areas using more refined data. Nevertheless, I do believe there is tentative supporting evidence for this model.

Aspects of Human Demography and Warfare

The interaction of past human demography and warfare is the underpinning of the model. My emphasis is the shift from tribal to chiefdom level organization, and to a lesser extent from chiefdom to state, so I focus on the features of these types of societies. A key point is that human populations will rapidly grow to reach the available carrying capacity in almost all situations. The arguments in support of this proposition are complex, as is the concept of carrying capacity. See Chapman (1988) and Dewar (1984) for good discussions of carrying capacity. These arguments have been presented elsewhere and there is no need to repeat them here (Bates and Lees 1979; Read and LeBlanc 2003). It is sufficient to state that the idea that human societies have mechanisms to control their populations well below the carrying capacity is without foundation. Human populations are capable of rapid growth and do grow in almost all situations when they are not constrained by the carrying capacity. Growth rates in excess of two percent are not unrealistic, and certainly rates above one percent could be, and were, regularly attained. In particular, tribally based farmers that are sedentary and store food are capable of significant growth. In the absence of new technologies or climate improvement, we would expect most such tribally organized societies to have their growth constrained by the carrying capacity except under rare circumstances. The failure to recognize this key aspect of the human condition has led to many incorrect models and explanations of human behavior. As assumptions about population growth are often implicit in many models, they must be carefully analyzed to see if they are realistic.

Responses to Carrying-Capacity Stress

There are a number of different responses societies make to carrying-capacity stress. These are sometimes misunderstood and are worth a brief discussion. Although treated separately, they would have functioned in concert. Social mechanisms to control growth certainly did exist in the past, but as discussed in LeBlanc (2003), and Read and LeBlanc (2003), among many others, they will not result in balance well below the carrying capacity, and their possible existence does not change the relevance of the following factors.

Starvation

Starvation certainly did occur in the past, although its effects were probably often disguised, because nutritional stress would have contributed to deaths from other causes rather than being the main cause of death. This has been shown to be the case in Europe, where death rates tracked the cost of grain, a proxy for availability of food (for example, Rotberg and Rabb 1983). Nutritional stress in the form of lowered birth rates, higher infant mortality, increased susceptibility to disease, and other stressors was a major factor in regulating population levels, but outright starvation would have invoked drastic efforts to overcome it.

In any case, while nutritional stress was common in the past, starvation could never keep population levels *well below* the carrying capacity in the long term. Deaths from famine will never exactly match the growth rate, so periodic famine will not produce a stable situation of a population so much below the carrying capacity that it is immune to nutritional stress. (See Read and LeBlanc 2003 for an extended discussion). So in non-state situations, no society seems to let starvation alone keep the population at or just below the carrying capacity without seeking other solutions. As noted, this does not mean that starvation, direct or indirect, would not have been a major factor in controlling population levels; it would have. The point here is that starvation would only control or limit population when it was near, or above, the carrying capacity. By the time a population was being limited by starvation the people would have long recognized the serious threat of their starving and would have responded in some way to the threat. People respond to carrying-capacity stress before they are decimated by starvation. Thus, starvation does not serve to reduce the population to the degree that there would be no response to nutritional stress.

Emigration

Far too commonly, it is assumed that resource stress can be relieved by emigration. Where would people go where there were not others with the same problem? The "solution" of emigration assumes that there is some place to migrate to where there will be sufficient resources. This must have been rare if in most places people were near the carrying capacity (LeBlanc 2003). People certainly moved, but they rarely did so peacefully, because other desirable places were already filled to carrying capacity. Small segments of a group can relocate, but it is hard to see how this can relieve a regional resource stress problem significantly for any length of time. Most emigration was really combined with warfare and needs to be conceptualized that way. That is, migration usually resulted in warfare with preexisting inhabitants in the new territory.

Apparent exceptions are the long-distance voyaging by the Pacific and Southeast Asian peoples, but this was done with only the faint hope of finding an empty land.[3] More often, people probably moved into inhospitable zones, such as malarial areas or very marginal areas as those with high risk for agriculture. In some cases the areas could be so marginal that the population was unable to reproduce itself, and thus became population sinks. Examples include the Nunu of Equatorial Africa (Harms 1987) and the Gidra of Papua New Guinea (Ohtsuka 1996); there are forager examples as well (for example, Davidson 1989). It is hard to imagine, and there are no known examples, of people leaving a peaceful, non-resource-stressed environment and moving to such inhospitable areas. That is, population sinks existed, but always within a larger regional context that included warfare. Probably the losers in conflict moved as the only alternative to annihilation.[4]

Intensification

An obvious solution to resource stress is to intensify production, thereby increasing the carrying capacity. Intensification should be seen as including the development of new technologies, as well as working harder and building productive facilities. Intensification requires increasing labor in almost all cases (some new technologies do not, but many, such as acorn processing do). This is the heart of the Boserup (1965) model. Intensification can be observed at all levels of sociopolitical complexity. Band-level Australian Aborigines replanted tubers and dug eel traps. Tribally organized California Indians shifted from high value resources to the intense processing of acorns, and manioc processing was undertaken in much of lowland South America. Terracing and irrigation systems were widely implemented over much of the world, usually, but not always, by complex societies.[5] Similarly, Hawai'ians built enormous fish pond/traps (Kirch 1984), and raised fields were extensively built in both Mesoamerica and South America (Denevan 2001; Pohl 1990; Turner and Denevan 1985).

Although intensification is almost ubiquitous among farmers in more complex societies, and even though it comes in myriad forms and represents great ingenuity and often massive levels of effort, it is not a long term solution to population growth.[6] Population will grow as these new resources become available. So, unless the rate of intensification keeps up with population growth, these efforts only postpone resource stress for a while. As intensification usually takes ever more effort to increase output, population will soon once again grow to the point it consumes the new production. It is possible that a confluence of factors—a series of new crops, some new technologies, and the like—might allow for intensification to continue for a long time. This may have been the case for the Aegean in the Early Bronze Age (Renfrew 1972). Overall, however, population growth probably caught up with major rises in the carrying capacity in a century or two at best. Moreover, as will be argued below, intensification required effort, so there was always a cost-benefit choice between intensification or seeking an alternative solution to the problem of increased population.

Most relevant to the argument being made here is that some areas are more amenable to intensification than others. While some intensification is probably possible almost anywhere, the labor effort to intensify would have been much higher in some places than others, and adjacent areas may have had different intensification potential. Even minor differences in hydrology or geology would make irrigation or terracing more costly, less productive, or almost impossible beyond some limits in some places, while these constraints may have been much more forgiving in an adjacent region or valley. Because intensification was unevenly applicable to an entire region, this would set up different cost-benefit choice options for different groups—a circumstance I return to below.[7] One of the alternatives to intensification, of course, was warfare. The differential ability to intensify among different zones may be more important than the absolute ability to intensify. Similarly, it is the rate that intensification could take place when compared with population growth that is relevant. Marked differences in the ability to intensify are more likely to result in intergroup competition than when everyone is similar. When the ability to intensify is low compared with the potential growth rate, we would expect more competition with other groups.

Warfare

A final option to population stress is warfare. One consequence of war would have been significant deaths. This does not mean that warfare functioned as a means to reduce population numbers, and warfare deaths may have been less significant than other effects, especially nutritional stress.[8] Some warfare deaths would have been direct, especially among men; other deaths would have been indirect, due to dislocations, losses of stored food resources, or fleeing in bad weather. Chronic warfare could be the cause of death of 25 percent of adult males and perhaps 5 percent of adult women, and perhaps an equal number of children.[9] Many tribally organized societies engaged in warfare regularly, most at least annually. We can characterize the warfare of such tribal societies as chronic and chaotic. Fighting consisted of raids and ambushes, with the dawn surprise raid a preferred tactic. Pitched battles did occur, often with hundreds of men involved, but generally battlefield leadership was weak. Most raids and ambushes resulted in only a few deaths, as did most pitched battles, but routs and massacres did occur. In spite of the low number of deaths in each event, cumulative warfare deaths were substantial. This is seen ethnographically from New Guinea to South America, and archaeologically in such places as California (see Feil 1987; Keeley 1996; and LeBlanc 2003 for extended discussions).

Rarely did one group have a technological advantage for long, and so each side raided, ambushed, and battled with deaths roughly equal. Since most tribal war is attritional, the larger the group, the more likely it would win out in the long run. Moreover, in order to keep one's group size large enough to survive, allies were needed. Tribal warfare was intimately intertwined with finding and maintaining allies. Failure of allies to support one in times of need was likely to result in rout and annihilation, or the disintegration of the social group. The inherent inability of tribes to maintain large cohesive groups and to manage them effectively in battle or raid made it hard for one group to gain the upper hand over their enemies. That is, in a given region, all tribes faced the same problem. They would all have grown to the carrying capacity, all would be trying to form and maintain alliances in order to survive, and warfare would be chronic. Classic examples of such situations can be found in highland New Guinea, among the South American horticulturists such as the Yanomamo, and areas of Africa and Southeast Asia; they are also found archaeologically in the American Southwest and eastern states, and in Europe.[10] Differences between tribal and chiefdom warfare are of interest. Tribal warfare tended to be almost continuous, or often annual. Once food stress became apparent to the population and starvation was a likely outcome, there were few mechanisms to stop competition. In contrast, the decision to go to war in chiefdoms was made by the elite, who had the option to choose not to fight. This may have resulted in some starvation or indirect deaths among non-elites. Nevertheless, it could lead to longer intervals without warfare. The political calculations of the elite entered the decision matrix and so warfare could be postponed or avoided. Conversely, chiefdoms could fight for reasons that did not help the population as a whole. Elites could see commoners as resources to be fought over because they could extract part of their production, where tribes saw land or some commodity, such as cattle, as the critical resource. That is, chiefdoms are interested in land indirectly in terms of what they can extract from the users, not in farming it themselves. So warfare sometimes appears less rational among chiefdoms in that immediate survival was not the main reason for going to war, but instead was for the aggrandizement of the elite. It should be noted, however, that a chiefdom that did not fight was likely to be eliminated by neighbors that did, so from the elite's point of view the warfare was for survival. For the commoner, it may have meant little more than one set of elites replacing another set. These factors tend to make it harder to predict when chiefdom warfare would take place or who would win.

Weak leadership and poor logistic abilities among tribes limited the type of combat that took place. Sieges, multipronged attacks, and the like were simply beyond the organizational capability of almost all tribes. In contrast, chiefdoms could effect some of these warfare methods. Tribes also lacked the supra-organization to plan for war. A chief could send out spies and collect data from a variety of sources to assess the enemy. Tribes had fewer mechanisms to collect such data. Tribes could not effectively amass the tools of war. Chiefs stockpiled weapons, built large and effective forts and war canoes, and by storing food within forts, maintained the ability to resist siege. That is, complex societies had many military advantages over less complex ones, so there was substantial benefit to being so organized. This factor certainly played an important role in the maintenance of complex societies, but it is not the particular focus here.

There is one other very common and important feature of competing, tribal polities and chiefdoms. Warfare resulted in buffer zones between groups. Such buffer zones play a number of important defensive roles. Buffer zones prevent destruction of crops because crops within a home territory can be destroyed only with much peril to the attackers. Because warfare was attritional, destroying the enemy's crops was a useful tactic. However, destroying crops takes time, and being deep in enemy territory is very dangerous, so taking time to devastate crops was not practical. However, if fields are planted at the very boundary of one's territory it is easy for the enemy to destroy crops while they are still growing, and so edges are rarely planted.

In addition, buffer zones serve as early warning system against surprise attacks. The greatest risk in launching a surprise raid is a lack of surprise. If a small group moves deep into enemy territory and is discovered before they can attack, the defenders can organize and counterattack. The attacking group will usually be smaller than the defending because men will have been left behind to defend against attacks from other quarters. As a consequence, defenders will outnumber the attackers and can devastate them.[11] Large buffer zones increase the danger to the attackers and increase the likelihood the defenders will discover the attackers in time. This is because the buffer zones are not left completely empty—they are patrolled and maybe even lightly hunted, and buffer zones are often observable from hill forts or other lookouts. They are, nevertheless, much less intensively used than land closer to the polity. Finally, buffer zones also lessen opportunities for disputes to arise, reducing the chances of wars starting at the wrong time and place.

Thus, where we have reasonable data, we find such buffer zones—often called no-man's-lands or empty zones—between competing groups. Examples are found among the Yanomamo (Chagnon 1968) and Highland New Guinea (Brookfield and Brown 1963; Heider 1979). Archaeological examples are also common. Buffer zones existed among the Maori—which were in some ways between tribes and chiefdoms (Allen 1994), in the American Southwest (LeBlanc 1999), Mesoamerica (Marcus and Flannery 1996), and the eastern United States (Milner et al. 2001) among many other examples.[12] The size of the buffer zones seems to be dependent on the nature of the crops. Standing crops such as corn seem to result in wider buffer zones than root crops such as bracken fern or sweet potatoes. In any case, buffer zones appear to be large given the territories of most tribal farmers. For example, in the American Southwest, allied clusters of communities were often separated by 20 miles from competing groups in the late prehistoric period, while the typical radius of an area they farmed was less than 10 miles, so that the buffer zones were wider than the farmed areas. If societies have circular territories and intensely use an area with a radius of A, and there is a buffer zone of width A between them, then over half the entire region is buffer zone. While this zone can be used to some degree, clearly the overall region's carrying capacity is greatly reduced, probably by at least a half. In the eastern United States, buffer zones seem to comprise well over half the entire region (see various chapters in Brose et al. 2001). Warfare and population growth result in the paradox that buffer zones significantly reduce the carrying capacity for a population that is already straining resources to their limit. Looked at from this perspective, any given tribal (and to a considerable extent, chiefdom as well) society has choices. It may try to limit growth, but this never works for long, so it is left with the alternatives just discussed of starvation, emigration, intensification, and conflict.

Beyond deaths, resources would have changed hands in warfare. Killing and taking another's resources went hand-in-hand. True replacement conquest (in contrast to subordination or control conquest), resulting in the elimination of one group and takeover by another group did occur over wide regions, and there are numerous archaeological and ethnographic examples. Most of the time this is a slow process, such as the well-documented case of the Nuer replacing the Dinka over a vast area (Kelly 1985). Even though there would have been shifts in boundaries and alliances and lots of deaths, in many instances the system changed little from a regional perspective. Some groups would replace others, some would fission, some would disappear, but the level of social complexity and the number and size of social units might be quite stable at the large scale. Tribal warfare of this chronic, but stable, kind is best attested in Highland New Guinea (Brendt 1964; Heider 1979; Reay 1959) or the Yanomamo (Biocca 1971). It is seen archaeologically among what Earle (1997) calls hill-fort chiefdoms, and in some periods in the Southwest (Haas and Creamer 1993; LeBlanc 1999), the southeastern United States (Milner 1999), and California (Lambert 1997; Lambert and Walker 1991) in North America.

However, the foregoing picture gives no mechanism for how social complexity could develop as a result of warfare. In particular, there is no incentive for enemy groups to coalesce or be conquered along the lines of Carneiro's model (see below). That is, most tribal warfare results in conquest of territory but not of people; one group simply replaces another, and so there is no change in social complexity. But, it is the consequences of chronic warfare that set the stage for potential changes in social complexity.

The Impact of Buffer Zones on Social Complexity

As noted, a particular and important consequence of warfare was the creation of no-man's-lands, or buffer zones. The creation of these zones stands out both for their importance and because they have been largely ignored in modeling ancient warfare. Chronic warfare seems commonly, if not always, to lead to such zones between competing polities. It also leads to the clustering of the sites that form a polity for mutual defense.[13] So, tribal and many chiefdom landscapes can be characterized as one of clusters of sites (strong alliances, or polities) separated by buffer zones, with flexible, ephemeral, and weaker alliances between these polities.

A dynamic of carrying-capacity pressure, warfare, intensification, and shifting boundaries would exist on the scale of a few generations. A very important point is that the buffer zones would have been largely empty, underutilized, or unutilized and fallow. As noted, buffer zones seem to have accounted for a significant amount of the land of a region. While it is hard to quantify the size, because the level of use would have tapered off as one moved away from the core area of each polity, it appears that such empty zones often contained 50 percent or more of all land in a region. The consequences of this significant empty land could have been profound.

Incidentally, failure amongst archaeologists to recognize the common existence of such buffer zones renders most regional estimates of carrying-capacity/population-size relationships fatally flawed. If population density is extrapolated from areas of known habitation to the entire region, and 50–60 percent of that region is unusable because of the need for buffer zones then the effective carrying capacity will be overestimated by 2–3 fold. Such a mistake is made, for example, by Allen (1997) for ancient Egypt.

Such a landscape of consequences and choices sets the scene for how conflict can result in increased social complexity. If by some means, two or more polities can be incorporated into a new polity, then buffer zones are not needed between them and they become usable. This results in an immediate increase in carrying capacity. When this happened, the enormous boost to the carrying capacity was much greater and quicker than intensification and must have been comparable to the most dramatic technological improvements. Because half a region's area could have been buffer zone, a doubling of the region's carrying capacity might have resulted. An additional benefit of combining territories could come about because a greater range of resources could be part of the larger, new system. If useful resources were unevenly distributed over the region, a larger system would be more likely to have more different types of resources within its boundaries than smaller systems (see Read and LeBlanc 2003).

The great gain in carrying capacity due to incorporating buffer zones into a new larger system would have been subject to the same problems of other gains in carrying capacity; the resultant population growth would eventually consume the increase. However, unlike intensification of agriculture by laboriously building productive facilities, the carrying-capacity gain due to buffer zone incorporation would have been very large and almost instantaneous.

It is this rapid and substantial change in carrying capacity that would have provided the opportunity for a new level of social complexity to become established. That is, the existing leadership, presumably war leaders, would have had a honeymoon period to develop a new social system to secure the benefits of being elite for themselves and their offspring. In order to become a new, stable social system, new rules and structures need to be devised. Very importantly, they need to be institutionalized. A doubling of the carrying capacity might have provided between three and eight generations of time to institutionalize leadership roles before resource stress would have occurred again. Thus, with luck, the newly established leadership may have evolved a new system that became stable.[14]

Elizabeth Arkush pointed out to me that there is still another factor related to buffer zones that would help an incipient leader gain support. Previous unoccupied buffer land would not have been "owned" by anyone. If the new leadership claimed these lands and parceled them out to their supporters, old allegiances and ties could have been broken and a new set of obligations and alliances developed in a very short time. While new leaders could reallocate land that had been previously owned by various individuals or social subgroups to attain the same end, especially among members of a defeated polity, this would presumably have resulted in considerable resistance and ill will. The benefit of allocating new lands, that is, unused buffer zone land, would have been that supportive members of the new and the old polity could be rapidly and meaningfully rewarded with almost no social cost.

Several factors affecting the ability to develop a new, stable social system would have existed at the same time. Potential external threats may have required the need for strong leaders, encouraging the system to stay large. The benefits of encompassing a patchy resource environment into one system would have done the same thing. Conversely, there are costs to large systems, both social and the more difficult task of defending a larger area, and so centrifugal forces would also have been at work. It is this interplay of forces that keeps the outcome of incorporating multiple polities into a new one from being automatic. Warfare may have resulted in the formation of larger, more complex political units that failed, which would then revert to their original sizes and complexity. So, a new, large system may or may not be able to overcome the forces of fission that will be at work.

Such a process of competing polities incorporated into one system with a subsequent increase in social complexity could be expected to repeat at various scales until some limit was reached. For example, a number of small polities could have subsequently grown into one system through a series of successful amalgamations on an island where no further polity-size growth was possible. Alternatively, there could be barriers that were too big to overcome, such as the water between islands, mountains or ridges, or stretches of desert that would all tend to limit how much any polity could grow. That is, if it was increasingly difficult to conquer areas, and similarly difficult to administer them, then a series of competing polities could emerge that would be unable to grow further.[15] Hawai'i provides a classic example, where single islands could be brought under the control of one chief, but multiple islands could not (until European technology enabled one polity to overcome the water barrier).[16] There are a few correlates of this model. As pointed out by Patrick Kirch (personal communication, 2002), it seems that the relatively more disadvantaged group tends to take over (conquer) the better off group. Or, the losers win. Those polities that are in locales that are least able to intensify will be more likely to compete with similar polities in that area, and a larger, better organized polity will eventually emerge. This polity will be able to take over adjacent land where there was a greater ability to intensify, as these localities would have had less warfare because of less competition over resources, and consequentially less skill and leadership for warfare. That is, we might expect a polity where intensification could easily take place to grow and ultimately take over relatively disadvantaged polities, but that seems to often not be the case. Instead, where intensification was a more rational option than trying to take territory, warfare skills would have been less developed than where warfare was the most rational option. Ultimately, those more skilled at war would conquer those more capable of intensifying.

Also, polity size matters. Two regions that are broadly equal in their ability to intensify will both reach carrying-capacity limits at nearly the same time. Unless extremely lucky, the smaller polity will not be able to conquer the larger polity, so we would expect the larger polity to win out eventually.[17] So, small polities that cannot expand due to geography are disadvantaged against their larger neighbors. If on the coast of Peru, each valley filled up, and perhaps each had equal potential to intensify, when it came to competition between them, the smaller valleys are unlikely to have been able to conquer the larger ones. So, the larger valleys would be able to conquer smaller polities, thereby get still larger, and conquer still more valleys. However, if the larger valleys were divided into competing polities, a fully integrated smaller valley may have been militarily stronger than any polity in a larger nearby valley, and been able to conquer a neighboring valley, one polity at a time. So there may have been two different processes at work. A somewhat smaller valley that first developed good military leadership and skills could conquer a somewhat larger, less organized valley, but there are limits to this. As discussed below, on the northern coast of Peru it was not the largest valley that became dominant, but it was not the smallest either. So there seem to be two principles at work: limitations to group size and limitations to intensification. Both predict which groups should win out, and one should expect a complex interplay of these two factors in any individual case.

Finally, it is worth considering the domino effect of one polity attaining, even briefly, a more complex social organization. Once one polity in a region does this, there is a high motivation for adjacent polities to follow suit. The new larger polity with more complex organization will have a significant military advantage. The other polities must reach the same level or be taken over one at a time. Thus, all polities in a region did not need to evolve from conquest directly. Warfare in one area that led to an increase in complexity may have been enough to cause it in an entire region.

The above discussion assumes a constant environment, but this was unlikely to have been the case for long. Resource stress would have been lessened by improved climate, and exacerbated by deteriorating climate. While climate is not the focus here, it was surely more important than most interpretations of the past admit. This is seen in the late prehistory of the eastern United States, where deteriorating climate had a dramatic impact on the social systems there (Drooker and Cowen 2001; Fitzgerald 2001).[18] What is relevant here is that in some cases the timing of climate shifts could have extended the time an emerging elite would have had to legitimize their new status (see below). In other cases climate change could have truncated the good times increasing the likelihood that the process failed.

To summarize, there are several aspects of these buffer zones that are significant: (1) buffer zones, also known as empty zones or no-man's-lands, are widely known both ethnographically and archaeologically; (2) buffer zones use up huge chunks of land and decrease the regional carrying capacity; (3) once incorporated into a polity, they provide a large, immediate boost in carrying capacity, and the resultant good times could enable elite status to be institutionalized; and (4) this would not be an inevitable outcome, but would depend on a host of other factors as well.

Circumscription

The present model bears some similarity to Carneiro's (1970) circumscription model for the origins of the state. He argues that states arose where agricultural land was limited by geography. He also applies this concept to chiefdom formation (1981). In places like the Nile valley, which are surrounded by non-farmable land, farm land was circumscribed. This, according to Carneiro, was unlike the Amazon or the eastern United States. Carneiro believes that in places like the Amazon there was no shortage of land, so for him, the opposite of circumscription is unlimited carrying capacity. In this he is incorrect. He also admits that "social circumscription" can exist in areas that have, in his mind, unlimited land. Such areas were those that were so highly populated that there is no empty place to move to, resulting in circumscription of farmable land. I believe almost all situations were of this kind. His model might be more reasonably formulated as contrasting circumscribed areas with those where the farmable area was very large compared with the size of the political units.

Carneiro argues that the war leaders would be appointed as political leaders, and the defeated would become slaves or subjects. There are primary differences in our models. I see "social circumscription" as being almost universal—most of the time, most people are surrounded by other people and usable land is limited. Carneiro does not recognize the importance of empty zones in enabling complex societies to take root. Moreover, he does not see the development of more complex systems as a stochastic process that can succeed or fail depending on local circumstances. Nor that circumscription, such as in the New Guinea highlands, does not automatically lead to more complexity, or that a key ecological factor may be the differential, not absolute ability to intensify agriculture.[19] I think what Carneiro may be seeing is that in some situations such as the Dinka-Nuer or the Yanomamo, any village or unit has a number of different places they can flee to when defeated. So starting with a territory of 22,500 km^2 the Nuer took over an additional 86,000 km^2 of Dinka territory without a more complex society developing. However, if a village or *nome* along the Nile were defeated, the linear placement of the settlements may have severely limited the number of social units one could move in with, thus increasing the likelihood the defeated people would be incorporated into the victorious polity.[20]

Circumscription, in the sense that competition results when no more intensification is practical, is part of the present model, although not key to it. I do not believe Carneiro would object to the present formulation, and he saw his original model as simply a first step in trying to figure out why warfare was such a key ingredient to the formation of state societies.

A Just-So Story of Chiefdom Formation

With these ideas in mind, one can paint a greatly simplified story of how a complex society could come to exist. Let us imagine a region with a series of competing tribal polities. Each polity would try to form alliances, but such alliances would be too weak to remain together for long. Suppose a particularly charismatic, inspiring individual comes along, perhaps a great warrior, but perhaps not, and is able to form a really effective alliance that is cohesive for even a short time. This alliance then has the potential to effectively defeat one or more neighboring polities and take over their territories. But more importantly, what if this leader(s) is capable of keeping the successful alliance together for a while? Suddenly, this group would have a greatly increased area, not primarily because it has captured new territory, but because the previously extant buffer zones both between allies and enemies are now available for use. It is also probable that these buffer zones had lain fallow for some time, if boundaries happen to have been stable for a while, and so the buffer zones might be particularly productive.

So, immediately after a successful conquest and consolidation of a group of tribally structured territories, the population would have been in a very favorable position. Warfare would presumably be reduced (not necessarily eliminated, as there might still be more enemies expected on the fringes), and carrying capacity possibly more than doubled, due to the new availability of the former buffer zones. Under such a situation, we would expect the population to begin to grow as constraints on growth would have been reduced. We might expect three to eight generations of good times resulting in population growth until the carrying capacity was again being approached and the good times would come to an end. It is this multigenerational span of the population being below the carrying capacity that may have been critical for the formation of complex societies.

It is useful to consider the problem of complexity from the point of view of the incipient elite. In a fully functional complex society, the elite have more wealth, and command the labor of many. They maintain this position with little overt threat of violence against those who do not acquiesce to being non-elite. This is accomplished, in part, by tradition. The elite are perceived by all as elite. They look and behave as if they are elite. That elite status is inherited is assumed by all. Or to put it another way, ideology and social practice legitimizes elites—non-elites accept the existence of elites and try to curry favor with them rather than deposing them. It works in part because it is self-perpetuating—sumptuary privileges and better access to wealth mean elites look and act differently from commoners. There are special clothes, burial practices, house types, ceremonies, and behaviors, such as showing deference, providing gifts or goods, and various other ways to demonstrate elite status. One important behavior is the public passing of elite status from generation to generation. Once in place, these differences tend to be self-fulfilling. The elite will command more and better quality food. As a consequence they will be bigger and healthier than commoners. The elite will command more and better quality clothing and ornamentation. As a consequence they will dress differently from commoners. They will command the resources to build larger houses, and have the ability to host feasts and other public events, which reinforce their status as powerful individuals.

In this situation the goal of non-elites is to become elite, or have their children become elite.[21] They try to be linked closely enough to elites so they are better off, both materially and in terms of status, than most other non-elites. There seems to be little thought of deposing the elites by non-elites, although there is plenty of competition among elites for the highest status positions. Once the concept that there are elites is established, the question becomes who gets to be elite, not whether there should be elites. Put another way, the concept of elites becomes institutionalized.

It is easy to see how such status differentiation can be maintained once well entrenched, but how does it get entrenched? It would seem that incipient elites would be expected to try very hard to institutionalize their positions as much as possible, and as quickly as possible. They would try to devise dress differences, create houses that were unique, and so on. Importantly, they would try and put into place the concept and practice of inheritance of their status. Thus, it is hard to see how developing and getting these institutions in place could take less than several generations. The newly emergent elites would need to maintain the new rules until everyone in the society grew up with them in place, so even the elderly could not talk about a time when status differences were not in place—a time when there were no elites.

Although there are several scenarios that come to mind that might lead to such a process, a charismatic leader taking control and being able to secure victory over surrounding enemies is quite likely. Because of the benefits gained from the elimination of empty zones, economic well-being would follow. If a threat of further conflict existed, this leader might have been able to argue for his continued leadership position to ensure everyone's security. In a time of plenty his taking resources from commoners would not be perceived as onerous, and the average person would probably have been better off (see Hayden 1995). As noted, the elites could buy allegiance and support by parceling out land in the former buffer zones to those who support them. The cycle of elite differentiation could have thus begun. A few generations later, the good times may have ended because of resultant population growth, but by then the behaviors may have been codified enough that the elites could maintain their position by tradition. Thus, leaders would emerge who capitalized on abundance, not scarcity, to institutionalize their status.

Such a scenario would be by no means assured. The leaders could overstep their bounds too soon and be deposed, especially if they did not have the benefit of learning "elite-craft" from older generations well schooled in its methods. Their enemies could be victorious either because the leader was not competent, or simply due to bad luck. Short-term fluctuations in climate could result in a decline in carrying capacity before several generations went by, and so on. That is, such a scenario may have been played out many times and only under certain circumstances would it work out that the newly emergent elites would retain power long enough for social differences to become institutionalized.

Additional Factors in the Emergence of Complexity

Any historic event that gave rise to a more stratified society must have been more complex than the picture painted above. Additional factors must have been at work, such as the existence of sufficient population densities to sustain elite-based systems. If there were not other constraints at work, we would expect all farmers to eventually become part of complex societies, something we know did not happen. On the other hand, there were long term benefits to belonging to a complex society that would have encouraged their becoming institutionalized and maintained. At least two such benefits can be envisioned. One relates to what other, nearby societies were doing. If one group becomes larger and better organized than its neighbors, it would have a continual military advantage. As discussed, it would be able to defeat any single neighbor. Thus, neighboring groups would be highly motivated to follow the same path of increased complexity, and amalgamate and form complex societies themselves.[22] If most societies in an area became complex, then it would be very disadvantageous for any group to revert to a smaller, tribally organized state, as it would be militarily disadvantaged. There may have been only one complex society in a region, due to environmental or topographic constraints, or simply because no individuals had enough charisma and intelligence to take advantage of the situation. The inherent centrifugal forces that would have existed in the one complex society could have resulted in its disintegration over time. For example, a weak or incompetent leader combined with food scarcity and a lack of dangerous neighbors might be enough for a subset of the complex society to break off and revert to a tribally based society, and the complex society might just crumble.

As mentioned above, another factor helping to maintain a complex system might be the nature of resource distributions within the territory of the complex society. If resources were patchy and unevenly distributed, then there would be additional benefits to being part of a larger society that incorporated these patchy resources into one system. That is, if each small tribal group's territory was a microcosm of each other small group's territory, there would have been no economic benefit to their combination, except for the aforementioned ability to utilize empty zones. But, if small group territories did not replicate one another, then their combination would have benefits. Foodstuffs and other goods could now move more easily from one zone to another, and the elites would likely facilitate such movement. Resources that became available in different seasons, necessary exotics such as stone for certain tools, or foods that would not all become scarce during drought or other weather changes, would all tend to increase the carrying capacity or reduce resource variability (which is much the same thing). Thus, these benefits would tend to compensate for the increased stresses and strains inherent in the complex society.

We should expect this complex matrix of benefits, drawbacks, and luck-of-the-draw in terms of inherited leaders' abilities, climate changes, and environmental variability, to result in a number of different outcomes to any single shift to complex societies.[23] But at the same time, we would expect the experiment to have been played out again and again, just as in a simulation model. Whenever the outcomes resulted in the elite maintaining their position for several generations and the underlying ecology was conducive to the maintenance of elite societies, we might expect the shift to more complexity to become institutionalized. That is, if it was realistically possible to sustain one in the region, we would expect the experiment to be run again and again until finally an elite society became established.

In other situations where the underlying factors did not favor the establishment of complex societies, these same experiments could repeatedly fail. Like Sisyphus pushing the stone uphill only to have it roll down before reaching the top, the process of attempting to form elites and their rapid dissipation could go on forever. Elite formation must need an underlying set of conditions for it to survive over time, and a set of particular circumstances for it to develop.

Warfare and conditions it sets up seem highly likely to be a prime mover, but not necessarily part of the underlying conditions necessary for elite systems to be maintained over the long term.[24]

A Few Examples

There are a few relatively well-researched examples of increases in complexity that can be examined with these ideas in mind. While I am not the expert in any of these areas, I think the broad trends are apparent. Other good examples probably exist, but they have yet to be accessible enough for the non-specialist to deal with them. The best examples we have of the process of changes in social complexity are with chiefdoms evolving into states, rather than tribes becoming chiefdoms. This is likely to be the result of the much higher archaeological visibility of chiefdoms and states compared with tribes, and not because the same process of competition and expansion was lacking among tribes.

Oaxaca

Kent Flannery and Joyce Marcus, and their colleagues, especially Redmond and Spencer, describe how the Oaxaca Valley held at least three competing chiefdom level polities, with clear empty zones between them around 700–500 B.C. (Marcus and Flannery 1996; Redmond 1983; Redmond and Spencer 1983). This case is discussed in much more detail in this volume. In short, the subsequent rapid move of one polity to take control of the heights of Monte Albán (which was initially defensible, and then later fortified) ultimately led to the consolidation of power in the valley. A major empty zone was removed and the new polity made use of the former empty land. It was earlier thought that the entire valley was unified at this time, but it now appears that conquest of outlying areas began by the Monte Albán polity prior to full valley consolidation (Spencer and Redmond 2001; Redmond and Spencer this volume). These outlying areas were less organized and had a different resource mix from the valley as a whole, and must have been separated from the Monte Albán polity by other buffer zones that could have been consolidated. So this process seems to be one where empty zones were turned into useful territory and the resource mix within the polity was increased, both of which would have been beneficial to population growth and good times for the polities' inhabitants. How the polities in each arm of the Oaxaca Valley formed initially is less clear. Did this result from tribal-level warfare? Also, it is not clear to me whether the polity in the northern arm—the apparent victor—occupied a less-favored portion of the valley than the other polities. So, this is a good example of regional consolidation as a result of warfare leading to a rise in complexity, but it is less clear as a test of some of the other propositions under consideration.

Egypt

The consolidation of power and the development of the Egyptian state seem to be a good example of the role of warfare, empty zones, and less favored regions ascending to power. According to Kemp (1989), and further discussed by Wenke (1997), as well as Bard (1994) and Trigger (1987), Egypt had a number of small clusters of farming communities, which evolved into completing polities with considerable buffer zones between them. These may be the origins of the 42 *nomes*, or administrative units, of Dynastic Egypt, and they seem to represent initial chiefdoms. In Upper Egypt, these polities were consolidated, in stages, apparently by warfare. In particular, one larger polity emerged from the consolidation of smaller polities around Nagada. This polity then conquered two other polities—those around Hierakonpolis and This—that had also consolidated. Did these latter two polities consolidate in response to the Nagada consolidation? The upper river became a single polity apparently after more conquest, and then the upper valley polity conquered the still politically divided delta. This led, in a few generations, to the formation of the classical Egyptian state with the attendant trappings of state-level organization.

Farming in the upper Nile River area would have been hard to intensify, when compared to the delta. The delta with its various ancient river channels and swamps was at that time a limitless resource for expansion, if enough labor was applied to it. In fact, intensification of farming in the delta continued to take place during Dynastic times, and in pre-Dynastic Egypt, it must have been a place where there were many opportunities for intensification. This was less the case in upper Egypt, where draining and canal building were not as useful or necessary. Thus, as population grew, it made sense not only to intensify in the delta but to conquer land along the upper Nile valley.[25] The upper valley polities that evolved from competition and conquest were the most likely to have the organization to successfully invade another's territory, and so the Nile valley population conquered the delta. As in other examples, the initial shift from tribally based clustered farming villages to larger chiefdom-based polities is much harder to characterize than the shift from chiefdom to state. It should be noted that some scholars such as R. C. Allen (1997) argue there was no population pressure during this span, but such arguments fail to consider the existence of buffer zones, or the trade-off between intensification and warfare.

Moche

The northern coast of Peru provides an interesting locale for examining some of these ideas. The Moche empire emerged from political consolidation in each of several river valleys along Peru's northern coast. These valleys were then incorporated into a simple state or very complex chiefdom (see Quilter 2002 for a recent overall synthesis). It has been argued that the Moche valley was at least partially taken over by a highland polity who were in turn driven out by an indigenous Moche polity (Billman 1999; see also Topic and Topic 1978).[26] After this victory, the Moche polity went on to conquer neighboring valleys with a resultant increase in social complexity. Of particular interest is that the Moche valley does not have the largest amount of irrigable land amongst these coastal valleys, but nevertheless emerged the victor. This would seem to be a case of good leadership and war organization born of necessity in the process of conquering and consolidating the entire Moche valley. This advantage was perhaps the reason this polity was subsequently able to conquer a nearby larger valley, which had not developed such war skills. Conversely, this might be a case of the less-favored valley winning out over the more favored one—the Kirch model. One suspects that ongoing research in these valleys will provide useful data on the role warfare played in the formation of the Moche empire.

On the far northern coast, the Jequetepeque and Seco valleys are so close that buffer zones seem to have included farmable land, where further south, inter-valley buffer zones would have been unfarmable. A large number of forts and fortified settlements in the Jequetepeque and nearby Zaña valleys may imply a more complex series of warfare events than in more isolated valleys related to the potential for valuable buffer-zone capture (Dillehay 2001). The Santa Valley may also be a case of intra-valley conflict finally consolidating the entire valley, removal of empty zones, and a resultant increase in complexity (Wilson 1997). Of course, after initial intra-valley conflict on the northern coast, there was external competition followed by multi-valley polities, and this was associated with warfare and ever-increasing social complexity. For example, sites in the politically consolidated Santa Valley are certainly clustered differently from the distribution of irrigable land, either for defense against attacks from other valleys or to form a line of defense against highland polities. It is interesting to note that this is the area Carneiro (1970) used in his initial theory of circumscription. There would seem to be considerable future potential for this region to provide further insight into the relationship between warfare and social complexity.

Okinawa

Political complexity came later to the Ryukyu Islands than it did to the Japanese Islands to the north (Pearson 1997). Survey data show that around A.D. 900 four site clusters existed on the southern one-third of Okinawa; these were probably organized as tribes. Each cluster had between 5 and 10 sites, and only a very few were located outside these clusters. Beginning around A.D. 1200, over 100 fortified castles were built. These were also clustered, and probably were the product of a dozen or so chiefdom-level organizations. Around A.D. 1350, "three centers emerged preeminent from the many contending chiefdoms of the previous period" (Pearson 1997:124). In the early 1400s, one of these complex chiefdoms defeated one rival and then 13 years later the other, consolidating power, which resulted in a state-like organization.

It is clear from the site distributions that the initial jump from tribes to chiefdoms was accompanied by a great reduction in the area of empty zones. However, iron became available around that time, and carrying capacity may have increased more from iron tools than from more available land. This may account for the increase in the number of polities, not a reduction as one might expect. Overall, there were multiple jumps in social complexity, accompanied by a reduction of empty zones, accompanied by considerable warfare and conquest. Further analysis might provide more insight into the role of empty-zone capture, and whether the less-advantaged polities won out.

Southeastern United States

The development of social complexity in the southeastern United States beginning about A.D. 800, provides additional examples of the processes under consideration. Some examples focus on single polities (Steponaitis 1978), others on larger areas (Anderson 1994; Anderson et al. 1986). Dye (this volume) considers several aspects of some of the better known examples, and demonstrates the intensity of warfare at this time. It appears that the same patterns can be seen in microcosm or regionally: consolidation of polities, elimination of buffer zones, and increased complexity. The formation of the initial Etowah chiefdom about A.D. 1000 is particularly interesting. Prior to this development there were "four contiguously-located, small scale social groups" represented by the Coker Ford, Cane Creek, Ellis, and Woodstock Phases (Little 1999). Within each site cluster/polity, villages were typically 2–5 km apart. Settlement location, walls, moats, defended entryways, and bastions point to significant warfare. The four polities were separated from each other by 33–55 km, and presumably they were competing with each other. A new larger polity centered on the Etowah site developed. Populations relocated, old buffer zones were eliminated, and new buffer zones were formed apparently in relation to polities in the adjacent Tennessee valley. The mound construction at Etowah implies the formation of a chiefdom at that time.

A similar process can be seen regionally with the development of more complex chiefdoms in the North Georgia region (Hally 1999). At A.D. 1000, sites are strongly clustered with typical clusters such as Hiwassee or Carters, consisting of several village sites, one or two of which had mounds that were presumably the residences of chiefs. Sites in each cluster are up to 10 km apart, but typically are only separated by 3–5 km. Given the large spacing between clusters, about 30+

km on average, the sites in each cluster would appear to represent simple chiefdom level polities. There is ample evidence for warfare between polities, and it is easy to see how eliminating buffer zones between the villages would have been beneficial. There were around 40 of these minor chiefdoms in this area that came and went, each typically lasting around 100 years, although the number and size of the minor chiefdoms remained relatively constant over a 600-year period.

We know from historical documents that in the mid-1600s some of these site clusters/chiefdoms were allied, or under the control of paramount chiefs such as the Coosa, or Ocute (Smith 2001). It is noteworthy that the spacing between minor chiefdoms within the zones controlled by known paramount chiefs was much closer together than was typical for most minor chiefdoms over most of this time interval. That is, it would appear that buffer zones were eliminated or reduced within the zones of the paramount chiefs, which would have increased local productivity. The closer spacing would have also made it easier to field large numbers of men. Interestingly the smaller paramount chiefdom—Ocute—was more tightly clustered that the larger Coosa chiefdom. One can surmise this was because the smaller group needed to be densely spaced for defense against the larger group. Thus, through time we see polities increasing in size and complexity and the concurrent reduction in buffer zones within them, all in the face of considerable warfare.

The area around Cahokia (Milner and Oliver 1999) presents a similar picture further to the northwest. The Cahokia area sites were tightly clustered with an empty zone between them and those in the Lunsford-Pulcher area. The spacing is only about 10–12 km between these clusters and a similar gap separates the Lunsford-Pulcher mound sites from the Maeys group further down the Mississippi. They all share Cahokia-style pottery and are in turn separated by an empty zone of over 30 km from a group of mounds sharing the Linn-Heilig-pottery style.[27] The distribution of the pottery styles and sites could be explained by the Cahokia group initially competing with the Lunsford-Pulcher group and subsequently conquering them, and then doing the same to the Maeys group. This would have resulted in common pottery styles and increased growth at Cahokia, both from tribute from Lunsford-Pulcher and Maeys peoples, and the elimination of the buffer zone between them. The Linn-Heilig group would not have been part of the chiefdom as evidenced by the wide buffer zone and different pottery. That is, these settlement and artifact data may show Cahokia in the process of expansion, with competing groups still nearby.

Polynesia

The various societies of Polynesia provide interesting examples of many of these ideas (see Kirch [1984] for more information on these examples and Polynesian warfare in general). Tikopia, a very small island of less than five km^2, seems to have contained three polities around A.D. 1600. One polity—the Nga Ariki—derived from an apparent migrant group that occupied the least productive zone on the island, conquered the other polities. From that time on, Tikopia was a single-polity chiefdom. This seems to be an example of the least favored and least intensifiable area producing the polity that wins out militarily.

At the other extreme, the Hawai'ian archipelago witnessed rapid population growth after being settled by long distance voyagers about A.D. 300–500. At first, occupation was limited to the well-watered, favorable windward sides of the various islands. Only after four to seven centuries of growth were all these locales filled up and occupation began in leeward areas.[28] Intensification started taking place soon after the population expansion into the leeward areas, especially via small-scale irrigation systems, but included terracing and fish ponds which required greater amounts of organized labor. There was more intensification potential, especially of pond-field irrigation systems, in the windward areas, but population grew all over. Kirch argues that for Hawai'i ". . . the most politically powerful and highly competitive chieftainships developed, *not* in areas where large-scale irrigation was feasible, but on the leeward sides of the islands" (1984:204), a pattern he sees for the Society Islands as well. As in other Polynesian societies, such as Samoa or the Marguesas (Roscoe 1992), it was difficult to bring entire islands into one polity for long, and multiple island systems were rarely attained, even briefly. Much of this may have been due to topography, with water barriers and high island ridges providing defensive features and limited communication that hindered the formation of larger polities. In particular, if there were natural buffer zones that were unproductive, then there was no carrying-capacity benefit to increased polity size.

New Zealand provides a still different insight. At European contact, numerous small polities were heavily competing with lots of buffer zones. The existence of 4,000–6,000 forts or *pa* demonstrates the level of conflict and how many polities there were, which is discussed in more detail by M. W. Allen (1996, this volume). The traditional view, put forth by Vayda (1960), was that warfare was over land. Additional land was available for farming, but it could have been brought into cultivation only by clearing virgin forest. Vayda suggests that this was a lot of work, and so warfare was a practical alternative. In contrast, Allen proposes that most of the good land, in the sense that it was located near other important resources, was already in production. The remaining land was either marginal for agriculture, due to the likelihood of frost, or not near other necessary resources. In either case, the option of simply moving to unoccupied land and farming was constricted and meant considerable risk of crop failure or inadequate diet. The choice between pioneering new land or capturing extant farmland seems to have been tipped toward capturing and defending good and well located land. It is interesting that no really large polities developed and social complexity remained minimal compared with other parts of Polynesia. Was this because clearing new land was always an alternative, keeping population density low? Was the short amount of time between the development of storage technology that Allen considers critical to the development of farming communities and European contact inadequate for the development of complexity? Or was the process truncated by a deleterious climate shift before it could happen? Was it because the staples were root crops that resulted in very small buffer zones that limited the benefit of capturing other polities? The shift to more complexity may have taken place had there been a few more centuries for the stochastic processes to unfold. Or alternatively, the formation of many small polities centered in hill-forts may have resulted in a stable situation much like in Highland New Guinea, precluding the formation of larger social units.

What Needs Explaining?

The above are some examples of complex societies developing from non-complex ones, and examples of jumps in complexity, from simple to complex chiefdoms, or chiefdoms to states. Why, and why not, do these jumps take place? How much is due to environmental constraints, how much to the ability to develop the requisite social mechanisms, and how much is simply due to the stochastic processes involved? For example, many times chiefdoms and city-states compete without reaching a higher level of social integration. These situations seem to result in what Renfrew (1986) termed peer-polities. Sometimes one of these peer-polities conquers another, but little comes of it—there is no scalar change the system. Such conquests are short lived, or they do not represent a change in complexity. Sometimes there is a minimal scalar change, but apparently not often. The Chimu state of Peru was technically an empire, but did not represent a significant scale-change from before. The Aztecs, too, conquered a number of other polities, but do not seem to have attained a level of organization more complex than many of the ones they conquered. In these instances, the system in a region apparently cannot develop beyond some threshold of size and organization. At least in some cases, this seems to be more a function of organization than of ecological determinants. For example, in Southwest Asia, Mesopotamian city-states finally gave way to empires, but only after a very long time. So while the model presented here can account for how a jump in social complexity might come about due to warfare, it does not explain why the process stopped in particular instances. A full understanding of the development of complexity is more than just how elites initially came to power.

Conclusion

Various paths to the development of complex societies must have existed. A path derived from the consequences of warfare appears to be one of these. Key to this model is that warfare was endemic most of the time in the past. The resultant buffer zones, combined with the need or benefit of strong war leadership, gave rise to situations that would be conducive to increased social complexity. The multigenerational benefit of having access to former buffer zones would provide the time needed to institutionalize the social environment for new, or new forms, of elites. This model also indicates the need to differentiate between mechanisms that maintain social complexity and those situations that initiate jumps in complexity. While the consequences of warfare may play a key role in increases in social complexity, it may have had a much smaller role in maintaining such complexity. The model proposed here results in testable implications allowing for reconsideration of the development of complex societies.

The present discussion also argues that any modeling of social complexity must include the demographic-ecological environment where it takes place. Population growth, resource stress, climate-environmental change, and warfare were omnipresent in the past, and multigenerational models that ignore these factors are unlikely to be very realistic. Models of the development of social complexity or explanations of shifts in complexity that invoke other factors as primary causes must show these omnipresent factors were either not at work or irrelevant.

Notes

1. While the original band, tribe, chiefdom, state typology of Service (1962) has been critiqued, modified and otherwise subjected to a great deal of revision and debate, as Earle (1987) notes, these concepts still have heuristic value. More elaborate schemas, such as that used by Johnson and Earle (1987), certainly also have value, but for the present discussion a simpler set of distinctions is adequate to make the points desired. Robert Carneiro (1981) provides a particularly useful discussion of the origins of the term chiefdom and misconceptions about the key aspects of chiefdoms.

2. That warfare was so common in the past is far from a universally held position. But the assumption that warfare was rare or absent in various societies was often based on negative evidence. Now that we are better able to recognize past warfare, and actually systematically look for it, it is clear that such assumptions were often wrong.

3. Obviously, new lands were successfully found. But the successful voyages are the ones we know about. Voyages from places like Tikopia, clearly related to population pressure, did not encounter empty places.

4. Reay (1959) discusses refugees as a result of conquest in the New Guinea Highlands.

5. The need to build terraces to increase carrying capacity is more common than often realized; see Donkin (1979) for their extent in the Americas.

6. Interestingly, because intensification increases population density, it increases a group's ability to keep others from expanding into its territory and makes it easier to expand into theirs.

7. It cannot be stressed too strongly that carrying-capacity limitations must be seen as trade-offs. For example, the Nuer could have significantly increased their farming yields, but cattle production was ecologically limited. However, the Nuer hate farming, especially the weeding, guarding and fertilization necessary to increase output, and they love cattle. Thus, the Nuer would rather fight for cattle and grazing land than farm more intensively. As the Nuer had considerable military advantage over the Dinka, they were able to expand at low cost. This is an example of those who chose intensification (the Dinka) losing to those who chose territorial expansion (Kelly 1985).

8. What was a rational option pursued by individual groups in a context of population stress may have reduced population numbers as a side effect. But this should not be seen as a deliberate and systematically pursued policy of population control.

9. Since these death rates are over an individual's lifetime, the male death rates work out to be somewhat less than one percent annually, and the adult female rate is less than one-quarter percent. Neither number is huge or insignificant. Warfare deaths would not solve resource stress and surely increased it by taking up land in buffer zones.

10. Of course, whether all such tribal warfare was the result of ecological factors, or whether revenge, attempts to gain power, and the like were also causes, is a matter of some debate. I believe there are enough cases where ecology clearly was the cause of warfare that one should be suspicious of cases in which it is argued the long-term ecological situation was not relevant, especially when the argument for non-ecological causes for warfare is based on negative evidence rather than on the demonstration that the societies involved were not under long-term environmental stress.

11. The inherent strength of the defense has long been recognized, and this is only one of many reasons why this is so. See Allen (2003) for a useful discussion of the advantages of defense.

12. Buffer zones also occur with chiefdoms, such as in pre-Classic Oaxaca or pre-Dynastic Egypt, and the late prehistoric societies of the eastern United States.

13. Alliance formation can also be expected under these circumstances. However, both alliances and buffer zones would not be static for long, and so only with very fine-grained chronometric control are they likely to be seen archaeologically.

14. Of course, a confluence of other events may have led to a society being well below the carrying capacity, such as new technology or benign climate cycle, and the same honeymoon may have existed for leaders in those circumstances. However, leaders with successful warfare experience would have been especially able to take advantage of such a honeymoon.

15. Conquest usually implies controlling the conquered people as well as their territory. With chiefdoms, this seems to be the case, and the local political system is often preserved.

With tribes, usually the losers are killed or flee, but a significant number may be incorporated into the victorious polity, but they lose their social identities in the process.

16. Polynesia demonstrates the full gamut of outcomes: large-scale consolidation in places like Hawai'i, partial consolidation in places like Samoa where single islands were rarely integrated for long, and New Zealand where a plethora of small-scale, simple chiefdoms were the norm. It would be interesting to understand why there were these different outcomes from very similar social systems.

17. This is particularly true for tribal warfare, which is highly attritional and in which leadership does not play a key role. With more complex societies, well-led and motivated smaller polities can defeat larger ones, up to a point. But overall, and over the long term, size does seem to matter.

18. See Fagan (1999), Lamb (1995), Leroy (1976), and Le Roy Ladurie (1971) for the importance of climate change and how rapid that change can be.

19. Most environments allow for some intensification, but some are much more amenable to it than others. So the cost of additional intensification will vary between areas. Where the cost is relatively low, it is the trajectory that will likely be taken; where it is high, warfare is more likely to be the chosen option.

20. Fleeing was not an attractive choice for the Dinka. When taken in they were usually stripped of their cattle and were considered at the bottom of the social strata. In addition, starvation, death from exposure, and so on accompanied such fleeing. Similar consequences occurred when polities were defeated in Highland New Guinea. When intensification in the form of farming facilities has been significant, people are very tied to their land, and fleeing is especially unattractive.

21. This is not easy, of course, because being elite is inherited, but such societies are somewhat fluid and there are opportunities, or perceived chances, to move up in status.

22. There are lots of good reasons for secondary processes to work, but the focus of this chapter is the primary emergence of complexity.

23. Such a luck-of-the-draw outcome may have been the case with the rise of Teotihuacan. By about 300 B.C. Cuicuilco and Teotihuacan were two major centers in the Valley of Mexico along with several smaller centers (which appear to have been competing). Cuicuilco was destroyed by a volcanic eruption, and Teotihuacan quickly became preeminent, resulting in major settlement-pattern shifts.

24. Underlying conditions seem to involve population and resource density, the amount of intensification, and the like.

25. This process would be comparable with the warfare vs. forest-clearing model of Vayda (1960) for New Zealand, only with a different set of options.

26. Coastal Peru is an area where warfare has been integrated into models of the origins of complexity, see for example Carneiro (1970), and various chapters in Haas et al. (1987).

27. One single-mound site lies between these clusters and had a different pottery style. It would be interesting to know if it was truly contemporary with the larger clusters.

28. While four to seven centuries may seem like a long time to fill up the islands, given my argument for populations to be at the limit of the carrying capacity almost all the time,

the Hawai'ian Islands would have been populated by a very small number of people, and have an area of 16,530+ km^2. Even at high growth rates it took a while to fill them up.

References

Allen, M. W. 1994. Warfare and Economic Power in Simple Chiefdoms: The Development of Fortified Villages and Polities in Mid-Hawke's Bay, New Zealand. Unpublished Ph.D. dissertation, Department of Anthropology, University of California, Los Angeles.

———. 1996. Pathways to Economic Power in Maori Chiefdoms: Ecology and Warfare in Prehistoric Hawke's Bay. *Economic Anthropology* 17:171–225.

———. 2003. Hillforts and the Cycling of Maori Chiefdoms: Do Good Fences Make Good Neighbors? Manuscript on file, Department of Geography and Anthropology, California State Polytechnic University, Pomona.

Allen, R. C. 1997. Agriculture and the Origins of the State in Ancient Egypt. *Explorations in Economic History* 34:135–154.

Anderson, D. G. 1994. *The Savannah River Chiefdoms: Political Change in the Late Prehistoric Southeast*. Tuscaloosa: University of Alabama Press.

Anderson, D. G., D. J. Hally, and J. L. Rudolph. 1986. The Mississippian Occupation of the Savannah River Valley. *Southeastern Archaeology* 5:32–51.

Bard, K. A. 1994. The Egyptian Predynastic: A Review of the Evidence. *Journal of Field Archaeology* 21:265–288.

Bates, D. G., and S. H. Lees. 1979. The Myth of Population Regulation. In *Evolutionary Biology and Human Social Behavior*, edited by N. A. Chagnon and W. Irons, 273–289. North Scituate, MA: Duxbury.

Billman, B. R. 1999. Reconstructing Prehistoric Political Economies and Cycles of Political Power in the Moche Valley, Peru. In *Settlement Pattern Studies in the Americas*, edited by B. R. Billman and G. M. Feinman, 131–159. Washington, D.C.: Smithsonian Institution Press.

Biocca, E. 1971. *The Yanoama: The Narrative of a White Girl Kidnapped by Amazonian Indians*. New York: Dutton Paperback.

Boserup, E. 1965. *Conditions of Agricultural Growth: The Economics of Agrarian Change under Population Pressure*. New York: Aldine, Hawthorne.

Brendt, R. M. 1964. Warfare in the New Guinea Highlands. *American Anthropologist* 66(4):183–203.

Brookfield, H. C., and P. Brown. 1963. *Struggle for Land: Agriculture and Group Territories among the Chimbu of the New Guinea Highlands*. Melbourne: Oxford University Press.

Brose, D. S., C. W. Cowan, and R. C. Mainfort Jr. (editors). 2001. *Societies in Eclipse: Archaeology of the Eastern Woodlands Indians, A.D. 1400–1700*. Washington, D.C.: Smithsonian Institution Press.

Brown, M. K., and T. W. Stanton (editors). 2003. *Ancient Mesoamerican Warfare*. Walnut Creek, CA: AltaMira Press.

Carneiro, R. L. 1970. A Theory of the Origin of the State. *Science* 169:733–738.

———. 1981. The Chiefdom: Precursor of the State. In *The Transition to Statehood in the New World*, edited by G. D. Jones and R. R. Kautz, 37–79. Cambridge: Cambridge University Press.

Chagnon, N. 1968. Yanomamo Social Organization and Warfare. In *War: The Anthropology of Armed Conflict and Aggression*, edited by M. Fried, M. Harris, and R. Murphy, 109–159. New York: Natural History Press.

Chapman, J. 1988. Putting Pressures on Population: Social Alternatives to Malthus and Boserup. In *Conceptual Issues in Environmental Archaeology*, edited by J. L. Bintliff, D. A. Davidson, and E. G. Grant, 291–310. Edinburgh: Edinburgh University Press.

Cohen, R., and E. R. Service. 1978. *Origins of the State: The Anthropology of Political Evolution*. Philadelphia: Institute for the Study of Human Issues.

Davidson, I. 1989. Is Intensification a Condition of the Fisher-Hunter-Gatherer Way of Life? *Archaeology in Oceania* 24:75–78.

Denevan, W. M. 2001. *Cultivated Landscapes of Native Amazonia and the Andes*. Oxford: Oxford University Press.

Dewar, R. 1984. Environmental Productivity, Population Regulation, and Carrying Capacity. *American Anthropologist* 86:601–614.

Dillehay, T. D. 2001. Town and Country in Late Moche Times: A View from Two Northern Valleys. In *Moche Art and Archaeology in Ancient Peru*, edited by J. Pillsbury, 259–283. Washington, D.C.: National Gallery of Art, Distributed by Yale University Press.

Donkin, R. A. 1979. *Agricultural Terracing in the Aboriginal New World*. Viking Fund Publications in Anthropology No. 56. Wenner-Gren Foundation for Anthropological Research. Tucson: University of Arizona Press.

Drooker, P., and C. W. Cowan. 2001. Transformation of the Fort Ancient Cultures of the Central Ohio Valley. In *Societies in Eclipse: Archaeology of the Eastern Woodlands Indians, A.D. 1400–1700*, edited by D. S. Brose, C. W. Cowan, and R. C. Mainfort Jr., 83–106. Washington, D.C.: Smithsonian Institution Press.

Earle, T. K. 1987. Chiefdoms in Archaeological and Ethnohistorical Perspective. *Annual Review of Anthropology* 16:279–308.

———. 1989. The Evolution of Chiefdoms. *Current Anthropology* 30:279–308.

———. 1997. *How Chiefs Come to Power*. Stanford: Stanford University Press.

Fagan, B. M. 1999. *Floods, Famines and Emperors: El Nino and the Fate of Civilizations*. New York: Basic Books.

Feil, D. K. 1987. *The Evolution of Highland Papua New Guinea Societies*. Cambridge: Cambridge University Press.

Fitzgerald, W. R. 2001. Contact, Neutral Iroquoian Transformation, and the Little Ice Age. In *Societies in Eclipse: Archaeology of the Eastern Woodlands Indians, A.D. 1400–1700*, edited by D. S. Brose, C. W. Cowan, and R. C. Mainfort Jr., 37–47. Washington, D.C.: Smithsonian Institution Press.

Haas, J. 1990. *The Anthropology of War*. New York: Cambridge University Press.

———. 2001. Cultural Evolution and Political Centralization. In *From Leaders to Rulers*, edited by J. Haas, 3–18. New York: Kluwer Academic/Plenum Publishers.

Haas, J., and W. Creamer. 1993. *Stress and Warfare among the Kayenta Anasazi of the 13th Century A.D.* Fieldiana Anthropology n.s. 21. Chicago: The Field Museum.

Haas, J., S. Pozorski, and T. Pozorski (editors). 1987. *The Origins and Development of the Andean State.* Cambridge: Cambridge University Press.

Hally, D. J. 1999. The Settlement Pattern of Mississippian Chiefdoms in Northern Georgia. In *Settlement Pattern Studies in the Americas*, edited by B. R. Billman and G. M. Feinman, 96–115. Washington, D.C.: Smithsonian Institution Press.

Harms, R. 1987. *Games Against Nature: An Eco-Cultural History of the Nunu of Equatorial Africa.* New York: Cambridge University Press.

Hayden, B. 1995. Pathways to Power: Principles for Creating Socioeconomic Inequalities. In *Foundations of Social Inequality*, edited by T. D. Price and G. M. Feinman, 15–86. New York: Plenum Press.

Heider, K. 1979. *Grand Valley Dani: Peaceful Warriors.* New York: Holt, Rinehart and Winston.

Johnson, A. W., and T. K. Earle. 1987. *The Evolution of Human Societies from Foraging Group to Agrarian State.* Stanford: Stanford University Press.

Keeley, L. H. 1996. *War Before Civilization.* New York and Oxford: Oxford University Press.

Kelly, R. C. 1985. *The Nuer Conquest.* Ann Arbor: University of Michigan Press.

Kemp, B. 1989. *Ancient Egypt: Anatomy of a Civilization.* London and New York: Routledge.

Kirch, P. V. 1984. *The Evolution of Polynesian Chiefdoms.* Cambridge: Cambridge University Press.

Lamb, H. H. 1995. *Climate, History and the Modern World*, 2nd ed. London: Routledge.

Lambert, P. M. 1997. Patterns of Violence in Prehistoric Hunter-Gatherer Societies of Coastal Southern California. In *Troubled Times: Violence and Warfare in the Past*, edited by D. L. Martin and D. W. Frayer, 77–110. Amsterdam: Gordon and Breach.

Lambert, P., and P. Walker. 1991. Physical Anthropological Evidence for the Evolution of Social Complexity in Coastal Southern California. *Antiquity* 65:963–973.

LeBlanc, S. A. 1999. *Prehistoric Warfare in the American Southwest.* Salt Lake City: University of Utah Press.

———. 2003. *Constant Battles: The Myth of the Peaceful, Noble Savage.* New York: St. Martin's Press.

Leroy, M. 1976. Ecological Instability, Population Change, and the Causation of War. *Peace and the Sciences* 2:41–51.

Le Roy Ladurie, E. 1971. *Times of Feast, Times of Famine: A History of Climate Since the Year 1000.* Translated by Barbara Brey. New York: Noonday Press.

Little, K. J. 1999. The Role of Late Woodland Interactions in the Emergence of Etowah. *Southeastern Archaeology* 18(1):45–56.

Marcus, J., and K. V. Flannery. 1996. *Zapotec Civilization: How Urban Society Evolved in Mexico's Oaxaca Valley.* New York: Thames and Hudson.

Milner, G. R. 1999. Warfare in Prehistoric and Early Historic Eastern North America. *Journal of Archaeological Research* 7(2):105–151.

Milner, G. R., and J. S. Oliver. 1999. Late Prehistoric Settlements and Wetlands in the

Central Mississippi Valley. In *Settlement Pattern Studies in the Americas*, edited by B. R. Billman and G. M. Feinman, 79–95. Washington, D.C.: Smithsonian Institution Press.

Milner, G. R., D. G. Anderson, and M. T. Smith. 2001. The Distribution of Eastern Woodlands Peoples at the Prehistoric and Historic Interface. In *Societies in Eclipse: Archaeology of the Eastern Woodlands Indians, A.D. 1400–1700*, edited by D. S. Brose, C. W. Cowan, and R. C. Mainfort Jr., 9–18. Washington, D.C.: Smithsonian Institution Press.

Ohtsuka, R. 1996. Long-term Adaptation of the Gidra-Speaking Population of Papua New Guinea. In *Redefining Nature: Ecology, Culture and Domestication*, edited by R. Ellen and K. Fukui, 515–530. Oxford: Berg.

Pearson, R. 1997. The Chuzan Kingdom of Okinawa as a City-State. In *The Archaeology of City-States*, edited by D. L. Nichols and T. H. Charlton 119–134. Washington, D.C.: Smithsonian Institution Press.

Pohl, M. D. (editor). 1990. *Ancient Maya Wetland Agriculture*. Boulder: Westview Press.

Quilter, J. 2002. Moche Politics, Religion, and Warfare. *Journal of World Prehistory* 16(2):145–195.

Read, D. W., and S. A. LeBlanc. 2003. Population Growth, Carrying Capacity, and Conflict. *Current Anthropology* 44(1).

Reay, M. 1959. *The Kuma: Freedom and Conformity in the New Guinea Highlands*. Melbourne: University Press of the Australian National University.

Redmond, E. M. 1983. *A Fuego y Sangre: Early Zapotec Imperialism in the Cuicatlan Canada*. University of Michigan Museum of Anthropology, Memoirs 16.

Redmond, E. M., and C. S. Spencer. 1983. The Cuicatlan Canada and the Period II Frontier of the Zapotec State. In *The Cloud People: Divergent Evolution of the Zapotec and Mixtec Civilization*, edited by K. V. Flannery and J. Marcus, 117–120. New York: Academic Press.

Renfrew, C. 1972. *The Emergence of Civilization: The Cyclades and the Aegean in the Third Millennium B.C.* London: Methuen.

———. 1986. Introduction: Peer Polity Interaction and Socio-political Change. In *Peer Polity Interaction and Socio-political Change*, edited by C. Renfrew and J. F. Cherry, 1–18. Cambridge: Cambridge University Press.

Roscoe, P. B. 1992. Warfare, Terrain, and Political Expansion. *Human Biology* 20(1):1–20.

Rotberg, R. I., and T. K. Rabb (editors). 1983. *Hunger and History: The Impact of Changing Food Production and Consumption Patterns on Society*. Cambridge: Cambridge University Press.

Service, E. R. 1962. *Primitive Social Organization: An Evolutionary Perspective*. New York: Random House.

Smith, M. T. 2001. The Rise and Fall of Coosa, A.D. 1350–1700. In *Societies in Eclipse: Archaeology of the Eastern Woodlands Indians, A.D. 1400–1700*, edited by D. S. Brose, C. W. Cowan, and R. C. Mainfort Jr., 143–155. Washington, D.C.: Smithsonian Institution Press.

Spencer, C. S., and E. M. Redmond. 2001. Multilevel Selection and Political Evolution in the Valley of Oaxaca 500–100 B.C. *Journal of Anthropological Archaeology* 20:195–229.

Steponaitis, V. 1978. Location Theory and Complex Chiefdoms: A Mississippian Example. In *Mississippian Settlement Patterns*, edited by B. D. Smith, 417–453. New York: Academic Press.

Topic, J. R., and T. L. Topic. 1978. Prehistoric Fortification Systems of Northern Peru. *Current Anthropology* 119:618–619.

Trigger, B. G. 1987. Egypt: A Fledgling Nation. *Journal of the Society for the Study of Egyptian Antiquities* 17:58–66.

Turner II, B. L., and W. M. Denevan. 1985. *Prehistoric Manipulation of Wetlands in the Americas*. British Archaeological Reports, International Series 232:11–30.

Vayda, A. P. 1960. *Maori Warfare*. Wellington: The Polynesian Society.

Wenke, R. 1997. City-States, Nation-States, and Territorial States: The Problem of Egypt. In *The Archaeology of City-States*, edited by D. L. Nichols and T. H. Charlton, 27–49. Washington, D.C.: Smithsonian Institution Press.

Wilson, D. J. 1997. Early State Formation on the North Coast of Peru: A Critique of the City-State Model. In *The Archaeology of City-States*, edited by D. L. Nichols and T. H. Charlton, 229–244. Washington, D.C.: Smithsonian Institution Press.

13

Archaeology, Cultural Anthropology, and the Origins and Intensifications of War

R. BRIAN FERGUSON

We are now well into the second decade of archaeology's discovery of war. To judge from the recent acceleration of publications and research topics, it seems certain to become a major field of study (Bray 1986; Carman 1997; Carman and Harding 1999; Martin and Frayer 1997; Owsley and Jantz 1994; Rice and LeBlanc 2001; Tkaczuk and Vivian 1989). The question is no longer whether, but whither, the archaeology of war? How will archaeological theory and findings develop? How will they relate to established interests in cultural anthropology? What new issues will archaeology raise? The potential theoretical impact of archaeology is great. As we see in this volume, within and across regional sequences there is tremendous recoverable variability—in whether there was a lot of war or little to none, ranging from raids to imperial conquest, and in clearly distinctive phases of military practice. That military variability goes along with variation in material circumstances and social and political structures, providing abundant raw material for theory on the causes and consequences of war. While ethnography remains much richer in coverage and detail, especially in non-material realms, archaeology has the advantage of very long time spans, compared to the usual ethnographic blink of an eye.

Although a great many ideas are raised in this volume, the over-arching concern is the connection between war and political consolidation. I will come back to that in closing. But this chapter goes in a different direction. While all the cases in this volume focus on prehistoric situations where archaeology shows war as unmistakably present, this chapter is concerned with two transitions: from the absence to the presence of war, and from prehistory to history. I argue two positions: ethnographic reports over the past five centuries do not represent the intensity of war in humanity's far distant past, and war as a cultural practice did not always exist. This is no assertion of some utopian idyll, of primeval flower children. Clearly, evidence shows interpersonal violence in some very early human remains, and collective lethal violence against other groups—war—has always been a possibility. Perhaps mammoth hunters had problems with each other; maybe Neanderthals and Cro-Magnons really did not get along. We do not know. But, I will argue, the preconditions that made war likely were lacking for most of humanity's really ancient history. If we stick with evidence rather than supposition, war was absent in many places and periods, it became much more common over time (although not in a straight line of increase), and in most very early archaeological traditions there are no signs of it at all. There was a time before war (also see Kelly 2000).

These claims are very controversial. In the past decade, the most prominent work by an archaeologist is Lawrence Keeley's *War Before Civilization: The Myth of the Peaceful Savage* (1996). This is a major book. It is the best, most comprehensive treatment ever of the *practice* of war by non-state peoples, a long overdue replacement for Turney-High's (1971) *Primitive War*. It is an effective antidote to the idea that such war was a harmless ritual, although whether this message will penetrate those non-academic circles where such misconceptions still run is another question. And it has been a great stimulus to a developing archaeological focus on war.

But there are problems with aspects of Keeley's book and other recent publications, most notably LeBlanc's, with Register (2003), *Constant Battles: The Myth of the Peaceful, Noble Savage*, Guilaine and Zammit's (2005) *The Origins of War: Violence in Prehistory*, and Otterbein's (2004) *How War Began*. Three important general issues are how the anthropology of war has been portrayed, the theoretical significance of Western contact in affecting indigenous warfare, and above all, the impression that has been given about archaeological evidence for war throughout the prehistoric record.

The first section of this chapter delineates the issues as framed by Keeley, LeBlanc, Guilaine and Zammit, Otterbein, and others. The second discusses the anthropology of war, and why the issue of Western contact has risen to prominence in that literature. The third, the substantive core of the chapter, is a preliminary overview of the archaeological record on the inception of war in many areas around the world. The fourth suggests reasons for the origin, spread, and intensification of war, including the impact of Western contact in Amazonia, and with special reference to the Yanomami.

The Issues

War Before Civilization is a general indictment of the anthropology of war. Keeley (1996; and see Keeley 2001:332, 342) claims that anthropologists have largely ignored what he calls "primitive warfare" (1996:4, 163), and have misrepresented it when they do discuss it, as "safe and ineffective" (1996:170), "undangerous, unserious, stylized, gamelike" (1996:41), and proposing "that nonstate societies were commonly pacifistic" (1996:25). He adds that a "handful of social anthropologists have recently codified this vague prejudice into a theoretical stance that amounts to a Rousseauian declaration of universal prehistoric peace" (1996:20). Keeley identifies me as a prime example of these tendencies (1996:20–22, 163, 203).

More consequential than what he has to say about anthropologists is the image he creates about the ubiquity and intensity of warfare in the archaeological record. I will not dispute here his characterization of ethnographic reports for the past couple of centuries. There is no doubt that the vast majority of nonstate societies practiced war, and war that produced high mortality over time. I do believe the *frequency* of war has been systematically inflated in standard data sets such as HRAF. Ember and Ember (1997:5) claim that 73 percent of non-pacified pre-state peoples make war constantly or every year—a remarkable proposition, but that is a subject for another investigation. More to the point for this volume, I *will* take issue with the projection of the ethnographic present throughout the archaeological past, the idea that recent measures of war by nonstate peoples are normal for non-state peoples through prehistory.

Keeley's position on this point is clouded by ambiguous phrasing, as in this passage:

> [N]othing suggests . . . that prehistoric nonstate societies were significantly and universally more peaceful than those described ethnographically. The archaeological evidence indicates instead that homicide has been practiced since the appearance of modern humankind and warfare is documented in the archaeological record of the past 10,000 years in every well-studied region. (1996:39)

Significant *and* universal? *Anytime* within the past 10,000 years?

Keeley never categorically states that war goes back indefinitely in time. But readers *take this to mean* that war is the norm throughout our prehistoric past (Gourevitch 1996; Simons 1997). For example, readers of the *New York Times* learned:

> The wonder of Lawrence H. Keeley's "War Before Civilization" is not the eloquent case the author makes that war has been a terrible thing ever since people started killing one another shortly after they first began to walk the earth. The surprising thing is that he has to make such a case in the first place. (Lehmann-Haupt 1996)

That interpretation is supported by quotes from Keeley such as, "War is something like trade or exchange. It is something that all humans do" (Pringle 1998:2040). Keeley also dismisses the idea that Western contact played a crucial role in the warfare ethnography records, saying it "merely brought some new weapons to fight with and new items to fight over," and claims that theorists who stress the importance of contact "deny the legitimacy of ethnography altogether" (1996:21).

Similar positions are advocated by others following Keeley's lead. LeBlanc and Rice (2001:5) speak of "a general avoidance of the topic" of war in anthropology. Walker (2001a:573) goes from noting the genuine lack of research on domestic and other "internal" violence among non-state peoples to imply that few anthropologists have studied war; and claims that "[t]he search for an earlier, less-violent way to organize our social affairs has been fruitless. All the evidence suggests that peaceful periods have always been punctuated by episodes of warfare and violence" (2001a:590). LeBlanc (1999:10–11) asserts that "the actual likelihood of there being a prehistoric interval of several hundred years' duration without any warfare seems small," and follows Keeley's dismissal of the impact of Western contact, stating "the colonial impact explanation seems close to being laid to rest." Several authors register varying degrees of skepticism about the significance of the Europeans' arrival for indigenous warfare (Bamforth 1994:95–97, 111; Lambert 2002:208; LeBlanc and Rice 2001:6; Walker 2001a:574).

Keeley's position on the ubiquity of prehistoric warfare has been affirmed and taken to a new level in LeBlanc with Register (2003). This book focuses more on archaeology, and is less critical of cultural anthropologists' research, though in passing it rejects an emphasis on European contact (2003:6). Its theoretical point is that the idea of non-state peoples being conservationists is a myth, arguing that population growth and resource depletion is what has made war so common—it is war for food (2003:9). That hypothesis is not relevant to this chapter. What is very relevant here is the assertion of the near universality of war throughout the archaeological record (see also LeBlanc, this volume).

> When there is a good archaeological picture of any society on Earth, there is almost always also evidence of warfare. . . . We need to recognize and accept the idea of a nonpeaceful past for the entire time of human existence. Though there were certainly times and places during which peace prevailed, overall, such interludes seem to have been short-lived and infrequent. . . . I realized that *everyone* had warfare in *all* time periods. . . . (2003:7–8, emphasis in original)

The editorial lead in a magazine exposition of his thesis reads: "Humans have been at each others' throats since the dawn of our species" (LeBlanc 2003:18).

Guilaine and Zammit (2005:ix–x, 20–22, 236–240 [French original 2001]) follow Keeley in emphasizing prehistoric violence, and portraying archaeology and anthropology as having artificially pacified the record. They do not assert that *all* prehistoric peoples had war, but argue that it was very common. They focus on Europe, especially France, and provide an almost overwhelming compilation of detailed brutality. Although the great majority of their evidence is from the Neolithic and later, they extrapolate this violence into earlier times where such evidence is lacking, with reasoning such as this: "The theory that warfare occurred in the Upper Paleolithic societies of the West seems entirely plausible, in view of the constant levels of aggression displayed by present-day hunting populations such as the American Indians" (2005:21). This is precisely the type of extrapolation this chapter argues against.

Now this debate has been joined, and complicated, by Otterbein (2004:10–15, 41–43, 98, 177–180, 199), a founding figure in the anthropology of war, who argues that there were two sociological starting points of war. The following is a very simple version of a complex argument: Raiding and ambush were a natural outgrowth of male-centered, big-game hunters who were already organized for cooperative killing. Such war existed for millions of years and was especially common in the Paleolithic. In some areas, a later shift to broad spectrum foraging broke up that pattern, and war disappeared. The absence of war provided the necessary stability for plant domestication to occur—domestication could not happen with war. Settled farmers could later take up war, for instance to control trade routes, but where that war was practiced, evolution to a state would not occur. For a state to emerge, war must be absent prior to the consolidation of "maximal chiefdoms," which are "inchoate states," although more typical chiefs use violence in internal factional struggles, repressions, and feuds. When states emerge, they reinvent war, and war spreads through secondary formations exposed to them. Among still-warring game hunters, domesticates can spread from their original centers, and long-time farmers can learn war by interaction with hunters, thus explaining the warfare of many non-state agriculturalists. Underlying this theory is Otterbein's long-established position that social organization for conflict is more important than conflict over scarce resources in generating war.

Otterbein's position is very different from those of Keeley and LeBlanc, and overlaps with mine, in that it recognizes great areas were without war for very long periods. The big difference between us is that he sees war as practiced by big-game hunters, and ending with a shift to more sedentary foraging, while I will argue the reverse: that war seems absent in the Paleolithic, and emerges first with more settled foragers (although most of them are peaceable). Evidence regarding that distinction will be noted as it comes up.

In asserting the deep antiquity of war, both Otterbein and LeBlanc rely heavily on the work of Richard Wrangham and others (see Wilson and Wrangham 2003; Wrangham 1999) on intergroup violence among chimpanzees. LeBlanc and Register (2003:86) argue: "If chimpanzees have a form of warfare, then it can be presumed that our forest-dwelling ancestors ('early hominids' or proto-humans) probably did too, because humans and chimps are so similar."

Intergroup violence among chimpanzees, and its implications for humanity, is a very large topic, which is evaluated in a book I am currently preparing. In that work I argue that the number of chimpanzee intergroup killings has been exaggerated, that where lethal encounters occur, they plausibly may be attributed to circumstances created by recent human activities, and that there is no basis for positing behavioral continuity of in-group/out-group hostility and killing in the transition from ape to human. Those issues cannot be discussed here, except to opine that chimpanzee behavior provides little support for the practice of war in humanity's distant past.

After discussing the chimpanzee material, LeBlanc and Register raise an idea with major significance. "If warfare has been part of the human condition for more than a million years (or six million years, depending on the start date), we just might be selected for behaviors that make us warlike" (2003:219–220). Although they go on to qualify the supposition, that idea succinctly identifies why the antiquity of war is such an important issue. Already, those who argue for a human biological propensity for war are citing Keeley in support (Fukuyama 1998:26; Gat 2000:165; Low 2000:213; Pinker 2002:56–57; Wilson 1998:341; Wrangham 1999:18)—despite the fact that Keeley (1996:157–159) himself disavows biology as "irrelevant." Now the circle is complete. While most archaeologists probably would agree with Underhill (this volume) that it is more productive to focus on the causes and consequences of war, rather "than endlessly debating whether inter-societal violence is an inherent part of human nature"—that debate is inescapable for archaeology. Like it or not, the archaeological record is central to this perennial question in Western culture.

The Anthropology of War and the Issue of Western Contact

Anthropological Visions

Whether archaeology, as a field, has willfully turned away from evidence of war, I leave to archaeologists to evaluate. In my reading, it seems variable. Clearly there was resistance to acknowledging war in the American Southwest (Solometo, this volume), but the issue of prehistoric war in the American Southeast has been actively discussed for many years (Dye, this volume). Without question, however, there is much more widespread interest in the topic today than even a decade ago. My first concern here is not with archaeology, but how Keeley characterizes the *cultural* anthropology of war of the past forty years.

To start, we can take up the claim that anthropology has ignored war. That was indeed true—forty years ago (Ferguson 1984a:6), not more recently. Compiling a bibliography of substantial anthropological discussions of war (including archaeology) in 1987, we quit around 1,500 citations, because there was no end in sight (Ferguson with Farragher 1988). The literature has grown by leaps and bounds since then. Even Otterbein's (1999) history of anthropological research on war was correctly criticized by Sponsel (2000) and Whitehead (2000) for ignoring entire areas of current research into war and other collective violence (and see Ferguson 2003). Tellingly, some international relations theorists are now looking for models of war in anthropology. Here is how one prominent political scientist characterizes anthropological research:

> For decades, anthropologists have been amassing a theoretically rich, empirically substantial, and methodologically self-aware body of statistical and case-study research on the relationship between war and culture in stateless societies and pre-industrial anarchic systems. (Snyder 2002:11)

Has anthropology portrayed war by non-state peoples as harmless, just a ritual or a game, with few casualties? Again, this once was true, long ago. Benedict (1959), Chapple and Coon (1942), Codere (1950), Leach (1965), Malinowski (1941), Naroll (1966), and Newcomb (1960), did say that primitive combat was largely a ritual without great consequence. Several other early writers, however, portrayed war as deadly serious struggle involving vital resources (Hunt 1940; Jablow 1950; Lewis 1942; Secoy 1953; Swadesh 1948). Otterbein (1999:794–799)—who critiques Keeley's history of the anthropology of war as inaccurate, and for having created his own "myth of the warlike savage" (1997)—does acknowledge a "myth of the peaceful savage," persisting as late as 1980. But besides those early citations I just listed, he provides no more recent cases of anthropologists promulgating that myth except to question the peaceable images about "Bushmen, Pygmies, and Semai" (1999:795–798). Each of those cases is a major debate in itself, and cannot be considered here.

In the present, two anthropological specialists on war and peace, Reyna (1994:55–56) and Sponsel (2000:837)—and only those two to my knowledge—argue that collective violence by comparatively egalitarian non-state peoples should be separated conceptually from the category of war, as defined by the practice of more centralized and hierarchical polities (though not necessarily states). Since the mid-1960s if not earlier, the vast majority of anthropological writers have agreed that among non-state peoples, war was very common and very consequential, both in casualties and in its impact on cultures. Few if any would fit the characterization on *War Before Civilization*'s dust jacket, that "for the last fifty years, most popular and scholarly works have agreed that prehistoric warfare was rare, harmless, unimportant, and . . . a disease of civilized societies alone."

As for my own view on war (since this has been made an issue), my first published research (Ferguson 1984b:269), on Northwest Coast warfare, was explicitly in support of Swadesh's (1948) view of it as lethal struggle for material gain, against Codere's (1950) view that it was ceremonial with few casualties.

> Northwest Coast warfare was no game . . . war was deadly serious struggle. Sneak attacks, pitched battles, ambushes, prolonged attritional campaigns, treacherous massacres, sporadic raiding—these were facts of life from before contact to "pacification" in the 1860s. . . . Warfare was, in large part, a contest over control of valuable resources. . . . Wars fought solely to capture ceremonial titles or crests seem to have been rare, despite the prominence given to this motive in ethnographies. (Ferguson 1983:133–134)

That work also cites archaeological evidence to claim that a war complex went back to about 1000 B.C.—although now I would push that to 2200 B.C., at least (see below). In discussing the theoretical significance of Western contact (1990:238) regarding war by Amazonian peoples, I wrote: "*It is an indisputable fact that warfare existed in Amazonia before the arrival of Europeans*" (emphasis in the original); and for North and South America, "Even in the absence of any state, archaeology provides unmistakable evidence of war among sedentary village peoples, sometimes going back thousands of years" (1992:113). Finally, prior to the publication of *War Before Civilization*, I (1997) had completed an essay all about evidence and theory regarding war before states.

Contact

So, what is all this talk about the critical role of contact with states, especially Western states? I was a graduate student at Columbia University in the 1970s, which was then the hotbed of anthropological theorizing on war (see Ferguson 1984a). In endless discussions, it became increasingly apparent that existing explanations of war were inadequate. They were overly abstract, and detached from its real practice. Ecological hypotheses looked best from a distance, breaking down on close inspection of behavior (a point relevant to recent theorizing in archaeology, where something very similar to the old cultural ecology has reemerged; see LeBlanc, this volume). Social structural theories went around in circles—does war create social patterns such as patrilocality, or vice versa? In the absence of compelling theory, there was a resurgence of the tautology that ruled anthropological theory for decades—and is still quite current—"they fight because it is part of their culture." At the same time, there was growing recognition of the importance of a historical perspective in general, of the critical importance of bringing in colonialism that had so often been ignored, and an awareness of the burgeoning ethnohistorical and regional literatures that matter-of-factly documented war as being highly responsive to changing contact circumstances. But history was paradigmatically excluded from anthropological theory on war. The goal of "Blood of the Leviathan" (Ferguson 1990) and *War in the Tribal Zone* (Ferguson and Whitehead 2000, orig. 1992) was to focus attention on historical connections, to begin theoretically mapping their dimensions and issues, and by doing so, create the foundation for a more realistic basis for explaining war.

Among anthropologists, there are significant differences in how the impact of contact has been conceptualized. Blick (1988)—who made the first broad statement on the issue—proposes a quantitative disjunction, between limited revenge fighting before contact and genocidal attacks after. I do not agree with either his general characterizations or the idea of a qualitative break. "Revenge" is more an idiom than a cause of fighting (Ferguson 1995a:354; cf. Ferguson 2005). Exterminative slaughter sometimes happens among non-state peoples, as in the northern Great Plains (Bamforth, this volume), and is remarkable even after contact, as in the rather extreme case of the Maori (Allen, this volume).

The position advocated by Neil Whitehead and myself is that Western contact generally transformed, frequently intensified, and sometimes generated war in extensive areas we call "tribal zones." For that reason, it is a mistake to uncritically project historically recorded war patterns into prehistory. Any effort to explain historic warfare should include historic conditions, although these by no means eliminate local factors engendering violence, or imply that there was no war before contact.

> For the anthropology of war, these findings suggest the need to reconsider current assumptions about the causes and practice of war in nonstate societies, which have been formed without reference to the contact-related variables identified here. What has been assumed to be "pristine" warfare now seems more likely to be a reflection of the European presence. This does not mean that nothing can be known about war outside the influence of Europe or other state systems. Archaeological data and judicious use of early reports from some situations can provide such information. The point, rather, is that we cannot discriminate precontact war patterns without a theoretically informed sensitivity to the influences of contact even in its earliest phases. (Ferguson and Whitehead 2000:27)

This is not much different from positions taken by some archaeologists dealing with this issue. Bamforth's (1994:112–113) thoughtful presentation of evidence of intense warfare on the prehistoric Great Plains concludes: "There is no doubt that contact period processes had profoundly negative effects on indigenous peoples and that an examination of those effects is necessary in any attempt to use post-contact information to illuminate precontact ways of life." Lambert's (2002:208–209) overview of North American archaeological evidence for war stresses the value of archaeology because it "focuses on a time before Western European expansion, colonialism, and other processes that altered the character and trajectory of many indigenous American societies." Walker (2001b) has detailed the massive, early and continuing, disruption and destruction of Native American people and societies on the Spanish borderlands of Florida. And even with all the prehistoric warfare in North America, a recently described study by Walker (Lucentini 2002:A9) of over 4,500 skeletons:

> found that those from after Christopher Columbus landed in the New World showed a rate of traumatic injuries more than 50 percent higher than those from before the Europeans arrived. "Traumatic injuries do increase really significantly. . . ." These findings suggest "Native Americans were involved in more violence after the Europeans arrived than before. . . ." Walker said that although part of the increased injury rate doubtless stems from violence by whites themselves, it probably reflects mostly native-on-native violence.

All these comments relate to North America. The two chapters in this volume that focus directly on the impact of Western expansion make the point even more forcefully. The Maori were hit with the full range of contact effects: new plants, animals, economic opportunities, tools, and above all, guns. They underwent massive sociopolitical change and reworking of cultural themes, leading to an explosion of warfare that killed about one-third of their population in thirty years (Allen, this volume). Peoples of East Africa were supplied with guns for slaving and the ivory trade, leading to not only massive mortality in raids, but forced displacements and ecological destruction, along with famines and diseases made worse if not caused by these changes (Kusimba, this volume).

The point of tribal-zone theory is that *everywhere* in the world where colonialism is impinging, recorded warfare cannot be taken as representative of precontact violence until and unless historical factors possibly encouraging collective violence are investigated. That is a major difference between the approach advocated here and that of Keeley, LeBlanc, Guilaine and Zammit, Otterbein, and many others, who continue to describe ethnographically reported warfare as if it represents an earlier phase of societal evolution. It may be that war is not dramatically increased by contact—the opposite may occur—but a lack of impact cannot be assumed.

It is unfortunate that the question addressed in some recent archaeological discussions is whether or not war existed before Western contact, or before states existed. To my knowledge, no one in contemporary anthropology suggests that it did not. Further, since I do not posit a qualitative break in the form of war before and after contact, I am not surprised to find prehistoric situations sometimes match or exceed the violence after contact. North American archaeology (and maybe beyond) seems inevitably headed for a conference titled something like "1250 A.D.," to comparatively examine the massive and widespread violence in the three centuries or so bracketing that date. But attention should also be given to the period from 1450 to 1550, or so, to ask if there was a lessening of actual violence in between this time and the first effects of Europeans. Only archaeology can reconstruct levels of violence from before and through contact, and could investigate—for instance—whether changing levels of violence accompany Western goods filtering in through trade networks, as MacDonald (1979) did for fort-building associated with protohistoric overland trade to the Pacific Northwest Coast.

Origins

But the archaeology of war must be very careful not to conflate *late* prehistory in North America or anywhere else with *all* prehistory. What sometimes seems lost in recent assertions that prehistoric warfare could be pretty terrible is the most significant question of all: can we identify an origin of war, or has it always been with us? Many have concluded that war is a relatively late human invention (Childe 1942; Ferrill 1985; O'Connell 1995; Roper 1969, 1975; Van der Dennen 1995:180–214; Vencl 1984:120–121). I am currently following in their footsteps, working on a global survey of archaeological evidence for war, from the earliest indicators up to the advent of historical records.

So what if no signs of war are found in early material? It is often said that "absence of evidence is not evidence of absence." Yet war leaves recoverable traces. Indicators of violence, or collective violence, in settlement and skeletal remains, weapons, and art have been reviewed elsewhere (Ferguson 1997:322–326; Lambert 2002:209–211; LeBlanc with Register 2003:58–64). By now they should be very apparent to readers of this volume. Yes, the chapters do raise cautions about evidence. Generally, the cultural presence of war is more visible than remains of actual violence (Arkush, this volume). Fortifications, nucleation, and movement to inaccessible locations all entail costs, and may be forsaken when war exists but only at low levels (Solometo, Allen, this volume). Even where war is intensive, central areas of cohesive war-making social groups may lack obvious signs of war, meaning researchers should look around the edges (Bamforth, Arkush, Connell and Silverstein, this volume). Skeletal material may be abundant, but unexamined for trauma, as in early China (Underhill, this volume). Yet when skeletons are examined, war signs show up, as in the North American Southeast (Dye, this volume), and in New Zealand, where violence is very clear in a total sample of fewer than a hundred (Allen, this volume).

These and other concerns understandably make many archaeologists reluctant to conclude that there was *no* war when they find no *indications* of war. Caution is always merited for any given case. What I argue in this chapter is that the early absence of evidence is not rare. It is a global pattern, and as such, gains probative weight. What is equally telling, is that around the world signs of war eventually do appear, clearly, and then continue through time, even when there is no corresponding improvement in the recovery of all physical remains. The complete absence of war indicators is followed by their clear presence. Looked at from these perspectives, I conclude, this absence of evidence should be seen as *negative* evidence. The simplest explanation is that war develops out of a warless background.

The next section is a summary of this work, up to its current point. Three caveats are in order. First, the research broke off before completing the west coast of North America, and several major world areas remain to be done. Second, these are preliminary findings; more research and reconsideration is anticipated for all regions. Third, this summary is very stripped down, leaving out details, dating issues, and most discussion of environmental, demographic, social, trade, and political conditions. All that will come (I hope) in a longer work. This summary focuses exclusively on evidence regarding the inception and early development of violence.

A Survey of Evidence for the Earliest Warfare

The Earliest Signs of Violence

Popular notions of the antiquity of war still seem to reflect Ardrey's (1961; 1966) dramatic portrayals, based on Dart's (1957:207) "blood-bespattered, slaughter-gutted" view of our past. Roper's pioneering survey of Pleistocene and Upper Paleolithic evidence contradicted that view, although she concluded "sporadic intraspecific killing probably took place" in the latter period (1969:448). Since then, additional, previously accepted cases of violence have been reconsidered and rejected (Binford and Ho 1985; Boaz and Ciochron 2001; Brain 1981; Ury 1999:34; White and Toth 1989, 1991). Not challenged (to my knowledge) is the Paleolithic individual Skhul IX circa 36,000 B.P.—once but no longer thought to be Neanderthal (Arensberg and Belfer-Cohen 1998:312)—from Mount Carmel, with what appears to be a spear thrust through its leg and hip (McCown and Keith 1939:74–75). Beyond Roper, at least nine sites from Europe to India, from 34,000 B.C. to 8,000 B.C. include signs of violence (Bachechi et al. 1997:137; Guilaine and Zammit 2005:50; Keeley 1996:37; Wendorf and Schild 1986:62, 74) (not including Jebel Sahaba or North America, below). At least one of those is Mesolithic (Sharma 1963). These finds in the growing corpus of skeletal remains essentially support Roper's earlier view—scattered interpersonal violence, but in circumstances that could include accidents, non-lethal intragroup conflicts, individual homicides, or executions. Neanderthal remains complicate the situation. There is much skeletal trauma, but usually not like that produced by combat (Berger and Trinkaus 1995), with two exceptions: the partially healed cut mark on the rib of Shanidar III (50,000 B.P.+), which Trinkaus and Zimmerman (1982:62, 72) call "the oldest case of human interpersonal violence and the *only* possible one among the Neandertals"; and the recently identified healed fracture from a blade-shaped object on the top of the skull of St. Cesaire 1, circa 36,000 B.P. (Zollikofer et al. 2002). There seems to be at least one clear case of cannibalism from 100,000 B.P. to 120,000 B.P. (De Fleur 1999:19), and even the earlier *Homo antecessor* circa 780,000 B.P. appears to be cannibalistic Fernandez-Jalvo et al 1999). The famous Krapina remains were judged *not* indicative of cannibalism by Trinkaus (1985) and Russel (1987a, 1987b), but White (2001) argues they are.

Yet cannibalism does not necessarily mean intergroup violence. The clear-cut case of Anasazi cannibalism (below) is *not*—all agree—indicative of war. And since the position of Neanderthals as human ancestors seems increasingly doubtful (and thus too *their* "antecessors" [White 2000:499]), the relevance of Neanderthal behaviors for *Homo sapiens* is questionable. Regarding the replacement of Neanderthals by *Homo sapiens*, there is no physical evidence to support the often suggested scenario that it took place through violence, rather than through some other form of competition.

Given the limited number and completeness of early human or hominid skeletal remains, and the amount of trauma reported—some apparently human-induced, most not, some maybe—patterns of Paleolithic violence remain enigmatic. The volume by Martin and Frayer (1997; and see Walker 2001a; Zollikofer et al. 2002) makes a compelling case for the need to consider the currently neglected issue of intragroup violence, such as club fights or domestic abuse, as a source of skeletal trauma. Defleshing prior to burial or reburial also leaves peri-mortem nicks and cuts that have nothing to do with violence. Is it possible that some of the reported trauma came from intergroup violence? Certainly. It is equally possible that none of them did.

Other claimed evidence for Paleolithic homicide or war is European cave art. Three representations at Pech Mere and Cougnac have lines which appear to go up to or through human-like forms (Leroi-Gourhan 1968:325, 1982:50). To Bachechi, Fabbri, and Mallegni (1997:136), who reproduce drawings of these figures, the lines suggest arrow shafts. To Kelly (2000:152–153), two of the images are "a portrayal of spontaneous conflict over resources," but by his definition, not war. For LeBlanc with Register (2003:5), they are "evidence of warfare." Guilaine and Zammit (2005:52–56) add other representations and see evidence of killings. For Otterbein (2004:71–73), they are proof of killings, and "the killings come at the peak of the hunting/warfare curve," although he then suggests they may represent an execution rather than battle.

Obviously, cave art is wide open to interpretation. Leroi-Gourhan (1968:323–325) sees them all as men "run through with spears." Giedion (1962:463–464) sees two of them as women, and one of unspecified sex, and concludes: "These figures depict no fight of man against man or of man against earthly foe. The 'arrows' that transfix the bodies of the masked or headless figures are magic projectiles." Either opinion is, of course, conjectural. For two reasons, however, I believe there is ample reason to question the consensus that these lines represent any sort of projectile at all. First, close examination of the representations (for good photographs and drawings, see Giedion 1962:462–467) shows that some lines are straight-ish, but others are decidedly curved or wavy. Compare this to the straight lines with exaggerated V-tips hitting large game, such as at Niaux (Giedion 1962:401–402). Second, in other cave art, from La Roche, Les Combarelles, and Abri Murat, similar lines go over, through, and around anthropomorphic figures, in ways that give no suggestion of projectiles (Giedion 1962:458, 459, 497). Perhaps the three representations are of a physical shooting, perhaps a shamanic one, or perhaps they are of something we cannot imagine. They do not prove the existence of human killings, and certainly not of war.

For evidence of collective violence, or war, the earliest accepted case remains the Nile Site 117, near Jebel Sahaba, very roughly estimated at about 12,000 B.P., where 24 of 59 well-preserved skeletons were associated with stone artifacts interpreted as parts of projectiles (Wendorf 1968:90–93; Wendorf and Schild 1986:818–824). This is a true outlier, without continuation, as that part of the Nile appears to have been abandoned soon after (Close 1996:47–50; Midant-Reyes 1992:63–64). The other exceptionally early evidence comes from northern Australia, where rock art suggests interpersonal violence between individuals or a few people from perhaps as early as 10,000 B.P., and group clashes from about 6,000 B.P. Here violence seems to continue thereafter (Tacon and Chippindale 1994).

Otterbein (2004:73–74) cites both cases in support of his theory that big-game hunters were warriors who gave up war as they moved into broad-spectrum foraging. The Australian case would support his association with big-game hunters, except that the art shows a progression from single fights to larger engagements. Site 117 is a different story. These were semi-sedentary people, alternately labeled Epipaleolithic or Mesolithic. For several thousand years, people of the Qadan culture had relied on catfish, water fowl, and wild grasses on the Nile's broad flood plain. These were broad-spectrum foragers, not big-game hunters, and their turn to war seems to have occurred as the Nile cut a new gorge and eliminated the flood plain (Close 1996:47–50; Midant-Reyes 1992:63–64).

The Middle East and Asia

The Middle East

This part of the world is very well known through archaeological work. In the Mesolithic, the Natufian people, semi-sedentary hunter-gatherers from 10,800 B.C. to 8,500 B.C., left extensive remains, including 370 carefully analyzed skeletons. Only two indicate any sort of trauma, and neither those nor anything else suggests military actions (Belfer-Cohen et al. 1991:412, 420–441; Henry 1985:376). Roper followed her article on the Pleistocene and Upper Paleolithic with a survey of evidence in the Middle East (1975). She accepted the prevailing view that the first clear evidence of war is the initial wall of Jericho, circa 7500 B.C., although she notes that this is the sole evidence in the Levant region until the sixth millennium (1975:304–310). Since then, however, Bar Yosef (1986) has argued persuasively that this first wall seems intended for flood control, rather than defense. Even Keeley (1996:38) acknowledges the general absence of war evidence in the Early Neolithic, although he does not consider the significance of that fact, instead treating it as a curious oddity.

Roper (1975:310–312) surveyed 18 sites from the seventh millennium, and the existing claims for war in five of them. She concludes none show "conclusive evidence" for war. I agree, except for Catal Huyuk, in Turkish Anatolia (6,250–5,400 B.C.), where the sum of evidence—particularly burials with daggers and maces (which Roper does not mention)—does support its presence (Mellaart 1967:68–69, 207, 209). Three older Neolithic excavations from northern Iraq, however, post-dating Roper's survey, clearly indicate war. The earliest is Qermez Dere (8250–7700 B.C.), with maces and enlarged projectile points (Watkins 1992:65, 68–69); the others, from roughly a thousand years later, have, in one, a major defensive wall, and in the other, maces and skeletons in association with arrowheads (Kozlowski 1989:27; Lloyd 1984:33). I take this time and place as the origin of a pattern of regular warfare that has continued down to the present day.

Roper's (1975:317–324) survey indicates regional differences in the sixth millennium. Settlements around Israel and Jordan remain without signs of war, but southern Turkey and northern Iraq and Syria have several clearly fortified locations from 5900–5200 B.C., some of which, such as Hacilar II, were destroyed with other indications of attack (see Mellaart 1975:115–118). In the fifth millennium, unambiguous indications of war become common across and around Anatolia, by the mid-millennium forming a continuous strip from northern Iraq through southern Turkey. In contrast, the Ubaid people of the Mesopotamian plains did know war, as evidenced by maces, but remained without the fortifications, settlement destructions, and militaristic art later characteristic of that area (Roper 1975:323–328; Stein 1994:38–40). Around 4300 B.C., on the Anatolian coast at Mersin, there appears to be a true fort, rather than a walled village, which was destroyed after about a century and reoccupied by Ubaid people (see Mellaart 1975:126–129). From then on, "[f]ortifications became the rule rather than the exception" (Roper 1975:329). Signs of actual fighting remain rather limited in the (poorly excavated) transition to Uruk after 3800 B.C. (Wright 1986:335), but by the time of rival city-states a thousand years later, a variety of evidence indicates intense and frequent war (Jacobsen 1976:77–79, 224).

From the Nile to Harappa

By 4500 B.C. if not earlier, there were several interacting areas of urbanization and state formation reaching from Egypt to the Indus and into Central Asia (Lamberg-Karlovsky 1981; Rowlands et al. 1987; Tosi 1979). Along the Nile, leaving aside Jebel Sahaba, the initial development of war is not visible, given the absence of an early archaeological record due to erosions, and classical archaeologists' interests in later periods. Evidence begins around 4300 B.C., with settled farming villages. In one of the northern Nile traditions, Merimda peoples had pear-shaped, Mesopotamian-style maces. Far to the south, people of the Khartoum Mesolithic of the mid-late seventh millennium made stone disks which are similar to disk-shaped maces used in its later Neolithic (5600–4300 B.C.) That style mace was also found in a second agricultural (4000–3500 B.C.) tradition of the middle Nile, which was the center of Egypt's later unification. After 3500 B.C. the pear-shaped mace replaced the disk (Fage and Oliver 1975:499–510; Midant-Reynes 1992:92–94, 127–131, 193). How much actual fighting was going on is unknown, and remains highly controversial even for the later development of Egypt (Savage 1997). But clearly war was present, though whether it developed locally or via external influence, and when, cannot be ascertained.

East of the Caspian Sea was a variously named area I will refer to as Namazga, after its best archaeological sequence. Agriculture spread into this area sometime before 6000 B.C., and small, undefended farming communities grew up amidst much more numerous Mesolithic sites (Dolukhanov 1986a: 124, 128–129; Kohl 1981:ix). Indications of war—settlements with ditches and towers—appear only in the Chalcolithic (radiocarbon dates vary greatly), just before major urban growth (Gupta 1979:56, 84–85). In the Bronze Age, from about 3000 B.C., large defensive walls become common, and by 2300 B.C. were spreading eastward along trade routes to Tajikistan and perhaps beyond (Kohl 1981:ix, xiv–xxii, xxix).

Further south, in the high country of Pakistan, early farmers were erecting village walls by 4000 B.C. (Miller 1985:39). To the east, down in the lowlands, at least some pre-Harappan settlements saw walls go up in their later phases, 3100–1900 B.C., and were subsequently occupied by people of the Harappan culture (Sankalia 1974:338, 342, 344, 357). For mature Harappa (2500–1800 B.C.), there is significant scholarly difference over the importance of war. Some see little, some a lot (for example, Jacobson 1986:160–162; Miller 1985:58). My reading of the evidence is that organized warfare was known, but less elaborated and practiced than in western or central Asia. In late Harappa, there are indications of intensifying warfare, although that evidence is accompanied by its own debates (Dyson 1982:421; Singh 1965:88–90, 121). But as Harappan civilization declined, evidence of widespread, very destructive wars becomes unmistakable, as narrated in the Rg Veda (Basham 1959:31–45; Singh 1965).

China and Its Environs

Like the Middle East, the Chinese archaeological record is massive, although, of course, mostly written in Chinese, and much of it has not been scrutinized for indicators of war (see Underhill, this volume). From the earliest Neolithic Peilikang phase, many villages and burials have been excavated, with no signs of violence. After 5000 B.C., distinctive regional Neolithics emerge. Among the Yangshao in the central Yellow River valley, many villages have surrounding ditches. Excavators interpret these as defensive, and some also have palisades. At least one late Yangshao village is surrounded by a rammed-earth wall (Chang 1986:87–90, 107–116; Needham and Yates 1994:241–242; Underhill 1989:229–230). One Yangshao skeleton has an embedded arrowhead, and another has been found from the Dawenkou Neolithic farther east, circa 5000 B.C. Underhill calls this "the only convincing skeletal evidence [for warfare] from the pre-Longshan period" (Underhill 1989:231), although again, few skeletons have been studied.

Regional Neolithics developed and expanded throughout the fourth millennium. By 3000 B.C., many distinctive features of Chinese civilization appeared in the extensive Longshan interaction sphere. In some regions of the later Longshan, there was war. Five locations after 2600 B.C. were surrounded by rammed-earth walls, with gates and guardhouses (Chang 1986:234–288; Liu 1996:264–272). Walls appear around settlements in Inner Mongolia, Yangzi, and Shandong regions around the same time, including a huge center in the latter, with major supplies of arrowheads (Chang 1986:248; Underhill 1994:202).

Even more unmistakable signs of war appear in Henan: skulls with scalp marks, bodies thrown down wells, new and deadlier weapons, etc. (Chang 1986:270–271; Liu 1996:264; Underhill 1989:231–235, this volume). Yet signs of war still show great variation, abundant in some areas, absent in others. Then comes the first known state, Erlitou (although Underhill, this volume, suggests earlier states may be found). As the Bronze Age proceeded to the Shang, war became a way of life (Yates 1999). Otterbein (2004:161–166) questions most of the evidence for war before Erlitou, seeing walls as efforts at flood control, and other indicators of violence as indicating internal political rivalries.

On the Korean peninsula, the early record is slim. I found no information bearing on war for the Chulman culture, Mesolithic people who became farmers. An agricultural Bronze Age people came in sometime between 1500 B.C. and 700 B.C., bringing Manchurian-style weapons (Barnes 1999:26, 160–161; Kim 1978). The Japanese record is better. Remains of sedentary complex hunter-gatherers, the Jomon, date from 11,000 B.C. onwards, in later times practicing some cultivation. Around 300 B.C., wet rice cultivators came to Kyushu from Korea, fusing with local cultures to become the Yayoi. From the beginning, the migrant villages showed numerous, clear, impressive defensive features and weapons of war. Of some 5,000 Jomon skeletons, ten show signs of violent death. Of about 1,000 Yayoi, there are more than 100 victims. Accounts from the contemporary Chinese court also document intensive war in Japan at the time of this transition (Barnes 1999:168–171, 218–220; Farris 1998:37–41, 1999:49–51; Imamura 1996:179–185).

Europe

Vencl, who more than anyone else has directed attention to archaeological signs of war in Europe (1984), concludes that there is no conclusive evidence of war up to and through Europe's Upper Paleolithic (1999:58), as does Dolukhanov (1999:77), despite the extensive archaeological record and the considerable social complexity of that period. Keeley (1996:37), LeBlanc with Register (2003:14), and others, however, do argue that there is persuasive evidence for war in the Upper Paleolithic in skeletal and other remains from Czechoslovakia. This is a critical point for their general arguments about the antiquity of war. Comparison of their claims with the empirical record, however, demonstrates that they are unsupported.[1]

As the herds of reindeer disappeared, a more settled forager's life developed through the ninth millennium. At a number of these Mesolithic locations, individual remains have been found with signs of violence, even killing. Constandse-Westerman and Newell (1982:75) surveyed Mesolithic skeletal material, and found of 59 mostly complete skeletons, five are associated with a "projectile," but conclude that other traumas are probably accidental. Three of the projectile instances are from around 4100 B.C., which is very late for Mesolithic, and well after the general shift to war discussed below. Guilaine and Zammit's (2005:75–77) survey shows eight Mesolithic sites in Europe, and four outside it (including Jebel Sahaba), but several of these have more than one burial with projectile injuries. One case worth special mention is the enigmatic "nests" of some 37 skulls, ochered and several with large depression fractures, from Ofnet in Bavaria circa 5500 B.C. (Frayer 1997), although Chapman (1999:105) concludes that these "indicate ancestral relations rather than a bloody incident." The separation and special interment of the skulls is not itself evidence of war, as such special treatment of one's own dead heads is common both archaeologically and ethnographically (Wright 1988). But the depression fracture seems difficult to explain as other than from violence. In sum, while it seems likely that some war was practiced in the European Mesolithic, many finds are ambiguous, and/or of single individuals, and still represent a small fraction of the osteological record (Chapman 1999:105–106). So while Vencl (1999:59) sees a broad, general shift toward war, Dolukhanov (1999:80) sees more limited and highly localized developments in response to particular conditions.

Northern Europe

After around 5500 B.C., agriculture spread across central Europe from the Black Sea to Holland. For an extensive time and area, most investigators see no indications of violent conflict, but rather exchange and fusion, among the scattered LBK farmers and Mesolithic people all around them (Barker 1985:139–147; Dennell 1985:135–136; Thomas 1999:150), although Keeley (1992; 1997) challenges that view. From around 4500 B.C., agriculture of the Tripolye culture spread, similarly without signs of violence with local Mesolithics, through eastern forests and steppes (Dolukhanov 1986b:117, 1999:81). But peace was not to last. By late LBK times, in its farthest penetration west (Belgium), palisades were put up around 4350 B.C. (Keeley 1997:312–314; Keeley and Cahen 1989). Enclosures of settlements became common across west and central Europe around the end of LBK, circa 4000 B.C. The purpose and meaning of enclosures is hotly debated, but a number incorporate clearly defensive features (Vencl 1999:68–69; Whittle 1985:85–86, 1988:1–6). Most significantly, at least four and possibly more later LBK sites, perhaps about 5000 B.C., include mass burials with unambiguous signs of violence—slaughters (Vencl 1999:60–64). To the east, Tripolye had fortifications, maces, and skeletons with trauma between 4400 B.C. and 3810 B.C. (Dolukhanov 1999:82).

Thus, across much of northern Europe, war shifted from a scattered and rare phenomenon to a common occurrence between 5000 B.C. and 4000 B.C. It never ceased thereafter. New, distinctive regional cultures developed in many areas in the fourth millennium. These people began building hill-forts and burying their dead with battle-axes (Dolukhanov 1999:83; Schutz 1983:75–77; Vencl 1999:66–70). Similar developments lagged by centuries in the farther reaches of northern and western Europe. In Denmark, 22 skeletons from a Mesolithic cemetery from about 4100 B.C. include one with an apparently lethal arrow wound and two with healed fractures suggestive of serious violence. Two centuries later agriculture had replaced hunting and gathering. By 3500 B.C., they had all the defensive features and battle-axes of central Europe (Albrethsen and Petersen 1976:14, 20; Andersen 1993:100–103; Price 1985:351). In southern England, major reliance on agriculture was dominant by roughly 3500 B.C., and ramparted villages were common by 3000 B.C. Around 2600 B.C., the heavily palisaded hill-fort of Hambledon Hill was destroyed in what appears to be fierce combat (Bradley 1991:51; Mercer 1988:89, 104, 1989, 1999).

Southern Europe

Closer to the Mediterranean, transitions to agriculture and violent conflict seem to be more variable, and sometimes obscure. Parts of Greece had a full Neolithic package by 6000 B.C. In Macedonia, early small-farming communities were undefended and near to water in low lands. By the final Neolithic about 4500 B.C. and 4000 B.C., settlements with formidable enclosures began to appear in elevated, defensible locations (Barker 1985:71–72; Kokkinidou and Nikolaidou 1999:92–96). In southern Italy, hundreds of Neolithic settlements on the Tavoliere plain and elsewhere were ringed by very substantial ditches from before 5000 B.C. to 3000 B.C. (Whitehouse 1987:358–359), representing perhaps the first pattern of regular warfare in Europe. However, further north in Italy over this time, settlements of farmers intermixed with hunter-gatherers, without such ditches (Barker 1985:65–67).

Iberia has dramatic evidence, but a complex pattern. The final phase of a long transition to a Neolithic life occurred by the third millennium. One cave at Alava, Spain contains remains of about 300 individuals, apparently deposited over time between 3800 B.C. and 2800 B.C. Nine have embedded arrow points, and many loose points are in the fill (Guilaine and Zammit 2005:152–154). A massive fortified site existed at Los Millares from 2500 B.C. to 1800 B.C.—but what enemy required such formidable defenses? Later settlements were smaller, on naturally defendable sites (Fernandez Castro 1995:17–23, 73 ff.; Monks 1997:13–17). Subsequent Neolithic and Chalcolithic remains display a variety of violent trauma, and there are extensive wall paintings that, in contrast to Paleolithic art, unambiguously depict armed-group clashes (Armendariz et al.

1994:215; Botella Lopez et al. 1995:70; Etxeberria et al. 1995:141–143; Guilaine and Zammit 2005:103–121, 156; Monks 1997:23–24).

France provides perhaps the best evidence for a late onset of war, somewhat ironically since this is the key area for Guilaine and Zammit. Brennan (1991) made a systematic direct examination of all available Middle (Neanderthal) and Upper Paleolithic remains from southwestern France (100,000–10,000 B.P.). These fragments represent 209 individuals, including a few widely known as supposed exemplars of violence. (Three other possible examples of violence were not available for examination). Of the total, she found a total of *five* fractures of any sort. Two Upper Paleolithic specimens had healed depression fractures on the skulls, but in a form consistent with an accident. Brennan (1991:206) concludes:

> There is little evidence in my data that traumatic injuries in these samples of Middle and Upper Paleolithic skeletons were common. The few traumas that are apparent can be as easily explained by accidental injury as by interpersonal violence. In fact the absence of a single parry fracture or wound to the left side of the head in my sample seems to belie some of the previously held notions in the literature of bestial behavior and violence for this time period.

Guilaine and Zammit (2005:49–50) acknowledge this study, and comment that if one were to go from the "evidence available," one would "conclude that aggressiveness was uncommon during this period." However, they choose another interpretation. Noting the few traumatized Cro-Magnon's found elsewhere in Europe (reported above under "The Earliest Signs of Violence"), they conclude that it was unlikely that they were peaceful.

Southern France shifts to cereal cultivation in the fourth millennium, and at the start of this transition, three sites show persuasive signs of cannibalism (Villa 1992:99; Villa et al. 1986). Skeletal trauma from projectiles becomes fairly common in the Neolithic (Cordier 1990). Guilaine and Zammit had two researchers compile an exhaustive list of all Neolithic arrow-inflicted wounds in France (2005:xii, 133, 241–251). The total number found from 5500 B.C. (late Mesolithic) to 3700 B.C. is just three individuals at three sites. But from 3600 B.C. to 2200 B.C., there are 41 sites, some with multiple victims. Although they minimize the significance of this dramatic research finding by observing that remains become more abundant as time goes on, the much wider occurrence of violence seems difficult to deny. Nevertheless, the percentages of victims remains quite small compared to other burial populations noted in this review. In tombs from 48 sites, comprising between 2,000 and 3,000 individuals, roughly 75, or under 4 percent have arrow wounds, including healed ones. Guilaine and Zammit argue that these may underrepresent actual violence. Certainly they might, but that makes three instances in which these authors argue *against* the evidence to speculate on the presence or intensity of war.

Bronze Age Europe

Dates for the Chalcolithic and Bronze Ages differ across Europe, but mostly fall into the range of 2300–700 B.C., with the Aegean area starting several centuries earlier (see Sherratt 1994). Much of the metal used in this period went into weapons, some for elite display rather than combat, some "ritually sacrificed" by being deposited in water. Weapons circulated over wide swaths of Europe and went through a succession of forms (Harding 1999; Kristiansen 1987; Osgood 1998; Randsborg 1992). It is not clear that this evident militarism is associated with an increase in actual fighting (Bridgford 1997:113–114; Robb 1997:136). Europe's first states, in Crete and Mycenaea, developed at the end of the Bronze Age, about 2000 B.C. and 1700 B.C. respectively, with much more emphasis on war in Mycenaea (Nikolaidou and Kokkinidou 1997; Wardle 1994). Both collapsed in the wave of widespread violence that swept from Egypt to middle Europe, around 1200 B.C., as the Iron Age, apparently, brought new and more powerful forms of making war (Drews 1993; Osgood 1998:77–83; Popham 1994; Randsborg 1992:199–201, 1999:191).

North America

A few preliminary comments must precede discussion of North America. First, my research ceased as I was working on the Pacific coast. That very extensive stretch will not be considered here, nor will the Great Basin, Arctic, and sub-Arctic. Second, as I was revising this chapter I learned of Lambert's (2002) excellent overview of North American materials. I find nothing to dispute in her assessments, but we do differ in that my overview is explicitly intended to highlight the increase in signs of war over time. Third, the North American material is more complicated than that of other areas already discussed, with very distinctive regional variants, and in some areas, more signs of collective violence at relatively early dates. Fourth, much of the following has been covered in greater detail by chapters in this volume. This survey looks for generalizations comparable to findings from other world areas.

About the earliest human inhabitants of the continent, we have been given two very different assessments of presence and prevalence of violence.

> The archaeological record gives no evidence of territorial behavior on the part of any of these first hunters and gatherers. Rather, they seem to have developed a very open network of communication and interaction across

> the continent. . . . [W]e find no sign anywhere in the archaeological record of even a *hint* of conflict or warfare. (Haas 1999:14)

> Proponents of simplistic materialist/ecological models that reduce warfare to competition over land and food will find little comfort in the evidence for frequent violent conflicts among earliest immigrants to the New World. These people lived at low densities and had ample opportunity to avoid violence by moving away from it but apparently were unable to do so. (Walker 2001a:591)

Two very early indications of violence are associated with the famous Kennewick Man, from 7000 B.C. to 5500 B.C., with a healed-over point (McManamon 1999), and his less famous approximate contemporary from Grimes Burial Shelter in Nevada, with obsidian embedded in his rib (Owsley and Jantz 2000). Besides Kennewick Man, Walker (2001a:588) provides reference to only one published work suggesting group violence, from Archaic Florida (Dickel et al. 1988)—a very significant case, but a late and singular basis for his generalization. Still, given the relative scarcity of skeletal remains this old, the number that have signs of violence must be taken as significant, and a mark against the perspective I argue here. The Eastern Archaic Woodlands is our next stop.

The East

Milner (1995, 1999) has been surveying the vast site literature for this region (and Dye, this volume). He (1999:120) notes some indications of violence for the Early Archaic about 8500–6000 B.C., but these "do not occur with any regularity" until the Middle and Late Archaic (6000–4000 B.C. and 4000–1000 B.C. [Fagan 1995:348]). An important early case is the one just mentioned (Dickel et al. 1988) from southern Florida, which is rather late at about 5400 B.C. to be classified as Early Archaic. A total of 168 individuals are represented in this very unusually well-preserved burial ground, and signs clearly suggestive of interpersonal violence occur in nine of them, including parry fractures, cranial fractures, and one embedded point. Another case is Mulberry Creek in Tennessee, 4000–3500 B.C. (Dye, this volume). But others see increasing cases of multiple traumatized individuals only in the Late Archaic, after 2500 B.C. (Gramly 1988:86; Munson 1988:12). Many cases of trauma are only single individuals, and so may not indicate war (Wilkinson and Van Wagenen 1993:198).

At least three Late Archaic areas do show clear evidence of war. Indian Knoll in Kentucky (4100–2500 B.C.) has 48 of 880 burials with embedded points, mutilations, or multiple burials (Webb 1974:147–155, 173–205). A few sites in central New York from about 2500 B.C. include skeletons with points and missing body parts (Ritchie 1980:77, 120). The 439 individuals from Tennessee

(2500–1000/500 B.C.) include 10 males with similar signs of violence, mostly from one location (Ostendorf Smith 1997; and see Dye, this volume). Yet Milner (1995:236) concludes that even later Archaic violence is limited compared to subsequent periods.

The Woodland Period after 1000 B.C. registers a clear decline in signs of violence in the great number of skeletal remains unearthed (Lovejoy and Heiple 1981:539; Milner 1999:122). But war did not disappear altogether, and Dye (this volume) still sees warfare as "widespread and endemic." Even among Hopewell people, usually characterized as peaceful traders, what appear to be trophy skulls are found (Owsley and Berryman 1975:50; Seeman 1988). In the middle Ohio Valley about A.D. 500, there is a shift from dispersed to nucleated and defendable sites (Dancey 1992). The arrival of the bow and arrow seems associated with more fighting in the seventh century (Nassaney and Pyle 1999), and sites in west-central Illinois show many signs of violence from the Late Woodland time on (Milner 1995:229). This long sequence creates problems for Otterbein's scenario of peace being structurally connected to broad-spectrum foraging and plant domestication. The Late Archaic was a time of increasing and more settled reliance on aquatic resources (Milner 1999:21), and the subsequent Woodland Period saw the domestication of sumpweed and sunflowers (Munson 1988:12–13; Watson 1988:40–43).

Yet the emergence of the Mississippian tradition by A.D. 800/900 still shows only limited preparations for violent conflict, although some settlement defenses appear as early as the eighth century (Morse and Morse 1983:237; Smith 1990). In the Southeast, at least, by A.D. 900–1050 there are indications of endemic warfare (Knight and Steponaitis 1999:10). A major increase in nucleation, palisading with sophisticated defensive features, and vast empty areas between centers begins after A.D. 1050 (Gramly 1988:91–93; Milner 1999:123–124), with the chiefly polities discussed by Dye (this volume). Around A.D. 1200, war clubs come to dominate over the bow and arrow, at least in combat around major centers (Dye 2002:128). In the twelfth century, similar defensive concentrations are seen in New York (Chapdeline 1993:197–201; Tuck 1978:326) and around that time, in Virginia (Roundtree and Turner 1998:279).

Late Prehistoric burials yield many individuals with embedded points and other trauma (Gramly 1988:87; Ritchie 1980:294). Around A.D. 1300, burials from Illinois of 264 fairly complete skeletons include 43 with such indications (Milner et al. 1991:583, 594). In a Michigan cemetery, nine percent of individuals have non-lethal depression fractures, mostly in females who may have been captives, and younger men are notably underrepresented (Wilkinson 1997:28, 35–38; Wilkinson and Van Wagenen 1993:193). In the central Mississippi/Ohio area after A.D. 1350, from an already nucleated base, there was additional concentration of populations, and abandonment of other areas, creating a vast "empty quarter" (Cobb and Butler 2002). Parallel variants are seen throughout the Southeast, giving rise to the sophisticated chiefly warfare recorded by the Spanish, although by then it existed in attenuated form (Anderson 1994:139–155; Dye 2002; Morse and Morse 1983:271–283).

The Great Plains

I found less information about early times for this area, but one detailed survey of remains from Texas, Oklahoma, New Mexico, Kansas, and Colorado suggests a late onset of war (Owsley 1989:131–133; Owsley et al. 1989:116–119). By my count from data charts, there are 173 individuals from all periods up through Woodland, and 447 from the late prehistoric (after A.D. 500 [Fagan 1995:139]). Of the former, the only indication of violent death is one woman, with two blows to the head. Of the latter, if one includes individuals in multiple burials where some individuals have embedded points, there are 74 cases of probable violent death, in one site accompanied by deliberate village destruction. After A.D. 1000, along the Missouri and Mississippi, Mississippian peoples surrounded large villages with ditches and palisades, and buried at least one chief with an ornate mace. There was a further nucleation accompanied by abandonment after A.D. 1350 (O'Brien and Wood 1998:288–292, 318–320, 331–333, 344). Fortification and Mississippian connections reached into northeastern Iowa from A.D. 1100 to A.D. 1200 (Alex 2000:134, 155, 182), but further west in Kansas and Nebraska there are no indications of fortifications or defensive locations (Krause 1970:106, 111; Wedel 1986:100).

Oneota people expanded from southwestern Minnesota through Iowa and much of Missouri and Illinois and environs after A.D. 1250, and especially after A.D. 1350, accompanied by fortified sites, skeletal trauma, and thunderbird iconography which in historic times is associated with war chiefs (Alex 2000:182–188, 200, 207–209; Bamforth, this volume; O'Brien and Wood 1998:345–347, 357). While a few individual skeletons show signs of violence before A.D. 1250 (Hollimon and Owsley 1994:351; Olsen and Shipman 1994:384), worse times were coming.

In the generally accepted picture, immigrants from the Central Plains tradition moved northward, initially without fortifications or other indications of war. But in the century after A.D. 1250, they and the previously resident Initial Coalescent people engaged in major fort building, some destroyed while under construction. Many, many skeletons indicate violent death, preeminent being the Crow Creek site, conventionally dated at A.D. 1325, where a minimum of 486 individuals were slaughtered (Hollimon and Owsley 1994; Kay 1995; Pringle 1998:2039; Willey 1990; Zimmerman 1997). Bamforth's contribution to this volume requires major revision of this view. War is detectable from A.D. 1000 on, associated with particular intervals of drought, not one long period, and Crow Creek's date cannot be specified more precisely than in the broad vicinity of A.D. 1400.

The Southwest

A great deal has been published on prehistoric warfare in the Southwest, especially over the past decade. LeBlanc's book (1999) is the most comprehensive, joined by a set of case studies (Rice and LeBlanc 2001). Despite an extensive earlier record, the first clear evidence of war I have seen dates from several centuries after the beginning of maize and squash agriculture, which occurred around 1500–1000 B.C. (Wills 1988:149). In southwestern Utah, within the Anasazi area, Weatherill's Cave 7 contains remains of some 90 individuals, most if not all of whom were slain, some mutilated. Artifacts place this within Basketmaker II, or between 500 B.C. and A.D. 500 (Hurst and Turner 1993:167, 170–171; although LeBlanc [1999:310] puts this at about A.D. 0, and Lambert [2002:220] puts it at "A.D. 400?"). Three other Basketmaker II sites may have been massacres, and there are numerous other signs of deadly violence (LeBlanc 1999:140–144). War signs decrease in Basketmaker III (A.D. 500–750), and come back in greater frequency in Pueblo I (A.D. 750–900). For Mogollon people, there are some defensible hilltop locations before A.D. 600 and more indications of war after A.D. 850; for Hohokam, there is nothing conclusive for war until the thirteenth century (LeBlanc 1999:129–149, 2000:94–95; Nelson 2000:326–327; Solometo this volume).

Violence among Anasazi from A.D. 900 to A.D. 1150/1250 is ambiguous and extremely controversial. Although one fringe location was fortified about A.D. 900 and abandoned after a massacre about A.D. 1000 (Eddy 1974:81), in the central areas of Chacoan Anasazi cultures there are no indications of war, suggesting the existence of a "Pax Chaco" (Lekson 2002:613–614). There are, however, non-lethal traumas, especially among women (Martin 1997) and signs of brutal killing interpreted alternatively as cannibalistic terror perpetrated by the political elite, or slaying and dismemberment of witches (Bullock 1998; Darling 1998; Kantner 1999; Turner and Turner 1999; Walker 1998). No one, however, seems to question that *some* cannibalism occurred, and that this was *not* in a context of war.

Signs of tensions—the abandonment of Chaco, opening spaces between groups around Kayenta—develop in the century after A.D. 1150, leading to tribal nucleation and movement into cliff dwellings around A.D. 1250. Abandonment of northern and some southern Anasazi areas and clustering of remaining settlements occur after A.D. 1275 (Haas 1990; LeBlanc 1999:264–270, 2000:45–54; Upham and Reed 1989). Rice and LeBlanc's (2001) volume of case studies, with a concentration on Hohokam and Sinagua regions, all concern the "narrow time frame, from the A.D. 1200s to the early 1400s" (2001:2), when there is the most evidence of war throughout the Southwest, although preceded by a century of increasing tensions. Hohokam areas, too, were abandoned by the late fourteenth century (Fish and Fish 1989:119–121; Wilcox 1989:163). Solometo (this volume) describes similar intensification of conflict on the Mogollon rim, from limited indications of war after A.D. 850, to clear intensification in A.D. 1150–1250, followed later by abandonment. Further south, in northwestern Chihuahua, the large center Casas Grandes was burned, with crushed bodies and deliberate destructions, then abandoned in A.D. 1340 (Ravesloot and Spoerl 1989:131–134). By the early fifteenth century, what remained of the entirely rearranged population seemed to engage in less war, though war was still being practiced when Coronado arrived (Creamer and Haas 1998:55–57; Haas and Creamer 1997:241–243; LeBlanc 1999:264, 305).

Section Conclusion

There are numerous regions of the world where good archaeological data are available for centuries or even millennia before any suggestion of war appears. This is so for the Middle East, Central Asia, the Indus, China, and Japan. Later in each of these areas, archaeological evidence of war becomes clear and continuous. For Egypt, the critical developmental period is lacking. Europe may be more complicated, with scattered instances of (possibly) collective violence in the Mesolithic, an initial and apparently peaceful spread of Neolithic traditions (with one probable exception from Italy), giving way to a widespread pattern of warfare from the fifth millennium on.

North America is even harder to summarize, with different and sometimes conflicting trends in different areas. Although there are a few very early indications of violence, in most areas there are either no suggestions of war in the earliest material, *or* signs of violence which appear quite limited compared to later prehistoric times. Lambert's (2002) review of the North American literature indicates that this generalization applies to regions I have not yet fully researched. I would note in advance of more complete discussion that the northern Northwest Coast stands out as the earliest start of a war pattern in North America, about 2200 B.C., that then continued in practice down to historic times (Ames and Maschner 1999:209–210; Cybulski 1992:156–157, 1994:80–81; Moss and Erlandson 1992:81). Although I have yet to go through all the material for Mesoamerica, South America (touched on below), Africa, Melanesia, and the

Pacific, my preliminary readings suggest little to contradict this picture of a relatively late emergence of war. Discussions of Palau (Liston and Tuggle this volume) and New Zealand (Allen, this volume) are consistent with that.

Although episodes of war are possible any time in human prehistory, there is no convincing evidence of collective intergroup violence any time before 10,000 years ago (except Jebel Sahaba), and in many parts of the world much more recently than that. I realize that evidence can be read in different ways, and many will not be convinced that war was absent. But I think it is difficult to disagree with the assertion that the presence of war, and its intensity, is highly variable. To claim that "war is something . . . that all humans do," or "*everyone* had war in *all* time periods" is contradicted by the evidence.

Another point of general agreement should be that, even though times of more war were sometimes followed by times of less war, the overall, long-term trend was for more war over time. Besides the evidence I have presented, that simple fact is apparent in this volume. In Palau, war appears in the record around A.D. 600. The Maori brought war with them to New Zealand, but war intensified greatly around A.D. 1500. In the U.S. Southeast, there were several long steps in war development beginning by 3500 B.C., but the intensity of war surged in the 500–600 years before contact. Looking at ancient times, we see in China war became more common over the course of the Neolithic, and still more common in the Bronze Age. Oaxaca is a particularly important case. Although the chapter by Redmond and Spencer in this volume picks up around 700 B.C., when there were already warring chiefdoms, Flannery and Marcus (2003) begin their article further back in time: the time frame of 8000–2000 B.C. is characterized by "warless societies," and signs of war first appear around 1540 B.C. but are then absent from 1100 B.C. to 800 B.C.—although Otterbein (2004:123–126) questions that earlier evidence of war. Later prehistory indicates much more war than earlier prehistory.

This is a critical point. Those who suspect war in earlier times when evidence is lacking are relying on two overlapping bases. One is theory about why war occurs. Theories are legion, and according to many, some war is always expected. The other basis—upon which most theory is drawn—is ethnographic observations of war over the past five-hundred years. A major point of this chapter, of course, is that Western contact frequently led to intensified warfare among observed peoples. But what the archaeological record demonstrates is that prehistoric warfare got much worse in later prehistory, *before* any outside contact. Thus, war among ethnographically observed peoples is doubly inappropriate for forming opinions about humanity's distant past.

The next section presents my ideas—tentative empirical generalizations—about how war developed out of a warless background, and why it became more common over the millennia and often intensified with Western contact. Then it ties all these issues together with a discussion of Venezuelan prehistory and the Yanomami.

The Spread of War up to the Ethnographic Present

Why War Became Common

In this condensed summary of early evidence of war, I have not discussed the material and social correlates of that development. I will not speculate on direct causes, but several general factors seem implicated as preconditions, which in variable combinations, make the origin and/or the intensification of war more likely. (Most of these are discussed in some detail in Ferguson 1997:334–337.) One is a shift to sedentary existence—though not necessarily agriculture—or at least to increased dependence on fixed sites. Another is generally increasing population within broad areas. Two others, although these seem less relevant in earlier North American sequences than in the Old World, are the development of social ranking and increasing trade, especially of status goods—although in North America the ambitions of chiefs are major factors in the later intensification of war. A fifth is the development of social institutions for bounding groups in conflict. Kelly (2000:44) and Boehm (1999:90–98) make a more specific claim, that it is the development of segmental kinship systems that enables war. Rice (2001) has found support for that idea in the American Southwest, and Flannery and Marcus (2003) in Oaxaca. Finally, a serious ecological reversal, involving climate change or anthropogenic resource degradation, is often implicated in the origin and/or intensification of war.

The general absence of these preconditions can explain why human populations did not develop cultural practices of war in earlier times. But over the millennia, these preconditions became more widespread, and war arose in more regions of the world, as described in the previous section. What happened after that, after war began in different areas but before there were any states around to influence things?

War spread. Not automatically, or quickly, as is sometimes imagined in parables of anarchy (Schmookler 1984). But eventually, spread it did, through some combination of contact stimulus and converging conditions. This is seen in contexts already discussed. In China, signs of war became more common through the extensive Longshan interaction sphere and beyond (Chang 1986:270–271; Liu 1996:264; Underhill 1989:231–235, this volume). In Japan, war was brought by immigrants from Korea, but then spread through the islands (Barnes 1999:168–171; Farris 1998:37–41; Imamura 1996:131). In far western and more northern Europe, the first cultivators replaced hunter-gatherers and made war without the peaceful centuries of earlier expanding farmers (Anderson 1993:102; Bradley 1991:50–52; Mercer 1988:89, 104, 1989, 1999). In the center of North America, the Mississippian period saw the rise of nucleated, fortified settlements after A.D. 1050, and over the next century or two this pattern spread outward in all directions (Chapdelaine 1993:200–201; Morse and Morse 1983:256, 263–266; Roundtree and Turner 1998:278–280). On the Pacific Northwest Coast, the war complex developed in the north gradually came to characterize more dispersed and less hierarchical southern groups (Ames and Maschner 1999:209–210; Coupland 1988:207–212). And as described by Allen (this volume), later Polynesian seafarers carried a warrior complex along with them to new islands. So even before states, war was becoming normal in ever broader areas of the tribal universe.

Then what happened once states appeared? In theory, successful states suppressed collective violence within their administration, although this varied in practice (Ferguson 1999:404–405). There are indications that ancient states fostered violence and war among non-state peoples around them. The rise and fall of states could create sweeping waves of war. The development of the Zulu state was followed by a spreading chain-reaction of terrible violence, known as the *mfecane*, although the growing European presence may have played a role in this horror (Cobbing 1988; Hamilton 1995). The collapse of Teotihuacan led to destabilization and war throughout northwest Mexico (Nelson 2000). In the Andean highlands, Arkush (this volume) describes "chain reactions" of war spreading out from political centers through peripheral areas.

Relatively stable, central states, the sources of our earliest histories, commonly saw themselves as surrounded by fierce "barbarians" (Ferguson 1999:418–420). This was not *merely* ideological projection. But the origins of such militarism are obscure. How much was an internal development? How much from state stimulus? Probably the best bet is that a pronounced military orientation developed as part of long-term interaction between emerging state centers and peoples of their peripheries. It is clear, however, that ancient states commonly fostered ethnogenesis and tribalization, and enlisted these "martial tribes" as "ethnic soldiers" to, among other things, project force farther into their hinterlands than encumbered state armies could manage economically (Goldberg and Findlow 1984). It also seems a safe bet that this, at least sometimes, spread intensive war far outwards.

Militaristic states, over time, replaced comparatively non-militaristic ones. In Peru, after 1000 B.C., several apparently theocratic states were conquered, incorporated and culturally transformed to fit the mold of expanding militarists (Pozorski 1987). After the decline of the relatively unmilitaristic Harappa, the Indus region became part of the endless wars of the Rg Veda (Singh 1965; Srivastava 1984). Finally, ancient states fostered war even distant from their frontiers. From the first century A.D., Roman, Arab and other demands for slaves sent waves of violence spreading inland from the east coast of Africa (Edgerton 1972:161; Kusimba, this volume; and see Lovejoy 1983). Sri Lanka experienced repeated, intensive warfare related to control of the expanded Indian Ocean trade of the ninth and tenth centuries A.D. (Gunawardana 2000:78–79). So the existence of ancient states further contributed to the prevalence of war among non-state peoples.

Then came the European expansion. Over all, European expansionism was *more* disruptive and "warrifying" than that of ancient states (Ferguson 1993). Whereas ancient states would move into contiguous areas, subject to a long history of interaction, Europeans crossed enormous distances and oceans. Doing this, they introduced new diseases, plants, and animals that massively disrupted contacted groups. Europeans had trade goods that were in great demand, and, especially later in time, military and transportation technology and techniques that could revolutionize warfare. European expansionists were not unique in seeking captive labor, but the vast extent of their operations was. The same goes for the European quest for land cleared of previous inhabitants. All of these aspects of European expansionism sent out shock waves that went far beyond frontiers, often preceding any Western observer. This area of impact Neil Whitehead and I call a "tribal zone" (Ferguson and Whitehead 2000). While Western contact did not *always* lead to more frequent or destructive warfare—sometimes the opposite occurred—case studies collected in *War in the Tribal Zone*, and many others, leave little doubt that in many, many parts of the world, European expansion after A.D. 1500 led to more war among non-state peoples, before any pacifying effect set in.

Amazonia and the Yanomami

To make this discussion of archaeology, history, and the temporal increase in war more unified and concrete, let us consider war among Amazonian peoples, and particularly the Yanomami of the Upper Orinoco region—long considered a type case of pristine, primeval warfare. Initial historical reports from the coasts and major rivers of northwestern South America document large settlements, some organized as chiefdoms, usually readily able to demonstrate substantial military capabilities (DeBoer 1981, 1986; Medina 1934; Morey and Marwitt 1974; Myers 1988; Whitehead 1988). How long had this pattern existed? Excavations of major settlements along the lower Amazon and middle Orinoco, the latter beginning around 2100 B.C., are remarkably free of war signs (Roosevelt 1980). One good sequence comes from a tributary of the Rio Apure, which itself flows into the Orinoco, about 500 km from ancestral Yanomami lands. Here chiefdoms and war appear together—after major population growth, along circumscribed agricultural land, in the contact zone between lowland and Andean peoples (where war was already well-established)—around A.D. 550. Chiefdoms did not appear on the middle Orinoco until A.D. 1100. By A.D. 1530 and the first historical accounts from the savanna near the Apure, powerful chiefs lived in large fortified villages, with extensive irrigation systems, and some were able to raise fighting forces reportedly exceeding ten thousand men (Roosevelt 1991; Spencer 1998:127–129; Spencer and Redmond 1992:135–137).

As researchers now mine long-neglected historical documents, especially for Venezuela and environs, we are getting a much clearer picture of extensive, interconnected political systems, with ties reaching west to the Andes, south to the Amazon, and north through the Caribbean (Arvelo-Jimenez and Biord Castillo 1994; Chernela 1993; Whitehead 1988, 1994). War was certainly an integral part of these systems, but how the war-making river chiefdoms related to more mobile peoples of the interior such as Yanomami—whether in symbiosis, conflict, or both—is at present a very open question. Within decades of first contact, these exposed peoples were involved in military resistance to the Europeans, and soon after that were ensnared in imperial rivalries and slave raiding (Whitehead 1988:71 ff., 1994, 2000). Even as early as the time of Hans Staden (1928), marooned in Brazil in 1550, war clearly reflected decades of major European influence (Ferguson 1990:241). These regional sociopolitical systems were destroyed and their peoples eliminated within the first century or so of contact (Hemming 1978:29–42; Whitehead 1994, 1999), long before any anthropologist was around to theorize their wars.

The ethnology of war has relied heavily on Amazonian cases, but as noted earlier, our theoretical paradigms ruled history out. When it is brought back in, *all* of the key cases upon which theory has been built have been obviously, dramatically impacted by the Western intrusion. Europeans directed native peoples to attack others who made trouble or who were allies of imperial rivals, or to produce purchasable captives, or just to divide and conquer. New diseases interpreted as witchcraft led to fighting, and Indians displaced from one region came into conflict with others. Western goods stimulated war as objects of plunder, and caused disputes over trade control (Ferguson 1990). Which brings us to the Yanomami specifically.

It is very common to hear it said that even in the mid-1960s, Yanomami lived unaffected by "civilization." This is why their warfare is so often claimed to represent the human condition as it existed in our evolutionary past. Both premise and conclusion are very wrong. Yanomami have been indirectly and directly affected by the European expansion since they became targets of other natives seeking captives to trade to the Europeans in the late 1600s.

A Spanish observer in the 1740s reported that along the Upper Orinoco, not far from Yanomami lands, local peoples were "peaceful" except for the recently intrusive Guaipunaves—slave takers for the Portuguese—who decimated local populations (although the possibility of anti-Portuguese bias must be considered in this account) (Gilij 1965 I:55, II:57, 289). By this time, the highland home of the Yanomami was being targeted by slave raiders coming from every direction—and they were still being victimized by raiders on a smaller scale a century or more later (Ferguson 1995a:77–82, 181–186). The Spanish established their first outpost on the Upper Orinoco in 1756. Over the next few years, they witnessed the diminishing Guaipunave enter into new violent conflicts with remnants of once powerful peoples from the Negro, who were fleeing the Portuguese there. By 1761, all the survivors were escaping the Europeans by moving into highland forests, leaving the Orinoco and other rivers nearly abandoned (Ferguson 1995a:82–85).

All early reports of Yanomami making war come from periods of specific and intense disturbance, either as targets of slave raids, or in situations of marked disparities in recently introduced Western goods (Ferguson 2001). The bulk of *Yanomami Warfare* (Ferguson 1995a) is devoted to detailing evidence that Yanomami wars over the past century or so are results of tensions associated with unequal distributions of steel tools and other Western manufactures. Yanomami of the Orinoco-Mavaca area in the mid-1960s—the subject of Chagnon's (1968) *Yanomamo: The Fierce People*—were additionally suffering massive, broad-spectrum disruption of their lives related to the presence of missionaries and other outsiders, which directly encouraged their unusually high level of interpersonal violence (Ferguson 2000). This is quite different from LeBlanc's claim (this volume) that Yanomami had chronic warfare because they had reached their carrying capacity.

Based on the connection of all known fighting to external factors, and my own historical ecological reconstruction of their pre-steel subsistence as more mobile and lower density (Ferguson 1998), I offered the "hunch" that before Columbus, war *between Yanomami communities* was "limited or even nonexistent" (Ferguson 1995a:75). Because Yanomami built no major structures, used few stone implements, and consumed the bones of their dead, we will never know for sure. Archaeologically, they are nearly invisible. Sometimes I do wonder if that hunch goes too far. But raising that possibility is, I believe, a useful caution for those who would project ethnographic war patterns into distant prehistory.

Conclusion

The issue is not whether there was war before civilization. No serious scholar doubts that there was. The issue is how to explain war, both specific wars and war in general as a part of the human condition, and how ethnology and archaeology can join forces in this quest. For those indigenous peoples once distant physically, technologically, economically, and militarily from expansionist Europe, the need to figure Western contact into explanation of post-contact war seems elementary. Archaeology has the ability to investigate pre-contact times, and to witness the effects of contact from its earliest phases. But that is only the beginning. Archaeology can investigate the military effects of ancient states on peoples around them and along their trade routes. Archaeology can address the question of how and why war spread outwards from its original centers, how its practice and elaboration changed over time, and what factors contributed to its genesis in the first place.

Archaeology and ethnology should join, where appropriate, in theory. A robust theory of war should be capable of explaining the origins of war, its transformation in European tribal zones, and everything in between. Regarding Northwest Coast warfare, I developed (1984b) a pre-contact model that grounded war in geographic and temporal variations of critical subsistence resources. With post-contact depopulation, that model no longer applied. Yet war went on, variably, and in some cases quite intensively. Those variations in practice can be explained primarily as efforts to increase supplies or profit from trade in Western goods, or to feed the slave trade which existed at contact but got worse later. An explanation of Northwest Coast warfare must attend to both archaeology and history.

That study was an effort to create a *testable* theory of war causation, aimed at explaining which groups attack, which groups are attacked, periods of intense war, and periods of peace. A somewhat modified, greatly elaborated, and avowedly scientific version of that approach was developed for the Yanomami case (Ferguson 1995a:21–58; and see Jones 1998; Steel 1998). For the Northwest Coast, explanation of prehistoric warfare was much more broad-brush than that of historically observed events, in part because there was much less archaeology to go on in the early 1980s. But we can never expect the same detail of sequences through archaeology as through history, and that poses a problem for theoretical unification.

One way to bring the long spans of prehistory together with history is through a programmatically modified version of cultural materialism (Ferguson 1995b:30–32). This modification preserves the principle of infrastructural determinism but in a non-reductionist way. Structure and superstructure are seen as vast conjunctures of variables with substantial causal autonomy. It also enables a theoretically consistent integration of an enormous number of linkages between war and society. A recent article (Ferguson 1999) is a compilation of these linkages in a systematic comparison of war and society among non-state peoples vis-à-vis among ancient and medieval states. More systematic comparisons of archaeological data with ancient and medieval states could bring new perspectives to questions such as those asked in this volume.

For instance, one generalization from the cases here is that war does not always lead to political consolidation. It can enforce or lead to fragmentation as well. That is no surprise from the perspective of ancient states, where unification and break-up frequently alternate over centuries. LeBlanc (this volume) offers a new and interesting hypothesis that consolidation of two polities formerly separated by buffer zones can lead to a much larger and more potent polity than its former peers. Some cases in this volume, especially that of Monte Albán, seem to support this idea, though others, such as the upper Belize River valley and the frontier between Aztec and Tarascan empires, suggest less vacancy at peripheries. More generally, the comparison of tribal peoples and ancient states (Ferguson 1999) makes the point that "the space between" polities is anything but empty. It is highly and variably patterned at levels of infrastructure, structure, and superstructure.

Looking at ancient states quickly reveals basic variations in political autonomy and consolidation. The older distinction between territorial conquest and hegemonic domination is a necessary starting point, but not nearly sufficient for understanding militarily based integration. Relations between dominant and subordinate centers vary along scales that range from alliance, through domination, to incorporation; and from trade, through tribute, to taxation. Often transitions occur as a gradual, incremental process, rather than a sudden event. These shifts may be difficult to distinguish archaeologically, but the possibilities should be kept in mind while framing hypotheses. Further, not only do political centers grow, they also decline in strength, and one of the recurrent themes among ancient states is the gradually increasing autonomy of what were once tightly dominated sub-polities.

Cases in this volume show some variations of consolidation (although pigeonholing cases is often tenuous): from tribal in the narrow sense of political unification without center or pronounced hierarchy (such as the northern Plains and Southwest, sometimes), through an array of small and large chiefdoms (as in the Southeast, Palau, New Zealand, and eastern Africa), through equal/independent or ranked/consolidated stratified peer polities (as with Maya), to various forms of expansionist states (as in Mexico, the Andes, and China). This shows that consolidation must be seen as a three-dimensional process, with the axis of power joining geographic layout. Again and again authors in this book have asserted that war was a result of chiefly (or higher) political ambitions. And it is most important to emphasize, that all those discussions of military success conferring prestige, and of the legitimating effects of militaristic iconography, involve hierarchical arrangements *within* the war-making polity. There is an internal/external dialectic in hierarchical politics.

It must also be emphasized that war is no sole, prime mover in political development. Many other cultural spheres are engaged. Because this volume is about societies that practiced war, it may give an unbalanced picture of war's importance in that process. Even in the cases here, there are variations in the significance of war, with Andean state expansionists appearing significantly less violent than Mesoamerican. Elsewhere there may be emergent ancient states with little if any warfare.

Previously I (1994:101–104) suggested that war and peace may have self-reinforcing tendencies which ramify throughout societies, so that there could be alternative militaristic and peaceable trajectories toward complexity. Consideration of ancient and medieval states (Ferguson 1999:400) added the idea that societies may differ in the extent to which the institutions of political, military, and religious leadership are separated, or unified. Taking all of this in suggests that there is no one, single path toward state formation. Our goal should be to develop a comparative political sociology of hierarchical intergroup relations. Those considering these issues might benefit from a text and area that is not often considered, Gottwald's (1979) massive, very anthropological study of Israel, 1250–1050 B.C.

Ancient and medieval states suggest other elements that could be a part of this political sociology (also see Andreski 1968; Otterbein 2004). How much is internal production rearranged to support armies, and/or as a consequence of military subjugation? To what degree are military organizations put to use in other kinds of labor? Does military administration spur development of a literate bureaucracy? Are there common and elite forces (or more tiers than that), and how does that articulate with domestic stratification—for example, are there military aristocracies, and is upward mobility into them possible? Do soldiers have to return home by season, or are they freestanding professionals? Are ethnic soldiers—units of culturally distinctive peoples—incorporated into large armies? Not all of these may be subject to archaeological investigation, but the questions must first be raised to find that out.

Disentangling this snarled thicket of causality is a labor for generations of scholars. One step we may plant firmly now is that war as a regular practice, war as a social institution, *had a beginning*. If it had a beginning, then war is not an inevitable expression of either human nature or the nature of societal existence.

To recognize an ancient beginning is to conceptualize the possibility of a future end to war. But we cannot deal with the origins of war if we continue to project observations from recently observed indigenous peoples backwards through time. The view espoused here is that the origin and early development of war should be approached in its own time, and its own terms—not blinkered by the ethnographic present.

Numerous times in this volume, authors have suggested that the wars they uncovered had three kinds of causes: struggle over important productive resources, the ambitions of political leaders, and local cultural beliefs which provide both justification and an impulse toward war. In closing I wish to highlight this consensus, which I believe would be seconded by a great many other archaeologists and cultural anthropologists.

War is a result of basic material concerns, filtered through an internal/external political system, pushed along by values that encourage militarism. In direct contrast to those biological explanations that are reinforced by a war-forever-backwards view, this simple, communicable conclusion has implications for how we understand war in the world today, from so-called "ethnic conflicts," to terrorism and the war in Iraq (Ferguson 2005). If we want to understand all this violence, we should begin by identifying who is calling the shots, what are their material and political interests, and how do they selectively employ cultural identities, symbols, and values in leading people into war. In my estimate, that—not "war is in our blood"—is the critical implication of the new archaeology of war.

Notes

1. LeBlanc with Register (2003:124) and Keeley (1996:37) rely on what Keeley calls "the celebrated Upper Paleolithic cemeteries of Czechoslovakia" to support the deep antiquity of war. Since their portrayals of the remains of these mammoth-hunters seems quite conclusive, it is important to consider those claims against current evidence and interpretations, for the findings from Predmosti, and the three clustered sites of Dolni Vestonice I, II, and Pavlov.

Keeley (1996:37) writes that these imply, "either by direct evidence of weapons traumas, especially cranial fractures on adult males, or by the improbability of alternative explanations for mass burials of men, women, and children—that violent conflicts and deaths were common." Hill and Wileman (2002:17) cite Keeley in referring to "the mass homicide in Czechoslovakia where groups of men, women and children—the males showing signs of cranial injuries—have been dated to between 34,000 and 24,000 years ago."

LeBlanc and Register (2003:124) provide the most extensive discussion of these findings, referring to Dolni Vestonice:

> The well-known "village" consisted of a very large structure obviously occupied by many families, similar to the Iroquois longhouses, surrounded by some smaller

> structures. The entire area was surrounded by a wall or fence of mammoth bones. Typically this sort of barrier is used ethnographically around the world for defense. A number of multiple burials—several people placed in the same grave at the same time—have been found at Dolni Vestonice, especially mass burials of fighting-age males, a number of whom also have wounds to the head. It is unlikely that several males in their prime would die from disease at the same time. They could have been killed in a failed mammoth hunt, but death from warfare is certainly more plausible. This "village" was located on a high point of land—hills provide a good deal of defense especially against spear-throwers, the best weapon of the times. Almost every line of evidence for warfare I would expect to find for this type of forager has been identified at Dolni Vestonice.

LeBlanc and Register (2003) do not cite any reference in support of these characterizations, but they seem to rely on Klima (1962), whose comments do support some of their claims. Additional research and analysis has occurred since then. What are more current understandings of these sites?

There is a mass burial at Predmosti, estimated to date from 27,000 B.P. to 25,000 B.P., as part of a very long sequence of occupations. It was excavated in 1894, using the crude methods of the time. The site was later destroyed by brick makers, and almost all the skeletal material was destroyed during World War II. What we know about Predmosti is from the report of the investigator. The mass grave is 4 m-by-2.5 m, including remains of 18–20 individuals, 12 of them children, all covered by rough limestone slabs (Allsworth-Jones 1986:152–153, unpaginated appendix entry 12; Svoboda et al. 1996:62, 141, 226). *There is no reason to assume that these people died or were buried at the same time.*

Jiri Svoboda believes that these represent "a pattern of gradual additions of bodies within a long-term burial area." He bases this conclusion on the fact that Predmosti has "disturbed and incomplete skeletons, with only portions of a few bodies in anatomic order. This is in strong contrast to the almost complete burials of Dolni Vestonice. . . . [implying] that earlier bodies were disturbed while adding new ones" (personal communication 2003). This can be seen by comparing the diagram of the Predmosti mass grave and photo of the DV triple burial in Svoboda et al. (1996:168–169). Mass burial, yes. Mass killing, highly unlikely.

There is no mass burial at Dolni Vestonice or Pavlov. There is one triple burial of two males and an individual of undetermined sex, but more likely female (DV 13, 14, 15, about 26,600 B.P., Klima 1987), three other individual skeletons, and numerous scattered remains (Sladek et al. 2000). Some skulls, such as that of DV 16 (Svoboda and Vlcek 1991:326) have small depressions, consistent with non-lethal fighting, (along with other post-depositional fractures) (Svoboda et al. 1996:147; Svoboda, personal communication 2003). Erik Trinkaus characterizes them as "pretty minor bumps on the head that. . . . [would not] have been noticed for more than a week or so. I do not find them very convincing of interpersonal violence—just general tough lives" (personal communication 2003). The exception is DV 12, with a *healed* 3 cm depression on its forehead (Trinkaus et al. 2000:1119). Whatever was going on, these are *not* people killed by blows to the head.

The strongest claim for violent death at Dolni Vestonice is not mentioned by Keeley or LeBlanc. Klima (1987:835), in his initial report on the triple burial, comments: "The remains of a thick pole, stuck deep into DV XIII's hip up to the coccyx support the contention of his forced death." Further analysis of the site, however, led to the conclusion that the pole was just a piece of a wood structure that was placed over the bodies and burned, then collapsed into the bodies (Svoboda et al. 1996:64, personal communication 2003).

As for the other lines of evidence cited by LeBlanc with Register (2003): there is no large structure, nothing like a longhouse at Dolni Vestonice, only small ones of about 4–5 m diameter, although at DV I, two of these seem connected. Except for those two, we do not know if these were contemporary or sequential occupations—the "village" is speculation. In this region, some such Upper Paleolithic structures are outlined (not walled) in stones or bones, such as one described at DV I, believed to have been occupied for about two years. However, those of DV II—the location of the triple burial—appear even more temporary; no outlines, only artifacts around a hearth. Although there are large deposits of mammoth bones at these and other Moravian mammoth-hunter sites, there is no surrounding wall of any sort at any of the locations. Although one part of Dolni Vestonice is on a projecting spur of land, its defensive value is questionable. The spur is on the lower slopes of a mountain, overlooking a river valley—like settlements in the region, probably to monitor migrating large game. If anyone wanted to win a spear-throwing contest with residents of Dolni Vestonice, all they would have had to do was walk a little farther uphill (Svoboda et al. 1996:146–147, 151–155, personal communication 2003).

References

Albrethsen, S. E., and E. B. Petersen. 1976. Excavation of a Mesolithic Cemetery at Vedbaek, Denmark. *Acta Archaeologica* 47:1–28.

Alex, L. M. 2000. *Iowa's Archaeological Past*. Iowa City: University of Iowa Press.

Allsworth-Jones, P. 1986. *The Szeletian and the Transition From Middle to Upper Palaeolithic in Central Europe*. Oxford: Clarendon Press.

Ames, K. M., and H.D.G. Maschner. 1999. *Peoples of the Northwest Coast: Their Archaeology and Prehistory*. New York: Thames and Hudson.

Andersen, N. 1993. Causewayed Camps of the Funnel Beaker Culture. In *Digging into the Past: 25 Years of Archaeology in Denmark*, edited by S. Hvass and B. Storgaard 100–103. Copenhagen: The Royal Society of Northern Antiquaries.

Anderson, D. G. 1994. *The Savannah River Chiefdoms: Political Change in the Late Prehistoric Southeast*. Tuscaloosa: University of Alabama.

Andreski, S. 1968. *Military Organization and Society*. Berkeley: University of California.

Ardrey, R. 1961. *African Genesis*. New York: Dell.

———. 1966. *The Territorial Imperative*. New York: Atheneum.

Arensburg, B., and A. Belfer-Cohen. 1998. Sapiens and Neandertals: Rethinking the Levantine Middle Paleolithic Hominids. In *Neandertals and Modern Humans in Western Asia*, edited by T. Akazawa, K. Aoki, and O. Bar-Yosef 311–322. New York: Plenum.

Armendariz, J., S. Irigarai, and F. Etxeberria. 1994. New Evidence of Prehistoric Arrow Wounds in the Iberian Peninsula. *International Journal of Osteoarchaeology* 4:215–222.

Arvelo-Jimenez, N., and H. Biord Castillo. 1994. The Impact of Conquest on Contemporary Indigenous Peoples of the Guiana Shield: The System of Orinoco Regional Interdependence. In *Amazonian Indians from Prehistory to the Present*, edited by A. Roosevelt, 55–78. Tucson: University of Arizona Press.

Bachechi, L., P-F. Fabbri, and F. Mallegni. 1997. An Arrow-Caused Lesion in a Late Upper Paleolithic Human Pelvis. *Current Anthropology* 38:135–140.

Bamforth, D. B. 1994. Indigenous People, Indigenous Violence: Precontact Warfare on the North American Great Plains. *Man* 29:95–115.

Barker, G. 1985. *Prehistoric Farming in Europe*. Cambridge: Cambridge University Press.

Barnes, G. L. 1999. *The Rise of Civilization in East Asia: The Archaeology of China, Korea, and Japan*. New York: Thames and Hudson.

Bar-Yosef, O. 1986. The Walls of Jericho: An Alternative Interpretation. *Current Anthropology* 27:157–162.

Basham, A. L. 1959. *The Wonder that was India*. New York: Grove Press.

Belfer-Cohen, A., L. A. Shepartz, and B. Arensburg. 1991. New Biological Data for the Natufian Population in Israel. In *The Natufian Culture in the Levant*, edited by O. Bar-Yosef and F. R. Valla, 411–424. Ann Arbor, MI: International Monographs in Prehistory.

Benedict, R. 1959. The Natural History of War. In *An Anthropologist at Work: The Writings of Ruth Benedict*, edited by Margaret Mead, 369–382. Boston: Houghton Mifflin.

Berger, T. D., and E. Trinkaus. 1995. Patterns of Trauma among the Neandertals. *Journal of Archaeological Science* 22:841–852.

Binford, L., and C. K. Ho. 1985. Taphonomy at a Distance: Zhoukoudian, "The Cave Home of Beijing Man"? *Current Anthropology* 26:413–441.

Blick, J. 1988. Genocidal Warfare in Tribal Societies as a Result of European-induced Culture Conflict. *Man* 23:654–670.

Boaz, N., and R. L. Ciochan. 2001. The Scavenging of "Peking Man." *Natural History*, March, 46–51.

Boehm, C. 1999. *Hierarchy in the Forest: The Evolution of Egalitarian Behavior*. Cambridge: Harvard University Press.

Botella Lopez, M. C., S. A. Jimenez Brobeil, J. A. Ortega Vallet. 1995. Traumatisms in Bronze Age Settlements in the Iberian Peninsula: Argar Culture. *Proceedings of the Sixth European Meeting of the Paleopathlogy Association*, 65–72. Barcelona.

Bradley, R. 1991. The Pattern of Change in British Prehistory. In *Chiefdoms: Power, Economy, and Ideology*, edited by T. Earle, 44–70. New York: Cambridge University Press.

Brain, C. K. 1981. *The Hunter or the Hunted? An Introduction to African Cave Taphonomy*. Chicago: University of Chicago Press.

Bray, W., (editor). 1986. Weaponry and Warfare. *World Archaeology* 18(2).

Brennan, M. U. 1991. Health and Disease in the Middle and Upper Paleolithic of Southwestern France. Unpublished Ph.D. dissertation, Department of Anthropology, New York University.

Bridgford, S. D. 1997. Mightier than the Pen? (An Edgewise Look at Irish Bronze Age Swords). In *Material Harm: Archaeological Studies of War and Violence*, edited by J. Carman, 95–115. Glasgow: Cruithne Press.

Bullock, P. Y. 1998. Does the Reality of Anasazi Violence Prove the Myth of Anasazi Cannibalism. In *Deciphering Anasazi Violence*, edited by P. Y. Bullock, 35–51. Santa Fe, NM: HRM Books.

Carman, J., (editor). 1997. *Material Harm: Archaeological Studies of War and Violence*. Glasgow: Cruithne Press.

Carman, J., and A. Harding. 1999. Epilogue: The Future Study of Ancient Warfare. In *Ancient Warfare: Archaeological Perspectives*, edited by J. Carman and A. Harding, 245–250. Phoenix Mill, UK: Sutton Publishing Ltd.

Chagnon, N. 1968. *Yanomamo: The Fierce People*. New York: Holt, Rinehart, and Winston.

Chang, K. 1986. *The Archaeology of Ancient China*. New Haven: Yale University Press.

Chapdelaine, C. 1993. The Sedentarization of the Prehistoric Iroquoians: A Slow or Rapid Transformation? *Journal of Anthropological Archaeology* 12:173–209.

Chapman, J. 1999. The Origins of Warfare in the Prehistory of Central and Eastern Europe. In *Ancient Warfare: Archaeological Perspectives*, edited by J. Carman and A. Harding 101–142. Phoenix Mill, UK: Sutton Publishing Ltd.

Chapple, E., and C. S. Coon. 1942. *Principles of Anthropology*. New York: Henry Holt.

Chernela, J. 1993. *The Wanano Indians of the Brazilian Amazon: A Sense of Space*. Austin: University of Texas Press.

Childe, V. G. 1942. War in Prehistoric Societies. *Sociological Review* 23: 126–138.

Close, A. E. 1996. *Plus ca Change*: The Pleistocene-Holocene Transition in Northeast Africa. In *Humans at the End of the Ice Age: The Archaeology of the Pleistocene-Holocene Transition*, edited by L. G. Straus, B. V. Eriksen, J. M. Erlandson, and D. R. Yesner, 43–60. New York: Plenum.

Cobb, C. R., and B. M. Butler. 2002. The Vacant Quarter Revisited: Late Mississippian Abandonment of the Lower Ohio Valley. *American Antiquity* 67:625–641.

Cobbing, J. 1988. The Mfecane as Alibi: Thoughts on Dithakong and Mbolompo. *Journal of African History* 29:487–519.

Codere, H. 1950. *Fighting with Property: A Study of Kwakiutl Potlatching and Warfare 1792–1930*. Seattle: University of Washington Press.

Constandse-Westerman, T. S., and R. R. Newell. 1982. Mesolithic Trauma: Demographical and Chronological Trends in Western Europe. In *Proceeding of the 4th European Meeting of the Paleopathology Association, Middleburg-Antwerpen 1982*, edited by G. T. Haneveld and W.R.K. Perizonius, 70–76. Utrecht.

Cordier, G. 1990. Blessures Prehistoriques Animales et Humaines avec Armes ou Projectiles Conserves. *Bulletin de la Societe Prehistorique Française*, 10–12:462–481.

Coupland, G. 1988. Warfare and Social Complexity on the Northwest Coast. In *Cultures in Conflict: Current Archaeological Perspectives*, edited by D. Claire and B. C. Vivian, 205–214. Calgary: University of Calgary Archaeological Association.

Creamer, W., and J. Haas. 1998. Less than Meets the Eye: Evidence for Protohistoric

Chiefdoms in Northern New Mexico. In *Chiefdoms and Chieftaincy in the Americas*, edited by E. M. Redmond, 43–67. Gainesville: University Press of Florida.

Cybulski, J. S. 1992. *A Greenville Burial Ground: Human Remains and Mortuary Elements in British Columbia Coast Prehistory*. Hull, Quebec: Canadian Museum of Civilization.

———. 1994. Culture Change, Demographic History, and Health and Disease on the Northwest Coast. In *In the Wake of Contact: Biological Responses to Conquest*, edited by C. S. Larsen and G. R. Milner, 75–85. New York: John Wiley and Sons.

Dancey, W. S. 1992. Village Origins in Central Ohio: The Results and Implications of Recent Middle and Late Woodland Research. In *Cultural Variability in Context: Woodland Settlements of the Mid-Ohio Valley*, edited by M. F. Seeman, 24–27. MCJA Special Paper no. 7. Kent, OH: The Kent State University Press.

Darling, J. A. 1998. Mass Inhumation and the Execution of Witches in the American Southwest. *American Anthropologist* 100:732–752.

Dart, R. 1957. *The Osteodontokeratic Culture of Australopithecus Prometheus*. Memoirs of the Transvaal Museum, No. 10.

DeBoer, W. 1981. Buffer Zones in the Cultural Ecology of Aboriginal Amazonia: An Ethnohistorical Approach. *American Antiquity* 46:364–377.

———. 1986. Pillage and Production in the Amazon: A View through the Conibo of the Ucayali Basin, Eastern Peru. *World Archaeology* 18:231–246.

De Fleur, A., T. White, P. Valensi, L. Slimak, and E. Cregut-Bonnoure. 1999. Neandertal Cannibalism at Moula-Guercy, Ardeche, France. *Science* 286:128–131.

Dennell, R. 1985. The Hunter-Gatherer/Agricultural Frontier in Prehistoric Temperate Europe. In *The Archaeology of Frontiers and Boundaries*, edited by S. Green and S. Perlman, 113–139. Orlando: Academic Press.

Dickel, D. N., C. G. Aker, B. K. Baron, and G. H. Doran. 1988. An Orbital Floor and Ulna Fracture from the Early Archaic of Florida. *Journal of Paleopathology* 2:165–170.

Dolukhanov, P. M. 1986a. Foragers and Farmers in West-Central Asia. In *Hunters in Transition*, edited by M. Zvelebil, 121–132. Cambridge: Cambridge University Press.

———. 1986b. The Late Mesolithic and the Transition to Food Production in Eastern Europe. In *Hunters in Transition*, edited by M. Zvelebil, 109–120. Cambridge: Cambridge University Press.

———. 1999. War and Peace in Prehistoric Europe. In *Ancient Warfare: Archaeological Perspectives*, edited by J. Carman and A. Harding, 73–88. Phoenix Mill, UK: Sutton Publishing Ltd.

Drews, R. 1993. *The End of the Bronze Age: Changes in Warfare and the Catastrophe ca. 1200 B.C.* Princeton: Princeton University Press.

Dye, D. 2002. Warfare in the Protohistoric Southeast, 1500–1700. In *Between Contacts and Colonies: Archaeological Perspectives on the Protohistoric Southeast*, edited by C. B. Wesson and M. A. Rees, 126–141. Tuscaloosa: University of Alabama Press.

Dyson, R. H. 1982. Paradigm Changes in the Study of the Indus Civilization. In *Harappan Civilization: A Contemporary Perspective*, edited by G. L. Possehl, 418–428. New Delhi: Oxford and IBHI Publishing.

Eddy, F. W. 1974. Population Dislocation in the Navaho Reservoir District, New Mexico and Colorado. *American Antiquity* 39:75–84.

Edgerton, R. B. 1972. Violence in East African Tribal Societies. In *Collective Violence*, edited by J. F. Short Jr. and M. E. Wolfgang, 159–170. Chicago: Aldine.

Ember, C. R., and M. Ember. 1997. Violence in the Ethnographic Record: Results of Cross-Cultural Research on War and Aggression. In *Troubled Times: Violence and Warfare in the Past*, edited by D. L. Martin and D. W. Frayer, 1–20. Langhorne, PA: Gordon and Breach.

Etxeberria, F., L. Herrasti, and J. I. Vegas. 1995. Arrow Wounds during Prehistory in the Iberian Peninsula with Regard to San Juan ante Portam Latinam. *Proceedings of the IXth European Meeting of the Paleopathology Association*, 141–145. Barcelona.

Fagan, B. M. 1995. *Ancient North America: The Archaeology of a Continent*. New York: Thames and Hudson.

Fage, J. D., and R. Oliver (editors). 1975. *The Cambridge History of Africa, Volume 1 from the Earliest Times to c. 500 B.C.* New York: Cambridge University Press.

Farris, W. W. 1998. *Sacred Texts and Buried Treasures: Issues in the Historical Archaeology of Ancient Japan*. Honolulu: University of Hawai'i Press.

———. 1999. Japan to 1300. In *War and Society in the Ancient and Medieval Worlds: Asia, the Mediterranean, Europe, and Mesoamerica*, edited by K. Raaflaub and N. Rosenstein, 47–70. Cambridge: Center for Hellenic Studies and Harvard University Press.

Ferguson, R. B. 1983. Warfare and Redistributive Exchange on the Northwest Coast. In *The Development of Political Organization in Native North America: 1979 Proceedings of the American Ethnological Society*, edited by E. Tooker, 133–147. Washington, D.C.: American Ethnological Society.

———. 1984a. Introduction: Studying War. In *Warfare, Culture, and Environment*, edited by R. B. Ferguson, 1–81. Orlando: Academic Press.

———. 1984b. A Re-examination of the Causes of Northwest Coast Warfare. In *Warfare, Culture, and Environment*, edited by R. B. Ferguson, 267–328. Orlando: Academic Press.

———. 1990. Blood of the Leviathan: Western Contact and Warfare in Amazonia. *American Ethnologist* 17(2):237–257.

———. 1992. Tribal Warfare. *Scientific American* 266(1):108–113.

———. 1993. When Worlds Collide: The Columbian Encounter in Global Perspective. *Human Peace* 10(1):8–12.

———. 1994. The General Consequences of War: An Amazonian Perspective. In *Studying War: Anthropological Perspectives*, edited by S. P. Reyna and R. E. Downs, 85–111. Langhorne, PA: Gordon and Breach.

———. 1995a. *Yanomami Warfare: A Political History*. Santa Fe, NM: School of American Research Press.

———. 1995b. Infrastructural Determinism. In *Science, Materialism, and the Study of Culture*, edited by M. F. Murphy and M. Margolis, 21–38. Gainesville: University Press of Florida.

———. 1997. Violence and War in Prehistory. In *Troubled Times: Violence and Warfare in the Past*, edited by D. L. Martin and D. W. Frayer, 321–355. Langhorne, PA: Gordon and Breach.

———. 1998. Whatever Happened to the Stone Age? Steel Tools and Yanomami Historical Ecology. In *Advances in Historical Ecology*, edited by W. Balee, 287–312. New York: Columbia University Press.

———. 1999. A Paradigm for the Study of War and Society. In *War and Society in Ancient and Medieval Worlds: Asia, the Mediterranean, Europe, and Mesoamerica*, edited by K. Raaflaub and N. Rosenstein, 389–437. Washington, D.C., and Cambridge: Center for Hellenic Studies, distributed by Harvard University Press.

———. 2000. A Savage Encounter: Western Contact and the Yanomami War Complex. In *War in the Tribal Zone: Expanding States and Indigenous Warfare*, (Second printing), edited by R. B. Ferguson and N. L. Whitehead, 199–227. Santa Fe, NM: School of American Research Press.

———. 2001. 10,000 Years of Tribal Warfare. *The Journal of the International Institute* 8(3):1, 4–5.

———. 2003. Introduction: Violent Conflict and Control of the State. In *The State, Identity, and Violence: Political Disintegration in the Post-Cold War World*, edited by R. B. Ferguson, 1–58. New York: Routledge.

———. 2005. Tribal, "Ethnic," and Global Wars. In *The Psychology of Resolving Global Conflicts*, edited by M. Fitzduff and C. Stout. Westport, CT: Praeger.

Ferguson, R. B., with L. E. Farragher. 1988. *The Anthropology of War: A Bibliography*. New York: The Harry Frank Guggenheim Foundation.

Ferguson, R. B., and N. L. Whitehead (editors). 2000. *War in the Tribal Zone: Expanding States and Indigenous Warfare* (Second printing with new preface). Santa Fe, NM: School of American Research Press.

Fernandez Castro, M. C. 1995. *Iberia in Prehistory*. Oxford: Blackwell.

Fernandez-Jalvo, Y., J. C. Diez, I. Caceres, and J. Rosell. 1999. Human Cannibalism in the Early Pleistocene of Europe (Gran Dolina, Sierra de Atapuerca, Burgos, Spain). *Journal of Human Evolution* 37:591–622.

Ferrill, A. 1985. *The Origins of War: From the Stone Age to Alexander the Great*. New York: Thames and Hudson.

Fish, P. R., and S. K. Fish. 1989. Hohokam Warfare from a Regional Perspective. In *Cultures in Conflict: Current Archaeological Perspectives*, edited by D. C. Tkaczuk and B. C. Vivian, 112–129. Calgary: The University of Calgary Archaeological Association.

Flannery, K. V., and J. Marcus. 2003. The Origin of War: New ^{14}C Dates from Ancient Mexico. *Proceedings of the National Academy of Sciences*, 100:1801–1805.

Frayer, D. W. 1997. Ofnet: Evidence for a Mesolithic Massacre. In *Troubled Times: Violence and Warfare in the Past*, edited by D. L. Martin and D. W. Frayer, 181–216. Langhorne, PA: Gordon and Breach.

Fukuyama, F. 1998. Women and the Evolution of World Politics. *Foreign Affairs*, September/October, 24–40.

Gat, A. 2000. The Causes and Origins of "Primitive Warfare": Reply to Ferguson. *Anthropological Quarterly* 73:165–168.

Giedion, S. 1962. *The Eternal Present: The Beginnings of Art*. New York: Pantheon.

Gilij, F. S. 1965. *Ensayo de Historia Americana* (3 books). Translated and preliminary study by A. Tovar. Caracas: Biblioteca de la Academia Nacional de la Historia.

Goldberg, N. J., and F. J. Findlow. 1984. A Quantitative Analysis of Roman Military Operations in Britain, circa A.D. 43 to 238. In *Warfare, Culture, and Environment*, edited by R. B. Ferguson, 359–385. Orlando: Academic Press.

Gottwald, N. K. 1979. *The Tribes of Yahweh: A Sociology of the Religion of Liberated Israel, 1250–1050 B.C.E.* Maryknoll, NY: Orbis.

Gourevitch, P. 1996. Misfortune Tellers. *The New Yorker*, April 8:96–100.

Gramly, R. M. 1988. Conflict and Defense in the Eastern Woodlands. In *Interpretations of Culture Change in the Eastern Woodlands during the Late Woodland Period*, edited by R. W. Yerkes, 85–97. Columbus: Department of Anthropology, Ohio State University.

Guilaine, J., and J. Zammit. 2005. *The Origins of War: Violence in Prehistory*, translated by M. Hersey. Malden, MA: Blackwell.

Gunawardana, R.A.L.H. 2000. Conquest and Resistance: Pre-state and State Expansionism in Early Sri Lankan History. In *War in the Tribal Zone: Expanding States and Indigenous Warfare*, edited by R. B. Ferguson and N. L. Whitehead, 61–82. Santa Fe, NM: School of American Research Press.

Gupta, S. P. 1979. *Archaeology of Soviet Central Asia, and the Indian Borderlands*, 2 vols. New Delhi: B.R. Publishing Corporation.

Haas, J. 1990. Warfare and the Evolution of Tribal Polities in the Prehistoric Southwest. In *The Anthropology of War*, edited by J. Haas, 171–189. Cambridge: Cambridge University Press.

———. 1999. The Origins of War and Ethnic Violence. In *Ancient Warfare: Archaeological Perspectives*, edited by J. Carman and A. Harding, 11–24. Phoenix Mill, UK: Sutton Publishing Ltd.

Haas, J., and W. Creamer. 1997. Warfare among the Pueblos: Myth, History, and Ethnography. *Ethnohistory* 44:235–261.

Hamilton, C. (editor). 1995. *The Mfecane Aftermath: Reconstructive Debates in Southern African History*. Johannesburg: Witwatersrand University Press, and Pietermaritzburg: University of Natal Press.

Harding, A. 1999. Warfare: A Defining Characteristic of Bronze Age Europe? In *Ancient Warfare: Archaeological Perspectives*, edited by J. Carman and A. Harding, 157–174. Phoenix Mill, UK: Sutton Publishing Ltd.

Hemming, J. 1978. *Red Gold: The Conquest of the Brazilian Amazon*. Cambridge, MA: Harvard University Press.

Henry, D. O. 1985. Preagricultural Sedentism: The Natufian Example. In *Prehistoric Hunter-Gatherers: The Emergence of Cultural Complexity*, edited by T. D. Price and J. A. Brown, 365–384. Orlando: Academic Press.

Hill, P., and J. Wileman. 2002. *Landscapes of War: The Archaeology of Aggression and Defense*. Charleston, SC: Tempus.

Hollimon, S. E., and D. W. Owsley. 1994. Osteology of the Fay Tolton Site: Implications for Warfare during the Initial Middle Missouri Variant. In *Skeletal Biology in the Great Plains: Migration, Warfare, Health, and Subsistence*, edited by D. W. Owsley and R. L. Jantz, 345–353. Washington, D.C.: Smithsonian Institution Press.

Hunt, G. 1940. *The Wars of the Iroquois: A Study of Intertribal Trade Relations*. Madison: University of Wisconsin.

Hurst, W. B., and C. G. Turner. 1993. Rediscovering the "Great Discovery": Wetherill's First Cave 7 and its Record of Basketmaker Violence. In *Anasazi Basketmaker: Papers from the 1990 Wetherill-Grand Gulch Symposium*, edited by V. Atkins, 143–191. Salt Lake City, UT: Bureau of Land Management.

Imamura, K. 1996. *Prehistoric Japan: New Perspectives on Insular East Asia*. Honolulu: University of Hawai'i Press.

Jablow, J. 1950. *The Cheyenne in Plains Indian Trade Relations*. American Ethnological Society Monograph 19: Seattle.

Jacobsen, T. 1976. *The Treasures of Darkness: A History of Mesopotamian Religion*. New Haven: Yale University Press.

Jacobson, J. 1986. *Studies in the Archaeology of India and Pakistan*. New Delhi: Oxford and IBH Publishing, Co.

Jones, T. 1998. Unification, Deduction, and History: A Reply to Steel. *Philosophy of Science* 65:672–681.

Kanter, J. 1999. Survival Cannibalism or Sociopolitical Intimidation? *Human Nature* 10:1–50.

Kay, M. 1995. *Hard Times at the Helb Redoubt: 1992–1993 Archaeological Investigations at the Helb Site (39CC208), Campbell County, South Dakota*. Fayetteville, AR: University of Arkansas.

Keeley, L. H. 1992. The Introduction of Agriculture to the Western North European Plain. In *Transitions to Agriculture in Prehistory*, edited by A. B. Gebauer and T. D. Price, 81–95. Madison, WI: Prehistory Press.

———. 1996. *War Before Civilization: The Myth of the Peaceful Savage*. New York: Oxford University Press.

———. 1997. Frontier Warfare in the Early Neolithic. In *Troubled Times: Violence and Warfare in the Past*, edited by D. L. Martin and D. W. Frayer, 303–319. Langhorne, PA: Gordon and Breach.

———. 2001. Giving War a Chance. In *Deadly Landscapes: Case Studies in Prehistoric Southwestern Warfare*, G. E. Rice and S. A. LeBlanc. Salt Lake City: University of Utah Press.

Keeley, L. H., and D. Cahen. 1989. Early Neolithic Forts and Villages in NE Belgium: A Preliminary Report. *Journal of Field Archaeology* 16:157–176.

Kelly, R. C. 2000. *Warless Societies and the Origin of War*. Ann Arbor: University of Michigan Press.

Kim, J. 1978. *The Prehistory of Korea*. Honolulu: The University Press of Hawai'i.

Klima, B. 1962. The First Ground-plan of an Upper Paleolithic Loess Settlement in Middle Europe and its Meaning. In *Courses Toward Urban Life: Archeological Considerations of Some Cultural Alternates*, edited by R. J. Braidwood and G. R. Willey. Chicago: Aldine.

———. 1987. A Triple Burial from the Upper Paleolithic of Dolni Vestonice, Czechoslovakia. *Journal of Human Evolution* 16:831–835.

Knight, V. J., Jr., and V. P. Steponaitis. 1999. A New History of Moundville. In *Archaeology of the Moundville Chiefdom*, edited by V. J. Knight Jr. and V. Steponaitis, 1–25. Washington, D.C.: Smithsonian Institution Press.

Kohl, P. L. 1981. The Namazga Civilization: An Overview. In *The Bronze Age Civilization of Central Asia*, edited by P. L. Kohl, vii–xxxviii. Armonk, NY: M.E. Sharpe, Inc.

Kokkinidou, D., and M. Nikolaidou. 1999. Neolithic Enclosures in Greek Macedonia: Violent and Non-Violent Aspects of Territorial Demarcation. In *Ancient Warfare: Archaeological Perspectives*, edited by J. Carman and A. Harding, 89–99. Phoenix Mill, UK: Sutton Publishing Ltd.

Kozlowski, S. K. 1989. Nemrik 9, A PPN Neolithic Site in Northern Iraq. *Paleorient* 15:25–31.

Krause, R. 1970. Aspects of Adaptation among Upper Republican Subsistence Cultivators. In *Pleistocene and Recent Environments of the Central Great Plains*, edited by W. Dort Jr. and J. K. Jones Jr., 103–115. Lawrence, KS: University of Kansas Press.

Kristiansen, K. 1987. From Stone to Bronze: The Evolution of Social Complexity in Northern Europe, 2300–1200 B.C. In *Specialization, Exchange, and Complex Societies*, edited by E. M. Brumfiel and T. K. Earle, 30–51. Cambridge: Cambridge University Press.

Lamberg-Karlovsky, C. C. 1981. Afterword. In *The Bronze Age Civilization of Central Asia*, edited by P. L. Kohl, 386–398. Armonk, NY: M.E. Sharpe.

Lambert, P. A. 2002. The Archaeology of War: A North American Perspective. *Journal of Archaeological Research* 10:207–241.

LeBlanc, S. A. 1999. *Prehistoric Warfare in the American Southwest*. Salt Lake City: University of Utah Press.

———. 2000. Regional Interaction and Warfare in the Late Prehistoric Southwest. In *The Archaeology of Regional Interaction: Religion, Warfare, and Exchange Across the American Southwest and Beyond*, edited by M. Hegmon, 41–70. Boulder: University Press of Colorado.

———. 2003. Prehistory of Warfare. *Archaeology* May/June, 18–25.

LeBlanc, S., with K. Register. 2003. *Constant Battles: The Myth of the Peaceful, Noble Savage*. New York: St. Martin's Press.

LeBlanc, S., and G. E. Rice. 2001. Southwestern Warfare: The Value of Case Studies. In *Deadly Landscapes: Case Studies in Prehistoric Southwestern Warfare*, edited by G. E. Rice and S. A. LeBlanc, 1–18. Salt Lake City: University of Utah Press.

Leach, E. 1965. The Nature of War. *Disarmament and Arms Control* 3:165–183.

Lehmann-Haupt, C. 1996. Even in Eden, It Seems, War was Hell. *The New York Times*, July 18, C 17.

Lekson, S. H. 2002. War in the Southwest, War in the World. *American Antiquity* 67:607–624.

Leroi-Gourhan, A. 1968. *Treasures of Prehistoric Art*. New York: Harry N. Abrams.

———. 1982. *The Dawn of European Art: An Introduction to Palaeolithic Cave Painting*. Cambridge: Cambridge University Press.

Lewis, O. 1942. *The Effects of White Contact Upon Blackfoot Culture*. Seattle: American Ethnological Society Monograph no. 6.

Liu, L. 1996. Settlement Patterns, Chiefdom Variability, and the Development of Early States in North China. *Journal of Anthropological Archaeology* 15:237–288.

Lloyd, S. 1984. *The Archaeology of Mesopotamia*, rev. ed. New York: Thames and Hudson.

Lovejoy, C. O., and K. G. Heiple. 1981. The Analysis of Fractures in Skeletal Populations, with an Example from the Libben Site, Ottowa County, OH. *American Journal of Physical Anthropology* 55:529–541.

Lovejoy, P. 1983. *Transformations in Slavery: A History of Slavery in Africa*. Cambridge: Cambridge University Press.

Low, Bobbi. 2000. *Why Sex Matters: A Darwinian Look at Human Behavior*. Princeton: Princeton University Press.

Lucentini, J. 2002. Bones Reveal Some Truth in "Noble Savage Myth." *The Washington Post*, April 15, A9.

MacDonald, G. 1979. *Kitwanga Fort National Historic Site, Skeena River, British Columbia: Historical Research and Analysis of Structural Remains*. Ottawa: National Museum of Man.

Malinowski, B. 1941. An Anthropological Analysis of War. *American Journal of Sociology* 46:521–550.

Martin, D. L. 1997. Violence Against Women in the La Plata River Valley (A.D. 1000–1300). In *Troubled Times: Violence and Warfare in the Past*, edited by D. L. Martin and D. W. Frayer, 45–75. Amsterdam: Gordon and Breach.

Martin, D. L., and D. W. Frayer (editors). 1997. *Troubled Times: Violence and Warfare in the Past*. Amsterdam: Gordon and Breach.

McCown, T. D., and A. Keith. 1939. The Stone Age Men of Mount Carmel. Oxford: Clarendon.

McManamon, F. 1999. The Initial Scientific Examination, Description, and Analysis of the Kennewick Man Human Remains. ParkNet, National Park Service, www.cr.nps.gov/aad/kennewick/mcmanamon.htm.

Medina, J. 1934. *The Discovery of the Amazon, According to the Account of Friar Gaspar de Carvajal and Other Documents*. H. Heaton, editor, B. Lee, translator. New York: American Geographical Society.

Mellaart, J. 1967. *Catal Huyuk: A Neolithic Town in Anatolia*. New York: McGraw Hill

———. 1975. *The Neolithic of the Near East*. London: Thames and Hudson.

Mercer, R. J. 1988. Hambledon Hill, Dorset, England. In *Enclosures and Defenses in the Neolithic of Western Europe*, edited by C. Burgess, P. Topping, C. Mordant, and M. Maddison, 77–87. Oxford: British Archaeological Reports, International Series 403(1).

———. 1989. The Earliest Defences in Western Europe, Part II: The Archaeological Evidence. *Fortress* 1(2):2–11.

———. 1999. The Origins of Warfare in the British Isles. In *Ancient Warfare: Archaeological Perspectives*, edited by J. Carman and A. Harding, 143–156. Phoenix Mill, UK: Sutton Publishing Ltd.

Midant-Reynes, B. 1992. *The Prehistory of Egypt: From the First Egyptians to the First Pharaohs*. Oxford: Blackwell.

Miller, D. 1985. Ideology and the Harappan Civilization. *Journal of Anthropological Archaeology* 4:34–71.

Milner, G. R. 1995. An Osteological Perspective on Prehistoric Warfare. In *Regional Approaches to Mortuary Analysis*, edited by L. A. Beck, 221–244. New York: Plenum.

———. 1999. Warfare in Prehistoric and Early Historic Eastern North America. *Journal of Archaeological Research* 7:105–151.

Milner, G. R., E. Anderson, and V. G. Smith. 1991. Warfare in Late Prehistoric West-Central Illinois. *American Antiquity* 56:581–603.

Monks, S. J. 1997. Conflict and Competition in Spanish Prehistory: The Role of Warfare in Societal Development from the Late Fourth to Third Millenium B.C. *Journal of Mediterranean Archaeology* 10:3–32.

Morey, R., and D. Marwitt. 1974. *The Guahibo: People of the Savanna*. Acta Etnologica et Linguistica no. 31. Vienna.

Morse, D. F., and P. A. Morse. 1983. *Archaeology of the Central Mississippi Valley*. New York: Academic Press.

Moss, M. L., and J. M. Erlandson. 1992. Forts, Refuge Rocks, and Defensive Sites: The Antiquity of Warfare along the North Pacific Coast of North America. *Arctic Anthropology* 29(2):73–90.

Munson, P. J. 1988. Late Woodland Settlement and Subsistence in Temporal Perspective. In *Interpretations of Culture Change in the Eastern Woodlands during the Late Woodland Period*, edited by R. W. Yerkes, 7–17. Columbus: Department of Anthropology, Ohio State University.

Myers, T. 1988. Spanish Contacts and Social Change on the Ucayali River, Peru. *Ethnohistory* 21:135–157.

Naroll, R. 1966. Does Military Deterrence Deter? *Trans-Action* 3(2):14–20.

Nassaney, M., and K. Pyle. 1999. The Adoption of the Bow and Arrow in Eastern North America: A View from Central Arkansas. *American Antiquity* 64:243–263.

Needham, J., and R.D.S. Yates. 1994. *Science and Civilization in China, Volume 5, Chemistry and Chemical Technology: Part VI Military Technology: Missiles and Sieges*. Cambridge: Cambridge University Press.

Nelson, B. A. 2000. Aggregation, Warfare, and the Spread of the Mesoamerican Tradition. In *The Archaeology of Regional Interaction: Religion, Warfare, and Exchange Across the American Southwest and Beyond*, edited by M. Hegmon. Boulder: University Press of Colorado.

Newcomb, W. W. 1960. Toward an Understanding of War. In *Essays in the Science of Culture: In Honor of Leslie A. White*, edited by G. Dole and R. Carneiro, 317–336. New York: Thomas Crowell.

Nikolaidou, M., and D. Kokkinidou. 1997. The Symbolism of Violence in Palatial Societies of the Late Bronze Age Aegean, a Gender Approach. In *Material Harm: Archaeological Studies of War and Violence*, edited by J. Carman, 174–197. Glasgow: Cruithne Press.

O'Brien, M. J., and W. R. Wood. 1998. *The Prehistory of Missouri*. Columbia: University of Missouri Press.

O'Connell, R. L. 1995. *Ride of the Second Horseman: The Birth and Death of War*. New York: Oxford University Press.

Olsen, S. L., and P. Shipman. 1994. Cutmarks and Perimortem Treatment of Skeletal Remains on the Northern Plains. In *Skeletal Biology in the Great Plains: Migration, Warfare, Health, and Subsistence*, edited by D. W. Owsley and R. L. Jantz, 377–387. Washington, D.C.: Smithsonian Institution Press.

Osgood, R. 1998. *Warfare in the Late Bronze Age of North Europe*. BAR International Series 694. Oxford: Hadrian Books.

Ostendorf Smith, M. 1997. Osteological Indications of Warfare in the Archaic Period of the Western Tennessee Valley. In *Troubled Times: Violence and Warfare in the Past*, edited by D. L. Martin and D. W. Frayer, 241–265. Amsterdam: Gordon and Breach.

Otterbein, K. 1999. A History of Research on Warfare in Anthropology. *American Anthropologist* 101:794–805.

———. 2004. *How War Began*. College Station: Texas A&M Press.

Owsley, D. W. 1989. The History of Bioarcheological Research in the Southern Great Plains. In *From Clovis to Comanchero: Archeological Overview of the Southern Great Plains*, edited by J. L. Hofman, R. L. Brooks, J. S. Hays, D. W. Owsley, R. L. Jantz, M. K. Marks, and M. H. Manhein, 123–136. Oklahoma Archeological Survey of the University of Oklahoma and the Louisiana State University, with the Arkansas Archeological Survey.

Owsley, D. W., and H. E. Berryman. 1975. Ethnographic and Archaeological Evidence of Scalping in the Southeastern United States. *Tennessee Archaeologist* 31:41–60.

Owsley, D. W., and R. L. Jantz (editors). 1994. *Skeletal Biology in the Great Plains: Migration, Warfare, Health, and Subsistence*. Washington, D.C.: Smithsonian Institution Press.

———. 2000. Biography in the Bones: Skeletons Tell the Story of Ancient Lives and Peoples. *Scientific American Discovering Archaeology*. January/February, 56–58.

Owsley, D. W., M. K. Marks, and M. H. Manhein. 1989. Human Skeletal Samples in the Southern Great Plains. In *From Clovis to Comanchero: Archeological Overview of the Southern Great Plains*, edited by J. L. Hofman, R. L. Brooks, J. S. Hays, D. W. Owsley, R. L. Jantz, M. K. Marks, and M. H. Manhein, 111–122. Oklahoma Archeological Survey of the University of Oklahoma and the Louisiana State University, with the Arkansas Archeological Survey.

Pinker, S. 2002. *The Blank Slate: The Modern Denial of Human Nature*. New York: Penguin.

Popham, M. 1994. The Collapse of Aegean Civilization at the End of the Late Bronze Age. In *The Oxford Illustrated Prehistory of Europe*, edited by B. Cunliffe, 277–303. New York: Oxford University Press.

Pozorski, S. 1987. Theocracy vs. Militarism: The Significance of the Casma Valley in Understanding Early State Formation. In *The Origins and Development of the Andean State*, edited by J. Haas, S. Pozorski, and T. Pozorski, 15–35. New York: Cambridge University Press.

Price, T. D. 1985. Affluent Foragers of Mesolithic Southern Scandinavia. In *Prehistoric Hunter-Gatherers: The Emergence of Cultural Complexity*, edited by T. D. Price and J. A. Brown, 341–367. Orlando: Academic Press.

Pringle, H. 1998. North America's Wars. *Science*, 27 March, 2038–2040.

Randsborg, K. 1992. *Hjortspring: Warfare and Sacrifice in Early Europe*. Aarhus: Aarhus University Press.

———. 1999. Into the Iron Age: A Discourse on War and Society. In *Ancient Warfare: Archaeological Perspectives*, edited by J. Carman and A. Harding, 191–202. Phoenix Mill, UK: Sutton Publishing Ltd.

Ravesloot, J. C., and P. M. Spoerl. 1989. The Role of Warfare in the Development of Status Hierarchies at Casas Grandes, Chihuaha, Mexico. In *Cultures in Conflict: Current Archaeological Perspectives*, edited by D. C. Tkaczuk and B. C. Vivian 130–137. Calgary: The University of Calgary Archaeological Association.

Reyna, S. 1994. A Mode of Domination Approach to Organized Violence. In *Studying War: Anthropological Perspectives*, edited by S. P. Reyna and R. E. Downs, 29–65. Langhorne, PA: Gordon and Breach.

Rice, G. E. 2001. Warfare and Massing in the Salt and Gila Basins of Central Arizona. In *Deadly Landscapes: Case Studies in Prehistoric Warfare*, edited by G. E. Rice and S. A. LeBlanc, 289–329. Salt Lake City: University of Utah Press.

Rice, G. E., and S. LeBlanc (editors). 2001. *Deadly Landscapes: Case Studies in Prehistoric Warfare*. Salt Lake City: University of Utah Press.

Ritchie, W. A. 1980. *The Archaeology of New York State*. Harrison, NY: Harbor Hill Books.

Robb, J. 1997. Violence and Gender in Early Italy. In *Troubled Times: Violence and Warfare in the Past*, edited by D. L. Martin and D. W. Frayer, 111–144. Langhorne, PA: Gordon and Breach.

Roper, M. 1969. A Survey of the Evidence for Intrahuman Killing in the Pleistocene. *Current Anthropology* 10:427–459.

———. 1975. Evidence of Warfare in the Near East from 10,000–4,300 B.C. In *War, Its Causes and Correlates*, edited by M. A. Nettleship, D. Givens, and A. Nettleship, 299–344. The Hague: Mouton.

Roosevelt, A. 1980. *Parmana: Prehistoric Maize and Manioc Subsistence Along the Amazon and Orinoco*. New York: Academic Press.

———. 1991. *Moundbuilders of the Amazon: Geophysical Archaeology on Marajo Island, Brazil*. Orlando: Academic Press.

Roundtree, H. C., and E. R. Turner III. 1998. The Evolution of the Powhatan Paramount Chiefdom in Virginia. In *Chiefdoms and Chieftaincy in the Americas*, edited by E. M. Redmond, 265–296. Gainesville: University Press of Florida.

Rowland, M., M. Larsen, and K. Kristiansen (editors). 1987. *Centre and Periphery in the Ancient World*. Cambridge: Cambridge University Press.

Russel, M. 1987a. Bone Breakage in the Krapina Hominid Collection. *American Journal of Physical Anthropology* 72:373–379.

———. 1987b. Mortuary Practices at the Krapina Neandertal Site. *American Journal of Physical Anthropology* 72:381–397.

Sankalia, H. D. 1974. *The Prehistory and Protohistory of India and Pakistan*. Poona, India: Deccan College.

Savage, S. H. 1997. Descent Group Competition and Economic Strategies in Predynastic Egypt. *Journal of Anthropological Archaeology* 16:226–268.

Schmookler, A. B. 1984. *The Parable of the Tribes: The Problem of Power in Social Evolution*. Boston: Houghton Mifflin Co.

Schutz, H. 1983. *The Prehistory of Germanic Europe*. New Haven: Yale University Press.

Secoy, F. 1953. *Changing Military Patterns on the Great Plains*. Seattle: University of Washington Press.

Seeman, M. F. 1988. Ohio Hopewell Trophy-Skull Artifacts as Evidence for Competition in Middle Woodland Societies circa 50 B.C.–A.D. 350. *American Antiquity* 53:565–577.

Sharma, G. R. 1963. Mesolithic Lake Culture in the Ganga Valley, India. *Proceedings of the Prehistoric Society* 39:129–146.

Sherratt, A. 1994. The Emergence of Elites: Earlier Bronze Age Europe. In *The Oxford Illustrated Prehistory of Europe*, edited by B. Cunliffe, 244–276. New York: Oxford University Press.

Simons, A. 1997. Two Perspectives on War and its Beginnings. *Current Anthropology* 38:149–151.

Singh, S. D. 1965. *Ancient Indian Warfare with Special Reference to the Vedic Period*. Leiden: E.J. Brill.

Sladek, V., E. Trinkaus, S. W. Hillson, and T. W. Holliday. 2000. *The People of the Pavlovian: Skeletal Catalogue and Osteometrics of the Gravettian Fossil Hominids from Dolni Vestonice and Pavlov*. Brno: The Academy of Sciences of the Czech Republic.

Smith, B. D. (editor). 1990. *The Mississippian Emergence*. Washington, D.C.: Smithsonian Institution Press.

Snyder, J. 2002. Anarchy and Culture: Insights from the Anthropology of War. *International Organization* 56:7–45.

Spencer, C. S. 1998. Investigating the Development of Venezuelan Chiefdoms. In *Chiefdoms and Chieftaincy in the Americas,* edited by E. M. Redmond, 104–137. Gainesville: University Press of Florida.

Spencer, C. S., and E. M. Redmond. 1992. Prehispanic Chiefdoms of the Western Venezuelan *Llanos*. *World Archaeology* 24:135–155.

Sponsel, L. E. 2000. Response to Otterbein. *American Anthropologist* 102:837–841.

Srivastava, K. M. 1984. The Myth of Aryan Invasion of Harappan Towns. In *Frontiers of the Indus Civilization*, edited by B. B. Lal, S. P. Gupta, and S. Asthana, 437–444. New Delhi: I. M. Sharma of Books and Books.

Staden, H. 1928. *Hans Staden: The True Story of His Captivity, 1557*. M. Letts, translator. London: Routledge and Sons.

Steel, D. 1998. Warfare and Western Manufactures: A Case Study of Explanation in Anthropology. *Philosophy of Science* 65:649–667.

Stein, G. 1994. Economy, Ritual, and Power in Ubaid Mesopotamia. In *Chiefdoms and Early States in the Near East: The Organizational Dynamics of Complexity*, edited by G. Stein and M. S. Rothman, 35–46. Madison, WI: Prehistory Press.

Svoboda, J., V. Lozek, and E. Vlcek. 1996. *Hunters between East and West: The Paleolithic of Moravia*. New York: Plenum Press.

Svoboda, J., and E. Vlcek. 1991. La Nouvelle Sepulture de Dolni Vestonice (DV XVI), Tchecoslovaquie. *L'Anthropologie* 95:323–328.

Swadesh, M. 1948. Motivations in Nootka Warfare. *Southwestern Journal of Anthropology* 4:76–93.

Tacon, P., and C. Chippindale. 1994. Australia's Ancient Warriors: Changing Depictions of Fighting in the Rock Art of Arnhem Land, N.T. *Cambridge Archaeological Journal* 4(2):211–248.

Thomas, J. 1999. *Understanding the Neolithic*. London: Routledge.

Tkaczuk, D. C., and B. C. Vivian (editors). 1989. *Cultures in Conflict: Current Archaeological Perspectives*. Calgary: University of Calgary Archaeological Association.

Tosi, M. 1979. The Proto-Urban Cultures of Eastern Iran and the Indus Civilization: Notes and Suggestions for a Spatio-Temporal Frame to Study the Early Relations between India and Iran. In *South Asian Archaeology 1977: Papers from the Fourth International Conference of the Association of South Asian Archaeologists in Europe*, edited by M. Taddei, 149–172. Naples: Instituto Universitario Orientale, Seminario de Studi Asiatici.

Trinkaus, E. 1985. Cannibalism and Burial at Krapina. *Journal of Human Evolution* 14:203–216.

Trinkaus, E., and M. R. Zimmerman. 1982. Trauma among the Shanidar Neandertals. *American Journal of Physical Anthropology* 57:61–72.

Trinkaus, E., J. Svoboda, D. L. West, V. Sladek, S. W. Hillson, E. Drozdova, and M. Fisakova. 2000. Human Remains from the Moravian Gravettian: Morphology and Taphonomy of Isolated Elements from the Dolni Vestonice II Site. *Journal of Archaeological Science* 27:1115–1132.

Tuck, J. A. 1978. Northern Iroquoian Prehistory. In *Handbook of North American Indians, Volume 15, Northeast*, edited by B. E. Trigger, 322–333. Washington, D.C.: Smithsonian Institution Press.

Turner, C. G. II, and J. A. Turner. 1999. *Man Corn: Cannibalism and Violence in the Prehistoric American Southwest*. Salt Lake City: University of Utah Press.

Turney-High, H. 1971. *Primitive War: Its Practice and Concepts*. Columbia: University of South Carolina.

Underhill, A. P. 1989. Warfare During the Chinese Neolithic Period: A Review of the Evidence. In *Cultures in Conflict: Current Archaeological Perspectives*, edited by D. C. Tkaczuk and B. C. Vivian 229–240. Calgary: University of Calgary Archaeological Association.

———. 1994. Variation in Settlements during the Longshan Period of Northern China. *Asian Perspectives* 33:197–228.

Upham, S., and P. F. Reed. 1989. Inferring the Structure of Anasazi Warfare. In *Cultures in Conflict: Current Archaeological Perspectives*, edited by D. C. Tkaczuk and B. C. Vivian, 153–16. Calgary: The University of Calgary Archaeological Association.

Ury, W. 1999. *Getting to Peace: Transforming Conflict at Home, at Work, and in the World*. New York: Viking.

Van der Dennen, J.M.G. 1995. *The Origin of War* (2 volumes). Groningen, the Netherlands: Origin Press.

Vencl, S. 1984. War and Warfare in Archaeology. *Journal of Anthropological Archaeology* 3:116–132.

———. 1999. Stone Age Warfare. In *Ancient Warfare: Archaeological Perspectives*, edited by J. Carman and A. Harding, 57–72. Phoenix Mill, UK: Sutton Publishing Ltd.

Villa, P. 1992. Prehistoric Cannibalism in Europe. *Evolutionary Anthropology* 1:93–104.

Villa, P., C. Bouville, J. Courtin, D. Helmer, E. Mahieu, P. Shipman, G. Belluomini, and M. Branca. 1986. Cannibalism in the Neolithic. *Science* 233:431–437.

Walker, P. L. 2001a. A Bioarchaeological Perspective on the History of Violence. *Annual Review of Anthropology* 30:573–596.

———. 2001b. A Spanish Borderlands Perspective of La Florida Bioarchaeology. In *Bioarchaeology of Spanish Florida: The Impact of Colonialism*, edited by C. S. Larsen, 274–307. Gainesville: University Press of Florida.

Walker, W. H. 1998. Where are the Witches of Prehistory? *Journal of Archaeological Method and Theory* 5:245–308.

Wardel, K. A. 1994. The Palace Civilizations of Minoan Crete and Mycenaen Greece, 2000–1200 B.C. In *The Oxford Illustrated Prehistory of Europe*, edited by B. Cunliffe, 202–243. New York: Oxford University Press.

Watkins, T. 1992. The Beginning of the Neolithic: Searching for Meaning in Material Culture Change. *Paleorient* 18:63–75.

Watson, P. J. 1988. Prehistoric Gardening and Agriculture in the Midwest and Midsouth. In *Interpretations of Culture Change in the Eastern Woodlands during the Late Woodland Period*, edited by R. Yerkes, 39–68. Columbus: Department of Anthropology, Ohio State.

Webb, W. 1974. *Indian Knoll*. Lexington: University of Kentucky.

Wedel, W. R. 1986. *Central Plains Prehistory: Holocene Environments and Culture Change in the Republican River Basin*. Lincoln: University of Nebraska Press.

Wendorf, F. 1968. Site 117: A Nubian Final Paleolithic Graveyard near Jebel Sahaba, Sudan. In *The Prehistory of Nubia, vol. II*, edited by F. Wendorf, 954–995. Dallas: Fort Burgwin Research Center and Southern Methodist University Press.

Wendorf, F., and R. Schild. 1986. *The Prehistory of Wadi Kubbaniya*. Dallas: Southern Methodist University Press.

White, T. D. 2000. *Human Osteology* (2nd ed.). San Diego: Academic Press.

———. 2001. Once were Cannibals. *Scientific American* 285(2):58–65.

White, T. D., and N. Toth. 1989. Engis: Preparation Damage, Not Ancient Cutmarks. *American Journal of Physical Anthropology* 78:361–367.

———. 1991. The Question of Ritual Cannibalism at Grotta Guattari. *Current Anthropology* 12:118–138.

Whitehead, N. L. 1988. *Lords of the Tiger Spirit: A History of the Caribs in Colonial Venezuela and Guayana, 1498–1820*. Dordrecht, Holland: Foris Publications.

———. 1994. The Ancient Amerindian Polities of the Amazon, Orinoco, and the Atlantic Coast: A Preliminary Analysis of Their Passage from Antiquity to Extinction. In *Amazonian Indians from Prehistory to the Present*, edited by A. Roosevelt, 33–54. Tucson: University of Arizona.

———. 1999. Native Society and the European Occupation of the Caribbean Islands and Coastal Tierra Firme, 1492–1650. In *A General History of the Caribbean*, vol. 3, edited by G. C. Damas and P. Emmer, 180–200. London: UNESCO.

———. 2000. A History of Research on Warfare in Anthropology—Reply to Keith Otterbein. *American Anthropologist* 102:834–837.

Whitehouse, R. 1987. The First Farmers in the Adriatic and Their Position in the Neolithic of the Mediterranean. *Actes du Colloque International du Centre National de la Recherche Scientifique* (Premieres Communautes Paysannes en Mediterranee Occidentale):357–365.

Whittle, A. 1985. *Neolithic Europe: A Survey*. Cambridge: Cambridge University Press.

———. 1988. Contexts, Activities, Events—Aspects of Neolithic and Copper Age Enclosures in Central and Western Europe. *British Archaeological Reports, International Series* 403(1):1–19.

Wilcox, D. R. 1989. Hohokam Warfare. In *Cultures in Conflict: Current Archaeological Perspectives*, edited by D. C. Tkaczuk and B. C. Vivian, 163–172. Calgary: The University of Calgary.

Wilkinson, R. G. 1997. Violence against Women: Raiding and Abduction in Prehistoric Michigan. In *Troubled Times: Violence and Warfare in the Past*, edited by D. L. Martin and D. W. Frayer, 21–43. Amsterdam: Gordon and Breach.

Wilkinson, R. G., and K. M. Van Wagenen. 1993. Violence Against Women: Prehistoric Skeletal Evidence from Michigan. *Midcontinental Journal of Archaeology* 18:190–216.

Willey, P. 1990. *Prehistoric Warfare on the Great Plains: Skeletal Analysis of the Crow Creek Massacre Victims*. New York: Garland Publishing.

Wills, W. H. 1988. *Early Prehistoric Agriculture in the American Southwest*. Santa Fe, NM: School of American Research Press.

Wilson, E. O. 1998. *Consilience: The Unity of Knowledge*. New York: Alfred A. Knopf.

Wilson, M. L., and R. W. Wrangham. 2003. Intergroup Relations in Chimpanzees. *Annual Reviews in Anthropology* 32:363–392.

Wrangham, R. 1999. Evolution of Coalitionary Killing. *Yearbook of Physical Anthropology* 4:1–30.

Wright, G.R.H. 1988. The Severed Head in Earliest Neolithic Times. *Journal of Prehistoric Religion* 2:51–56.

Wright, H. T. 1986. The Evolution of Civilizations. In *American Archaeology, Past and Future*, edited by D. J. Metzer, D. D. Fowler, and J. A. Sabloff, 323–365. Washington, D.C.: Smithsonian Institution Press.

Yates, R.D.S. 1999. Early China. In *War and Society in the Ancient and Medieval Worlds: Asia, the Mediterranean, Europe, and Mesoamerica*, edited by K. Raaflaub and N. Rosenstein, 7–45. Cambridge: Center for Hellenic Studies and Harvard University Press.

Zimmerman, L. J. 1997. The Crow Creek Massacre, Archaeology and Prehistoric Plains Warfare in Contemporary Perspective. In *Material Harm: Archaeological Studies of War and Violence*, edited by J. Carman, 75–94. Glasgow: Cruithne Press.

Zollikofer, C., M. Ponce de Leon, B. Vandermeersch, F. Leveque, and J. Carman. 2002. Evidence for Interpersonal Violence in the St. Cesaire Neanderthal. *Proceedings of the National Academy of Sciences* 99:6444–6448.

Contributors

Elizabeth N. Arkush is a research associate at the Cotsen Institute of Archaeology, University of California, Los Angeles.

Mark W. Allen is assistant professor of anthropology at California State Polytechnic University, Pomona.

Douglas B. Bamforth is associate professor of anthropology at the University of Colorado, Boulder.

Samuel V. Connell is a research associate at the Cotsen Institute of Archaeology, University of California, Los Angeles, and a post-doctoral fellow at the Central Identification Laboratory in Hawaii (CILHI).

David H. Dye is associate professor of archaeology at the University of Memphis in Tennessee.

R. Brian Ferguson is professor of cultural anthropology at Rutgers University, Newark, and has published extensively on the subject of war.

Chapurukha M. Kusimba is associate curator of African archaeology and ethnology at the Field Museum in Chicago.

Steven A. LeBlanc is director of collections at Harvard's Peabody Museum of Archaeology and Ethnography, and has recently published Constant Battles: The Myth of the Peaceful, Noble Savage (2003, with K. Register).

Jolie Liston is project director at the International Archaeological Research Institute, Inc., a not-for-profit research company in Honolulu, Hawaii.

Elsa M. Redmond is a research associate in the Anthropology Division at the American Museum of Natural History, New York.

Jay E. Silverstein is a fellow at the Central Identification Laboratory in Hawaii (CILHI).

Julie Solometo is assistant professor of anthropology at James Madison University, Harrisonburg, Virginia.

Charles S. Spencer is curator of Mexican and Central American archaeology at the American Museum of Natural History

H. David Tuggle is senior archaeologist with International Archaeological Research Institute, Inc.

Anne P. Underhill is an associate curator in anthropology at the Field Museum in Chicago.

Index